P9-DFZ-121

"THE DEFINITIVE BIOGRAPHY OF JACKIE . . . AS ACCURATE AS WE'LL EVER HAVE."
—*Wilmington Sunday News Journal*

—Jackie's relationship with her father, the dashing and notorious womanizer, Black Jack Bouvier

—How Jackie broke off with her first fiancé to marry John Kennedy

—How she handled John Kennedy's obsessive extramarital sexual life

—The treatments she and John regularly got from the infamous "Dr. Feelgood"

—The quarrel they had just before Dallas

—Her decision to marry Aristotle Onassis and their life together

—The legendary shopping sprees, the need for money, the famous friends and enemies, the children and how they turned out

—And everything, *every*thing, else, about

A Woman Named Jackie

"Lifts the veil on the queen of Camelot . . . Heymann has succeeded in getting 825 people to talk and acquired access to FBI, CIA, Secret Service and White House files."
—*USA Today*

C. DAVID HEYMANN is the author of several major biographies, including *Poor Little Rich Girl: The Life and Legend of Barbara Hutton.*

A Woman Named
JACKIE

by
C. David Heymann

A SIGNET BOOK

SIGNET
Published by the Penguin Group
Penguin Books USA Inc., 375 Hudson Street,
New York, New York 10014, U.S.A.
Penguin Books Ltd, 27 Wrights Lane,
London W8 5TZ, England
Penguin Books Australia Ltd, Ringwood,
Victoria, Australia
Penguin Books Canada Ltd, 10 Alcorn Avenue,
Toronto, Ontario, Canada M4V 3B2
Penguin Books (N.Z.) Ltd, 182–190 Wairau Road,
Auckland 10, New Zealand

Penguin Books Ltd, Registered Offices:
Harmondsworth, Middlesex, England

Published by Signet, an imprint of New American Library,
a division of Penguin Books USA Inc.

This is an authorized reprint of a hardcover edition published by Lyle Stuart, Inc.

First Printing, June, 1990
13 12 11 10 9 8 7 6 5

 REGISTERED TRADEMARK—MARCA REGISTRADA

Printed in the United States of America

To Eugene L. Girden, Esq.,
and Judge Harold R. Tyler, Jr.,
two of the finest lawyers
I have ever known.

I have been through a lot and I have suffered a great deal. But I have had lots of happy moments as well. I have come to the conclusion that we must not expect too much from life. We must give to life at least as much as we receive from it. Every moment one lives is different from the other. The good, the bad, hardship, the joy, the tragedy, love and happiness are all interwoven into one single indescribable whole that is called LIFE. You cannot separate the good from the bad. And, perhaps, there is no need to do so either.

—Jacqueline Bouvier Kennedy Onassis

Please call me Jackie—that ghastly name.

—Jacqueline Bouvier Kennedy Onassis
to James Fosburgh, 1961.

1

Arrangements had been made for the expectant mother to have her baby in a New York clinic, but the child was late in coming. One week after the estimated date of arrival, when nothing had happened, the restless father-to-be drove his wife to East Hampton for the weekend; they spent the next weekend again at his family's summer residence—and the next. The baby refused to appear. Altogether five weeks elapsed and the mother, though big and a bit uncomfortable, was so reconciled to the delay that she accompanied her husband on yet another East Hampton weekend.

She felt fine on Saturday, but when she woke up the following day she was in acute pain. Since her doctor was also spending the weekend on Long Island and there was no time to get her to New York, the mother was rushed to a small but efficient hospital in nearby Southampton. There, on July 28, 1929, six weeks later than expected, she gave birth to an eight-pound baby girl. The child, their first, had dark fluffy hair, a snub nose, generous lips and large, luminous eyes. The Bouviers named her Jacqueline ("Jackie") Lee.

Her mother, at twenty-two, was a slim, petite brunette with a pretty face and an endearing manner. Janet Lee Bouvier was described by friends as "highly ambitious, smart, aggressive as hell, a daredevil horseback rider who believed in hard work and self-reliance." As if to enhance her background she described herself as "one of the Lees of Maryland." Actually her grandparents were lace-curtain Irish immigrants who had fled the potato famine and made fast money in America, not unlike the Kennedys of Boston.

The child was named after her father, Jack Bouvier, whose full name was John Vernou Bouvier III. He was thirty-eight, a stockbroker, and until his marriage the

1

previous year, had been considered one of social New York's most sought-after bachelors. Tall, muscular and exotic-looking, with shiny black hair, broad cheekbones, pencil-line mustache and widely spaced dark blue eyes, he had a deep, year-round suntan and a medley of sobriquets, including "The Sheik" and "The Black Prince," but most appropriately "Black Jack"—a reference not to his swarthiness so much as his penchant for beautiful young women. Janet, sixteen years his junior, fit the pattern perfectly.

The East Hampton residence where Jack and Janet Bouvier had awaited the birth of their child was called Lasata, an American Indian name meaning "Place of Peace." Built along the lines of an English manor house and resembling something out of an F. Scott Fitzgerald novel, the fourteen-acre estate was located on Further Lane, in those days a sandy stretch of road that ran parallel to the sea. Lasata belonged to "the Major," John Vernou Bouvier, Jr., Jackie's grandfather, a respected lawyer who later retired from the bar and joined his bachelor uncle M. C. (Michel Charles) Bouvier's lucrative stock brokerage firm, eventually inheriting much of M. C.'s considerable wealth.

Formal and fastidious, the Major used a walking cane and wore the high starched collar, pince-nez eyeglasses, three-piece suits and pointed waxed mustachios so fashionable among gentlemen of his age and station. To his wife, the former Maude Frances Sergeant, and his children, he must have seemed remote, pompous, sometimes stern, sometimes brash and boastful. Jackie's grandfather was a chauvinist, an American patriot who belonged to any conceivable group, society or organization that marched under the Stars and Stripes, from the Chamber of Commerce to the American Legion. A *belles lettres* dilettante and professional curmudgeon, the Major cranked out a constant stream of notes to local newspaper editors on such civic-related subjects as tax collection and mail delivery. In his spare time he created slogans and verses for various occasions, and inserted them in books and in presents for his children and grandchildren.

Jackie's father, born in 1891, was the eldest of the Major's five children. His brother, William Sargeant Bouvier, "Bud" to his siblings, was born in 1893, followed by Edith, 1895, and the strawberry-blond twins,

Maude and Michelle, ten years later. As befitted their social station, the family spent the summer months and most weekends in East Hampton, the remainder of the year first in Nutley, New Jersey, and later in Manhattan. The boys attended the best schools, though neither performed with particular distinction. Jack, expelled from Phillips Exeter for instituting a weekly poker game in the student dining hall, persevered at less prestigious prep schools, matriculating at Yale in 1910 and graduating four years later. Jack's brother Bud also entered Yale and was graduated in 1916. Both boys finished near the bottom of their class.

Tom Collier, Jack's companion at Yale, recalled him as "funloving and bold, the original East Egg party boy. He certainly wasn't the studious type. I don't remember him ever cracking a book or studying for an exam at Yale. He ran track during his sophomore year but gradually lost interest in the sport and began chasing girls instead. He could walk into a room full of women, and ninety-five percent of them wanted to be with him—he was *that* charismatic. But he was confused about it. Once he'd been with a woman, he lost interest in her and moved on to the next. He treated them poorly. At night he'd take one girl up to his bedroom, and the next morning a totally different girl would emerge. He'd have them lined up beforehand, maybe three or four a night, and he'd kick them out as he used them up. He maintained interest in a girl only if she didn't succumb. But ultimately they all succumbed."

Edith Bouvier, Black Jack's sister, had married a lawyer, Phelan Beale, and the lawyer had gone into partnership with the Major to start the New York law firm of Bouvier, Caffey and Beale. Phelan Beale had a number of acquaintances in the brokerage business, one of whom steered Jack Bouvier, just out of Yale, to a job opening with the Wall Street brokerage firm of Henry Hentz & Co., of which Herman B. Baruch, brother of financier Bernard Baruch, was senior partner. Black Jack started as a trainee and within months rose to the position of broker. With his youthful charm, his bravado and his love of money, the fledgling stockbroker seemed ideally suited to his new profession.

The only discernible obstacle in his path was the war in Europe, a war in which the United States was becoming more involved by the day. To his patriotic father's immense disappointment, Jack Bouvier refused to enlist immediately, waiting until the last possible moment before volunteering for service. In August 1917, several months after America's entry into World War I, he was commissioned a second lieutenant in the U.S. Army Signal Corps. While Bud, having signed up early in the campaign, distinguished himself for valor in the trenches of France, Jack fought his "toughest battles"—as he wrote to a friend—"in the smoke-filled, honky-tonk back-alley bars and brothels of North and South Carolina, waiting for this dirty little war to end. . . ."

Jack resumed his post with Henry Hentz & Co. in 1919 and three years later, with his family's blessing, decided to go into business for himself. On January 6, 1922, Black Jack accepted loans from his great-uncle M. C. Bouvier of $40,000, $30,000 from Herman B. Baruch, and $10,000 from his brother-in-law Phelan Beale, a total of $80,000, all at 6 percent per annum. He used the money to acquire his own seat on the New York Stock Exchange.

The terms of the loan stipulated that if Jack made more than $13,500 a year, he would pay the three men the excess as their interest. He agreed that his personal expenses would not exceed $6,500 per year until his debt was liquidated. "The remaining $7,000 of the $13,500 permitted to be drawn by me are for purposes of interest payments and office expenses." The promissory note further stated that Jack was "not to allow any loss to run against me more than three-eighths of a point. . . . Any violation of this agreement on my part may be followed by the sale of my Stock Exchange membership."

Black Jack became what is known in the trade as a stock specialist, a "broker's broker," meaning a broker who buys and sells a select line of stock for other brokerage firms; among the stocks he handled were Kennicott Copper, Texas Gulf Sulphur, Colorado Fuel and Power, and Baldwin Locomotives. He did well, dressed in expensive continental suits, purchased a new car and rented a luxury apartment at 375 Park Avenue. His personal living expenses far exceeded the relatively meager amount allotted by the loan agreement, and he failed to reduce substantially the principal on his loan. He was earning money—his commissions averaged $75,000 per year over the next five years—but he spent too much, and he didn't keep a very close eye on where the money went.

Louis Ehret, son of a New York real estate baron and a friend of Black Jack, observed that Jack had no sense of responsibility when it came to money or financial affairs. "He spent money with a will," said Ehret. "He gambled, he drank, he pissed it away on women. During his bachelor days he gave nightly parties at 375 Park Avenue, inviting half of New York. It was never a case of Black Jack trying to fleece anyone. He was simply naive about money. He spent it in all directions. When a check came in, he didn't bother about its intended final destination; he simply used it to pay off his latest debt. Equally astounding was the fact that he got away with it. His three creditors, for example, not only didn't foreclose on him, they offered him a second loan—in 1925 he increased his debt by another $30,000."

Louis Ehret attended many of Black Jack's Park Avenue soirées and observed first-hand his friend's uncanny success with women. "All these women fluttered around him like love-hungry moths," said Ehret. "He met them everywhere—at country clubs, tea dances, bars, nightclubs, restaurants. He had this incredibly macho way of sauntering up to a beautiful woman and staring her down. It was like an athletic contest. The two players would lock eyes and stare until one or the other gave way. Jack invariably won, the girl never knowing quite what to do, finally looking away out of pure embarrassment. Jack got off on this. It was a way of flaunting his masculinity, of dominating the woman. It worked. They were all dying to go to bed with him. And it didn't matter to him who they were or where they came from, whether they were single or married, rich or poor. Some of Jack's girls belonged to renowned families with lots of prestige and money. Others were less socially eminent, less wealthy, less inhibited and often more fun. By and large they were all the same to him."

There were frequent hints of forthcoming engagements, bits and pieces in the gossip columns and society pages linking Black Jack to this debutante or that socialite. His family looked on with growing apprehension as he went around creating emotional havoc, cutting a wide romantic swath among the serried ranks of society's most eligible females. His frenzied, sometimes ostentatious demeanor did not quite fit in with the conventional and conservative East Hampton code by which most of the natives lived.

Black Jack was not the only Bouvier whose life-style deviated from the accepted norm. For the twins, Maude and Michelle, life was one long round of parties, dances, post-deb functions, and horse and dog shows, but their older sister Edith, now with three of her own children, indulged in several eccentricities that even Black Jack must have found dismaying. A frustrated *chanteuse* and opera singer, she spent more than $50,000 to train and refine her voice, and ended her marriage to Phelan Beale by engaging in affairs with a succession of male vocalists and voice coaches. She transformed her East Hampton house, Grey Gardens, into a literary salon, taking in and feeding writers, musicians and artists, while hopelessly trying to regenerate their flagging careers. She dressed in what can best be described as pre-hippie Bohemian floppy hats, silk scarves, long flowing robes and gowns in the manner of Isadora Duncan.

The family's gravest cause for concern, however, was Bud Bouvier, who had returned from the war with a serious drinking problem. He and his brother were now constantly bickering, Jack being the more forceful and aggressive, and Bud the more vulnerable. Both brothers drank heavily, Bud certainly to excess—the result, he explained, of seeing half his platoon cut down in battle.

Bud had another good reason to seek oblivion in drink. His marriage to Emma Louise Stone, a strikingly attractive blonde from East Hampton, had ended in divorce while their only son was still little. Unable to hold down a steady job, Bud was being sued for back alimony, and the ensuing publicity was disconcerting to a family obsessively concerned with public image. Treating Bud's alcoholism as a personal disgrace rather than a serious illness, his father threatened to cut him off, and at one point, after Bud was arrested for speeding and drunk driving, described him as "a contemptible parasite and a dirty nuisance."

It was in the midst of these tawdry events that Black Jack surprised everyone by announcing his romantic interest in Janet Norton Lee. Janet was in her early teens when the James T. Lees spent their first summer in East Hampton. She was the second of three sisters—Marion,

Janet, Winifred—brought up in the Glittering Twenties like the daughters of many newly affluent New York parents. Janet lived in a large house with servants, attended Miss Spence's School, learned the social graces, made her debut at Sherry's, spent one year at Sweet Briar College and another at Barnard, owned her own automobile (as did both her sisters) and rode her own horses.

The Bouviers considered themselves socially superior to the Lees, although both families belonged to the Maidstone, East Hampton's prestigious private country club. The Bouvier social stock had risen because of successful pairings in the family with members of such well-established American clans as the Drexels, Dixons and Pattersons. By comparison the Lees were relative newcomers. James Thomas Lee, a short, balding, physically uninspiring man, had put himself through City College and Columbia University Law School (from which the Major was a fellow alumnus). He then made a fortune as a property and finance entrepreneur, parlaying his intelligence and business acumen into position and title—for forty years, he served as president and Chairman of the Board of the New York Central Savings Bank. Unlike the Bouviers, he made his money the hard way—through his own efforts.

The late Truman Capote observed that "if the Lees were made to appear in some way inferior, the supposedly aristocratic but decadent Bouviers could only profit from a touch of Irish grit. The Bouviers were poseurs. They looked like money, breeding and power, but they weren't. Jackie's grandfather, the Major, had put together and published a fantasy of Bouvier genealogy tracing the family to French aristocracy. He gave them a coat of arms and invented family members who were never members of the family. It was a work of art, a total fabrication. On the other hand, the confidence it instilled greatly helped the Bouviers to realize their social ambitions. Believing themselves to be aristocrats, they felt and behaved like aristocrats. Jackie—and her various kin—adopted the loftiest of aristocratic principles, noblesse oblige, and tried to adhere to it."

The "fantasy of Bouvier genealogy" referred to by Capote was a volume entitled *Our Forebears*, which the Major issued privately in 1925 and reissued several times thereafter, the final edition emerging in 1947, a year before the Major's death. He dedicated the book "To my grandchildren and to those who may later add to their joyous company," and sent copies to assorted genealogical and historic societies, as well as to each member of his family. The significance of the chronicle, as Capote points out, was that it showed the Bouviers to be of French aristocratic descent, tracing their ancestral roots to one François Bouvier (c. 1553) "of the ancient house of Fontaine near Grenoble." The problem was that the noble sixteenth-century François Bouvier, a landowner and "Counsellor in Parliament," with his own crest and coat of arms, had nothing at all to do with the family's true forebear, a gentleman of the same name but much lower station, who lived two centuries later and kept an ironmonger's shop in Grenoble, and whose wife was a simple domestic.

Major Bouvier's genealogical study was studded with errors, oversights and exaggerations of every kind. Jackie's branch of the family owed its existence not to French aristocrats but to the petite bourgeoisie—drapers, tailors, shopkeepers, farmers and small-time merchants. The Major, constitutionally ill-equipped to settle for the mediocre or mundane, even took liberties with the history of his own grandfather, Michel Bouvier, the original owner of what was to become a common given name in the family and the first Bouvier to emigrate to America.* According to *Our Forebears,* Michel had arrived in Philadelphia from the French village of Point-Saint-Esprit in 1815 and prospered as a cabinet-maker, a manufacturer of veneers, and a speculator in real estate. There was nothing said about his meagre beginnings, the fact that he had started as an impoverished, uneducated carpenter

---

Our Forbears makes the claim that André-Eustache Bouvier, Michel's father, was among the French soldiers who fought under George Washington at the Battle of Yorktown in 1781, afterwards returning to France. There is no historical support for this assertion, which appears to be one more invention on the part of this fanciful family genealogist. It did, however, enable the Major to gain entrance to the Society of the Cincinnati, composed of supposed descendants of officers who served in the American Revolution. The Major, Bud and Black Jack all proudly displayed boutonnieres in their lapels signifying membership in the society. The name "Bouvier," incidentally, means "ox-herder" in French, again reinforcing the petty bourgeois origins of the family.

whose one-man operation had been in constant danger of collapse. Major Bouvier also referred in his genealogy to the intimate friendship between Michel Bouvier and Joseph Bonaparte, when in truth they barely knew each other. Napoleon's brother, having arrived in America the same year as Michel, had once merely ordered a few pieces of furniture from Bouvier's little carpentry shop.

Major Bouvier was not alone in his wish to rewrite history. The parents of Janet, James and Margaret Lee, harbored their own legacy of well-kept family secrets. By the time Janet turned fifteen, her mother and father were no longer living together. Although never officially divorced, they occupied separate quarters on different floors in one of James Lee's Manhattan apartment buildings. James blamed the estrangement on his wife's Irish-born mother, who shared Margaret's apartment and constantly interfered in the marriage. But the root cause of their separation was Margaret Lee's love affair with a man named William Norris, a New York City attorney whose wife was as adamant as James Lee in refusing to grant a divorce. The strain of the arrangement, coupled with the need to keep it hidden from view, caused those concerned a great deal of pain and anxiety. By common consent, Janet had been cast in the thankless role of family go-between. As such, she represented the sole means of communication not only between her parents, who wouldn't speak to each other, but between them and her sisters, who couldn't speak. It was partially in an effort to extricate herself from this impossible situation that she set out to marry Jack Bouvier.

According to at least one family member, Jack Bouvier was actually Janet's second choice. Little Edie Beale, the daughter of Edith and Phelan Beale, the one-time blond "Body Beautiful" of the Maidstone Club and the first-born of the Major's eleven grandchildren, insisted that from the moment Janet set eyes on him, her first choice had been Bud Bouvier.

"Of the two brothers, Bud was the more simpatico," said Edie. "He had the elegance and sensitivity that Jack lacked. Jack simply never grew up. He wasn't at all introspective. His only concern in life was himself, the fulfillment of his own drives and needs, whether that meant hanging out at '21,' attending a prize fight at the

Garden, or chasing after women. Everything in Jack's cosmos revolved around the bedroom.

"Jack was divinely decadent and Janet was painfully proper. They were like fire and ice. I doubt she ever really wanted to marry him. She adored Bud, but because Bud was divorced and an alcoholic, her parents wouldn't allow it. So she wound up with Jack. I don't think he was any more anxious than she. It was just something he did to prove to himself he could do it. He didn't want to marry her. He wasn't in love with her and she wasn't in love with him. She was in love with Bud Bouvier."

Beyond the largely imagined importance of his family name—he was a member of East Hampton's inner circle, but only on the fringe of what Mrs. Astor would define as high society—Jack Bouvier had little to recommend him as a proper husband for an up-and-coming clubwoman like Janet Lee. To add to his insatiable womanizing and an unwavering attraction to bookies and gambling casinos, he demonstrated what James Lee regarded as a total lack of solid business sense. He was a dreamer and schemer, a speculator, a man who owed dozens of people thousands of dollars in unpaid debts, and always with a need of further loans. Black Jack's personal expenses invariably equaled or exceeded his earnings. Money burned holes in his pockets. He spent for the sheer pleasure of spending. At one point, on the verge of financial ruin, he owned no fewer than four automobiles, including a black Lincoln Zephyr, and a maroon Stutz which was frequently driven by a chauffeur in matching maroon livery.

James Lee easily discerned the truth about his prospective son-in-law's questionable financial practices. Peter Bloom, a bookkeeper for Lee, had previously held the same position in a firm owned by Bernard Baruch.

"Jack Bouvier borrowed money from everybody," said Bloom. He accepted a number of loans from the Baruchs—not just to acquire a seat on the Stock Exchange but to keep the business going and to help support some of his more spectacular vices, gambling and women for example. His promissory notes kept passing across my desk, only they were all going one way. I mean there was no attempt on his part, so far as I could tell, to make good on any of them."

Whatever the extent of his reservations about Jack

Bouvier, James Lee did nothing to oppose his daughter's engagement in the spring of 1928. Given Black Jack's string of broken engagements and unfulfilled commitments, this intended marriage seemed in jeopardy even without parental intervention. Janet's father assured his closest associates that despite their engagement, the couple would never walk down the aisle together. But before summer's end, he would be proved wrong.

The wedding took place in St. Philomena Church, East Hampton, on July 7, 1928, before a gathering of bankers, attorneys, financiers, stockbrokers and their families, swarms of fetching girls and ambitious young men—a formidable representation of wealth and influence. An uncertain but sober Bud Bouvier, two days out of a private sanatorium named Silver Hill in New Canaan, Connecticut, served as best man. And Margaret Lee, Janet's mother, made one of her rare public appearances in the company of her estranged husband.

The East Hampton Star proclaimed it the social event of the season. The half-dozen bridesmaids donned jonquil-yellow chiffon gowns and green straw hats. The matron and maid of honor, Janet's sisters, were mirror reflections in green chiffon and yellow hats. The scene inspired one New York society reporter to rhapsodize, "Have you ever glimpsed the loveliness of a bed of nodding green and gold jonquils in the sunshine? Surely you've all seen a stately bride bedecked in satin, lace and silver? Combine these effects and you'll have a glowing pictue of Mrs. John Vernou Bouvier III, stepping into the sunshine from the door of quaint St. Philomena's Church yesterday with her attendants about her."

After the ceremony, five hundred guests attended a midday reception at the sprawling estate James Lee had rented for the summer on Lily Pond Lane, not far from Grey Gardens. Couples danced on the porches and lawns to the music of the Meyer Davis orchestra. The gaiety of the afternoon was suddenly shattered by a loud argument inside the house between the groom and his newly acquired father-in-law, the first of many arguments to come. Soon afterwards the newlyweds slipped away to spend their wedding night at New York's Savoy Plaza Hotel. The following morning they boarded the *S. S. Aquitania* for a five-week European honeymoon.

Halfway across the Atlantic, the groom instigated an

apparently innocent but distracting flirtation with Doris Duke, the tall and angular sixteen-year-old tobacco heiress, who was en route to Europe with her mother. "The world's wealthiest teenager," as the press dubbed her, was flattered by the attentions of her fellow passenger. There was nothing more to it, Black Jack would tell friends, not even a kiss to encourage the friendship. Janet, however, evidently thought otherwise. She demonstrated a quick and violent temper by shattering a large ornamental wall mirror outside their cabin. Harmony was restored only after the honeymooners reached their hotel in Paris.

2

Black Jack Bouvier once told Louis Ehret that his secret ambition in life was to earn $5 million by age thirty-nine and then retire to a sunny village on the Riviera with a yacht and an all-female crew. According to Edie Beale, Jack's favorite expression went: "If somebody wants something from you, make him pay for it." As Edie perceived him: "Uncle Jack never cared much for high society; that was Janet's domain. Jack cared more about money. In essence he was the complete mercenary—nothing in life is free—and his attitude rubbed off on his children."

Money was almost certainly the central issue for Jack on October 24, 1929, the day of the crash on Wall Street. The Stock Market catastrophe followed closely a far more crushing personal tragedy: Bud Bouvier's death at age thirty-six from cirrhosis of the liver. Holding himself partly to blame for his brother's dismal end, Black Jack traveled to the Santa Ynez Valley in California, where Bud had spent his final days, to retrieve his body and bring it home to East Hampton.

Ten weeks after Bud's death, on December 22, 1929, Jacqueline Lee Bouvier was baptized at the Church of St. Ignatius Loyola in New York. Bud Bouvier had been the original choice to be Jackie's godfather at the ceremony. Instead, Janet Bouvier asked her father to fill the role. But on the appointed day at the appointed hour, James T. Lee found himself marooned in a taxicab in the middle of a traffic jam miles from the church. A last-minute substitution had to be made, and this time the honor fell to Miche Bouvier, Bud's nine-year-old son, who later defined the moment as "my appointment with destiny."

Black Jack's animosity towards "Old Man Lee," as he now referred to him behind his back, increased in direct proportion to his own mounting financial anxieties. Since

13

most of Jack's fiscal sources had gone the way of his own small reserve, the Crash, and the onset of the Great Depression, left him nearly at the monetary mercy of his father-in-law.

Well aware of Black Jack's erratic financial history, James Lee agreed to render aid in the form of non-interest-bearing loans and a rent-free apartment, but only under certain stringent conditions. First, Jack would have to agree to reduce his exorbitant spending and cut back on his flamboyant life-style. Secondly, he would have to be willing to give up some of the luxuries he had come to accept as necessities, including all but one of his automobiles, his numerous club memberships, his predilection for continental fashion. There could be no more cavorting, no gambling, no drinking, no investing or speculating in high-risk stocks. As a gesture of his willingness to comply, he would have to submit a monthly profit-and-loss statement to James Lee's bookkeepers, accounting for every dollar spent or saved.

While his personal resources continued to dwindle, Black Jack moved his family into a posh eleven-room duplex at 740 Park Avenue, an apartment building owned and managed by Janet's father, by coincidence only a block from a similar duplex owned by Jack's father, the Major, at 765 Park Avenue. Bristling with indignation over the prospect of remaining forever financially dependent upon his in-laws, Jack began spending substantial sums of borrowed money to refurbish and remodel their new apartment. His immediate plans called for a renovated kitchen, the addition of several deluxe bathrooms (with gold-plated fixtures), the construction of a new nursery. He ordered a number of walls torn down, others repaneled, at the same time drawing up blueprints for the transformation of an extra maid's room into a small gymnasium equipped with weight-reduction equipment, sauna, belt vibrator, rubbing table, built-in sunlamps. He hired a trainer and a masseuse to keep him in shape, a cook, two maids, two grooms for the family stable at Lasata, and an English nanny, Bertha Newey, to look after Jacqueline. While the apartment was being redecorated, he took his wife on a second European honeymoon, leaving baby with her new nanny. Upon their return a month later, they embarked on still another vacation, this time to White Sulphur Springs, Georgia, taking baby and nanny along.

Whereas Janet's father subsidized their New York apartment, it remained for the Major to underwrite Rowdy Hall, Jack and Janet's long-term summer rental at 111 Egypt Lane, East Hampton. The two-story wood-frame colonial was the site of Jackie's second birthday party, attended by some twenty little boys and girls. The significance of the occasion is that it marked the debut of Jackie's name in print, apart from the obligatory announcement of her birth. A reporter for *The East Hampton Star* covered the latest event: "Little Jackie Bouvier, daughter of Jack Bouvier and the former Janet Lee, will not make her bow to society for another sixteen years or more, but she was a charming hostess at her second birthday party given at the home of her parents, 'Rowdy Hall,' on Egypt Lane. The party featured games and pony rides for the children, followed by Jack Horner pie and birthday cake."

Less than a month later, Jacqueline, in a white bonnet and white doeskin gloves, was again cited by *The Star*, this time for "showing" her first pet, a shaggy black Scotty pup named Hootchie, at the annual East Hampton Village Fair dog show. "Little two-year-old Jacqueline Bouvier," read the account, "toddled to the show platform and exhibited with great pride a wee Scotch terrier of about her own size." Although Jackie won a prize, the reporter seemed more impressed with the quality of Black Jack Bouvier's dark suntan. "Mr. Bouvier is so deeply tanned with East Hampton suntan," she wrote, "that he much resembles one of those handsome Egyptians you see careening along in their Rolls-Royce cars in Cairo, in the land of the Nile."

On March 3, 1933, the family was completed with the birth of Jacqueline's sister, Caroline Lee, named after Caroline Maslin Ewing, her great-grandmother on her father's side, best known for her work as the organizing spirit behind the New York Foundling Hospital.

Jack Bouvier set the tone by calling his youngest daughter Lee; everybody insisted on calling her older sister Jackie, although as a child she disliked the name and far preferred Jacqueline.

With Lee's arrival, Jackie suddenly graduated from babyhood at the ripe age of three-and-a-half. She moved

into a room of her own, and Lee inherited the nursery
and the nanny, Bertha Newey. They shared a playroom
in their Manhattan duplex filled with handmade toys and
dolls and stuffed animals from F.A.O. Schwarz. Jackie's
favorite was an old rag doll named Sammy, who accompanied her everywhere and with whom she had long
imaginary conversations.

A frequently recounted story took place less than a
year after Lee's birth. While walking in Central Park
with her infant sister and English nanny, Jackie wandered off by herself. A police officer spotted her alone,
strolling unconcernedly down a path. She stepped up to
him, looked him in the eye and stated firmly, "My nurse
and baby sister seem to be lost." Jackie was retrieved
from the nearest stationhouse by her mother.

One of her mother's most engaging stories concerning
the childhood of Jackie and Lee illustrates a key difference in their personalities. As a child Jackie was blunt,
direct and matter-of-fact; Lee wa polite, even diplomatic.
The story was that in their apartment house, an elevator
operator named Ernest was endowed with a crest of
blond hair which jutted above his forehead. One morning
little Lee, skipping into the elevator, said: "Ernest, you
look pretty today."

Ernest was about to thank Lee when Jackie interrupted: "How can you say such a thing, Lee? It isn't
true. You know perfectly well that Ernest looks like a
rooster."

Another of Jackie's traits was boisterousness. Her teachers at Miss Chapin's School on East End Avenue in
Manhattan, where she was enrolled after a year in Miss
Yates's pre-school class, were unanimous in their impression that Jackie, though highly intelligent, was actually a
problem child.

In her mother's opinion, Jackie was hyperactive and
imperious in school primarily because she was bored:
"Jackie's intellectual ambition ran ahead of her chronological age. She was extremely precocious, reading books
like *The Wizard of Oz*, *Little Lord Fauntleroy* and *Winnie
the Pooh* before she even began kindergarten at Miss
Yates's. One day, when she was six, I found her reading
a book of short stories by Chekhov. I asked if she understood all the words. 'Yes,' she said, 'except—what's a
midwife?'

"Her problem at Chapin was sheer boredom. Jackie would finish her classroom lessons before any of the other children and, lacking things to do, would make a nuisance of herself. She could be audacious and demanding, even show-offy, a handful for those in charge of her."

Boredom was only part of the problem. The real reason Jackie didn't care for the all-girl school at first was that, as in many select private schools in New York, its students were required to wear a traditional blue-linen jumper uniform, and Jackie had always rebelled against regimentation.

One day a classmate told Jackie's mother that Jackie was "the very worst behaved girl in school," and that her teachers sent her to see Miss Ethel Stringfellow, the headmistress, "almost every day."

"What happens when you're sent to Miss Stringfellow?" Jackie's mother asked.

"Well," said Jackie, "I go to the office, and Miss Stringfellow says, 'Jacqueline, sit down. I've heard bad reports about you.' I sit down. Then Miss Stringfellow says a lot of things—but I don't listen."

A conference was arranged between the headmistress and Jackie's parents, at which Miss Stringfellow told them she was especially anxious to channel the girl's intelligence and her efforts because "she has the most inquiring mind we've had in this school in thirty-five years."

After discussing the situation with the Bouviers and learning among other things that Jackie was "mad" about horses, Miss Stringfellow had an inspired idea on how she could reach her boisterous student.

The next time Jackie appeared in her office, the headmistress told her, "I know you love horses and you yourself are very much like a beautiful thoroughbred. You can run fast. You have staying power. You're well built and you have brains. But if you're not properly broken and trained, you'll be good for nothing. Suppose you owned the most beautiful race horse in the world. What good would he be if he wasn't trained to stay on the track, to stand still at the starting gate, to obey commands? He couldn't even pull a milk truck or a trash cart. He would be useless to you and you would have to get rid of him."

The horse metaphor worked: Jackie understood. She

had been only a year old when her equestrienne mother first placed her on a pony. The Bouviers owned seven ponies and hunters and boarded them first at Lasata and later at the adjacent East Hampton Riding Club, a private stable managed by Arthur G. Simmonds, an English-born veterinarian who became Jackie's riding master. Arthur's son, Martin Simmonds, remembered riding and playing with Jackie when both were "little whippersnappers," as did Martin's older sister, Queenie Simmonds-Nielson.

"My dad was fussy where the members took their horses when they rode," said Martin Simmonds, "but most of them would ride on trails through the woods. We owned about eighty acres of land. There were three rings and vast stretches of open field. Every August the club sponsored its own horse show. The East Hampton Horse Show became an important stop on the way to the National Horse Show at Madison Square Garden. From the age of five, Jackie competed regularly on the Long Island horse-show circuit. She began riding in lead-line events and worked her way up. She was damned plucky. She'd get tossed on her butt while taking a jump and a moment later she'd be scrambling to climb back on.

"On the other hand, she always seemed a bit of a snob. I can remember her arriving for her riding lessons in her grandfather's Duesenberg and the chauffeur jumping out and holding open the door, and after the lesson her Mademoiselle used to brush her off with a little whiskbroom. In front of the stables stood a clubhouse which my mom ran, where the ladies had tea and cucumber sandwiches in the afternoon. Jackie and her Mademoiselle often stayed for tea. Most kids her age just wanted to climb on a horse and ride off into the sunset. Jackie seemed to love the ritual of the sport as much as the riding. Like her mother, she had the patience to master the finer points of horsemanship."

Queenie Simmonds-Nielsen recalled that her father, Arthur Simmonds, gave Jackie her first lessons in the ring: "Jackie spent an entire summer just walking around the ring on her horse so she would have a seat. The following summer she began to trot. It was a long time before she was allowed to canter or jump. My father taught riding in the classic manner. You not only had to learn how to ride but also how to school a horse. My father had these sayings—a horse always knows his rider's character, and training the horse trains the rider. In a sense, Arthur Simmonds, rather than any of her school teachers, was the first great moral influence in Jackie's life.

"Jackie's mother was also a superb rider, one of the best in the club, and had much to do with her daughter's interest in horses. Jackie's father came to the club occasionally to watch his daughter ride, but wound up spending all his time on the telephone, calling up the Stock Exchange. His only concern seemed to be business.

"Janet was definitely the driving force in terms of riding. For many years she was a junior master of the Suffolk Fox Hounds. Each summer they hosted two or three drag hunts in East Hampton. There were foxes on Long Island at that time—there still are—but in those days they would merely drag the scent. Otherwise they were quite formal about it. Dicky Newton of Watermill was master of fox hounds. He was very, very English. It was tally ho, and all that sort of thing. People were delighted to have us ride across their property. They'd come out and wave as we rode by. Jackie also took part in the hunt. But she and I would only ride to the first check and be brought back in by a groom. The first check is where the entire group comes together for the first time. It was exhausting exercise for a child, but Jackie always seemed ready to ride on.

"That's the quality I remember most vividly about Jackie—her fierce competitive edge," Queenie added. "My father ran a special event for the kids called a paper chase. He'd cut up a stack of old newspapers and then take off very early in the morning and scatter the strips of newspaper in strategic locations along the trail. We used to try and follow this paper chase on horseback until we came to the end, where there would be a prize waiting for the winner.

"There was another contest for children as well: a gymkhana or egg race. You had to ride a horse from one place to another holding a wooden spoon with an egg balanced on it. The tiny tots would walk their ponies, the older kids would trot. The winners received cups. You could always tell from the expression on Jackie's face whether she'd won or not. She was so intent on winning that she permanently soured her sister on the sport. The

Bouviers owned this piebald pony, Dancestep, that once rolled over and nearly crushed Lee to death. Between that incident and Jackie's aggressive attitude, Lee opted for her bicycle and gladly forgot about horses."

Samuel Lester, a childhood friend of Martin Simmonds, exercised horses at the East Hampton Riding Club: "I used to walk and exercise the horses. Jackie would bring her horse in, or her mother would bring hers in, and I'd walk them. This was when they still boarded their horses at Lasata. I didn't get paid for my work. I did it because I liked to ride horses.

"Jackie's mother owned a magnificent chestnut show horse named Danseuse, which she later gave her daughter as a present. I can still see Jackie in her pigtails and riding outfit—top hat, Ascot tie, coat with contrasting collar and trousers to match the collar, long leather boots—putting Danseuse through her paces. She exercised the horse by the hour and was soon bringing home blue ribbons by the boxload.

"Jackie was a fast learner. She thrived on competition, often performing better in the actual horse show than in practice sessions. The larger the crowd, the more proficient her ride. Her entire family turned out for the shows—all her little cousins, her mother in a riding outfit of her own, her father in a white gabardine suit, her Bouvier grandfather in his Panama straw hat. If Jackie happened to lose an event, her facial muscles would tighten into knots. Her mouth and jaw would pull as taut as a rope. She wasn't happy unless she won, unless she beat all the other little kids."

Jackie never disclosed the point at which she first became aware of the cracks, stresses and strains that were eventually to tear apart the Bouvier marriage. It took years before she admitted even to herself that something could possibly be wrong with the marriage and with parents who did their best to keep their traumas and tensions under wraps. Held in check by the iron grip of good manners and an unshakable resolve never to lose face, Jackie refused to betray her feelings, not even later when her parents went their separate ways and she and her sister became sacrificial lambs in a tormenting divorce struggle.

Despite Jacqueline's refusal publicly to acknowledge

the rupture in the marriage, the widening rift between her parents was to play a vital part in the formation of her character and personality. It had reached the point where even outsiders could see that below the surface of this *Social Registrite* union there were differences that could never be resolved. At the core of their difficulties lay the timeless problem of money—their mutual inability to live within their means, Black Jack's unending failures on the stock market. Although he made a substantial profit after the repeal of Prohibition by investing in liquor shares, he lost it all again by gambling at the race track and in a rash of indefensible stock and bond investments. Attempts to conceal the extent of his losses only tended to deepen the dilemma. Yet he found it increasingly difficult to share his private burden with a woman as ambitious, pushy and seemingly materialistic as Janet Bouvier, particularly given his financial dependence on her father.

Nor was it a simple matter to hide his marital discord from his immediate family. His parents, while generally supportive, constantly intervened by offering unsolicited advice. The twins, responsible for introducing Jack and Janet in the first place, also found themselves thrust into the middle. Lee Bouvier was sheltered by virtue of her youth, but Jacqueline had no insulation at all. The angry silences that increasingly passed between her parents too often erupted into full-blown altercations. Whenever an argument loomed, Jackie was exiled. "Why don't you go and exercise your pony?" became a common refrain for getting her out of harm's way.

The caring for her horses represented one mode of escape; she had others, including a pet rabbit that lived in her bathtub in New York, and her father's harlequin Great Dane, King Phar, with whom she often romped through her grandmother's vegetable garden at Lasata.

Edie Beale recalled that her cousin enjoyed playing imaginative games: "Jackie, Lee and Shella, the daughter of Aunt Michelle, played together on the grounds of Lasata and imagined they saw medieval warriors and knights weaving around the hedges; they created dramatic epics, written and directed by Jackie, enlivened by real makeup and grown-up clothes. In these childhood dramas Jackie always assumed the role of a queen or princess, while Lee and Shella played the parts of her ladies-in-waiting.

"Jackie never outgrew the princess role. She was an odd mixture of tomboy and dream princess. She climbed trees but had a fairy princess complex. She even had a crown, part of a circus costume that she wore during these childhood performances. It was a game, but she took it seriously. Then one day she announced her intention to run away from home to become 'Queen of the Circus.' And in a way I suppose she did. It's amazing how Jackie's dream world later materialized for her, and also how unhappy it seemed to make her."

The "Queen of the Circus" motif was evidently a recurring symbol for Jackie. At fourteen she wrote a string of tongue-in-cheek predictions for each member of the family. For herself she foresaw a future as the circus queen who, though admired "by the world's greatest men," married "the man on the flying trapeze," in certain respects perhaps a prefiguration of John F. Kennedy.

Aunt Michelle recalled the tomboy aspect of Jackie's evolving personality, how she struggled to keep up with Michelle's son, Scotty, a churlish, husky boy two years older than Jackie: "On Sundays, Jackie chased Scotty from room to room and up into the fruit trees that shaded Lasata. They competed in tennis and baseball, raced each other in the Maidstone swimming pool, formed their own secret society called 'The Blood Brothers.' Scotty's sister, Shella, was the third member. They built a clubhouse and painted a sign with the name of the society in black letters only because they couldn't find any red paint."

Scotty was the family cut-up and clown, a supreme mischief-maker whose greatest pleasure was to throw firecrackers and sand at people when they weren't looking. He was the proverbial "bad boy," "a little twerp" in the words of a bemused relative. Once he was "banished" from the Maidstone Club for swinging by a rope from the rafters and alighting on a table of elderly club members during a formal dinner dance. Yet such antics were precisely what endeared him to Jackie, the two cousins being the youngest black sheep in a flock overburdened with the type.

Jackie's other favorite cousin during these years was Miche Bouvier, in many respects practically an older brother to Jackie. Explaining how he and Jackie had grown close, he said: "My father died in 1929. Four years later my mother remarried a professional U.S. Army officer. They were very often in far places of the world. So I spent summers, quite a number of them, with the family in East Hampton, sometimes with my grandfather, sometimes with Jackie's family."

By the mid-1930s, Jack and Janet Bouvier had given up Rowdy Hall and were using Wildmoor as their summer home. Overlooking acres of potato fields and sea grass, Wildmoor belonged to the Major and had been the family residence at East Hampton prior to Lasata. Jack and Janet were currently accorded rent-free access to the house.

Miche remembered the automobile trips they took from New York to East Hampton on what was then the Vanderbilt Parkway: "Jackie's father had a very fine memory and as he drove us out, he told stories about his boyhood and his college days and about my father. He told the kinds of stories kids like to hear.

"Smithtown, which was then on the route to East Hampton, was the midway point. We used to stop there for pistachio ice-cream cones. Then we'd be back on the road and Jack would resume his childhood tales. He'd get so caught up in them that we'd invariably be stopped for speeding. Janet became upset. I liked Janet. We got along. But she and Jack didn't always get along."

John H. Davis, the son of Aunt Maude and the eventual author of well-received family histories of the Bouviers as well as the Kennedys, was the same age as Jackie. In discussing her past, he recalled that she frequently escaped her familial problems by visiting Edith and Edie Beale at Grey Gardens.

"She had great feeling for Aunt Edith," said Davis. "Edith was a welcome respite from the pressures Jackie experienced in her own household. There were good reasons for these pressures—Black Jack's extramarital flings; his growing financial problems. In addition to his other burdens, he was attempting to support Miche at this juncture, trying to put Miche through boarding school. It was a responsibility he willingly assumed after Bud's death.

"His problems weren't simple. Stockbrokers are either investors or gamblers. Black Jack was a gambler, an in-and-outer—he bought on Tuesdays, sold on Fridays. He was impetuous. He and my father shared the same brokerage office: they maintained separate firms but at the same address. My father frequently provided Jack with new customers, though they had opposing philosophies. My father was conservative in outlook. He and Jack endlessly debated but never resolved the question of long-term versus short-term investments. They agreed on only one thing—Joseph P. Kennedy, the first chairman of Franklin D. Roosevelt's newly established Securities and Exchange Commission, was to blame for all their misfortunes. Kennedy, father of the future President of the United States, had recently outlawed all the techniques and regulations that had enabled him to amass millions on the stock market. Regardless of their differing fiscal philosophies, they both loathed Kennedy and were outraged by his tactics. That John Kennedy's father should contribute to the troubles that beset Jackie's father was one more twist in her complex history.

"When it came down to it, a major source of irritation between Jack and Janet Bouvier had to do with their respective social orientations. Jack didn't give a damn about the so-called '400.' He was a hedonist. He wanted to enjoy himself. Janet cared about nothing but the '400.' She was Irish and she could never live that down. She was very nouveau. She was a 'learned lady,' as somebody once put it. And they are the worst kind, and the most vigorous in adherence to the rules. She had to learn to be a lady. Her parents would look up in the books the ways in which one had to behave. Janet wasn't born to the manor. She had to learn, and that's why she became so good at it. She wouldn't break the rules. Her head ruled her heart completely, while with Black Jack it was the other way around.

"Jackie fell somewhere in the middle, and her parents constantly placed her in the middle. As a result, she gravitated toward Aunt Edith. On Saturday afternoons when Edith listened to the opera on the radio, Jackie sometimes listened along. And on Sundays Edith often joined the rest of the family for brunch at Lasata. It didn't take much in the way of encouragement to get her to sing. At the slightest hint or suggestion, she would warble her way through her entire repertoire: Puccini, Cole Porter, Kurt Weill, Wagner, Verdi, what have you.

Jackie loved it, she absolutely loved it. Edith, being both the family outcast and an *artiste manqué,* was somebody with whom Jackie could finally identify.

"Edith encouraged Jackie to find her own mode of expression. But the Major had a more direct influence. He composed the first of many successive birthday poems to Jackie when she was one. He did this with all his grandchildren. They were sentimental poems with classical allusions that were meticulously correct in rhyme and meter."

Davis also remembered, "We were encouraged to respond in like manner. Jackie began writing poetry and short stories at the age of seven or eight. She also sketched and decorated her written work with line drawings. Her early poems dealt with nature, the turn of seasons, walks along the shore. Her short stories usually concerned the family pets. One of her tales, 'The Adventures of George Woofty, Esq.,' was about her pet terrier's imaginary romance with Caprice, a sleek, black Bouvier-des-Flandres female dog that Jackie's father had given her because of the similarity in names. It was the kind of writing you would expect of a wistful, gifted, lonely little girl."

For all her escape mechanisms, Jackie found it impossible to shut her eyes completely to the rapidly disintegrating marriage of her beleaguered parents. At night her bedroom walls would vibrate with the hammering of her parents' quarrels, their angry words reverberating through the house. Perhaps Jackie didn't understand the full meaning of the words, but she followed their harangues as they berated one another to the point of exhaustion. Sometimes, as she later confided to her mother, she would sneak out into the dark hallway, where she could make out actual words—her mother's loud ultimatums, her father's fierce denials and acid denunciations. For hours she would stand and listen, silently praying for the resolution she knew would never come.

Judith Frame, an acquaintance of the Bouviers during this period, remembered Jackie as "an inscrutable child— you never knew what she was thinking or how much she knew of her parents' problems. She was a beautiful child, a replica of her father—the same wide-spaced, flashing eyes, dark coloration, prominent cheekbones. She and her sister were always impeccably dressed, often in matching outfits. They had these 'musical dresses'—green linen with rickrack, a musical scale and notes running across the front of each dress.

"It was no secret that the Bouviers weren't getting along. Janet quickly grew weary of Jack's poker nights, business trips and nights out with the boys. These were euphemisms for nights out with the girls. It wasn't uncommon to see Jack and Janet together at a private dinner party in East Hampton, and see him again a few hours later at the Devon Yacht Club on Gardiners Bay with another girl on his arm and Janet nowhere in sight."

Judith Frame recalled a well-documented story that at one of the Bouvier parties in East Hampton Janet saw her husband disappear into the bushes with somebody's wife—just took her by the arm and wandered off. On another occasion she caught him in a deep embrace with a girlfriend of hers named Tammy Welch. "It meant nothing," he told Janet. "We were just joking," he added.

"Black Jack was lethal, absolutely lethal. He was extremely handsome and knew it. He used to strut around the Maidstone like a barnyard rooster, fixing his hair, gazing in mirrors, parading for the women. He was the Don Giovanni type—seductive, charming, dangerous. He carried himself as if all eyes in the world were upon him. I don't know how tall he was. Six feet maybe, but he looked much bigger. It was the way he entered a room, the way he moved. Of course all this posturing may well have been a cover-up for some deep-seated insecurity on his part—it's hard to say. He used to go speeding up and down the roads in his convertible drawing attention to himself, disappearing in a haze of champagne and dust.

"It reached the point where Janet refused to be seen in public with her husband. They'd be invited to somebody's house and at the last minute she'd feign illness, or make up some other obvious excuse why she couldn't go. She refused to deal with all the whispering that went on behind her back. She had too much pride. Yet she didn't have enough pride to simply ditch her husband—not until half the world knew about their problems."

Anthony Cangiolosi, a young caddy at the Maidstone during the club's heyday, also had observations about Jack Bouvier's compulsive lusting. "He was a womanizer, quite a womanizer," said Cangiolosi. "When you get caddies bullshitting, you hear all about that business.

The Maidstone had one of the top eighteen-hole golf courses in the country. And to be a member of the place you had to be blue-blue-blue, or at least have pretty good credentials.

"I was about twelve years old when I started caddying there, and I just happened to get stuck with Black Jack, which is what the caddies called him. After the first time around, he kept asking for me. Whether he tipped decently or not on a given day depended on the stock market. If the market was up we got a quarter, if it was down we got ten cents. Jack was closer to his money than bark on a tree. That's how close he was. But his old man was worse. The Major was so tight he wouldn't even hire a caddy. Whenever he played a round he'd have Jackie or one of his other grandchildren caddy for him.

"The decent part about caddying for Black Jack is that he never played more than nine holes. There was a greenskeeper's shack at the ninth hole where he'd take the ladies to go to bed with them. He'd dismiss the caddy. 'That's all, caddy—you can take the bags back to the clubhouse.'

"Of course you'd pretend to go back in, but instead you'd dump the clubs someplace, usually in the rough, and double around for a peek through the window of the shack. And there they'd be, naked as jaybirds. What I remember most clearly about Black Jack was his hair. He must've used axle grease on his hair because it was just about as slick and flat as you could get it.

"To be honest, you'd be lucky if you made it past the fifth hole with Black Jack. He'd usually knock off after a few holes, and he and the woman would take a hike into the woods. He was a fast worker.

"Once in a while he'd play in a foursome. But it was usually women he played with, and he had some beautiful-looking women. They were members of the club and they were married. You'd caddy for Black Jack and some guy's wife, and three days later you'd caddy for the woman and her husband. And you'd say, 'Oh shit!' If I'd had any brains when I was younger, I'd have bought a camera."

One of Black Jack's occasional golf partners was Virginia Kernochan, an understated, demure woman several years younger than Janet. In early June 1934, Virginia accompanied the Bouviers to a horse show at the Tuxedo

Park Riding Academy, ostensibly to watch Janet compete against other top club riders. In the course of the afternoon, Black Jack did one of his by-now famous disappearing acts, taking Virginia with him; they reappeared four hours later during the final event of the day.

A United Press photographer spotted Black Jack and the two ladies as they were preparing to leave. Agreeing to pose for the camera, Janet, still in riding gear, hoisted herself atop the rail and was joined there by Virginia, while Black Jack for his part stood off to Virginia's side, tenderly holding her hand. Because Janet happened to be looking the other way she didn't see the hand-holding episode, but the publication of this particular photograph in the following day's New York *Daily News* left little to the imagination; society columnist Maury Paul (the original Cholly Knickerbocker) soon speculated in print that the Bouviers and Miss Kernochan were "having a grand old time."

While Janet knew about her husband's hyperactive premarital sexual adventures and found his appeal to other women tantalizing, she had no intention of continuing to condone such behavior. Nor did her father. Not wanting Janet to repeat the same mistake he had made in his own marriage, James Lee gave her the name of a leading New York divorce lawyer and urged her to make an appointment. Janet resisted at first, convinced she could still salvage the relationship and make her rakish husband see the damaging effect his flagrant womanizing had upon their marriage.

The campaign to domesticate Black Jack soon faulted. Franklyn Ives, an insurance executive, had rented the house next door to Wildmoor on Appaquogue Road during the summer of 1936 and was privy to some of the events that would lead to a final dissolution. "I happened to be there in early May that year, putting the property in shape for the season," said Ives. "The summer crowd hadn't yet arrived, and East Hampton looked like a ghost town. On a Friday toward the middle of May a Ford convertible pulled into my neighbor's driveway and three men climbed out. It was Jack Bouvier and a couple of stockbroker friends of his.

"Black Jack was very cordial. When they saw me standing there, he and his cronies came over and introduced themselves. I'd heard about the Bouviers from the owners of the house I was leasing. I knew there were two cute little girls with lots of pedigreed dogs, an attractive mother who loved horses, and a stockbroker father who was experiencing a bit of financial difficulty. But that was only part of the story.

"Within an hour of Black Jack's arrival another car drove up and three girls jumped out—all in their young twenties, all remarkably good-looking. One of the three—a statuesque redhead with a breathtaking figure and wonderful legs—was obviously with Jack.

"I soon learned that Wildmoor, with its six bedrooms and impressive vistas, was used as an off-season retreat by Black Jack's male friends, who would pack their tackle boxes and tell their spouses they were going off for a little fishing, when in reality they were going off to free-spirited weekend parties at Wildmoor, which usually included a crowd of young single women.

"During the summer the situation was reversed. The wives would be down in East Hampton all week with the children, while the men would be stuck at their jobs in New York. After work, Black Jack would throw parties for many of the same people at his duplex on Park Avenue, never telling anyone that the place actually belonged to his father-in-law. Everyone thought he was swimming in money.

"The redhead with the fabulous legs turned out to be a showgirl at a nightclub. She and Jack were sort of an item that summer, although he had a number of other girls on the line. He and his wife had become intimate strangers. They shared the same house but not the same bed. When they talked they quarreled. They had nothing left to say to each other.

"Over the next three or four months, I became friendly with Black Jack. To the extent that I knew him, I'm not convinced he was fully aware of the consequences of his actions. He struck me as a man of contrasts and extremes, a person deeply divided by the most basic of human emotions: love and hatred; kindness and brutality; sensitivity and callowness. He was one of those characters on the New York social scene other people talked about. There were dozens of stories flying around. I once heard that he was bisexual, that he occasionally went off with men, that he and Cole Porter were lovers. I don't know whether this story is true or not. I do know

that he and Cole Porter were in the same class at Yale. I
also know that Jack had trouble keeping his fly zipped
and that one of his favorite New York watering holes was
Cerutti's, a gay bar on Madison Avenue. There was a
marvelous pianist at Cerutti's named Garland Wilson.
But I suspect Jack may have gone simply to imbibe the
atmosphere."

The Bouvier marriage was probably most succinctly
portrayed by Alexandra Webb, a socialite who moved in
the same circles as Jack and Janet. "Janet married him,"
Webb insisted, because his name appeared in the Register. He married her because her father operated a bank.
She was a bitch and he was a bastard, and in the end
both were disillusioned."

3

Jack Bouvier embarrassed his wife once too often. On September 30, 1936, when Jackie was seven, her mother demanded a six-month trial separation. The only member of her husband's family Janet still trusted was the Major. She agreed to let Jackie's grandfather draw up the separation papers, granting to her temporary custody of the children and giving their father weekend visitation rights. Jack Bouvier was also required to pay his wife $1,050 each month "for her support and maintenance and for the support and maintenance of Jacqueline and Lee."

Black Jack moved out of the Park Avenue duplex and into a small but sunny room at the Westbury Hotel, Madison Avenue and 69th Street. Although he maintained a brave front, he was presently faced with a new onslaught of financial worries, not only wife-and-child support but a lawsuit that had been filed against him by the estate of M. C. Bouvier to recover thousands of dollars in outstanding debts (including a $25,000 loan extended in 1930), not to mention a $40,000-plus attachment lawsuit filed by the Internal Revenue Service for back taxes.

Despite these troubles, Black Jack carried off his weekend visits to the children with his customary dash and élan. They shared a secret signal—an alternating series of long and short honks on his automobile horn—and at the first blast Jackie (her father's nickname for her was "Jacks") would come running and fling herself into the front seat beside her father. Lee ("Pekes") was not far behind.

They had several favorite activities and places to go, including the Bronx Zoo and Belmont Park, where Black Jack proudly introduced his daughters to the jockeys in the paddock before the day's races. There were horse-and-buggy rides through Central Park, shopping expeditions down Fifth Avenue, visits to the Metropolitan Museum of Art. Or Black Jack might invite some of his children's friends to join them for lunch at Schrafft's, followed by a movie and ice-cream sundaes. Other times, they drove uptown to Baker Field, Columbia University's athletic stadium, to row the afternoon away in the outdoor rowing seats set up for sculling practice. Baker Field was also good for watching baseball tryouts in the spring and football practice in the fall.

Because the family canines were now all kept on Long Island, Jack had made arrangements with several pet shops in Manhattan to "borrow" their dogs. On Sundays, he and his daughters would often march into a store, pick out a clutch of the saddest, sorriest-looking pooches they could find, leave a deposit and take them for a brisk walk in Central Park. Later, they would return the dogs and redeem their deposit.

Once, Black Jack convinced Janet to let him have the girls on a Friday morning so he could give them a tour of Wall Street. John Ficke, a bookkeeper in Jack Bouvier's small brokerage firm, brought the girls over to the Stock Exchange that morning. "There were two balconies down there, one for the ordinary riff-raff, the other for the brokers and their guests," said Ficke. "Jack had made special arrangements to reserve the latter balcony just for his daughters. He'd been bragging about their pending visit for weeks, so there was plenty of hoopla on the Stock Exchange floor when they finally showed. Here were these two adorable little girls up there by themselves in front of the entire Exchange, and everybody knew they belonged to Jack. The place erupted in wild cheers and applause. The girls loved it. They did little curtsies to the crowd, and the place broke up again. Black Jack couldn't have been happier if Wall Street had accorded him a tickertape parade—he was proud as hell of those kids."

Judith Frame would recall just how much "Jackie enjoyed herself during these visits with her father. All week long, she looked forward to her weekends and the time she would have with him. Her father was the closest person in her life. She seemed to glow in his presence. As a child, she was more in tune with her warmhearted, outgoing father than with her coolly methodical, less emotional mother, although later on I think this pattern reversed itself.

"A contributing factor in all this was Jackie's closeness to the Bouvier family, as against the Lees. She identified with the Bouviers, considered herself one of them, and until she moved away, remained very much under their thumb. And the Bouviers, with the possible exception of the Major, considered Janet the chief culprit in the affair. They blamed her for breaking up the marriage. They blasted her for everything she'd ever done or said. They did a real number on Jackie. If you keep telling a child the reason she can't have her pony is because of her mother, the child eventually begins to resent her mother.

"Janet had the added misfortune of being a perfectionist. It became her responsibility to discipline the girls, teach them manners, tell them to sit up straight, drink their milk, brush their teeth and go to bed on time. She was practical-minded, down-to-earth. In her conventional mold, Janet dressed conservatively and behaved the same way and encouraged a similar mode for her daughters. 'Money does not grow on trees,' she constantly reminded them.

"Their father by contrast indulged them—took them to the zoo and out for ice-cream sodas, or trooped them over to Saks, Bonwit Teller, Bergdorf Goodman and De Pinna for new clothes and jewelry. However strapped for funds he happened to be, he was uninhibitedly extravagant and generous when it came to his daughters. There was a world of difference in the way Jack and Janet wanted the kids brought up. Their mother wanted the girls to conform to the standards of acceptable society; their father encouraged them to stand out and be noticed. It was a matter of style, not a question of right or wrong. But of course Janet became the ogre, while Jack, as far as the children were concerned, could do no wrong."

Black Jack initiated the reconciliation that brought the family together again in April 1937. Janet had little hope of the marriage succeeding but agreed to try for the sake of the children. That summer they rented a cottage overlooking the sand dunes of East Hampton.

One version of ensuing events appears in a sworn deposition made in 1939 by Bertha Kimmerle, hired by Janet to replace Bertha Newey as Jacqueline and Lee's governess. Bertha Newey's enforced departure during a critical period in Jackie's childhood created additional stress. Jackie had begged her mother to rehire Miss Newey, but the episode leading to her discharge had created animosity on both sides. Mrs. James T. Lee, it seems, had paid an unannounced call on her grandchildren at their Manhattan duplex, became enraged at some imagined slight and tried to slap Jacqueline in the face. Bertha Newey, attempting to protect the child, stepped forward and absorbed the blow herself. She then, "very properly" she felt, returned it to Mrs. Lee.*

Miss Kimmerle, an employee of the Bouviers from August 1937 to December 1938, when she too was fired by Janet Bouvier, testified that within a week of her arrival she noticed that relations between the couple were hostile. Jackie's mother was "a lady who unmistakably has a will, and was generally engaged in doing what she wanted, when she wanted and where she wanted. It was thus a matter, if not daily at least of frequent occurrence, that Mrs. Bouvier was not home, and the children, consistently without their mother, were always in my company.

"On the other hand Mr. Bouvier was left in the house quite alone, but his love for the children, and their very joyous love for him, I could easily see. Both were devoted to him, and both sought his company whenever it was possible. . . . This was particularly so in the case of Jacqueline . . . an unusually bright child with a passionate fondness for horses. Little Lee was a lovable little mouse, not as high-strung or as alert as her sister, but strong, sweet and affectionate."

The Kimmerle deposition went on to say that Jacqueline and Lee seemed more reserved in their mother's presence than in the presence of their father. This may have been due to Mrs. Bouvier's frequent bouts of tem-

---

*Bertha Newey's actions are described in her own words in what is also a sworn deposition, portions of which appear in John H. Davis's, *The Kennedys: Dynasty and Disaster*, pp. 177–186. The same volume contains sections of depositions by Bertha Kimmerle and Bernice Anderson, a maid in the Bouvier household, whose testimony is discussed later in this chapter. The depositions were to have been used by Jack Bouvier in his divorce struggle with Janet, but since the divorce went uncontested at a hearing in Nevada, the depositions were never introduced. These documents are currently in the possesion of Mrs. Maude Davis, Jackie's aunt and the mother of John H. Davis.

per. "Indeed," claimed Miss Kimmerle, "I had not been in their home more than ten days when Mrs. Bouvier gave Jacqueline a very severe spanking because the little girl had been too noisy in her play. She would spank Jacqueline quite frequently and became often irritated with the child, but for no reason that I was able to see."

Miss Kimmerle recalled an incident that took place on Sunday, September 26, 1937. "Mrs. Bouvier called her father over to the house. I could gather that she was mad because Mr. Bouvier had not, while in town, gotten himself a lawyer for some purpose. I do know that when the three, that is, Mrs. Bouvier, Mr. Lee and Mr. Bouvier, were together in a very noisy argument, little Jacqueline raced upstairs to me and said: 'Look what they are doing to my daddy!' and at the time Jacqueline was in tears."

It was a lost summer for Jackie. Martin Simmonds saw her whenever she arrived for lessons at the East Hampton Riding Club. "There are no secrets in East Hampton," said Martin. "Everybody knows everybody else's business. Everybody knew about the Bouviers. Their difficulties spawned the worst rumors. All the kids knew and some made a point of needling Jackie. But when she didn't want to hear something she didn't listen. She had a lot of grit for a little girl."

Fanny Gardiner, a founding member of the East Hampton Riding Club, "felt sorry" for Jackie. "I'll never forget the Jackie I knew then," she remarked. "She was a wistful child, wandering around the riding club like a motherless kitten, talking to the grooms and caring for the horses. She went through the motions of childhood; she climbed trees, skipped rope and played hide-and-seek with her cousins. But you somehow sensed she was a thousand miles away, existing in a world of manufactured dreams."

In September, their marriage about to collapse, the Bouviers accepted an invitation to spend ten days in Havana with Earl E. T. Smith and his then-wife, Consuelo Vanderbilt. Smith, a partner in the Wall Street investment firm of Paige, Smith & Remick, socialized with Black Jack from time to time. "My wife and I played golf with Jack and Janet," Smith reminisced. "The four of us were friendly. When we realized their marriage was headed for the rocks, we invited them to join us in Havana. We thought if they were away from New York and in company with friends, they might possibly work out their differences."

Havana, for all its pre-Castro glitter, served only as Black Jack's Waterloo. Before the end of the month, the Bouviers were back in New York, once again living apart. This time the couple agreed to call it "a permanent separation." Black Jack told anyone who would listen that he had wanted to salvage the marriage but his wife had refused.

From the Hotel Alcazar in Miami Beach, where he vacationed over Christmas of 1937, Jack wrote a long and rambling letter to his father-in-law, asking Mr. Lee to help him reconcile with Janet, at the same time accusing his wife of having fallen in love with another man. He identified "the other man" as Earl E. T. Smith and traced the betrayal to their visit with the Smiths in Cuba. Although the letter never accuses Janet of having had an outright affair with Smith, the implications are clear enough:

> My dear Mr. Lee,
>   I am writing to ask you for aid and guidance in a situation that is so vital to both Janet and myself and our two kiddies, that it has almost reached staggering proportions. As Janet undoubtedly told you by now, she believes or even knows that she's in love with Earl Smith which is a death blow in itself but something I had coming to me for a long time. However all this falling in love Janet did was done under the most ideal surroundings with Smith giving her no quarter with his persistency. . . .
>   Our trip outside of everything else was terribly hectic. Of course at the minute Janet has not very much feeling left for me. And I think most of it is due to the fact that in a rage of insane jealousy which finally culminated at the end of ten days by Mrs. Smith making insinuations to me, I said something in front of [Mrs. Smith], which I'd not have done if I'd been myself. . . .
>   I may deserve to lose Janet because I haven't ever been much of a husband, and perhaps this is a boomerang and I'm only getting what I deserve. But I still love and adore her . . . and I'm not letting her break up her home, her children's lives, as long as there is a fighting chance of my preventing it.

On the verso of the signature page, almost by way of a postscript, Black Jack wrote in pencil: "Jacqueline & Lee suggest that we forgive and forget now that we're practically all even and give them a little dual control for a change."

Earl Smith's reaction to the letter, years after the fact, was one of mild shock. "I'm flattered," he said, "but I never knew Janet was supposedly in love with me. I was married at the time and very happy with my wife. Besides, I liked Black Jack. I got along with him, or thought I did. It sounds like he was just looking for someone to pin a rap on. There was never an affair, I swear. In fact I didn't see Janet again for decades after their visit."

James T. Lee ignored the letter. He had come to detest Black Jack and wished for nothing more than the legal dissolution of his daughter's marriage. His main regret was that he still occasionally encountered Black Jack at the Maidstone Club, and in order to distance himself from the family, requested that the club lease him a new cabana as far away from the Bouvier cabana as possible.

Other members of the Lee family felt a similar degree of resentment. In 1936 Winifred Lee, Janet's younger sister, had married Franklin d'Olier, Jr., a Philadelphia businessman who described Black Jack as "a man of questionable character," while Winifred said of him: "There's no excuse in the world for Black Jack. He was a terrible guy. He was the bottom. He was the worst man you could possibly find."

In June 1938, Black Jack rented the same East Hampton house he and Janet had shared the summer before. He urged her to spend the summer with him and make a last-ditch effort to save their marriage. Janet refused. Instead she rented a house for herself and the girls in Bellport, forty miles from East Hampton.

According to Bertha Kimmerle's deposition, Janet wasn't around much that summer. She made frequent out-of-town trips with the new men in her life, leaving Jackie and Lee in the custody of their governess and a maid. Under no circumstances, she told the servants, were they to allow Black Jack in the house.

According to the deposition, the merest mention of her husband's name sent Janet into a frenzy. She went so far as to instruct Miss Kimmerle that if either of the children cried for their father, they were to be spanked.

Normally not a cruel or unreasonable woman, Janet evidently felt that she was somehow locked in mortal combat with her estranged husband for the affection of their children. Bernice Anderson, the family maid, stated in her deposition that Jacqueline frequently threatened to run away to her father's house. "Once, when her mother was away," said the maid, "Jacqueline asked me to help her find her father's number in the telephone book as she was so unhappy and wanted to talk to him without delay."

The separation agreement, now somewhat altered, called for the girls to spend the month of August with their father. But the good times they had so eagerly anticipated never materialized. There were several impediments, not least of which were the children themselves, particularly Jackie. The once bright, confident, energetic youngster had changed. She grew shy, and to hide her shyness, she adopted a rather aloof, almost regal manner. She became an observer rather than a participant.

To add to the anxiety created by the separation of her parents, Jackie noticed a change in conditions at Lasata. Although she was too young to understand its significance, the older members of the family realized that the Major had acquired a mistress, a woman more than thirty years younger than himself. Mrs. Mabel Ferguson was an attractive Englishwoman living in New York and working for the British Consulate. In addition to seeing a good deal of each other, they carried on a voluminous correspondence. The Major adorned his flowery, Victorian letters with naughty limericks, original love poems and amusing speculations on the nature of love, sex and marriage. He gave her gifts of clothing and lent her money that he never recovered. "He fell in love with her," said Edie Beale, "and when grandmother found out about it, her heart shattered. The affair killed her."

"The golden summers" of Lasata, as John Davis called them in his family history, were over. Four of the Major's five children would be divorced; one had died. The Major, long viewed as the family's most stalwart and enduring member, had all but deserted his devoted wife. A dominant and conquering man, he had completely humiliated her.

"Grandmother Maude had always been the glue that

held everything together," said Edie Beale. "It never really mattered who the various offspring married—they were all immediately inducted into the family. But the divorces, the drifting apart, the philandering—all those factors played a role in the chopping down of the family tree.

"It reached the stage where every member of the family hated every other member. They were ghastly to each other. They would sit around bickering about whose child was the most brilliant, the most beautiful, the most popular. It was obnoxious. It created a wall of animosity and antagonism that separated the various factions of the family."

Bouvier Beale, Edie's lawyer brother, saw the situation in much the same light: "The Bouviers always fought. Everyone was at loggerheads. There was no softness in that family, no love lost anywhere. Those Sunday get-togethers at Lasata were pure torture. Everyone would congregate, shake hands, then ten minutes later they'd be at each other's throats. After about three hours they'd shake hands again and leave. This went on weekend after weekend. If anyone held it together it was Grandmother Maude, but after a while it all just fell apart."

By September, Jackie and Lee were back with their mother. They had vacated the Park Avenue duplex for a smaller apartment at One Gracie Square, near Miss Chapin's School. Jackie was taking ballet lessons three times a week with Miss O'Neill at the old Metropolitan Opera House, and social dance classes once a week at the Colony Club with the fashionable Miss Hubbell, a class in which the boys wore Eton jackets or neat blue suits, the girls their finest party dresses. She also had Danseuse to ride on weekends and after school; her father had agreed to pay for feed and board at Durland's, a stable on West 66th Street.

Such amenities notwithstanding, the situation at home worsened. Bernice Anderson, having moved into the Gracie Square apartment with Janet and the girls, claimed that Mrs. Bouvier drank excessively, took sleeping pills, rarely rose before noon and seemed perpetually nervous and depressed. Janet's high-strung demeanor must have had a disquieting influence on the children. For the first time Jackie's academic performance at school slipped.

She and her mother had frequent shouting spells, while Lee went off on uncontrollable crying jags.

By mid-1939, Janet had retained her own divorce counsel in the person of William Evarts of the law firm of Milbank, Tweed and Holt. Evarts immediately advised Janet to hire a private investigator to gather evidence of indiscretion on her husband's part; adultery, he explained, represented automatic grounds for divorce in New York State and would guarantee Janet a generous divorce settlement.

Evarts referred her to a top man in the field, and Janet called him. Within weeks the investigator came up with a name: Marjorie Berrien, a young socialite and the latest of Black Jack's numerous conquests. He also discovered the identities of several of the women Jack had dated while still cohabiting with his wife, including those in attendance at Black Jack's off-season parties in East Hampton.

Armed with names, dates, times, locations and even photographs of the women in question, Janet's attorney approached the press. On January 26, 1940, the New York *Daily Mirror* published an article under the bold headline, "SOCIETY BROKER SUED FOR DIVORCE," implicating Black Jack in a series of adulterous affairs and citing Marjorie Berrien as one of his steady companions.

By virtue of its sensational slant, the article received extensive media coverage. It was picked up by the major news services and reprinted in practically every tabloid and newspaper between New York and California, stigmatizing Jacqueline and causing her keen embarrassment. It wasn't so much that she was shocked by the infidelities and casual relationships of her social set but rather the trauma of seeing her father attacked in print and having to suffer the inevitable name-calling by classmates and friends.

Because Janet had entered into an active social life of her own, and because her lawyer feared a possible challenge to her divorce suit (Black Jack had gone to the trouble of gathering the sworn depositions of many of their household employees), it was decided she would seek a divorce in Nevada on grounds of "extreme mental cruelty." On June 6, 1940, two months after the death of Maude Sargeant Bouvier (Jackie's grandmother), Janet and the children boarded a train at Grand Central Station and forty-eight hours later arrived in Reno, Nevada.

With the exception of several afternoon excursions to Lake Tahoe and a series of legal conferences with her Reno attorney, George Thatcher of Thatcher & Woodburn, Reno's leading (and most expensive) law firm, Janet spent the next six weeks as a paying guest at the Lazy-A-Bar Ranch, riding hoses with Jackie and taking frequent dips in the resort swimming pool with Lee.

On July 22, at 9:30 a.m., Janet, George Thatcher and Ruth Peigh, whose husband owned the Lazy-A, drove up to the side entrance of the Washoe County District Courthouse in Thatcher's black Rolls-Royce. Janet wore a crisp white suit, white pumps and a neat white bow in her glossy black hair. They entered the building through the rear and climbed a flight of stairs to the courtroom on the second floor.

It was a closed hearing, with only three courtroom personnel in attendance: the clerk of the court, a court stenographer and District Judge William McKnight. Jack Bouvier was represented in absentia by Charles Cantwell, a local attorney whose sole contribution to the proceeding was a broad smile, possibly in anticipation of his legal fee. Janet was spoken for by her lawyer and Mrs. Peigh, whose testimony was needed to establish the fact that Janet had been a legal resident of Washoe County "for no less than six weeks." Following Mrs. Peigh's brief testimony, Janet took the witness stand and answered several perfunctory questions before offering a fuller statement on the failings of her marriage:

> My husband and I separated at the end of September 1936 to April 1937, and for over a year before this he neglected me. Once he left home for several days without telling me where he was. It was very upsetting, and when I would remonstrate with him about his conduct he used to fly into rages and swear and curse at me, and he used harsh language. In April 1937 we effected a reconciliation, but after this his conduct was the same, and during the last period he used to make very insulting remarks about my father in particular and the rest of my family, and in September 1937 we separated finally. . . . It made me very sick and nervous.

The hearing lasted no more than twenty minutes, the terms of the divorce having previously been negotiated by opposing lawyers. The final agreement called for Jack Bouvier to give Janet $1,000 per month—one-half as alimony, the other half for the continuing maintenance and support of the children. Beyond this basic figure, some fifty dollars less per month than the amount paid during the separation, he was now also responsible for "all necessary medical, surgical and dental expenses and the school tuition for each of the children during their respective minorities," including "day or boarding school, preparatory school, college and university, as well as instruction in cultural or physical accomplishments not included in school tuition." Finally, he agreed to pay $2,500 outright to cover Janet's legal fees and expenses.

In return, Black Jack was granted visitation rights with the children on alternate Saturdays and Sundays, one day during the week (after school hours), one-half of Christmas and Easter vacations and six weeks each summer (August 1—September 15). The one unavoidable drawback was Janet's inalienable right to remarry and relocate, in which case seeing his daughters could become a serious difficulty for Jack. When this situation actually arose, and Janet remarried and moved away, Black Jack felt compelled to issue a public statement on the case. "Women are all the victors in my generation," he said.

4

Jacqueline was nearly eleven when her parents divorced—old enough to be aware of the collapse of her world, but too young to absorb its full significance. Instinctively she blocked herself off, creating a refuge into which she could escape. Blocking became her main line of defense, her means of dealing with the trauma and stigma of the breakup. She taught herself how to participate in events without becoming part of them, how to observe without being seen. She became a voyeur, an onlooker; she developed an inner core, a private self that no one could ever know or touch.

Outwardly, the quality of her life remained basically unchanged. She threw herself into many of the same activities that had sustained her in the past. She read more than ever, delving into romantic literature, devouring *Gone With the Wind* and the complete works of Lord Byron as well as a biography of the poet by André Maurois. She commenced collecting her own library of books on the dance and doggedly continued her ballet lessons. She listened to music, wrote poetry, painted and sketched. In 1941, she scored a double victory in the junior horsemanship competition at the Madison Square Garden National Championships. In full American Indian regalia, she won first prize in the Costume Class at the East Hampton Riding Club. Later she wore an old-fashioned lace dress and drove a horse and buggy in East Hampton's annual fund-raising parade sponsored by the Ladies' Village Improvement Society.

Jackie remained a moody but determined child, sullen one minute and cheerful the next. Her determination showed in the smallest gestures. When she placed a stamp on an envelope, she pounded the stamp into place with her fist. If she happened to enjoy a book, she insisted on reading the author's entire *oeuvre*. She had, as Stephen

43

Birmingham noted in a portrait of her, an uncanny influence over people, "a strange ability to get people to do what she wanted, to go with her where she wanted to go, to play the games she wanted to play. 'Guess the name of the song I'm thinking of,' she said to a group of friends one morning in East Hampton. All day long the friends sat around her, guessing and guessing, trying to come up with the name of the song—for Jackie."*

Despite her resolve and drive, Jackie felt powerless to do anything about the complex problems that had destroyed the marriage of her parents. She and Lee were now nothing more than pawns in a fiendish chess match between a pair of disillusioned and feuding adults. As both sides attempted to cling more tightly to the children, Jackie struggled to maintain her own equilibrium.

Black Jack Bouvier continued to win favor with his daughters by allotting them a monthly allowance above and beyond the payments mandated by the divorce agreement. Liberated from the constraints and pressures of marriage, the fifty-year-old Bouvier vacated his room at the Westbury Hotel and moved into a two-bedroom apartment at 125 E. 74th Street, where he resumed the carefree life-style he had savored prior to marriage. The only difference between then and now was that he could presently enjoy some of the privileges and joys that came with fatherhood.

While Black Jack dated some of the youngest and most beautiful women in New York, Janet worked diligently at expanding her own horizons. Through Mrs. Eugene Meyer, a friend living in Washington, D.C., and the wife of the man who owned the *Washington Post* and *Newsweek*, she met Hugh Dudley Auchincloss, Jr., a big, toddling teddy-bear of a man with smiling eyes and a pleasant disposition. A graduate of Groton, Yale and the Columbia Law School, Auchincloss practiced law in New York from 1924 to 1926, when he became a special agent in aeronautics with the newly formed aviation section of the Commerce Department in Washington. He then served in the Western European Division of the Department of State under President Herbert Hoover, resigning in 1931 to form the investment-banking firm of Auchincloss, Par-

*Stephen Birmingham, *Jacqueline Bouvier Kennedy Onassis*, 1969, p. 35.

ker & Redpath with headquarters in Washington and branch offices in New York and other major East Coast cities. Though younger by seven years than Jack Bouvier, Hughdie—as friends affectionately called him—was infinitely more mature and stable, emanating a solidity and strength of character that Janet hadn't found in her first husband.

The Auchinclosses were of Scottish descent. The first member of the family to settle in America, in 1803, had established a flourishing business importing and distributing yarn. Subsequent generations invested in nitrate and railroads or went into banking and real estate, while others moved to New York or Rhode Island and made advantageously bountiful marriages. One can fairly hear the woof and tweet of history whistle through the names of the ramified Auchincloss tribe: Bundy, Grosvenor, Rockefeller, Saltonstall, Tiffany, Vanderbilt and Winthrop among others.

Hughdie's father, Hugh D. Auchincloss, Sr., married Emma Brewster Jennings, daughter of Oliver B. Jennings, a founder along with John D. Rockefeller of Standard Oil. A substantial share of his mother's inherited wealth was later passed down to Hughdie. The Auchinclosses possessed personal wealth and social standing in far greater abundance than anything the Lees or Bouviers had ever imagined. Yet like most patrician families of New England background, they subscribed to a credo that called for hard work, philanthropy and keeping a low profile.

For all his credentials, Hughdie had a somewhat spotty record at the altar. By the time he met Janet, he had been twice married and divorced. His first wife, Maria Chrapovitsky, was the daughter of a Russian naval officer; his second was Nina Gore Vidal, the alcoholic daughter of Thomas P. Gore, a blind Senator from Oklahoma, and the mother of writer Gore Vidal (then still known as Eugene Vidal, Jr.). Hughdie had three children of his own—Hugh Dudley III (nicknamed Yusha, a Russian approximation of Hugh), a product of his first marriage; Nina Gore ("Nini") and Thomas Gore from the second.

"I'd been living with my father at Merrywood, the family estate at McLean, Virginia, when he started dating Janet in 1941," said Yusha Auchincloss. "Janet visited us at Merrywood during Christmas vacation that year and brought along Jackie and Lee. I was a couple of years older than Jackie, but she was so bright and perceptive for her age that any chronological difference between us immediately disappeared."

Janet and Hughdie continued to see each other on a regular basis, often on weekends when he would stay in a New York apartment he maintained at 950 Park Avenue. In March 1942, he brought Yusha along and father and son spent more than a week with Janet and her two daughters.

"Although the idea of marriage undoubtedly crossed my father's mind," said Yusha, "he kept the thought to himself. He certainly didn't say anything to me. His divorce from Nina Gore in September 1941, following a protracted legal battle, still hung heavy on his mind. And then there was the war—the United States had finally joined the Allied war effort. Father wanted to play a role. The Office of Naval Intelligence assigned him to its planning unit at Kingston, Jamaica, and ordered him to report no later than mid-June 1942. Janet drove down to Merrywood with Jackie and Lee to see him off.

"The plot to get married wasn't hatched until the day before it occurred. It was strictly an eleventh-hour decision induced in part by the notion that in time of war people are entitled to act on impulse; they're permitted, even encouraged, to fulfill their fantasies.

"The ceremony took place on the morning of the day Father left for Kingston. Janet and Father stood next to a fountain at the edge of what had once been a croquet lawn, a large clearing in the middle of the forest. I was best man. Jackie and Lee attended. The only other guests were Wilmarth and Annie Lewis, my father's brother-in-law and sister. The ceremony lasted no more than fifteen minutes. Later in the day, Janet drove Father to Union Station in Washington, where he boarded a military train and then a transport ship for Kingston."

Hugh Auchincloss's return came sooner than expected. In September his mother died, and the military reassigned him to a routine War Department desk job in Washington. By then there were five children living in the house—Tommy, Nina, Jackie, Lee, and Yusha—with two still to come. Janet, Jr., was born in 1945, Jamie two years later. It was to Janet's credit that she somehow managed to accommodate so many disparate lives all thrown together under one roof.

The transition from New York to Washington and Newport, where Hugh Auchincloss owned a second ancestral home, Hammersmith Farm, proved less complicated than Janet had expected. She was relieved to have found a man she not only admired, but one who could also provide for her and her girls. Hugh Auchincloss had money and properties to spare, including boats, automobiles, servants, horses, paintings and all the other accoutrements of wealth and power. He belonged to the best clubs—Bailey's Beach and the Newport Country Club in Newport; the Metropolitan Club in Washington; the Chevy Chase Country Club in Chevy Chase, Maryland; the Knickerbocker Club in New York. He was on the A-list of Washington's most punctilious social arbiter, Rose Miriam, and regularly attended parties given by Laura Curtis, Pauline Davis, Virginia Baker, Gwen Cafritz and other top Capitol Hill hostesses. More important, he seemed to have many of the qualities Janet appreciated in a man; he was responsible, gentle, courtly and devoted. If he appeared a bit staid and set in his ways, nobody minded very much. He was known, for example, to repeat his favorite stories at stupefying length. There was the one about the train journey through Bulgaria when he was attacked by fleas and used itching powder instead of the proper flea powder. Then there were the codfish cakes, which he claimed were the true test of the *cordon-bleu* chef; he could do a lengthy monologue on codfish cakes. Even Janet found him tedious at times. Once when Jackie asked her mother, "What movie star does Uncle Hughdie remind you of?" Janet offered the name Harpo Marx—"except he's a little better than Harpo because he can say, 'Yes, dear.' "

Uncle Hughdie—Jackie's nickname for her stepfather—also tended to be a little absentminded on occasion, as when he emerged from his cabana at Bailey's Beach and belly flopped into the crowded swimming pool only to discover that while he had removed his clothing, he had forgotten to don his bathing suit.

His most discernible vice, perhaps his only vice, was an intense interest in pornography. Hugh Auchincloss owned a complete library of rare pornographic books, slides, films and manuals. This trove featured illustrated and photographic material on nearly every facet of human sexuality, including pederasty, sado-masochism, bondage, dominance, submission, homosexuality, bisexuality, transsexuality, bestiality and scatology. For years he frequented Washington's two main neon-lit "strips"—Ninth Street, N.W. and Fourteenth Street, N.W.—in search of sex-specialty shops that catered to his particular reading and viewing needs, spending a small fortune on sexually explicit books and films, "French" postcards and other forms of hard-to-find erotica. Ninth Street likewise offered a number of busy, high-priced bordellos whose clientele included some of the leading political figures of Washington. Hughdie became a familiar client in these establishments, pursuing the same wide range of interests among prostitutes that he did in pornography.

Hugh Auchincloss solved several problems which had beset Janet and her daughters, and helped them all to take a more relaxed and confident view of the world. Evidently Janet was ecstatic with her new marriage. Her sister, Winifred d'Olier, characterized Hugh Auchincloss as "one of the finest, most marvelous gentlemen you'd want to know. Compared to Black Jack Bouvier, he was an absolute saint."

No sooner had Jackie and Lee arrived at Hammersmith Farm than they were shipped off to spend the latter half of the summer with their father at East Hampton. Edie Beale recalled Jackie arriving without any summer clothes: "Janet had just remarried and hadn't yet had time to pack up Jackie's belongings. My mother went through the attic at Grey Gardens and pulled out all my old clothes and sent them to Lasata for Jackie. The poor darling wasn't exactly tickled at having to wear hand-me-downs, but her father had no intention of splurging on a new wardrobe."

According to John Davis's Kennedy family biography,* Jackie's father discovered a new romantic interest that summer, the young wife of a British army officer stationed in Washington and working at the Pentagon. The lady, whose identity Davis doesn't divulge, met Black Jack while visiting friends in East Hampton. Despite the presence of his daughters, Bouvier made no effort to

*See John H. Davis, *The Kennedys: Dynasty and Disaster,* pp. 192–193, 195–196.

conceal his attachment to the officer's wife. "I first became aware of her existence," writes Davis, "when, upon entering the men's section of the Bouvier cabana at the Maidstone Club one day, I beheld Uncle Jack entwined with this lovely lady on the floor of the shower room. Soon she became virtually a member of the family."

Within days, the married lady had moved into Black Jack's summer rental and was busy preparing meals and keeping house for Jack and his daughters. She attended Sunday brunches at Lasata. She became Jack Bouvier's steady companion at dinner parties and country club functions. The couple enjoyed shocking staid East Hamptonites by putting on public displays of their mutual infatuation. As John Davis describes it, "They walked arm-in-arm, they held hands, they hugged and kissed unabashedly, they made love wherever they found themselves: in the Bouvier cabana, at Jack's house, behind the dunes." What Jackie, at the impressionable age of thirteen, made of all this can only be surmised. But one can safely assume that she returned to Merrywood at the end of her vacation in a state of confusion.

Black Jack and his paramour remained together until the following June, when the British officer and his wife returned to England. Several months after her departure, John Davis tells us, she surprised Jack with the news that she had given birth to twins, a boy and a girl, "reminding Jack she hadn't been living with her husband nine months before their birth, she had been living with him." Black Jack was the father, but the lady and her husband had decided to raise the children as their own.

Jack Bouvier had neither the inclination nor the finances to debate the issue. Although he never laid eyes on the children, other members of the Bouvier family did, including Jackie, whose curiosity would not rest until she saw them for herself. During a brief 1949 trip to England, she visited her father's former sweetheart and the two children he had purportedly sired. Jackie later noted in a letter to her father that the boy and girl looked remarkably like him.

The possibility, indeed the probability, that she had a half-brother and half-sister living in England filled Jackie with horror. According to John Davis, she became particularly concerned in the mid-1950s when John Kennedy began seriously to consider running for President. Jackie understood the effect that such a disclosure might have on her husband's political future and decided at all costs to keep the facts secret.

"Nobody mentioned the twins until I revealed their existence in my Kennedy book," said John Davis. "And by then they were both dead, victims of a macabre coincidence. The boy met a tragic and untimely death in an automobile accident in Morocco, the girl was mysteriously murdered while living in Trinidad."

In September 1942, Jackie returned from her summer vacation in East Hampton and moved into Merrywood. The Georgian-style, ivy-covered brick mansion stood on 46 verdant acres high on the Virginia shore across the Potomac from Washington, and boasted a host of luxurious features: an Olympic-size swimming pool (its bath house modeled after a Swiss chalet), indoor badminton court, two stables, riding paths, brooks, ravines, hills and valleys, four-car garage (with automatic car-washing apparatus), eight bedrooms, banquet-style kitchen (equipped to serve three hundred or more), wine cellar, separate quarters over the garage for the servants. There were so many bathrooms that one visitor lightheartedly suggested the house had originally been built for the Crane family of Chicago, among the first and foremost plumbing supply manufacturers in the United States. There were also many impressive public rooms, including a semi-circular game room at one end of the house that Nina Gore, Janet's predecessor, decorated with round furniture and used for bridge parties. Janet's top priority on becoming Mrs. Auchincloss was to redecorate both Merrywood and Hammersmith Farm, and to this end she retained the services of New York interior decorator Elisabeth Draper.

"Janet brimmed with energy," said Mrs. Draper. "She was a perfectionist, very selective, very meticulous in everything she did, from the way she sat to the way she wiped her lips after a meal. She was very attentive to detail and had a light touch, which helped when it came to redecorating Merrywood. Hughdie's former wives had filled it with thick carpeting and hunks of Gothic furniture. The windows were mullioned and covered with shutters, the walls lined with dark wood paneling. Janet retained the earlier formality but made it far more liveable.

"The best thing about Merrywood was the sound of

the Potomac below. There were large rocks down there which gave just enough ripple to the river. You could hear it most clearly from the main third-floor bedroom, the room Jackie chose as her own, a low-beamed boudoir about twenty feet by twelve feet, which sat a bit apart from the rest of the house."

There was another room across the hall from Jackie's bedroom which had been occupied by Gore Vidal, whose departure at age sixteen coincided roughly with Jackie's arrival. Of his six years at Merrywood, Vidal has said: "It was a peaceful . . . life, a bit Henry Jamesian, a world of deliberate quietude removed from the twentieth-century tension. It was a life that gave total security, but not much preparation for the real world."*

Although they didn't come face to face until 1949, Vidal left behind several long-sleeved dress shirts which Jackie wore while riding. At first, horseback riding was the only family activity in which she took part. She spent many of her early days at Merrywood alone in the privacy of her bedroom expressing her lonely thoughts and feelings of solitude in poems and drawings that she sent to her father in New York or committed to sketchbooks.

She also wrote her father letters (which he in turn shared with other members of the family) describing some of the problems she faced in adapting to her new surroundings. She contended that Uncle Hughdie had no sense of humor and complained of having to stand at attention before meals in order to recite, prayer-like, the Auchincloss motto which began, "Obedience to the Unenforceable," and ran on for what seemed hours. She would apparently recite the motto in an almost inaudible whisper but would then be forced to repeat it—louder and with greater conviction.

Another Auchincloss peccadillo was Hughdie's parsimony. During the winter months, he insisted on keeping

---

*Merrywood served as the setting for Gore Vidal's novel *Washington D.C.* (1967), where it was called Laurel House. Regarding Jackie, Vidal told *Playboy* Magazine (June 1969): "I was unaware of her until the Forties, when I began to get reports from friends visiting Washington that she had introduced herself to them as my sister. I was, pre-Kennedy, the family notable. In 1949, we finally met and I allowed her claim to be my sister to stand. Anyway, I certainly know what her childhood was like, since it was pretty much the one I had endured."

all the frozen foods and ice cream on long tables set up on the back porch of Merrywood. That way he could save money by shutting off the deep freeze. But it was imperative to remember that when the temperature shot above a certain point the food had to be returned to the deep freeze and the deep freeze turned back on. When the temperature dropped again, the process was reversed.

Besides writing to her father, Jackie sent frequent notes to her grandfather, the Major, expressing a vague sense of displacement and complaining about Holton-Arms, the conservative girls' day school, then in downtown Washington, where she had been enrolled for eighth grade. She found the other girls at school unfriendly, the curriculum bland and uninspiring.

Nor did she care for the social dance classes her mother made her take in Washington with Miss Shippen, famous among well-bred Maryland and Virginia girls. Jackie felt she had mastered all the social etiquette and dance steps she would ever need; her mother felt otherwise. Janet forced her to take not only the classes but to attend the dance parties for boys and girls Miss Shippen gave during vacations.

For the 1942 Christmas party, Jackie donned her first adult evening gown: blue taffeta, full-skirted, puff-sleeved. Gold kid slippers completed the costume and, as her feet had outgrown the rest of her, she appended a brief caption to a photograph of herself that she placed in one of her mother's family albums: "Jacqueline's first evening dress. This was lovely blue taffeta and I had a pair of gold track shoes and a really chic feather cut."

In the summer of 1943, Jackie spent her first uninterrupted stretch at Hammersmith Farm in Newport. Hughdie explained that his family had built the estate in 1887 not in the fashionable Bellevue Avenue with its imposing lineup of marble mansions but on ninety-seven acres of outlying farmland because "the Auchinclosses didn't care to follow in the footsteps of the Vanderbilts and Astors; we wanted to forge our own identity."

The main house contained twenty-eight rooms, thirteen fireplaces, a wraparound brick terrace and an elevator. It stood at the end of a long driveway, its tiered roof crowned with gables and cupolas, its views comprised of glistening Narragansett Bay with its yachting and sailboat activity on one side, perfectly manicured lawns and emerald pastures on the other. On the farm were stables for work horses and ponies, barns for bulls and Hughdie's Black Angus cows, pens and coops for sheep, goats and chickens.

Inside, the house was sunny, spacious, filled with plants and flowers from the formal gardens scattered about the property. The furniture was sturdy and old-fashioned. Animal heads ornamented the walls. In the high-ceilinged Deck Room, so named because it looked out on water and resembled the deck of a ship, an array of modern, Oriental and animal-skin rugs and carpets covered the floor, while a stuffed pelican frozen in simulated flight was suspended from the ceiling. In the downstairs rooms and corridors, the walls were white, the carpets red. To match this color combination, Jackie suggested that henceforth all family dogs should be black: they were.

As at Merrywood, Jackie staked out an isolated bedroom on the third floor. It faced the bay and at night she could hear the foghorns blowing at sea and feel the cool summer winds. Her mother, aided by Elisabeth Draper, decorated the room in yellow wallpaper topped with a hand-painted flower frieze bordering the white-washed ceiling. The cane and white wood furniture—desk, dressing table, night table, bureau, bookshelf and rocking chair—made the room seem quaint and feminine. There were twin beds with matching cane inlaid headboards and a small shelf for Jackie's childhood collection of miniature porcelain animals.

Elisabeth Draper recalled that when Hugh Auchincloss inherited Hammersmith Farm from his mother, "The house wasn't in good condition. It was run down, and it wasn't easy to find help to put the place together. Hammersmith Farm had once accommodated a staff that included sixteen house servants and thirty-two gardeners and farm hands. But in 1943 they were on war footing and only a few of the workers who used to look after the property had survived both the draft and the economy drive. There were no men around and the upkeep on Hammersmith Farm was prohibitive. But they refused to sell it. Hugh Auchincloss had been born in the house and was determined to die there when his time came. So they decided to renovate and refurbish and care for it themselves, using whatever materials and furniture were at hand.

"Most of the wood furniture pieces were inherited. They were in effect their own antiques. All the closets and storage rooms had to be searched to see what 'leftovers' could be salvaged. Janet's main objective in redecorating and refinishing the house was to retain the sentiment of the old country farm. It had a country farm atmosphere inside as well as out. Hammersmith Farm couldn't have been occupied by artificial people. There was nothing ostentatious or phony about it."

Because of the shortage of wartime manpower, Janet set out to reduce the number of formal gardens at Hammersmith Farm, including two of five greenhouses on the property. She divided the remaining farm labor among the children. Since Hammersmith Farm supplied the local naval base with milk and eggs, Yusha inherited the job of milking the cows and Jackie daily fed more than two thousand chickens. Everybody helped to clip the hedges, trim the flower beds, prune the fruit trees and mow the lawns. Wartime restrictions limited the number of telephones in the house to one. They kept the phone in the basement, and the girls worked in shifts answering it.

Jackie's latest batch of letters to her father reflected her quickly evolving sensibility. Where several months earlier she had registered only complaints, she had recently come to grips with her new surroundings. She enjoyed the responsibilities that had been thrust upon her as well as the advantages available as a result of her mother's remarriage into a family of privilege. She reported taking several long hikes with Hughdie. She mentioned the pleasure she derived from all her new siblings. Although she missed the hue and cry of New York, she found the rural settings of Merrywood and Hammersmith Farm completely relaxing. She had even begun to enjoy Holton-Arms and had uncovered an inspiring teacher at school in the person of Miss Helen Shearman. Miss Shearman taught Latin, and, much to her own surprise, Jackie "fell in love with the subject."

While it seemed almost inevitable that Jackie should come to appreciate her new situation, her father had difficulty accepting this fact. He turned to the bottle for solace, feeling abandoned by his daughters. He blamed Janet for their desertion.

"It drove him crazy," said Louis Ehret. "I remember

dropping by his apartment one evening and finding him stretched out on his sofa. He was wearing nothing but blue boxer shorts and a pair of black patent leather shoes. He'd been drinking martinis all day at the Stock Exchange Luncheon Club, and he looked awful.

"Somewhere along the line he'd developed that famous Wall Street saying—'Take a loss with Auchincloss'—and although he kept repeating it that evening, his real anger was directed at Janet. It seems that at Janet's subtle prompting Jackie and Lee decided to spend Christmas of 1943 with the Auchinclosses in Virginia. This marked the first time they hadn't joined their father and the Bouviers at Lasata for the traditional festivities. Throughout the holiday season Black Jack had been extremely subdued and even the Major, although there were many other grandchildren around, sorely missed Jackie and Lee.

"I sat there that night—this was early January 1944—watching him twist and turn on the sofa, listening to his truculent rant against Hugh and Janet, especially Janet, how she'd 'stolen the kiddies' from under his nose and 'conned poor Hugh into her conjugal bed.'

"When he drank too much, a darker, violent side of his personality tended to emerge. He began talking about World War II and about 'this kike and that kike.' He was anti-Semitic. It was a kind of suburban prejudice, because he was also anti-Irish ('this mick and that mick'), anti-Italian ('this wop and that wop'), even anti-French ('this frog and that frog'). When he drank he hated everyone, including himself.

"When he finished, I pointed to his head and told him he ought to see somebody because something had obviously gone awry.

" 'There's nothing wrong with me,' he said. 'It's the world that has problems.'

" 'I don't doubt that,' I told him. 'But you need help.' "

It came as no surprise to Ehret to learn several months later that Black Jack had voluntarily committed himself to the alcohol rehabilitation program at Silver Hill, the same sanatorium where Bud Bouvier had sought refuge sixteen years earlier. With its fine Hitchcock furniture, grass tennis courts, lush lawn, nearby lake and white pine woods, Silver Hill had the relaxed, exclusive air and overall appearance of an expensive country club. The patients were predominantly middle-aged, neurotic and well-to-do. A single room in the main house cost a thousand dollars per month, excluding medication and psychiatric care. Black Jack spent eight weeks at Silver Hill in 1944 and was again a patient in 1946 and 1947. Despite these and several other concerted efforts to reduce his drinking, he never completely beat the habit.

In 1944, with two years' study at Holton-Arms behind her, Jackie enrolled as a boarding student at Miss Porter's School in Farmington, Connecticut. Farmington (as the school is usually called) hadn't changed much from what Miss Sarah Porter, a girls' school headmistress in the classic New England mold, intended when she founded it in 1843. Despite the founder's parochial background, the school had always catered to the rich and worldly, to girls whose parents wanted them to graduate polished but also educated.

The atmosphere at Farmington in Jackie's day was distinctly high-minded, correct, superior, competitive, snobbish, cold and arbitrary. The all-girl student body was required to take Friday afternoon tea with the teachers, and to attend Sunday-night lectures by visiting scholars in the school chapel. On Saturdays, the older girls were permitted male "callers"—Farmington girls usually dated boys from Harvard, Yale and other Ivy League colleges—but the callers weren't allowed to enter the dormitories. Nor were the girls permitted to leave the school grounds during term time without special permission. There was no smoking, no drinking, no cardplaying. There was even a regulation concerning the type of fiction the girls were allowed to read in their spare time. They were not permitted to peruse popular romantic novels, or "penny dreadfuls" as they were known in the women's magazines of an earlier epoch.

Those who attended Miss Porter's with Jackie remember her in her first year as a temperamental, standoffish, rather shy teenager who liked to take long walks by herself around the periphery of the campus, an area called "The Loop" which was lined with old houses and tall oak trees. One of the houses along this route belonged to Wilmarth and Annie Lewis, Jackie's Auchincloss relations. Wilmarth, also known as "Lefty," was a celebrated Walpole and Blake scholar. Annie, an alumna of Miss Porter's, owned a valuable collection of eighteenth-century prints. Jackie liked to visit the couple and borrow art books from their private library. Now and again she brought a friend along and they would stay for dinner, preferring home-cooked food to the mediocre fare served at school.

The dormitories for the then approximately hundred-and-fifty girls at Farmington consisted of plain old-fashioned three- and four-story houses, very much like the private homes located along The Loop. During her first year, Jackie shared a comfortable, cheerily wallpapered room with Susan Norton, a debutante-to-be from a well-to-do New England family. Also in Jackie's class were her cousin, Shella Scott, and former Chapin classmate Nancy Tuckerman ("Tucky"), whose parents, Roger and Betty Tuckerman, had been friendly with the Bouviers in East Hampton. While not as intellectual as Jackie, Tucky shared Jackie's sense of humor. She was reserved, tactful, and knew how to keep a secret. As Jackie's roommate during the next two years she would have to keep many secrets; in time she would become Jackie's closest and most devoted female friend.

"At age fifteen my cousin was prissy, bookish and bossy," said Edie Beale, also a former graduate of Farmington. "She wrote Mother long letters from school examining in great depth every course they made her take. I only saw her once during this period—we were both shopping for shoes in New York. Jackie was too much, *de trop* in French—a perfectly horrible child. That's why her classmates nicknamed her Jacqueline Borgia.

"Jackie always knew how to get what she wanted. She was a master manipulator. Her greatest concern seemed to be money, primarily because she didn't have any. Her stepfather had money and her stepbrothers and stepsisters were well looked after. But Jackie, although she grew up in luxurious surroundings, depended on the $50 monthly allowance her father sent to school. At a place like Farmington, where great wealth was taken for granted, fifty dollars didn't go very far. If you didn't board your own horse at school, you were considered an outcast. This created problems for Jackie because neither her mother nor her stepfather would pay the extra $25 a month to board Danseuse at Farmington. And her father couldn't be expected to fork out more than he already did. So Jackie wrote to Granddad asking if he would stand treat and, by way of a bribe, enclosed copies of her latest poems. He sent the money and the horse followed."

Jackie devised still another scheme involving Danseuse. After the mare arrived at Farmington, it developed that Jackie had no blanket for the horse and no money to buy one. She resolved the problem by writing her mother that Danseuse "is wearing a stolen blanket which I snitched from another horse." A check for a new horse blanket arrived from Merrywood in the next mail.

Among Jackie's fondest Farmington memories were the weekend visits by her father. Miche Bouvier, who sometimes accompanied Black Jack, recalled Jackie's classmates "practically swooning at the sight of her handsome father. They were convinced he looked like Clark Gable playing Rhett Butler in the movie version of *Gone With the Wind*. His skin was so dark that at least one student thought he was black. But in general they just mooned over him, and although this pleased Jackie it also embarrassed her."

Tradition at Farmington demanded that visiting parents take their daughters for steak luncheon at the Elm Tree Inn, followed by an afternoon of school-sponsored activities. Black Jack once partnered Jackie in a father-daughter tennis tournament. He drove up to watch her compete in the Farmington horse shows. He even subscribed to *Salmagundy,* the student newspaper, because his daughter was a staff member and contributed occasional cartoons and poems.

He particularly enjoyed watching her perform in school plays. She joined "The Farmington Players," a student theater group that staged a Christmas tableau and two full-length plays each year. In her junior year she played the male role of Mr. Bingsley in a theatrical production of Jane Austen's novel *Pride and Prejudice*. At other times she performed in the so-called "germans," song-and-dance spectaculars that were a specialty at Farmington. At the end of her junior year, she both wrote and performed in the farewell german, choosing as her theme that of a circus coming to town. The presentation featured Jackie's favorite childhood symbol—a circus queen, this one drawn across stage in a chariot while holding aloft a maypole around which danced a corps of gaily costumed circus clowns and ballerinas.

"She made good use of her acting ability and flair for

the dramatic," said Lily Pulitzer, who attended Farmington at approximately the same time as Jackie. "The way she walked and moved derived from an interest in the stage. She also seemed highly intellectual. I never saw her without a stack of books in hand, even when she wasn't studying. I had the distinct impression that in those days she preferred books to boys. She didn't date very much at Farmington. When she went out it was usually in a small group, or with boys whose parents were friendly with her parents. She joked about winding up like Miss Shaw, one of the school's many spinsterish housemothers—'unwed and unloved.' "

For others at Farmington, Jackie seemed "the perfect nonconformist." She rebelled against school rules as well as social mores. She smoked cigarettes in her dormitory room, filched freshly baked cookies from the school kitchen, wore conspicuous hairstyles and too much makeup to school functions, on one occasion dumped chocolate pie upside down in a much-despised teacher's lap. She even dressed differently from her classmates, eschewing the cashmere sweaters, plaid skirts and white poplin raincoats so popular at school, in favor of nondescript, less conservative skirts and all-season capes. Whatever the latest fashion trend, she could be counted on to dress in defiance of it.

Her most daring and perhaps rebellious act occurred when she agreed to pose for a classmate's camera; the resultant series of snapshots showed Jackie with bared shoulder, lascivious pout, head thrown back and wavy dark hair spilling over an eye in imitation of screen siren Veronica Lake.

When one of these snapshots fell into the hands of Ward L. Johnson, Farmington's headmaster, he notified Jackie's mother expressing dismay at how anyone as bright as Jackie (she maintained an "A–" average at Farmington) could behave so poorly. Jackie reacted by embellishing her letters home with irreverently comic sketches of the headmaster. She made the mistake of mailing one of her illustrated letters to her Bouvier grandfather, who responded immediately with a note of reproach: "I discern in you more than passing evidence of leadership, but before leading others we must guide ourselves. . . . Don't be pretentious or labor under a false impression of indispensability. To do so spells the prig, male or female. . . ."

When Jackie graduated from Miss Porter's in June 1947, her entry in the class yearbook reflected an undiminished sense of rebellion. Next to "ambition in life," the graduate wrote: "Not to be a housewife." As much as anything, the statement seemed to be directed against her mother, against everything her mother stood for and believed in. Jacqueline had no desire to be a homemaker or clubwoman, concerned only with outward appearances and the mordant rituals of high society. The material reality of that way of life might have held promise for other graduates of Miss Porter's, but not for Jackie.

Eilene Slocum, a close friend of Janet Auchincloss and a member of one of Newport's most formidable clans, observed that Jackie and her mother were always quite different: "They were different and yet Janet had a greater influence than has generally been acknowledged. Janet's drive for excellence rubbed off on Jacqueline. They were different insofar as Jacqueline had far greater aspirations than her mother. She never wanted to be an ordinary woman or lead an ordinary life, in ordinary circumstances among ordinary people. She would never have been content merely to raise a family and attend fund-raising affairs. From the beginning she was enormously ambitious. In her way one of the most ambitious young people I've ever known."

Noreen Drexel, whose cabana at Bailey's Beach Club in Newport adjoined the Auchincloss cabana and whose husband, John Drexel, was related to Black Jack Bouvier, agreed that Jackie "even when young gave the impression of a person going places. She had a uniqueness. She was intellectually ahead of herself. She wrote stories for children and then read them to the children in the neighborhood, my own children included. You had the sense that she could have been an excellent teacher or perhaps an important author. The only future I would never have predicted for her is First Lady. She didn't have the personality that goes with the job."

5

One of the few enduring traditions that high society retained after World War II was the Coming Out party, supposedly the presentation or introduction of one's daughter to one's friends, and hence to society. Considering her apparent reservations when it came to emulating her mother's life-style, it seemed odd that Jackie should express interest in her own Coming Out party. Yet it was Jackie who approached Uncle Hughdie and asked whether she could make her debut at Hammersmith Farm. Hugh Auchincloss readily agreed, and Jackie's mother made the arrangements. What made the party unique was that Janet planned it as a tea, an afternoon dance reception for three hundred, and scheduled it for the same day in June that Jamie Auchincloss, born five months earlier, was christened at Newport's Trinity Church. The engraved invitations summoned guests to the Auchincloss residence "To meet Miss Jacqueline Lee Bouvier and Master Jamie Lee Auchincloss."

The second stage of Jackie's debut took place in July with a formal dinner-dance at the Clambake Club, an old and venerable Newport institution. This time Jackie shared the honors with Rose Grosvenor, one of three daughters of the Theodore Grosvenors, Newport neighbors and distant relations of the Auchinclosses. The Club, perched atop rocks overlooking the Atlantic, had been festooned with hundreds of flowers cut from the Auchincloss and Grosvenor gardens, the terrace (used for dancing) strung with strand after strand of tiny blue lights.

As they stood in the receiving line together, Rose Grosvenor, blond, blue-eyed, dimpled, made an ideal foil for tanned, glowing Jacqueline. Rose wore the more expensive outfit, a white Dior original, but it was Jackie's simple frock (the same she'd worn to the Hammersmith Farm tea reception) that the newspapers dubbed "a designer's dream" and described as "a lovely white tulle gown with an off-the-shoulder neckline and bouffant skirt." The "dream," Jackie admitted years later, came off a New York department store rack and cost less than fifty-nine dollars.

The true sartorial marvel that evening, however, turned out to be Lee Bouvier, who at fourteen already possessed a woman's figure and the desire to flaunt it. Sylvia Whitehouse Blake, one of Jackie's closest Newport friends, noted that "Jackie didn't care a whit about fashion in those days. She and I ran around in shorts and sneakers all summer. The only time we dressed up was during Tennis Week, Newport's social highlight, but even then we weren't exactly your typical *Vogue* fashion-plates. Lee, on the other hand, shorter than Jackie but more rounded with a classically attractive heart-shaped face and tiny, delicate features, never left the house unless dressed for Ascot."

Lee's attire the night of her sister's Coming Out party seemed sharply at odds with her usual. She wore a tight, strapless gown of pink satin, sprinkled generously with rhinestones and set off with elbow-length black satin mitts, fingerless, tethered by a pointed strap over the middle finger. Amidst the prim and proper throng of young Newport socialites, Lee stood out. Janet Auchincloss blanched at the sight of her daughter's outfit. Jackie, also shocked at first, found it amusing once she calmed down. The stag line converged on Lee *en masse*. It marked the first and last public occasion on which she would upstage her older sister.

Later Jacqueline occasionally borrowed Lee's "siren suit," as both called it, and claimed to be wearing it when Igor Cassini, the Hearst gossip columnist,* named her the year's Number One Debutante, an honor he bestowed upon Lee in 1950, the year of her debut at the Junior Assemblies. Igor's allusion to Jackie read as follows:

*Igor Cassini, known to his friends as "Ghighi," had taken over the Cholly Knickerbocker column from Maury Paul. Appearing daily and Sunday in the Hearst flagship, the *New York Journal-American*, he was syndicated in hundreds of newspapers around the country.

America is a country of traditions. Every four years we elect a president, every two years our congressmen. And every year a new Queen of Debutantes is crowned . . . The Queen Deb of the year for 1947 is Jacqueline Bouvier, a regal brunette who has classic features and the daintiness of Dresden porcelain. She has poise, is softspoken and intelligent, everything the leading debutante should be. Her background is strictly "Old Guard." . . . Jacqueline is now studying at Vassar. You don't have to read a batch of press clippings to be aware of her qualities.

Igor Cassini's assessment appeared faulty in at least two respects: Jackie was neither particularly dainty, nor was her background "strictly" Old Guard, unless one overlooked the fact that she was in name a Bouvier. Nevertheless, to be crowned Deb of the Year in 1947, before the advent of coast-to-coast television, was tantamount to becoming the high priestess of café society, a focus and target for dozens of news-hungry media gossips. It meant instant stardom and recognition, and in some cases a good deal of unwanted attention.

"I named a Queen Debutante every year," said Igor Cassini. "I usually tried to choose one of the prettier, flashier society girls. Jackie wasn't flashy, and she didn't make her debut at any of the classic cotillions, such as the Christmas Ball, the International Ball or the Junior League Ball. I had seen her and met her briefly but I didn't come to know her until her marriage to Jack Kennedy. Yet I felt something very special in her, an understated elegance which she later lost but at the time still had. Although shy and extremely private, she stood out in a crowd. She had that certain something. I don't know precisely what word to use to describe this quality: beauty, charm, charisma, style, any or all of the above. Whatever it happened to be, she had it."

Jackie's selection as Debutante of the Year helped stimulate her until-then dormant social life but did little to endear her to her freshman classmates at Vassar, many of whom resented and simultaneously envied the title. Jackie did her best to downplay both the accolade and the attitude it engendered. But for the better part of a year the gossip and society columnists continued to write about her. In December 1947, Elsa Maxwell noted in her column: "Jacqueline Bouvier . . . is being besieged with offers of all sorts and demands for interviews and pictures—but her conservative family is staying away from all publicity." Walter Winchell exclaimed: "Jacqueline Bouvier's poise! What a gal! She's the beautiful daughter of Mrs. Hugh Auchincloss. Blessed with the looks of a fairy-tale princess, Jacqueline doesn't know the meaning of the word snob!"

Charlotte Curtis, the future writer and *New York Times* editor, entered Vassar a year ahead of Jackie but later lived next door to her in the same dormitory. "We were both at Main Hall," she recalled. "We saw each other all the time. I knew about the Deb of the Year title, but I don't remember her ever bringing it up. I think it rather embarrassed her. She certainly had no desire to become another Brenda Frazier, the socialite whose Coming Out party was her one claim to fame.

"Unlike Brenda Frazier and others of her ilk, Jackie had brains. She also had a great deal of poise for somebody so young. On the other hand, she didn't seem particularly thrilled with Vassar. She used to refer to it as 'that goddamn Vassar.' There was such a lot of intellectual and political ferment on campus what with it being 1948 and an election year. Vassar was a wonderful institution for that sort of thing. It was an extremely open college and one that tolerated all different kinds of ideas.

"It was Truman versus Dewey, but Henry Wallace was also running for President and there was a good deal of talk about Communism. There were two student newspapers—the conservative *Vassar Chronicle* and the liberal *Vassar Miscellany News*—and the student body and faculty were evenly divided between them. Jackie with her social background was perhaps too sophisticated and blasé to be drawn into the dogfight. Also, it was a time when she had just discovered an interest in men and dating, not in the name or political party of the next President of the United States."

Charlotte Curtis's roommate at Main Hall was Selwa Showker, the future "Lucky" Roosevelt, long-time journalist and Chief of Protocol during the Reagan Administration. "I knew Jackie and very much liked her at Vassar," said Mrs. Roosevelt. "She had a quality of real innocence. Even then she had that breathless way of talking.

It wasn't a put-on—it's how she spoke. She also had this wonderful little sense of humor. There was a twinkle in her eye. I suppose the tragedies she experienced in later years took it away, but she had it then. She possessed great beauty. I don't think she's as beautiful now, also because of the tragedies. But as a girl she had natural beauty and very exotic coloring.

"In addition to her other qualities, Jackie was extremely modest. I remember when we received our grades, I would say, 'Oh, Jackie, I got an "A–" in political science and an "A–" in economics.' Jackie didn't say much. And I said to myself, 'Oh, dear, she probably received a poor report and doesn't want to say so in front of anybody.' So as we were walking along, I said, 'Jackie, did you not receive a very good report?' She said, 'Oh, it was all right.' It turned out she made Dean's List and had straight 'A's.' Here she'd done much better than any of us yet hadn't said a word.

"I don't think any reporter or biographer has ever succeeded in capturing Jackie's essence. There's an elusive quality about her, an inexplicable shyness. She doesn't reveal herself and was always very protective of her inner self. I consider myself somewhat sensitive and I think I have insights about her from those days that have never left me, but it would be presumptuous to say that I knew her better than anyone else did, despite the fact that she visited my dorm room practically every night. And obviously when she attended Vassar she was less protective of herself than in subsequent years when she became a public figure.

"I know certain things about her. She was very intellectually curious. For example, she constantly asked me about my family. I was of Lebanese extraction and had grown up in a small town in Tennessee. These aspects of my life fascinated Jackie. She wanted to know all about how my father stowed away on a boat as a young boy to come to America. She wanted to know about Lebanon. I had pictures of my family in my room and Jackie would scrutinize the faces and ask questions about the various members of my family, almost like a reporter gathering material for a story. She had a way of focusing on a person that left one dazzled; it was most flattering.

"The most disconcerting quality about Jackie was her two-headed personality. On the one hand she had this almost starlike quality—when she entered a room you couldn't help but notice her, she was such an exquisite creature. At the same time, she seemed so very private. She kept a photograph of her father in her room, and we all used to go in and say, 'Oh, what a handsome man!' We all thought he looked just dreamy. But she never spoke about him, never even mentioned her parents' divorce. She refused to talk about the boys in her life. She dated frequently. You never saw her around campus on weekends. But she never named names, never disclosed herself.

"It seemed strange because the rest of us would talk about our dates. We were all in and out of love a hundred thousand times. Every guy we met we thought, 'This is it!' Of course it wasn't. But you discussed it with your friends, you hashed it out and compared notes. Maybe we talked about it so freely because we were innocent. Our mores and attitude toward morality predated the so-called sexual revolution. We were basically naive."

Jackie's Deb of the Year laurels gained her a considerable social following at Vassar. Young gentlemen flocked to Poughkeepsie, seventy-eight miles up the Hudon River from New York City, to see and meet this newly crowned glamour girl. On weekends she traveled to the leading men's colleges or went to an occasional debutante affair in such society exurbs as Glen Cove, Rye, or Greenwich, Connecticut. Or she stayed with her father in New York, met her beaux under the Biltmore clock, fox-trotted through subscription dances at the Plaza and St. Regis with a beardless stag line known for decades as "the St. Grottlesex set." Other times she journeyed back home to Merrywood to visit her mother and stepfather, where she would invariably be joined by Yusha Auchincloss, then an upperclassman at Yale.

"She adopted me as a friend and confidant, a kind of big brother," said Yusha. "She confided in me more than in any of her girlfriends. We corresponded regularly and when we were together at Merrywood or Hammersmith Farm I ran errands for her, drove her around, introduced her to my friends, fixed her up with schoolmates. It was a transitory period in her life. She liked playing the field, meeting a variety of types—varsity swimmers at Yale,

Harvard pre-med candidates, up-and-coming New York lawyers and stockbrokers."

Although Jackie went to parties and dated frequently, she later classed many of her college-aged escorts as "beetle-browed bores" and maintained she could never have married any of them, "not because of them, but because of their lives."

Despite her refusal to focus on anyone in particular, Jackie proved proficient at the dating game. Jonathan Isham, a student at Yale when Jackie went to Vassar and one of her more frequent escorts, suggested that she treated dating very much as a game of skill, a means of sharpening her social abilities: "She was so much brighter and better-read than the people around her that she sublimated it. She sometimes came across as a wide-eyed, sappy type. It was pure defense. When I'd take her to the Yale Bowl, and it'd be fourth down and five to go, she'd say to me, 'Oh, why are they kicking the ball?' I'd say, 'Come on, Jackie, we'll have none of that.' She wasn't a dissembler—I don't want to imply that. But she was and I think probaby still is quite fey. Jack Kennedy used that word to describe her, and I believe it fits."

Peter Reed, a friend of Jackie's from Newport, acknowledged that she "enjoyed playing the ingenue. It was her way of protecting herself. She had a reputation for being a bit tight-assed around men. She talked a lot about animals and antiques. But everybody liked her. She had a delightful, offbeat sense of humor.

"I used to take her to dances at Bailey's Beach and at the Newport Country Club. I also dated her several times on the college circuit. There was a ridiculous rumor going around that I'd bedded down with her. I wish it were true. It would have made a nice memento. But it isn't. You couldn't get to first base with Jackie.

Columbus "Chris" O'Donnell, former director of Resorts International, Atlantic City, N.J., also recalled Jackie from her college days: "My sister, Nuala, wife of Senator Claiborne Pell of Rhode Island, used to be quite friendly with Jackie. We all were. I dated her on occasion but always very informally.

"Although she went out with men, I'd have to classify her as a loner. She didn't run with the gang. She was an unusual girl—very selective, otherworldly, good-looking, bright, impossible to know.

"Her future husband, Jack Kennedy, was a notorious womanizer. But Jackie was never sexually adventuresome. The minute you turned into her driveway after a date, she'd tell the taxicab driver to hold the meter. 'Hold your meter, driver,' You knew you weren't getting past the front door. And you were lucky to get a peck on the cheek."

At first when she started dating, Jackie's father took the matter lightly. His early letters to her at Vassar reflect an attitude of gentle, but good-natured caution:

> I suppose it won't be long until I lose you to some funny looking "gink," who you think is wonderful because he is so romantic looking in the evening and wears his mother's pearl earrings for dress-shirt buttons, because he loves her so. . . . However, perhaps you'll use your head and wait until you are at least twenty-one.

But soon, as Jackie demonstrated a preference for passing her weekends at Yale or Princeton rather than in New York with her father, his letters became more demanding. On one occasion, after spending the weekend at Yale and missing Sunday night curfew at Vassar, Jackie received an angry missive from her father that began: "A woman can have wealth and beauty and brains, but without a reputation she has nothing." Subsequent notes warned of the necessity of "playing hard to get" and of "not giving in." Citing his personal experience as evidence, Black Jack wrote that the more a woman refused his advances, the more attracted to her he felt; conversely, he lost respect for the damsel the instant she relented.

Besides admonishing her on the perils of moral impropriety, he expressed disappointment in Jackie's failure to make Daisy Chain, Vassar's honorary society for "Big Women on Campus," placing the blame on her lack of involvement in school activities. He suggested she spend less time in company with potential suitors and more time in school, taking advantage of the college's many opportunities.

Jackie pointed out that, despite her weekends away from school, she had made Dean's List, earning her highest grades in two of Vassar's most difficult courses—

Florence Lovell's History of Religion and Helen Sandison's lecture series on Shakespeare. For the latter she had committed to memory the entire text of *Antony and Cleopatra*, which she promised to recite during her next visit with her father. She also offered to help him redecorate his East Side apartment and apparently complied by going to Bloomingdale's in New York and charging hundreds of dollars' worth of fabrics and draperies to her father's account.

The death of Jackie's Bouvier grandfather in January 1948, following complications from a prostate operation the summer before, gave rise to new confrontations. The Major's last will and testament contained some unpleasant surprises, particularly for Black Jack who received no inheritance whatsoever, his accrued loans canceling his share of the estate. The Major's British-born mistress, on the other hand, received an outright bequest of $35,000. The largest legacies went to the twins, Maude and Michelle, in the form of stocks, bonds and the deed to Lasata, which they later sold rather than pay maintenance and upkeep on the property. Edith Beale, least well off in the family, received a trust fund worth $65,000, with Black Jack appointed chief trustee. Each grandchild, Jacqueline and Lee included, inherited $3,000 in trust.

Black Jack's management of his sister's trust fund led to conflict on all fronts. Edith and Edie Beale soon accused him of a variety of sins—losing capital by making a series of poor investments on their behalf, reducing the principal of their inheritance by gambling it away at the racetrack, misappropriating their money for his personal use.* Janet Auchincloss also entered the fray, demanding that her former husband invest Jackie's and Lee's funds in U.S. Treasury Bills rather than in stocks or securities.

While her elders hashed it out (Janet eventually had her way), Jackie accepted an invitation to spend July and

*According to Edie Beale, Black Jack reduced the principal of her mother's inheritance from $65,000 to $58,000. Her brother, Bouvier Beale, maintains that Black Jack replaced the difference and defends the Major's appointment of Black Jack as Edith's trustee: "Grandfather had no faith in my mother's ability to handle her own finances. He was right to question her abilities. She went through

August (1948) with three friends on a tour of Europe. Two of Jackie's companions that summer, Helen and Judy Bowdoin, were stepdaughters of Edward F. Foley, Jr., then Under Secretary of the Treasury. The fourth member of the group was Julia Bissell, of Baltimore. Helen Shearman, Jackie's former Latin teacher at The Holton-Arms School, agreed to chaperone the girls on the trip.

Helen Bowdoin (today Mrs. Helen Bowdoin Spaulding) still sees Jackie on occasion and recalled vividly the circumstances surrounding their European junket: "My sister and I had been to Europe with our parents before the war, but we were little girls then and didn't remember much. Our parents were friends of the Auchinclosses and when my stepfather suggested that Jackie accompany us, she immediately acquiesced. They had to procure her father's permission because we had planned to take the trip during the period she usually spent with him. Janet Auchincloss convinced Miss Shearman to chaperone us. It was Jackie's first trip abroad."

Judy Bowdoin (Mrs. Judy Bowdoin Key) remembered their voyage as "the most grueling and tightly scheduled seven weeks I've ever spent. Everything had been prearranged, every minute accounted for. Nothing had been left to chance. We boarded the *Queen Mary* and from that moment we were treated like plebes at West Point.

Edward Foley had pulled strings to have the girls admitted to a Royal Garden Party at Buckingham Palace during their stay in England. "But it poured that day," said Judy Bowdoin. "Hundreds of guests, the women in cartwheel straw hats and elbow-length white gloves, the men in dinner jackets, had to seek shelter under the refreshment tents. It turned into a mob scene. There was a reception line under one of the tents and we were greeted by King George VI and Queen Elizabeth. Sir Winston Churchill also put in an appearance. Jackie went through the reception line twice to be able to shake Sir Winston's hand a second time."

---

money like water. I was asked to step in and take over for Black Jack but I wouldn't touch it. Mother was too argumentative. She and Grandfather argued continually. Mother was hard-assed, a tough nut. She had a fractious, powerful personality. Grandfather didn't like Mother as much as he liked the twins, which is why he left them more money than he left her."

After London and a tour of the English countryside, the girls headed for Paris, the medieval castles of Provençal, two days at Juan-les-Pins on the French Riviera (where they again encountered Churchill); Zurich, Lucerne, Interlaken and the Jungfrau in Switzerland; Milan, Venice, Verona, Florence and Rome; then back to Paris and the boat-train to Le Havre.

"One more day in a drip-dry blouse and I'll just die," Jackie told her travel companions. But on the whole she enjoyed herself thoroughly and vowed to return. "I've had a glimpse, next time I want to soak it all up," she informed her mother.

An opportunity to return presented itself sooner than expected. At the beginning of her sophomore year, she read a notice on a Vassar bulletin board describing the Smith College Junior Year Abroad program. The program, open to candidates from other schools as well, featured three or four European locations. Jackie hoped to attend the Paris program run in conjunction with the Sorbonne.

She had several reasons for wanting to join the program other than merely longing to return to Europe. First and foremost, Jackie had grown weary of Vassar's highly charged and ultra-competitive atmosphere. She was tired of rules that banned men from campus during the week and restricted the number of weekends students were permitted away from school during the semester.

Even while awaiting a response to her Junior Year Abroad application, she informed her father of her intention to drop out of school in favor of a career as a photographer's model. She had the face and figure for modeling and had recently appeared in amateur fashion shows in Newport and East Hampton to raise funds for charity. She had also received a small fee from *Life* when she appeared as one of several models in a photographer's layout of a Vassar College charity fashion show.

Her father opposed the idea vehemently, pointing out that only "a woman on the make" would consider entering the field of modeling. He hadn't sunk thousands of dollars into her education, he complained, to have her become a photographer's model.

He felt equally unsympathetic toward the latest man in Jackie's life, Colonel Serge Obolensky, a distinguished White Russian prince and social specialist who had, among other accomplishments, successfully restored the social status of no less than half-a-dozen New York hotels, including the Plaza, the St. Regis and the Sherry-Netherland. Known to gossip column readers as "the best waltzer in New York," Obolensky occasionally took Jackie dancing.

Jack Bouvier hastened to remind his nineteen-year-old daughter that the prince, then in his mid-sixties, was old enough to be her grandfather.

Jackie countered by pointing out that many of her father's female escorts were young enough to be his daughter.

Black Jack's current flame, Sally Butler, an employee of Pan American Airlines in Miami, wasn't too much older than Jackie. Grace Lee Frey, a friend of Sally's, described the Floridian as "strikingly beautiful with very long hair, which Black Jack suggested she cut in a style reminiscent of Norma Shearer. Sally did it, and it made her look even younger. At some point Bouvier went out to California with Sally to meet her parents. Her parents adored him but not as a marriage partner for their daughter. The age difference unnerved them."

Although they never legalized their union, Jack Bouvier and Sally Butler had a longtime off-and-on romance. Once when Sally was visiting her paramour at East Hampton, Jackie and her father became embroiled in a fierce argument. Jackie had apparently asked Sally whether a certain dress she wanted to wear looked better with pearls or with a gold chain she had been given by her father. Unaware of the chain's history, Sally suggested the pearls. At first Jack said nothing. Suddenly he exploded. He grabbed the pearl necklace from around Jackie's neck, shouting at her as the necklace broke and dozens of pearls spilled across the floor. He continued to yell until Jackie donned the gold chain and changed into another dress.

Confrontations of this sort were compounded by an increasing sense of alienation between Jackie and the Auchincloss side of her family. As disconcerting as she found her father's stormy behavior, she felt even more at odds with the socially entrenched lives of her mother and stepfather.

Jonathan Tapper, for many years the family major-domo, regarded Janet as "a highly critical woman who expected perfection and got it. She had restored Hammersmith Farm to the kind of grandeur usually associated with the manor houses and plantations of the antebellum South. By the late 1940s, she had amassed a staff of twenty-five. She had one maid whose only job was to empty wastebaskets. She had a special fetish about the kitchen. Everything had to be spotless. The cook used to complain because she couldn't cook and not have utensils sitting around on the counters. Janet would come in and tell the cook to get rid of them. She would say about the kitchen floor, 'I want it to be as polished as a ballroom floor.' If a bottle on the bar wasn't full, we were instructed to throw it out. She didn't want to give people the impression of being poor.

"Janet sometimes overdid it in terms of trying to prove herself. She believed in decorum, and possibly this had something to do with trying to hide her nouveau background. There were more servants at Hammersmith Farm than there were rooms in the house. Hugh Auchincloss didn't entirely approve but was powerless to do anything about it. Jackie found the excess appalling. There were so many servants to feed at mealtime that she and Lee were lucky to get a sandwich for lunch. Then there was the backstairs overhead—the staggering bills for electricity, linens, food and toiletries necessitated by such a large staff. Jackie kept telling her mother that so many servants could only 'ruin' the two youngest children—Jamie and Janet Jr. Jackie and her mother couldn't agree on anything."

Others familiar with the inner world of the Auchinclosses told similarly dismaying tales. Newport doyenne Eloise Cuddeback thought Hugh and Janet "tedious and boring." "They were boring," she said, "because they didn't have any desire to include the rest of civilization in their own little socially correct cosmos. People who live in a cloistered universe, who do everything and go everywhere together because that's their security blanket, are difficult to take, and often make for an unstimulating evening."

Another Newport neighbor, author Alan Pryce-Jones, considered Hugh Auchincloss "a stuffed shirt with no sense of humor. To his credit he had less interest in country club life than Janet. Janet thrived on Bailey's Beach. She could be rather enchanting but also quite horrifying. She had a vicious temper. She once pulled a knife on a maid during an argument and threatened to use it. She put the fear of God into her children. She did it so they'd measure up. They grew up with a benign, laid-back stepfather and a mother capable of explosive, temperamental outbursts. No wonder Jackie wanted to study in Paris."

Following her acceptance into the Junior Year Abroad program, Jacqueline faced her most difficult hurdle: she had to convince her parents that the time spent in France would have educational benefits. The Sorbonne appealed to Janet's snobbish sensibility but appeared less attractive to Black Jack, although he deemed it a far better choice for Jackie than dropping out of school entirely. The trip would take her away from him but, he reasoned, the rival Auchincloss clan would also be denied her presence. Besides, it would give him the opportunity to grow closer to Lee. More outgoing, less independent and self-willed but also subject to fewer emotional swings than Jackie, Lee (who had followed her sister to Miss Porter's) made a good companion, consulted her father more and listened to his advice even if she didn't always heed it.

Jackie's year in France started mid-August 1949 with an intensive six-week language arts program at the University of Grenoble in the south of France, during which time she boarded with a French family and spoke only French. She enjoyed the experience so thoroughly that when she arrived in Paris she turned her back on Reid Hall, the dormitory where most of the Sorbonne's American students lived, and moved in with the De Rentys.

Countess Guyot de Renty lived in a large apartment at 78 Avenue Mozart in the 12th *arrondisement* and rented rooms to students. The Countess and her late husband, fighters in the French Underground during World War II, had been deported to Germany and placed in separate concentration camps; the Count did not survive. But his wife and their two daughters pulled through. Jackie had befriended one of the daughters in the United States. Claude de Renty, Jackie's age, had attended Mt. Holyoke College in Massachusetts and had invited Jackie to visit her in France. Now they were living together.

Jacqueline wrote to Yusha Auchincloss describing the De Rentys: "They are the most wonderful family. I feel exactly as if I'm in my own house—heavenly mother—Claude, daughter, my age—divorced daughter Ghislaine and her four-year-old son Christian—and two American girls who just finished Milton." Jackie happened to know one of the two American girls, Susan Coward, from New York.

Removed from the clamorous environment of Vassar and the tug-of-war of her divorced parents, Jackie blossomed. In later years she referred to her Paris hiatus as "the high point of my life, my happiest and most carefree year."

"Jacqueline was very gay, very easy to satisfy," reflected Countess de Renty. "She seemed to appreciate everything we tried to do for her. And it couldn't have been easy for a girl accustomed to the comforts of America, because in 1949 there were still severe postwar restrictions in France. She had an 'alimentation card' with which to buy bread and meat when she stayed here. Her mother sent 'Care packages' containing sugar, coffee and other foodstuffs hard to come by.

"Like most French residences, the Avenue Mozart apartment had no central heating. During the winter months Jacqueline did her homework in bed wrapped like a mummy in scarf, mittens, sweater and earmuffs. There was a single bathroom containing an antique tin tub for all seven of us, but hot water was rare. The alternatives were either a cold shower or the bidet. Americans aren't used to the French bath habits. One chilly day when Jacqueline was trying to take a hot bath, the water heater exploded shattering the bathroom window. Jacqueline seemed unfazed by the accident. She was fearless, a trooper in the truest sense of the word.

"The three girls—Jacqueline, Susan Coward and Claude —often went out together weekends. Claude introduced them to her friends. Jacqueline would go to the opera, theater, ballet. Tickets were inexpensive. She adored the Louvre. She liked putting on a fur coat and going to the middle of town and being swanky at the Ritz. She also enjoyed the lovely, quiet, studious world of the Sorbonne. She extracted the best from all worlds and managed to live for the moment. I introduced her to an artist we knew, a Bohemian type who escorted her to all the underground cafés and jazz clubs. He took her around on his motorcycle, and on Saturdays they visited the art galleries and antique shops.

"Jacqueline was unpretentious both in life-style and in fashion. She dresesd casually. Perhaps the attainment of power changed her in later years, but at that time she remained completely unsoiled. Her one shortcoming was an inability to draw close to people. She was secretive. She made charming small talk but never divulged her inner thoughts. She wasn't superficial, just difficult to pin down."

Jackie's tendency to camouflage her true feelings seemed most apparent in her relationships with men. One of her steady dates in Paris, Ormande de Kay, an aspiring American screenwriter living abroad, characterized Jackie as "very appealing in one sense and very self-protective in another."

"To be honest," admitted de Kay, "I lusted after Jackie's roommate, Sue Coward, but she was interested in a guy called George. I remember seeing them kiss one night under a lamppost and feeling ruffled. I used to telephone the apartment hoping that Jackie would be out, but then if she wasn't. . . . Well, theoretically I was her boyfriend, or one of her boyfriends.

"I'm no longer friendly with her but in those days she was full of enthusiasm. And she was extremely attractive. I used to stun all my French acquaintances with her—they were absolutely staggered by her beauty.

"We did all the usual and expected things that young couples do in Paris—traveled by Métro, queued up at the neighborhood cinema, walked hand-in-hand along the Seine, hung out at places named Flore, Deux Magots, Dome and Coupole where we hoped to catch a glimpse of Camus or Sartre. When I had money, which wasn't often the case, I'd take her to a nightclub in Montparnasse. But she didn't seem to care whether you had money or not. She had just as good a time sitting at a sidewalk café and watching the people drift by.

"She had one disturbing feature, namely that little-girl manner of hers. She still has it to some degree. The older she gets the more maddening it becomes. But it was pretty disconcerting even then. It consisted of that by-now familiar teeny-weeny voice and a kind of lost expression on her face. I always attributed it to her mother. Ordinarily a nice and intelligent woman, Janet Auchincloss occasionally resorted to a similar mode of behavior—the damsel-in-distress act taken to the extreme. It's a Southern routine, the routine of being both dumb and attractive to men. That's the way you get the man, by playing stupid. Apparently it works."

Another man Jackie saw during her year at the Sorbonne was George Plimpton, who was completing a graduate degree in English literature at Cambridge University. When Jackie visited London over the Christmas holidays, she and George ran into each other.* Thereafter they rendezvoused whenever George turned up in Paris, once (according to a letter Jackie wrote for the twenty-fifth anniversary issue of *The Paris Review*, a literary journal cofounded and edited by Plimpton) "in an airless hole of a nightclub on the boulevard Raspail." George, "rather pale in a black turtleneck sweater," told Jackie "how the blue notes of saxophones through smoke-filled haze ushered in the dawns" for him, and how he "would walk the gray Paris streets in the first light back to a strange bed."

Jackie concludes her memory of that meeting: "Your evenings sounded exotic to one who was spending hers swaddled in sweaters and woolen stockings, doing homework in graph-paper cahiers."

Contrary to her claim, Plimpton recalled Jackie as having enjoyed a rather tumultuous social life in Paris. "Not that she didn't study," he ventured, "but she obviously managed to get around. She seemed to know everyone in Paris. She knew many of my friends: Peter Matthiessen, Bill Styron, Clement and Jessica Leigh-Hunt Wood, John Marquand, Jr. She knew the French intellectuals and the British bankers who spent their weekends hunting pheasant in the French countryside. She knew everybody but nobody knew her."

In February 1950, during semester break, Jackie received a visit in Paris from her mother and stepfather. She'd never written them about the lack of creature comforts in the De Renty apartment—the tin tub and the absence of heat—and at first they were both taken aback. Elegant by French standards, the flat didn't quite live up to Janet's expectations. Jackie, strong-willed as ever, assured them that the apartment met her needs; she had no intention of moving out.

---

*It was on this junket (December 1949) that Jackie met the children of her father's wartime mistress, her purported half-brother and half-sister whose identity she vowed to keep secret.

After a week in Paris, the Auchinclosses took Jackie and her roommate Susan Coward on a tour of Austria and Germany—Vienna, Salzburg, Berchtesgaden (where they visited the ruins of Hitler's summer retreat), followed by Munich and the nearby Dachau concentration camp. Hughdie, according to Janet, "wanted Jackie to see more of the Continent than just Paris and the Côte d'Azur. He wanted her to understand the significance of World War II and to realize that Europe wasn't all glamour and glitter and gold."

At the end of the school year, Jackie undertook another excursion, this one across France in company with Claude de Renty. "Jacqueline left before I did, and I caught up with her at Lyon," said Claude. "I borrowed my sister's car and we took turns driving, stopping for picnics, swimming, sightseeing. Our destination was Saint-Jean-de-Luz and along the way we lodged with friends or camped out. Among the places we stayed were Auvergne, Toulouse, Montauban, Charente, Bordeaux, Landes and Nantes. The entire trip, including a week at Saint-Jean-de-Luz, lasted a month.

"Like any two young girls, one of our primary topics of conversation happened to be men. Jacqueline rarely spoke in specifics. I knew several of her boyfriends in Paris because I'd introduced them. Others were strangers to me. None of her attachments seemed very serious. There had been a high-ranking staff advisor to Premier Georges Bidault with whom she'd gone horseback riding several times in the Bois de Boulogne and out to dinner, but I don't think it ever reached the amorous stage.

"Jacqueline had enormous strength of character, but she also had her weaknesses. It wasn't always easy for her. When you're the kind of person who wants only to be strong—well, she suffered from this. She couldn't accept her own frailties. Nor could she deal with frailties in others. She couldn't tolerate weak men. She wasn't the kind of woman who could coddle a man emotionally. If she didn't esteem and admire a man, if she didn't look up to him, she dropped him immediately."

Jackie's final venture in Europe that summer was a three-week trip to Ireland and Scotland with Yusha Auchincloss. "I'd signed on for a tour of duty with the U.S. Marines," recalled Yusha, "but decided to take a little vacation first. I invited Jackie to come along. Neither of us had ever been to Ireland or Scotland before. It seemed an appropriate place to go, since I was half Scottish and Jackie half Irish. We rented a drive-away and put up at small country inns. Jackie's favorite activity was to stop and talk to strangers, whether shopkeepers, pub crawlers, tinkers, tramps or farmers. She was endlessly fascinated by ordinary people and the stories they had to tell."

Jackie and Yusha returned to the United States aboard the *Liberté* and were met at the pier in New York by Jack Bouvier. To Black Jack's immense disappointment his reunion with Jackie lasted only two days before she rushed off to Merrywood to register for her senior year of college at George Washington University in Washington, D.C. After her year in Paris she had no intention of returning to Vassar, "a schoolgirl among schoolgirls," particularly as George Washington had agreed to accept all her previous college credits and allow her to graduate in two semesters as a French literature major.

Early in 1951, while studying for her mid-year exams, Jackie was reunited with Ormande de Kay, her former escort in Paris. With the outbreak of the Korean War, De Kay, a petty officer first-class in the Naval Reserve, had been called up and assigned to a destroyer then still in mothballs in the Naval Yard at Charleston, South Carolina.

"One day," he said, "the ship's telephone rang and over the public address system I was directed down to the gangplank. It was a woman from Washington, Mrs. Eve Tollman, a famous hostess, who said that I must come up there because they were having a party and then there was going to be a ball to celebrate the 200th anniversary of the founding of Georgetown, and they were expecting the most beautiful girl. 'Wouldn't you say she's the best-looking girl in Washington?' she asked her husband. 'Yes,' he said.

"That sounded fine to me, so I hitchhiked to Washington and went to the Tollmans in Georgetown. At the party they had five-star generals and Supreme Court justices and ambassadors, and everyone seemed to be standing around waiting for this girl to arrive. Finally she appeared, and to everyone's amazement, including my own, we rushed into each other's arms. The girl turned out to be Jacqueline Bouvier. And so off we went, and she was the belle of the ball. With that sort of reintroduction I felt somehow obligated to have a kind of romance with her. I used to hitchhike up from Charleston and spend my weekends at Merrywood."

It was also at this juncture that Jackie entered *Vogue's* 16th Annual Prix de Paris, a writing contest open to college seniors, offering the winner a one-year trainee position with the magazine—six months in Paris and an equal stint in their New York offices. Contestants were required to submit four technical papers on fashion, a personal profile, the blueprint for an entire issue of the periodical and an essay on "People I Wish I Had Known" (in the world of art, literature, music, ballet—people no longer living).

So determined was Jackie to win that she audited a secretarial typing course at George Washington University and spent a great deal of time working on her essay. She chose Sergei Diaghilev, Charles Baudelaire and Oscar Wilde as the people she most wished she had known. Her diligence paid off. Jackie won the contest, defeating some 1,280 entrants from 225 accredited colleges. She was flown to New York to have her photograph taken for *Vogue* by Horst P. Horst, and to be introduced to the magazine's editors, many of whom recognized the winner's name from her previous title as Debutante of the Year.

"I was with her the day they notified her," said Ormande de Kay. "I remember seeing this telegram that had been opened on the hall table at Merrywood and naturally I couldn't resist reading it. It was from somebody at *Vogue* announcing to Jackie that she'd won the Prix de Paris. I suddenly realized for the first time that behind that dopey exterior—the one she displayed for the benefit of the men in her life—there lurked quite a good mind."

Although her mother heralded the victory, Hugh Auchincloss felt less certain that Jackie should accept the prize. He believed that another lengthy stay in Paris might permanently alienate his stepdaughter from her homeland; she might decide to settle in Paris for good. He converted Janet to his view, and they joined forces to persuade Jackie to decline the award.

In exchange they agreed not only to let Jackie spend the summer of 1951 in Europe but to have Lee join her, and to foot the bills for both of them. The trip would serve as a dual graduation present: Jackie had earned her bachelor's degree at George Washington University; Lee had graduated from Miss Porter's and in September would matriculate as an art history major at Sarah Lawrence College.

To trace their summer travels through England, France, Italy and Spain, the sisters pasted up a scrapbook of Jackie's curlicued drawings and rhymes and Lee's anecdotal stories, which they entitled *One Special Summer* and presented to their mother at the end of the trip. Discovered among family memorabilia, the scrapbook was published in 1974 by Delacorte Press and excerpted in *Ladies' Home Journal*. Despite the book's girlish, sometimes juvenile tone, it remains the most complete record we have of that eventful expedition.

Beginning with an unblinking commentary on her experiences aboard the *Queen Elizabeth*, Lee writes about the interested Lebanese she met on the voyage out: "Jackie has warned me about the quirks in the sex lives of Near Easterners!!" Then there was the proboscidate Persian who whirled Lee round the dance floor ("The only thing I could see . . . was his nose"), while Jackie waltzed gracefully with the sexy purser.

The girls stayed in England long enough to lease a Hillman Minx and ferry it to France, where they promptly stripped the car's gears. In Paris, Jackie introduced Lee to some of the friends she had made during her year at the Sorbonne, including Claude de Renty, who immediately noted key differences between the sisters: "Jacqueline was dark, serious, moody and extremely curious about the world. Lee, blond and very much the kid sister, appeared perhaps easier to get to know. She was easygoing and affable but far less profound than Jacqueline. Jacqueline possessed an intensity that Lee clearly lacked."

Men and social activities figure prominently in *One Special Summer*. Lee recounted their meeting, at a French army base, "the two best-looking officers this side of Paradise. They wore blue berets and had lovely gold cords twinkling underneath their arms." From Jackie we hear about some "awfully nice English and Spanish boys" they befriended, as well as Jackie's encounter with a Spanish journalist who "had just finished a series of articles on [D. H. Lawrence's] *Women in Love*" and wanted to read them to her if only she "would come to his office that night."

In Venice, where Lee attempted but failed to find somebody to give her voice lessons, Jackie took private sketching sessions with a young and dashing Italian artist. Lee noted that "Since we've been in Venice, Jackie has really gotten terribly interested in ART. Of course we have been going to museums all along, but now she seems to want to learn as much about it as she can, and has found this teacher who has had a lot of experience, and she takes sketching lessons from him every day."

The teacher, whose photograph appears in *One Special Summer*, looked the epitome of every romantic American girl's European dream. Tall and lean, he carried sketch pads under his arm and wore his Italian-cut jacket draped across his shoulders. Standing next to him (in the same photograph) in clinging dress, sandals and sunglasses, Jackie appeared bemused and charmed by her handsome artist-companion.

The sisters rounded out their summer tour by visiting art critic and collector Bernard Berenson at *I Tatti*, his spacious estate in Settignano, outside Florence (his advice to Jackie: "Marry someone who will constantly stimulate you—and you him"), followed by a week's stay at Marlia, a picturesque villa that once belonged to Napoleon's sister, Ellsa Baciocchi Bonaparte, when she was Duchess of Lucca, and which now belonged to the Count and Countess Pecci-Blunt. By coincidence their son Dino was a friend of John F. Kennedy.

"What took place at Marlia," said Roderick Coupe, an American writer currently residing in Paris, "surely didn't make the pages of any book by the Bouvier sisters. Let me add that Dino's mother, Countess Anna Pecci-Blunt, who is now dead, was one of the great figures of her period—a rather terrifying, highly amusing, very brilliant woman. She was extraordinary. So was her villa, which was best known for its vast surrounding park.

"What happened to Jackie and Lee could only have happened in Europe where people take seriously such traditional values as manners and social etiquette. They apparently left the villa without saying goodbye to the Countess. They were leaving the villa very early in the morning to return to America and didn't want to wake her up. The Countess thought it terribly rude; she thought these two American girls had no manners at all, and she put the word out on them. Jackie and Lee were mortified. They had thought it more polite not to bother the Countess so early in the morning. They later apologized, but it put a definite damper on the trip. This unintentional slight, like something out of Henry James, marked them for several years to come."

6

Jackie's return to the States in the late summer of 1951 renewed the bitter hostilities between her father, who wanted her to live with him in New York and accept a part-time job in his small brokerage operation, and her mother, who promised to procure Jackie a better position in the Washington, D.C., area. Jackie weighed the alternatives while staying at Newport, dating various members of the Bailey Beach social set. One of her steady dates, Steven Spencer, took her flying in his private, single-engine plane. Another, Bin Lewis, was a frequent tennis partner. A third, John Sterling, golfed with her at the Newport Country Club.

"I hadn't seen Jackie since before her junior year abroad," said Sterling. "She'd changed considerably, lost that girl-next-door chubbiness. Tall and imposing at 5 feet 7 inches, with high cheekbones and sensuous lips, she looked and moved like a woman. Yet she remained as cool and aloof as the Jackie of old, an absolute ice princess.

Jackie herself has described this period as one of "pure frustration." She felt her future had been mapped out for her. She complained to Sterling that the only thing expected of her was "to marry well." That's all she'd ever really been trained to do, and that's what all the women she knew were doing—"just like their mothers before them."

The one concrete decision Jackie made at Newport was to settle in Washington rather than with her father in New York. Black Jack's drinking, his gambling, his erratic behavior made communication between them impossible. Father and daughter argued more than ever. His complaints were the same ones he'd levied against Jackie in the past. He accused her of contacting him only when she needed money, of being overly extravagant, of dating men whose intentions were unclear and of ignoring him while pandering to the Auchinclosses. At other times he tried to buy her affection by giving her unlimited use of his charge plates at New York's leading department stores. He offered to absorb all her medical bills but only if she consulted doctors and dentists in New York, as opposed to Washington or Newport.

Elaine Lorillard, wife of tobacco scion Louis Lorillard and a resident of Newport, joined Black Jack for cocktails at his apartment about this time and was amazed by the number of photographs of Jackie that lined the walls and sat on tables and bureaus: "There were photographs and oil paintings of both Lee and Jackie, but there seemed to be more of Jackie. She was everywhere. And Black Jack talked about her non-stop. He longed for her and felt disappointed by her choice of Washington as a temporary home. But then he began to reason that perhaps she might find more interesting work in Washington."

It was Uncle Hughdie who opened the door to an interesting job by suggesting that Jackie consider a career in journalism. One of his close friends was Arthur Krock, Washington correspondent for *The New York Times,* who offered to help Jackie find a suitable position.

What happened next has become part of the Kennedy lore, a story which has developed in the telling, one of those pleasant little Jackie anecdotes that has helped shape the legend. Krock telephoned Frank Waldrop, editor-in-chief and part-owner of the *Washington Times-Herald* (now defunct), who once hired ex-Ambassador Joseph P. Kennedy's daughter Kathleen ("Kick") as a secretary and sometime columnist. Another former *Times-Herald* columnist employed by Waldrop was Inga Arvad, a suspected Nazi spy whose wartime involvement with a young Naval officer named John F. Kennedy would in later years create a scandal.

"Are you still hiring little girls?" Krock asked Waldrop and added without waiting for an answer: "I have a wonder for you. She's round-eyed, clever and wants to go into journalism."

He also mentioned casually that "the little girl" he had in mind was the stepdaughter of Hugh Auchincloss, a name well known to Waldrop. He agreed to see Jackie.

The *Times-Herald,* founded by the eccentric and very

wealthy Eleanor "Cissy" Patterson,* was probably the least influential newspaper in Washington. Its editorial style was distinctly rightwing; prior to our entry into World War II, it espoused isolationist views that won few friends in a town strongly supportive of Franklin Roosevelt. Waldrop himself was a southern conservative whose blunt, crusty, hard-hitting manner tended to intimidate youthful reporters. But, Hugh Auchincloss assured Jackie, she would gain an invaluable education working for the newspaper, especially for an editor as dedicated and knowledgeable as Frank Waldrop.

"The old *Times-Herald* building was at 13th and H Streets," said Waldrop. "Jackie turned up in my office at the beginning of December 1951. I was accustomed to having these youngsters come and want to get on the paper because it was very exciting, very intriguing, a great place from which to scout around town and have fun. Jackie was just another one. They came and went. I was curious to see if she really wanted to make a career in journalism, so I asked her if she wanted to learn the business or just hang around a newspaper until she got married. If she did want to make a career, I told her I'd give her the kind of assignments that would help; if she didn't, I'd find a place for her anyway but at least she wouldn't be taking somebody's job who did want to make a career of it.

"She said she wanted a career. She admitted she didn't type well and knew nothing about reporting but wanted to learn. I believed her. I told her to come back after Christmas and we'd talk about it again. She came back after Christmas and apologized. She said she was sorry because she had at first said she wanted to make a go of it, but that she had become engaged over Christmas and therefore she supposed I wouldn't want to hire her at all. It was a very honest, very ladylike thing to do. And so I said, 'Well, tell me about him. You didn't say anything

*Cissy Patterson was the granddaughter of Joseph Medill, who owned the *Chicago Tribune,* and the sister of Joseph Patterson, founder of the New York *Daily News*. The *Washington Times-Herald* was the first major American newspaper to be edited and published by a woman. After Cissy Patterson's death in 1948 at age 67, the *Times-Herald* was operated by an executive board of seven who had been named in Cissy's will as the new owners of the newspaper. Frank Waldrop was among the seven.

about this fellow before Christmas. Where did you meet him, who is he?' And then it emerged that it was somebody she'd met only recently. 'Oh hell,' I said, 'that doesn't mean a thing. Come on down here Monday morning and get to work.' "

The press announcement of Jackie's engagement appeared within days of her joining the *Times-Herald* staff; it said that Jackie's fiancé, John G. W. Husted, Jr., had attended Summerfield School, England, and graduated from St. Paul's, Concord, New Hampshire, and Yale University, had served in World War II with the American Field Service attached to the British Forces in Italy, France, Germany and India. Husted's family, from Bedford Village in Westchester County, was in the banking business, while John worked for Dominick & Dominick, a leading banking investments firm in New York.

Jackie and John Husted had been introduced by Mary deLimur Weinmann, at the time a girlfriend of Yusha Auchincloss: "Because of my friendship with Yusha I used to dine occasionally at Merrywood. I'd known Jackie since 1948. She had a very active mind when young and couldn't sit still. She was also very shrewd, a trait she evidently inherited from her mother. I remember the way Janet sat at the dinner table with all those children around her, everybody jabbering away at once except for Janet. She'd sit there smiling quietly to herself. Her mind seemed to be floating, but she knew exactly what was going on. Jackie was the same way. She seemed to be out of it at times, but it was all an illusion. She knew precisely what was happening.

"I wasn't terribly close to Jackie. She didn't make friends easily. But I was close enough to fix her up. I'd told John Husted about her, and one weekend late in 1951 he drove down from New York for somebody's party in Washington. Jackie was also there and that's when I introduced them.

"John was tall, well-built, urbane, very handsome in a WASPish way, and Jackie was a knockout in her own, very individual fashion. I felt they might hit it off, but I never imagined it would go as far as it did. I was amazed. It was love at first sight for John. I drove back to New York with him at the end of the weekend and he was absolutely entranced. He couldn't stop talking about her. The next thing I heard they were engaged."

John Husted, who today lives on Nantucket and remains friendly with Jackie, "friendlier than when we were engaged," found it "perfectly natural" that he and Jackie should meet in the first place. "Hugh Auchincloss had been a great friend of my father's at Yale," he explained. "Jackie's mother and my mother had known each other for years. My sister Anne and my sister Louise were both at Farmington during the same period as Jackie. So you might say we had a lot in common.

"I was immediately impressed by Jackie's originality, her sensitivity. She was also quite beautiful with those great wide-set eyes and dark brown curls styled in a feather cut. She looked like a deer that had suddenly emerged from the forest and seen its first human being. She had this expression of eternal surprise etched on her face.

"She introduced me to her father and we spent an afternoon together. We had Yale, the brokerage business and New York in common. He said he thought Jackie might be a little difficult at times, but he had nothing against her marrying me—if that was her desire. He wanted nothing more than to see her happily married and living in New York, where she belonged.

"Frankly, I wouldn't have cared what anybody had said. I had fallen in love with her. One evening I telephoned Merrywood and told her I thought it might be nice to get engaged. 'Meet me at the Polo Bar in the Westbury Hotel at noon on Saturday, and I'll know you accept,' I said. The Polo Bar used to be one of Black Jack's favorite haunts. It was a place where young people met for drinks. If you had a tiny apartment, you almost had to meet there.

"Anyway the day arrived and I went over there. It was snowing and I must've waited for several hours. No Jackie. I was about to leave when finally she came sailing in, and over a couple of drinks we agreed to become engaged. A few weeks later Hugh Auchincloss threw an engagement party for us at Merrywood, and it was there that I gave her a sapphire-and-diamond engagement ring that had belonged to my mother."

Two of the guests at the party were journalist Philip Geyelin, who later joined the *Washington Post,* and his wife Cecilia Parker Geyelin, daughter of Hugh Auchincloss's partner in the brokerage firm of Auchincloss, Parker &

Redpath. According to Cecilia, the party was very bleak. "I didn't feel the place was exactly brimming over with joy and love and anticipation," she remarked. "People seemed guarded and cool, and the principal characters— Jackie and John Husted—barely appeared to know each other. They hardly spoke to each other, and when they did Jackie would merely nod her head and smile.

"Of course, Jackie was truly the product of a mother who must've said to her, 'Darling, don't act more intelligent than the men in your life because it frightens them away. There are other ways to skin a cat.' That would account for Jackie's demure little smile that day. But still, I couldn't figure out what she and John Husted were doing together."

Mary deLimur Weinmann also had reason to doubt the sincerity of Jackie's wedding plans. A few weeks after the engagement party, Jackie called on Mary to thank her personally for the introduction to John Husted. "She wore gloves," recalled Mary. "She removed her left glove to show me her engagement ring and I noticed that her fingernails were green. She explained that they had turned green from the developing bath she used in the darkroom at the *Washington Times-Herald*. She immediately launched into a lengthy and very detailed account of her job at the newspaper. She went on and on. Finally, almost as an afterthought, she mentioned that they had scheduled the wedding for sometime in June, and that of course I would receive an invitation. Everything considered, she seemed rather blasé about it."*

*Shortly after Jackie's visit, Mary deLimur Weinmann went to Rome with her parents and there encountered Lee Bouvier: "Lee had gone to Italy with her mother during semester-break supposedly to learn how to sing. But she had not been as attentive about singing as she might have been, and Janet was tearing out her hair. Jackie was always prodding her to sing. 'Sing, Lee, sing,' Jackie would say, and Lee would sing. But Lee wasn't serious about singing—she just wanted to be in Rome. I was headed to Paris and since I happened to be a few years older than Lee, Janet asked whether she could send Lee along, I didn't mind. Another girlfriend of mine also made the trip. At the last minute we decided to detour by way of Kitzbühel, Austria, to do some skiing. None of us had ever been on skis before. Lee soon found a young ski instructor who was willing to devote himself to her. She wasn't as inquisitive or as deep as Jackie, but Lee was absolutely divine-looking at that stage. The boys loved her and she them."

Far more than marriage, Jackie's immediate concern appeared to be her career. In a matter of weeks she'd worked her way from the position of "gofer," fetching coffee and running errands for various editors, to that of city room receptionist. Then when one of his regular columnists resigned and Frank Waldrop decided to fill the post with a full-time Inquiring Photographer feature, Jackie volunteered for the position.

Previously the Inquiring Photographer had been an irregular item in the newspaper, a rotating assignment shared by several reporters and photographers. Betty Fretz, a reporter with the *Times-Herald* who occasionally filled in as Inquiring Photographer, reflected on the post: "We used to joke about being in the dog house when we were assigned to the Inquiring Photographer spot. The photographers hated it even more than the reporters. They preferred to sit in a bar someplace rather than snap mugshots of people standing on street corners answering stupid questions. Nobody could fathom anyone wanting the job and agreeing not only to pose the questions but take the pictures."

In convincing Waldrop to give her a try, Jackie claimed she could handle a camera, although she had only used a Leica before. The cumbersome, professional photographer's Speed Graflex was an unfamiliar tool. She secretly signed up for a crash course in news photography to learn how to use the larger model.

Following a brief tour of police stations and hospital emergency rooms to acquaint herself with the ins and outs of urban existence, Jackie was turned over to Betty Fretz and staff photographer Joe Heilberger for on-the-job training.

"She interviewed people and I helped her put the copy together," recalled Fretz. "She didn't know how far to stand from the subject when taking their picture, so Joe Heilberger stretched himself out on the floor to measure off six feet and told her to take all her photographs from that distance."

Appraisals of Jackie's performance and dedication to the job were mostly negative. Estelle Gaines, a city desk reporter for the *Times-Herald,* found Jackie seriously wanting in terms of newspaper background: "I always felt she was just passing time. She landed the job only because she was the stepdaughter of 'Take-a-Loss with

Auchincloss,' She was untrained and very scared. She was awkward in movement as well as assignment. It was so obvious that she couldn't handle a camera. Her photographs were perpetually out of focus. She tried to befriend several of the photographers on the paper but they were a very fast and tough crew.

"She once asked some of the fellows in the photo unit what they wanted for Christmas. When they suggested it comes in a bottle, she promised to oblige. She wrapped the bottle beautifully in a fancy box listing all their names. When they unwrapped it at the office Christmas party, they found a bottle of milk. Had she followed up with a real bottle of Cutty Sark or J&B, the prank would've been worth pulling. But she didn't, and it simply didn't come off.

"Most of the female reporters and editors on the paper frightened her. Very few of us were intrigued by the Washington and New York social scene. We didn't socialize with Jackie, because she wasn't one of us. Her idea of fun consisted of an evening at 'The Dancing Class,' a snobby subscription dance series held at the posh Sulgrave Club, a place where none of us would be caught dead.

"Jackie was primarily interested in covering those listed in the Blue Book or the Green Book. One of her few female contacts on the staff was Achsah Dorsey Smith, the society editor. She was kinder to Jackie than most of us because she had a better understanding of Jackie's background. The rest of us had grown up on the crime beat. We weren't likely to serve Jackie tea and crumpets. It wasn't that we were unkind. It's just that we were competitive and too busy for social chatter."

Jack Kassowitz, assistant managing editor of the *Times-Herald,* became Jackie's supervisory editor and an occasional luncheon companion. But in retrospect he too would take a dim view of Jackie's professional commitment: "She was just out of college and a socialite, somebody impressed with the world of journalism but unwilling to make the necessary sacrifices. She was a poor little rich girl—wealthy family but no money of her own. She was living at Merrywood to save on rent and she owned a second-hand black Mercury convertible that she drove to and from work.

"She behaved like a social climber. She enjoyed dancing, fancy restaurants and meeting people who were famous and had money. She seemed innocent and a bit naive on the surface, but she knew exactly where she was going and what she was doing—and it had very little to do with the newspaper business.

"As a reporter she was at best mediocre. I did her editing and had to rewrite almost everything she submitted. At first I came up with most of the topics for her column; she eventually devised some of her own. It was a lighthearted column and the questions were pretty silly. A typical one might be, 'What's your secret ambition'—or, 'Should a tall woman marry a short man?'

"Her job consisted of going out and interviewing eight or ten people, snapping their pictures, then putting it all together. She did better with children and celebrities than with the average man or woman on the street. In the real world of the Great Adventure, she found it difficult to approach strangers. There were days when she simply refused to go out; the smallest rainstorm provided an excuse not to have to leave the premises.

"In the grim atmosphere of a hot, cluttered city room it was pleasant enough to look up and see an attractive girl like Jackie. Her looks were her main contribution to the newspaper. Many of the reporters and photographers were after her, but she constantly deflected their invitations to dinner. I assume she desired bigger game or simply didn't care to date her colleagues. When they realized she wasn't available to them, they ganged up on her. They would say, 'What's a nice girl like you doing in a place like this?' Or, 'We're all thinking of taking a powder and going out to your pool this afternoon, how about it?'

"Over lunch I once asked her to describe her ideal man. She said she hated *perfect* men. She found them boring. 'I look at a male model,' she said, 'and am bored in three minutes. I like men with funny noses, ears that protrude, irregular teeth, short men, skinny men, fat men. Above all, he must have a keen mind.' She didn't say it, but I suppose it helped if he also had a lot of money."

Jack Kassowitz's memories of Jackie may well have been tarnished by an unpleasant experience in 1955, after she'd married John F. Kennedy and left the *Times-Herald.* "She and Kennedy were vacationing in Nassau aboard his father's yacht, and I was also down there," said Kassowitz. "I sent my business card with a bouquet of roses. Jackie snubbed me. I wasn't invited aboard. Never even heard from her. No response. Nothing. She didn't seem to want to remember the people she'd known on the way up."

Even former college chums such as Lucky Roosevelt remained apprehensive when it came to Jackie's so-called career ambitions. "There's an awful lot made of her reportorial life, which in reality amounted to zilch," said Mrs. Roosevelt. "She went around with her little camera and took pictures. But having been a reporter all my life, I can tell you there's a vast difference between that kind of amateur activity done largely for fun and being a serious reporter where you start out as a copy girl and work your way up. It was just an opportunity for her to find out if she really wanted to go into journalism, the way we all try things when we're young. But I don't think one can call oneself a journalist on the basis of eighteen months as an Inquiring Photographer."

Despite her detractors, Jackie soon had her own by-line and received a moderate salary increase from $42.50 to $56.75 weekly. Frank Waldrop sized her up as "somebody who did her job. She was useful or she wouldn't have been there."

The questions she devised showed a whimsical turn of mind: "Do the rich enjoy life more than the poor?" "Chaucer said that what women most desire is power over men. What do you think women desire most?" "Do you think a wife should let her husband think he's smarter than she is?" "If you were going to be executed tomorrow morning, what would you order for your last meal on earth?" "Would you like to crash high society?" "How do you feel when you get a wolf whistle?"

Several of her queries now seem almost eerily prophetic: "Which First Lady would you most like to have been?" "Would you like your son to grow up to be President?" "Should a candidate's wife campaign with her husband?" "If you had a date with Marilyn Monroe, what would you talk about?" "What prominent person's death affected you most?"

Jackie's newspaper ambitions sometimes took her in odd directions. One day she told a sports writer acquaintance she wanted to interview Ted Williams in the locker room the next time the Boston Red Sox came to town to play the Washington Senators.

"You can't do that," said the writer.

"Why not?" she asked.

"Because you can't," the writer insisted.

"I don't understand," said Jackie.

"Take my word for it. It's just not done," said the writer.

Instead of Ted Williams, Jackie settled for a half-dozen players on the last-place Washington Senators. The team, which had lost ten games in succession when Jackie marched into the locker room at Griffiths Stadium, went on a sudden winning streak. The manager of the ballclub attributed their change of luck to Jacqueline Bouvier.

But after a certain point Jackie began to lose her enthusiasm for the job. Angele Gingras, a society reporter who started at the *Times-Herald* at about the same time as Jackie, recalled how Jackie would complain that the editors were "pushing" her around, forcing her to use certain questions and interview certain political types. "One day she perched on my desk," said Angele, "and began to remonstrate against 'God,' our name for Frank Waldrop, and against all the other powers at the top. 'If I have to interview that boring Munthe de Morgenstern one more time, I am going to quit this job,' she railed. Morgenstern, dean of the diplomatic corps in Washington, apparently held great favor with Waldrop.

"The job became something of a grind for Jackie, although she managed to maintain a sense of humor about it. One afternoon I happened to run into her on the street. She was wandering around with her camera slung over her shoulder searching for interesting-looking people to photograph and interview. My job as a society reporter required the same dedication—I was always running along the streets, waving at taxis to take me to various luncheons and teas.

"Jackie knew I had lived in France for a while, so she grinned and asked me how business was going—as one lady walking the Washington equivalent of the Boulevard des Italiens to another. I laughed, knowing she was referring to the 'Never on Sunday' girls who patrolled that Parisian thoroughfare.

"Of course there was a trace of irony beneath the humor. Not only did she feel that the newspaper was

exploiting us—we were being overworked and underpaid—
but there was a sense of personal indignation. Jackie
realized that the editors considered her the Junior League
type, useful but not essential. They took her lightly because she wasn't reporting hard news. Her female colleagues denigrated her because she traveled within the
social set. Some of these women could be pretty bitchy.
They spread rumors to the effect that Jackie was sleeping
with this guy and that guy. People at the paper who'd
never even met her had stories to tell. The stories weren't
true. I don't mean that she didn't fall in love and do her
share of petting and so forth, but she wasn't sleeping
around. That much I can practically guarantee."

Jackie's first few months at the *Times-Herald* were
spent commuting back and forth between Washington
and New York, where she passed her weekends with
John Husted. Occasionally Husted visited her in Washington, staying at Merrywood and accompanying his intended on interview rounds for her daily column. He
frequently found her in a playful, vibrant mood, full of
laughter and practical jokes, the latter almost always
directed against her sister Lee, whose weekends home
from college invariably brought out the boys. Jackie enacted one such burlesque on a Sunday morning while Lee
and a male friend lounged lazily around the house, reading the newspaper. Suddenly a grotesque figure, draped
from head to foot in white silk sheets and emitting a
highpitched whine, ran through the living room. Moments later the defrocked apparition reappeared. It was
Jackie, inquiring in her most dulcet stage whisper whether
anyone had seen "poor Aunt Alice—her dementia seems
to be acting up again."

Jackie's sense of fun was at best mercurial. There were
moments when she could be as arch and stentorian as an
aging schoolmarm. Early in 1952, John Husted brought
Jackie home to Bedford to spend the weekend with his
parents. On Saturday evening while they were leafing
through some old family photograph albums, John's mother
asked her prospective daughter-in-law if she wanted to
have a childhood snapshot of John. "Mrs. Husted," said
Jackie, "if I want any photos of your son I can take my
own."

By March 1952 the relationship, which John Husted

characterized as "chaste," had started to cool. Janet
Auchincloss had made discrete inquiries and learned that
the young man earned only $17,000 per annum at Domi-
nick & Dominick, and although this figure was by no
means inconsiderable considering the year, it struck Janet as far too small a salary on which to support a family.
Janet expressed her opinion not to Husted—"She was
too polite to talk money to me," he said—but to her
eldest daughter.

Financial considerations notwithstanding, Jackie's wan-
ing interest in her fiancé seemed to be based primarily on
psychological factors. John Husted surely had the makings of the classic American husband: upright, depend-
able, prone neither to wild partying nor to gross indiscretions.
He would return from work in time for dinner and be a
kind and devoted father. He would remember birthdays
and wedding anniversaries with generous gifts and ultimately be a good provider. But the man Jackie wanted to
marry would fall into a different category. Like Black
Jack Bouvier, he would have to be vintage boyfriend—
experienced, entertaining, guileless. If it happened that
the man in question also had money (preferably of the
family-fortune variety), so much the better. Jackie had
nothing against inherited wealth.

While still engaged she began dating other men, among
them John B. White, a former *Times-Herald* features
writer who by 1952 had gone to work for the Department
of State. White, the son of a southern Episcopalian minister and a one-time beau of Kathleen Kennedy, had
been introduced to Jackie by socialite Noreen Drexel and
felt "immediately drawn to her. She had all those elfin
qualities that men seek in women."

Although White couldn't recall Jackie ever mentioning
her engagement to John Husted, "I had the distinct impression she felt weary of shuttling back and forth to
New York. After a while she started spending her weekends around Washington, and she and I went out occasionally. We discussed her Inquiring Photographer column,
which I thought represented the best escapist literature
then being produced in the District of Columbia. There
was no notion that she'd ever keep on doing it or even
keep on in journalism, but she did have a knack for the
column. She was good at dredging up questions. She was
curious-minded and gifted at gaining people's confidence—

she elicited frank answers from her interview subjects. And she loved to talk with her high-class friends about questions to put to people in her column. It interested her friends as well. I suggested several questions. All her friends did. And at various times she interviewed her friends and relatives in the column and put her own questions to them.

"I always felt that Jackie had many different kinds of talent. She showed me a charming present she'd made for her mother's birthday, *The Red Shoes,* a dear little book, a fairy tale for children that she'd written and illustrated and put together. It was an offshoot of the scrapbooks she'd done as a child, and it was a beautiful piece of work. It was so attractive I told her I wanted to take it and try to find a publisher for it. She balked at the suggestion but finally let me borrow the book. I brought it up to Boston on a visit and carried it around to some friends in publishing who all thought it looked great but couldn't see how you could market it. I thought afterwards what a pity that it never got published.

"After she cut back on seeing John Husted, she commenced throwing these parties at Merrywood. She'd have them whenever her parents left town. The guests, many of them bigwigs on the Washington scene, were mostly in their fifties and sixties. I'm nearly a generation older than Jackie, but these people were two generations removed. She handled them beautifully. But she didn't have many friends her own age. I became curious and asked a friend of hers, Mary deLimur Weinmann, about it. Mary confirmed that Jackie had very few girlfriends and missed the comradeship of equals, that she dealt splendidly with older men and women but not with contemporaries.

"It seemed very odd indeed, so one weekend I took her down to New York and introduced her to some girls I knew. I told her the reason. I said, 'You should have girlfriends your own age.' I left her alone with them for a few hours. The girls were very interested and pleased with Jackie, but she didn't feel the same way. She just couldn't cement onto women of her age bracket. I think it was because she didn't like to open up. She was good at getting others to talk about themselves, but she wouldn't talk about herself, which is something young people demand. Older people don't mind relating their experiences, in fact relish the opportunity because usually nobody pays them much heed."

Another place John White took Jackie was St. Elizabeths, the federal mental hospital in Washington's Congress Heights adjoining Bolling Air Force Base overlooking
the Anacostia River. The grounds of the hospital, 400
acres of rolling grasslands densely wooded with elms,
oaks and maples, had once been part of an arboretum
and the trees still bore identification plaques in English
and Latin.

"I'd once written a newspaper series on St. Elizabeths,
with its 7,000 mental patients," explained White, "in the
course of which I became friendly with the hospital's
director, Dr. Winfred Overholser. I thought Jackie might
enjoy meeting him and also seeing the grounds, which
were not only very tranquil but had a vertiginous view of
Washington.

"We drove up there and Jackie loved the view and
found the institution intriguing. Those were the days
when Ezra Pound, the famed American poet, was incar-
cerated at St. Elizabeths and noted writers like T. S.
Eliot, H. L. Mencken and Katherine Anne Porter went
out to pay him homage.

"We didn't see Pound but the day we visited we came
across three old fellows sitting side-by-side on a bench
facing Washington. They were utterly motionless and
still, catatonic I think. Jackie and I sat on a second bench
and watched them and wondered what secrets lurked in
their minds, whether they were perhaps sharing thoughts.

"When I introduced Jackie to Dr. Overholser, she
engaged him in a fascinating discussion on the subject of
Hercules. She wondered why a man in a myth would
have so many difficulties all his life and why he had all
those fits of temper which continually got him into trouble. She asked Dr. Overholser whether Hercules had a
diagnosable case of mental illness. Overholser seemed to
feel Hercules belonged in a place like St. Elizabeths,
that he was certifiably schizophrenic.

"Jackie enjoyed talking about people and motives from
a psychological point of view. She and I played a game
once in a while in which I wrote down a list of names of
women, names in history or literature who had certain
qualities in common with Jackie. Then I'd read them off
and she'd comment on them. It was the only way I could
ever get her to talk about herself, even indirectly.

"The first name on my list, for example, was Joan of

Arc. But Jackie rather quickly dismissed her. She admired Joan of Arc's persuasiveness and felt she herself had the same quality, but she wasn't prepared to meet Joan of Arc's untimely and tragic end.

"Another name was Sappho, the Greek poet. Jackie very much liked this idea except Sappho was supposedly a lesbian and she wasn't into that at all. But she thought she would like to have lived long ago and been unique, the very best in the world at her trade of poetry. And she approved the notion of living on a small remote island, as did Sappho.

"Jackie had no use for the Biblical Eve. She thought Eve handled herself poorly. Jackie didn't care for anything that wasn't well done. She had the same general reaction to Pandora. She admired Pandora's desire to bring good things to the world but felt she could've been more direct about it. Pandora became the unwitting victim of a good deal of evil and a little bit of good. The unwittingness didn't appeal to Jackie, who as much as possible wanted to be in control of events.

"The two women she most identified with were Madame de Maintenon and Madame Recamier, the great seventeenth- and eighteenth-century *salonistes* of France. Both women were extremely attractive and had a gift for bringing out wit in others, particularly men. They didn't like women hanging around a lot. So the men would gather at their salons and just regale each other. It's a delightful idea, along the more contemporary lines of Gertrude Stein and Alice B. Toklas or the Algonquin Round Table.

"Jackie relished the thought of running a salon and of inviting highly intelligent people into her home. Good conversation was precious to her. She had a great knack for inspiring it and loved to see people enjoying themselves and being bright. Her parties at Merrywood had the makings of a salon, and she obviously fostered that ideal during her reign at the White House.

"Jackie herself mentioned Eleanor of Aquitaine because a book had come out on her which she'd read. Eleanor was right in the middle of the big events of her day and she was the trusted friend of the men who shaped these events. More than anything, Jackie took pleasure in dealing with and being close to men who were doing important things, not necessarily as advisor so much as confidante. Jackie wanted to be the confidante of an important man. Even then her interest in people tended to be in direct proportion to their importance and their ability to amuse. If a person was good and decent and all those wonderful things, that was all right, but much more vital to her was somebody who happened to be powerful and charming regardless of his or her character. Power and charisma seemed to override all other qualities in her estimation of people."

As John White readily discovered, Jackie was quite a powerhouse in her own right. "One afternoon," he said, "we decided to drive down to Fort Washington in Virginia, the site of several minor skirmishes during the War of 1812. It was just an excuse to spend a few hours in the country. On the way back to Washington, we found ourselves ensnarled in a massive traffic jam.

"We both had separate dinner appointments that evening, and we were running late. Traffic was tied up for miles. I was content to be a bit tardy but Jackie wasn't, and for the first time I saw a streak of real ferocity in her. It was my car and I was driving, but she began to take charge.

" 'Back up here and go down that little road,' she said at a certain moment. She knew the neighborhood because we weren't too far from Merrywood, so I decided to listen to her. But once I followed her first direction she started giving me all sorts of orders—'Turn right, turn left, stay on your side of the road.' She even put her hands over mine on the steering wheel to make sure I made the turns she wanted, and I thought what a huge, strong, peasant hand that is. That's not a ladylike hand at all. It's a big, strong, powerful hand. And I suddenly realized I was dealing with something I hadn't even suspected. She was one tough cookie, really tough!

"That undigested, renegade toughness lay at the very core of Jackie's personality. And I suppose it intimidated lots of people. It intimidated me—I certainly never tried anything with Jackie, although I tried things with almost everybody else. I don't know, maybe I felt protective of her or something. Maybe I felt it would be opening up more than she or I could handle.

"I do remember holding hands with her once. And again I had that feeling of what a big strong hand, how out of character with this fadeaway voice and this apparent fragility—but this creature is not in the least fragile. I had the feeling she had not had much, if any, sexual experience. But she wasn't particularly afraid of it. She wasn't prudish. When that came, she would deal with it in the same ham-handed fashion."

Among Jackie's other idle relationships during this period were Godfrey McHugh, an Air Force major ten years her senior, and William Walton, a correspondent for *Time* and a paratrooper in World War II. Both men were bachelors. She met McHugh through her mother and her sister, and was introduced to Walton by John White.

"I took Jackie to meet Bill Walton because he was a dear, close friend," said White. "And I thought he would do her good. He was smart and wise, extremely attractive in manner, quick-minded, knowledgeable, a fellow with a wry, dry wit."

Although then still a journalist, Walton was on the verge of drifting into a second career as an artist. His stark yet luminescent Cape Cod landscapes appealed to Jackie. And like Jackie, Walton had an affinity for powerful big-name celebrities. His closest friend during the war had been Ernest Hemingway. "His parties," said White, "were almost dauntingly impressive. You felt a little embarrassed to be in the same room with some of these people, they were so big."

Jackie started attending Walton's galas and reciprocated by inviting him to hers. Walton and White sometimes lunched together or met for late-afternoon drinks. On one occasion, Jack Kassowitz joined the group for cocktails and noticed that Jackie followed "the highbrow conversation as avidly as a spectator at a tennis match, chortling and chuckling whenever Walton or White made an impressive conversational point—and even when they didn't."

Godfrey McHugh, meanwhile, a popular "extra man" on Washington's dinner party circuit, was a tireless globetrotter who, by the time he met Jackie, had traveled around the world on countless military and personal expeditions. "That's why Jackie enjoyed being with me," he said. "She loved listening to stories of my travels and the people I'd met. And I enjoyed the company of sophisticated and pretty girls. Jackie was more than pretty. She had incredible allure, what they used to call animal magnetism. She didn't speak much, but when she did you listened."

Still another member of Jackie's burgeoning legion of male admirers was Charles Bartlett. Bartlett's interest in Jackie dated to 1948, when he first arrived in Washington, an ambitious and talented correspondent for the *Chattanooga Times*. In 1949, he invited her to his brother David's wedding at East Hampton, L.I., where, so the story goes, he nearly succeeded in introducing her to his friend John F. Kennedy, Representative from the 11th Congressional District of Massachusetts, the Boston district which had sent twice-convicted former Mayor James M. Curley to Washington just before Kennedy.

Bartlett, a native of Chicago and a graduate of Yale, had met Jack Kennedy soon after the war, when his family wintered at Hobe Sound and the Kennedys were practically next door at Palm Beach. "I knew Jack's tastes in women and I thought he'd appreciate Jackie because she wasn't like anyone else," said Bartlett. "At the same wedding reception I introduced her to former heavyweight boxing champion Gene Tunney. They stood in one corner and Jack in another, talking politics as usual. Neither could be distracted or detached, and by the time I managed to intervene in Jackie's tête-à-tête, Jack had already departed."

The next opportunity for an introduction came in May 1951. Charles Bartlett had married Martha Buck, well-to-do daughter of a steel industry magnate; they were living in Georgetown, awaiting the birth of their first child. Although Charles Bartlett has always taken credit for introducing Jack and Jackie, the true matchmaker seems to have been his wife.

"Martha was the one who finally got Jack and Jackie together. insisted Lewis Buck, Martha's uncle and her father's business partner. "She did it because Charlie was still interested in Jackie. He'd take her out to lunch and then bring her home for dinner. Charlie and Jackie would be drinking in the living room while Martha, slightly pregnant, was in the kitchen preparing dinner. Martha eventually got fed up with the arrangement and called her father and said, 'What am I going to do?'

"Her father said, 'Bring home somebody for Jackie. Introduce her to some guy.' And that's what happened.

It was John F. Kennedy. She arranged that now-historic dinner party, invited Jack and Jackie and several other couples so it wouldn't look too contrived. She pushed Jack and Jackie together on the couch, served them cocktails and *hors d'oeuvres* and let them drink their heads off. Charlie had nothing to do with it."

John Kennedy's recollection of the eventful evening, evoked during a 1957 *Time* magazine interview, was that Jackie, then still a college senior, appeared to have more substance than most of the young women he had encountered, a deeper sense of purpose in life than merely flaunting her beauty. "So I leaned over the asparagus and asked her for a date." To which Jackie commented that the Bartletts hadn't served asparagus that evening.

In fact, the evening ended on a somewhat disparaging note. Charles Bartlett recalled that after dinner "everyone repaired to our small backyard to play what was then commonly known as 'The Game,' actually a form of Charades in which two opposing teams, working against time, act out a given word or phrase, syllable by syllable. The team guessing the word first wins. The Kennedys were as proficient at 'The Game' as they were at touch football—and just as competitive. But Jackie, being super bright and having studied pantomime at Miss Porter's, was in a league by herself.

"Jack seemed duly impressed and when it came time to leave, he walked her to her car which was parked in front of the house. He was saying something about wanting to take her someplace for nightcaps when there was a sudden commotion. Our fox terrier had raced ahead of them and made an unexpected leap through an open window of the car, landing with a howl in someone's lap. The mysterious stranger, it turned out, was an ex-boyfriend of Jackie's who happened to live nearby; he'd been on his way home when he spotted her car and decided to plant himself in the back seat as a sort of practical joke. Jackie was as surprised as anyone to find him there. She turned a deep red, and then she recovered herself and made the introductions. Jack became flustered. He excused himself and left, quickly.

But he seemed interested because he telephoned the next day and started asking questions. Then we heard nothing from him until the fall. As for Jackie, she spent the summer in Europe with her sister Lee."

Jack and Jackie didn't meet again until the following winter when Jackie was already engaged to John Husted and working at the *Times-Herald,* and Kennedy was busy preparing for his Senatorial contest in Massachusetts against Republican incumbent Henry Cabot Lodge. Again it was Martha Bartlett who instigated the meeting, this time by convincing Jackie to invite Kennedy as her escort to another dinner party at the Bartletts' home.

"We didn't think much of Jackie's fiancé," said Charles Bartlett. "He was a nice fellow, but he didn't seem to be worthy of her hand."

The dinner went well. The first time they went out together, not long after this meeting, Kennedy took Jackie dancing in the Shoreham Hotel's Blue Room. They had a chaperone: Dave Powers, Kennedy's political aide from Boston. The evening's conversation alternated between politics and baseball.

Thereafter the encounters between Jack and Jackie followed a curious private pattern—"spasmodic" was her word for it. "He'd call me from some oyster bar up on the Cape with a great clinking of coins, to ask me out to the movies the following Wednesday . . .," she said. Although campaigning in Massachusetts, Kennedy spent Tuesday through Thursday of each week in Washington, and it was on those days they were free to meet. On occasion Jackie visited him at his Boston apartment-cum-office in Bowdoin Street, brushing past his two secretaries, Evelyn Lincoln and Mary Gallagher, both of whom wound up in the White House with Kennedy.

By April they were dating more regularly, but limited their public appearances, preferring small dinner parties at the homes of close friends or relatives. They often went to the Bartletts for evenings of bridge, Chinese checkers or Monopoly. Others in their select circle at this point included Senator and Mrs. Albert Gore, Senator and Mrs. John Sherman Cooper (who were actually courting at the same time as the Kennedys), and Jeff and Pat Roche (Jeff Roche, a close friend of Charles Bartlett, was a Hearst newspaperman from New York). Other times they dined and spent the night at the Georgetown home of Jack's brother and sister-in-law, Bobby and Ethel Kennedy.

"Then there were the evenings," according to Jack's former Choate roommate Kirk LeMoyne (Lem) Billings, "when they would simply neck in the back seat of Jack's car and afterwards he would drive her home along the Potomac and over Key Bridge to Merrywood. One night his car broke down halfway out her driveway. He trudged back to the house, where Jackie gave him the keys to her stepfather's car. The next morning Hugh Auchincloss found his prized blue Bentley missing and an old, brokendown convertible with Massachusetts plates blocking the driveway.

"Not long after they started dating seriously, Jack found himself in an even more awkward situation. Once while nuzzling with Jackie in the car, they were interrupted by a state trooper. They were parked on a secluded side street in Arlington when the trooper drove up, climbed out of his patrol car and shined his flashlight into the back seat of Jack's convertible. By this time Jack had managed to take off Jackie's brassiere. Apparently the trooper recognized Jack because he apologized and retreated. But Jack had visions of possible headlines: U.S. SENATOR MAULS TOPLESS INQUIRING PHOTOGRAPHER. CAMERA GIRL BUSTED WITH TOP DOWN. 'She may be engaged but at least she's not married,' he said. 'Now *that* could be unpleasant.' "

Although he didn't know all the details, John Husted had few illusions concerning Jackie. "At first after our engagement," he noted, "her letters were very frequent and very romantic. But soon she began writing that her mother thought we were rushing into something, that we had our whole lives ahead of us and we ought to perhaps put off our plans a bit.

"Next I received this strange letter in which she said, 'Don't listen to any of the drivel you hear about me and Jack Kennedy. It's all newspaper talk and doesn't mean a thing.' This came at a time when we were seeing less of each other, so I began to get the picture. Then I received a letter saying she felt we should definitely postpone the wedding. You didn't have to be Einstein to know what that meant."

Toward the middle of March, Jackie invited John Husted to Merrywood for the weekend. As he recounted it, he arrived before she did and was greeted by young Nina Auchincloss, sitting in the library in her little blue Potomac School uniform practicing her spelling. Nina entertained the visitor for an hour until Jackie appeared and took over, while Nina retreated upstairs to her bedroom. Jackie seemed completely untroubled and even ebul-

lient at first. After several minutes, she and John Husted
went upstairs and serenaded the bewildered Nina. Husted
joined Jackie and her family for dinner that evening and
spent the weekend in the same spacious guest room where
he usually stayed when visiting her.

At noon on Sunday she drove him to the airport for his
return flight to New York. As they entered the airline
terminal, Jackie silently slipped the engagement ring off
her finger and dropped it in the side pocket of his
suitjacket. "She didn't say much and neither did I,"
recalled Husted. "There wasn't much you could say.

"A few weeks later I received a letter from Hugh
Auchincloss. Hugh liked me and I think felt badly that it
hadn't worked out. He said as much in his letter and
closed by quoting that famous line from Tennyson, 'Tis
better to have loved and lost than never to have loved at
all,' then added, 'P.S. And I ought to know.' And I think
he did because he'd been married twice himself before he
married Jackie's mother."

Jackie felt a sense of relief at having ended her engagement without difficulty. Janet, overjoyed at the outcome,
returned the engagement presents and placed an announcement in the press stating that "by mutual consent" both
parties were disengaged and once again eligible.

Although initially disappointed, John Husted quickly
recovered. In 1954, the society page of *The New York
Times* reported his marriage to Mrs. Ann Hagerty Brittain,
daughter of Mrs. Raoul H. Fleischmann and the late
Sherward Hagerty of Philadelphia. It was Mrs. Brittain's
second marriage; her first had ended in divorce. Her
stepfather was president and publisher of *The New Yorker*
magazine. And like Jackie, Ann had studied at Miss
Porter's School.

Ormande de Kay encountered John Husted at New York's
River Club "not long after Jackie shed him for Jack. It
brought to mind a letter I'd received from Jackie after I'd
shipped out during the Korean War. The letter, written in
January 1952, had bounced around from one Naval post
office to another, and didn't catch up with me until early
spring. She wrote, 'I want you to be the first to know that
I've found the love of my life, the man I want to marry.'
It was John Husted. By the time the letter reached me,
she had dropped Husted and was chasing Jack."

When Jackie first apprised John White of her interest

in Kennedy, he told her he thought no good would come of it. "I'd been a friend of Jack's from my days with his sister Kathleen," attested White. "We had double-dated on a number of occasions. I knew what a womanizer he was. I told Jackie I didn't think he'd make a very good husband, that he was nice to play around with but nobody to bring home to Momma.

"I think for Jackie the desire to conquer JFK was first of all the money, then the challenge and finally the fact, as far as I could see, that she had very little experience dealing with love and didn't know what to expect. In this area she had much less knowledge than her sister Lee. Jackie was tougher but also much more innocent than her younger sister. She maybe just thought that JFK wasn't the worst bargain in the world. And certainly the idea that he was on the way up appealed to her.

"I'd known other girls who had dealt with him. I used to hear their stories. Some of them would say to deal with such raw power and such open contempt—being checked off in a little black book—was a hell of a challenge. They thought they might break through to him. And the fact that he was such a cold fish also played a role. He had warm blood but a cold heart. Most of these women had dealt with other men and regarded JFK as an oddity to be treasured. He was different—totally cold and ruthless toward women, which I suppose many of them found charming. It was almost the idea of being able to say the next morning you were drunk and didn't know what you were doing.

"I don't think Jackie cared much about JFK's morals. We discussed Jack a bit later on, and by then Jackie understood the situation and was willing to accept the risk. More important to her than his morality was that he be at the center of events and that he acquit himself well and give her a decent role in the drama. It's fair to say they both lived up to their ends of the bargain.

"It all might have turned out quite differently for Jackie. She might have been more like her father. She talked about Black Jack and seemed to worship him, though with certain apprehension and reservations. She probably recognized in herself some of her father's qualities. I had the feeling that she felt with a little more guts she might take off for Paris or some such place and become totally independent, but instead she settled for security. Black Jack was a constant threat, a temptation resisted."

7

In November 1952, following the election of Dwight Eisenhower as President and John Kennedy as Democratic Senator from Massachusetts, John Davis met his cousin Jackie for lunch at Washington's Mayflower Hotel. As Davis describes it in *The Kennedys*,* their conversation soon moved from trivial family matters to the more interesting subject of Jackie's ongoing relationship with John Kennedy—how the Senator (according to Jackie) went daily to a hairdresser "to have his hair done," how he sulked "for hours," if, at a party or reception, nobody recognized him or took his picture. Joking about introducing Jack Kennedy to Aunt Edith Beale and her newly acquired menagerie of forty cats, Jackie noted that Kennedy was highly allergic to animals, especially to horses and cats. "Imagine me with someone allergic to horses!" she quipped. Her other memorable comment that afternoon: "The Kennedys are really terribly bourgeois."

Bourgeois or not, the youthful Senator evidently possessed certain qualities that appealed to Jackie: looks, charm, biting wit, and an impossibly wealthy father. Jack Kennedy was also exceptionally eligible, frightfully ambitious, and of the same religious background as Jackie. In political terms he defined himself as "an idealist without illusions." Asked what he thought were his best and worst qualities, he rated curiosity his best; worst was his irritability, his impatience with the boring, commonplace and mediocre. Beneath his glittering, outgoing exterior, there seemed to be an insularity and loneliness that Jackie not only recognized but shared. Deep within him was "a pool of privacy," which she herself also had. She compared herself and Jack to "icebergs," the greater part of

*See John H. Davis, *The Kennedys: Dynasty and Disaster*, pp. 150-151.

their lives submerged, and insisted they both "sensed this in each other, and that this was a bond between us."

She had read a newspaper interview in which Jack Kennedy had elaborated on the kind of wife he wanted. "Something nice," he said. "Intelligent, but not too brainy." This description disturbed her far less than the fact that she differed so drastically from the type of woman he usually dated—seductive, outgoing, curvacious. While not self-conscious about it, she was highly aware of her more athletic, flat-chested figure.

Jackie concentrated on molding herself into a warm, enthusiastic, lighthearted companion, a girl with a love of art, music and literature. Her most attractive feature to men was her ability to become "a bewitching lighthouse beacon of charm," and when the beam was on, the light was bright. When she liked a man, she focused on him to the exclusion of everything else in the room, taking him in with her wide-set eyes, listening to him "with a shining, breathless intensity."

For Jack Kennedy, the light was always on. Jackie informed Mary Van Rensselaer Thayer, a journalist friend of her mother's, that from the beginning she realized Jack "would have a profound, perhaps a disturbing influence" on her life. In a flash of perception she also understood that here was a man who, despite what he told interviewers, did not really want to marry. The realization had demoralized her. She envisaged heartbreak, but decided that such heartbreak might be worth the pain and effort.

Jackie's plan of action was as meticulously plotted as any of Jack Kennedy's subsequent political campaigns, very little left to chance. When she learned that he sometimes brought his lunch to work in a paper bag and ate alone in his Senatorial office, she made a point of dropping in on him at lunchtime with a hot box-lunch for two. She used her newspaper column to excellent advantage, asking questions calculated to nudge Jack in the right direction. "Can you give any reasons why a contented bachelor should marry?" she asked a group of tourists in front of the Lincoln Monument. Another day she took her cue from Irish author Sean O'Faolain and asked a dozen passers-by what they thought of his view that "the Irish are deficient in the art of love?"

One morning Frank Waldrop suggested that Jackie

interview John Kennedy for her column. He realized
Kennedy had taken Jackie to the Eisenhower Inaugural
Ball in January 1953; she had covered it for the *Times-
Herald*. But he didn't know the full extent of their rela-
tionship, or that she had co-hosted a cocktail party
Kennedy had thrown on the eve of the Ball.

"Go on up there and interview the fellow," Waldrop
told Jackie. "Tell him I sent you. But don't get your
hopes up. He's too old for you—besides, he doesn't want
to get married."

Jackie rolled her eyes but said nothing. With the help
of reporter Estelle Gaines, she interviewed not only Senator Kennedy but also Vice President Nixon, a pair of
freshman members of Congress and several U. S. Senate
pages. She asked the pages, "What's it like observing
politicians at close range?" and conversely, of the politicians, "What's it like observing the pages at close range?"

Kennedy's response, while inconsequential, contained
a touch of humor: "I've often thought that the country
might be better off if we Senators and the pages traded
jobs. If such legislation is ever enacted, I'll be glad to
hand over the reins. . . ."

Jackie's pursuit of the vibrant Senator did not go unnoticed on the Hill. William "Fishbait" Miller, Congressional Doorkeeper, remembered "Jackie Kennedy when
she was Jackie Bouvier and a scared little newspaper girl
trying to act dignified and grown up . . . would come to
me to help her get some pictures for her column, which
simply involved asking a question a day."

Fishbait offered to help Jackie in her romance with
Kennedy. First, he warned her to "keep hands off" the
party's "most glamorous and eligible man." Then he
said, "But if you really want him, Jackie, I'll help you get
him."

"Fishbait, you nut," she replied. "If I need help, I'll
advertise."

Another unsolicited offer of assistance came from Lem
Billings, but not until he, too, tried to dissuade her. "I
took her aside at a party," he said, "and attempted to
teach her 'the facts of life.' In general terms, I described
Jack's physiological problems—his bad back, his Addison's disease—and talked about some of the women in
his life, emphasizing the dangers of getting involved with
somebody older who was already set in his ways. I also

went into Jack's political ambitions, his desire to become President, and what that might mean with regard to her own future. 'In this town,' I said, 'you don't count unless they play "Hail to the Chief" when you enter the room. If they don't do that, you're nothing but a spear carrier around here.'

"Having said all that, I told her how important she could be in terms of Jack's career. I told her she stood head and shoulders above all the other women he'd known. 'Most of them don't have minds of their own,' I said. 'They only want to please him, to be the perfect hostess. They read *Time, Newsweek, U.S. News & World Report,* the number-one fiction and nonfiction best-sellers. That's all you need in Washington. With that you're able to talk to anyone about anything, to get through dinner or a cocktail party without making an ass of yourself, so long as you don't mention sex or religion. But as we both know, that's not what Jack needs. He needs a woman with social flair but also somebody with intelligence and character, like yourself. If you want me to talk to him, I will.' "

Although she declined the offer, Jackie had good reason to question the future. Gradually her newspaper job had begun to take second place to her relationship with Kennedy. She demonstrated her devotion (and literary skill) by helping him edit and write several Senatorial position papers on Southeast Asia and a term paper in art history for Teddy Kennedy, Jack's youngest brother, then still an undergraduate at Harvard.* She translated several books for Jack, including the work of Paul Mus, a French writer whose field of expertise was France's involvement in Vietnam. She ran his errands, carried his briefcase when his back ached, accompanied him to political dinners, helped him shop for clothes (until Jackie came along, Kennedy took little interest in men's fashion) and relaxed with him by going sailing or to the movies (he insisted on seeing only Westerns and adventure films, neither of which appealed to Jackie; she went anyway).

---

*Dependence on the skill of others, academic and otherwise, became an early and repetitive pattern in Ted Kennedy's life. During his freshman year at Harvard (1950), he convinced a schoolmate to take his final exam for him in Spanish. Exposed, they were both expelled but reinstated a year later.

Early in the relationship, in fact while still engaged to John Husted, Jackie spent a long weekend with Jack at the Kennedy oceanfront estate in Palm Beach. Rose Kennedy was away and Jackie didn't meet Jack's mother but sent her a thank-you letter anyway, signed Jackie. "I thought it was from a boy," Rose Kennedy wrote in her autobiography. It was the first she had heard of Jack's new friend.*

The first time Jackie actually saw her future mother-in-law was the summer of 1952 when she spent several days in Hyannis Port, Cape Cod, at the Kennedy compound. Though she knew Bobby and Ethel and had been introduced to Jack's sisters, the prospect of meeting Rose Kennedy and her formidable husband made Jackie anxious.

She thought she started off poorly because her evening gown was a shade too dressy for a country weekend dinner. Jack teased her about it in an affectionate way. "Where do you think you're going?" he said. Rose Kennedy came to her defense. She said, "Oh don't be mean to her, dear. She looks lovely."

Though they went out of their way to include Jackie in their activities, the whole family together, driving, vital, secure in all-for-one and one-for-all spirit, could not fail to overwhelm a newcomer to their close-knit ranks. Jackie was swept along by the frenzy and energy of the clan as they rushed headlong and without pause from one activity to another.

"How can I explain these people?" she later wrote. "They were like carbonated water, and other families might be flat. They'd be talking about so many things with so much enthusiasm. Or they'd be playing games. At dinner or in the living room, anywhere, everybody would be talking about something. They had so much interest in life—it was so stimulating. And so gay and so open and accepting. . . ."

According to family friend Dinah Bridge, the Kennedys were equally impressed by Jackie's performance: "She was put through her paces, I should think you could say. And she stood up extremely well to the Kennedy barrage of questions. It was quite a barrage. You had to know the form to keep up, you know, because the jokes went so fast, and the chitter chat. But she did extremely well."

*See Rose Fitzgerald Kennedy, *Times to Remember*, pp. 346–348.

Subsequent visits, however, were more stressful. She began to suspect and notice, without admitting it even to herself, that there was an element of reserve in the Kennedy attitude towards her which kept her apart and which, in spite of all the wonderful welcoming noise, made her feel as if she were on probation.

The rampant activity she experienced on her first visit seemed, if anything, to accelerate. The competition—in touch football, tennis, swimming, sailing, softball, golf, even dinner table conversation—was almost *too* fierce. Jackie compared the family compound to Boy Scout camp, her own reception to a sorority hazing. She referred to Jack's sisters—Eunice, Jean and Pat—as "the Rah-Rah Girls" and described their compulsive game-playing as "the remnant of a second childhood," observing that when they were bored with conventional sports they took either to the trampoline for gymnastics or to the beach for calisthenics and jogging. "When they have nothing else to do," she told Lee, "they run in place. Other times they fall all over each other like a pack of gorillas."

Jack's sisters needled Jackie mercilessly and bombarded her with sarcasm and a loud, boisterous humor that was highly unnerving. They referred to her as "The Deb," ridiculed her "Babykins" voice, forced her to play touch football, upbraiding her whenever she ran in the wrong direction or dropped a pass. When she told them her name was pronounced "Jac-lean," Eunice observed under her breath, "Rhymes with queen." They also laughed when she refused to eat peanut butter-and-jelly sandwiches on an afternoon sail and instead brought pâté and quiche and a bottle of white wine. The sisters were led by Ethel, who had always prided herself on being "more Kennedy than thou." When Jackie confided, somewhat ingenuously, that she had once hoped to become a ballerina, Ethel pointed to her shoes and said, "With those feet of yours? You'd be better off going into soccer, kid."

Jackie struggled to keep up with the blistering Kennedy pace until finally she decided to revert to her old style and her more tranquil and reflective manner. "It's enough for me to enjoy a sport without having to win, place or show," she told Jack when he tried to convince her to join his crew for the annual Labor Day Hyannis Port Yacht Club Regatta. She and Joe Kennedy watched the race through binoculars from a private jetty in front of the compound.

"Joe soon became Jackie's most ardent supporter," said Lem Billings. "He admired her because of her individuality. She wasn't afraid of him. She cajoled him, teased him, talked back to him. He was the moving spirit behind the entire clan. He shaped his children's lives, their relationships, their thoughts. By conquering him, she was conquering his son."

To win Joe Kennedy to her side, Jackie played upon his social insecurity, dropping hints about her illustrious background, flaunting her French Catholic ancestry, her highly developed sense of style, while hiding the tough and ambitious Irish Catholic side of her character. She sensed immediately that what appealed to Joe, despite the taunts of his daughters, were her refinement and polish. Every one of the Kennedy men married women more socially prominent than themselves. Joe married Rose because her father, John Francis (Honey Fitz) Fitzgerald, was a U.S. Representative and Mayor of Boston. Climbing the social ladder, attaining a measure of historical respectability, getting out of the East Boston slums: those were the conditions that motivated Joe Kennedy. His inability as an Irish Catholic to crash the Boston Brahmin establishment is what drove him to move his family to New York. Later he impressed every Irishman in America by gaining political favor with the British bluebloods during his ambassadorial stint at the Court of St. James's.

Jackie had all the vital social ingredients that Joe Kennedy thought would help Jack attain the presidency: Miss Porter's, Vassar, the Sorbonne, Debutante of the Year, the Prix de Paris, Merrywood and Hammersmith Farm. If nothing else, she gave the impression of having great wealth, dispelling the notion that she might possibly be a golddigger. Her wealth was largely an illusion because in reality Jackie was almost penniless. But nobody knew that until after the marriage. Joe Kennedy's only concern at the moment was the twelve-year age difference that existed between Jack and Jackie. He realized that a failed marriage could be fatal to Jack's political future. He also realized that Jackie's experiences in life—her sophistication and maturity—made her seem older than other girls her age. If there were to be problems in the marriage, they would stem from other causes.

"Joe Kennedy not only condoned the marriage, he ordained it," claimed Lem Billings. 'A politician has to have a wife,' he said, 'and a Catholic politician has to have a Catholic wife. She should have class. Jackie probably has more class than any girl we've ever seen around here.'

"After that I expected a proposal any day, although it was hard to imagine Jack actually saying 'I love you' to Jackie and asking her to marry him. He would have liked it to happen without having to say the words. He wasn't exactly the candy-and-flowers type.

"Still, by the early spring of 1953 it was clear that the relationship had progressed further than any of the others he had indulged in in the past. He and Jackie were most certainly on intimate terms. She didn't want his friends to know they were sexually involved. Jackie couldn't be attracted to a man unless he was 'dangerous,' like her father. It was Freudian. Jack knew about her attraction to Black Jack and even discussed it with her. She didn't deny it.

"My guess is that Jackie enjoyed sex but primarily as a by-product of a deeply emotional relationship. Sex is the most sophisticated of games, and Jackie was highly sophisticated. She enjoyed the drama inherent in relationships. It bothered her that Jack was still dating other women, but it also intrigued her. She kept her own options open, retaining a measure of independence by managing to be seen with all manner of eligible young (and older) men. She warmed to the challenge, playing 'hard to get,' not always being there when Jack telephoned her and not always being available when he reached her.

"By this point, Jackie had visited Hyannis Port on several occasions and had gradually grown closer to the other members of the clan, including Jack's sisters. If they still resented Jackie, it was because of Jack. After Joe Jr.'s death on a secret bombing mission during World War II, Jack became the family's major symbol of hope. His sisters opposed every girl interested in marrying him.

"The Kennedys thought of themselves first, everybody else second. Anybody admitted to the inner sanctum, whether friend or spouse, had to first prove his or her loyalty. Their suspicion of outsiders had been reinforced both by the outside world's resistance to them and a series of family tragedies—Joe Jr.'s death during the war; the death in 1948 of Kick Kennedy in an airplane crash over France; the prefrontal lobotomy performed on Rosemary Kennedy and her permanent internment at St. Coletta's, a convent in Jefferson, Wisconsin."

Having succeeded in charming Joe Kennedy, Jackie next arranged a meeting between Jack Kennedy and her father. The introduction of the two Jacks took place in February 1953 over dinner in a New York restaurant. According to Jackie, "They were very much alike. They talked about sports, politics and women—what all red-blooded men like to talk about."

Black Jack subsequently told Louis Ehret that aside from needing a haircut, young Mr. Kennedy seemed "a decent chap—not what I expected. I thought he'd be more like his old man. At any rate, Jackie's madly in love with him."

James Rousmaniere, one of Jack Kennedy's Harvard roommates, also heard about the meeting—from Kennedy's perspective. "Black Jack was really a very unfortunate man and Jacqueline tried to live him down most of her life," said Rousmaniere. "He was pretty bad. His drinking was legendary. There was a sense of buried drama about him, brewing clouds.

"By the time Jack Kennedy discovered him, Black Jack was in a state of slow but visible decline. Although he still followed the Market, he was about to sell his seat on the Exchange. He had become a recluse. Jackie didn't pay him much heed anymore and neither did Lee. So Jack Kennedy made a real attempt to get to know him, even before he and Jacqueline were married.

"He visited his future father-in-law in New York on several occasions. Black Jack took him to the Stock Exchange Luncheon Club and then gave him a tour of Wall Street. Another time, Jack dropped in on him at home. They were alone and they watched a prize fight together on television. Black Jack seemed lonely and Jack made the effort to stretch his visit. Black Jack was drunk or at least drinking. Kennedy himself drank relatively little, but Black Jack got him drinking a bit that evening and they ended up having a fine time."

On April 18 Black Jack Bouvier paid his first visit to Merrywood. His daughter Lee had dropped out of Sarah Lawrence College, had taken art and voice lessons in

Italy, had worked briefly for *Harper's Bazaar* in New York, had seriously considered but ultimately rejected the opportunity to take a screen test for Paramount Pictures, and finally at age twenty was about to undertake a new project—marriage. The young man in question was Michael Temple Canfield, the adopted son of Harper and Brothers publisher Cass Canfield. A Harvard graduate and Marine combat veteran, Michael had dated Lee sporadically since her debutante days. He had recently accepted a post with the American Embassy in London, and it was there that he and Lee hoped to settle.*

The wedding was to be held at Washington's Holy Trinity Church, the reception at Merrywood. Jack Bouvier, however great the ordeal, felt obliged to venture into Auchincloss territory and give his daughter away. Although he carried off the first part of his mission with great restraint, he soon began to experience pangs of regret. Touring the spacious grounds of Merrywood and the mansion itself, he couldn't help but think of his own modest apartment in New York. The contrast between the two residences, the difference between his rival's wealth and his own limited means, had never before been so dramatically drawn. The realization that he hadn't been able to give his daughters nearly as much as Hugh Auchincloss had given them left a permanent scar.

The effects of the marriage were equally hard on Jackie, Lee's maid of honor, in that they reminded her of her own precarious position—that of the as yet unmarried older sister. But by the middle of May, Jack Kennedy had made what for him amounted to a declaration of love—he proposed. He told Jackie that he had actually decided the year before to marry her. He had wanted to wait, he said, but knew all along that she was the one.

"How *big* of you!" Jackie shot back.

Formal announcement of their engagement would have to be delayed. *The Saturday Evening Post* had scheduled

---

*One persistent rumor had it that Michael Canfield was the illegitimate issue of a union between a certain married English noblewoman and the Duke of Kent (the younger brother of the King) The Canfields had supposedly adopted him to prevent a scandal from rocking the British Royal Family. According to Cass Canfield, Jr., Michael's brother, "The rumor is just that—a rumor. It has no basis in fact and started because Michael somewhat resembled the real son of the Duke of Kent."

a story, "Jack Kennedy—The Senate's Gay Young Bachelor," and Kennedy didn't want to proclaim his defection
from the ranks until the magazine hit the newsstands. In
addition Jackie had agreed to accompany a friend, Aileen Bowdoin (today Aileen Bowdoin Train), to the Coronation of Elizabeth II in England.

Aileen, older sister of two of the girls with whom
Jackie made her first trip to Europe, had conceived the
idea for the expedition: "I suddenly became infected with
the Coronation-and-travel bug, so I called Jackie. 'Will
you go to the Coronation if I can arrange rooms and
passage?' I asked. Jackie, who was immediately bitten by
the same bug, said she would have to check with her
editor. She called me back the following day. The editor
wanted her to cover the Coronation for the newspaper.

"My father George Bowdoin in New York had a great
friend, Alex Abel-Smith, whose wife was one of Queen
Elizabeth's ladies-in-waiting. They would be staying at
Buckingham Palace during Coronation week, so they
agreed to give us their flat in London. Then my father
knew the director of U. S. Lines, and we were able to
obtain a last-minute cabin aboard the *S.S. United States*."

Jackie's articles on the Coronation, including a series
of quick, catchy pen-and-ink sketches, made the front
page of the *Times-Herald.* She covered everything from
the Duke and Duchess of Windsor's dogs kenneled aboard
the *United States* (they traveled with their own portable
fire hydrant) to Perle Mesta's Ball at Londonderry House.
An avid celebrity watcher, Jackie observed Lauren Bacall
waltzing with General Omar Bradley (Humphrey Bogart
paced the sidelines), was introduced to the young Marquess of Milford Haven (who told her that a special mark
had to be made on the crown of St. Edward the Confes-
sor so that it would not be placed the wrong way round
on the Queen's head), conversed with the Pasha of Marrakesh at a U.S. Embassy dinner dance. When she wasn't
partying, Jackie could be found roaming the streets of
London interviewing American tourists, British house-
wives, cockney factory workers, students from Caribbean
islands. The interviews formed the basis for an article on
the commoners' view of the Coronation.

After a week in London Jackie received a telegram
from Jack Kennedy (ARTICLES EXCELLENT, BUT
YOU ARE MISSED)—it was one of his rare romantic

messages—followed by a transatlantic telephone call. Jack had just returned to Washington from his sister Eunice's wedding to Sargent Shriver in New York and wanted to tell her about it. He then asked whether she could buy "a few" out-of-print books for him in London—mostly volumes on history and legislation as well as some Aldous Huxley—and when she agreed, he proceeded to reel off a list of titles four pages long. Jackie had to purchase an extra suitcase and pay a hundred dollars in excess baggage fees to get the books back to the United States.

Aileen Bowdoin noted that "not many people realized Jack Kennedy had proposed to Jackie before we left. While we were over there, she tried to decide whether or not to marry him. It was a difficult decision. She was her own person and the Kennedy family, as everyone knows, consists of some pretty rugged characters. As much as she cared for Jack, she felt that she'd lose her independence and separate identity to the family. Her job at the *Times-Herald* had nothing to do with it . . . it was a question of joining that family and being taken over by them."

For over a year Jackie had wanted nothing more than to marry Jack Kennedy, but the reality of the situation filled her with trepidation. She needed more time. After two weeks in London, she decided to spend an additional two weeks in Paris.

One of the people whose advice Jackie sought in Paris was John P. Marquand, Jr., son of the celebrated New England novelist and himself an emerging writer whose first novel, *The Second Happiest Day*, had been published the year before.

"We knew each other," said John Marquand, Jr., "through my wife Sue Coward. Sue had been Jackie's roommate in Paris when they were both at the Sorbonne. Another connection we had was that Sue's first cousin was Michael Canfield, who was married to Lee. Jackie and I were closest before she became the Cleopatra of her age. We kept up a steady correspondence but I destroyed most of it a long time ago—I just didn't want to have it around.

"When Jackie turned up in Paris following the Coronation, we went out to dinner several times. I don't know that I played any role as a sounding board, but I do know that rumors began to circulate that we were lovers, that I was the one who deflowered Jackie. This ludicrous story was given credence by Kitty Kelley in that book of hers on Jackie [*Jackie Oh.!*, 1978, pp. 27–28], in which she quoted some unidentified source as having claimed not only that I was Jackie's first lover, but that afterwards she said something like, 'Oh! Is that all there is to it?'

"I have no idea where Kitty Kelley got all this—I refused to be interviewed by her—but it reflects on me a whole lot more than it does on Jackie. I mean what kind of an asshole would go around making claims on the maidenhead of Jacqueline Kennedy Onassis? When Kitty Kelley reported this story, people were calling me up and riding me about it. I was appalled. I approached Jackie and she said, 'Let's not talk about it. Forget it.' Anyway, it's bullshit, totally apocryphal, categorically untrue."

Jackie and Aileen opted to fly home rather than return by boat. They departed Orly Airport on June 14 and were scheduled to touch down in Boston late that night. Seated across the aisle from Jackie on the airplane was Zsa Zsa Gabor. Zsa Zsa later recalled, "Twenty-four hours on the plane she kept asking me—it was no joke— 'What do you do for your skin?' And I never bothered to ask her name. She wasn't the most glamorous nor the most beautiful woman. She had kinky hair and bad skin."

Although Jackie didn't realize it, Zsa Zsa Gabor and Jack Kennedy had once been an item. Jackie said nothing about Jack, but as they neared the United States coastline she became increasingly uneasy. She began to wonder if he would be at the airport to meet her.

The Hungarian-born actress departed the airplane before Jackie, zipped through customs and found Jack Kennedy in the waiting room, leaning casually against a counter. When Kennedy saw Zsa Zsa, he embraced her and lifted her off the ground. "My darling sweetheart, I've always been in love with you," he said. Moments later Jackie entered the waiting room and spotted Jack with Zsa Zsa. Jack put the actress down and smiled as Jackie stepped forward. He then introduced the two women.

"Miss Bouvier and I spent hours together on the plane," Zsa Zsa told Kennedy. "She's a lovely girl. Don't dare corrupt her, Jack."

"But he already has," Jackie whispered.

8

The day after her return from Europe, Jacqueline Bouvier went to see her boss, Frank Waldrop, and with mock contrition handed in her resignation. "She told me I'd been right in suspecting she might end up married rather than a professional reporter," said Waldrop. "She was hamming it up, but I said I was disappointed because her articles on the Coronation showed promise. Then I said, 'Who's the lucky fellow?' 'John Kennedy,' she responded. '—And this time it's for real.'"

The official announcement of Jack and Jackie's engagement on June 24, 1953, was followed by two engagement parties, one given by the Auchinclosses at Hammersmith Farm, the other by the Harringtons, friends of the Kennedys, in a big house they owned at the edge of the Hyannis Port Golf Club. Larry O'Brien, political aide to John Kennedy and a member of the fabled "Irish mafia," arrived at the Kennedy compound several days prior to the Harrington party.

"My wife and I were sitting around with Jack and Jackie," O'Brien recalled. "We were all in casual attire, swim suits and Bermuda shorts, when two young businessmen in three-piece suits appeared. They were from Van Cleef & Arpels, the exclusive New York jewelry store. They were delivering Jackie's engagement ring. Jack slipped it on her finger. It was a twinned square-cut emerald and diamond. My wife and Jackie had fun exchanging it, putting it on and admiring it. Jack was so pleased that he invited the two men to stay and join us for a swim."

They reenacted the ring ceremony for the benefit of the guests at the Harringtons, enjoyed a sit-down luncheon and took part in the usual pranks and party games, including a scavenger hunt during which a school bus was abducted and a policeman's hat stolen.

121

Jackie returned to Hyannis Port a week later for what she hoped would be a leisurely vacation of tennis, reading, sketching and sailing. Instead she was introduced to a *Life* magazine photographer and told that she and Jack would spend the next three days posing for hundreds of shots to be used with a cover story on their romance. When she balked, Jack's sisters advised her it was for the good of his career.

During July, Jackie accompanied Jack to Worcester, Mass., the site of a recent tornado, where he presented a check for $150,000 from the Joseph P. Kennedy, Jr., Foundation to Assumption College, which had been severely damaged by the storm. Aboard their chartered plane sat a dozen reporters and photographers. Asked by one if she felt she had much in common with the Massachusetts Senator, Jackie replied that they had some things *too much* in common: "Since Jack is such a violently independent person, and I, too, am so independent, this relationship will take a lot of working out."

The bride-to-be was a frequent guest at Hyannis Port that summer. When not beleaguered by the press, she and Jack skippered the *Victura* (Kennedy's 24-foot sailboat), read poetry aloud, or strolled along the beach. Jackie even joined the family for an occasional game of touch football, retiring permanently a year later when a burly Harvard classmate of Ted Kennedy's accidentally broke her ankle when he tripped over her.

In mid-July Jackie's mother invited Rose Kennedy to Newport for lunch and to discuss the wedding plans. Jack and Jackie were also in Newport that weekend. Before lunch the four drove to Bailey's Beach Club. Janet and Rose were dressed up—cartwheel hats, white gloves, silk dresses and pearls. Jack wore an old undershirt, cut-offs and a pair of bedroom slippers.

"The two mothers were in the front of the car and we were sitting in the back seat, sort of like two bad children," Jackie reported. "Anyway [after we reached the club], Jack and I went swimming. I came out of the water earlier; it was time to go for lunch, but Jack dawdled. And I remember Rose stood on the walk and called to her son in the water, 'Jack! . . . Ja-a-ck!'—and it was just like the little ones who won't come out and pretend not to hear their mothers calling—'Ja-a-ck!' but he wouldn't come out of the water. I can't remember whether she started down or I went down to get him, but he started coming up, saying, 'Yes, Mother.' "

Over lunch Janet Auchincloss let it be known that what she wanted was a small, very exclusive wedding for Jackie—no pictures, no press, no crowds, just a discreet notice in the Newport and Washington newspapers and a few close family friends.

"Look, Mrs. Auchincloss, your daughter is marrying a political figure, a Senator, a man who may one day be President," protested Jack Kennedy. "There are going to be photographers whether we like it or not. So the idea is to show Jackie to best advantage."

When arbitration bogged down, Jack unleashed his father on Janet. Joe Kennedy flew to Newport. The minute Jackie saw the Ambassador step off the airplane, striding defiantly toward them, she realized her mother didn't stand a chance.

The ceremony Joe Kennedy negotiated with Jackie's mother would take place in Newport but it would be more along the lines of a media event than a society wedding.

Both sides remained wary of the other. Janet Auchincloss found the Kennedys gauche, venal and hard-nosed; she told friends that Jackie was marrying "down, not up." Joe Kennedy struck her as abrasive, abrupt and hairtrigger-tempered, "the kind of man who will rip your head off if he doesn't get his way."

Reflecting on the Auchinclosses in particular and Newporters in general, Joe Kennedy told Red Fay, a wartime chum of Jack's: "They don't even know how to live up there in Newport. Their wealth is from an era gone by. Most of them are just keeping up a front and owe everybody. If you pulled the carpets up most likely you'd find all the summer dirt brushed under there, because they don't have enough help to keep those big places running right. The food is generally second-rate. I tell you they don't know the first thing about living up there as compared to the way we live down here."*

---

*Joe Kennedy's comments appeared in the original draft of Fay's *The Pleasure of His Company* (1966), a book about his friendship with John F. Kennedy. Jackie requested that this passage, as well as many others, be excised prior to the book's publication. Under pressure from the Kennedy family, Fay complied.

In August, Jack Kennedy took off with Torbert H. "Torby" Macdonald, a former college roommate (and a future Massachusetts member of the House of Representatives), on a two-week Mediterranean pleasure cruise, leaving Jackie behind to work out the final wedding arrangements. Jackie's mother was enraged. "No man in love does something like that," she told her daughter. "If you're in love with a girl, you want to be with her."

Although she denied it, Jackie was alarmed by Kennedy's need for what he called "a last fling." Estelle Parker, a fashion designer with boutiques in Palm Beach and Newport, described a scene in which, while fitting Jackie for her trousseau, she was obliged to listen to a lengthy outpouring of premarital anxiety.

"She had several concerns," said Estelle Parker, "starting with men who can't settle down. She wanted to know what I thought of husbands who cheat on their wives. I felt she was talking to me because she couldn't talk to her mother and didn't want to talk to any of her mother's friends.

"I knew she wasn't too crazy about the Kennedys. She realized that if she married into that family she would be expected to cater to their every whim. Kennedy women were treated like second-class citizens. They would virtually pick up Rose Kennedy by the scruff of the neck and physically remove her from the room when the talk turned serious. Jackie wasn't prepared to tolerate that sort of treatment.

"She seemed confused, undecided. At the same time that she refused to play second fiddle to the Kennedys, she worried about her lack of experience as a homemaker. She knew nothing about housekeeping. She had grown up with maids and cooks. She knew about place settings and flower arrangements, but she couldn't boil an egg. She had quit her newspaper job and was trying to learn something about running a household. When I was fitting her in Newport, she asked if I could put together a few household hints to help her along.

"My husband and I filled a large looseleaf notebook with all sorts of information, telling her what to keep in the refrigerator, like cold cuts and beer for the Senator and his political pals, how to make cut flowers last, how when changing beds you simply place the top sheet on the bottom. Of course some years later when she became

First Lady, she had her sheets changed three times a day, but at the beginning she was more moderate. When I saw her again two years later, she still had the notebook in her possession and told me she was using it. 'Without it I would have been lost,' she said."

The best-kept secret concerning Jackie's wedding was fashion designer Ann Lowe, a black American who for fifty years quietly sewed clothes for some of the leading women in American society. Janet Auchincloss, always cost-conscious, hired her to outfit the entire Jacqueline Bouvier/John Kennedy bridal party. Jackie made frequent trips to New York that summer for fittings and alterations, never telling anyone who was responsible for designing her wedding gown.

Lois K. Alexander, director of the Harlem Institute of Fashion and a friend of Ann Lowe's, recalled that a flood in Ann's Lexington Avenue workshop just days before the wedding created havoc: "Ten of fifteen gowns were completely ruined. The fifty yards of ivory silk chiffon from which the wedding dress was made, the bridesmaids' pink silk faille and red satin had to be replaced by the supplier. The bridal gown, which had taken more than two months to make, was completed in two days of cutting and three days of sewing. An estimated $700 profit turned into a $2,200 loss because Ann refused to discuss the accident with the Auchinclosses."

While Ann worked feverishly to complete the dresses, the Kennedys celebrated the imminent wedding in rousing fashion, starting with a bash at Boston's Parker House for 350 of Jack's political associates and campaign supporters. The clan then turned its Hyannis Port compound into a sort of amusement park for friends and relatives. For a week before the September 12, 1953, nuptials, the lawns teemed with activity, highlighted by an outdoor birthday party for the senior Mr. Kennedy. Each of his "children" gave him a sweater and popped them, one atop another, over his head.

The scene then switched to Newport, where Anthony and Jane Akers, friends of the Auchinclosses, hosted a cocktail party in honor of Jack and Jackie. Two days before the wedding, Hugh Auchincloss gave a bachelor dinner for eighteen at the Clambake Club. Jack Kennedy keynoted the affair with a champagne toast to his absent future bride ("to my future bride, Jacqueline Bouvier") and then invited everyone to throw their glasses into the fireplace.

"I'd told Jack beforehand that this was the protocol at such functions," said Red Fay. "But I was surprised he went through with it because the glassware consisted of these beautiful crystal goblets that belonged to Hugh Auchincloss and had evidently been in his family for generations. He winced when eighteen glasses shattered in the fireplace. After we disposed of those glasses, the waiter replaced them with another set of Auchincloss's fine crystal and refilled them. Jack stood up and said, 'Maybe this isn't the accepted custom but I want to again express my love for the girl I'm going to marry. A toast to the bride,' Everybody downed their bubbly and a second time the glasses went flying into the fireplace and were destroyed. Hugh Auchincloss appeared badly shaken. As a result of the second toast, the third set of glasses to come to the table could have fitted very nicely into the rack at Healy's ten-cent restaurant."

The bridal dinner was also held at the Clambake Club. There, the night before the ceremony, the wedding attendants received their gifts—Brooks Brothers umbrellas for the fourteen ushers, monogrammed silver picture frames for the ten bridesmaids. The bridegroom then gave a tongue-in-cheek speech, disclosing his motivation for marrying Jackie—he had wanted to remove her from the Fourth Estate. She had become too perspicacious a reporter and, as Inquiring Camera Girl, menaced his political future.

Jackie teased back. As a suitor, she stated wryly, the Senator was in certain respects a failure. During their courtship he had written her no love letters and but a single postcard, which he had sent from Bermuda. She held it aloft and read its message aloud: "Wish you were here. Jack."

Mary deLimur Weinmann attended the bridal dinner and remembered Jack giving Jackie her wedding present. "It was a diamond bracelet," she said. "And I was sitting next to her when he came by with it and sort of dropped it in her lap. She was so surprised."

For Jackie, a dark shadow over the wedding was cast by her father. In preparation for the event, Black Jack spent the month of August sunning himself and exercising at the Maidstone Club in East Hampton. He took weeks to select a suitable wardrobe, a perfectly tailored cutaway, his father's pearl stickpin, shoes and gloves of the finest imported leather. He booked a room at the Viking, Newport's top hotel, while his twin sisters and their husbands chose the nearby Hotel Munchener King.

"The Auchinclosses controlled the social arrangements for the wedding," recalled Jack Bouvier's sister Michelle, "and they saw to it that Jackie's father was effectively excluded from active participation. Janet made certain that his role was kept at a minimum, that he attended none of the preceremony dinner parties. Jack was crushed. He had expected to be invited to at least several of the functions. But he wasn't. Except for the few minutes he spent with her at the wedding rehearsal, he never even saw Jackie. Consequently, the ceremony began to assume epic proportions in his mind. He was determined to make his grand entrance in style. He would escort his daughter down the center aisle and give her away: that was one privilege they could not possibly take away."

At Hammersmith Farm, on the dawn of the wedding day, Jackie was serene and purposeful. With Janet and Lee to assist her, she put on her wedding gown and a rosepoint lace veil that had belonged to Janet's mother. It didn't seem to matter that the veil, which Janet had worn the day she married Jack Bouvier, had endured two previously unsuccessful marriages.

The gown itself was criticized by at least one fashion expert as "an atrocious mass of tissue silk taffeta, with excessive ornamentation of ruffles, tucks, stitchings and flowers," an opinion Jackie tended to share. She had wanted a more modern, streamlined wedding gown but in the end acceded to the wishes of the groom. Jack Kennedy had asked her to wear "something traditional and old-fashioned." For luck, she also wore a blue garter.

The situation at the Viking Hotel that morning was anything but serene. Black Jack's twin sisters had dispatched their husbands—John E. Davis and Harrington Putnam—to help him prepare for the wedding. When they arrived they found him half-clothed and half drunk, an empty highball glass and a bottle of whiskey close at hand. His speech was slurred and he could barely stand, much less walk a straight line.

The two men telephoned their wives and reported his condition. Maude and Michelle then called Janet Auchincloss to say that while Black Jack had apparently taken a few drinks, they felt he could still pull himself together in time to walk Jackie down the aisle.

Janet immediately objected. She had no intention of being embarrassed in front of so many people on the most important occasion of her daughter's life. Jackie's stepfather would replace Black Jack. If Black Jack dared to show himself at St. Mary's Roman Catholic Church, Janet would have him forcibly ejected. Although the twins tried to reason with her—it was Jackie's wish to be escorted by her real father—Janet had already made her choice.

As reported in *The New York Times*, more than 3,000 spectators thronged St. Mary's later that morning for a glimpse of the 36-year-old groom and his 24-year-old bride. Police circled the crowd with a rope and pulled them back toward the opposite side of the street as Jackie's limousine delivered her to the front of the church.

Saint Mary's, which had been decorated with pink gladioli and white chrysanthemums, overflowed with more than 750 invited guests. Jackie's young half-brother and half-sister, Jamie and Janet, Jr., served as page and flower girl. Bobby Kennedy was best man and Lee was matron of honor. Joe Kennedy had asked the Archbishop of Boston, Richard Cushing, to conduct the Nuptial high Mass, assisted by Monsignor Francis Rossiter and several other high-ranking clergymen, including the Very Reverend James Kellor of New York, head of the Christophers movement, and the Very Reverend John J. Cavanaugh, former President of Notre Dame. Luigi Vena of Boston, a tenor, sang "Ave Maria," "Panis Angelicus" and "Jesu, Amor Mi," his melodious voice contrasting sharply with Cushing's grinding monotone as he ended the formal Mass by conferring on the newlyweds an apostolic blessing from Pope Pius XII.

The one moment of levity in an otherwise traditional ceremony was provided by none other than John White. "When Jackie first became engaged to JFK, I bet her she wouldn't go through with it," said White. "She even gave me 2-1 odds. If for any reason she didn't marry him, she'd pay me two dollars; if she did marry him, I'd give her a dollar.

"I actually expected to win but then the wedding invitation arrived. I remember receiving invitations from both sides—Jack and Jackie—which somewhat amused me. There was so little overlap in their groups of friends that neither side would assume that anybody could belong to the other side as well.

"I drove up to Newport for the wedding, and the first I saw of Jackie she was walking down the aisle on the arm of Hugh Auchincloss. So I waved my dollar bill at her, and while people around me started to laugh, nobody but Jackie understood the significance of the gesture. She gave me a big smile as she sailed by."

Sylvia Whitehouse Blake, one of Jackie's bridesmaids, was impressed by the "splendid way in which she comported herself, her ability to rise above the problems of the day, namely the enforced absence of her father. I was totally unaware, as a bridesmaid, of the fact that he was drunk at the Viking Hotel, or whatever it was that we've all since heard. And she certainly didn't cry or let on, even though the books all say that she was terribly upset. But I suppose it must have been a very traumatic experience for her—to be so fond of her father and yet know that he was not very happy."

Another wedding guest, Eilene Slocum, had been told of Black Jack's presence in Newport and wondered what had become of him. "How could you not wonder," she remarked, "—he wasn't there to give Jacqueline away. Hugh Auchincloss had taken his place. People buzzed, particularly at the reception afterwards at Hammersmith Farm. There were more than 1,300 people at the reception, a strange combination of Irish politicians and many of Hugh and Janet's Republican family friends, and a high percentage of both were aware of Jack Bouvier's absence.*

"Otherwise it was one of those 'perfect' weddings—a sunny, windswept day, horses and cattle grazing in the pasture, everybody radiant and fit, several huge tents set up across the back lawns. Meyer Davis, who had played at Janet's first wedding, fiddled madly away. The children —mine, Noreen Drexel's and the two young Auchinclosses —did the Mexican Hat Dance for the benefit of the newsreel cameras.'"*

---

*Ken McKnight, who served in the Department of Commerce during the Kennedy Administration, said of the wedding reception: "The help (chauffeurs, etc.) were at a tent by themselves and the

After signing the wedding register, Jack and Jackie joined the receiving line while their well-wishers queued to congratulate them—senators, governors, socialites, stock brokers, political aides, a large cross-section of all the families involved. It took them two-and-a-half hours to file by.

Shining, easily the star of the show, Jackie stood next to Jack, who looked relaxed, perhaps deceptively so. But guests who saw him at close range, noticed that his face bore scratches and bruises, the result of an early morning touch football scrimmage with some of his cronies. He wore them well as he smiled for the photographers and danced with his bride under a blue-and-white striped marquee. Jackie then danced with her stepfather, helped the groom cut the four-foot-tall wedding cake, tossed to the bridesmaids her bouquet of pink and white spray orchids, and disappeared to change for the first leg of their honeymoon.

In the privacy of her own bedroom, Jackie's self-control finally gave way. Tears filled her eyes (more than anything she had wanted her father to be present on this special day), but by the time she rejoined the wedding party in her gray Chanel suit (she wore Jack's diamond bracelet and a diamond pin she had received as a wedding present from her father-in-law), she had composed herself again. She embraced her mother, her sister and as many close relatives as she could reach, expressed her gratitude to Uncle Hughdie for filling in for her father, and in a storm of rice and confetti, drove to the airport with Jack, where they boarded a private plane for New York.

They spent their wedding night and the following day in the honeymoon suite at the Waldorf-Astoria, and early on the third morning flew to Mexico City on their way to Acapulco. Arriving at the airport in Mexico City, they were confronted by a team of Mexican immigration officials. Their passports were in order but Evelyn Lincoln, Kennedy's secretary, hadn't included their birth certifi-

---

caterer made a mistake by giving them the Moët Vintage that was supposed to be for the guests. Instead guests got the cheaper stuff. After the wedding, the chauffeurs of 500 cars were 'bombed' and with only one road back to town they had the worst traffic jam in Newport's history."

cates. After a three-hour delay, they were permitted to proceed to their final destination.

Acapulco had been Jackie's idea. Several years earlier she had briefly visited the resort with her mother and stepfather and had seen a villa that stuck in her mind as the place she most wanted to spend her honeymoon. The house, constructed of pink stone, staggered up from the blue-green Pacific on various levels against a red-clay cliff. What Jackie didn't know was that the villa belonged to Don Miguel Alemán, President of Mexico and an old acquaintance of Joe Kennedy's. Recognizing the villa from Jackie's detailed description, Joe Kennedy contacted Alemán and learned that *El presidente* would be only too glad to accommodate the newlyweds. He gave them full run of the property for as long as they wanted to stay.

Jackie's first act on settling in was to write her father a long and loving letter, saying she knew how pressured he must have been and that, as far as she was concerned, she still really felt that he was the one who had accompanied her down the aisle.

The letter meant a great deal to Black Jack. Although he didn't show it to anyone, he told people about it, including Yusha Auchincloss.

"I'd been introduced to Black Jack by Jackie," explained Yusha, "and over the years we had established a close relationship. After Jackie's wedding, I felt sorry for him and I decided to give him a ring. This was a week or two after his return to New York. He felt better by then. The newspapers said he became ill, and that's why he couldn't give Jackie away. Actually he'd been scared and nervous what with all the crowds and media people at Newport, and everybody conjecturing about him and Janet.

"Incidentally, it wasn't true that he and my father didn't get along. If anything, my father tried to smooth the way between Black Jack and Janet. But it proved impossible because there was so much hostility there already.

"Jackie's letter of forgiveness helped restore Black Jack's confidence. Whatever the cause, he had failed to meet his paternal obligations and this was a burden he would have to bear. But knowing that he hadn't lost face with his daughter made a difference. And then after they returned from their honeymoon, Jackie visited her father in New York and they hashed it all out again. She told him that he hadn't been invited to the prenuptial festivities because he wouldn't have felt comfortable at any of them; nobody thought he even wanted to attend."

Jackie wrote another letter from Acapulco, this one to Rose Kennedy detailing their daily activities: a deep-sea fishing expedition on which Jack had caught a nine-foot sailfish that Jackie intended to stuff and mount as a memento of their honeymoon; Jack's Berlitz Home-Guide studies in Spanish, and his often amusing attempts to converse in that language; her difficulty on water skis; their marathon tennis matches at the Villa Vera Racquet Club. She enclosed a lengthy, tightly constructed poem she'd composed for Jack in imitation of Stephen Vincent Benét: "He would find love/He would never find peace/ For he must go seeking/The Golden Fleece. . . ." There was no mention in the letter of the party they attended at the neighboring home of Mexican architect Fernando Parra, at which Jackie found her husband on the terrace surrounded by three glamour girls, each competing with the others for attention. What distressed her was that this represented only one of a number of such incidents that took place during their honeymoon.

After a fortnight in Acapulco they flew to San Francisco to visit Jack's friends, Red and Anita Fay. The Fays discerned a growing tension between the newlyweds. Red Fay attributed the trouble to "the pressures of public life—not to mention those of an old shipmate and his wife—[which] too often intruded on the kind of honeymoon any young bride anticipates."*

Jack Kennedy had a habit of going off on outings without Jackie. One afternoon, he and Red Fay went to a professional football game, leaving the two ladies to fend for themselves. Anita took her guest to lunch and then on an exhaustive automobile tour of the Bay area. Jackie didn't enjoy herself. She resented being left behind with somebody she barely knew, and resented even more her husband's all-too-obvious interest in other women. Jack Kennedy, who described himself to Red Fay as "both too old and too young for marriage," flirted shamelessly with every attractive and interesting female who came his way.

*Paul B. Fay, Jr., *The Pleasure of His Company*, p. 163.

9

In mid-October 1953, back from her Mexican honey-moon, Jackie Kennedy met her friend Selwa "Lucky" Roosevelt for lunch at the Occidental Restaurant in Washington, D.C. As Lucky recalled it, "I had married before Jackie and accompanied my husband, Archie Roosevelt, to Turkey, so we missed her wedding. We caught up with each other over lunch. She seemed very bubbly and excited. She and Jack had appeared on Edward R. Murrow's "Person-to-Person," which was then the most popular program on prime-time television. I remember Jackie saying to me in the course of our luncheon, 'Oh Lucky, isn't it wonderful to be so happy and in love.'

"It seemed touching at first but then I began to wonder. She and Jack didn't have a home of their own as yet and were dividing their time between her parents' house in Virginia and the Kennedy homes at Hyannis Port and Palm Beach. She said they were looking for a house because they planned on having children—'And if you have children you ought to have your own place.'

"I thought it a bit odd that they were living with their in-laws and what a strain this must have put on them. What did having children have to do with owning a home? If you're married, you ought to be out on your own."

In New York at a dinner party given by Charles and Jayne Wrightsman, Palm Beach acquaintances of the Kennedys, Jackie encountered another old friend, Jeanne Murray Vanderbilt, with whom she had often gone horse-back riding as a child. "After dinner," said Jeanne Vanderbilt, "Jackie and I found ourselves in Jayne's bedroom. Jack Kennedy was in Washington and Jackie was in New York by herself. She looked a bit lonely, a bit lost. It seemed she might be having problems adjusting to her new situation, especially given the size and nature of

133

the Kennedy family. She knew that the Murrays were a sprawling Irish-Catholic clan, so she said to me, 'Jeanne, you come from a large family. How do you handle them?'

"I didn't know what to tell her. I mentioned the importance of maintaining one's own identity. I said, 'You can't change them, so don't try to change yourself.' Something to that effect."

Such advice, while well-intentioned, was easier given than followed: remaining true to oneself among the Kennedys created as many problems as it resolved, particularly when compounded by the intense togetherness of the tribe. Jack and Jackie spent a great deal of their time with the rest of the family, much more time than Jackie would have liked.

She and Jack spent Christmas of 1953 with his parents in Palm Beach and Jackie caught a further glimpse of some of the family's less attractive characteristics. As a Christmas present she had given Jack an expensive oil painting set. "Almost immediately," said Lem Billings, "all the Kennedys descended upon it, squeezing paint out of the tubes, grabbing brushes, competing to see who could produce the greatest number of paintings in the least amount of time. They went at it from early morning until late at night, starting outdoors, and then when it became too warm, they all retreated into the house dripping paint and turpentine across floors and carpets. Jackie was stunned. She stood there with her mouth hanging open, ready to explode."

Having come of age on a strictly controlled budget and within the bounds of an equally stringent behavioral code, such arrogance and waste on the part of her in-laws shocked Jackie. The financial resources of the Kennedys, variously estimated at between $100 and $750 million depending on the year and source, seemed almost inexhaustible. Joe Kennedy had amassed a fortune and had done so through a series of deals that would be frowned upon today but were more common among brokers and financiers of another day—from vast imports of "medicinal whiskey" from Scotland at the height of Prohibition, to shrewd stock manipulations and cutthroat business transactions involving the purchase and sale of assorted companies and corporations. His earnings seemed to come from every corner of the marketplace: real estate, oil, utilities, shipyards, motion pictures, movie theaters, stocks and bonds, the Merchandise Mart Building in Chicago (which he owned), Hialeah Race Track in Florida (of which he was one of the majority stockholders). He had worked his way through Harvard and at one point in his career had been the youngest bank president in the country. While obsessed with the accumulation of wealth, his real objective was to gain social prestige for himself and his family. In 1925, he established a million-dollar trust fund for each of his children, and by the mid-1940s the trusts had swelled in value to ten times that figure.

For all their wealth and recklessness, the Kennedys were notoriously parsimonious. Judge James Knott, former director of the Palm Beach Historical Society, considered them "incredibly frugal. I don't mean frugal in a strict financial sense, I mean they were ungiving—they never entered wholeheartedly into the social life of Palm Beach. They never entertained. They were a large clannish family, led by a man who was no social jewel. Joe Kennedy didn't have public vivacity or wonderful anecdotes he wanted to share. He was just a businessman, very successful and clever, but without social aspirations or habits of any kind. He had been Ambassador to Great Britain but certainly wasn't ambassadorial. He held several other minor government positions—chairman of the U.S. Maritime Commission, member of the Hoover Commission, but he rarely talked about these experiences. He belonged to the prestigious Everglades Club but didn't partake socially. I remember him visiting Bradley's on occasion, Palm Beach's famous gambling casino, though he never wagered. He told me once he didn't like to lose."

George Vigouroux, owner of art galleries in Palm Beach and New York, confirmed Judge Knott's point of view: "Every penny Joe Kennedy earned went to the family, or into their sundry political campaigns. Since they never entertained they didn't care what their homes looked like. They were in dire need of repair. Joe would paint the front of the house but not the back or sides, because people saw only the front. No matter how much money he had, Joe Kennedy remained essentially what he had always been: the son of an independent-minded Irish immigrant saloonkeeper.

"Rose Kennedy was an even greater penny-pincher. Here was a woman who attended Mass every day of the week and never put more than a single dollar bill into the collection plate. Father Jeremiah O'Malloney of St. Edward's in Palm Beach tolerated her because the family had a name. But he was disgusted with Rose's paltry donations and would castigate her in front of the entire congregation. She couldn't have cared less. She and her daughters packed their own lunch to the weekly church picnic, rather than buy what the church had to offer in the way of food. She would storm around her house turning off light switches to save electricity, mark the liquor bottles to prevent the help from knocking the stuff off behind her back, dock the servants a dime for every bottle of Coca-Cola they took from the pantry between meals. The servants were miserably paid. Their name for the Kennedy home was 'The House of the Minimum Wage.'

"Rose remained friendly with Palm Beach socialite Mary Sanford primarily because Mary had a heated swimming pool. Until Joe Kennedy's stroke in 1961, he refused to install a similar unit in his own swimming pool. Rose would go to Mary's house and would invariably arrive at lunchtime. The amusing part is that she enjoyed swimming in the buff. Mary would be entertaining friends over lunch when suddenly the nude form of Rose Kennedy would appear and make a mad dash for the swimming pool. Mary's guests never knew quite what to make of it, and Mary had long since stopped bothering to explain."

More shocking perhaps than their monetary priorities was the chauvinistic attitude shared by the men in the Kennedy family, from Joe Sr. down to the youngest of his sons. Joe Kennedy was a tireless pursuer of women. The best known of his extramarital adventures was his involvement with Gloria Swanson. In the late 1920s, he formed a movie company, Gloria Productions, which produced the first talkie for the "Queen of Hollywood." He seduced her in the privacy of his Palm Beach estate while his wife sat in another room, and Swanson's husband, the Marquis Henri de la Falaise, went fishing for the day. He took her in the manner of "a roped horse, rough, arduous, racing to be free," she wrote in her autobiography.* "After a hasty climax he lay beside me, stroking my

*See Gloria Swanson, *Swanson on Swanson*, pp. 356–357.

hair." Somehow, Gloria knew that this "strange man *owned me.*" He took her along when he and his wife traveled to Europe and maintained her in a private bungalow on Rodeo Drive in Beverly Hills. Throughout their three-year affair, she lived in fear of becoming pregnant. Kennedy wanted to have a child by her, and he pointed out to her that in an entire year his wife hadn't become pregnant either, "proving" that he had been "faithful" to Gloria. Their relationship ended when Kennedy replaced her with Nancy Carroll, an actress who bore a striking resemblance to Swanson. It was only later that Gloria discovered that the bungalow and a number of extravagant gifts Kennedy had given her, including a car and a fur coat, had been secretly charged to her expense account.

Joe Kennedy's egocentric and callous treatment of women could be astonishingly cruel. Marianne Strong, a literary agent and public relations expert, recalled an incident involving Joe Kennedy and two teenage models he took to dinner at La Caravelle in New York: "My late husband and I knew that Joe Kennedy frequented La Caravelle, was even rumored to be part-owner of the restaurant, so it came as no surprise to find him seated next to us. He had these two very beautiful and slim girls on either side, and it soon became clear that he was pleasuring one of them under the table. He had his hand in her panties and a hard, ugly smirk on his face. And while he was doing that, he was eating dinner with his other hand.

"My husband summoned the maitre d'. 'We didn't come here to be entertained,' he said. 'Can we please be moved.'

"The hapless maitre d' couldn't find an empty table anywhere in the room. We could either stay and shut up or leave. We stayed and endured the remainder of Joe Kennedy's performance."

Doris Lilly, the vivacious, bright-eyed, former *New York Post* society scribe, likewise endured an unpleasant evening at the hands of the Kennedy patriarch. "Joe Kennedy represented the height of vulgarity," she remarked. "He was horny, that's all he was. He went after every girl he ever saw. He went after me. He took me out one night for dinner at '21.' It was the middle of summer and it was hot. Nobody had air conditioning in those days. I had all this wine with dinner and I wasn't used to it. Then he took me to El Morocco and gave me more to drink. Eventually he brought me back to my apartment building. We were standing in the lobby and he said, 'What's that over there?' 'Where?' I said. I turned my head and he clamped his mouth over mine, kissed me, and I ran upstairs and threw up. He was so disgusting. He was a disgusting man. He wanted me to go to Saratoga with him and I told him I was sick and so he sent a doctor to my house.

"He had a number of girlfriends. I knew a girl who was his mistress for years. She was a showgirl. Joe bought her an apartment at Beekman Place in New York, which is where all the rich men kept their mistresses. It was the ideal area because there was very little traffic and nobody to spot you on the street. He supposedly didn't mind spending money on his girlfriends because he gave her lavish gifts of jewelry.

"She told me Rose didn't care how many women Joe kept as long as she had her family. The only time Rose had sexual relations with her husband was for the purpose of reproduction. She was that devout a Catholic. Once she had her family she was no longer interested. So the fact that he had women on the side didn't mean anything to her. Many people talked about 'the long-suffering Rose.' It's not true. Rose didn't object to Joe's women as long as they didn't interfere with her personal life or with her family."

"Joe Kennedy's life was an intricate balancing act," suggested Slim Aarons, a society photographer for *Holiday* and *Town & Country* and other fashionable publications. "He lived among the rich but wasn't really one of them. He wasn't into the social scene. He had three interests: politics, golf and women. He was a powerful man who didn't mind hurting people, or at least didn't worry about it. That was the secret to his success.

"I used to visit him in Palm Beach. He'd let me photograph him down there but only if we didn't attach a dateline to the shot. He wanted people to think he lived year-round in Hyannis Port. It was bad politics to be associated with Palm Beach, especially in those days when money alone was the common denominator. Blacks weren't allowed in the village after 7 p.m. The country clubs were mostly restricted. Palm Beach was a downer for anyone whose son wanted to be President of the United States.

"Joe Kennedy fooled around with dames all the time. During one stretch that I spent in his Palm Beach home, he had a 25-year-old girl with him. She left the same day Father Cavanaugh of Notre Dame came. Father Cavanaugh left and Rose arrived. Rose departed and the 25-year-old girl returned. I always felt that Joe's womanizing represented an active rebellion against the restrictive morals he associated with Irish Catholicism. He wanted to show the world that he was liberated, free of those restraints. He loved to flaunt his women in front of others. And no woman was off limits—not your wife, your daughter, the girlfriends his sons brought home to dinner. There was a kind of inevitability to it. If you were young and attractive and female and you came into contact with the Kennedys, you could be certain that one or the other of the men would try to lure or force you into bed."

Joe Kennedy's womanizing, while shocking to many, merely titillated Jackie, who had the experience of her own father against whom to measure the actions of her father-in-law. She and Joe established a closeness that she shared with few. They had a similar sense of humor, on one occasion jointly chasing a servant out of the family dining room by throwing half-eaten lamb chops at her. Jackie listened when the Ambassador told her about Jack's early shyness in the political arena. "I never thought he had it in him," said Joe Kennedy. She criticized her father-in-law when he voiced what she considered racist views on blacks and Jews, pointing out that he saw the world only in terms of absolutes, black and white, rather than the way it was—a subtle mixture of grays. He appreciated her candor. "She's the only one around here with any gumption," he told his wife.

"The Ambassador," said Lem Billings, "enjoyed talking about his female conquests. For hours he would tell Jackie about Gloria Swanson, Marion Davies and countless others past and present. He and Jackie shared personal feelings and private jokes. Whenever she and Jack had marital problems, she would unburden herself to Joe. He admired her for her strength, the fact that she always maintained her own identity. She was the one person who could stand up to the old man and get away with it."

Despite her closeness to Joe Kennedy, her relations with Rose, whom she found "scatterbrained" and "overbearing," deteriorated rapidly. Langdon Marvin, a long-time consultant and aide to Jack Kennedy, was privy to the first stirrings of trouble between the two ladies, both of whom wanted to dominate the spotlight.

"In the fall of 1953, around Halloween, I visited the family at Hyannis Port," said Marvin. "I was dating Gloria Emerson, the writer, and we both flew up for the weekend. We arrived late and they were already at dinner. To my immense surprise, we were offered, although it was obvious we weren't supposed to linger over it, a rum cocktail. Old Joe didn't like people drinking his liquor, which was strange seeing as he was making something like fifty cents on every bottle of whiskey sold in the United States. Jackie said to me, 'Langdon, I'm so glad you came. This is the first drink I've been allowed in this house since we got back here.' I found this rather sad. Somebody who's married to a truck driver, living in a cold water flat on Eleventh Avenue in New York, can decide whether she wants a beer before or after dinner. In this case there were limitations. And since Jackie was then living with the Kennedys, she was at their beck and call.

"I remember that weekend as being bitterly cold, the more so because Rose and Joe refused to turn up the heat. I had to wear three pairs of socks and as many borrowed sweaters. When Jackie mentioned our discomfort, Rose glared at her. 'We'll watch a movie,' said Rose, 'it's warmer in the basement.' So after dinner we all trudged down to the basement to watch a film in Joe's screening room. I wasn't particularly in the mood but knew better than to argue with any of the Kennedys. First we saw home movies of Jack's and Jackie's wedding, followed by a somewhat drab gangster film starring Edward G. Robinson. Needless to say, the basement was by far the coldest room in the house.

"The next day, Saturday, Jackie showed me a political cartoon book she'd been working on in her spare time. I remember one cartoon about a senator's wife learning to tell if the Senate was still in session by the light in the Capitol and the flag over the chamber. There was another of Jack looking very grim with all sorts of spiky hairs growing on his legs, saying, 'I demand my marital rights.'

"We were skimming the book and watching a touch

football game in progress on the lawn. Every few plays a bunch of Kennedys would fall to the ground and start wrestling among themselves. Jackie seemed almost offended. She became more offended when Rose Kennedy approached and said, 'Jackie, why don't you and Langdon join the rest of the group. The exercise will do you both some good.' Without batting an eye, Jackie parried: 'It's about time somebody around here started exercising his mind rather than his muscles.'

"It was no secret that they deplored one another. Jackie constantly poked fun at Rose. She found hilarious Rose's habit of pinning little notes to her clothes to remind herself of some chore or task she had to perform. And Rose was just as amused by Jackie's trick of running the water faucet whenever she went to the bathroom to drown out the sound of her bodily functions.

"Everybody knows the story of how Rose, aggravated by Jackie's penchant for sleeping late, inquired of Mary Gallagher, who was then Rose's secretary, if Jackie was coming down soon. 'You might remind her that we are having some important guests for lunch and it might be nice if she would join us.' When Mary delivered the message, Jackie responded by doing a mean-spirited imitation of her mother-in-law's nasal brogue and made a point of staying in bed until the 'important' guests had come and gone.

"The next time I saw Jackie after Halloween was January 1954. I went down with Gloria Emerson to Palm Beach. Jack's parents were away, but there was trepidation because Rose was expected. She arrived in time for lunch the following day and sat at the head of the table. A few minutes later Jack came down the stairs and wandered into the living room. There on the wall, where his mother's prize Renoir had once hung, Jackie had mounted this huge, stuffed, bronzed sailfish that Jack had hooked on their honeymoon. Jack joined us for lunch but said nothing. Finally after dessert we all headed for the living room. Well, Rose took one look at that monstrous fish hanging on her wall and nearly passed out. She left the room without a word, found the maintenance man, accused him of the dirty deed and fired the unfortunate fellow on the spot."

Nine months after the fish incident, with Jackie in Europe and Jack about to undergo back surgery in New

York, the Senator asked Langdon Marvin to arrange a house party in Northeast Harbor, Maine, where Langdon's parents owned a summer cottage. Langdon knew exactly what Jack meant by "house party," and although he very much cared for Jackie, it wasn't his place to question Jack's actions. He did as asked.

He recalled the circumstances: "There were seven of us at the house party, including myself, my Harvard classmate Joe Driscoll, Grace Ferro, Sally Alexander, Jack and two others. The girls were all elegantly attractive. I laid down one rule for the group: always travel in odd numbers—three or five or seven in the house or indoor swimming pool, never two or four or six. That way nobody would ever be able to pin anything on Jack, and thus on me.

"I booked the entire second floor of the old Kimball House. Mrs. Kelly, the concierge, was told that Jack would occupy his own room. On our first night we went to the Pot-and-Kettle Club, a very exclusive outfit in Bar Harbor. Jack was on crutches because of his back. The next day we watched the sailboat races, and that evening we went to the Bar Harbor Country Club dance. Jack didn't dance, but by then word had spread that a U. S. Senator was in town and that he wasn't alone.

"Today this might not mean anything but in those days it did. We were subjected to an awful lot of espionage—people listening in on the switchboard, room service crashing into Jack's room with two breakfast trays instead of one, hotel maids inspecting the sheets. They did everything but look under the beds. And the town was suddenly crawling with reporters asking questions and bribing hotel personnel.

"The next morning we had a little conference and we decided the situation called for Jack to take Mrs. Kelly, an elderly widow with a walking cane and snow white hair, to morning Mass at the nearest Catholic church. Jack was still groggy from the night before, so we plopped him into a bathtub filled with cold water, dressed him in a suit and delivered him to the lobby. There was Mrs. Kelly with her car in the driveway. Jack climbed in and off they went, followed by a caravan of reporters and photographers. After that we had no more problems—no espionage, no press, no room service barging into our rooms.

"How did Jackie deal with Jack's philandering? The truth is I never asked. I assume she knew. I'm positive she knew. But she never confronted me with any hard evidence.

"I can only guess that it caused a great deal of tension. I have no idea if there's any medical evidence for it, but I sometimes wondered if it wasn't the reason for all those miscarriages and other related problems that Jackie had. She suffered a miscarriage during their first year of marriage. Her doctor told her that if she remained so high-strung she might have trouble bearing children. That made Jack nervous and probably induced him to have more affairs. He wanted a large family, no fewer than five children, but realized very early in the marriage that this just wasn't going to happen."

10

"Jackie once described Jack Kennedy to me as somebody with a minuscule body and a huge head," said Truman Capote. "She said this in a moment of anger. I don't think she realized what she'd walked into when she married him. He was in constant competition with his old man to see who could nail the most women. Jackie wasn't prepared for quite such blatant womanizing. She hadn't expected to find herself stranded at parties while her husband went off with somebody new. Nor did she expect to become the object of derision among those females in her own circle who knew, as did almost everyone, what was happening."

Jackie herself put a somewhat softer edge on it when she confided to a friend: "I don't think there are any men who are faithful to their wives. Men are such a combination of good and evil."

Capote put it far more bluntly: "All those Kennedy men are the same—they're like dogs, they have to stop and pee on every fire hydrant."

Capote recalled a small dinner party he attended in New York approximately two years into the Kennedy marriage: "It took place in an apartment on Park Avenue, and the Kennedys were there. So was Babe Paley. * The ladies, including Jackie and Babe, had left the table after dinner and the men were supposed to be having brandy and cigars, and some high roller from Texas was recounting his experiences with $1,500-a-night call girls in Las Vegas. He knew their telephone numbers and their specialty—sucking cock, rim jobs, around the world. He knew how well they did it, how long, how deep, how big a cock they could take and what they could do with it that nobody else had ever done. That's how he talked. It

*Wife of William Paley, Chairman of the Board of CBS.

144

was nauseating, a real stomach-turner. And Jack Kennedy was lapping it up, practically taking notes. He did write some names and numbers on a scrap of paper. Later when he and Jackie were leaving, she asked him what we'd discussed. 'Politics,' he said, 'plain old politics.' But Jackie knew the score. She knew everything."

Gore Vidal also felt that Jackie knew and tacitly approved of, or at least closed her eyes to, Jack's meanderings; Vidal termed the Kennedy marriage "an eighteenth-century affair: a practical union on both sides." He further suggested that Jackie, as well as Lee, had been raised to play the modern equivalent of the classic courtesan role.

Senator George Smathers of Florida, who shared a Washington *pied-à-terre* with Jack at the Fairfax Hotel, originally opposed his friend's marriage: Jack asked me what I thought of Jackie. I didn't just offer my opinion. He asked what I thought of him marrying her. I had this horses-and-porcelain opinion of Jackie, and I told him I thought he could probably do better. What I meant was that they weren't well-suited, not outwardly at any rate. I was wrong in telling him because Jack could be contentious. He told her what I'd said and she brought it up at the White House after she became First Lady. We were dancing at some Presidential function and she whispered into my ear: 'I bet you and Jack wish you were back in Italy by yourselves.' Then she brought up what I'd said about her almost ten years earlier. I don't think she ever really forgave me, maybe because she associated me with Jack from his wild bachelor days."

George Smathers acknowledged that Jack Kennedy inherited his "womanizing complex" from a demanding father who "wouldn't accept second-best from any of his sons." Smathers agreed that Joe and Rose "procreated only for children, which is why Joe did so much fooling around. My feeling was that Rose, like Eleanor Roosevelt, hated sex, couldn't tolerate it. Joe was chauvinistic, a tremendous skirt-chaser, and Jack had an equally active libido. When it came to women, Jack had an unusually short attention span. He enjoyed variety. He loved adventure. 'Live each day as if it's your last'—that became his philosophy. He could be very serious, very earnest, but he also possessed a highly developed sense of fun. It was a gift, maybe his greatest gift, the ability to make the most out of every experience. I don't think I've known anybody who went about it in quite the same way."

James Rousmaniere regarded Jack during his undergraduate years at Harvard as "an odd admixture of serious scholar and fun-loving, girl-crazed fool." Rousmaniere described the dormitory parties Jack gave at Winthrop House: "Two hundred students would crash a suite normally meant to hold no more than twenty. Jack used to hire Snowball, a legendary Cambridge bartender best known for a lethal concoction called green dragon punch. One sip of this magic potion and you were halfway to paradise.

"Jack was always very successful with girls. Very. All he had to do was snap his finers. He never had only one girlfriend at a time; he had many. But he had his favorites. The three he talked about in those days were Olive Field Cawley, who later married Tom Watson, president of IBM; Charlotte McDonnell, whose sister Anne married Henry Ford II; Frances Ann Cannon of Cannon Mills fame, who married author John Hersey. There were also giddy romps with any number of coeds, models, stewardesses, showgirls and nurses. He had an unending supply. Every time he went to New York for a weekend he returned with ten new names. I used to rib him by saying, 'Jack, you ought to find yourself a nice Catholic girl and settle down.' His response: 'Introduce me to one, and maybe I will.' "

According to Langdon Marvin, an "almost incestuous atmosphere" pervaded the Kennedy household. "What I mean," said Marvin, "is that the Kennedy men passed their women around like community property, preyed off each other's dates, traded them like baseball cards. Jack, for example, went out with a number of Joe Jr.'s former girlfriends. There were Stella and Ana Carcano—always known as Bebe and Chiquita—daughters of Miguel Angel Carcano, the Argentinian Ambassador to England. Joe Jr. dated Chiquita; Jack visited the family's cattle ranch in Buenos Aires and socialized with both sisters. They eventually married Englishmen: Bebe, Lord Edmund; Chiquita, Lady Astor's youngest son, Jakie.

"Then there was Pat Wilson, Joe Jr's last girlfriend, a ravishing young English widow who had been married to the Earl of Jersey, divorced him and married Robin Wilson, who was killed in World War II. Jack squired

Pat around at the same time he was seeing the famous English tennis star Kay Stammers.

"When Jack met a girl he wanted, he didn't waste time on preliminaries or social amenities. He let them know straight out what he expected of them. If he happened to sit next to a comely gal on an airplane, he'd arrange a date with her and then bring her back to his hotel room. Or he'd make a date with the stewardess and do likewise. When he was finished with the girl, he usually gave her telephone number to his father or one of his brothers, and they did the same for him."

Kennedy spent part of the summer of 1940 in Southern California, sharing an apartment in the Hollywood Hills with actor Robert Stack, who later made his mark as FBI crime fighter Eliot Ness in television's "The Untouchables." In his 1980 autobiography, *Straight Shooting,* * Stack leaves little doubt as to Kennedy's early prowess with women: "I've known many of the great Hollywood stars and only a very few of them seemed to hold the attention for women that JFK did, even before he entered the political arena. He,d just look at them and they'd tumble."

Susan Imhoff, a former flight attendant, encountered Jack in the fall of 1940: "He was then attending graduate courses at the Stanford School of Business Administration in Palo Alto, and I was attending a junior college near San Francisco. We met at a party on Nob Hill. Jack owned a brand-new, dark-green Buick convertible with green leather seats. After the party he drove me home and asked me out for the following evening. He was attractive, tall and slim, bright-eyed with a healthy crop of copper hair and a boyish smile.

"Jack was cute and smart and wise, but he was also stubborn, bossy and arrogant. He talked endlessly about his father, with whom he seemed unusually close. I know he had a bad back because even then he slept on a plywood bed board and couldn't drive for more than an hour without having to stop and stretch.

"Because of his back he preferred making love with the girl on top. He found it more stimulating to have the girl do all the work. I remember he didn't enjoy cuddling

*See Robert Stack, *Straight Shooting*, pp. 72–73.

after making love, but he did like to talk and he had a wonderful sense of humor—he loved to laugh."

Susan Imhoff wasn't Kennedy's only female companion during his brief graduate school career. Edward Folger, a part-time Stanford graduate student, cited the names of Nancy Burkett and Harriet Price, "two of the sexiest and most popular coeds on campus," as also having dated Jack. "He used to take them dancing at the Mark Hopkins and the St. Francis Hotel in San Francisco, or they would dine at L'Omelette, an 'in' restaurant in Palo Alto.

"Jack Kennedy had two sides—formal and British versus informal and very American. He would take a girl dancing at a fancy hotel to impress her, but at heart he preferred 'hanging out.' He liked to dress casually in old tennis sweaters, chinos, loafers without socks, and he was often lax about manners. He didn't have any really, in the sense of letting women go through the door first or opening a door for them or standing up when an older woman entered the room. His table manners weren't much better. He wolfed down his food and then left the table while others were still eating. He did the same thing when the conversation ceased to interest him. He would simply get up and go without a word. He was generally nice to people, but heedless of their feelings.

"I suppose there's something appealing to women about a brusque and forceful figure. At Stanford the girls flocked after him. On big college weekends, they would turn down other dates in the hope that he might ask them out. He invited Harriet Price to that year's Berkeley-Stanford football game. Afterwards they went to Del Monte—to the Del Monte Lodge—where they spent the night with other student couples, a Stanford tradition in those days. At night there was always a formal dinner-dance and the next morning everyone headed for the beach at Carmel. I recall what an utterly attractive couple Jack and Harriet made. But then the Japanese attacked Pearl Harbor and America entered the war. Jack Kennedy quit Stanford and enlisted in the Navy."

Inga Arvad, a tall, full-bodied Danish journalist, was working as a columnist for the *Washington Times-Herald* late in 1941, when her friend Kathleen Kennedy introduced her to her brother Jack, who was then an ensign at the Pentagon in the Office of Naval Intelligence (ONI).

Jack Kennedy was immediately attracted to the flaxen-haired, blue-eyed Nordic beauty who, at twenty-eight (four years his senior), seemed far more worldly and experienced than any of his former girlfriends.

Inga was indeed an interesting woman. Born in Copenhagen in 1913 and educated in London, Brussels and Paris, she married a young Egyptian diplomat and then divorced him prior to her twentieth birthday. She won a beauty contest in France and became the Berlin correspondent for a large Danish newspaper, quickly gaining favor with the German High Command and successfully conducting interviews with the likes of Hermann Goering, Joseph Goebbels and eventually Adolf Hitler, who invited her as his personal guest to the 1936 Olympic Games in Berlin. When the German foreign ministry suggested that Inga work for the Third Reich as an undercover agent in Paris, she instead returned to Denmark, accepted a supporting role in a low-budget motion picture and married Paul Fejos, the film's Hungarian-born director.

Sharing a sense of adventure, the couple spent two years shooting nature documentaries in the Dutch East Indies before arriving in Singapore where they met Axel Wenner-Gren, a Swedish financier who had made a fortune manufacturing vacuum cleaner parts and anti-aircraft guns. Nobody seems to know exactly what happened next, but within weeks Fejos found himself in the Andes conducting an archaeological expedition to the Inca ruins of Machu Picchu, financed by Wenner-Gren, while Inga and the Swede set out aboard his 300-foot yacht on a trip around the world. Their voyage terminated at New York, where in 1940 Inga enrolled in a graduate program at the Columbia University School of Journalism.

It was Arthur Krock, a consulting professor at the School of Journalism, who later found Inga a position with Frank Waldrop at the *Times-Herald*. "Krock was our unofficial procurer," reflected Waldrop. "He sent us Kathleen Kennedy, Inga Arvad and Jackie Bouvier. Inga had by far the most talent of the three. She could capture in 300 words, insights into character and personality that most reporters today spread across two pages of newsprint. Her column—'Did You Happen to See?'—appeared three times a week and consisted of interview-profiles of semi-prominent Washingtonians, mainly in political circles."

Ensign Kennedy called his new playmate Inga-Binga, Bingo, and the Scandalous Scandinavian, and they frequently doubledated with John White and Kathleen Kennedy, both of whom were then also at the *Times-Herald*. What Jack Kennedy didn't realize at first—what nobody realized—was that Inga had become the subject of an intensive physical and technical FBI surveillance operation. Because of her earlier ties to leading German officials and her romance with Axel Werner-Gren, a suspected Nazi operative in his own right, the Department of Justice had reason to believe that Inga Arvad might be a German undercover agent.

"When I first heard that Inga was suspected of spying for Germany," said Frank Waldrop, "I realized that the Allies couldn't possibly lose the war. I'm willing to be put on record anywhere, anytime, that if Adolf Hitler was stupid enough to have Inga Arvad operating as a spy, he goddamn well deserved everything that happened to him. Inga was a bright, good-looking kid from Denmark trying to get along in the world, just like the rest of us. Yet here comes J. Edgar Hoover with his endless flow of files and dossiers, bugging her telephone, planting a microphone under her pillow, intercepting her mail, ransacking her apartment, tailing her as if Mata Hari herself had set out to seduce and compromise the future President of the United States.

"That's how it started. Once they had Jack Kennedy in their telescopic lens, they brought ONI into the operation. Jack was transferred out of Naval Intelligence and sent to the Navy Ship Yard at Charleston, South Carolina. Inga visited him there on several occasions. The FBI, on order from both President Roosevelt and Attorney General Francis Biddle, bugged their hotel room. Now they had tapes of Inga and Jack making love. This suited President Roosevelt immensely. Roosevelt had wanted to find something that would give him more leverage to twist Joe Kennedy's tail. The President felt betrayed by Joe Kennedy. He'd sent Joe to England as Ambassador and Joe became an appeaser and apologist for British Prime Minister Neville Chamberlain, compounding his crimes by advising members of Parliament that Roosevelt was nothing but a puppet for the Communists and Jews, and augmenting this appraisal with the view that democracy in Great Britain was finished and that fascism would soon take hold. They brought Joe Kennedy back to the U.S. but they had to have some way to subdue him. Enter Inga Arvad."

The FBI probe ultimately revealed as much about the Kennedys as it did about Inga. Federal agents discovered, for example, that Joe Kennedy's children shared their father's isolationist tendencies. Joe Jr., while a student at Harvard, had joined fellow undergraduates on the Harvard Committee Against Military Intervention in Europe, a reactionary group that petitioned influential government officials and held rallies opposing American entry in the European war effort. More explicit were the Bureau's charges against John F. Kennedy, accusing him of voicing "anti-British and defeatist sentiments and blaming Winston Churchill for getting the United States into the war. . . . It also appears that Kennedy had prepared for his father at least one of the speeches which his father had made, or was intending to make, in answer to criticism of his alleged appeasement policies. . . . In addition Jack Kennedy stated that in his opinion England was through, and his father's greatest mistake was not talking enough, that he stopped talking too soon."

Political considerations notwithstanding, the bulk of the FBI files on Inga Arvad examine her relationship with John Kennedy, noting that she saw him in Charleston on weekends, registering at different hotels and traveling under the assumed name of Barbara White. On February 9, 1942, Federal agents filed the following extract: "Surveillance maintained upon subject [Inga Arvad] from the time of her arrival in Charleston, S.C. . . . until her departure therefrom . . . to return to Washington D.C. [During subject's stay in Charleston], Jack Kennedy, Ensign, U.S. Navy, spent each night with her in her room at the Fort Sumter Hotel, engaging in sexual intercourse on numerous occasions. . . . She called him 'Honey,' 'Darling,' 'Honeysuckle,' 'Honey Child Wilder,' and said, 'I love you.' "

The same files contain lengthy transcriptions of telephone conversations between Jack and Inga. While unrevealing in terms of Inga's supposed espionage activities, they do tell us something of Jack Kennedy's current state of mind (February 5, 1942):

J—I heard you had a big orgy up in New York.
I—I'll tell you about it. I'll tell you about it for a

whole weekend if you'd like to hear about it. My husband [Paul Fejos] had his little spies out all over the place.

J—Really?

I—No, he didn't. But he told me all sorts of things about you, none of which were flattering. He knew every word you had said to your father about me. It made me look like shit, it amused me very much.

J—What does he mean by "every word I said to my father about you?"

I—Somebody who knows your family very well and also knows my husband, but I don't know who it is. The person has known you since you were a child and I think they live in New York.

J—What about it?

I—He said, "Jack Kennedy shrugged his shoulders and said, 'I wouldn't dream of marrying her; in fact, I don't care two bits about her. She's just something I picked up on the road.' " It's very amusing, darling. Tell me, when are you [shipping out]?

J—I'm not leaving for quite a while yet. What all did your husband say?

I—Why he said I could do what I wanted. He said he was sad to see me doing things like this. I'll tell you about it and I swear that he is not bothering us and that you need not be afraid of him. He is not going to sue you though he is aware what he could do by suing you.

J—He would be a big guy if he didn't sue me.

I—After all, he's a gentleman. I don't care what happens, he wouldn't do something like that. He's perfectly all right.*

The first person to inform Jack Kennedy of the FBI investigation was Langdon Marvin: "I originally learned of the FBI tap on Inga from a friend of mine who was an

*Presumably Inga was referring in this conversation to the possibility of Paul Fejos, to whom she was still legally married, naming JFK as corespondent in a divorce suit. The conversation further reveals that while JFK was undoubtedly sexually drawn to Inga, he had no serious intention of marrying her.

FBI special agent during World War II. This friend was in on the tap and told me about the tapes of Jack and Inga-Binga making love. He wanted to know what, if anything, I knew about Inga. I told him I knew very little.

"I only knew that she was one of a number of nice-looking, young women who lived at what I called the Peacock Palace, otherwise known as Dorchester House, at 2480 16th Street NW.* I called it the Peacock Palace because all the hallways in the building were lined with mirrors. You couldn't help but primp and pose as you headed for the elevators. Jack briefly shared an apartment in the same building with 'Kick' Kennedy. It was a big party building. A friend of ours, Alfredo de la Vega, also lived there. He had a thicker carpet than anybody else. He'd invite everybody to play knee football in his living room. You had to play on your knees and you had to cross the wall-to-wall living-room carpet to score a touchdown.

"Jack's father blew up over the Inga Arvad affair. There was some scrounging around and eventually Joe had to pull strings to get Jack out of ONI and into active sea duty. The Charleston Ship Yard was only a temporary assignment. The Director of ONI wanted to cashier Jack right out of the Navy, but Joe Kennedy knew people in Washington. One of them was James Forrestal, who became Secretary of the Navy, and another was J. Edgar Hoover. Joe Kennedy was a Special Service Contact for the FBI, in other words an unpaid informant. He knew Hollywood inside out and he began naming names, turning in Communist sympathizers and supporters in the motion picture industry. Joe understood that Hoover wielded tremendous authority and that his files on Inga Arvad could have a deleterious effect on his son's future.

"Ten years later, after he beat Henry Cabot Lodge in the Massachusetts Senatorial race, Jack became alarmed over the FBI files. 'That bastard, I'm going to force Hoover to give me those files,' he said to me. I said, 'Jack you're not going to do a thing. You're not going to ask for them. You're going to forget they exist. You're

---

*In the course of the FBI investigation, Inga Arvad moved to an apartment at 1600 16th Street NW. It was at this address that most of the FBI surveillance was conducted.

going to let them collect dust. You can be sure there'll be
a dozen copies made before he returns them to you, so
you will not have gained a yard. And if he knows you're
that desperate for them, he'll realize he has you in a
stranglehold.' "

On March 2, 1942, Jack Kennedy visited Inga in Washington. The purpose of the house call was ostensibly to
end their relationship, a fact later reflected in a brief FBI
internal memorandum:

> Due to the fact that Jack Kennedy . . . left town
> only one hour . . . after having seen Inga Arvad, it
> is believed Kennedy has broken off relations with
> Arvad, giving the reason that some friend of his
> [Langdon Marvin] has told Kennedy the Naval au-
> thorities [and the FBI] were watching him and ap-
> parently had a microphone in her room. . . .

On March 6, Jack Kennedy evidently experienced a
change of heart. His telephone call to Inga from Charleston
was duly recorded by the FBI:

> J—Why don't you come down this weekend?
> I—What a question. Don't you remember that
>   we talked it over Sunday?
> J—I know it.
> I—Oh, you don't think it's going to stay?
> J—Life's too short.
> I—Oh, Kennedy! . . . You're not giving up what
>   we promised last Sunday, are you?
> J—No, not till the next time I see you. I'm not
>   too good, am I?
> I—I think you're perfect, dear. We'll probably
>   meet again.
> J—You mean next week?
> I—I'm not coming. I don't know. I'm not trying
>   to be stubborn. I'm only trying to help you.
>   You know that don't you?
> J—I figured it out. . . .
> I—I still love you as much as always and always will.

In the end, it was the war that came between Jack and
Inga. Jack Kennedy was transferred to a PT-boat squadron and assigned to active duty in the Pacific. Inga,
having at last divorced her second husband, left the *Times-*

Herald and moved to New York, where she took up with the elderly Bernard Baruch, spending several months in his luxurious beach house at Sands Point, L.I.

Jack wrote to Inga from the Solomon Islands ("Knowing you has been the brightest part of an extremely bright 26 years") and near the end of the war even returned to her, this time in Hollywood, California, where she had taken a job as a gossip columnist with the North American Newspaper Alliance. But by then their romance had cooled, and both were involved in other relationships.

In 1947, Inga married Tim McCoy, 64, a retired star of cowboy movies who operated his own traveling wagon show and rodeo. The McCoys bought a horse farm near Nogales, Arizona, settled down and raised two sons. After Jack Kennedy's assassination, Inga was approached by a number of book publishers to document her affair with Jack. Although offered substantial sums of money, she refused. She died of cancer in 1973, a femme fatale of yesteryear but, for all intents and purposes, Jack Kennedy's first great love.

Although the FBI failed to uncover any meaningful connection between Inga Arvad and the architects of Nazi Germany, the Bureau did establish the foundation for an ongoing investigation into the personal life of John F. Kennedy. Few of his future liaisons or passing encounters would go unnoticed or uncharted. The FBI's "social" files on John Kennedy, only recently released in their entirety, contain information on, among others, a series of short involvements in the years immediately following World War II.

According to some of the names in these files, it appears that Jack Kennedy shared his father's affinity for Hollywood stars and starlets. In 1945, while passing through Paris, he called on Hedy Lamarr, the Viennese-born actress whose nude appearance in *Ecstasy* (1932) helped launch her film career. In her 1966 autobiography, *Ecstasy and Me: My Life as a Woman,* she writes that Kennedy telephoned to ask her for a date. She invited him to her apartment and he arrived an hour later bearing a bag of fresh oranges. Since citrus fruit was nearly impossible to obtain in postwar Paris, the gift was much appreciated. Jack and the beguiling Miss Lamarr spent a most pleasant evening together.

Less famous than Lamarr but equally charming was Angela Greene, a Powers Agency model-turned-actress. Jack and Angela dated off and on from 1944 to 1946, when she married wealthy Los Angeles realtor Stuart W. Martin. Angela recalled Jack taking her to some of New York's leading nightspots—Sardi's, The Stork Club, El Morocco—but typically never having enough cash to make it through the night. When they attended Mass at St. Patrick's Cathedral he had to borrow money from her for the collection box. Angela spent several days with Jack at Hyannis Port and was as astounded as every other visitor by the degree of family rivalry and Joe Kennedy's constant sermons on the necessity of finishing first, whether in a Presidential race or a game of Monopoly ("Which they played as if they really owned the property," she was quoted as saying).

In one FBI report, Jack is reported to have escorted Susan Hayward around Hollywood, while in another he is mentioned as being seen in company with Joan Crawford. Others with whom his name was linked were starlet Peggy Cummins, former ice-skating champion Sonja Henie (whom he termed a "real heartbreaker") and Lana Turner. There is no mention of Olivia de Havilland in the files, though Jack met her in 1945 at a Beverly Hills party thrown by motion picture producer Sam Spiegel. Jack saw her again at a dinner party given by Gary Cooper. A few days later he went to her home for afternoon tea. Chuck Spalding, Jack's friend and a New York advertising executive, went along for encouragement.

"Jack was just fascinated with Olivia," said Spalding. "He put himself out to be as attractive as he could be. He leaned toward her and fixed her with a stare and he was working just as hard as he could, really boring in. . . . Finally we get up to leave, he is still working on her to come out to dinner. But she had another date and wouldn't break it. Then, taking his leave, Jack, unable to take his eyes off Olivia, put his hand on the doorknob and walked straight into the hall closet. Tennis rackets and tennis balls and everything came down on top of his head. . . .

"Later that night, we went to dinner at a restaurant and Olivia was there with the writer-artist Ludwig Bemelmans. Jack said, 'I can't understand it. Just look at that guỹ! I know he's talented, I know he's got great ability, but really! Do you think it was my walking into the closet? Do you think that's what really did it?' "

Joan Fontaine, Olivia's younger sister, was similarly given the rush by Jack. To fend him off; she told him stories of how his father had also propositioned her in her home. Jack listened and then said, "I only hope I'm the same way he is when I reach his age."

Jack Kennedy's most serious entanglement with an actress during this period involved Gene Tierney. They first met in 1944 at a party thrown by California socialite Betsy Bloomingdale. Their two-year relationship started in 1946 when Kennedy, still wearing his U.S. Navy lieutenant's uniform, again visited Hollywood and the set of Gene's latest movie *Dragonwyck*. While playing a scene she turned and found herself "staring into what I thought were the most perfect blue eyes I had ever seen on a man. . . . He smiled at me. My reaction was right out of a ladies' romance novel. Literally, my heart stopped."

Gene was on the verge of getting divorced from fashion designer Oleg Cassini and was facing the trauma of having to institutionalize a retarded daughter, a situation for which Jack, because of his sister Rosemary, had great empathy. He and Gene started dating, mainly in New York whenever Gene went East. By now she was telling family and friends she had met a fellow who was not only a national war hero (thanks to the publicity generated by John Hersey's laudatory *New Yorker* account of JFK's *PT-109* adventures),* but who was also running for Congress and would surely be President someday. "That was

---

*John Hersey was engaged to Frances Ann Cannon, JFK's former girlfriend, when he first met Jack during the war, heard his *PT-109* story, researched and wrote it up. "It developed," he said, "that the Kennedys did a reprint of the article and ran an excerpt in *U.S. News and World Report* without copyright notice and without my permission. I wrote JFK and asked if he'd heard of the copyright acts. He wrote me a charming letter back saying he would be very glad as recommpense for his error to give me the reprint rights to *Why England Slept*, a terrible book he'd written based on his senior thesis at Harvard. Of course he was elected President and of course *Why England Slept* was reprinted, but I never heard anything more about it. Joseph Kennedy, meanwhile saw to it that the *PT-109* article ran in *Reader's Digest* and even used it as a campaign brochure for his son. When they cast the film version in 1963, Jack wanted Warren Beatty to play his role; it went instead to the less glamorous Cliff Robertson."

his goal," she writes in a personal memoir. "He talked about it in a way that was unselfconscious." Gene noted that while Jack seemed to have little of the romantic in his blood, 'he gave you his time, his interest. He knew the strength of the phrase 'What do you think.' "

On a week's holiday at Cape Cod, where she, too, met his family, Gene recollected that Jack picked her up at the station "wearing patched blue jeans. . . . I thought he looked like Tom Sawyer." On another occasion, "It was for Jack that I first wore one of the ankle-length New Look dresses made famous by Dior." Jack's reaction to the dress: "Good God, Gene, what's that?" Her rueful reminiscence notes that Jack just shook his head when she talked about high fashion. "He later married a very stylish lady, but I think it's fair to say that clothes were not his weakness."

Neither apparently were divorced Episcopalian movie stars. One day over lunch, without warning, he said, "You know, Gene, I can never marry you." At the end of their meal as he was about to leave the restaurant to catch a plane, she said in a soft voice, "Bye-bye, Jack."

"What do you mean. That sounds kind of final," he said.

"It is," she responded.

The ill-fated romance was "sweet," said Gene from a later vantage point; she remembered Jack as "a serious young man with a dream" and as a person who "took life just as it came."*

Rumor has it that Jack Kennedy was once "secretly" married to a woman he dated in the 1940s, Palm Beach socialite Durie Malcolm, whose family he had known since his youth. Jack dated Durie in 1939 and again at the beginning of 1947, when he took her to the Orange Bowl game in Miami. It was the same year that Durie married Tom Shevlin, a former Yale football star and scion to a lumber fortune.

---

*JFK also pursued Austine "Bootsie" McDonnell, the estranged wife of gossip columnist Igor Cassini, hence Gene Tierney's sister-in-law. Bootsie later married William Randolph Hearst, Jr., whose oral history at the JFK Library stipulates that Jack Kennedy was "very popular and very handsome and very high-spirited and very much sought after by the girls, I can tell you that." See also Gene Tierney with Mickey Herskowitz, *Self-Portrait*, pp. 141–157.

While intense enough to capture the fleeting attention of the Palm Beach society watchers, the relationship between Jack and Durie never culminated in marriage. The story, which broke in 1962 when Kennedy was President, purported that the two had been surreptitiously married in 1939 and divorced in Reno in 1948, but that the divorce had been invalidated, and that Archbishop Cushing had obtained a Papal annulment of the marriage in early 1953. Based on an erroneous entry for Durie, discovered by a researcher in a family genealogy (*The Blauvelt Genealogy*), the marriage rumor gained currency and was used by arch-conservative, radical and racist publications in an effort to attack Kennedy politically.

The FBI files contain material not only on the Durie Malcolm-Jack Kennedy matter, but on an alleged romance in 1951 between JFK and Alicja Purdom, wife of British actor Edmund Purdom, which came to light ten years later when an Italian weekly carried an article on Alicja's supposed relations with Kennedy.

The article, as translated by the FBI, states that Alicja Purdom, born Barbara Maria Kopczynska in 1926 at Lodicz, Poland, was engaged to President Kennedy and that she could have become the First Lady of America, except that the marriage had been opposed by the President's father because she was a Polish-Jewish refugee who entered the United States in 1939. She lived with her mother in Boston until 1951, when she moved to New York City, which is where she and Kennedy had their romance. The article further suggests that a $500,000 payoff settled a lawsuit she filed against Kennedy.

Launching its own investigation, the FBI concluded that a lawsuit had indeed been instituted against John Kennedy ("the gist of [which] appeared to concern an affair between JFK and 'a woman,' as a result of which the woman became pregnant"), but that the entire record of the suit had been sealed by a New York court. Supposedly the sealed court records contained incriminating photographs of JFK and Mrs. Purdom, as well as other documentation that could have been harmful to the President.

The FBI files include a 1963 memorandum from J. Edgar Hoover to then-Attorney General Robert Kennedy, which reads in part: "When the suit was filed in New York just prior to the President's assuming office, you apparently went to New York and arranged a settlement of the case out of court for $500,000."

In a recent interview, "the woman" in question (now Mrs. Alicja Corning Clark, the widow of Singer Sewing Machine heir Alfred Corning Clark) admitted knowing JFK in 1951 ("I knew the entire family"), but denied ever having been engaged to him or instituting a lawsuit against him, although she admitted having had dealings "with some corrupt lawyers." She also stated she never received a payoff from the family.

Such confusion is understandable considering the profusion of women in John Kennedy's life, particularly at that stage in his career. Joan and Clay Blair, Jr., in their encyclopedic account *The Search for JFK,* list a number of his girlfriends, including a pair of nurses, Ann McGillicuddy and Elinor Dooley, both of whom were involved with Jack toward the end of the war. There was also Pamela Farrington of Boston, a fashion model with black hair and sapphire eyes, a frequent travel companion who enjoyed sunbathing in the nude. When Kennedy ran for the Senate in 1952, his aides became frantic over a photograph in circulation showing Jack lying next to the naked and very-well-built Pamela on a deserted Florida beach. The candidate merely snickered at the snapshot and remarked, "Yes, I remember her. She was great!"

John Sharon, from 1950 to 1952 an aide to Congressman Charles Howell of New Jersey (Sharon subsequently became an aide to Adlai Stevenson), came to know Jack and began to socialize with him: "Congressman Kennedy had the office right next door to ours on the fifth floor of the Old House Office Building. . . . And frequently . . . we went out double-dating at night. He was interested in a girl I was dating. Her name was Hermila Anzaldua. We had a double-date at his house for dinner one night. . . . I arranged to get him a date with a gal named Lolita Delosorios. It was then that he asked me which of the two girls I was dating. And I informed him, and he smiled . . . and concentrated his attention on the other girl, which I thought was very gentlemanly."

"Gentlemanly" wasn't quite the term that occurred to television news commentator Nancy Dickerson when describing JFK. "He had great sex appeal," she granted, "but he was the complete male chauvinist. He saw women primarily as objects of pleasure. He didn't denigrate them, but he didn't exactly idealize them either. I remember when he came to take me out one night and he didn't come into the house; he stayed in his car and simply honked his horn. I didn't like it, and he never did it again.

"We dated before he married Jackie. Besides being young, rich and handsome, he was overpowering—you couldn't help but be impressed by him. But sex to Jack meant no more than a cup of coffee. I've been quoted as saying that before, and it's true. He used to tell his friends that unless he had sex at least once a day he developed a severe migraine and couldn't sleep at night. I'm certain the pursuit meant more to him than the act itself."

During his congressional years, Kennedy was rarely at a loss for female companionship, although the word among many Georgetown women was that he was a disappointment as a sexual partner and had a predisposition for making love with one eye on the clock. George Smathers told Kitty Kelley: "Just in terms of the time he spent with a woman, he was a lousy lover. He went in more for quantity than quality." Kennedy himself once bragged to reporters: "I'm never through with a girl until I've had her three ways."

Pulitzer Prize-winning historian Dr. Margaret Louise Coit* met John F. Kennedy in the early spring of 1953 while researching a biography of Bernard Baruch. "John Kennedy was the golden lad of liberal politics, the most eligible bachelor in New England," she said. "Every girl in Massachusetts and Washington, D.C., wanted to date him, and I wasn't any exception."

An hour in Kennedy's busy senatorial office and a quick spin around town with the Senator left Margaret Coit in a state of breathless excitement: "In his office he kept signing these glossy glamour-boy photographs of himself to send to his constituents, taking telephone calls, dictating letters to five or six staff members, perusing legislative reports, skimming newspapers, reading his mail, all the while carrying on a conversation with me. He had enormous drive and energy. At one point he asked me how Bernard Baruch had made his fortune. 'The same

---

*Margaret Louise Coit's *John C. Calhoun: American Portrait* won the Pulitzer Prize for biography in 1951.

way your father made his fortune,' I said. 'You should ask
your father.' He changed the subject. He pointed to his
bookshelves overflowing with books. 'Ask me about any
of them,' he said, 'I've read them all.'

"He drove me to the boarding house where I was
staying. As we passed the White House he turned unusually serious, almost solemn. 'One day that's going to be
my home,' he said. I looked at him. I thought he'd gone
crazy. But I was young and impressionable, and when he
invited me to an at-home engagement party to be held a
few days later for his sister Eunice and Sargent Shriver, I
jumped at the opportunity.

"Richard Nixon, Alice Longworth and Stuart Symington
were among the guests at the party. Kennedy's sisters
were also there, looking very spiffy and stylish. Their
hair was frosted. It was the first time I'd ever seen
frosting on hair.

"Kennedy and Symington spent the entire party standing in a corner, discussing politics. I felt neglected. He'd
invited me to his home but hadn't said a word to me.
Then toward the end of the party, he took notice and
came over to me. He grabbed me in the hall, and put his
arm around me. We were in public and I felt slightly
embarrassed, but I didn't say much."

Margaret Coit saw Kennedy once more, several days
later. He again drove her home, and this time she made
the mistake of inviting him in. 'A friend of mine had
warned me not to get caught alone in a room with Joe
Kennedy, but nobody had said anything about Jack," she
remarked. "I invited him in because he seemed tired. I
thought he might want to sit and rest for a few minutes."

As they sat together on the living room couch, Jack
suddenly lunged at Margaret. They struggled, and she
managed to fend him off. "Don't be so grabby," she
scolded. "This is only our first date."

Kennedy persisted, pawing her again. "Let me talk to
you," said Margaret. "I have standards, just like your
sisters. You wouldn't want me to do anything you wouldn't
want your sisters to do, would you?"

Kennedy allowed as how he didn't care what his sisters
did. He grabbed her a third time. "What about your
priest?" said Margaret. "What will you tell him?"

"Oh, he'll forgive me," said Kennedy. He grinned,
pressing her to the couch. She managed to wriggle free,

and got up to cross the room for a glass of water from the kitchen. Kennedy complimented her on her well-formed legs. When she returned to the couch, he resumed where he had left off.

"This is only our first date," Margaret reiterated. "We've got plenty of time."

Kennedy raised his head and looked deeply into her eyes. "I can't wait," he said in a cold, mechanical, robot-like voice. "I'm going to grab everything I want. You see, I haven't any time."

The same relentless approach worked better with some of Jack's other girlfriends. While courting Jackie Bouvier he was involved with at least three other women: Ann McDermott, who had come to Washington to find a job in government; Noël Noël, a long-term intimate of Philip Graham of the *Washington Post* and a sometime companion of JFK; Florence Pritchett, a bright, engaging and elegant member of café society, whose friendship with Jack lasted from the mid-1940s until the end of Camelot.

"Flo Pritchett and Jack had a wonderful relationship," said Lem Billings. "If you were down, there'd be nobody you'd rather be with because she just always said something that made you smile. Flo was the one person who could be counted on to amuse Jack. She was great company. When he wasn't feeling well, when his back hurt or he felt depressed, she was the one he wanted to see.

"Before meeting Jack she'd been married to Richard Canning, son of the bubble gum king. If she hadn't already been married and divorced, I suspect Jack would have gladly married her. Instead she became the second wife of Earl E. T. Smith and lived next door to the Kennedys in Palm Beach. After that there were stories of secret interludes between Jack and Flo, feverish encounters on the stretch of sand connecting their respective homes. Although I never personally witnessed any of these meetings, I don't for a second doubt that they occurred."

11

By early spring of 1954, Jack and Jackie Kennedy were living in a small, rented, nineteenth-century townhouse at 3321 Dent Place in Georgetown. The house stood in the center of a row of nearly identical residences; an ambassador and a retired admiral lived across the street, but the block also included rooming houses and student apartments. Students lived in the neighborhood because Dent Place was only four blocks from Georgetown University; a block from their house was a public park where Jack and his brother Bobby sometimes played touch football.

One night a week, Jack drove to Baltimore to take a speed-reading course with an instructor from Johns Hopkins University. Jackie, a natural speed reader, registered for an American History survey course with Professor Jules Davids at the Georgetown University School of Foreign Affairs. She and Jack discussed her course assignments over breakfast each morning. They gave small dinner parties at home, on one occasion for eight including Jackie's mother. "I think I could entertain a king or queen with less apprehension than my mother, when there are other guests present," said Jackie. They hired a full-time cook, Mattie Penn, and gave larger dinners at Merrywood, where they stayed whenever Jackie's parents left town.

But it wasn't, as Jackie later put it, quite what she had in mind. "During our first year of marriage, we were like gypsies living in and out of a suitcase," she said. "It was turbulent. Jack made speeches all over the country and was never home more than two nights at a time.

"To make matters even more restless, we had rented a house in Georgetown for six months and, when the lease ran out, we moved to a hotel.

"We spent the summer, off and on, at Jack's father's

house in Hyannis Port. Ours was the little room on the first floor that Jack used to have by himself. It didn't take me long to realize it was only big enough for one.

"That first year I longed for a home of our own. I hoped it would give our lives some roots, some stability. My ideal at that time was a normal life with my husband coming home from work every day at five. I wanted him to spend weekends with me and the children I hoped we would have.

"One morning the first year we were married, Jack said to me, 'What food are you planning for the 40 guests we're having for lunch?'

"No one had told me anything about it. It was 11 a.m., and the guests were expected at one. I was in a panic. As soon as I could gather myself, I tore up to a little Greek place (in the neighborhood) that made wonderful casseroles.

"The luncheon was a success—casserole, salad and raspberries. I vowed never again to be disturbed when Jack brought home unexpected guests."

In spite of Jackie's earlier vow that she would never end up living the life of a suburban housewife, she now seemed to aspire to little else. "The main thing for me was to do whatever my husband wanted," she remarked. "He couldn't—and wouldn't—be married to a woman who tried to share the spotlight with him.

"I thought the best thing I could do was to be a distraction. Jack lived and breathed politics all day long. If he came home to more table-thumping, how could he ever relax."

Her first priority was to make sure her husband ate three healthful meals a day, rather than the fast-food diet he had endured as a bachelor. In her desire to become a good hostess, Jackie spent both time and effort learning the vintage years of great wines. According to friends, Jack soon began to take pride in his wife's gourmet tastes.

After dinner, he began smoking an occasional Cuban cigar, which he said helped him digest his food. "It also," said Jackie, "made him less critical of my cigarette smoking."

Jackie took on the task of organizing her husband's wardrobe. His casual attitude toward clothes was well known. Ted Reardon, Jr., his senatorial administrative assistant, recalled an occasion when Kennedy, not yet married, dressed for an important political roast in a spotless Brooks Brothers blue serge jacket, a solid brown tie and an old faded pair of black trousers. Reardon expressed dismay at the color combination, but Jack couldn't understand his objection.

At the time of his marriage, Jack's wardrobe left little to choice. Igor Cassini, a guest at the wedding, remarked in one of his gossip columns that as of 1954, "Kennedy owned four usable winter suits plus two that he hadn't had time to have fitted. (His wardrobe might have been more extensive were it not for his habit of checking out of a hotel and leaving a suit behind in the closet.)"

Jackie changed all that. "I brought a certain amount of order to Jack's life," she claimed. "We had good food in our house—not merely the bare staples that he used to have. He no longer went out in the morning with one brown and one black shoe on. His clothes got pressed, and he got to the airport without a mad rush, because I packed for him."

Jackie's efforts on his behalf were not without humor. To be able to take over on cook's night out, she signed up for a cooking course. Her first opportunity came the day the course ended. "Evelyn Lincoln called and said Jack was leaving the office, so I started everything," she said. "I'd heard those silly stories about the bride burning things and I just knew everything was going right when suddenly, I don't know what went wrong, you couldn't see the place for smoke. And when I tried to pull the chops out of the oven, the door seemed to collapse. The pan slid out and the fat splattered. One of the chops fell on the floor but I put it on the plate anyway. The chocolate sauce was burning and exploding. What a smell!!!!! I couldn't get the spoon out of the chocolate. It was like a rock. The coffee had all boiled away. I burned my arm, and it turned purple. It looked horrible. Then Jack arrived and took me out to dinner."

Jackie's would-be contributions weren't all domestic. Although shy and retiring in public, she did what she could to fulfill the role of senatorial squaw by following the Senate debates, joining the gallery whenever Jack gave an important speech, reading the *Congressional Record* and answering bales of her husband's office mail. She attended political rallies and receptions, as well as cocktail parties and luncheons. She joined the Ladies of the Senate Red Cross (she learned how to fold bandages) and a Senate wives cultural group that raised funds for local museums and music societies. She didn't enjoy the ladies' groups but stayed with them, at least temporarily, for Jack's sake.

What's more she helped mold Jack into a more effective public speaker. Kennedy at first lacked basic skill and confidence, though he had studied at Boston's Staley School of Oratory. He slouched when he spoke and often kept his hands in his pockets. He tended to talk on and on, usually much too quickly, never knowing when to take a breath or how to make a point. His voice was rasping and high-pitched. Drawing on her theater training at Miss Porter's and her natural bent for the dramatic, Jackie slowed him down, helped him modulate his voice and give clearer expression to his thoughts. She demonstrated how certain hand gestures could make him appear more relaxed. She taught him the benefits of body language and trained him to harness his overabundant energy.

Jackie attempted to reinforce her role in any number of ways. Helen McCauley, a former Green Book member of Georgetown society, recalled Jackie's bridge-playing efforts. "I received a telephone call from a girlfriend saying that Mrs. Kennedy felt her husband played a pretty fair game of bridge, and she was worried that her game wasn't up to snuff. She wanted to play more regularly so she could improve. My friend knew that I had a weekly game with Ann Covington and Ann Clark, whose husbands were both in government, and that we were looking for somebody to replace a fourth lady who had recently moved. The problem was that we played international match points and were all rather advanced players. My friend went back and explained this to Mrs. Kennedy, who in turn said she would play for any amount that anyone wanted just so she could perfect her game. I asked Ann Clark what she thought and she said, 'Oh, that's just like being hired to play.'

"Well, my husband had just died and I was lonely and so I told my friend, 'Tell Mrs. Kennedy that I'll try to find two other ladies and she can join that game.' And that's what I did, and we met once a week at Mrs. Kennedy's house, and she was utterly charming. The first thing she said to me was, 'You must tell me everything I do wrong.' I corrected her as we went, and her game improved. She was a quick study. She was also quite modest. I learned later that she was a tournament Scrabble player, one of the best in the country. But, anyway I always admired her for going to such lengths to be able to play bridge at her husband's level."

To keep up with him, Jackie also took golf lessons. Hugh Sidey, White House correspondent for *Time* and author of a John F. Kennedy biography, tells of something that happened at the Hyannis Port Golf Club in the summer of 1954: "It was the seventeenth hole, and Jack watched Jackie flail away in a sandtrap until he could not watch another time while the ball fell back at her feet. 'Open the face of the club, follow through,' he called from his golf cart. 'Let me show you,' he said finally, taking the club. He gave a couple of professional-looking practice swings, raised the club in a graceful arc, then brought it down smoothly and powerfully. The ball rose two feet and dribbled back into the sand. Kennedy looked down calmly, handed the club back to Jackie, said, 'See, that's how you do it.'"*

For all her wifely efforts, Jackie's marriage to John Kennedy was marked by pain and tragedy. On October 11, 1954, he was admitted to the Hospital for Special Surgery-Cornell University Medical Center in Manhattan to undergo X-ray and other preliminary medical examinations. His physicians wanted to determine the exact cause of a chronic and excruciating lower back condition that had required spinal surgery in 1944.

Langdon Marvin saw Jack during the first week of his hospital stay and found him in a surprisingly placid state of mind. "He successfully masked his suffering," said the visitor. "He had hung a poster of Marilyn Monroe in short shorts and tight sweater on the wall above his head; stuffed animals were strewn about the bed; somebody had installed a small tropical fish tank and filled it with goldfish. Jackie dropped in every few hours to keep Jack company and relate the latest tidbit of gossip. She had moved in with Jack's sister Jean, and although the circumstances were far from ideal, she seemed to enjoy being back in New York. At the Helena Rubenstein

*See Hugh Sidey, *John F. Kennedy, President*, p. 247.

beauty salon on Fifth Avenue, she discovered a new hair stylist, Kenneth Battelle, the same Kenneth she would use for years. In those days Kenneth was just starting out, and Jackie was simply a young lady from Washington, D.C., on an extended visit to New York.

"Despite Jack's condition, it wouldn't have surprised me to learn that he'd bedded at least one of his dozen or so nurses. They had their eye on him, and Jackie had her eye on them. Jack's main conern, however, seemed to be politics—the matter of the Senate vote to censure Joe McCarthy, the red-baiting junior Senator from Wisconsin whose Committee on Un-American Activities had poisoned the political atmosphere. Jack's father was friendly with McCarthy. He had contributed to McCarthy's campaign fund, just as he had once contributed to FDR's campaign fund. His daughter Eunice had dated McCarthy. And Bobby Kennedy had served as the committee's chief counsel. Personally, Bobby always struck me as the junior G-man type. But Jack felt he couldn't justifiably come out against McCarthy. Under the circumstances, I think he regarded his hospital stay as something of a mixed blessing—unfortunate but well-timed."

The Kennedy family's personal physician, Dr. Sara Jordan, of the Lahey Clinic in Boston, opposed the idea of major back surgery. She was concerned—and rightfully so—that Jack's adrenal insufficiency (due to a well-documented case of Addison's Disease) might produce shock, infection and other serious post-operative complications. Surgery would entail more than the usual range of risks. For her part, Jackie agreed to go along with whatever Jack decided. "I'd rather be dead than spend the rest of my life on crutches," he told her, opting for a surgical remedy.

On October 21, a team of four Cornell physicians, headed by Dr. Philip Wilson, performed a double-fusion operation on Kennedy's spine in the hope of stabilizing and strengthening his back. The delicate operation seemed to go well, but within days infection set in and Jack's condition worsened. For three weeks he remained on the hospital's critical list.

Charles Bartlett visited Jack in mid-November: "He'd passed the crisis by then, but he remained hospitalized and very, very ill. Jackie was magnificent with him. She had this almost uncanny ability to rise to the occasion.

She sat with him for hours, held his hand, mopped his brow, fed him, helped him in and out of bed, put on his socks and slippers for him, entertained him by reading aloud and reciting poems she knew by heart, bought him silly little gadgets and toys to make him laugh, played checkers, Categories and Twenty Questions with him. Once his health improved sufficiently, she encouraged friends to visit as often as possible. Anything to distract him from the pain."

Jackie's spunk and resilience in the face of her husband's medical problems gained her the grudging respect of Jack's family. Among her other assets, she proved herself adept at handling social and political figures of prominence. Adlai Stevenson telephoned Jack to cheer him up and in return received an endearing letter from Jackie, saying that his call had absolutely "transformed Jack." Lyndon Johnson, who had just become Senate Majority Leader, received a similarly enchanting letter in response to a telegram. To Bernard Baruch, who stopped by the hospital only to be turned away by an overprotective nurse, she wrote: "If you only knew how crushed we are to have missed you—I know Jack is miserable—because he would have adored to have seen you—but I am sure I am much more—because I would rather meet you than anyone in the world—and now I feel that you are a ship that has passed in the night." Answering a letter of encouragement from President Eisenhower to her husband, she wrote: 'You did more for him than any doctor could possibly do."

One evening at a small New York dinner party, Jackie encountered Grace Kelly and prevailed upon the actress to return with her to Jack's hospital room. "I'm the new night nurse," Grace whispered into Kennedy's ear. The patient smiled but was so groggy from medication that by the next morning he could hardly remember having had a visitor.

Near the end of December, his doctors suggested that Jack might mend faster in the familiar surroundings of one of his father's homes. Departing the hospital on a stretcher, accompanied by Jackie, a private nurse and a personal attendant, he was transported by ambulance to LaGuardia Airport, where the group boarded a plane for Miami. There they were met by a second ambulance that took them to the Kennedy estate in Palm Beach.

Within two months, he was back in New York and back at the Hospital for Special Surgery. The infection had flared again, necessitating a second operation to remove a metal plate implanted during the previous operation. Kennedy was discharged three weeks later and returned to Palm Beach. For the next month, the nurse looked after him and, before leaving, taught Jackie how to dress his wound.

George Smathers visited Jack in Palm Beach. "I went down there with my brother," he said. "Jack had dropped maybe forty pounds. His sister Eunice joked about it. 'It's nothing serious, just Jackie's cooking,' she said. He was on his stomach because he couldn't bear any weight on his back. Jackie had gone shopping that day, so he asked me to change his dressing. I removed the gauze and found this huge, open, oozing, very sickly-looking hole in the middle of his back. 'Look at this,' I said to my brother, who leaned over to have a peek. 'God, there's green stuff coming out of it,' he said. It was truly a gruesome sight. The pills they'd prescribed obviously weren't worth a damn because he was in a great deal of pain. It was so bad he couldn't sleep at night, and he would drift off during the day.

"I realized then that I'd misjudged Jackie. Anybody who could look at that festering wound day after day and go through all that agony with her husband had to have backbone. Jack himself knew it. 'My wife is a shy, quiet girl, but when things get rough, she can handle herself pretty well,' he said of Jackie. It must have been a trying period for her. She was living with her in-laws, which is never easy for a bride. In a sense her appearance betrayed her. She wasn't fragile. She was tough. Joe Kennedy recognized her potential from the start. It's true he had lusted after the Auchincloss connection and realized that Newport was a rung above Boston on the social ladder. But primarily he wanted somebody for Jack who had the guts and the presence of mind to make the run with him for the presidency."

As Jack regained his strength, Jackie encouraged him to read and write and paint. The painting, which he did in bed, came to a halt when Rose Kennedy began complaining about the laundry bills. Instead he embarked on a book he had wanted to write on the subject of political courage, continuing the project after he and Jackie moved into Merrywood several months later. One visitor to the Auchincloss residence noted that Jack couldn't yet sit up but he could use a writing board and wrote almost upside down in bed.

Jackie, who helped shape the overall theme of the book, did much of the initial research, scanning numerous historical volumes sent over by the Library of Congress, taking notes and writing out long passages. The book focused on eight important figures (including John Quincy Adams and Daniel Webster) and their achievements in the face of daunting obstacles. He titled it *Profiles in Courage* and in it gave Jackie her proper due:

> This book would not have been possibble without the encouragement, assistance and criticisms offered from the very beginning by my wife, Jacqueline, whose help during all the days of my convalescence, I cannot ever adequately acknowledge.

Profiles was published in early 1956 to rave reviews, a number of which were evidently planted; a lavish promotion budget, provided by Joe Kennedy, helped it hit the major best-seller lists. The book also captured that year's Pulitzer Prize for biography, an award that thrilled Jack Kennedy. Writing, he told friends, might well have been his chosen career had his older brother survived the war. He had once told Margaret Coit about his brief stint as a reporter for International News Service, the Hearst press association, adding that he would rather win a Pulitzer than become President of the United States.

The prize, however, raised questions as to Kennedy's actual participation in the writing of the book, and even raised some questions concerning his earlier volume, *Why England Slept,* a onesided defense of his father's controversial isolationist stand during World War II. It, like *Profiles in Courage,* had been a contender on the best-seller lists.

Blair Clark, Kennedy's friend and former roommate at Harvard, remembered attending a luncheon at the Blackstone Hotel during the 1956 Democratic Convention in Chicago at which John Kennedy's written works came up as a topic of conversation: "There were a number of people at our table, including Jack Kennedy and newspaper columnist Joe Alsop, and we were discussing the flap about whether Jack had actually written *Profiles in Courage*. Partially as a joke, I said, 'Well, of course, Jack, you remember when you and I met in Widener Library at [Harvard], and you asked me to rewrite sections of *Why England Slept*.' He became furious at this comment. But in truth he did ask me to rewrite sections of his first book. I suppose he trusted me because I was editor of the *Harvard Crimson*, the student newspaper, and at his behest I'd helped him procure a spot on the staff.

"As I recall, it was the spring of 1940 when I bumped into Jack at Widener. He'd been on leave in England for a semester, putting together his senior thesis. He had it with him when I saw him in the library, and he wanted me to look it over and make some revisions. I spent three or four sweltering afternoons with the manuscript. I might have written a few paragraphs that were original, but mostly I rewrote and edited. Frankly I was surprised he found a publisher for it."

Blair Clark wasn't the only person to contribute to the shaping of the manuscript. Much more pervasive was the role played by Arthur Krock who, we now know, took the completed thesis and reworked it into publishable prose. Krock, a confrere of Joe Kennedy's, then suggested that Henry Luce, with whom Kennedy was also very friendly, be drafted to write a preface to *Why England Slept*. A few words from the founder of *Time* could help the book's commercial viability.

But Joe Kennedy went one step further. To insure the book's appearance on the best-seller list, he sent representatives scurrying around the country to buy out the stock in every bookstore that carried it. Tom Hailey, a college student hired on a part-time basis to perform odd jobs around the Kennedy compound at Hyannis Port, remembered an incident that took place in the early 1940s. "I spent a week in the attic and basement of Joe Kennedy's house counting copies of *Why England Slept*," said Hailey. "They were stacked from floor to ceiling in boxes, cartons and crates. I'd never seen so many books in one place before, all by the same author. I counted maybe thirty to forty thousand copies of the volume."

Joe Kennedy understood the publicity value inherent in bestsellerdom and prestigious literary prizes such as the Pulitzer, and imparted this knowledge to his sons.

Jack Kennedy, despite stern and vociferous pronouncements to the contrary, apparently had little to do with the final version of *Profiles in Courage,* much less than he was willing to admit.

Although hesitant to take credit for his part in the project, Ted Sorensen, who by now was working for Jack, wrote major portions of the various drafts. Another important voice belonged to Jules Davids, Jackie's former Georgetown Universiy American History professor; it had been Jackie's idea to bring Davids into the enterprise.

"Sorensen and I did much of the work on *Profiles in Courage,*" claimed Davids. "Arthur Schlesinger, Jr., James MacGregor Burns and Arthur Holcombe also made contributions. Alan Nevins wrote the preface and offered some suggestions. But Sorensen and I shaped the thing and wrote most of it. You could almost call it a government paper, a position paper, with sundry drafts and revisions prepared by editors, aides, research assistants, secretaries and advisors."

Jackie assumed responsibility for trying to locate a publisher for the project. Angele Gingras, who hadn't seen or spoken to Jackie since their days at the *Washington Times-Herald,* bumped into her in the spring of 1955 at Lord and Taylor in New York. Jackie began asking Angele about publishers.

"We were both in the department where you order material for clothes and we pulled up chairs and sat there gabbing for an hour," said Angele. "Jackie described her husband's back problems. Then she mentioned *Profiles in Courage.* She said Jack was doing the writing and she was helping him. She hoped to find a publisher and wanted to know about literary agents, whether one should have one and whether I could recommend any. She also wondered about making multiple submissions; that is, sending the manuscript to more than one publisher at a time, a common practice today, but not done in those days. I advised her to deal directly with the publishers, one at a time."

Jackie turned to Cass Canfield at Harper and Brothers, mainly because his son, Michael, was married to her sister Lee. Canfield read an early draft of the manuscript, found it sketchy but interesting, offered Kennedy a moderate advance and assigned the book to editor Evan W.

Thomas, the son of American Socialist leader Norman Thomas.

In due course, Canfield and Thomas visited the Kennedys at Merrywood. Jack's back, according to Thomas, "was still so sore he couldn't pick up the manuscript from the table next to his chair. After that meeting, we communicated mostly by telephone. If Jack didn't write *Profiles in Courage,* he nevertheless knew the book's contents backwards and forwards. He could respond to queries about individual pages, paragraphs, even sentences. The one thing I remember about Jackie is that whenever Jack and I had an honest editorial disagreement, she invariably sided with her husband. It's difficult to say who did what with respect to the book. There's no doubt that Ted Sorensen proved extremely helpful. Whether this meant that Jack wasn't the book's sole author remains a question that may never be answered."

The *Profiles in Courage*-Pulitzer Prize-JFK controversy arose again on the Mike Wallace ABC television show of December 7, 1957, when columnist Drew Pearson specifically charged that it was a national scandal that Kennedy had been awarded a Pulitzer for a work he hadn't written. Jack Kennedy watched the program and early the next morning called Washington attorney Clark Clifford, whose office had handled several minor legal matters for the Kennedy family. "I'm coming over immediately," he informed Clifford.

"While Jack sat opposite me," recalled Clifford, "his father telephoned and said, 'Sue the bastard for $60 million!'

" 'That isn't quite the way to go about it,' I told him.

"Jack and I flew to New York and we spent a couple of days up there working with the ABC people and we took along a lot of notes that Jack had written when he was laid up with the back operation. We persuaded them to make a retraction on the following week's program, though I'm certain they were still dubious about the book's authorship. I know Drew Pearson had his doubts. But Jack and his father seemed happy with the results.

"I really had no idea why they were so agitated at first. Later I did, because it was either while we were in New York or on our way back to Washington that I realized Jack was getting ready to run for President and that's why they'd been so upset. It would have been a heavy burden to carry if, in running for President, somebody had officially charged him with the misrepresentation of calling himself a successful author when he hadn't even written the book."

After seven months' absence, John Kennedy resumed his senatorial duties. He would not use crutches in public, refused a wheelchair and walked unaided, but still felt soreness in his back. He went to a new doctor in New York, Janet G. Travell, who ordered him to wear a specially designed back brace, sleep on an extra-firm, cattle-tail hair mattress, relax in a rocking chair and use corrective shoes, one a quarter of an inch higher than the other.

"The lumbar fusion didn't solve John Kennedy's back problems," said Dr. Travell. "A non-surgical program utilizing some of the methods I proposed in addition to a regimen of calisthenics and exercises proved far more beneficial. I recommended massages, hot baths and heating-pad treatments. Of course I had the advantage of hindsight. It's easy to look back and say, 'Well, the operation didn't work. It should never have been done.' But at the time they felt they had to do something for him, and surgery seemed the most logical step.

"Once, after I finished examining Jack, Jackie asked me if it was possible to give him a shot of something that would provide total relief from pain. I said, yes, there was such a shot but it would eliminate all sensation below the waist. Jackie frowned, and Jack grinned; he said: 'Well, we can't have that, can we Jackie?' "

By mid-June, Jack felt up to throwing a gala at the Kennedy compound in Hyannis Port for some 400 state legislators, state house officials and members of Congress, as well as their spouses. The affair served to announce Kennedy's return to office and hinted at bigger political events soon to come. Jackie played hostess, flashing her broad smile but feeling vaguely ill at ease. She resented her husband taking her by the arm and thrusting her forward with the words, "I want you to meet my wife . . . Jackie." She disliked political functions and particularly disliked the people who attended them.

Mrs. John F. Kennedy took a decidedly snobbish view of politics. To her mind the men were uncouth cigar-chomping jackals, their wives were humdrum and predictable—they behaved as if they were always on television, went through all the usual motions, said and did all the expected things. According to Jackie, the women talked about nothing but draperies and slipcovers, children and grandchildren, diets and cookbooks. They exchanged recipes and made simpering comments about "the good people back home," the masses whose collective vote determined whether their husbands returned to Washington.

"Jackie was no Elsie de Wolfe or Maharani of Cooch-Behar, but she had more sophistication than most of these political wives," said Truman Capote. "She was naive in certain respects, shrewd in others. She couldn't tolerate those women. She made fun of their dowdiness and slobbering devotion to their husbands' political careers. 'They're such pigeons,' she used to say.

"Jackie's kind of sophistication came from growing up in New York, attending the best schools and taking frequent vacations abroad. It was acquired, not inherited. It didn't come from the home. But it put her in a separate category in terms of women whose husbands chose careers in public service or government. She had more flair, more taste, more imagination than they did.

"I would sit around the Carlyle bar with her and listen to all these cute little sagas about her family—how she took her young stepsister Nina shopping for her first training brassiere, and how years later at Nina's wedding to Newton Steers, Jr., Jackie stepped into an empty bathtub fully clothed to demonstrate the practical benefits and correct use of a douche bag ('Better use vinegar, the white kind,' she advised Nina. 'And do you know you can burn your insides out if it's not properly diluted?'). Now, really, can you picture Eleanor Roosevelt, Bess Truman or Mamie Eisenhower explaining the fine art of the female douche?"

In the late summer of 1955, in connection with Kennedy's service on the Senate Foreign Relations Committee, Jack and Jackie departed on a two-month tour of Europe. The trip, which included ten days in Poland and an audience with the Pope, was to be a working vacation. In Rome they were entertained by Clare Boothe Luce, the American Ambassador to Italy, at a dinner party attended by French Premier Georges Bidault. Afterwards, Kennedy and Bidault were eager to talk, but there was a language barrier.

Jackie was called upon to act as interpreter. Later, Bidault wrote to her. "Never," he said, "have I encountered so much wisdom invested with so much charm."

In Paris Jackie met up with her sister Lee and accompanied her to antique shops and fashion shows. One evening at a social gathering they were introduced to American social historian Cleveland Amory, who was in Paris working on a never-to-be-completed Duchess of Windsor book. "I was working with the Duchess on this project, and the two sisters were extremely curious about her," said Amory. "They asked all sorts of questions. The next day I asked the Duchess about Jackie. She knew all about the Kennedys, and she said, 'Oh, it must be so difficult being married to a man like that. I wonder how she keeps him in check.' She said this with raised eyebrows, insinuating that the Kennedys were having problems."

Jackie seemed to have one main method of keeping her husband "in check," or rather of trying to keep him that way. She sulked a lot. JFK couldn't stand it when anybody sulked—it drove him mad. But Jackie exercised other methods of control as well.

By all accounts, she was among the best of the "put-down artists." She enjoyed deflating certain male egos with her sharp wit. Toward the end of their European junket, accompanied by British playwright Sir William Douglas-Home, the Kennedys attended a party in the South of France aboard the yacht of Aristotle Onassis, the Greek shipping tycoon. Also aboard that afternoon was Sir Winston Churchill. Unlike his father, Jack Kennedy gradually developed admiration for Churchill. He dressed formally for the occasion and was very solicitous of the old man, hoping to make an impression. But Churchill, evidently under the weather that day, hardly noticed the Senator. As the Kennedys were leaving the yacht, Jackie pointed to her husband's white dinner jacket and said, "I think he thought you were the waiter, Jack."

Back in the States that October, the Kennedys started the gradual process of moving into a more permanent residence. They acquired one of the homes in the Kennedy compound at Hyannis Port, one of three whose back yards joined, each lived in by members of the Kennedy family. In addition, Jack Kennedy paid the final installment on a total purchase price of $125,000 for

Hickory Hill, a white brick Georgian manor on six acres of woodland in McLean, Virginia, two miles from Merrywood. Once the Civil War headquarters of General George B. McClellan, the house stood at the top of a steep incline, with a long U-shaped driveway that ran past the front door. There were stables and orchards on the property, and a swimming pool at the bottom of the hill to the rear of the house, useful if Jack meant to adhere to Dr. Travell's recommended exercise routine.

To control the occasional muscle spasms that he still suffered in back and neck, Kennedy took regular injections of Novocain, and 25-50 mg. of oral cortisone every twenty-four hours. Moreover, although he and his political aides publicly denied that he suffered from Addison's disease, he was being treated for it and had been for some time. His ailment had been managed fairly successfully on a program of desoxycorticosterone acetate (DOCA) time-release pellets of 150-300 mg. implanted every three months in a tiny incision in the muscles of his thighs. DOCA, a synthetic form of cortisone, in conjunction with the cortisone tablets he took on a daily basis, tended to stimulate not only his underactive adrenal glands (the major cause of Addison's disease) but his sexual drive as well.

"There was a touch of the comical to it," said Dr. Gerald Ehrlich, a specialist in psycho-sexual conditioning and disorders. "Give a man large doses of cortisone and he often becomes miraculously, wonderfully priapic, or at least rampant. In Kennedy's case, all that cortisone over a prolonged period probably did increase his sexual drive. More vital to the enterprise than his physical needs, however, were the psychological pressures that drove him to such behavior, the need to prove himself, the compulsive risk-taking, the sense that societal rules didn't apply to him."

While Jackie Kennedy set about redecorating their new house, paying particular attention to the nursery, her husband resumed his recently dormant extramarital love life. The FBI files indicate that from mid-1955 to the end of 1959, he maintained a suite on the eighth floor of Washington's Mayflower Hotel. One anonymous FBI informant refers to the suite as "Kennedy's personal playpen" and notes that he attended a Mayflower party at which Senator John Kennedy and Senator Estes Kefauver, another distinguished philanderer, and "their respective dates made love in plain view of the other partygoers. When they were done, the two Senators simply exchanged mates and began anew."

Similar charges were levied against John F. Kennedy by Robert Parker in his 1987 book, *Capitol Hill in Black and White,* an anecdotal memoir by the former maitre d' of the Senate dining room.* In the mid-1950s, Parker worked for Harvey's, a popular Washington restaurant practically next door to the Mayflower. "Unlike most other Senators," writes Parker, "Kennedy rarely ate there. At first, he used to drop in to order dinner, which I carried to his love nest . . . at the Mayflower Hotel. After a while, he started phoning in his order, and I and the other waiters, depending on how many friends JFK was entertaining, would carry the food to room 812 and serve it. . . . Kennedy always seemed to be having parties there. Sometimes he would be alone with a woman; sometimes it would be a small affair with a few men and their dates. He or an aide would call me early in the morning and ask me to get the room ready. I would set up the bar, prepare the snacks, and see that there was plenty of ice."

Besides the more intimate gatherings, Jack Kennedy threw large bashes at the Mayflower for celebrities such as Audrey Hepburn, Betty Grable, Judy Garland, Marlene Dietrich (with whom Jack's father claimed to have been on intimate terms while vacationing on the Côte d'Azur in 1939), Bing Crosby and Frank Sinatra. Sinatra, an indefatigable source of names and telephone numbers of attractive and available women, invariably received the red-carpet treatment from Kennedy. "JFK would order a load of lobsters . . . and Harvey's would cook and serve them with all the trimmings," writes Robert Parker. Kennedy further reciprocated by unlocking a number of political doors for Sinatra, arranging introductions to some of the most influential men on the Hill.

A link between Sinatra and Kennedy had been established in 1955 by the marriage of Peter Lawford, a member of Sinatra's notorious "Rat Pack," and Pat Kennedy, Jack's sister, a union that Joe Kennedy strongly opposed. "If there's anything I think I'd hate as a son-in-law, it's

*Robert Parker, *Capitol Hill in Black and White,* pp. 84-85.

an actor," the Ambassador said on meeting Lawford. "And if there's anything I think I'd hate more than an actor as a son-in-law, it's an English actor."

Although Joe Kennedy and Peter Lawford remained largely at odds with one another (Lawford rarely stayed at his father-in-law's house when visiting Hyannis Port or Palm Beach), the English actor became a fast and faithful supporter of the future President, providing him every imaginable amenity from dates with actresses and show-girls, to a California safehouse where Kennedy could carry out his West Coast assignations. Like Langdon Marvin and other JFK followers and employees, Lawford often acted as the beard for Jack, distracting the press and providing a convenient front for Jackie's benefit.

Not that Kennedy couldn't fend for himself. He culti-vated the majority of his own affairs, adopting a course of such high visibility that he sometimes appeared to be flaunting his latest conquest. Lance Morrow, a reporter for *Time* and author of *The Chief: A Memoir of Fathers and Sons*, quotes Bobby Baker, a protégé of Lyndon Johnson, as having seen Senator Kennedy in the fall of 1955 emerge from a movie theater on G Street with a stupendous-looking blonde. "She was stacked, and she was six feet tall," Baker informed his cronies.*

The blonde may well have been burlesque queen Tem-pest Storm, whose hair color seemed to change from performance to performance and whose physical attri-butes were more than a little intimidating. Kennedy met Tempest in 1955 when she performed at Washington's Casino Royale, and continued to see her that year when-ever she appeared in the area. She described their relation-ship as stormy but sexually satisfying, commenting that Kennedy seemed to be almost insatiable in bed.

Philip Nobile (writing as V. De Foggia) penned an article, "JFK and the Teenager," for the July 1985 issue of Penthouse's *Forum*, of which he was then editor, suggesting that Kennedy was likewise involved during the mid-1950s with a Radcliffe student who later worked briefly in Washington. Kennedy apparently made no pre-tense of his affair with the coed, often driving his auto-mobile right up to her Radcliffe dormitory and parking it outside. He saw her whenever he visited Boston. McGeorge

*Lance Morrow, *The Chief: A Memoir of Fathers and Sons*, p. 100.

Bundy, a Harvard dean and subsequently National Security Adviser under Kennedy, reportedly warned Jack "about being so obvious." Reckless and overly confident, Kennedy ignored Bundy's advice.

"There may not have been many witnesses to Jack Kennedy's love life, but there was enough circumstantial evidence to convict him a thousand times over," said Marianne Strong. "Before becoming a literary agent, while still society editor for the *New York World-Telegram,* I remember seeing him and Vivi Stokes Crespi huddled together in a corner at a party in the old Ambassador Hotel on Park Avenue. They were paying a lot of attention to each other. Jackie wasn't there. Jackie and Vivi had been friends during their deb years, which is the reason I noticed this rather strange party tableau in the first place."

Emile de Antonio, a filmmaker of note and a mainstay on the New York arts scene, knew a number of the women Kennedy associated with during this period. "I was in JFK's class at Harvard, class of '40," remarked De Antonio, "and I can vouch for the fact that he went with a lot of high-placed women. Power being the supreme aphrodisiac of our age, JFK was able to explore and realize his wildest fantasies. That's the main reason the family didn't want an investigation of JFK's assassination. While in office, he became involved with many socially prominent women—for obvious reasons the Kennedys didn't want this information made public.

"This is not to say that all his relationships with women were sexual in nature. He had platonic relationships as well. I knew one of his friends, a Boston girl named Kay-Kay Hannon, who's now married to Douglas Auchincloss, a relation of Hugh Auchincloss. Kay-Kay was once married to Shipwreck Kelly, the one-time husband of Brenda Frazier. She was also married to a member of the King ranching family of Texas. Jack knew her both early and late in his career. They were close, but how close I don't know. What people say when they're together depends on a special kind of chemistry. If you want to talk about everything that's on your mind, including the problems you have with your wife, you obviously look to somebody special. I'm not convinced JFK shared these thoughts with anybody. Possibly this was Jackie's domain. She probably knew him better than anybody else did, and ultimately this may have been the glue that held them together."

Ormande de Kay visited the Kennedys at Hickory Hill in early May 1956. "It was the first I'd seen of Jackie since her marriage," he said. "There were maybe six for dinner. Jackie was pregnant and expecting in September. She and her mother had been decorating the house. There were swatches of material and samples of wallpaper on the coffee table. It was impossible to tell how Jack and Jackie were getting along. He made a passing reference to the impossible traffic jams every morning between McLean and Washington, D.C., and she said very little.

"After dinner, he revealed the Kennedy family's political plans, which are fascinating in retrospect. They were going to put all three brothers in the Senate. Jack was already a Senator so he was concentrating on attaining higher office, maybe Vice-President in the coming election. They were going to get Bobby elected Senator from New York. And they were grooming Teddy to move to Arizona where he would face Barry Goldwater. They apparently didn't think too highly of Goldwater.

"Of all the people to marry, I thought it strange indeed that Jackie should select an ambition-bitten politician. Poliics seemed so remote from Jackie's background. And then Jack Kennedy was such a womanizer, just like Jackie's father. Both were the kind of men who would spawn with anything that twitched. I had to believe that this was part of her fatal attraction to Jack, the idea that she would succeed where her mother had failed—she would take the full measure of her polygamous husband and bring him to heel."

Appearing as part of a panel on CBS-TV's "Face the Nation" for July 1, Senator Kennedy said, "I am not a candidate for Vice-President, and I doubt if I will be nominated for Vice-President." He then gave four reasons for believing he would not be put on that year's Democratic Party ticket with Adlai Stevenson: he was Catholic; at 39, he might be considered too young; a Southerner would probably be sought to balance Stevenson's strength in the Northeast; and his vote on certain bills had been unpopular. But, he quickly added, he would be honored and "of course . . . would accept if nominated."

Three weeks later, he flew to Los Angeles to record his narration of a twenty-minute film on the history of the Democratic Party, commissioned to serve as a preface to the keynote speech at the forthcoming Democratic National Convention in Chicago. It was scheduled to be shown immediately preceding the keynote address of Governor Frank Clement of Tennessee.*

The film was organized by Dore Schary, chief of production at Metro-Goldwyn-Mayer, and was written by Norman Corwin. There was a rumor in political circles that the production was financed by Joe Kennedy, hence the selection of Jack to be its narrator, but in fact the film was ordered by the Democratic National Committee, and the choice of Jack Kennedy to be its spokesman came about in a Tinker-to-Evers-to-Chance fashion. When Corwin finished the script, he and Schary discussed the casting of a narrator. They agreed that it should be a political figure, rather than an actor—but which political figure? It happened that Corwin was on his way to have lunch with an old friend, Edward R. Murrow, and he suggested to Schary that perhaps Murrow, fresh from Washington, might have some good ideas on that score. Murrow did. He suggested Governor John Winant of New Hampshire, a handsome Lincolnian figure, but quickly withdrew that notion and came up with the name of Senator Jack Kennedy, whom he characterized as "young, bright, charismatic, and definitely on his way up." When Corwin asked about Kennedy's availability, Murrow replied, "He'll probably be eager to do it. It can only boost his stock in the party."

Corwin relayed Murrow's nomination to Schary, who endorsed it and passed it on to Paul Butler, chairman of the National Committee. Kennedy accepted the role without hesitation, and flew out to meet Schary and Corwin

---

*When the film was shown at the convention, it was carried by NBC, ABC and Mutual, but CBS chose to cut away to the convention floor for interviews with delegates. Since the film was positioned as part of the keynote presentation, the Democrats were angry with CBS, and issued a strong protest. The cut was taken as an insult not only to the Democrats, but to the convention, the TV audience, and Senator Kennedy. The Senator, however, was unruffled.

at Schary's home in Brentwood. Over dinner they discussed the script. Jack suggested two minor changes, one of which was to delete an allusion which might be construed as relating to his father. He said, with a chuckle, that it would be prudent for a film on the noble history of the Party to hurry on past the point.

True to form, Jack did not make the trip to Los Angeles alone. His companion, though she did not accompany him to the dinner at Schary's, was a rich and well-connected society belle who called herself "Pooh" but was known to intimates simply as "P." "She was stunning but not particularly brilliant," said Langdon Marvin. "The way she looked, she didn't have to be. Jack was fascinated by her. She was apparently very uninhibited, or as old Jack-in-the-Box put it, 'She'll eat anything in the goddamn room. Anything.' "

With Jackie, who was now seven months pregnant, Kennedy arrived in Chicago for the August 13 opening of the Democratic Convention feeling that he had perhaps an outside chance of being chosen as Stevenson's running mate. While Jack and his two brothers occupied adjoining suites in a downtown Chicago hotel, Jackie stayed in Sarge and Eunice Shriver's Lake Shore Drive apartment. The luxury apartment came with Sargent Shriver's job as manager of Joe Kennedy's Chicago Merchandise Mart.

In her delicate condition and in the middle of a week-long Chicago heatwave, Jackie nevertheless attended a "unity" breakfast at the Palmer House Hotel for the New England party delegates, and went to various functions at the convention itself, including her husband's nomination address for Adlai Stevenson. A photographer took a picure of Jackie and Jean Kennedy, recently married to New York businessman Stephen Smith, standing on their seats in the convention box, excitedly waving "Stevenson for President" pennants.

Although she tried to share in the excitement, Jackie admitted she never truly understood what all the shouting was about. She lacked the Kennedy family's political savvy and understanding, and although she would later attain it, it had not yet become part of her persona. The one person at the convention who took pains in trying to explain the mechanics of the event to her was Josefa Moss, the sister of Lyndon Johnson. When Josefa died of cancer in 1960, Jackie wrote to Lady Bird Johnson recalling Josefa's presence at the convention—"and over those hectic days—I became so fond of her. She was the one thing I looked forward to every day—going back to that frenzied arena."

On the second night of the convention, Jackie accompanied her husband to Perle Mesta's "champagne party for campaign wives" at the Blackstone Hotel, a rowdy, raucous bash where Jackie knew almost nobody. "I was too shy and unsure of myself," she later admitted. A reporter for a Boston newspaper described her as standing by herself in the middle of the fray, a bit wide-eyed "like a little girl at a grown-up party. . . . She didn't seem ill-at-ease, exactly. But she was out of things, not really part of what was going on."

Perle Mesta, "the hostess with the mostest," didn't remember Jackie from her London Coronation Ball in 1953 and didn't seem overly impressed with either of the Kennedys. In an interview following the party, she said: "I wasn't prepared for Jack Kennedy to be wearing brown loafers with a tuxedo." She referred to Mrs. Kennedy as "a beatnik," observing that she hadn't even bothered to put on a pair of stockings.

Jackie didn't forget the slight. When she became First Lady in 1961, she remarked that Perle Mesta's parties were "too obvious" and that Perle too often comported herself "like a distiller's wife." Perle Mesta gave few Washington parties during the Kennedy Administration and, for the first time in years, wasn't invited to attend any given at the White House.

In 1952, while working as Inquiring Camera Girl at the *Washington Times-Herald,* Jackie wrote to newspaperwoman Bess Furman, expressing her feelings concerning the press: "I'm so in love with all that world now—I think I look up to newspaper people the way you join movie star fan clubs when you're ten years old." Once Jackie found herself the object of pursuit rather than the pursuer, her sentiments were quick to change. She had become wary of the press soon after marrying John Kennedy; by 1956, she regarded the media as her personal enemy.

Maxine Cheshire, a young and ambitious reporter for *The Washington Post,* tried to interview Jackie at the Democratic National Convention. "It was shortly after the convention had turned to Stevenson that I spotted Jackie sitting in the Kennedy box on the convention floor," writes Cheshire. "I wanted her reaction, but she wanted nothing to do with me once she heard me mention the word 'newspaper.'. . . . When she got up and left the box and started across the floor, I followed her. And when she ducked down the stairway that led to the underground parking garage, I was in pursuit. And when she saw, on the garage floor, that I was still after her, she hiked up her dress and broke into a run."*

The "extra weight" of Jackie's pregnancy was no apparent handicap, for within moments she had outdistanced the *Post* reporter. And that was the last Maxine Cheshire saw of her that day.

Jackie was in attendance again during the vice-presidential balloting. Adlai Stevenson, attempting to infuse excitement into the convention, had decided after his first-ballot victory to let the delegates choose his running mate rather than designate one himself. The tactic came as a shock to the Kennedy camp, which had still hoped for Stevenson's support and sanction.

The only time Jacqueline became directly involved in any tactical maneuverings was the hectic night before the vice-presidential ballot, when she joined Teddy, Bobby, Sargent Shriver, Jean Kennedy Smith, Ted Sorensen, Charles Bartlett, Connecticut State Chairman John Bailey and others in Jack's hotel room. "I don't remember Jack being there exactly but I remember a lot of commotion and Bobby saying that we must try to get all the votes for the next day," she recalled afterwards. "I remember Bobby asking me if I knew anyone in Nevada or some other states. I can remember being there a lot that night. I think when something like that starts and gains momentum, then you want it, yes. . . ."

George Smathers remembered the telephone ringing in his hotel room at 2:30 in the morning: "It was Jack, asking me to nominate him for Vice-President. I told him to get Connecticut Governor Abe Ribicoff. He said he already had Ribicoff, but he wanted me to second the nomination. 'Kefauver has it wrapped up,' I told him. He insisted on running, said it would be wide open. I finally agreed, just to get some sleep.

"When I walked out there the next day at 8:00 a.m., the convention center was half empty. I didn't know what

---

*See Maxine Cheshire, *Maxine Cheshire, Reporter*, pp. 49–50.

the hell to say. When Jack started in Congress, he was still basically a young upstart, a whippersnapper with big ideas and a weathy father. Advancing to the Senate, he was not especially industrious or influential as a legislator, and seemed excessively preoccupied, for such a junior Senator, with higher office. The ambition was unmistakable, but it was an ambition almost totally devoid of any purpose for the country. The object of winning was simply to win. I didn't think he stood a chance of getting the vice-presidency. Well, I started talking about John F. Kennedy as World War II hero—*PT-109* and all that. The guy hadn't done anything politically really. So next I talked about his distinguished family. I repeated this bit three or four times. Suddenly I felt an excruciating pain in my back and chest. I thought I was having a heart attack—right out there on television in front of the world. It was Sam Rayburn, the convention's chairman, poking his gravel into my ribs to let me know that my two minutes were up. 'McCormack's here,' he whispered into my ear. John McCormack was to give the other seconding speech, and I was glad as hell to get away from the microphone.

"McCormack's speech seemed even more disorganized than mine, and if Bobby Kennedy hadn't shoved him onto the platform, he wouldn't have given it. In the end Jack lost and Estes Kefauver won, but Jack came much closer than expected. Joe Kennedy, who'd been vacationing on the French Riviera, thought Jack fortunate to have lost. 'Stevenson can't take Eisenhower,' he said, 'Jack's better off without it. If he runs with Stevenson, they'll blame the loss on his being a Catholic. Besides, if you're going to get licked, get licked trying for first place, not second. He's better off running for the top spot in '60.'

"It's worth noting that after the convention Joe Kennedy paid to have a study conducted of the sentiment regarding Catholics in the United States—could there be a Catholic President? The study concluded there could. Considering Jack's rather limited political credentials, he had performed superbly, placing himself in a position where he could eventually become the first Catholic President.

"When it was over our group met briefly in Jack's hotel suite. Jack stood on the bed and made an impromptu speech. Jackie shed some tears as he spoke. I was amazed she had taken the loss so seriously. After all it had been a last-minute effort. The significance of the '56 vice-presidential business was that JFK worked for all of 24 hours and came within 30½ votes of winning the second spot. Frankly, I think he ran only because Stevenson threw down the gauntlet on the convention floor. Jack couldn't resist a challenge. None of the Kennedys could.

"Prior to the convention, Jack, Teddy and I had formulated plans to do a little sailing afterwards off the coast of Italy. At the time it seemed a fun thing to do. But given Jackie's reaction to the convention and her advanced state of pregnancy, I had my doubts.

"Jackie insisted we go. 'You guys should take that trip,' she said. 'You all worked so hard, especially Jack. He deserves a rest.'

"So we went, but Jack should have known better. Jackie had suffered a miscarriage only the year before, which meant there might be complications. Also, she'd nursed him back to health following his back surgery. Now that she needed him he seemed to be deserting her."

12

Immediately following the 1956 Democratic Convention, Jack Kennedy returned to Boston with his wife and waved off reporters at Logan Airport, claiming exhaustion on his part and overexertion on hers. "I have nothing to say," he said. "I've been in the news enough."

Jackie had decided to spend several weeks relaxing at Hammersmith Farm with her mother and stepfather. Jack and Teddy, meanwhile, were soon headed toward Paris. They spent their first night at the Hotel George V and the next day traveled to Val-sur-mer on the French Riviera, where Joe Kennedy had leased a villa for the season. Among the Ambassador's houseguests were Clare Boothe Luce and the William Douglas-Homes. Sir William told Jack how proud he had made his father by his close race for the vice-presidential nomination. "In two years," said Sir William, "the only name they'll remember from the convention will be yours."

Jack had gone to Val-sur-mer to seek his father's counsel before deciding on a future political course. But while on the Riviera, he received advice from a completely unexpected source: Winston Churchill. Aristotle Onassis sent a message from Monte Carlo, inviting Jack to join him aboard his yacht. Winston Churchill was with him. Recalling his unsuccessful meeting with Churchill the year before and wanting a second chance, Jack departed at once.

Receiving him with open arms aboard the yacht, Onassis led Jack to Churchill, who sat in a lounge chair in his favorite spot on deck. Clearly aware of Kennedy's strong showing at the recent Democratic Convention, Churchill asked him about his presidential prospects in the future. "It's difficult to say," Kennedy replied. "You know, I am a Catholic." "You can always change your religion," Churchill noted. Then he added: "But if I were you, I would play up the Catholicism. Don't give the impression you're trying to hide it. Flaunt it. People will admire you for your courage if you flaunt it."

Jack returned to Val-sur-mer and relayed Churchill's advice. "That's the first sound judgment I've ever heard the man offer," said the Ambassador.

Jack and Teddy connected with George Smathers a few days later in Cannes and there chartered a forty-foot sailing vessel that came complete with skipper and galley cook. Other deckhands included "P," Jack's current socialite mistress, and a sultry French starlet recently linked by gossip columnists to Aly Khan.

Although George Smathers denied the presence of women on the cruise, a *Washington Star* correspondent later interviewed the boat's skipper who reported seeing "several young women aboard." Another journalist apparently met and interviewed a friend of "P's." The friend confirmed that "P" was "the mystery woman who kept JFK company on his post-convention Mediterranean cruise." The same friend confided that Jack gave "P" a book (presumably *Profiles in Courage*) containing the following inscription: "To P—/In memory of times together/In past and future/John Kennedy."

On August 23, while still recuperating from the strain of the convention, Jackie suffered an internal hemorrhage and severe abdominal cramps. Her mother rushed her to Newport Hospital. In an effort to save the baby, doctors performed an emergency Caesarean. The infant, an unnamed girl, died before drawing her first breath.

When Jackie regained consciousness following the surgery, the first person she saw, sitting by her bed, was Bobby Kennedy. Her mother had reached Bobby at Hyannis Port, and he had tried in vain to contact Jack by transatlantic telephone. Jack's boat, it appeared, lacked a ship-to-shore radio. Bobby immediately drove to Newport to take his brother's place. It was Bobby who informed Jackie of her infant's death. Many years later Jackie learned that her brother-in-law had also arranged for the burial of the dead child. "You knew that, if you were in trouble, he'd always be there," she ventured.

It was not until August 26, three days after the tragedy, that Jack reached Genoa and spoke directly to Jackie. His first reaction was one of mild annoyance. After the call, George Smathers set him straight: "You better haul ass back to your wife if you ever want to run for President." Jack flew home two days later.

The day after he arrived at Newport, with Jackie still confined to a hospital bed, Kennedy attended a dinner party given by Louis and Elaine Lorillard at the Clambake Club. "I sat him on my right, and he was a charming and jovial dinner partner," said Mrs. Lorillard. "He didn't reveal the slightest hint of a rift with Jackie. We all knew about the stillbirth from the newspapers. But Jack insisted Jackie was doing well and would be up and out in a day or two."

Despite Kennedy's outward calm, his marriage had reached a turning point. A hospital spokesman attributed the stillbirth (her second unsuccessful pregnancy in as many years) to "nervous tension and exhaustion following the Democratic Convention." Charles Bartlett blamed it on Jackie's not sleeping the night before the vice-presidential race. Rose Kennedy placed the blame on Jackie's nicotine addiction (she chain-smoked when she became nervous), while Janet Auchincloss held Jack Kennedy responsible ("He should have been there for you," she told Jackie).

The situation was exacerbated by several factors, not least of which were two other Kennedy family births. On August 25, two days after the death of Jackie's child, a daughter, Sydney Lawford, was born to Pat Kennedy and Peter Lawford. She was their second child and first daughter. And on September 9, Mary Courtney Kennedy was born to Ethel and Robert Kennedy. She was their fifth child and second daughter. These joyful births in the wake of Jackie's tragic loss only served to heighten her personal sense of failure and despair.

"Though the Kennedys never mentioned it to her face," said Peter Lawford, "there was always the uncomfortable feeling in the air when she was around that, as far as childbearing went, she had rather let them down. Behind her back they would say things. They would suggest she was maybe too 'high born' to have children. I mean babies were literally popping out of these women, while Jackie had her share of problems.

"It was ironic. Pat and I had our second child only two days after Jack and Jackie lost theirs. But we weren't in Chicago for the '56 convention. Pat stayed home in Santa Monica during her final months of pregnancy. It was

Jackie who went and stood up for Jack during his head-to-head battle with Senator Estes Kefauver. If anyone played the high-born aristocrat it was Pat, not Jackie.

"What's more, Jackie had to bear the brunt of the burden by herself. Jack, to his eternal discredit, just couldn't grasp the situation—the miscarriage she had endured previously, the stillbirth, the medical consultations, the need for 'C' sections, the blood transfusions, the prolonged hospital recoveries. It was something he couldn't face and to my mind, much as I loved and admired him, it represented a profound failing on his part, a grave weakness."

When Jackie regained her strength sufficiently to leave the hospital she returned to Hammersmith Farm. In her present frame of mind she had no desire to go to Hickory Hill, which she had decorated and planned with a baby in mind. Its emptiness only reinforced her sadness and disappointment, and reminded her of all the nights she had been left there by herself while her husband went out politicking or womanizing or both. "It was all wrong," she declared of that tenuous period.

"As often happens in times of turmoil, Jack and Jackie's differences in outlook, interests and manner became more obtrusive," said Lem Billings. "They were both bitter, disillusioned, withdrawn, silent as if afraid that conversation would deepen the wound. In that sense, they were both repressed; they couldn't talk directly. To her sister Lee, Jackie confessed that she suspected she was physically incapable of childbearing. But within earshot of Jack, she blamed the misfortune on her grinding participation in the '56 Democratic National Convention. Jack reacted to this kind of talk by turning his back and getting out on the campaign stump for Stevenson and Kefauver."

The breach between Jack and Jackie widened. Rumors of an impending divorce began to circulate and eventually reached the gossip columns. Jack Kennedy sold Hickory Hill (at cost) to his brother Bobby. Jackie went to New York to visit Lee, who had separated from Michael Canfield the year before and whose marriage would eventually be annulled.

"There was certainly talk of a divorce between Jack and Jackie," acknowledged Peter Lawford. "But it was only talk. *Time* reported a meeting between Jackie and

Joe Kennedy in New York at which Joe purportedly offered her a million dollars to stay married to Jack. There was a meeting, but there was no such offer. In fact, when Jackie saw the *Time* story, she telephoned Joe and said, 'Why only one million dollars, why not ten million?' She was laughing. The same rumor made the rounds in 1960. This time the story had it that Joe had offered her the money to stay with Jack through the campaign. Neither version is correct. They met and Joe undoubtedly told Jackie that Jack loved her, even if it didn't always appear that way. He probably spoke about his own marriage to Rose and gave her the old line about sex and love being two separate and distinct entities for a man.*

"I'm inclined to believe that the womanizing wasn't an important issue for Jackie. Her father, grandfather and father-in-law were all ladies' men. She didn't like it, but it wasn't enough to cause her to seek a divorce. She'd witnessed the effect of her parents' divorce and didn't want a repetition. I'm not saying she didn't become a bit cynical about marriage. Perhaps if she'd been able to have children earlier in the marriage, it might have made a difference. It might have drawn them closer sooner.

"But what truly distressed Jackie was Jack's career. She didn't care for politics, had been brought up to think of most politicians as con men and crooks, and found the atmosphere of politics at odds with her own interest in literature and the arts. It's possible had Jack not achieved his goal in 1960 that Jackie might either have pushed him into another career or left him and moved to Europe. I suppose we'll never know."

Although Jackie's meeting with Joe Kennedy had nothing to do with the exchange of money, Jackie did present

---

*Lady Mary (May) Sommerville Lawford, the mother of Peter Lawford, contradicts her son. In her posthumously published autobiography, "Bitch!": The Autobiography of Lady Lawford (as told to Buddy Galon), p. 77, she states: "Old Joe Kennedy offered his daughter-in-law a check. The check was for one million dollars! The payoff: to remain married to Jack. Jackie Kennedy was a clever girl; such a good businesswoman. She said, 'Make it tax free and it's a deal.' " Interviewed by the present author prior to the publication of that book, Peter Lawford said. "My mother used to spread vicious and often untrue rumors about the Kennedys, particularly Jackie. So did I, I'm afraid. Don't believe everything you read."

several demands she wanted met, including a partial with-drawal from the often-suffocating embrace of her in-laws. During vacations and summers it had been the custom of all the Kennedys—Jack's brothers and sisters, and their children, and whatever other relatives (and family friends) happened to be around—to have dinner every night with Jack's mother and father. But now Jacqueline said, "Once a week is fine. Not every night." Joe consented.

He also agreed that Jack and she should move back to Georgetown, and within days he found a rental for them at 2808 P Street NW, where they stayed from January to May 1957, when they bought 3307 N Street NW, a red-brick, slant-set Federal townhouse built in 1812. The main floor contained a long, high-ceilinged, double-fireplaced drawing room. An inner window looked out on a bricked backyard, shaded by shiny-leaved magnolia trees. Down a narrow hall were the dining room, kitchen and a tiny passageway anteroom. At Joe Kennedy's insis-tence, Jack gave his wife a free hand in decorating the house, and Jackie took full advantage of the offer.

Despite these and several other concessions (Jack could no longer take telephone calls during the dinner hour), Jackie continued to suffer pangs of resentment. At Palm Beach that winter, she annoyed Rose Kennedy one after-noon by playing a particular Cole Porter album over and over again. She deliberately shocked Rose by appearing at lunch in strawberry-colored linen shorts, a sleeveless yellow silk shirt, bright blue Capezio slippers with embroid-ered pearls and a belt painted with bats and the words BATS IN YOUR BELFRY.

Her behavior in the days following the loss of her child was unpredictable. Jack Kennedy, who once described his wife as "fey," characterized her mercurial tempera-ment by drawing a wavy line across a sheet of paper; through it he drew a bold straight line to represent his own even-tempered disposition. Jackie more or less con-firmed this assessment, saying of her husband: "He is a rock, and I lean on him for everything."

"I remember a round-table discussion at Hyannis Port when the topic was whether or not to run for the presi-dency in 1960," said Lem Billings. "Bobby, who had said publicly that Jackie was 'poetic, artistic, whimsical, pro-vocative, independent and yet very feminine,' made a comment about whether she would be up to the campaign and whether her love of ballet, fox hunting and eighteenth-century antiques and prints might not alienate the average voter. Jackie insisted she would do whatever they wanted her to do in the hope of bolstering Jack's chances.

" 'Now that she's ready to campaign,' said Jack, 'the question should be—is the campaign ready for Jackie? For that matter, is America ready for Jackie?'

"Jack was joking but Jackie became visibly upset. She jumped up from her chair and bolted out of the room. Jack went after her and brought her back. One of Jackie's problems was that she could dole it out but she couldn't take it. She was too thin-skinned for her own good."

It was shortly after this incident in early 1957 that a reporter overheard a Kennedy family row from a nearby table at Le Pavillon in New York. Jacqueline asked for the check, saying to Bobby Kennedy, "I'm going to walk out on you. Every Kennedy thinks only of the family! Has anybody ever thought about my happiness?"

"No question, the Kennedys were impossible at times," said Geore Smathers. "Rose Kennedy and Jackie never got along very well. Jackie compared Rose to 'a dinosaur without a brain in her head.' Then there were Jack's sisters, always bragging about how much capital the family controlled, how powerful Joe was, how much influence he had, and how Jack would be elected President in 1960. They could drive you bananas with that kind of prattle. They undoubtedly drove Jackie crazy, and she probably drove them up the wall as well."

Igor Cassini recalled the difficulties Jackie had on certain social occasions, "especially at those famous Kennedy parties—wild, brawling soirées with people falling or being shoved into swimming pools. And not just at Hickory Hill during Camelot. I mean the parties that took place at Hyannis Port and Palm Beach when Jack was still a Senator.

"I recall a party the Kennedys attended at the Palm Beach estate of Charlie and Jayne Wrightsman. I was then married to Charlene Wrightsman, Charlie's daughter from a previous marriage. Jack Kennedy had courted Charlene during his young, still insignificant days. Charlie, who was a Taft Republican, more to the right than Louis XIV, had made it clear that he found JFK unsuitable. But Jack and Jackie, mainly through my efforts, became friendly with Charlie and Jayne. The Kennedys were aware, needless to say, that if Charlie could be persuaded to change his stripes, he would perhaps become a significant contributor to Jack's future campaign. And that is precisely what happened. Charlie became a great JFK fan and gave the Kennedys considerable financial support and constant gifts.

"At this particular party all the Kennedys, with the exception of Jack and Jackie, became very rowdy. Bobby, Teddy, Stephen Smith and Peter Lawford got a bit tipsy and started playing touch football in the Wrightsman living room. A dozen Baccarat glasses and a priceless set of signature chairs were demolished in the process. The Wrightsmans later discovered that Peter Lawford had made several phone calls to California leaving them with a hefty unpaid bill.

"Jackie just couldn't deal with this kind of behavior. It made her extremely nervous, set her on edge. You could see her visibly cringe. She would bite her fingernails and wring her hands. It was an overreaction but she couldn't help herself."

On the positive side, Jackie was present with her husband when some leading Democratic politicians were debating the choice of a city for their 1960 convention, the one at which John Fitzgerald Kennedy would receive his party's endorsement for the highest office in the land. At a lull in the debate, someone asked Jackie her choice of city.

"Acapulco," she replied, without thinking, and all the men laughed at what they thought was Jackie's idea of a joke.

All, that is, except Jack. He gazed at her for several moments, and then he took her hand in his and held it tightly. She smiled brightly, perhaps a bit too brightly, and then he smiled, too—a wide, wondrous, understanding grin.

The year 1957 continued to be a period of dramatic highs and desultory lows, a duration that severely taxed Jackie's inner resources and sense of self.* In March, to

*According to Kitty Kelly, *Jackie Oh!*, pp. 75–78, Jackie's fractured existence induced her to undergo a session of electroshock therapy at Valleyhead, a private psychiatric facility in Carlisle, Mass., whose doors closed in 1977. This charge appears to be untrue. Her

198   C. DAVID HEYMANN

her delight, she learned that she was again pregnant. This time she decided to avoid all the anxiety-provoking activities and pressures that had hampered her previous pregnancy.

"Jackie tried to restrict herself to the decoration of their recently purchased N Street home," said Elisabeth Draper, Janet Auchincloss's interior decorator. "I'd helped her with Hickory Hill, and she invited me to have a look at the new property, though she hired New York decorator Mrs. Henry 'Sister' Parish to do the actual work.

"Jackie had high hopes for the N Street house. 'Bessie,' she said to me, 'this is going to be it. No more traveling around.' Of course she'd made the same vow on moving into Hickory Hill. I felt badly for Jackie—she and Jack had moved from house to house. It gave their marriage a kind of temporary quality, a sense of 'nothing is permanent.' I don't know how to say it exactly—every home she had ever lived in was like a one-night stand.

"But this time it was going to be different. Jack gave her *carte blanche* in terms of decorating the place. He

---

source is the anonymous wife of an anonymous anesthesiologist who worked only weekends at Valleyhead. Kelley hints that the session took place in 1957 but gives no exact date. But what makes her story particularly implausible is that Jackie was not under the care of a psychotherapist on a regular basis at this time, and even by Kelley's admission, she "was well into her forties and living in New York" when she began seeing a psychotherapist. It would have been nearly impossible for a person not under the direct and ongoing care of a licensed psychologist, psychiatrist or psychoanalyst to receive electroshock treatment at Valleyhead, or at any other responsible institution for that matter. More incredible is Kelley's apparent suggestion that eletroshock therapy is or was administered on a one-time, come-at-your-own-convenience basis. Had Jackie undergone electroshock therapy, she would have been subject to a series of treatments administered over a duration far more extensive than the single weekend Kelley claims Jackie spent at Valleyhead. According to Lyle Stuart, the original publisher of *Jackie Oh!*, Kelley claimed she went to Valleyhead with a concealed tape recorder to interview staff members. The fact remains that she failed to name a single staff member who actually saw Jackie Kennedy at Valleyhead. Futhermore, not a single relative or friend of Jackie's was found who would or could verify the author's reports. In short, although it has long been accepted as fact by the popular press, Kelley's contention that Jackie underwent electroshock therapy seems to be one more example of unsupportable myth.

didn't have much to do with it. Like most men, he was more fundamental. He didn't get interested in pretty little ornaments.

"Jackie did. She loved surrounding herself with beautiful objects—fresh flowers in simple arrangements, French drawings, candle-fitted *doré* wall fixtures, pink-gilt porcelain cups and saucers used for cigarettes and as ashtrays, embroidered linens, terrycloth towels, caned Louis XVI dining chairs, fragile Louis XV drawing room chairs, blond wood marquetry tables, rare tapestries, softly colored fabrics. We'd decorated Hickory Hill largely in blue and white satin, attractive but not very practical. It hardly seemed appropriate for John Kennedy to come home from work and have to put his feet up on a footrest lined with white satin. Jackie wanted to make their new home as much his as hers—in other words, less precious. She went about it as methodically as she did everything— notating every shade of color in a little notebook, listing every piece of furniture, studying hundreds of carpet and drapery samples, making scale drawings of the nursery on the third floor. She wasn't the kind of person to sit back and let the interior decorator take over."

Early in July, as work on the house progressed, Jackie received an upsetting telephone call from Yusha Auchincloss. Yusha had paid one of his periodic visits to Jackie's father in New York and had come away convinced that the one-time *bon vivant*, now an angry and frustrated recluse, was seriously ill. Jackie flew in to see him. He complained bitterly about her lack of concern in recent years, save when she herself needed something, but he gave no indication of being sick. Jackie returned to Hyannis Port, where she had been spending the summer.

He was, in fact, a very sick man but did not know that he had cancer of the liver. On July 27, experiencing acute pain, he was admitted to Lenox Hill Hospital for a series of tests. Jackie again flew in, but, still not knowing the extent of his illness and "thinking that he was all right," decided to spend her birthday with her mother in Newport.

A telephone call the morning of August 3 informed Jackie that her father had lapsed into a coma. Shocked that they had not been kept apprised of his condition, she and Jack made immediate arrangements to fly to New York. Miche Bouvier was waiting at the hospital for them when they arrived. They were an hour too late.

Black Jack's last word, according to a nurse, had been "Jackie." He was 66 at the time of his death.

Jackie was deeply upset and weighed down by remorse for not realizing sooner the severity of her father's illness. She felt burdened by the fact that she had not been there to comfort him in his final hours, and she reproached herself for failing to be more attentive to his needs. Grim and downcast, she took charge of the funeral arrangements.

She sent Miche Bouvier and Aunt Maude to select a coffin, but went herself to see one of Black Jack's women friends who owned a photograph of him she thought suitable for publication, then sat down and composed the obituary. She asked her husband to take text and photographs to *The New York Times* with specific instructions to hand the items personally to the managing editor.

She selected St. Patrick's Cathedral for the funeral service, notifying only immediate family members and a dozen or so of her father's closest business and personal associates. White wicker baskets filled with brightly colored summer blossoms lent the small funeral an informal air. Before closing the coffin, Jackie removed a link bracelet she was wearing, a graduation present from her father, and placed it in his hand. The closed coffin was then covered by a thick blanket of yellow daisies and white bachelor's buttons.

"I cried when Jack died," said Jackie's cousin Edie Beale. "I broke down at the funeral. Nobody else cried. Jacqueline didn't cry. She never showed anything. I don't care for people who mask their emotions. Jacqueline didn't shed a tear at St. Patrick's and she didn't shed any at the family plot in East Hampton when we went to bury him.

Among the mourners at St. Patrick's were seven or eight of Jack Bouvier's old flames. They hadn't been formally invited but came of their own accord. They were dressed in black from head to toe and sat together like family in the last pew. Actually, they were more like a fan club than family. I've heard women say that once you'd been with Black Jack Bouvier, no other man would do."

13

A life for a life: on November 27, 1957, the day after Thanksgiving and four months after the death of Jack Bouvier, Jacqueline Kennedy gave birth at New York's Lying-In Hospital, Cornell University Medical Center, to a perfectly healthy baby girl. Delivered by Caesarean section, Caroline Bouvier Kennedy weighed 7 lbs. 2 ozs. and looked, according to her father, "as robust as a sumo wrestler."

Baby Caroline was three weeks old when Jackie draped her in the same soft robe she had worn at her own christening and, with the beaming father in attendance, took her to St. Patrick's Cathedral to be baptized by Cardinal Cushing of Boston. For her parents, Caroline's birth represented something of a triumph. Jackie was ecstatic, and Jack, having ultimately blamed himself for his wife's previous failures, felt relieved and reassured. The mood of their marriage took a distinctly upward swing.

Accompanied by Maud Shaw, the tiny, gray-haired British nanny hired to care for Caroline, they returned to Washington and moved into their new Georgetown home. Jackie had acquired an oil painting of Arabian horses by Shreyer, which her father had bequeathed to her in his will. In addition to an ornate writing desk for Lee, the will stipulated a number of small cash bequests to his nephews and nieces, and a token provision of $1,000 for "each grandchild yet to be born." Jack Bouvier divided his estate equally between Jackie and Lee, each receiving roughly $80,000 after taxes. Her inheritance, far less than it might have been had her father managed his funds efficiently, nevertheless enabled Jackie to buy her husband an exorbitant Christmas present—a sleek white Jaguar sports car which he found too ostentatious and promptly traded in for a new Buick.

For perhaps the very first time in her marriage Jackie felt comfortable in her own home, sufficiently insulated from the powerful grasp of the Kennedy family and far enough removed from her own critical and domineering mother to develop a true sense of identity and independence. Jack and Jackie regularly entertained friends at dinner, though never more than six or eight at a time, took in occasional movies, and even attended the April in Paris Ball at the Waldorf-Astoria in New York.

Whatever feelings of inferiority Jackie had about her performance in the political and public arena, they had no doubt been magnified by her two successive failures at childbearing. But the birth of Caroline gave her a new sense of confidence. She finally admitted to herself that the Kennedys were public figures who fed on publicity, and that while she needed to preserve some degree of privacy in her own life, she would also have to learn to make accommodations to the family into which she had married.

She told a reporter, "I wouldn't say that being married to a very busy politician is the easiest life to adjust to. But you think about it and figure out the best way to do things—to keep the house running smoothly, to spend as much time as you can with your husband and your children—and eventually you find yourself well adjusted . . . The most important thing for a successful marriage is for a husband to do what he likes best and does well. The wife's satisfaction will follow."

Jackie agreed to pose with her sister Lee for a fashion layout in the December 1957 issue of *Ladies' Home Journal,* an article which even to Jack's amusement quoted Jackie as saying: "I don't like to buy a lot of clothes and have my closets full. A suit, a good little black dress with sleeves and a short evening dress—that's all you need for travel."

What the magazine's readership didn't know was that following their modeling session, Jackie and Lee demanded they be given the clothes in which they had been photographed. Bruce Gould, then editor of *Ladies' Home Journal,* recalled the proposition: "They made us commit ourselves to give them the dresses they had worn. It was tit for tat, don't you know. . . . Both these girls hadn't very much money, and they liked to dress well. They didn't really have enough money to dress as they would like to dress, and as a matter of fact, when Jackie became First Lady, the President raised hell with her because of all the money she spent on her clothes. Very likely that's why she eventually married Onassis. She was mad about clothes, and one way or another was determined to get them."

Jackie's fashion splurges apparently started long before she reached the White House. "Jack began complaining about her spending soon after their marriage," remarked George Smathers. "She had a fetish for expensive clothes. Also for household furnishings. I understood the household business. Nothing was more important to her than having a nice home. It was practically pathological, and probably dated to her childhood when she was shuffled from one household to another—from town to country, from her father's apartment to her mother's—and not allowed to take roots. The beginning of her marriage to Jack had been a continuation of that process. Her passion for houses, for decorating and furnishing them, for moving in and out and starting over again, persisted for years.

" 'She's breaking my goddamn ass,' Jack used to say about her spending. She would buy clothes and furnishings and hide the bills and then try to pay for them out of her monthly allowance. Jack didn't notice the bills at first. But when she couldn't pay, the bills would go to the family accounting office at 277 Park Avenue, New York. The Kennedys employed a battery of comptrollers, accountants and tax experts to look after their finances. One day, Joe Kennedy went through a sheaf of financial statements and discovered the amounts of money being spent by his children and their spouses. That evening he let loose. 'Where the hell would you people be without me?' he shouted. 'You have no conception of how difficult it is to make money, nor do you have any idea of the value of money.'

"Soon after, Joe said to me, 'Jack may know how to balance the federal budget, but he doesn't understand much about personal finances. I'm baffled as to why he doesn't take more interest in the estate situation. He doesn't know how his own trust works. You're his buddy, and you're a lawyer—you straighten him out.'

"So I took an hour with Jack and went over his finances, showed him that his trust yielded a certain amount every month and that he had to set spending limits. But I didn't get through to him. As a matter of fact, I don't really think he knew—ever knew—a great deal about it, or cared greatly. All that happened was he started haggling with Jackie over the bills. In that sense, they had an entirely average marriage—she spent and he seethed.''

Her spending and privacy remained major issues in the Kennedy household. When Jack, already deeply involved in his campaign for re-election as Senator of Massachusetts, agreed to admit a *Life* photographer to baby Caroline's nursery, Jackie put up the first of many objections against such intrusion. She relented in the end, but only after Jack promised her a trip to Paris in the summer of 1958. He also agreed to restrict the use of baby pictures in the future.

Both before and after the Paris vacation, Jackie played an active role in Jack's state-wide campaign, an excellent training ground for what lay ahead. Because of Bobby Kennedy's current position as Chief Counsel of the Senate Labor Rackets Committee (JFK would serve on the same committee), the management of Jack's current campaign fell to his brother Ted. Also at the helm was Larry O'Brien. Recognizing Jackie's potential, O'Brien made her his special charge.

"As time went on and we got into political activity, I discovered that this was all very new to her," he explained. "She hadn't had any involvement of that nature—Massachusetts-type politics . . . the hand-shaking, back-slapping and so forth, which is all rather traditional. She was willing to be involved in whatever way she could, but by the same token it was my judgment that you shouldn't take a person who's completely removed from that sort of activity and has no background or experience in it and just take a plunge, so to speak. We kind of moved along recognizing that she had to become acquainted with the people, acquainted with the procedure, acquainted with the politics generally, and that this would take time.

"Jackie did some things around the state on her own that year—receptions that we put together, visitations of one sort or another—and at other times joined Jack as he campaigned. Additionally, she participated in the production of a 30-minute television program illuminating Jack's continuing career and home life, an early example of a new form of political propaganda.

"On the whole, she was a refreshing change from the usual candidate's wife because she did not bother to put on a phony show of enthusiasm about everything she saw and every local politician whom she met. The crowds sensed that and it impressed them. When Jackie traveled with the Kennedy bandwagon, the crowds were twice as big.

"I heard all the stories about how much Jackie supposedly hated politics. My impression is that she was amused and even somewhat intrigued by politics, by the people and by the sheer spectacle of it. What is politics, after all, if not street theater carried to the extreme? There were some very funny and delightful moments. I remember one involving 'Mugsy' O'Leary, a *Last Hurrah* type from Boston, who was hired as Jack's chauffeur. One day Mugsy drove Jackie to do some shopping. They were late for a political rally she had promised to attend, and Mugsy didn't know how to get her out of this chic boutique. Finally he stuck his head in the door and shouted to her: 'Come on, Jackie, for Chrissake move your ass.' "

Jackie's ability to speak French, Spanish and Italian proved invaluable. William DeMarco, an old-time Democratic district leader, recalled Jackie's appearance at the Michelangelo School in Boston's Italian-dominated North End: "The greatest thrill of my life was the day Jacqueline Kennedy addressed a crowd of about 800 people at the school when her husband ran for the Senate. The gracious lady stood up before the big crowd, and the Italian people, the elderly people who were there, didn't know who she was. But when she opened her mouth and introduced herself in Italian, fluent Italian may I say, as the wife of Senator Kennedy, all pandemonium broke loose. All the people went over and started to kiss her, and the old women spoke to her as if she was a native of the North End. And I think her talk is actually what cemented the relationship between Senator Kennedy and the Italian-Americans of the district. They figured that not only was he the representative of the district, he was one of them.

"During the Columbus Day parade, Jackie marched the streets with Jack, and people thought they were the ideal Italian-American couple. You couldn't tell the Italian-American people of the North End that the Kennedys were Irish. No, they were Italian because Jackie spoke the language so well."

Lem Billings felt Jackie's particular strength lay in her ability to guide and advise Jack in ways that his aides and assistants couldn't. "O'Brien and O'Donnell and Powers and the rest of them couldn't always be counted on to give the most honest appraisal. They were like fight managers, cornermen who tell the fighter he's behind or ahead on points, depending on what they think will spur him on. Jackie could afford to be more objective, more truthful. One of her assets was an acute ability to judge people. She could smell a phony a mile away and wasn't afraid to tell Jack he was being had. She would also tell him when she thought he was making a mistake. He once got into a row with an important European journalist. Jackie ended it by giving Jack a good swift kick under the table.

"In many ways Jackie emerged as chief architect of the entire Camelot image. But one important point that seemed to elude her had to do with friends and enemies in the world of politics. When Jack was irked by a particular politician, Jackie would dutifully share his attitude, and if the opportunity presented itself, she would give the offender a cold stare. But she came to learn that the person in question wasn't necessarily an enemy, and that in politics one may have seeming antagonists who are not foes, but only colleagues with whom one may some time or other be called upon, or forced by circumstance, to work."

A prime example of Jackie's naiveté in this area occurred on a snowy March evening in 1958. Dean Acheson, a former Secretary of State, was waiting on a platform in New York's Pennsylvania Station when a porter invited him to step out of the cold and into the stationmaster's office. He found there an elegantly attired, attractive young woman whom he knew from Georgetown, Jacqueline Kennedy.

Jackie and Acheson sat down to have a cup of coffee, waiting for the train to arrive. Jackie began to assail Acheson for a statement he had made in a recent book, *Power and Diplomacy,* criticizing a speech that Jack Kennedy gave in the Senate—in 1957. JFK's speech called on France to grant Algeria immediate independence and demanded that the United States censure France in the

United Nations, in the event independence wasn't forthcoming. Acheson felt that this was a disrespectful way to treat "America's oldest and most sensitive ally."

Jackie tore into Acheson not merely for these comments, but because the statesman had recently told her stepfather, Hugh Auchincloss, that Joe Kennedy was "a social-climbing bootlegger who had been ostracized by Brahmin Boston and had later retaliated by buying his spoiled son a seat in Congress."*

Acheson listened to Jackie's complaint and then pointed out that they were likely to be spending some hours together—they had looked at their tickets and found that their seats were next to each other.

"We can either spend our time fighting, or we can be pleasant," said Acheson.

"All right, let's be pleasant," responded Jackie.

After a lengthy delay the train left New York but did not reach Washington until 7:00 o'clock the next morning. Acheson and Jackie passed their difficult night alternately engaged in conversation and falling in and out of fitful sleep.

Once back in Washington, Jackie resumed their discussion by letter, asking Acheson "how one capable of such an Olympian tone can become so personal when attacking policy differences?" Acheson wrote back, suggesting that as far as he knew, "the Olympians seem. . . . to have been a pretty personal lot."

Jackie had the last word. Writing to thank Acheson for his letter, she said she saw now that the best way to make a point was "to attack" one's opponent—"but this means you make an enemy of every one you disagree with, for harsh words do not leave much room for future concilia-

---

*Acheson's comment about Joe Kennedy "buying " JFK a congressional seat refers to a $500,000 loan Joe made in 1952 to John Fox, publisher of the *Boston Post,* thus inducing the paper to endorse JFK rather than its first choice, Henry Cabot Lodge. On another occasion Acheson referred to Joe Kennedy as "a prototypical Wall Street wheeler-dealer, a corrupt money man whose political mentor was Honey Fitz Fitzgerald, the disreputable former mayor of Boston and the father of Joe Kennedy's bride." In April 1960, Acheson wrote Harry Truman that he hoped to block JFK's nomination for President: "Maybe we should all give Jack a run for his money—or Joe's." Despite their differences, Acheson served as a foreign affairs consultant to JFK during the Kennedy administration.

tion. Life becomes so dreary when every day you add a new name to the list of people who won't speak to you."

Another lesson Jackie gradually learned was the importance of establishing her own connections among the combative female ranks of Washington society. "Jackie had always resisted cultivating friendships with other women," said Lem Billings. "She reflected an aura of fragility which seemed to attract men more than women, and which at the same time reduced every man she met to pure jelly. Then she met the feisty and irrepressible Alice Roosevelt Longworth. Alice was the first woman whose political voice Jackie admired. Alice used to have Jackie in for tea. She'd call up and ask Jackie to drop everything and come over at once, and Jackie would go. They'd sit around a table—Alice, Jackie and a few other select guests—and eat thin bread and butter. It was the kind of ceremony Jackie normally detested. At first she went only because Alice was such a powerful figure in Washington society. Jack forced her to go. 'You don't stand up Mrs. Alice Longworth and live to talk about it,' he told her. Gradually Jackie learned to appreciate Alice. She was such an entertaining figure, so histrionic and pleasantly eccentric, that you couldn't help but be amused."

At one of Mrs. Longworth's teas, Jackie encountered Mrs. Herbert Lehman, wife of the former New York State governor. Mrs. Lehman, who with her husband maintained a suite at the Washington Sheraton, also gave formal tea parties which Jackie occasionally attended. Her other contact in this group was Mrs. Richard Neuberger, whose husband was a U.S. Senator from Oregon. When he died in 1960, Maurine Neuberger was first elected to fill her husband's unexpired term and then to a full Senate term of her own. The Neubergers lived a block from the Kennedys, and the two couples took turns hosting each other at dinner parties.

Jackie had also remained friends with Mrs. John Sherman Cooper, who gave her several tips she had picked up while campaigning with her husband in Kentucky. "I remember her telling me that she carried little cards with her and that whenever she left a city or town she'd write a note," said Jackie. "She told me to do this while campaigning . . . Right away when you leave write a little note—'Dear so-and-so, thank you for this or that,' because otherwise everything piles up and you forget."

It was Lorraine Cooper who taught Jackie the importance of remembering names and faces. Jacob Javits, the late New York Senator, met Jackie at a bipartisan political function in 1958. "She had a gift for connecting names and faces," Javits recalled. "It's an ability most politicians develop along the way, only she developed it to a much more significant level. She could meet somebody once and remember them forever. I don't mean some anonymous housewife in a reception line in Iowa. I'm talking about minor political officials—a mayor, governor or convention delegate. She also struck me as unusually polite and well-spoken. I thought if JFK intended to make a run for the presidency, Jackie would be a major asset and vote-getter."

Jackie herself sent mixed signals regarding her newly adopted role. Early in 1958, she said: "Politics is in my blood. I know that even if Jack changed professions I would miss politics. It's the most exciting life imaginable—always involved with the news of the moment, meeting and working with people who are enormously alive, and every day you are caught up in something you really care about. It makes a lot of other things seem less vital. You get used to the pressure that never lets up, and you learn to live with it as a fish lives in water."

But when the mask slipped it revealed an entirely different personality. One day a reporter saw the Kennedy car parked in front of a convent in Lowell, Mass. Jack was inside introducing himself to the Mother Superior and the nuns ("They vote, too," he had reminded his wife). Outside, sitting in the back of the car, was Jackie, looking tired and bored, grimly flipping the pages of a fashion magazine.

On another occasion, while a Kennedy motorcade inched its way through the crowded streets of downtown Boston, she buried herself in the back seat of the limousine and furtively read General Charles de Gaulle's memoirs—in their original French. Another time she was observed reading Proust's *Remembrance of Things Past*. Then there were the mornings when she simply refused to go campaigning for Jack and instead insisted on taking long solo walks by the Georgetown canal.

If anything prevented Jackie from being a more enthusiastic campaigner, it was her inherent fear and distrust of the press. "Nothing disturbs me as much as interviewers and journalists, she told Yusha Auchincloss. "That's the trouble with a life in the public eye. I've always hated gossip column publicity about the private lives of public men. But if you make your living in public office, you're the property of every tax-paying citizen. Your whole life is an open book."

"Jackie hated Jack Anderson and Drew Pearson, who were always running anti-JFK reports, or so she felt," said George Smathers. "She didn't seem to care that this was their job. She had surprising antipathy toward the press in general, and as time passed, her bitterness increased. She forgot that she herself had once been an inquiring photographer avidly pursuing public figures. Now that the press was pursuing her, she labeled it an invasion of privacy."

Mary Tierney, a reporter for the *Boston Herald-Traveler,* covered Jackie during both the 1958 Senatorial re-election campaign and John Kennedy's 1960 race for the presidency, and found her "a tough nut to crack." Jackie's disdain for the press was immediately evident to Tierney. "She had this inane smile that seemed to have been fixed in place by a plasterer. I thought of her as an appendage to the Kennedy family. She was a little actress, but without her lines she was lost. I mean she's one of those people you say 'hello' to and she's stuck for an answer. You ask her three questions and she's really bent out of shape. She was only allowed three questions by the press each campaign stop, a rule imposed by Larry O'Brien.* 'Just three questions,' he said. I said, 'God, we don't want to tax her brain.'

"Jackie didn't go for full-fledged interviews unless she could control them. I thought she was a dummy, to be honest about it. I didn't think she was capable of talking about too much of anything, no less political affairs. She had that breathless approach and just didn't seem too interested. She hated campaigning. She would ride in a separate car, or she would be with Jack in a car and then fade into the woodwork when he stopped to work the crowd. She didn't have that feeling for campaigning that he did. He liked the pressing of the flesh. It was his time.

---

*Larry O'Brien denies ever having placed a limit on the number of questions allowed Jackie but admits she was reticent and might possibly have imposed such a moratorium on her own.

He had charm and popularity. He just had it. He had this appeal and everybody clamored to shake his hand and be near him.

"Jackie looked down her nose at the average person in politics. She certainly didn't care for the Irish mafia that surrounded Jack. They weren't good enough for her. She didn't care about people like that. She's a snob. I think she campaigned because it was expected of her. For somebody who had been an inquiring photographer at one time, she was a very cold person. She didn't have a warm bone in her body.

"She was a very strange lady. She was a nerd, a big zero. She wasn't stupid in an intellectual sense—she happened to like Adlai Stevenson because he was an intellectual—but she took no interest in politics per se. She began to enjoy it once she reached the White House, but not before. Her marriage was a matter of convenience. She wanted the supposed glamour, and the Kennedys wanted that non-Irish quality, the added dimension. All that Irish business—the pub-crawling, the story-telling, the singing, the ward politics—bored the ass off Jackie.

"I remember once in the campaign when we all drove up to Worcester together. It was cold that day and Jackie wanted to wear her mink coat, but Jack told her it wouldn't be appropriate. Worcester was a working-class town. So she wore a blue tweed coat instead and pouted the entire way there.

"She returned to Boston by herself. I drove in a car with JFK and another reporter. Jack was running for re-election as Senator but had the presidency in mind. He wanted to run up a big plurality in the Senatorial race to convince the party leaders that he was presidential material. All he talked about during the trip was the presidency. He wanted it very badly, but there seemed to be this unspoken concern with regard to Jackie's role in a nationwide campaign. If going from Boston to Worcester troubled her, how would she feel about trekking to Wyoming or Mississippi or New Mexico?"

Although she restricted her long-distance jaunts at first, Jackie seemed to fare better on the national tour than she did during Massachusetts outings. She accompanied Jack to a Democratic Party fund-raiser in Los Angeles in the spring of 1958. Joseph Cerrell, who later became executive director of the Democratic Party in California, recalled the effect of Jackie's presence.

"I had met her first at the Chicago convention in '56," he said, "but this was the first I'd seen of her in California. I had the feeling she didn't care particularly for California but wanted to put in an appearance for her husband's sake. Anyway, I remember her causing a considerable stir because it was the first time Californians had seen anybody sporting a hemline above the knee. Her glamour and her unconventional beauty attracted attention and enticed the news media, for whom the couple had become a symbol of youth and vitality—a new symbol for a New Age. They looked more like movie stars than most movie stars."

Jackie and Jack spent their fifth wedding anniversary at a midwest Democratic conference in Omaha, Nebraska, and attended a Jefferson-Jackson Day fund-raiser in Des Moines, Iowa. Closer to home again, Jackie accompanied her husband to a rally in Baltimore, an event covered for NBC-TV by Nancy Dickerson. After the rally, Nancy hitched a ride back to Washington with the Kennedys.

"Jack drove his usual 90 m.p.h. and Jackie began to feel queasy," said Dickerson. "So we traded places—she stretched out in the back seat, and I sat up front with Jack. I suspected Jackie's nausea had more to do with the crowds at the political rally than with Jack's driving. She didn't particularly like the crowds that surged around her in campaigns. They frightened her, made her ill."

A somewhat similar incident occurred during the winter of 1958. James Rousmaniere, then working in New York, received a telephone call from Jack Kennedy. "Fordham University Law School is giving me an honorary degree," said Kennedy. "Jackie and I are flying into New York tomorrow. Meet us at LaGuardia and we'll drive in together."

Rousmaniere met them at the airport. It was snowing, and it had obviously been a rough flight up from Washington because Jackie wasn't feeling well.

"We put her in the back seat of the car," said Rousmaniere. "The weather and heavy traffic had reduced the roads to slush. The drive into New York seemed interminable. Within half an hour Jackie was vomiting all over my back seat. It was a terribly embarrassing situation for her through no fault of mine, and I'm sure it gave her a lasting memory of me she wanted to forget."

Jackie later told Larry O'Brien she had learned more about human nature during her first year on the campaign trail than she had learned from all her previous experiences combined. "She joined us on the traditional election-eve tour of the Boston wards, which in those days culminated at the G and G Delicatessen on Blue Hill Avenue in Dorchester," said O'Brien. "She shared a bag of chocolates with me, and, since she didn't think she should be seen smoking, I would hold a cigarette for her and she would take furtive puffs from time to time. We were exhausted but happy. Jack, Bob and Ted climbed atop a table and sang 'Heart of My Heart'—offkey but exuberantly."

In the end, their efforts were rewarded. John Kennedy beat a Boston lawyer named Vincent Celeste by a margin of more than 874,000 votes, a record three-to-one ratio. The national media gave excellent coverage to Kennedy's sweeping victory. He had taken a giant step toward 1960.

14

One week after JFK's re-election as Senator, during a private dinner with Joe Kennedy and other Kennedy family members at Le Pavillon in New York, Lem Billings made a witty but caustic remark about Jack. Jack was not present. The Ambassador, usually amused by a good joke, did not laugh, and instead sharply rebuked him, then explained that he must never again talk that way about Jack in public. "LeMoyne," he said, "you are one of the people who must understand this. You can never know who might be listening. From here on, you must think of Jack less as a friend and more as a potential candidate for President of the United States." He paused and then added: "I will tell you right now that the day is going to come when you will not call Jack 'Jack.' You will call him 'Mr. President.' "

Word of Jack Kennedy's intention to pursue the presidency spread quickly. Nancy Tenney Coleman, a Hyannis Port neighbor of the Kennedys, attended a circus ball at New York's Plaza Hotel during the 1958 Christmas holiday. Among the guests were Loel and Gloria Guinness, Mary Sanford, Spanish pretender Prince Juan Carlos, the Duke and Duchess of Windsor, New York Governor Nelson Rockefeller, Averell Harriman and Jack and Jackie Kennedy.

"I was dancing with Charlie Bartlett," said Nancy Coleman. "I hadn't seen JFK in a long time, so I said, 'Let's go over and say hello to Jack.' That's when Charlie told me about Jack's plan to run for the presidency. I couldn't believe it. I said, 'Charles, you've got to be kidding. He's not going to run for President.' Charlie said, 'Oh yes, he is.' 'Well, I'll ask him myself,' I said. He said, 'Oh Nancy, please. He'll know I told you.' 'So what?' I said. 'I'm an old buddy of his. I'm an old friend.' We had grown up together on the Cape. He had a wonderful sense of humor. He was fun. He was just a nice normal person. You never thought in a thousand years he was going to be President.

"So, I stopped him on the dance floor. I always called him Ken to his face. I said, 'Ken, somebody told me you're going to run for President. I don't believe it.' He had an Upmann cigar in his mouth, even though he was on the dance floor. He took the cigar out and said, 'I'm not only going to run for President, I'm going to win.'

" 'My God, Ken,' I said. 'You'll ruin the streets of Hyannis Port. The tourists will be up there in droves. The town will never be the same.' And, actually, once he became President, that's just what happened."

According to George Smathers, JFK's presidential candidacy was orchestrated from beginning to end by Joe Kennedy. "It became Joe's run for the roses as much as Jack's," said Smathers. "Joe Kennedy masterminded the whole campaign, just as he had masterminded Jack's initial entry into politics after Joe Jr.'s death. 'We're going to sell Jack like cornflakes,' he boasted. He'd begun lining up political bosses as early as 1957, starting with Mayor Richard Daley of Chicago. He was probably one of the first to use polls. He hired Lou Harris, and Harris used to sit around with his slide rule at $500 an hour. But that information was an invaluable tool. Joe Kennedy was also the first to understand the public relations aspect of politics. He understood that what you did was to merchandise a concept and he had enough experience in Hollywood and the motion picture business to grope around in that whole area, which has now become common practice.

"The 1960 campaign was Joe's show entirely, yet he managed to organize it from behind the scenes. Because of his past record, he was forced to stay out of the limelight. But he called the shots, and you could sense his influence and imprint on many of Jack's ideas."

Peter Lawford visited Palm Beach with Frank Sinatra early in 1959 to do some preliminary planning for the presidential campaign. Sinatra, already deeply committed to Kennedy, had temporarily renamed the Rat Pack the "Jack Pack" and in a similar vein referred to Peter as "brother-in-Lawford."

Lawford recalled that Sinatra stayed with Morton Downey, Joe Kennedy's oldest friend in Palm Beach, while he himself stayed with Frank and Betty McMahon. McMahon, a Canadian oil man, was a member of Palm Beach's horsey set.

"Joe Kennedy ran the campaign from an outdoor enclosure next to the swimming pool," said Lawford. "He called it 'the bullpen.' There was no roof on the structure. Inside were a telephone and a deck chair. Joe spent his mornings on the telephone barking orders at frightened minions and employees. What seemed odd about the arrangement was that he made his calls in the nude, which was the reason for the enclosure. And this is the same man who castigated me for not wearing anything on my feet while playing golf in Palm Beach with Jack.

"Joe Kennedy was the world's greatest hypocrite. His philosophy was quite simple: 'Do as I say, not as I do.' But his great gift, his genius if you will, was that he could simplify a problem rather than make it more complex, as most of us do. He would see one road instead of many and he would follow the road. Most of us, including myself, are victims of our imagination. Not Joe. He had a concept of destiny."

During Sinatra's visit, Joe Kennedy outlined the role he hoped the singer would play, namely that of fundraiser and quasi-social director. Sinatra's value to any political campaign had to be the wide spectrum of people he knew, not just in the entertainment field but in the world of big business and industry, real estate, even gambling and racketeering. On the lighter side, Joe wanted Sinatra to record a campaign song for Jack. They settled on "High Hopes" and convinced Sammy Cahn and Sinatra's personal arranger, Jimmy Van Heusen, to rework the lyrics.

"Then Joe turned to me," said Peter Lawford. " 'You've got to find some way to shut down your mother,' he said. 'Her public denunciations aren't exactly aiding the cause.' My mother, Lady May Lawford, was outspoken to say the least. Her latest outburst, this one against my wife, had been picked up and printed by Walter Winchell: 'Patricia Lawford is a bitch, a real bitch. She has millions but lets Peter pay all their bills. Their million-dollar dream estate in Santa Monica, previously owned by Louis B. Mayer, boasts a marble swimming pool, rose gardens and a screening room with red leather walls. But the house and every stick of furniture in it belong to my son.' Something to that effect.

"My mother and Joe Kennedy were mortal enemies. But what could I do about it? 'She's my mother, Joe. I can't kill the woman, I said. 'No,' he responded, 'but I can.' Then he said: 'Slip her some cash, pay her off. She'll quiet down. If you don't, I will.'

"Joe Kennedy plainly didn't know my mother. No amount of money in the world would have bought her silence. When Jack campaigned for President in Los Angeles, she rented an elephant and rode it down Wilshire Boulevard with a sign urging voters to support Richard Nixon."

Not long after his visit to Palm Beach, Frank Sinatra invited Joe Kennedy to join him at the Cal-Neva Lodge, a log-cabin-type nightclub-resort hotel overlooking the picturesque north shore of Lake Tahoe. The state line ran down the middle, with the gaming tables and slot machines on the Nevada side and food and dancing in California. Sinatra owned a share in the lodge, as did Chicago mobster Sam Giancana. It became known as a place where motion picture celebrities and underworld crime chieftains could rub shoulders and come and go at will.

Peter Lawford was also present at Cal-Neva when Joe Kennedy arrived: "Over the next two years he came out maybe a dozen times. He always came alone. Frank saw to it that he enjoyed himself.

"Besides the fun, the reason he came was to see a fellow named Norman Biltz. Biltz owned property on the lake. He was very wealthy himself, and had access to lots of other money as well. He was called 'the King of Nevada.' He was a tough old bird. He controlled both Republicans and Democrats in the state, though he himself was a Republican. But it didn't matter to Biltz whether you were one or the other.

"He told fascinating stories about Nevada politics and what went on, as I say, in both parties. He'd been married twice before, but his wife at that time, and until his death, was Esther Auchincloss, the sister of Hugh Auchincloss. Now you can take it from there; it was Jackie who arranged the first meeting between Biltz and Joe Kennedy.

"Hugh Auchincloss was the epitome of cheap. He contributed all of $500 to Jack's campaign. He normally contributed $10,000 to the Republican party presidential candidate. It's true he allowed Janet to throw fund-raisers for JFK, but he would have preferred it had Jack been Republican. Biltz was diferent. He and Joe Kennedy had much in common in their great power and drive. They were both full of themselves, charming scoundrels, I suppose you could say. Before Biltz was done, he had raised more than $15 million towards Jack's campaign and lined up people like Wilbur Clark, owner of the Desert Inn in Las Vegas and head of the Nevada Democratic delegation. Joe Kennedy must have kicked in $30 million of his own money. Others contributed, including several Mafia figures. Marilyn Monroe gave $25,000, as did other stars. It was the most highly subsidized presidential campaign ever run in this country. That, the women's vote and Jackie Kennedy figured as major factors in the race."

Joe Kennedy, master manipulator and strategist, also brought the Kennedy ladies into the grand picture, initiating the famous ladies' teas that had become so popular during JFK's various campaigns in Massachusetts, and seeing to it that the ritual continued on a national basis. Joe Alsop, who felt the turning point in Jack's career was the series of life-threatening operations he had endured in 1955, attached great importance to the part in the presidential campaign played by the Kennedy women. He was impressed by their old-fashioned good looks, their "great long legs," their wonderful heads of hair, the whole group sort of "attacking the voters en masse." Alsop could remember nothing like it in any previous political campaign. He thought it an "extraordinary performance."

Langdon Marvin visited the Kennedys in Palm Beach early in 1959 and was amazed by how "optimistic they all seemed about Jack's presidential prospects, especially the women in the family. Rose, Eunice, Pat, Jean and Ethel were huddled in the kitchen over a chocolate layer cake they were rapidly devouring, excitedly hatching plans for the upcoming campaign. Whenever one or the other had what seemed like a promising idea, they would all scamper into the living room to check it out with Bobby, who was Jack's campaign manager."

"They were political animals, the whole clan, with a true desire to affect the course of modern-day history," said Slim Aarons. "If you wanted their friendship you had to be willing to back them to the hilt. When JFK began actively campaigning, I received a telephone call from Chuck Spalding. Chuck had become director of the campaign in New York State. He wanted me to give some campaign talks for Jack. I said I couldn't. I had a number of pending photo assignments that I couldn't put off. Among other incidentals, I had a family to support. 'But Jack needs you,' said Chuck. 'I appreciate that fact,' I said, 'but I really do have commitments.' After that they dropped me like a hot potato.''

Throughout 1959 and the first half of 1960, when she became pregnant again, Jackie joined Jack on many of his campaign outings, starting with New Hampshire and continuing into Wisconsin, West Virginia, Virginia, California, Oregon, Ohio, Rhode Island and New Jersey. In later months she returned to some of the states she had visited previously and added Maine, Delaware, Tennessee, Kentucky, Maryland, North Carolina, New York and Pennsylvania to her itinerary. She spoke Spanish in New York City, French in Eau Claire, Italian in Syracuse and a smattering of Polish in Milwaukee. She taped messages in foreign languages for radio and television. She appeared on a number of television interview programs, including the "Today" show with Dave Garroway. She gave luncheons at her home in Georgetown. She visited supermarkets and spoke to shoppers over the public address system. She and Jack traversed the country aboard *Caroline*, a converted twin-engine Corvair purchased earlier by Joe Kennedy at a cost of $350,000. The use of a private airplane gave them an immense advantage over the opposition, which had to depend upon the often erratic schedules of commercial airlines to deliver them to their destinations.

"There were two phases to the campaign," recalled Larry O'Brien. "First we had to win the Democratic nomination; then, we had to beat Richard Nixon. The first part came easier to Jackie because she wasn't pregnant. And by then she had become a seasoned traveler, learning to subsist on 'fast foods' and to live on the road with only three dresses—one for morning, one for afternoon, one for evening—and one hat for church. Her jewelry consisted of a string of pearls. She also took a traveling iron and a sewing kit. By this point she had learned how to hustle a crowd, force herself onto a platform in front of 5,000 screaming strangers, shake 10,000 hands without collapsing of fatigue."

"You shake hundreds of hands in the afternoon and hundreds more at night," Jackie noted. "You get so tired you catch yourself laughing and crying at the same time. But you pace yourself and you get through it. You just look at it as something you have to do. You knew it would come and you knew it was worth it.

"The places blur after a while, they really do. I remember people, not faces, in a receiving line. The thing you get from these people is a sense of shyness and anxiety and shining expectancy. These women who come up to see me at a meeting, they're as shy as I am. Sometimes we just stand there smiling at each other and just don't say anything."

Jackie's first major trial didn't come until March 1960. Kennedy was driving hard for victory against Hubert Humphrey in Wisconsin's presidential primary. Word arrived from Washington that a vote was imminent in the Senate on civil rights legislation. It was a vote he couldn't afford to miss.

"You go back to Washington and vote, Jack," said Jackie. "I'll carry on for you."

Carry on she did. Accompanied by Ted Kennedy, she journeyed from town to town, giving short speeches at each stop. In Marshfield, she told seventy-five people at a luncheon in the Charles Hotel: "We've been working so hard in Wisconson, and I know that if you do see fit to support my husband you will find you haven't misplaced your trust. In recent years he has served on the Senate Labor and Public Welfare Committee and in that capacity has done as much for workers in this country as any U.S. Senator. He will continue to do everything in his power if elected President."

In Neillsville, she spoke on a local radio show and said simply: "He has served his country fourteen years in the Navy and in Congress. He cares deeply about the welfare of this nation, and as President will make the greatest contribution to its future."

At Fairchild, she stopped at an elementary school to visit some kindergarten children, as well as their teachers and parents. She told the children they made her miss Caroline, and assured the adults that her husband's hope and concern were the nation's youth.

Public reaction to Jackie's overall efforts ran the gamut. Edmund Nix, District Attorney of Eau Claire County, remembered a rash of bad press when Jackie was spotted "walking down the street smoking a cigarette." Nix personally felt that Jackie "did a very fine job, made quite a good impression" filling in for Jack.

Jerry Bruno, an advance man for JFK, thought Jackie "extremely helpful in Wisconsin. In Kenosha, my hometown, John Kennedy was delayed at the American Legion Home when he was supposed to be downtown at a coffee-and-tea reception. There was an overflow crowd at the reception. The crowd was lined up for blocks. Jackie mounted the rostrum and gave a speech. Alan Ameche, the professional football player, was there. Between Ameche and Jackie, they kept that crowd entertained until Kennedy finally arrived.

"Jackie didn't love campaigning, but she didn't mind it either. Her mind focused a good deal on Caroline. She mentioned how much she missed her daughter. 'I wonder how Caroline's getting along,' she would say. She was furious with a certain *Milwaukee Journal* reporter who kept writing stories about a possible breakup between Jack and herself. He was a political reporter who seemed to pay more attention to gossip than politics. He made frequent reference to rumors that they were on the verge of divorce. It used to make her blood boil. She was also furious about the fact that this reporter kept raising the religious issue. If there were 10,000 people at a rally, he would write that 9,900 of them were Catholic. No matter where we went in Wisconsin, this bloke would report that 99 percent of the audience was Catholic. Jackie finally couldn't take it any longer. She said, 'I wonder if that guy does an individual poll at each function on the issues of this campaign. How else could he gather his statistics?' "

Frank Thompson, an old friend of JFK, described an amusing incident that took place in Wisconsin. "They were all in Madison," remarked Thompson. "Ivan Nestinger, later Undersecretary of HEW, was the mayor and was driving Jack around in a very small car on an extremely cold day. Jackie had gone off by herself to do some campaigning among the black churches on the outskirts of Madison. Toward evening they picked her up and she squeezed into the back seat between two other people, and Jack, seated in the front, said, 'Jackie, how did you do?' She said, 'Oh, I did very well. I met the loveliest minister of the loveliest black church, and he has all kinds of financial troubles. I thought it would be nice to help him out, so I gave him $200.' Jack said. 'Well, that was nice.' Then, on a quick second thought he added, 'Goddammit, it wasn't my money, was it?' "

When the Wisconsin Primary votes came in, and Kennedy beat Hubert Humphrey by 106,000 votes, it appeared that Jackie's presence might have given her husband the margin of victory. Jackie would never make such a claim. She attributed the win to Jack's valor under fire. The press attributed it to the large percentage of Catholic voters in Wisconsin. West Virginia, a predominantly Protestant state, would be the more-important test.

Charles Peters, editor of *Washington Monthly,* was one of JFK's political organizers in West Virginia. When informed by Bobby Kennedy that Jackie would be joining the primary campaign in his home state, Peters vehemently opposed the idea. "I felt Jackie would compare unfavorably with Muriel Humphrey, Hubert's wife, who was down-to-earth and much more like West Virginians. I thought Jackie far too glitzy. In fact I thought JFK a bit glitzy for West Virginia. So did my mother, who was also a Democratic Party organizer in West Virginia, and who didn't think they should enter the primary race. But they did, and in retrospect they were quite right to do so.

"I was in charge of Kanawha County, the largest county in the state. I went out campaigning with Jackie twice. She seemed quite pleasant about her role. You sensed a light restraint on her part but not much more. I suspected from what I'd heard that she wanted to campaign. She wanted to help. She was definitely eager by this time to get into the White House.

"What amazed me most, I think, was the way people reacted to Jackie. I first got the sense through Jackie's emerging popularity, of what was happening in American society. There was no question that instead of identifying with the woman who was like them—Muriel Humphrey— they identified with the Princess. You could just tell they wanted Jackie. They had a wondrous look in their eyes when they saw her. After the dowdiness of Eleanor Roosevelt, Bess Truman and Mamie Eisenhower, they were looking for an aristocratic image. And the Kennedys did a superlative job of merchandising that image.

"Their campaign was extremely well organized. JFK had a politically subtle mind, and Joe Kennedy was the

master of con-man hustle. The Kennedys all had a deep
desire to rise socially and perceived how rising socially
could help them politically, first in Massachusetts and
then nationally. I think Jack Kennedy's motive for marrying Jackie was that she gave him class. At least there
was the perception of class, since her background was
actually the same as theirs.''

Kennedy's victory in the West Virginia primary represented a major turning point in his campaign. "At that
moment we realized he could win it all," said Charles
Peters. "If he'd lost, we knew he could lose it all. It was
clear that there was a great deal riding on it. Never
before had so much ridden on something so small as a
primary in a state like West Virginia.''

What struck JFK's entourage was Jackie's lack of post-
victory exuberance. The night of the primary Jack and
Jackie, accompanied by their friends Ben and Toni
Bradlee, headed for a cinema in downtown Washington.
They wanted to see *Suddenly Last Summer* but arrived
after the movie started, so they wandered across the
street to an X-rated movie theater. They saw *Private
Property,* the "sexploitive" story of a wayward wife and
her torrid affairs with milkmen, repairmen, delivery boys
and anybody else who stumbled her way.

When the film ended, the foursome returned to the
Kennedy home on N Street. The moment they opened
the door, the telephone started to ring. It was Bobby:
Jack had won handily in West Virginia. He immediately
called his father and then alerted his crew to ready the
Caroline for immediate departure. Accompanied by the
Bradlees as well as Steve and Jean Smith, Jack and
Jackie flew to Kanawha, West Virginia, to personally
thank their supporters. "I think we have now buried the
religious issue once and for all," Kennedy told reporters
at the Kanawha airport.

The victory celebration took place at the Kanawha
Hotel. As champagne flowed and music played, Jackie
slipped out a back door, located the car that had brought
them from the airport, crept into the back seat, and sat
there weary and alone, waiting for the return trip to
Washington.

Jackie's malaise and ennui became apparent at other
points in the campaign. Elizabeth Gatov, a Democratic
Party leader in California, noticed at once that Jackie

"really didn't like politics very much and she didn't really like politicians or people connected with it. She came out to California several times with JFK and I found out quickly that she didn't want to go into a room that was full of people. . . .

"My own feeling was that she was really shy about these kind of people, that she couldn't relate easily to the types of individuals that you find in the political context. She wasn't comfortable with them and so when she was with JFK I'd try to find a couple of people—attractive, rather urbane men—to spend that period of time with her . . .-and help make it as pleasant and as easy for her as possible."

Clara Shirpser, another California political organizer, expressed a similar reaction to Jackie's seeming loss of interest in the campaign: "The big Kennedy reception at the Fairmont Hotel in San Francisco had lines of people stretched all through the lobby from the sidewalks to meet Jack Kennedy and shake hands with him. Jack and Jackie were both here. About a half-hour had gone by and Jackie had not appeared. I was standing in the receiving line near Jack. Everyone was saying, 'Where's Jackie? Where's Jackie?'

"I turned to Jack. I was near enough so I could talk to him and I said, 'Everyone is asking about Jackie. Why isn't she here?' He said, 'She evidently doesn't want to come down.' I said, 'I really think you ought to get her here. After all, you want to create good will.' He said, 'Will you go up and ask her?' I said, 'No, she wouldn't pay any attention to me.' He said something like, 'I've got news for you, she doesn't to me, either.'

". . . So I said, 'Please send someone to whom she'll pay some attention. Really, we ought to get her down here.' I think Jack finally went himself. Jackie did come then, but in a sulky mood, and she was almost uncommunicative. Somebody would say something nice to her and she would brusquely say, 'Thank you.' 'No,' or 'Yes.' She was not gracious, not friendly. She was one of the hardest campaign wives to get along with I have ever known in my life. She just liked the privileges and not the responsibilities."

Whatever else Jackie might have been, she was controversial. She had as many supporters as she did critics. Thus while some people felt she was much too stiff and formal and standoffish, there were others who admired her and valued her character and her carriage and her demeanor. Though several of her detractors accused her of losing as many votes as her husband gained, her numerous fans pointed out that she had played a significant role in JFK's dramatic ascent.

If she didn't always enter directly into the political turmoil, Jackie nevertheless managed to make her presence felt. She kicked off a nationwide campaign of women "Calling for Kennedy" by placing a conference call to eleven women in eleven states. She helped organize "The Women's Committee for New Frontiers," which met on several occasions during the campaign to discuss such topics as health care for the aged, unemployment, and public school education. She charmed Dr. Benjamin Spock and Reinhold Niebuhr (a Protestant theologian and philosopher) into supporting her husband's presidential bid. Following the advice of Mrs. John Sherman Cooper, she wrote "Campaign Wife," a weekly column for women which the Democratic National Committee distributed to various newspapers. She also doggedly defended her husband's political honor, reading the manuscript of a projected biography of Kennedy by historian James MacGregor Burns, then criticizing it in a long and angry letter.

The journalist Peter Lisagor never forgot the reception he received following his grilling of JFK on a segment of *Face the Nation*. "When it was over," he said, "Jacqueline looked at me as though I had crawled out of some hole and had struck with fangs and poison at the heel of her husband." She proceeded to berate him for asking JFK such "absolutely horrible" questions.

Jackie's importance to John Kennedy's campaign should not be underestimated. Always photogenic, mysterious, reserved and unpredictable, she made an undeniable impact on the American psyche. She was noticed more than any other of the Kennedy women, primarily because she was different; she wasn't "the girl next door" and she knew it—and she didn't try to sell herself as one. She defied political tradition by admitting that she rarely cooked and wasn't particularly interested in the mechanics of housekeeping. She made it clear that a governess looked after Caroline and that there were other servants in the house as well. She was refreshingly frank. She indicated she had campaigned with her husband because if she hadn't she never would have seen him. She said she found it unnerving to go downstairs for breakfast and discover a dozen men in rumpled suits sitting around the table smoking cigars and talking campaign strategy. She admitted spending money on clothes, not the $30,000 per year that *Womens Wear Daily* claimed she spent—"I couldn't spend that much unless I wore sable underwear" —but she confessed to having purchased several Hubert de Givenchy and Balenciaga creations and to frequenting a number of other European couturiers. She was different not only in manner but in appearance. In the middle of the campaign, her mother said to her, "Why can't you look more like Muriel Humphrey or Pat Nixon?"

Even her sense of humor set her apart. It was naughty, lascivious, risqué. Francis Lara, a French journalist stationed in Washington from 1959 through 1966, found Jackie's sensibility "very European. She was a merciless tease, loved exchanging quips and barbs—nothing malicious, just ticklish humor usually of a sexual nature. I would say to her, 'Ben Bradlee told me you were seeing So-and-so.' I would name somebody famous like Cary Grant. She did the same to me. She always laughed everything off. She was very smooth, clever, calculating. She knew what she was doing."

Jackie's sense of humor is perhaps best illustrated by the store-bought Valentine's Day card she sent Arthur Krock in 1959. On the face of the card was a sketch of a shapely blonde in a low-cut semitransparent sheath, her body contorted into a position reminiscent of Betty Grable's historic World War II rear-view pin-up pose. The printed message on the card read. "OKAY, Mr. Valentine, NOW UNSCREW ME!!" Underneath Jackie had written: "Love from a Front Runner's wife, Muriel Humphrey of course."

15

The closer John Kennedy seemed to come to the presidency the more frenetic became his random search for women. The FBI files on Kennedy make reference to "a pair of stewardesses that the subject is seeing in California." Another item points to the John Kennedy-Frank Sinatra connection: "Kennedy and Sinatra have in the recent past been involved in parties in Palm Springs, Las Vegas and New York City. Regarding the Kennedy-Sinatra information, *Confidential* magazine is said to have affidavits from two mulatto prostitutes in New York." Another notation in the files alleges that during 1957-1958, Kennedy made several trips to Havana, Cuba, to visit Flo Pritchett Smith, wife of Earl E. T. Smith, American Ambassador to Cuba under Eisenhower. Other meetings between Flo and Jack during this phase apparently took place in Miami and Palm Beach during Flo's visits to the States.

In September 1958, Jack Kennedy and George Smathers attended a party at the Italian Embassy in Washington. Another guest at the same party was Sophia Loren. Jackie was out of town and Sophia appeared to be by herself. Jack was interested. Instead of approaching the actress directly, he waited on the patio and sent Senator Smathers to do his bidding.

Smathers poured on the charm. He confronted Sophia and explained in a soft Southern drawl that his friend, Senator Kennedy, soon to become President Kennedy, wanted Miss Loren to join him in his Georgetown home for a late supper. The champagne, he added, was already on ice.

Another guest, reporter Maxine Cheshire, happened to be standing next to Sophia Loren and inadvertently overheard both the proposition as well as the actress's polite but firm refusal. Since Sophia's English was still a bit spotty in those days, Smathers thought she hadn't understood him. He asked again, and again she rebuffed him.

Cheshire could see Kennedy out on the patio, impatiently rocking back and forth on his heels. He would not take "no" for an answer, and he sent Smahers back for a second try.

This time Sophia looked to Cheshire for help, as if imploring the reporter to somehow make Smathers understand her lack of interest in him or his friend. From Sophia's reaction, Smathers got the impression that Cheshire, whom he had never seen before, was some sort of chaperone or translator assigned to the actress during her stay in Washington. Smathers smiled at Sophia and said, in an unmistakably exasperated tone, "Oh, what the hell, you might as well bring your friend along. We'll make it a foursome."

Another actress who managed to sidestep Kennedy was Jean Simmons. Her former husband, Stewart Granger, in his autobiography, recalls the time Jean came back from location shooting in Boston for a 1958 movie called *Home Before Dark*. "She told me of this very attractive senator who had wooed her with flowers and eventually ended up practically breaking down her bedroom door." With a grin, Jean added that "he had such a lovely smile I nearly let him in." Bridling, Granger asked if she knew his name. "Yes, he's a very important Senator called John Kennedy." Adds Granger: "I'd never heard of him."*

Jack fared better with Pamela Turnure, a 21-year-old Georgetown debutante who looked a great deal like Jackie, was equally aloof and even sounded like her. Pam took a secretarial job in Jack's senatorial office and later joined his presidential campaign team. Photographer Bob Phillips, who traveled in the same circles as Pam, described her as "bright, attractive, well-groomed, well-spoken. She dated a number of men I knew and gave some lovely parties. I never went out with her myself but we did become close friends. Even so, she never mentioned Kennedy to me in any context other than employment. I didn't know the romantic details until much later."

Pam's frequent late-night meetings with Jack were of more than passing interest to her Georgetown landlords,

*Stewart Granger, *Sparks Fly Upward*, pp. 380-381.

a strict Catholic couple, Leonard and Florence Kater. They were outraged. They set up tape recorders at several strategic locations, including a basement air vent that led straight to Pam's bedroom on the second floor. The results were as incontrovertible as the photographs they took at 1:00 a.m. on July 11, 1958, of John Kennedy emerging from Pam's apartment. Copies of the candid snapshots went not only to the FBI but to newspapers, magazines and television stations. With rare exception—a brief article appeared in the *Washington Star*—the Katers were ignored. J. Edgar Hoover added their photographs to his already bulging files on John Kennedy, but refused to meet personally with them.

The Katers took their campaign to the streets and began showing up at JFK's political rallies with hand-fashioned signs denouncing the candidate as an adulterer. They followed him to Independence, Missouri, when he called on former President Harry S. Truman. They telephoned Joseph Kennedy, who brusquely dismissed their complaint, and they went to Boston to see Richard Cardinal Cushing. When all else failed, Mrs. Kater picketed the White House.

Pam Turnure had long since vacated her apartment in the Kater house, and, on John Kennedy's recommendation, moved into the Georgetown home of Mary Meyer. Mary, the sister of Toni Bradlee, was a free-lance artist. A graduate of Vassar, Mary happened to be friendly with Jackie Kennedy. Until Jackie became First Lady, she and Mary often took morning strolls together around Washington.

"Mary Meyer found herself unwittingly drawn into a web of intrigue," said James T. Angleton, chief of counter intelligence for the CIA and a confidant of Mary's. "Pam Turnure was living with Mary and seeing John Kennedy on the sly. Mary knew about the relationship. But she also enjoyed a friendship with Jackie Kennedy. When the Kennedys entered the White House, JFK suggested that Pam become Jackie's press secretary. 'Why do I need a press secretary?' Jackie asked. Pam had no experience working with the press. But Jackie finally relented, realizing she could thereby keep an eye on Pam. What she didn't count on was Jack dropping Pam and taking up with Mary Meyer."

Deirdre Henderson, another young and attractive woman

who worked on Kennedy's presidential campaign team, couldn't decide whether to be insulted or relieved that she hadn't been propositioned by her employer. "I started working for him in 1958," she remarked. "I was interviewed first by Ted Sorensen and then by Kennedy. Afterwards, Kennedy told me to step into another room and type out a list of what I considered the ten most important foreign policy issues of the day. My list apparently met with his approval because he asked if I wanted to be his speech writer. I didn't think I knew enough for that. 'Why don't you let me do research for you?' I suggested. He finally hit upon the idea of sending me to Boston to become his liaison with the intellectual community.

"I moved into an apartment in Cambridge and threw a cocktail party to get Kennedy together with some of the Harvard and M.I.T. crowd who later joined his administration, many in key positions. It was perhaps the most important cocktail party of the campaign, because it was there that Walt Rostow came up with the term 'the New Frontier' and started pressing it on Kennedy. It eventually became his tag line. I can honestly say that in my presence Kennedy always acted the perfect gentleman. He never tried anything with me. But he did something during the campaign that rather surprised me. He learned that one of his top aides, a married man, was having an affair with a young female staffer. For some reason this bohered him. He telephoned the aide and proceeded to berate him. Considering Kennedy's personal history and reputation, this struck me as a bizarre method of handling the situation."

One of Kennedy's less publicized friendships seems to have been with Lady Jean Campbell, the daughter of the Duke of Argyll and the granddaughter of the powerful British press magnate Lord Beaverbook. Russell D. Hemenway, a campaign manager for Adlai Stevenson, considered himself a close associate of Jean's and frequently saw her in the mid- to late 1950s in company with Kennedy. "She was a voluptuous brunette in her early twenties, independent, bright, on the whole a rather uncomplicated girl. She became the companion of Henry Luce, left him to become Norman Mailer's third wife, and somehow managed to sandwich JFK between the two. I never knew the full extent of the relationship. I saw them together at New York dinner parties and at places like the Stork Club and they both looked very comfy."

Less intense but longer lasting was Jack's relationship with Joan Lundberg, a California divorcée with two children whom he met in Santa Monica late in 1956 and continued to date sporadically through 1959. According to Joan, she and some friends visited a Santa Monica bar called the Sip 'n' Surf and there she saw the Lawfords sitting with John Kennedy. Determined not to lose the opportunity to meet him, she glided over to the juke box which stood next to his table and began a conversation on the obvious excuse of getting him interested in the record she was about to play.

Kennedy left before she did, and shortly after his departure, she received a telephone call from him at the bar. He invited her to a party at the Lawfords. When she arrived at the party, she discovered he had invited several other women as well, but to her delight, he chose to spend the night with her.

She later said she attracted him because of her strong resemblance to his sister Pat, a likeness that helped them travel together, since they were frequently mistaken for siblings. She spent time with him both at the Lawfords' home and on the campaign trail. Because she was supporting her two young children, Kennedy paid her travel expenses. Joan claimed their relationship ended when friends of the Lawfords began to ask questions, and she was subsequently banned from the Lawford residence.

During the presidential campaign, most of JFK's female companions were drawn from that transient pool known in his camp as "the Kennedy girls," the models, hostesses and college cheerleaders recruited in every city, county and state by the candidate's advance men to add sparkle and zest to the race. Janet DesRosiers, the stewardess aboard the *Caroline,* felt that had Jackie done more campaigning with Jack, the opportunity and need for such dalliances would have been greatly reduced.

"The trouble is that Jackie didn't enjoy campaigning," said DesRosiers. "She found the pace too hectic and didn't care to rub shoulders with Mr. and Mrs. John Doe. When she did campaign, she remained aloof, quiet, alone. She was very reserved. I think Jack might have tried to encourage her more. She represented a large part

of the Kennedy image-making machine, and it must have
been disconcerting for him that she didn't accompany
him more often or generate greater enthusiasm or buoy-
ancy when she did accompany him.

"One of my functions as stewardess, which could not
have pleased Jackie very much, were the neck and shoulder massages I gave JFK every day. Give somebody a
massage and people automatically assume there's something going on. But somebody had to do it. He worked
himself into knots, toiling interminable hours, rising at 4
a.m. to shake hands at some remote airplane gate in
subzero weather. The man gave as many as thirty speeches
a day, seven days a week, three weeks at a clip.

"He had voice and back problems. The massages helped
his back. David Blair McCloskey, a Boston University
professor, was his speech therapist and voice coach. Mc-
Closkey gave him exercises to strengthen his vocal cords
and ordered me to keep him quiet once he boarded the
plane. I gave him a pad, and he communicated by pen."

Preserved for posterity by Janet DesRosiers, several of
JFK's midair notes provide intimate glimpses of his fixation on sexual fulfillment. Expressing himself on the possibility of defeating then-Vice President Richard Nixon in
the national election, he wrote: "I suppose if I win, my
poon days are over"—"poon" being a familiar Navy term
for sexual activity. Another day he scribbled: "I suppose
they are going to hit me with something before we are
finished"—an apparent reference to his expectation that
the Nixon camp would try to exploit his extramarital
affairs. On the back of a business envelope, he coldly
noted: "I got into the blonde." He also expressed his
plans in case he failed to win the Democratic nomination:
"If I lose—around the world in 180 days." He evidently
had in mind an expanded version of the Mediterranean
bacchanalia that had followed his 1956 defeat at the
Democratic National Convention in Chicago.

Regardless of how tight JFK's schedule happened
to be, he always made time for Frank Sinatra. On
February 7, 1960, flying from Texas to Oregon, Kennedy
decided to detour slightly by way of Las Vegas, where
Sinatra was currently playing the Sands Hotel.

Blair Clark, then working for CBS-Radio as moderator
of his own nightly news program, was aboard the *Caroline*
on this particular flight: "There were only five or six

news people on the plane—a couple of guys from the wire services, somebody with *The New York Times,* Mary McGrory and myself. We all figured, how bad can it be to catch Sinatra at the Sands?

"Once we reached the hotel, Mary and I were invited to Sinatra's suite for drinks while the singer finished dressing for his show. He had his entourage along—Dean Martin, Sammy Davis Jr., Joey Bishop, Peter Lawford. They had just completed filming *Ocean's 11,* and Lawford went on at great length describing the plot.

"After a while we went downstairs to the Sands Lounge. We were seated at Sinatra's table, and people kept coming and going, jumping up and sitting down. There were all these bimbos and showgirls standing around. And then there was one woman, quite attractive, with blue eyes and raven hair, whose name was Judith Campbell (Exner). It didn't mean a thing to me at the time; years later the pieces begin to fall into place."

Exner, 26 and divorced, was a failed Hollywood actress but a successful West Coast party girl. She and Sinatra had enjoyed a tempestuous fling, and it was Frank who passed her along to Kennedy. Although JFK wined and dined her the following day on the patio of Sinatra's hotel suite, their sexual involvement did not begin until March 7 (the day before the New Hampshire primary), when they rendezvoused at the Plaza Hotel in New York.

In the course of their relationship, which lasted until mid-1962, there were many encounters—in Las Vegas, Los Angeles, Chicago, Miami Beach, Palm Beach, Palm Springs, Washington, and New York. They met in hotels, motels, Jack's home in Georgetown (while Jackie vacationed in Florida), and on a number of occasions in the White House. Kennedy apparently lavished Exner with gifts, including a large diamond-and-ruby brooch and a $2,000 check to cover the cost of a new black diamond mink coat she had bought for herself. In addition they were in constant telephone contact. The White House logs revealed countless calls between them during Kennedy's first eighteen months in office.

The most intriguing aspect of their affair was the subsequent revelation of Exner's ties to the Mafia, particularly to figures such as Chicago crime boss Sam Giancana and his California lieutenant, John Roselli, both later recruited by the CIA, along with Florida Mafia chief

Santo Trafficante, in an ill-conceived plot to assassinate Cuban dictator Fidel Castro and at the same time compromise President Kennedy.

Attempting to capitalize on her relationship with JFK, Exner wrote a book in 1977, *My Story,* in which she traces her friendship with both Kennedy and Giancana (to whom Frank Sinatra also introduced her), admitting that Giancana became her chief benefactor, housing her and giving her valuable presents, yet wondering whether he might not somehow be using her "because I was the President's girl?"

Exner's next version appeared on February 29, 1988, when *People* magazine published an article, "The Dark Side of Camelot," by Kitty Kelley, essentially an extended interview with Exner, in which the former party girl "now dying of cancer" admits not only having lied in her book but also before a 1975 U.S. Senate Select Intelligence Committee investigating the failed Castro assassination caper. Exner's latest story had it that in addition to "sexually servicing" JFK, she had been his personal courier regularly delivering envelopes from Kennedy to both Giancana and Roselli, and less often back to Kennedy. Presumably, according to Exner, these parcels contained secret communications between Kennedy and the Mafia soliciting their intervention in the West Virginia primary, and, later, as prospective "hit men" in the Castro plot. Exner also claims in *People* (she and Kelley split a fee of $100,000 for the piece) that she arranged a number of personal meetings between Kennedy and Giancana, at least one of which she herself attended.

Despite numerous flaws and inconsistencies in Exner's several accounts, the fact remains that while dating Kennedy she did maintain ties to the Mafia, and that Kennedy, aware of those ties, nevertheless continued to see her.* We know also from FBI documents and wiretaps that JFK had direct contact with Mob figures Meyer Lansky and Joe Fischetti, and very likely benefitted politically from Mafia money and muscle in Texas, Illinois and West Virginia.**

---

*A discussion of some of these flaws and inconsistencies follows in the source notes section (chapter 15) at the back of this book.
**FBI documents indicate that Sam Giancana, eager to dispose of a

"Judith Exner liked to flatter herself," contended Peter Lawford. "She began to believe she meant something to Jack. She thought he cared for her. But Jack wasn't the type to confuse sex with love, not even when it involved somebody as glamouous and famous as Marilyn Monroe."

Jack and Marilyn first met at Peter and Pat Lawford's home in 1957 but saw little of each other until 1959 when JFK arranged to spend several uninterrupted days in Palm Springs with Marilyn. It was there that their affair began.

Peter Lawford had been aware from the beginning of the possible dangers, as well as the potential benefits, that their relationship might bring. Since products are often sold by star endorsement, Marilyn's closeness could be a boon to Kennedy's campaign. Conversely, his friendship could affect her future happiness. The other possibility, of course, was the peril of exposure. Nobody would elect for President a man known to be cheating on his wife and humiliating his family. There was concern among JFK's aides, particularly when they learned that Marilyn Monroe planned on being with him during the 1960 Democratic National Convention in Los Angeles, while Jackie remained behind in Hyannis Port.

Aside from the selection of Lyndon Baines Johnson as his running mate, John F. Kennedy's first-ballot victory in Los Angeles on July 13, 1960, afforded few surprises. Bobby Kennedy had arrived in town a week early and established a command post in a four-room suite at the Hotel Biltmore. Joe and Rose Kennedy moved into Marion Davies's Beverly Hills mansion. Joe had a battery of telephones installed poolside and did his best to keep out of sight, allowing Rose to represent him at the actual

---

federal surveillance operation directed against the Giancana Chicago crime syndicate, tried to curry favor with JFK by dispatching illegal Atlantic City casino operator Paul "Skinny" D'Amato to West Virgina with instructions to distribute bribes to local sheriffs and other poll officials. The same documents, however, make clear that D'Amato's influence was at most minimal. The most important factor in the West Virginia primary was probably the presence in JFK's camp of Franklin D. Roosevelt, Jr. It had been Joe Kennedy's idea to recruit the late president's son, whose family name was revered throughout the state. President Roosevelt had been the one to give the miners the right to organize and earn a decent wage.

convention (the chant among JFK's opponents went: "Jack and Bobby run the show, while Ted's in charge of hiding Joe"). Jack Kennedy reserved his own suite at the Biltmore but also sublet actor Jack Haley's penthouse apartment at 522 North Rossmore Boulevard, as well as a second apartment at the same address, a mere ten-minute drive from the convention site, the Los Angeles Memorial Sports Arena.

As expected, Jackie remained in Hyannis Port, content to follow the proceedings on a small, rented television set, relieved to be spared the pressure and chaos that had marked the Democratic Convention at Chicago four years earlier. She also spoke daily with her sister Lee, who attended the convention with Prince Stanislas "Stas" Radziwill, the roly-poly, mustachioed, Polish-born nobleman she had married in March 1959. Stas, twenty years Lee's senior, had emigrated to England in 1946 and entered the construction and real estate business. Like other members of the family, he had been recruited to campaign for JFK and gave speeches in Boston, Newport, Los Angeles, San Francisco and Milwaukee. During the convention, the Radziwills occupied a suite at the Beverly Hilton.

California Democratic Party chief Joe Cerrell observed that Frank Sinatra remained "extremely busy behind the scenes" organizing a $100-a-plate fund-raising dinner at the Beverly Hilton attended by nearly 3,000 JFK supporters, including Hollywood stars Janet Leigh, Tony Curtis, Angie Dickinson, Milton Berle, George Jessel, Rhonda Fleming, Judy Garland, and the entire Rat Pack. Jack sat next to Judy Garland at the head table, while Sinatra sat at the end of the same table with the other Democratic candidates—Adlai Stevenson, Stuart Symington and Lyndon Johnson.

Sinatra and his Pack were highly visible during the convention, opening it on July 11 with a jazzy rendition of the national anthem, then prowling the sports arena floor in an effort to influence undecided delegates. He and Peter Lawford took turns bartending at a cocktail party organized by Joe Kennedy at the Davies mansion. He lined up comedian Mort Sahl to deliver one of his satirical monologues before JFK's acceptance speech.

"There was an atmosphere of euphoria and exuberance in L.A. during that eventful week," said Peter

Lawford. "The Eisenhower administration had been like an enormous national tranquilizer. Finally the Democrats had a candidate who could inject some excitement and idealism back into the American bloodstream."

The accusations that John F. Kennedy was too young, too Catholic ("He's such a *poor* Catholic," Jackie told columnist Arthur Krock), too rich and too sickly, continued to be heard long after his nomination. When Lyndon Johnson grumbled that he "wouldn't be pushed around by a forty-three-year-old boy," he meant JFK. Eisenhower referred to him as "that young fellow." Dr. Janet Travell recalled the attempted burglary of Jack's medical records from her New York office and the subsequent disclosure by the Johnson camp that despite his age, JFK had a mysterious ailment (Addison's disease) which could prevent his completion of even a single term in office.

Betty Carson Hickman, a member of Lyndon Johnson's Senate staff, remarked that "every delegate [at the convention] was provided by the Kennedy group with anything they wanted for their entertainment including liquor and women sent to their room. It was felt that the campaign was bought by Joseph Kennedy for Jack: that was the general feeling, I think, of everyone. It was a regrettable thing that it was that way."

The one unmentionable theme both among members of the press and Kennedy's political adversaries was his philandering. As Betty Carson Hickman explained it, "There was sort of a gentleman's agreement in Washington that you don't talk about my private life and I don't talk about yours. . . . I'm grateful now that it's coming to light. Not for the people that are already gone—I hate to see it brought out because of their children—but I think now our politicians are realizing they have to live a cleaner life and uphold the morals a little better, which I think they should."

In her book on their relationship, Judith Exner writes of a meeting with Jack in a suite at the Beverly Hilton on the opening night of the convention, at which he attempted to talk her into participating in a *ménage à trois,* introducing her to "a tall, thin, secretarial type in her late twenties, with brownish hair and rather sharp features." When Exner resisted, Kennedy told her, "I know you; I know you'll enjoy it."*

*Judith Exner, with Ovid Demaris, *My Story,* pp. 164-165.

Apparently Frank Sinatra had tried to interest her in the same sexual activity. She had refused then, and she refused now.

What spare time Kennedy managed during the remainder of the convention was spent primarily with Marilyn Monroe, whose marriage to playwright Arthur Miller was about to dissolve. She had also recently engaged in a highly publicized affair with Yves Montand, her co-star in the aptly titled film *Let's Make Love* (1960), who keenly disappointed her by ending the affair. He did not want to leave his wife, Simone Signoret. Marilyn had hoped for more than a fling. Now she looked to John Kennedy.

On the second night of the convention, Marilyn joined Kennedy for dinner at Puccini's, a local restaurant owned by Frank Sinatra and a handful of silent partners. They were accompanied by Peter Lawford and Ken O'Donnell.

"Of all his 'other' women, Marilyn was perhaps the best for him," opined Lawford. "They were good together. They both had charisma, and they both had a sense of humor. Marilyn was saying that night that Jack's performance was 'very democratic' and 'very penetrating.' She also came up with that wonderful line, 'I think I made his back feel better.'

"Jack liked to pat and squeeze her. He was touching her here and there under the table when this bemused expression suddenly crossed his face. Marilyn said later he had put his hand up her dress and discovered she wore no underwear."

Marilyn was part of the crowd of 100,000 that jammed the Los Angeles Coliseum on July 15 to hear Kennedy give a rousing acceptance speech. She attended a skinny-dipping party at the Lawfords that night, and a day later turned up at the victory bash Joe Kennedy gave for his son at Romanoff's.

"There were a lot of mixed emotions at the Romanoff's restaurant affair," reflected George Smathers. "Members of the Kennedy camp felt betrayed because JFK had chosen Lyndon Johnson as his running mate. Without Johnson, Jack would never have won the election, yet the Kennedy people were relentless in their criticism of LBJ.

"Much of it had to do with the simple fact that he came from Texas, a region that conjures up images of cowboys, ten-gallon hats, guns, rodeos, outdoor barbecues, chili dogs, Texas ranger *machismo* and the Alamo. From that point of view, LBJ seemed the quintessential Texan: big, loud, brash, stubborn, pushy, vulgar and combative. Nobody in the Kennedy family and none of Jack's followers recognized any of his positive points. He had remarkable energy, an intensely analytical mind, rare comic gifts, and a Populist bent that made him eager to make life better for the masses of people. He was gregarious, friendly, sharp as a whip and probably the best legislator this country has ever had."

Having spent an extra day in Los Angeles to be with Marilyn Monroe, Jack Kennedy flew into Boston on July 17, greeted some 13,000 supporters at Logan Airport, switched planes and flew on to Cape Cod.

In anticipation of his arrival, Jackie had completed a drawing of JFK attired as George Washington, sailing into Hyannis Port aboard the *Victura* and being greeted at the pier by dogs, cats, children, grandmothers, a marching band (bearing a banner that read "WELCOME BACK, MR. JACK"), the inevitable hordes, as well as Jackie and Caroline.

Earlier that day, two hairdressers arrived at her home to shape her hair in the "high bouffant style she likes," preparatory to the arrival of her husband's plane at Barnstable Municipal Airport in Hyannis that evening. She then held a 45-minute press conference on the front porch of Joe Kennedy's house, fielding questions from a large excited choir of international newspaper, radio and television correspondents. The interview continued for another ninety minutes when a somewhat smaller group followed Jackie back into her own house, yelling questions as they walked.

By mid-afternoon Jackie was resting in her bedroom. Two days earlier, JFK had made arrangements with Hyannis Port neighbor Larry Newman to bring his wife to the airport to meet his plane. Somebody else in the Kennedy camp had asked Frank Morrissey, an old family crony, to do the same thing. Morrissey drove up from Boston and arrived shortly before 6:00 p.m. He encountered Newman.

"Don't worry about Jackie," said Morrissey. "I'll take care of her."

"Good luck," said Newman.

Morrissey entered the house and was directed to Jackie's bedroom on the second floor. He went up and started to talk to her. Momentarily, her voice loud for a change, Jackie could be heard throughout the house.

"Get out! Out! I don't want anything to do with you!"

On his way back to the car, Morrissey passed Newman.

"She seems to have changed her mind," said Morrissey. "She says she doesn't want to go."

Newman went up to her room and found her sitting on her bed. She had thought about it, she said, and she no longer wanted to go.

"I'm not going out there because Jack's plane will land and I'll be met by some Democratic Party committee-woman with a bouquet of tired red roses. Then Jack will head for the fence and I'll be left standing in the middle of the airport all by myself."

"Well, Jackie, I'll tell you what," said Newman. "Once you get to the airport, you're never going to be without somebody at your side because I'll be there until the last dog barks."

"Oh, all right, I'll go," said Jackie, resigned to her fate.

Joined by her fifteen-year-old half-sister, Janet Auchin-closs, Jackie and Newman drove to the airport and arrived in time to meet the plane. When it landed she quickly boarded, reappearing with her husband framed behind her in the airplane's open doorway as a roar went up from the crowd that was straining against a fence and police barricades.

"Kiss him, Jackie," shouted several photographers in unison. Kennedy broke off and went to the fence to shake hands. A Democratic Party committeewoman appeared and handed Jackie a bouquet of red roses before vanishing into the crowd. Jackie cast a knowing look at Newman. The two stood in the middle of the tarmac watching as Jack electioneered along the fence.

"What did I tell you?" said Jackie.

"And what did I tell you?" said Newman.

"Come on," she said. "Let's go home."

News of Jack and Marilyn Monroe had filtered back to Jacqueline. She brooded about her husband's latest affair and purportedly told her friend Walter Sohier, a George-town socialite, she wasn't certain if Jack's recent nomina-tion "signaled a beginning or an end."

She visited Truman Capote in New York. "Thank God, I'm pregnant," she told him. "I get to miss all those dreadful chicken dinners."

"She had no desire to resume the campaign," confirmed Capote. "She felt she'd contributed her share. She had helped Kennedy win the Democratic nomination. He and Lyndon Johnson would have to defeat GOP nominees Richard Milhous Nixon and Henry Cabot Lodge, Jr., on their own."

Lem Billings visited the Kennedys at Hyannis Port and helped mediate an argument between Jack and Jackie over her future role in the race. "Jack told her that Pat Nixon would stand behind her husband, and that if she didn't do the same he couldn't possibly win. All she had to do was smile and talk about Caroline."

Billings left and Norman Mailer arrived, intent on interviewing JFK for a soon-to-be-celebrated *Esquire* article, "Superman Comes to the Supermart," which subsequently reappeared in his book, *Presidential Papers*. Mailer, inappropriately attired in a formal black suit (and "sweating like a goat"), found himself in Jackie's yellow and white living room with a group that included Arthur Schlesinger and his wife; Stas Radziwill; *Saturday Evening Post* writer Peter Maas; campaign photographer Jacques Lowe; and JFK press secretary Pierre Salinger. Jackie offered him a drink—iced verbena tea with a sprig of mint—and made halting conversation with the author. Mailer sensed Jacqueline's controlled exasperation at having to entertain this small cordon of invaders. He found her distant, detached, moody and abstracted. After the piece came out, Jackie wrote him a note, a sort of "thank-you-for-your-good-words" letter; and he wrote her back saying, "Thank you for your praise."

Hostessing and writing letters seemed to be the extent to which Jackie wished to become involved at this stage of the presidential sweepstakes. To Arthur Krock she wrote that she hadn't so much as read the Democratic platform and had no intention of doing so. She gave a successful luncheon for some sixty Washington newspaper editors and reporters, and managed a Sunday buffet for representatives of various civil rights groups.

After the Republican convention, Lyndon and Lady Bird Johnson arrived in Hyannis Port for a visit with the Kennedys. While the two men conferred with several of

JFK's advisers, Jackie gave Lady Bird a tour of the house. Afterwards, Jackie said: "I feel so totally inadequate, so totally at a loss. Here I am at the time Jack needs me most, and I'm pregnant, and I don't know how to do anything."

"Well, you know what?" responded Lady Bird. "This is a charming house and it has your touch all over it. If I were you, I'd find one or two reporters and have them in and talk about your home. You could do that."

Accompanied by Betty Carson Hickman, the Johnsons returned to the Kennedy home the following day. According to Hickman, "Jack Kennedy could not have been more gracious. He came over three or four times. 'Betty, can I get you more coffee? What can I do?' And he was very gracious to everyone. But Jacqueline didn't even speak to Lady Bird.

"She hardly acknowledged that we were in the room and . . . went off to another part of the house . . . and was just above it all. To me, that was not being a lady. That sort of thing really disturbed me and I was afraid that the Johnsons wouldn't be treated with the respect they were due."

In the final analysis, the two people most responsible for Jackie's reemergence in the race were Joe Alsop, the columnist, and Joan Braden, the wife of liberal California newspaper publisher Tom Braden. Alsop visited Jackie at Hyannis Port that summer and found her in a highly agitated state, worried not only about her pregnancy but about the continuing onslaught of publicity, the unrelenting assault by the media upon her tightly guarded privacy. She expressed reservations about becoming First Lady, complained that she had nothing in common with Lady Bird, railed against the press for revealing that she had bought her maternity wardrobe at Bloomingdale's and had paid $34.95 for a new silk tea dress off the rack at Lord & Taylor.

Jackie told Alsop she was appalled at some of the personal questions asked by members of the press, and disgusted by the photographers who chased "poor little Caroline around with flashbulbs, wanting to turn her into a ghastly little Shirley Temple." She was similarly fed up with the Kennedy sisters—"They adore Jack and would do anything to get their names in print."

Alsop made Jackie understand that in trying to avoid

publicity she was only drawing more attention to herself, that she would be noticed whether she became First Lady or not. Even if she were plain Mrs. Kennedy of New York, London and the Riviera, people would know where she bought her clothes, he said. But what had that to do with her private self?

Running for President, according to Alsop, was the only game "worth the candle." He told Jackie she had no respect for power, probably because it had come so suddenly without her having had to work for it—power by marriage. But if everything worked out, she would welcome the power and hopefully use it for the things she cared about.

Joan Braden, introduced to the Kennedys by Joe Alsop, played a more direct and practical role in Jackie's reawakening: "I suggested six things Jackie could do to help in the race. Jack and Bobby said yes to all of them but didn't know how to persuade Jackie. I only convinced her because we were both equally pregnant. The only difference was that I didn't lose babies, and she did, so it became essential that she not exceed the limits of her endurance. I was used to working while pregnant. My husband and I were the models for the television series *Eight Is Enough*. As a result I not only mapped out Jackie's duties during the second phase of the campaign, I helped her fulfill them.

"If we had national television offers, for example, I often made the decisions—would she do this show or that show; will she appear here or there? Then I would accompany her to the TV studio, or if she did it from home I would stay there with her. When Jackie wouldn't talk to the press, which she refused to do on a number of occasions, they could come to me. I had been in and out of the press and I'd written newspaper articles; and my husband, of course, was in the business. I lived in that world, and many of our friends were in radio and television. Jackie didn't have that experience, although she'd been an inquiring photographer. But that's not reporting. If somebody like columnist Joe Kraft wanted to ask Jackie a question, he would just as often call me and ask it.

"During the campaign Jackie told me on several occasions she was afraid of losing the baby. She had flown through very inclement weather to campaign with Jack in Delaware and Maine. I didn't think it would make much

difference if she missed some other states. Jack's aides
saw New York as pivotal and wanted her to make the
trip. There was a tremendous amount of pressure on her.
I told her not to go. Her obstetrician, Dr. John Walsh,
advised against it, but Jackie said, 'If I don't go and Jack
loses, I'll never forgive myself.'

"She went. She spoke Spanish in Spanish Harlem,
Italian in Little Italy, and French in a Haitian neighborhood. JFK carried New York. I went along. We stayed at
the Waldorf. Jackie didn't go to everything. To relax one
afternoon, she and Bill Walton went gallery hopping on
Madison Avenue. That's the kind of thing she loved to
do. She was still unknown enough so she could do this
without creating a mob scene. And nobody knew Walton
of course. I remember at a campaign luncheon in New
York, Jack and Jackie were sitting about five seats apart,
and Jackie said, 'This is the closest I've come to lunching
with my husband in months. I haven't seen him since
Labor Day.'

"The highlight of the campaign for Jackie was the
ticker-tape parade through New York's financial district
where, perched with Jack on the back of an open car, she
experienced both fear and exhilaration as a huge crowd
jostled and shoved and flung themselves into their path.
Being on Wall Street reminded Jackie of her father. She
said later he would have been proud of her."

The climax of the campaign for John F. Kennedy could
only have been his four nationally televised one-hour
"debates" with Richard Nixon in September and October
1960. While debates have been a political tradition in the
United States since the time of Lincoln and Douglas,
these were the first presidential debates in history to be
broadcast on television. In a political race as close as this
one, the outcome of the debates all but determined the
winner of the election.

On September 26, Langdon Marvin accompanied Jack
to Chicago for the first debate. "The trip reminded me of
a scene out of the movie *The Candidate,* with Robert
Redford," said Marvin. "That film must have been based
in part on Jack's campaign, particularly in terms of
sexuality.

"We had recently returned from New Orleans, where
Jack spent 20 minutes making love to stripper Blaze Starr

in the closet of a hotel suite while her fiancé, Governor Earl Long, held a party in the next room. In the closet, Jack found the time to tell Blaze the story of President Warren G. Harding's making love to his mistress Nan Britton in a White House closet.

"The night before the debate, Jack said to me, 'Any girls lined up for tomorrow?' So I made arrangements to have a girl waiting for him in a room at the Palmer House. I took him down there about 90 minutes before airtime, rode up in the elevator with him, introduced him to the girl (she'd been prepaid for her services), then stood guard in the corridor outside the hotel room. Jack evidently enjoyed himself, because he emerged fifteen minutes later with an ear-to-ear grin on his face.

"During the debate he looked the picture of self-assurance and good health. Nixon, meanwhile, looked like an escaped convict—pallid, perspiring, beady-eyed. Jack was so pleased by the results he insisted we line up a girl for him before each of the debates."

Mary Tierney recalled covering a series of TV listening parties that Jackie hosted during the debates, which were attended by national committeewomen and their husbands and the State Chairmen and Co-Chairmen of Citizens for Kennedy-Johnson, as well as friends, relatives and members of the press.

"Jackie was pregnant at the time, and we all had to sit there and watch her reactions to the debate," said Tierney. "She did a lot of hand-wringing. She was like a silly schoolgirl, saying, 'What do I say? What do I do?' It was so ridiculous. She was such a jerk.

"We'd ask her, 'Well what do you think, Jackie?' And she'd say, 'Well . . .you know.' She took the most inane, baby doll approach to this thing."

Jackie also participated in a television interview conducted by actor Henry Fonda in which she apparently performed with a bit more verve. Dorothy Schiff, then owner-publisher of the *New York Post,* told Kennedy she thought Jackie had done well on the show. Kennedy agreed that his wife performed better on television than in personal interviews. Recounting her meeting with JFK for the benefit of a biographer, Schiff remarked: "He was utterly cold in his remarks about her, and I had a feeling he had very little interest in her except as she affected his campaign.''*

In one of Jackie's last interviews before the election, she was asked by Betty Beale whether she intended, if she became First Lady, to continue to jump into her car and rush down to Middleburg, Virginia, where she rode to hounds at the Orange County Hunt Club.

Once again proclaiming her independence, Jackie said, "That's one thing I won't give up."

On November 8, Election Day, Jack and Jacqueline went together to the polling section at the West End Library in Boston. Jackie wore a small gold pin fashioned as a donkey (the Democratic Party symbol) with a sapphire for an eye and tiny diamond chips for ears. JFK gave an identical pin to Lady Bird Johnson as a token of appreciation for her help in the campaign.

Over Bloody Marys, Jackie later informed Arthur Schlesinger that she had cast only one vote—for Jack: "It is a rare thing to be able to vote for one's husband as President of the United States, and I didn't want to dilute it by voting for anyone else."

Because of her pregnancy Jackie actually had voted by absentee ballot; she had accompanied her husband to the polls only for the benefit of the press. But contrary to what she told Schlesinger, she had also voted for Eddie McLaughlin for lieutenant governor. Tip O'Neill, a steadfast Kennedy backer, expressed acute disappointment over Jackie's failure to support him for Congress: "I was crushed, and I couldn't understand how she could do that to me." Other Democrats ignored by Jackie felt similarly let down.

Jackie's political hardness extended to members of her own family. For example, her stepsister Nina Auchincloss's marriage to Newton Steers, a campaign aide to Richard Nixon, temporarily severed family ties. Steers remembered a conversation between Jackie and Nina on the subject of politics: "Jackie was still talking to my then-wife, who, probably because of me, told Jackie that she would have to support Nixon. 'You mean you're voting for Milhous?' said Jackie. She seemed astounded. One of the national weeklies later ran an article on the rift,

*Jeffrey Potter, Men, Money & Magic: *The Story of Dorothy Schiff*, p. 261.

referring to me as 'A Republican in the Kennedy circle.' JFK didn't appreciate our sentiments. We saw him the night before he became president, and never laid eyes on him again until his funeral. We saw him on television but that was it. We were never invited to the White House. I daresay if I hadn't been politically involved, my wife would have gotten in on some of the Kennedy Camelot hoopla, but she didn't."

Jackie described the period between the closing of the polls and the moment of victory as "the longest night in history." She and Jack, Ben and Toni Bradlee, and Bill Walton had a quiet dinner at home in Hyannis Port, discussing art instead of politics. After dinner they settled in the living room to watch the returns slowly come in over television. Jackie spent part of the evening studying a stack of photographs taken of her and Jack during the campaign for use in case they won. They were joined by Ted Sorensen, while next door at Bobby's house, the rest of the family and aides were gathering reports by phone from workers across the country before they were registered by the television news commentators.

At 10:20 p.m., when early returns indicated a substantial lead for Kennedy, Jacqueline whispered, "Oh Bunny, you're President now."

"No . . . no . . . it's too early to tell," said Jack.

By 11:30, with Nixon pulling even and then slightly ahead, Jackie went to bed. Jack followed at 3:00 a.m., the election still undecided. But at 5:45 a.m., the Secret Service moved to establish security and surround the Hyannis Port house and compound. When he awoke at 7:00 a.m., John Fitzgerald Kennedy was President-elect, the youngest in history, his victory margin so slim—less than 115,000 popular votes out of the nearly 70 million cast—that Robert Kennedy, standing on his sofa in stocking feet, told reporters it was nothing less than "a miracle."

"Everyone, including myself and Janet Auchincloss, called JFK 'Mr. President,'" said Hughdie Auchincloss. "When he was elected we went from Jack to Mr. President overnight."

There were those, however, who resisted the formal title, particularly those who had known the President-elect from boyhood. Pharmacist Robert Green recalled the transition period in Palm Beach during those few exhilarating months, when Jack was selecting his cabinet and recuperating from the campaign. "Nothing had really changed about him. He was a completely natural guy. He still drove over to Green's for a hamburger at the lunch counter. He'd grab a couple of sports magazines from the rack and thumb through them while eating, then put them back. He never had any money with him. I told him it was on me, my contribution to the war chest.

"Jack always had great finesse. He could stick it to somebody and make them love it. He was that way both before and after he was elected President. The only difference was that after the election he was always surrounded by these Secret Service goons. But the crowd at Green's still called him Jack. One day when he was President-elect he came in for his hamburger. His Secret Servicemen couldn't believe it when we called him Jack. 'He's Mr. President,' one of them told me. 'Maybe to you he is,' I said, 'but to me he's Jack.' "

Marty Venker, a former Secret Service agent, remarked that before Kennedy learned to trust his Secret Service detail, he was forever "trying to lose them. They would turn their backs and he would jump into his convertible and take off. Then they'd have to drive all over Palm Beach looking for him.

"On one occasion he had his valet, an old black man named George Thomas, wrap him in a blanket and place him in the back seat of his car. The agent on duty stopped the car at the front gate. Kennedy stirred and the agent saw the blanket move. He drew his gun, put it to Thomas's temple and said, 'You ever do anything like that again and I'll blow your fucking brains out.' "

On another occasion JFK did manage to elude the Secret Service. The agents called in the FBI and finally turned to Palm Beach Police Chief Homer Large. Homer, a trusted Kennedy family associate, knew exactly where to find Jack. He was next door in Earl E. T. Smith's swimming pool. He and Flo Smith were alone, and as Homer put it, "They weren't doing the Australian crawl."*

---

*According to Earl Smith, "JFK wanted to appoint me ambassador to Switzerland, but Fidel Castro objected because the U.S. and Cuba no longer maintained diplomatic relations and Switzerland represented the U.S. in Cuba. Since I had been ambassador to Cuba under Eisenhower, Castro claimed my appointment to Switzerland

The imminent prospect of entering the White House didn't diminish JFK's need for new female conquests. Involved with Flo Pritchett Smith, Judith Exner and Marilyn Monroe, he now added movie and television star Angie Dickinson to his illustrious list. Although Angie has never publicly confirmed a relationship with Kennedy, she has made remarks of a suggestive and coy nature.

"He's the only presidential candidate who has ever turned me on," she said. "Naturally it was said, *printed*, that we were lovers. Even if I deny it now, I won't be believed."

On television's syndicated *PM Magazine*, she recently said of JFK: "He was wonderful. That's all I'll say. It would be bad manners to say more."

A widely circulated magazine called *Celebrity Sleuth* reports that Angie still keeps a photograph of the late president on her bureau with the following inscription: "Angie. To the only woman I've ever loved."

Other references abound. Betty Spalding, the former wife of Chuck Spalding, speculated that the relationship with Dickinson might have been serious, but that "he was going to be President, and he certainly couldn't take Angie Dickinson to the White House with him." Jackie Kennedy biographer Frieda Kramer *(Jackie: An Intimate Biography*, 1979) makes clear reference to "a lovely blonde actress, later to become the wife of a celebrated composer, who excited Jack's interest for a time." (Angie Dickinson later married composer Burt Bacharach.) Judith Campbell Exner writes of a meeting with the actress at which Angie exclaimed: "Judy Campbell! John has told me so much about you." Exner inferred that she meant John Kennedy.

Slim Aarons, a frequent visitor to Palm Springs, recalled that "Angie and JFK disappeared for two or three days in Palm Springs during the period before JFK as-

---

represented a conflict of interest. So my name was withdrawn, which was just as well because I didn't see eye-to-eye with JFK politically." Several books on the Kennedys have suggested that JFK wanted to send Earl Smith to Switzerland so he could have Flo to himself, an unlikelihood as Earl's wife would undoubtedly have accompanied him.

sumed office. They stayed in a cottage and never emerged. Everyone knew about it."

Joe Cerrell "didn't know that much about JFK's personal life, but I was privy to information about his relationship with Angie Dickinson. I knew about it at the time."

In a profile of Angie Dickinson published in the usually staid pages of *TV Guide,* the actress admitted she always found "powerful men attractive." She cited Frank Sinatra as an example and spoke frankly of her relationship with John Kennedy: "From the moment I met him, I was hooked, like everybody else. He was the sexiest politician I ever met. . . . He was the killer type, a devastatingly handsome, charming man—the kind your mother hoped you wouldn't marry."

For Jackie "the new era" started with new trepidations. She had overheard her husband ask a Secret Service man what degree of safety he thought possible for the President and his family. "Well, obviously there are plenty of loopholes," the agent responded. "If somebody wants to do it, he can do it."

Walter P. Reuther, President of the United Automobile Workers, and Jack Conway, future Deputy Director of the Office of Economic Opportunity, visited the Kennedys at Hyannis Port that fall. It was a crisp day, but the sun was warm, and the labor men sat on the beach talking with Jacqueline. "She really was obsessed," Conway said later, "with the whole idea of the change in her life, the change in Kennedy's life, and how do you protect against assassination." Reuther, himself wounded by mob gunmen in 1948, tried to assure her that the Secret Service used the most sophisticated law enforcement methods and strategies and that she had nothing to fear.

Jackie's obsessive need to protect her identity was probably what motivated her to start writing an autobiography at this point. By telling her own story, she hoped to dissuade others from tackling the subject, while also reinforcing many of the myths that had surrounded the Bouvier family, the greatest being that they were descendants of an upper-class French clan of the same surname.

Family intimate Mary Van Rensselaer Thayer jumped at the opportunity of working with Jackie on the project, and *Ladies' Home Journal* offered to pay $150,000 for

North American first serial rights, the first of four installments to appear the same month as Kennedy's inauguration. Doubleday would later publish a booklength version.*

Mary Bass Gibson, then executive editor of the *Journal*, remembered seeing "the first few chapters and thinking they were delightful. They described Jackie's childhood and her riding in horse shows, her poetry, her love of nature, her love of her father, things that were extremely appealing about Jackie Kennedy. And, of course, they were going to wind up with her husband's election and inauguration as President.

"It was intended to be an upbeat story, not a 'tell-all.' But I didn't realize until well into the project that Jackie herself was doing the writing. She used yellow lined paper and did not move out of bed. Mary would pick up the completed pages and go over them. Copy would come in each month, just barely making the press dates. Only Mary's name appeared in the byline, but it was Jackie's story and Jackie who wrote it. For better or worse, this is probably the only extended autobiographical work she will ever produce."

Jackie kept at the project until Thanksgiving, which she celebrated at home in Georgetown with Jack and Caroline. After dinner, Kennedy prepared to leave for the airport where his private plane was waiting to take him and his aides to Palm Beach. Jackie, whose baby was expected in three weeks, had spent much of the afternoon arguing with her husband. Reporters and photographers standing by the front door of the house watched it open and Jack depart.

The *Caroline* was halfway to Florida when an urgent radio message reached the plane: "Mrs. Kennedy has gone into early labor and has been rushed by ambulance to Georgetown University Hospital."

At the airport in West Palm Beach, Kennedy learned his wife was to undergo an emergency Caesarean operation. He immediately boarded the press plane that had accompanied the *Caroline* and returned to Washington. They were still airborne when news crackled through that Jackie had been delivered of a baby boy, John Jr., tiny at

*The Doubleday edition, a biography titled simply *Jacqueline Bouvier Kennedy*, by Mary Van Rensselaer Thayer, was published in 1961.

6 lbs. 3 ozs. and in need of incubation, but active and in satisfactory health.

On regaining consciousness, Jackie dismissed the pain and discomfort and asked to see her baby. As she was being wheeled into the nursery, a news photographer burst from a storage closet in the hospital corridor and aimed his camera at her. When Jackie saw him, she cried out, and a pair of Secret Service agents appeared, pounced on the intruder, confiscated his camera and exposed the film.

The photographer episode made the press, but an incident occurred on the Sunday following the birth that has remained buried to this day. Thomas L. Souder, then a lieutenant with the Seventh Precinct of the Washington, D.C., Police Department, was in charge of police security during Jackie's stay at Georgetown University Hospital. On the Sunday in question, Lieutenant Souder was Acting Police Captain.

"We had several policemen in and around the hospital," recalled Souder. "But it was a nurse who first spotted this fellow in his late teens or early twenties walking around a grassy area under Jackie's window. Her room was on the fifth floor and the windows were open.

"The nurse called the police, and a patrol car intercepted him. He was carrying a package containing five sticks of dynamite. When I got there, the package was on the ground and the cops had placed this man under arrest.

"I called the Army Bomb Squad and when their people carted off the explosives, I called Deputy George Waldrodt, Acting Chief of Police. What did they want me to do with the perpetrator? Waldrodt said he would get back to me. He telephoned a few minutes later. 'Send him downtown,' he told me. 'We'll want to interrogate him. Then send me a report by messenger, and forget it ever happened. Don't make any carbons, don't make any copies, don't mention it—now or ever.'

"They swept it up the line and under the rug. They never booked the guy, because that would have entailed all sorts of unwanted publicity. My guess is that somebody upstairs talked it over with Secret Service, Secret Service discussed it with the President-elect, and the President-elect said something like, 'I don't want any unnecessary noise. It'll only frighten Jackie.' And that was the end of it, until now—28 years later."

Blissfully unaware of the situation, Jackie slowly regained her strength. For the first five days she was too exhausted to leave her bed and began to recover only when they removed the baby from his incubator. Jack Kennedy returned to Palm Beach, and Jackie caught up with a week's backlog of newspapers. In the *Washington Post* she read that she had been rushed to the hospital for her Caesarean when she began "to hemorrhage." Through Pierre Salinger she sent word to the *Post* that the use of that particular phrase was in questionable taste. Maxine Cheshire, who had written the story, complained to her editor that Jackie was beginning to sound like something out of a 19th-century novel—too aristocratic to want to be described in such clinical terms.

A week after giving birth, Jackie sat pensively, alone, wrapped in a long black suede coat, on the enclosed roof of the hospital. Another patient happened along and recognized Jackie from her picture. "Excuse me, aren't you Mrs. Kennedy?" she asked. Jackie bowed her head and sighed resignedly. A few minutes later she returned to her room.

Feeling stronger, Jackie resumed her autobiography and went about the delicate business of selecting a personal White House staff, including her own dressmaker. Although Lady Bird Johnson had offered to have Stanley Marcus (of Nieman-Marcus fame) send Jackie sketches for an inaugural gown, Jackie had already ordered hers from Ethel Franco, head of the designer fashion salon at Bergdorf Goodman. Yet Jackie realized she would need her own couturier in the White House and began to think of suitable names. The only prerequisite was that he be an American, either native or naturalized. Her friend Oleg Cassini, a man of Russian ancestry who was raised in Florence, Italy, and arrived in America in 1936, came to mind. She sent for him. He interrupted a vacation with Jill St. John in Nassau, and arrived at Georgetown University Hospital bearing a portfolio of sketches.

Although Jackie admired Cassini's skill as a fashion designer, it was his continental manner that especially appealed to her. It helped that he had made a generous contribution to JFK's West Virginia primary campaign fund, and that along the way he had earned Joe Kennedy's everlasting gratitude by introducing him to a bevy of attractive young women. But the most weighty consideration from Jackie's standpoint was Ambassador Joe's offer to pay all her clothing expenses should she opt for Cassini.*

Jackie wanted to be dressed, she later wrote to Cassini, as if "Jack were President of France." She realized she was "so much more of fashion interest than other first ladies," but she didn't want her husband's administration "plagued by fashion stories of a sensational nature." She insisted she didn't want to be "the Marie Antoinette or Empress Josephine of the 1960s" and that she didn't wish to "seem to be buying too much." She therefore insisted on approving any publicity Cassini put out and requested that he "make sure no one has exactly the same dress as I do. . . . I want all mine to be original and no fat little women hopping around in the same gown." Above all, she demanded "protection"—"as I seem so mercilessly exposed and don't know how to cope with it. I read tonight I dye my hair because it is mousy gray."

On December 9, the day John Jr. was baptized in the small chapel at Georgetown University Hospital, Jackie kept an appointment with Mamie Eisenhower for the traditional housekeeping briefing of the incoming mistress of the White House. Jackie's Secret Service agent had phoned ahead and asked that the White House have a wheelchair waiting for Mrs. Kennedy when she arrived, as she was still subject to spells of dizziness and exhaustion. Envisioning herself having to push her successor through the long corridors of the mansion, Mrs. Eisenhower instructed her staff to keep the wheelchair out of sight in a closet, and make it available only if Jackie asked.

She didn't ask. She felt too self-conscious. She also felt ill at ease in the presence of her hostess. When she left, Jackie looked not only weary but upset. She told Letitia Baldrige, her new social secretary, that the place looked like "a hotel that had been decorated by a wholesale furniture store during a January clearance."

*Mortimer M. Caplin, former Director of the Internal Revenue Service under President Kennedy, told the author that Joe Kennedy once asked him, "With all the dresses Jackie has to wear for special occasions, are they deductible?" Caplin thought Joe Kennedy was jesting. But he wasn't because he raised the same question with his own accountants.

That same day Jackie took her children—John Jr. and three-year-old Caroline—to the Kennedy home in Palm Beach, determined to stay in seclusion until the January inauguration, and perhaps beyond.

But it was not to be. On Sunday morning, December 11, two days after Jackie's arrival, an incident took place that again involved explosives, but this time in such a way as to preclude secrecy. At 9:50 a.m., a car that was being driven along one of Palm Beach's oceanfront boulevards slowed down and came to a halt across the street from the Joseph P. Kennedy estate. Inside the house were members of the Kennedy family, among them the President-elect, his wife and their two young children.

According to Secret Service files, the driver of the car was a retired 73-year-old postal clerk from Belmont, New Hampshire, named Richard P. Pavlick, who had previously made threats against the life of John F. Kennedy and whose name was already familiar to those guarding the next president. Pavlick's car, it would later be learned, contained seven sticks of dynamite (three additional sticks were found in his motel room) that could be detonated by the simple closing of a knife switch. Pavlick's intention, as detailed in a rambling and disjointed statement, was to wait until Kennedy entered his car, then drive his own car forward into Kennedy's, close the knife switch, and blow up himself, JFK, the Secret Service agents, and anyone else who happened to be there.

Undetected, Pavlick watched the front of the house. He somehow knew that shortly before 10:00 a.m., Kennedy would be going to Sunday Mass. He saw the President-elect's car. A Secret Service agent sat behind the wheel, another stood beside the rear door. Minutes later the front door of the house opened and John Kennedy emerged, flanked by other members of his Secret Service detail, as well as Jacqueline, Caroline, several nieces and nephews, and John Jr. in the arms of the family nurse Luella Hennessey. The would-be assassin watched them embrace and laugh. And in that instant Pavlick was struck by a passing impulse, of remorse, guilt, even fascination. He did not, he later said, "wish to harm Mrs. Kennedy or the children. I decided to get him at the church or some other place." Kennedy waved to his family, stepped into his car and went on his way. Pavlick drove off in the opposite direction. His plan never materialized. On Thursday, December 15, he was arrested for reckless driving and turned over to Secret Service agents, who charged him with attempted murder and unlawful possession of dynamite. He subsequently spent six years in various federal prisons and mental institutions.

The incident had a chilling effect on everyone but Kennedy. A few days later, local pharmacist Robert Green passed Jack on the street and threw an arm around him. Three Secret Service agents went for their guns. Nobody was more shaken up than Jackie. "We're nothing but sitting ducks in a shooting gallery," she lamented. "From that day," said Lem Billings, "she was convinced that sooner or later they would all be blown to smithereens."

16

On January 16, 1961, six weeks after leaving for Palm Beach, Jackie returned to Washington, D.C., aboard the *Caroline*. She was by herself. All the Kennedy women and her own mother were in the receiving lines at the "Reception for Distinguished Ladies" at the National Art Gallery. Dressed in a black-and-white tweed suit and wearing a little red turban, Jackie slid into the front seat of a green sedan, driven by a member of the Secret Service, and headed for her Georgetown home. She had left her children behind in Palm Beach.

Her house was in disarray, crates and boxes and suitcases scattered everywhere, clothes piled on top of clothes, ornaments and books spread across couches and settees. Tish Baldridge directed traffic downstairs; Jackie's Spanish-speaking maid, Providencia "Provy" Parades, appeared to be in charge of the rest of the house.

The first bold designs for Camelot were beginning to take shape in Jackie's mind. While in Palm Beach she had tried to put the Pavlick incident into perspective by focusing on the immediate task of preparing for the White House. Chief usher J.B. West had sent albums of elaborately annotated photographs of many of the Executive Mansion's 132 rooms, which she studied and analyzed until she was familiar with every detail.

She had spoken at length about the White House with Sister Parish, who had been her interior decorator on the N Street house as well as her home at Hyannis Port. Sister arrived in Washington with ideas and a great many samples of furnishings, carpeting and wallpaper.

"I'd only seen photographs of the interior of the White House," said Mrs. Parish. "I didn't get inside until the day before Inauguration Day. We walked from room to room, opening closet doors and peeking into dark corners. My first reaction was that something had to be done. There was a great deal that I didn't like, much that would have to be discarded and replaced.

"The private living quarters were in terrible shape—spots on the carpets, falling plaster, handprints on the walls, peeling wallpaper, tattered draperies. All this could be easily repaired. The greater problem had to do with the formal public rooms. Most of the furniture that had been originally there was gone. The formal rooms contained a hodgepodge of tables and chairs. The furniture lacked historic relevance. It wasn't furniture that had belonged to any of the Presidents. It was stuff the White House had picked up along the way.

"I told Mrs. Kennedy that to do the White House justice, it would have to be restored from top to bottom. To accomplish a project of that magnitude required the cooperation of a committee, maybe even several committees. Otherwise it would take years to finish. I suggested that Mrs. Kennedy make this her pet project.

"She asked me to select the people I thought would be right for such a committee. That's how it all began. I chose the original committee. Other members were recruited at a later date. The original committee evolved into a whole organization. There were meetings all the time, mostly at the White House. Mrs. Kennedy was included in everything. There were few meetings that she didn't attend. She became a kind of overseer, coordinating with everybody, which wasn't easy because there were so many fragile egos involved. Occasionally the meetings became quite explosive."

Jackie's other major concern had been the inauguration, including what clothes to wear to the various functions. Although Bergdorf's designed her dress for the swearing-in ceremony, Oleg Cassini created a long, fawn-colored wool coat with a sable collar (to wear over the dress) and a matching sable muff (fashion doyenne Diana Vreeland's suggestion) for her hands. It was Halston who devised the fur-trimmed pillbox hat that Jackie wore on the back of her head. The pillbox, which actually had been around for years, helped boost "Her Elegance" (as *Womens Wear Daily* dubbed Jackie) to the top of every best-dressed list in Europe and the United States, giving rise to "the Jackie look," a revolution in style that included low heels, cloth coats in bright colors and Chanel-type suits. The "Jackie look" was the beginning of the Courrèges look or the so-called "little girl look." In short, a flaring baby doll appearance as adopted by a grown woman. In many ways Jackie was the original Youthquaker.*

"The common misconception about her is that she wanted to become a fashion trendsetter," said Oleg Cassini. "Nothing could be further from the truth. Jackie basically had her own carefully directed style. She dressed for herself. She wanted to be noticed, not copied. But it was clear from the beginning that anybody with Jackie's exotic beauty and high visibility was bound to have a profound influence on fashion."

Cassini designed the gowns Jackie would wear to the other inaugural functions, for the most part following precise instructions that Jackie herself provided. Matching footwear (size 10 1/2) was ordered from Eugenia of Florence. Tish Baldridge, once employed at Tiffany's, arranged to have them lend Jackie a sparkling diamond ensemble for the occasion. Jackie requested that her Palm Beach masseuse (a Swede once quoted as saying that Jackie had the coolest skin she had ever touched) fly to Washington, as well as Kenneth, her devoted hair stylist. Kenneth brought along his assistant, Rosemary Sorrentino, who had been straightening Jackie's hair since she had been a customer of Michael Kazan.

One task to which Jackie applied herself with mixed emotions was the compilation of a list of relatives, now comprising five families, to be invited to the inauguration and to several private gatherings scheduled to follow the swearing-in ceremony. The Bouviers, Auchinclosses, Lees, Fitzgeralds and Kennedys were as incompatible as the tribes of Babylon, and Jackie dreaded the prospect of contending with them all at once. To the family list she

---

*I'll give you two examples of the influence Jackie exerted on the fashion industry," said Halston. "On Inauguration Day when she wore the pillbox hat I designed for her, it was very windy and when she stepped out of the limo she put her hand up to the pillbox to keep it from flying away. She put a slight dent in the hat. The dent appeared in every photograph. Women started putting dents in their pillboxes and deigners even started designing them that way. On another occasion, JFK bought her a leopard coat for $3,000. I designed a matching hat. She wore the ensemble for the cover of *Life*. There was such a rush on leopard skin coats that the price jumped to $40,000 per coat and the animal soon went on the endangered species list where it remains today."

added the names of old school chums, favored social acquaintances, relatives of political assistants and aides, important personal and business acquaintances. With each invitation went an elaborate itinerary of Inauguration Day events and detailed instructions on how to reach the various vantage points. Jackie was meticulous about arrangements to collect relatives and friends from train stations and airport and deliver them to their hotels and to the functions, preparing special lists of those who, because of age or illness, qualified for official White House cars. Three buses were chartered to transport their guests around Washington.

Jackie's carefully laid plans were partially disrupted by a driving snowstorm that hit Washington the day before the inauguration, closing the airport and forcing thousands of visitors to abandon their cars and taxis and trudge on foot to their hotels. Three hundred National Guardsmen were deployed to plow the streets and clear a route for the following day's parade along Pennsylvania Avenue.

At 8:00 p.m. on the evening of the 19th, Jack and Jackie (accompanied by Bill Walton) attended a reception for Eleanor Roosevelt before being driven through the swirling snow to a pre-inaugural concert at Convention Hall, then on to the National Guard Armory for an all-star variety show arranged by Frank Sinatra and Peter Lawford. Ten thousand guests paid $1,000 apiece to help defray the Democratic Party campaign deficit and catch a glimpse of the new First Lady shimmering in white organza. Two hours late in starting, the gala featured performances by Harry Belafonte, Louis Prima and Keely Smith, Ella Fitzgerald, Bette Davis, Leonard Bernstein and Sir Laurence Olivier. Ethel Merman, although a staunch Republican, belted out "Everything's Coming Up Roses," while Sinatra followed with "That Old *Jack* Magic."

By the end of the show, Jackie had visibly wilted. She excused herself and was driven home, "so tired I could have slept in a suit of armor." Jack, who could not have been wider awake or more excited, joined the stars at a dinner thrown by his father at Paul Young's restaurant, arriving at N Street only an hour before sunrise.

Inauguration Day dawned bitterly cold. The President-elect was fully dressed when, at 10:40 a.m., the bubbletop presidential Lincoln limousine pulled up to his house. As he made his way to the front door, he called out to Jackie, who was still upstairs applying her make-up, "Jackie, for heaven's sake!" His exasperation faded when she appeared at the top of the stairs looking glamorous yet dignified, her outfit striking in its simplicity.

Accompanied by Speaker Sam Rayburn, the Kennedys reached the North Portico of the White House to pick up President and Mrs. Eisenhower. Eisenhower sent word that he hoped his successor and the new First Lady would join them first for coffee. Also in attendance were the outgoing Vice-President Richard Nixon and his wife, incoming Vice-President Lyndon Johnson and his wife, Senator Henry Styles Bridges (Chairman of the Republican Policy Committee) and other members of the Inaugural Committee. It was not a convivial gathering. Jackie felt uncomfortable and unhappy when she found herself seated next to Pat Nixon who ignored her and remained locked in conversation with Senator Bridges.

At 11:40 a.m., in the freezing cold, President Eisenhower and John F. Kennedy, followed by their wives in a second car, were driven to the Capitol for the swearing-in ceremony. At the Capitol, the Kennedys were led into a small room for a few private moments together. Jackie emerged first. All eyes were on her as she slipped into place in the stand between Mamie Eisenhower and Lady Bird Johnson.* She seemed in a daze as she watched the ceremony unfold: Robert Frost, blinded by the glare of the sun, aborting a poem he had written for the occasion and instead reciting one from memory; Cardinal Cushing intoning his prayers and the Chief Rabbi his benediction; Chief Justice Earl Warren administering the oath of office, and the thirty-fifth President (having discarded his overcoat in spite of the cold) repeating the oath in a firm voice free of strain; the President's inaugural address; Marian Anderson's rendition of "The Star-Spangled Banner." When it was over Jackie, whose idea it had been to incorporate Frost and Anderson into the ceremony, stepped forward and gently stroked her husband's cheek.

*No less than eight once and future First Ladies were present at JFK's inauguration: Edith Wilson, Eleanor Roosevelt, Bess Truman, Mamie Eisenhower, Lady Bird Johnson, Pat Nixon, Betty Ford and Jacqueline Kennedy.

"You were wonderful," she whispered. The next day she said: "I couldn't kiss him in front of all those people."

Following the ceremony, Jack and Jackie were whisked off to the official inaugural luncheon at the old Supreme Court Chamber in the Capitol, while other members of the family boarded buses to attend a buffet luncheon given by Joe and Rose Kennedy in the Mayflower Hotel's East Room. John Davis recalled a succulent spread of lobster, shrimp and smoked salmon "on a large banquet table in the center of the room surrounded by round tables set for six and eight. Each of five families settled into separate sections of the room. Joe Kennedy looked us up and down as though we were aliens from another solar system. He didn't say a word. The three Kennedy sisters—Eunice, Jean and Pat—spoke only to each other. Nobody would talk to Hugh Auchincloss."

Miche Bouvier concurred that "very few people mixed. I tried but without success. The room divided into two main groups—the Bouviers, Lees and Auchinclosses on one side, the Kennedys and Fitzgeralds on the other. Then it broke down into individual families. Joe Kennedy looked as if he'd just as soon be elsewhere, which as far as the Bouviers were concerned was fine."

The same crowd materialized at 5:00 p.m. for a family reception in the White House, following the afternoon's major event, the inaugural parade, which Jackie left after less than an hour. Exhausted and cold, she had gone home to the White House to prepare for the five inaugural balls still to be endured. She had commandeered the Queen's Room on the second floor while a White House maintenance crew renovated the presidential living quarters, installing a new nursery, pantry, utility kitchen and family dining room.

Jackie rested while her relatives flocked into the State Dining Room. "The Bouviers arrived first," said Edie Beale, "followed by the Lees, the Auchinclosses, then the others, the Kennedys arriving last because they had endured the cold the longest. We all reached for the hot coffee or tea, the spiced punch, the champagne, the cocktails, anything to thaw out. Then we returned to our respective clans.

"I walked over to Hugh Auchincloss. He had never met me before and didn't know me from Adam. 'I know all about you,' I told him. I almost spat in his face. I told him off for Jack Bouvier's sake, for Jackie's father.

"The Kennedys all looked very unhappy. I couldn't understand how, having finally attained their dream, they could be so morose. They seemed hyper and morose at the same time. I've never seen so much unhappiness in one room before.

"I went up to Joseph P. Kennedy, the patriarch, and told him that I'd almost been engaged to his eldest son, Joe Jr. I knew Joe Jr. from a Princeton house party. He was visiting Princeton, and so was I. So I told his father that if the almost-engaged had become a reality, and if Joe Jr. had lived and gone on to become President of the United States, then I, little Edie Beale, would now be a First Lady, and not cousin Jackie. He walked away from me shaking his head.

"I had wanted to meet Ethel Kennedy but I met Joan Kennedy instead. She was polite, harmless and naive. I didn't care for JFK's sisters, but Joan Kennedy was very sweet and kind. She didn't pull rank the way his sisters and Ethel did.

"Although JFK put in a token appearance at the gathering, Jackie remained sequestered in her room supposedly disappointed that Lee hadn't come to the inauguration. Lee couldn't come. She had been in some sort of automobile accident and was recuperating in Switzerland.

"Frankly, I wasn't overly impressed by John Kennedy. He was rather rude to me. On the only occasion that I tried to make conversation with him he looked straight through me. You know, the glassy-eyed stare."

An hour into the party, Janet Auchincloss marched upstairs to see what had become of her daughter. She found Jackie sitting up in bed, attendants and White House staff members scurrying about, a heating pad tucked beneath her lower back.

"Aren't you going to join us?" asked Janet. "Some of your relatives have traveled thousands of miles just to shake your hand. They haven't seen you since your wedding day."

"I can't," Jackie responded dolefully, "I just can't."

Miche Bouvier, the only family member invited to her room, understood Jackie's dilemma: "If you'd recently undergone a Caesarean section and then frozen your butt off at an inauguration speech and had to freeze your other end off watching an endless parade and then you had to get dressed to attend five or six balls that night, you'd also want to catch a few hours of sleep."

Rosemary Sorrentino and Kenneth worked away on Jackie's hair. "I'd straightened it the day before," said Rosemary. "Now it was a matter of brushing and styling it. After Jackie and her mother stopped bickering about the family gathering, Mrs. Auchincloss started complaining about her daughter's hair. She didn't approve of her hair-do, and tried to persuade her to change it. Failing, she turned to Kenneth and asked him to urge the change upon Jackie. But the new First Lady's mind, as well as her sweeping chignon, were set."

While his wife started dressing, John Kennedy showered and changed and briefly attended by himself a small dinner party at the home of George and Jane Wheeler, loyal Kennedy supporters. Among the guests were Angie Dickinson and Kim Novak, whose escorts to the inauguration were Red Fay, newly appointed Under Secretary of the Navy, and architect Fernando Parra. Fay, his wife in Europe, had agreed to squire Angie at Jack's behest.

The President returned to the White House and found Lyndon and Lady Bird Johnson waiting for him in the Red Room. Five minutes later, Jackie floated through the door in a rustle of chiffon, her spectacular white, silver and diamante-studded, Cassini-inspired ballgown loosely covered by a fine-webbed cape trailing nearly to her ankles. The President gave an approving nod. "Your dress is beautiful," he said. "You've never looked lovelier."

Jackie's regal appearance captivated those who filled the ballroom at the Mayflower Hotel for the first of the evening's five inaugural balls. She made no less an impression on the crowd at the Statler-Hilton, site of the second ball. She and the Johnsons had barely settled themselves in the presidential box when the President excused himself. Frank Sinatra was hosting many of the performers from the previous night's gala at a private party on a higher floor in the same hotel. Kennedy dashed upstairs for a second fleeting meeting with Angie Dickinson, returning to his seat thirty minutes later looking slightly winded and carrying a *Washington Post* under his arm as if he had just stepped outside to pick up a copy.

"Anything interesting going on in the world tonight?"

Jackie asked him. He smiled sheepishly; she shot him an icy glare.

Their third destination was the armory where more than a thousand guests gave them a twenty-minute standing ovation. Rose Kennedy later wrote of the "wave of love and admiration" that "engulfed" the President and First Lady. But neither the President's mother nor the President realized that the smile on Jackie's face was forced and fixed. She looked so appealing, so radiant, it would have been difficult to believe, even had she admitted it, that she was once more beginning to fade. Determination (coupled with a Dexedrine tablet she had taken earlier in the day) kept her afloat until Ted Kennedy suggested that they move on to the next function. It was midnight when Jackie, like Cinderella, proclaimed her evening at an end. "You go on, Jack," she said. "I'll have to go back."

Before calling it quits, President Kennedy attended two more balls and a party at the home of Joe Alsop. The Alsop "do" was also the last stop for a half-dozen Hollywood starlets imported for the inauguration by Peter Lawford.

According to Lawford, "All six wanted to be with the President. They arranged a lineup as they would at Madame Claude's brothel in Paris, and Jack chose two of them. This *ménage à trois* brought his first day in office to a resounding close."

17

Jackie awoke early the next morning to the sickening smell of fresh paint and the pounding of hammers. The Eisenhowers had removed their furniture and paintings, and her own hadn't arrived yet from N street. The emptiness depressed her, and the White House workmen with their tools, paint and ladders did little to enhance the atmosphere. She remained in bed. She did not expect company and gave a start when somebody knocked at the door. Her husband entered the room followed by his first official visitor, former President Harry S. Truman. Seeing the First Lady under the covers, Truman smiled, waved and quickly retreated.

Jackie spent the afternoon discussing White House restoration plans with Sister Parish, Bill Walton, David E. Finley (chairman, Fine Arts Commission) and John Walker (director of the National Gallery of Art and an old friend of the Auchinclosses). When they were done she joined her husband in one of the upstairs sitting rooms. Attempting to light the fireplace, the President and First Lady were soon engulfed by smoke and soot. Kennedy ran to the window but couldn't open it. "The windows haven't been opened in years," J. B. West explained. With difficulty the chief usher managed to pry open a small side window and a gust of frigid air sent Jackie scurrying from the room.

Conditions in the White House were hardly up to the standards one might expect of the First House of the land. Jackie discovered that her shower didn't work and the toilet didn't flush. There were no wastebaskets or bookshelves. "Didn't Eisenhower read?" she inquired. She also wanted to know why a Secret Service agent had to be posted outside the door whenever she used the lavatory. "At least let them fix the toilets," she muttered.

On Sunday, January 22, the Kennedys gave their first

informal dinner party at the White House, inviting the Franklin Roosevelts, the Joseph Alsops, the Tom Bradens and the Leonard Bernsteins. Bernstein, his usual ebullient self, embraced Jackie and planted a moist kiss on the side of her face, a gesture she didn't always appreciate. Seeing her annoyance, the President said to Bernstein, "Don't I get one?" Bernstein complied. The Kennedys broke out the champagne and caviar, a gift from Soviet Premier Nikita Khrushchev, and later led their guests on a cheerful tour of their new home.

"The house was empty," said Roosevelt, "and they were very far from settled in. Jackie said to me, 'Oh, do you know what I've just discovered? There are twenty calligraphers all writing away in the cellar.' I remembered them from my father's day but imagined they had long been replaced by a printing press. Yet they obviously hadn't, because all those copperplate press cards, copperplate menus, the whole thing was still there."

Joe Alsop, who also hadn't visited the White House in years, found that it now resembled the presidential suite in the Muehlebach Hotel in Kansas City—there wasn't a pretty thing in it, and there wasn't anything that wasn't fake or phony; whatever furniture remained after the Eisenhower administration was all reproduced from originals.*

Alsop recalled a moment when they were upstairs in the presidential living quarters, an area comprising seven rooms. In one of the rooms he noticed a pair of what looked like portholes in the wall. He said to Jackie, "What the devil are those?" They were located on either side of a door. J. B. West came in, and Jackie, too, asked, "What are those portholes for?" West pulled them open. They turned out to be President and Mrs. Eisenhower's his-and-hers built-in television sets. The chief usher explained that the Eisenhowers didn't like to watch the same TV programs but liked to watch their programs together, so they'd have their dinner on trays, one here, one there, and the portholes would be opened and they would watch—Ike a western, Mamie a soap opera or a situation comedy.

On Monday, Jackie's first full working day, she met

---

*When she first moved in, Jackie compared the White House to Lubyanka, the infamous Soviet prison.

the members of the White House domestic staff. They
were brought in three at a time while she perched on a
corner of a large desk in the First Family's quarters. She
wore jodhpurs, a white silk blouse and low brown boots,
and looked, according to one of the upstairs maids, like
the mistress of the mansion come to inspect her slaves.

"How can she see what she's looking at, with all that
hair falling in her face?" whispered chief housekeeper
Mabel Walker, a White House employee through five
administrations. Jackie overheard the comment and Mabel was the first to go, eventually replaced by Vassar
graduate Anne H. Lincoln, a friend of Jackie's, and until
her promotion an assistant to Tish Baldridge.

Although the staff occasionally questioned Jackie's dedication to the job, the new First Lady (she detested the
title and insisted on being called Mrs. Kennedy) showed
herself to be assertive, ambitious and industrious. She
wrote frequent, often detailed memos to various White
House personnel, and these became the official guidebook for the administration of the Executive Mansion.
West realized at once what it took others much longer to
understand: "Jackie's wish, murmured with a 'Do you
think . . .' or 'Could you please . . .', was as good as a
command. When she told you to jump, you jumped."

"If there's anything I can't stand, it's Victorian mirrors—
they're hideous," she wrote to West. "Have them removed and relegated to the junk heap."

Other memos followed in rapid succession:

"No Mamie pink on the walls except in Caroline's
room, no Grand Rapids reconditioned furniture, no glass-
and-brass ashtrays or trinkets—I intend to make this a
grand house . . ."

"Maud Shaw won't need much in her room. Just find a
wicker wastebasket for her banana peels and a little table
for her false teeth at night . . ."

"I can't teach the maids anything—nor have time to—
when they are that scared, as they are too panicky to
remember. The only way they will get to be good maids
. . . is to be around the family and house enough so that
some of the terror leaves them . . ."

"Something must be done about the window shades
throughout the WH. They are enormous and they have
pulleys and ropes. After pulling them down I feel like a
sailor taking in a sail."

During the early days, Mrs. Kennedy roamed the corridors of the mansion, discovering "treasures" and banishing "horrors," making certain that the family quarters received primary attention. A Truman-renovated guest room located over the Grand Entrance Hall made way for Caroline Kennedy's pink rosebuds, white-canopied bed and handmade rocking horses. An adjoining guest room became John-John's blue-and-white nursery, with white crib and playpen, and menagerie of stuffed animals.

"I want my children to be brought up in more personal surroundings, not in the state rooms," Jackie told J. B. West. "And I don't want them to be raised by nurses and Secret Service agents."

Through John Walker and David Finley, the Kennedys were able to borrow paintings, prints and lithographs from both the National Gallery and the Smithsonian. Jacqueline also discovered the hoard of furniture and domestic items that had been stored in the White House since Theodore Roosevelt's day. No catalogue of the stored furnishings existed, so Jackie embarked on what she called "spelunking missions" to see what could be salvaged. Aubusson rugs were brought up from the basement. Marble busts of past presidents were located in a men's room. She discovered the *Resolute* desk that found its way into the Oval Office. Bellange chairs and a pier table were recovered from a government warehouse and restored. The first inventory of all items in storage and on display was begun. The public areas and rooms were filled with imaginative flower arrangements created by Jackie's friend Bunny Mellon, who also volunteered the funds for a new White House rose garden. Pastel and polka-dot linens were ordered for the upstairs bedrooms. A housekeeping memo outlining the daily responsibilities of the staff was placed in circulation:

> All 18 bedrooms and 20 baths on second floor must be tidied; 147 windows kept clean; 29 fireplaces laid ready for lighting; 412 doorknobs polished; 3,000 sq. feet of floorspace on 2nd story waxed and buffed; half an acre of marble mopped and remopped; carpeting vacuumed three times a day (morning, noon, and night); 37 rooms on ground floor dusted twice daily (morning and evening).

Jackie laid down several other edicts as well, including the suspension of afternoon tours of the White House, which she deemed too disruptive for the work force doing the renovation work. "How can they plaster and paint with hundreds of tourists running about?" she asked in a memo to the chief usher. A White House staffer insisted that the real reason was that Jackie and her children took afternoon naps and couldn't rest with the hordes tramping through the mansion. With regard to naps, Jackie insisted her sheets be changed both before and after. She likewise insisted on a fresh supply of bath and hand towels three times a day.

A new central air-conditioning system had to be installed in the family apartment at a cost of $85,000 and the bills cleared with Bernard L. Boutin, director, General Services Administration. Boutin found Jackie "extraordinarily efficient in the way she managed to procure whatever she needed. I'd been told that she was naive, but she wasn't the least bit naive. I think that would be the least descriptive term for her."

Within the first month she exhausted the $50,000 allocated by the White House budget for the renovation of the First Family's quarters. She turned to West and Boutin and pointed out that the presidential apartments had been set up for an elderly couple (the Eisenhowers) and not for a youthful set of parents with two young children. In this manner she secured an additional government outlay of $125,000 for decoration purposes and vowed to raise supplementary funds on her own. By revealing her plight to wealthy friends Jayne Wrightsman and Bunny Mellon, Jackie found the necessary backing to complete her private living quarters.

After she moved into her own tastefully decorated bedroom (it contained a separate-but-attached bed for the President, though they maintained individual bedrooms), she issued a statement on what she expected her primary role to be: "I think the major role of the President's wife is to take care of the President and his children." Off the record she told journalist Charlotte Curtis, her former dormitory-mate at Vassar, that she didn't know if she could make it. "The White House is such an artificial environment," she said. "It's a snake pit. If I don't take care of myself, I'll go mad."

"Jackie wore so many masks she was impossible to

decipher," said Charlotte Curtis. "With her elevation to the position of First Lady, she became ever more elusive, more secretive, more dramatic. Probably she felt more vulnerable. Certainly she was a stationary target for the press, a much larger target than she had been as a Senator's wife."

Acutely aware that her privacy was at risk, Jackie forced members of the White House staff to sign a letter of agreement pledging never to write or talk about their years of employment with the Kennedys. The document had no true legal force (it was signed under obvious duress) and in the end only created resentment and negative publicity. Nor did it prevent staffers from writing of their experiences in the White House; if anything, it encouraged them.

Jackie expounded on her policy of secrecy in a lengthy memo to Pam Turnure, which began: "I feel strongly that publicity in this era has gotten completely out of hand—and you must really protect the privacy of me and my children—but not offend (the press)."

She continued:

"My press relations will be minimum information given with maximum politeness. . . .

"I won't give any interviews—pose for any photographs, etc.—for the next four years. . . ."

J. B. West, recipient of more intra-house memos from Jackie than anyone else, received a number of notes concerning the privacy of her children while playing on the South Lawn. Jackie had personally researched the subject and discovered the exact point through the high iron fence surrounding the White House where tourists and news photographers could take pictures of Caroline and John Jr. at play.

She drew a diagram of the lawn.

"If you stand in the children's playground—you will see that lots of people can take photographs from the place marked X," she memoed to West.

Then after asking him if he could have a "solid wall" of shrubs or trees planted at X, she added:

"Who will be the first President brave enough to build a brick wall?"

Jean-Paul Ansellem, Jackie's Washington hairdresser— she flew Kenneth down from New York only on special occasions—appeared at the White House on the average of three times a week and remembered Jackie's favorite topic of conversation as being "news leaks"—"She wanted to know how the people at *Womens Wear Daily* knew what she was going to wear to a function before she wore it."

"Jackie demanded total devotion," recollected Zella West, the widow of J. B. West. "When she had a problem she would call my husband at home at all hours. But many of these problems were of her own making. For example, she and Sister Parish had barely completed the presidential apartments when she brought in another decorator, a Frenchman named Stephane Boudin, and thus began a whole new decoration scheme. The rooms had to be completely repainted and reappointed."

"Jackie and the President had leased Glen Ora, a seven bedroom, 400-acre weekend and vacation retreat in Middleburg, and Jackie stripped the entire interior of the house and redecorated it as though she owned it. When the owner (Gladys Tartiere) saw the alteration, she insisted the Kennedys restore it to its original condition. She refused to renew her lease with the Kennedys.

At government expense, Jackie installed many of her own employees in the White House—her personal maid, her secretary, her husband's valet, the children's governess, a press secretary, a masseuse. This created problems insofar as their salary came out of the White House payroll, meaning that permanent staff members had to be terminated or work at greatly reduced wages. When J. B. West suggested that the Kennedys might want to absorb the additional expense of these employees, Jackie responded: "We don't have that kind of money. My husband is a federal employee, just like the rest of the White House staff."

West and others felt that Jackie snubbed the press, especially its female practitioners, and was too choosey when it came to selecting which official White House functions to attend. She found little or no time for the Girl Scouts of America, the Muscular Dystrophy Association, the Commission for the Blind and Physically Handicapped, the DAR, the A.S.P.C.A. or the American Red Cross. "Give them to Lady Bird," she instructed Tish Baldridge. During her first year in the White House, Jackie asked Mrs. Johnson to substitute for her on more than fifty separate occasions.

Herbert H. S. Feldman, a British attorney and author who met Jackie in 1961, described her as "hard, tough, self-serving, with no great ambitions towards personal achievement but a great love for the limelight, publicity and applause. Her mouth betrays her. It is like that of a shark. Indeed, the Kennedys and the Bouviers were a well-matched lot."

Another Jackie detractor, newspaperwoman May Craig, criticized her static face, steel armature, unpredictability and fawning love of the famous. As proof of the latter she cited Jackie's reluctance to meet with the student reporters from Miss Porter's and Vassar, two of the schools she herself attended, while extending an invitation for tea to George Balanchine, director of the New York City Ballet ("She looked like a pussycat," he said afterwards), as well as Greta Garbo, who arrived at a very small and private White House dinner with the Kennedys and Lem Billings. Garbo and Billings had met several years earlier on the French Riviera.

"Jackie wasn't just spinning her wheels," explained Billings. "She was picking these people's brains. That's how she operated. She invited accomplished artists so she could get the names of other accomplished artists who would perform at the White House."

Her method worked. Balanchine arranged to have Margot Fonteyn and Rudolf Nureyev perform at a state dinner, while Garbo planted a seed by mentioning Pablo Casals, the great Spanish cellist living in self-imposed exile in Puerto Rico. Although Casals had vowed never again to perform in a country that recognized Generalissimo Franco, he made an exception when the Kennedys personally invited him to play at the White House for the Governor of Puerto Rico and Mrs. Muñoz-Marin. The key to Casals's acceptance was the timely intervention of his American representative, attorney Abe Fortas, who passed along the presidential request and made final arrangements for the master cellist's one-day stay in Washington.*

*The Governor of Puerto Rico supplied the White House with a list of prominent Hispanics living in the U.S. whom he wanted invited to the Casals concert. JFK invited all but one: José Ferrer. In 1952, the year he won an Academy Award, Ferrer was brought up before the HUAC. "Maybe they felt that two suspect lefties like Casals and

The calibre of White House performers and the quality of Jackie's well-planned entertainments won her high marks in many quarters. So too did her beauty and style. Fashion critic Hebe Dorsey remarked that "Jackie's style changed the existing fashion, helped to break down a certain Puritanism that had always existed in America and which insisted it was wrong to wear jewelry, wrong to wear fancy hairdos, wrong to live elegantly and graciously, wrong to wear tailored clothes, fur coats, skirts that fell above the knee.

"Jackie intuitively knew what to do. She was casual but contemporary. She had great charm. And then too she learned as she went along, and although she tends to downplay it today, is probably more elegant now than ever."

Under Jackie's aegis Washington became a brighter, gayer, more intellectual, more romantic and fun place to be. The grand dinners she gave in the White House stood in direct contrast to the loud, crowded cocktail parties politicians were used to attending in the homes of such dowagers as Gwen Cafritz and Perle Mesta. Jackie soon emerged as the town's top hostess, throwing numerous affairs with equal success, a twist party one night and a starched-shirt shindig the next. She eliminated much of the posturing, informality and, with the help of Robert Meyzen and Roger Fessaguet, co-owners of Caravelle, hired a French chef, René Verdon, and a pastry chef, Ferdinand Louvat. Attacked by the press for employing "foreigners" at the White House and for printing state dinner menus in French, Jackie directed the President to rush Verdon's and Louvat's naturalization papers through channels.

Testy and overdramatic ("I would have died for President Kennedy," Verdon wrote to this author), René was not universally appreciated. Liz Carpenter, press secretary to Lady Bird Johnson, noted: "He was a prima donna. He was a French chef, and most of them come with a hell of a lot of blood pressure. They can make good sauces, but the employer has to put up with them. . . . He had a hard time getting on with the help."

---

myself were too many for one dinner at the White House," said Ferrer. In retrospect, JFK's decision to exclude Ferrer seems disrespectful as well as cowardly.

Haute cuisine aside, what gave these White House dance-and-dinner functions their special tone was the guest list. It was studded with the names of persons both gifted and celebrated, most of them from the worlds of art, music, dance, theater, film and literature. Guests ranged from Carl Sandburg to Igor Stravinsky, from Aaron Copland to Isaac Stern, from Tennessee Williams to Andrew Wyeth. One evening was given over to American Nobel laureates, another to commemorating Mount Vernon. And the after-dinner entertainments featured symphony orchestras, opera singers, ballet troupes, Shakespearean actors, poets and jazz musicians.

Jamie Auchincloss, Jackie's half-brother, was convinced that what endures from the Kennedy era are "those dazzling evenings of culture fostered and inspired by Jackie. She wasn't so much a creative spirit as a maker and shaker. She realized the potential of her position and the opportunities it presented, and she successfully exploited both.

"It's true there were aspects of the job she never embraced. She became frustrated with some of the very superficial functions where there was a lot of ass-kissing and glad-handing. But when it came to the arts, she was determined to do for this country what no First Lady had ever done.

"Jackie's forte was her ability to take an idea and run with it. An example that I remember and admire her for took place in 1961. I had gone into a record store in Washington and asked the manager what piece of fairly recent American orchestral music he could recommend, and he mentioned *The Grand Canyon Suite*, composed by Ferde Grofé. I bought the record and played it late at night during one of Jackie's visits to Hammersmith Farm. I was sitting in the Deck Room, and Jackie was painting a picture at the other end of the room and she said, 'What is that music?'

"I told her what it was and showed her the album cover, and then six weeks later I went back to boarding school and picked up my copy of *Time* and read that Jackie and the President had entertained Ferde Grofé in the White House and *The Grand Canyon Suite* was performed that evening for their guests. And the record I bought for $2.99 became a best-selling album because of playing it one night while Jackie was painting in the same room.

"Every move Jack and Jackie made was magnified a thousand times by the harsh glare of publicity. An example: My father owned a rare book of portraits of American Indians by George Catlin which Jack happened to see while recuperating from back surgery at Merrywood in 1955. When they reached the White House, Jackie asked the Smithsonian whether they had any Catlin paintings. It turned out they had just about the only real collection of Catlins in the world, and they made them available to the White House and this became the art that decorated the First Family's private quarters. Again, the publicity generated about a hitherto obscure artist made George Catlin one of the best known American artists—simply by telephoning the Smithsonian and saying, 'Send over a painting.' "

The knowledge that she was the focus of so much public scrutiny undoubtedly contributed to Jackie's recurrent seizures of anxiety. At times she attempted to defuse her anxiety with touches of sardonic humor, as when she reported two female wire-service reporters to the Secret Service, insisting that "two strange Spanish-looking women" were after her. The two correspondents, it turned out, were Fran Lewine and Helen Thomas. "The word filtered back to us, as intended," writes Thomas in *Dateline: White House*. "It was a brilliant carom shot since Fran is Jewish and I'm of Arab descent." An agent accosted the two women in front of the White House. They produced their press passes and were promptly arrested.

Once when Jackie turned up at the White House with a new German shepherd puppy, the press asked her what she would feed it. "Reporters," she shot back.

And at a crowded White House press reception for the Shah and Empress of Iran, a *Womens Wear Daily* correspondent asked the First Lady if she read that paper. Jackie replied, "I try not to."

She could also be somewhat less than humorous. When she was photographed toppling off her mount during a horse show, she telephoned Jack long distance and asked him to have the photo "killed." He refused ("Jackie," he said, "when the First Lady falls on her ass, it's news. . . .").

She once ordered the Secret Service to confiscate film

from press photographers who took pictures of the First Family without her permission. She stuck out her tongue at a group of tourists visiting the White House, then warned a *Boston Globe* reporter who had witnessed the incident that she would have him banned from the White House if he mentioned it in print.

After reading a newspaper account of Charlie, their Welsh terrier, Jackie stormed out to find White House kennel keeper Traphes Bryant. "Don't you ever give another thing to those damn nosey reporters," she yelled. She scolded Tish Baldridge for being overly cooperative with select members of the press: "Your first responsibility is to the family, not to the White House."

Pierre Salinger noted, "As the deluge of publicity continued unabated, Jackie's anger mounted to the point of ferocity. Because I was the President's press secretary I bore the brunt of her outrage."

Jackie's anger was vented in a series of handwritten notes to Salinger:

" . . .I thought you had made an arrangement with the fotogs not to take the children playing at WH. They have had all the pictures of Macaroni [Caroline's pony] they need. I want no more—*I mean this*—and if you are firm and will take the time, you can stop it. So please do. What is a press secretary for—to help the press, yes—but also to protect *us*."

After receiving the memo Salinger appealed to the White House photographers to respect Jackie's wishes, and for several months they did. Then one day the newspapers were again filled with snapshots of the children at play—made by an amateur who had sold them to the Associated Press. Another note from Jackie arrived at Salinger's desk:

"Don't worry—a nice calm memo: Your policy of no peep shows has worked marvelously all fall. Now if they get away with this I am afraid they will start up in full force again. So could you berate the fotog of the AP for buying it—if it was taken by a tourist. Guards should be told to watch for people photographing through grilles. The guards at the gate could have stopped this. If necessary, have one man patrol up and down outside by the S.W. [southwest] gate.

Cecil Stoughton, official White House photographer during the Kennedy administration, understood Salinger's dilemma: "Jackie had a running battle going with Pierre over keeping the children out of the press, even though they were always in the press. The President understood the political advantages of having the children photographed, whereas Jackie saw it as an invasion of their privacy. Pierre would schedule photo sessions for the children when Jackie was out of town, then blame the President when Jackie went after him. Jackie felt she couldn't do anything, say anything, go anywhere, without public knowledge. To her, the White House signified losing control of her life, becoming the butt of political comment and political gossip.

"A lot of people in the press found it difficult to believe that Jackie had ever been a reporter-photographer. She identified so little with the media, it seemed implausible she had once worked for a newspaper. I always felt her newspaper job was kind of a playgirl hobby: it gave her entrée into select circles."

Jackie's shyness and obsession about privacy became a central and controlling factor during her first year in the White House. She did her best to shun the White House press corps and ignored their pleas for personal interviews. She escaped the press and the pressure of the White House by spending as much time as possible away from Washington. When forced by her husband to respond to the press ("Poor Jack," she once said. "He thinks if I ignore them he'll be impeached"), she resorted to what her staff called "the PBO"—polite brush off.

She demonstrated this technique on April 11, 1961, at the annual White House Luncheon for Ladies of the Press, a group of some 200 reporters and editors from every state in the Union. Mrs. Kennedy chose the East Room for the buffet luncheon, the State Dining Room being too small to accommodate all the ladies at tables. It marked the first time René Verdon had prepared the food for a large gathering.

Jackie welcomed the ladies one by one as they filed past her into the chamber. She greeted Doris Fleasons with a lukewarm "Why, Doris, what are you doing here?" More disparaging was her reception of Angele Gingras, her former colleague at the *Times-Herald*. Garnett Stackleberg, a friend of Angele's, remembered the occasion because she happened to be standing behind Angele on line.

"Angele had helped Jackie quite a bit in the early days," said Garnett. "But as we walked through the receiving line and reached Jackie, she gave Angele about two fingers as they shook hands, two limp fingers and a stiff 'Hello,' not the least little sign of recognition, no 'Oh, hello Angele, how are you?' That was Jackie for you.

"I thought she enjoyed the power and the glory and the clothes and the standing around at parties and all that, but she was contemptuous of the press. She posed a lot. It was all theater. She was good at playing the role. She was even better at putting down the press. I'm certain Angele couldn't have been very pleased by the way Jackie handled her."

Hope Ridings Miller, editor of *Diplomat* magazine, characterized the luncheon as "lovely but tense because there were place cards indicating where everyone would sit. Jackie sat between somebody from *The New York Times* and somebody from *Time*, which angered the other girls.

"My impression was that she wasn't terribly interested. She was blasé, as though going through the motions. She was nice to me but only because I didn't cover the White House on a regular basis. It was the press corps she couldn't stand."

The Bay of Pigs fiasco took place a week later and marked the administration's first political setback. The President, more conscious than ever of public relations, encouraged Jackie to be more tolerant in her dealings with the press. According to reporter Esther Van Wagoner Tufty, his pep-talk had little effect:

"The first reception at the White House following the Bay of Pigs was for the President of Tunisia, Habib Bourguiba, and his wife. There were a number of female reporters in the Blue Room cocktail party before dinner, and Jackie was doing her utmost to ignore us, walking around with her gold cigarette case and small gold cigarette lighter, which she would hand to the nearest man when she wanted to smoke.

"The President noticed her giving us dirty looks. He went over to her and took hold of her very hard by the left arm. He marched her over to us and in his most charming voice told her to 'say hello to the girls, darling.'

After she whispered hello he released her arm and you could still see the imprint of his hand in her flesh.

"What made it particularly difficult dealing with Jackie was her totally unpredictable nature. At times she proved quite thoughtful. I went into the hospital for surgery in 1962 and received a handsome bouquet of roses from her. Other times she treated us like dirt. She repeatedly referred to the female members of the press corps as 'harpies.' In one memo I happened to see, she suggested 'keeping the harpies at bay by stationing a couple of guards with bayonets near them.' Frankly, I could never figure out exactly what her problem was with the press. You know, if you don't want your privacy violated don't become First Lady. That's how I see it.'"

Jackie didn't quite see it that way. Her war of independence with the press never ceased. The conduct of reporters at White House state dinners distressed her to the point where she suggested they be allowed to view the dining room before dinner only (" . . . but briefly and from a distance"). She didn't want them to return after dinner: "That is when they ask everyone questions and I don't think it is dignified to have them around. It always makes me feel like some social-climbing hostess. Their notebooks also bother me, but perhaps they should be allowed to keep them as, at least, you know they are press but I think they should be made to wear big badges and be whisked out of there once we all sit down to dinner." In a separate memo, she suggested that members of the press "be permitted to attend important receptions but be kept out of sight behind the pillars and potted palms. They are too intrusive. They surround our guests and monopolize them. Nobody could get near John Glenn the other night. Also, the minute the photographers have finished shooting, they are to be ushered out the front door, so the Marine Band can strike up 'Hail to the Chief.'"

Lem Billings admitted that Jack and Jackie often quarreled, sometimes quite bitterly, over her brusque treatment of reporters and photographers. The First Couple also argued about her personal expenditures, especially in light of his decision to donate his $100,000 annual salary to charity. He thought it would look bad if he accepted it, given his father's wealth. Jackie was annoyed by his seeming dependence on his father's advice. During the Bay of Pigs invasion, he phoned the Ambassador every hour on the hour. Jackie became disillusioned. But the business about the reporters remained paramount in her mind.

"In a way you couldn't blame her," said Lem. "No matter what she did they crucified her. They crucified her for taking tennis lessons, using a government helicopter to fly to Glen Ora, swimming in shark-infested waters off Florida, refusing to attend certain White House teas and luncheons, leaving Washington whenever her mother-in-law came to town, dancing the Twist with Secretary of Defense Robert McNamara, being present at one of those soirées at Bobby and Ethel's house when everyone wound up in the swimming pool with their clothes on, subverting White House tradition by doing away with tails and top hats at formal functions, eliminating the old-fashioned 'U'-shaped banquet tables for forty, in favor of round tables for no more than a dozen. Jackie did for Washington and the White House what the Modernists did for poetry—streamlined it, cut it to the bone. By force of will she hauled the weighty mechanism into the twentieth century, and all they could do was write and print gossip about her.

"Granted there were times when she exceeded permissible bounds. Once when the Congressional wives gave a lunch for her, she ducked out to attend a performance of the London Royal Ballet in New York. On another occasion she missed a press luncheon by feigning illness, then slipped out to spend the afternoon at the National Gallery of Art with André Malraux, France's Minister of Culture.

"Once she failed to appear at a reception for several thousand exchange students on the South Lawn. In that instance when a reporter asked Tish Baldridge the reason for Jackie's absence, she replied, 'Same old sinuses.' The reporter snooped around and soon learned that Jackie didn't have sinus trouble: she just felt like going fox hunting that day."

The ladies of the press enjoyed making Jackie their target. They bought long-range binoculars, rented cabin cruisers and followed her when she traveled aboard *Honey Fitz,* the 96-foot presidential yacht. They watched her through their binoculars, and she watched them back through hers. They shadowed her to Glen Ora, to

Newport, to Hyannis Port, to Camp David, the presidential hideaway in the Catoctin Mountains of Maryland, and, toward the last, to her new Atoka, Virginia, estate on Rattlesnake Mountain, the home Jack built for her after their Glen Ora lease expired.

Jackie gradually began to enjoy her position on the pedestal and to understand more fully what she meant to the American people, though she never fully came to grips with the press. She continued to resent them as deeply as ever. They were the bane of her existence, the thorn in her crown. She had few problems with men, children or animals. But she remained constantly on edge and antagonistic when it came to female journalists.

18

Jackie's other major problem during her White House years was the Secret Service, which kept her in a constant state of agitation, informing her of kidnap plots against her children, a Cuban pilot's plan to assassinate her husband, a convicted rapist who wrote Jackie letters (intercepted by the Secret Service) declaring his undying love and promising to "surprise" her on Jackie's next visit to New York. "There was a lot of romantic swill about the Secret Service," she would later tell friends. "Their finest hour was supposedly Jack's assassination, when they protected Lyndon Johnson, who wasn't the target anyway, while Jack got killed. The most dangerous thing about them was that if you didn't know better, you might even feel safe with those guys around."

It was easy to be lulled into a false sense of security by the Secret Service. They were a small, elite group and a tight-knit organization whose members were called "protectors." They were dauntingly visible, purposely intimidating-looking, physically powerful, and muscular, with their weapons bulging in order to scare off potential troublemakers. Many times the protector was the only human being with whom the President or First Lady came into contact. Members of the First Family became dependent upon them, came to trust them. They even confided in them. Jackie's supervising agent was Clint Hill. She and Clint took long walks together along the beach at Hyannis Port. He hovered over her, followed wherever she went.

Secret Service agent Marty Venker observed that working the perimeter security detail for President Kennedy was generally considered the best assignment in Secret Service history. "Those fortunate enough to work this detail," said Venker, "soon understood the meaning of Ted Sorensen's timeless quip: 'This administration is going

283

to do for sex what the last one did for golf.' Young agents newly assigned to Kennedy simply couldn't believe what they were seeing though they quickly learned to keep their comments to themselves. Kennedy enjoyed having them around. They not only procured for him but partied with him. They were young, handsome, well-educated fellows who enjoyed women and drinking and drugs. This was the James Bond era, and Kennedy was intrigued by the whole mystique of the Secret Service. He identified with us and knew we would never betray him. There was an unspoken agreement within the Agency that went something like, 'You protect my ass and I'll protect yours.' They weren't going to talk about his sexual proclivities because they were doing more or less the same thing. That's not to say they didn't wonder about his behavior. After all, he was President of the United States. They couldn't fathom that this sort of thing was actually going on in the White House. They'd say, 'God damn, people are going to find out about this.' But nobody dreamed of talking or going to the press. To do so would have been to betray not only the President but the Agency. There would have been an immediate closing of ranks. Any agent who talked would have been off the detail by sundown, and, since it was the plum detail, nobody talked. And had an agent talked, every other agent would have clammed up or denied the stories.*

"Being with Kennedy was like attending a traveling fraternity party. It was always party, party, party. There was this feeling that nothing could ever go wrong. You boarded Air Force One and you were in another world. The plane, which Jackie decorated, was as plush as a mansion. You asked for a barbecued steak and you were served a barbecued steak. It wasn't warmed-over airplane food; it was barbecued before your eyes—steaks three inches thick! The President had his own bedroom facilities where he often entertained women when Jackie wasn't aboard. I was told Jackie was bored by the whole White House experience and enjoyed going off on her own. And of course Kennedy encouraged her to go so he could party.

*Although JFK's Secret Service agents did not talk to the press, several of them apparently filed confidential reports on the President's sexual activities with their home office. Copies of these reports were provided the author under the Freedom of Information Act.

"On arriving at hotels on presidential trips, the President would immediately conduct two meetings, one of a political nature with his Chief of Staff, the other with the head of the Secret Service detail, usually the advance agent who had been in that particular city or country for at least two weeks prior to the President's arrival. So there were two orders of business: political and social. Kennedy invariably met with the advance agent first, which provides some indication of his personal priorities. He didn't want to know about security but about broads. The agent was supposed to set up dates for the President. If he was new to the job and wasn't aware of this fact, Kennedy let him know pretty quickly. He'd say something to the effect of 'You've been here two weeks already and still don't have any broads lined up for me? You guys get all the broads you want. How about doing something for your Commander-in-Chief?' It was said in a semi-jocular vein, but he meant it. Those in the know knew enough to have the broads lined up for him. Naturally every local beauty wanted to fuck the President. It was her patriotic duty. If we were on foreign soil, they did it for the adventure or novelty of the experience. Think how much fun they had telling their friends they'd just been laid by the President of the United States.

"Of all the Presidents in recent history, Kennedy was the most randy and the most brazen. He was brazen not only about women but about political affairs. He always left doors open, even to the Oval Office. He'd be conducting a top-secret meeting and the door would be wide open. You could see and hear everything.

"His parties when held at the White House usually took place in and around the swimming pool. Because of his bad back, the pool was heated to more than 90 degrees Fahrenheit. His father had commissioned French artist Bernard Lamotte to paint a mural of the harbor of St. Croix for the swimming pool. They installed stereo speakers for music and a special lighting mechanism. One flip of the switch and it was high noon at St. Croix. Another flip of the switch and it was midnight with the moon and stars shining in the darkened ceiling above. A door to the pool had been changed from clear to frosted glass to prevent anyone from spying on the President. The parties often involved Kennedy and two or three women. A pitcher of daiquiris would be prepared in anticipation and chilled in a portable refrigerator; little Vienna sausages wrapped in bacon would be kept in a portable heater. The waiters and household staff would either be dismissed for the day or told to stay away from the swimming pool. When Jackie was away, riding the elevator could be hazardous to one's health. The kennel keeper was on his way to the basement one evening. Just as the elevator door opened, a naked blond office girl came running out of the elevator, practically bowled him over, then stopped and asked if he knew where she could find the President. But even among the staff of the White House there was a conspiracy of silence to protect Kennedy and keep Jackie from divining his secrets.

"The President would keep tabs on his wife by having his Secret Service agent maintain radio contact with Jackie's agent. In this way, he always knew her whereabouts. He would be partying in the pool, and Jackie would be landing at Andrews Air Force Base. Kennedy and the girls would keep at it until the last possible moment when Jackie entered the White House grounds."* Naked bodies scattered every which way. An agent or usher rushed in gathering up the drinks and highball glasses and any other telltale evidence. Kennedy would remain in the swimming pool presumably doing his back exercises, while the women would be ushered out of the White House through the back door.

"There were several amusing accounts as to how Jackie nearly caught him in the act. Everybody knows the one about the White House maid who found a pair of black silk panties in the President's bed. Thinking they belonged to Jackie, she returned them to the First Lady. The next time Jackie saw her husband, she handed him the panties and said, 'Here, find out who owns these. They're not my size.'

"I heard another story that I know to be true because I was friendly with the agent involved in the incident. It doesn't concern Jackie but it does have to do with Kennedy's womanizing. When he used the pool, he always posted an agent outside the door. 'Nobody comes in,' he said. 'You understand that? Nobody.' One day Ken

---

*"Lace" was the code name the Secret Service used to identify Jackie. The President's code named "Lancer," had obvious sexual connotations.

O'Donnell appeared at the door to the pool. He explained to the agent that he had an appointment to see the President. 'I'm sorry, sir,' said the agent, 'but you can't go in there.' O'Donnell glared at the agent. 'Are you telling me I can't see the Chief?' he thundered. 'Those are my orders, sir,' said the agent. 'Nobody comes in.' 'You're nothing but a Secret Service agent, a little twerp,' said O'Donnell, 'and I'm going in there.' He barged past the agent into the swimming pool area and found Kennedy relaxing in the pool with two young ladies. All three were nude. Kennedy was furious. He jumped out of the swimming pool and started yelling at O'Donnell: 'You dumb prick! When an agent tells you to stay out, you stay out of here—now get lost!' Sticking up for the agent in front of the agent was what won Kennedy the Agency's loyalty.

"My supervisor, Tony Sherman, related an episode that took place in Puerto Rico. Tony worked in the Presidential Protection Division, the elite section of the Secret Service, and was privy to quite a few Kennedy stories. This one involved a relatively new agent assigned to the presidential detail in late 1961.

"The new agent was standing guard outside Kennedy's San Juan hotel suite when suddenly the door to the suite opened and the President emerged wrapped in a bath towel with an unlit cigarette in hand. The agent on duty could clearly see a blonde lying naked in Kennedy's bed. Kennedy asked the agent for a light. The agent began fumbling around in his pocket and pulled out the first item that felt like a book of matches. Unfortunately he had removed a rolled-up, unused condom which he proceeded to place in the President's outstretched hand. When Kennedy saw what he had been handed he began laughing hysterically, unrolled it and showed it to the girl lying in bed who also began howling. For several weeks the agent worried he might lose his job, but of course the President took the incident as a joke and nothing came of it."

President Kennedy was aided in his extramarital activity not only by the Secret Service but by members of his immediate staff. Doris Lilly was approached by one of Jack's henchmen while staying in Palm Beach in the spring of 1961.

"I was down there writing for the *New York Post,*" she

related. "President Kennedy held a press conference at his father's house on the beach, so I went over there. We had met only once, ten years earlier, on an airplane to Europe. This was before he married Jackie when he was still a Congressman. We stayed up all night talking. I told him I had once dated his father. At the end of the flight we exchanged telephone numbers, but we somehow never connected.

"I arrived halfway through the press conference. I saw him staring at me. He seemed to be trying to remember from where he knew me. Meanwhile he continued to answer questions. After the press conference, once the television cameras were off, reporters were allowed to step forward for further questions. So I started to walk toward him, but there were fifty reporters between us and after trying unsuccessfully to squeeze in I decided to leave.

"I returned to my hotel room and a few minutes later I received a telephone call from one of JFK's top aides. The President remembered me and wanted to set up an appointment. He had something he hoped to discuss and he wanted me to meet him at a place called The Swordfish Motel. That was the name of it. I was supposed to meet him there within the next hour. The caller didn't know what the President wanted to talk to me about but suggested it was probably very important. I knew what it was all about, and I said that I couldn't go. The caller kept insisting I wouldn't be disappointed. I knew exactly what was expected of me. I'd have had to be dumb, deaf and blind not to know. But I never went and wasn't sorry about it."

JFK's "daily dose of sex," as Garry Wills refers to it in *The Kennedy Imprisonment* (1981), became a more conspicuous part of his legacy than any single political achievement. Women were Kennedy's fatal character flaw; he could not resist them. He could not forego the opportunity to meet Jayne Mansfield, a Hollywood sex symbol often compared in appearance and style to Marilyn Monroe. Jayne, whose acting skills were negligible, nevertheless had ambition and brains and perhaps a more realistic view of men than her more celebrated rival.

"Jayne looked like a dumb blonde but was by no means stupid," said Peter Lawford, who introduced her to his brother-in-law during one of Jack's trips to California. "There were three meetings that I know of—one in Beverly Hills, one in Malibu, one in Palm Springs. Jayne, whose marriage to Mickey Hargitay was floundering during this period, used to call Jack 'Mr. K.' Jack spoke of her sexual prowess. She had the best body in Hollywood, long legs, large firm breasts and a minuscule waistline. But she couldn't make it with a man unless she was bombed.

"Jayne was far more casual about men than Marilyn Monroe. Marilyn threw herself into relationships body and soul; Jayne took them as they came. She could be dating a baseball player, a bartender, the President of the United States—to her they were all men and men were all the same.

"The time they met in Palm Springs Jayne was pregnant with Maria, her fourth child, and Jack wasn't aware of it until they got together. She was visibly pregnant. Her condition apparently turned him on, which surprised me."

Raymond Strait, Jayne Mansfield's press agent for ten years, confirmed at least two of the Jack and Jayne encounters in his book on the late actress, *The Tragic Secret Life of Jayne Mansfield* (1974). The President, writes Strait, once told Jayne that her voice was very similar to that of his wife's. "Jayne [was] insulted, but she never let on to him. She didn't sound like her, she complained [to me]. Jackie didn't sound like anything."

Jayne Mansfield registered one other complaint against Kennedy. She told Lawford there was "a coldness to him, a hard, flat coldness which must make his personal life with Jackie less than satisfactory."

A week after rendezvousing with Kennedy in Palm Springs, Jayne was sitting with Strait at the Polo Lounge in the Beverly Hills Hotel when she received a telephone call. "Jayne had been drinking a little and feeling giddy," writes Strait. "I didn't know who she was talking to until she became argumentative . . . on the telephone. She ended the conversation by saying, 'Look, you'll only be President for eight years at the most. I'll be a movie star forever!' She hung up the phone."

Another Lawford-inspired fling involved a high-priced New York call girl named Leslie Devereux. She, too, thought Kennedy "mechanized and cold, with hard glazed eyes and a high-powered smile. Peter Lawford never explained the situation, just gave me an address and told me to meet him there. It turned out to be the Hotel Carlyle. We went upstairs together to a penthouse duplex and there stood the President of the United States. He smiled and said, 'All right, Peter. Disappear.'

"I saw him four or five times at the Carlyle. It was all pretty standard sex at first, later it got more kinky. I'd been with a number of powerful politicians and one thing they always liked was mild S&M. So we did a little of that—I tied his hands and feet to the bedposts, blindfolded him and teased him first with a feather and then with my fingernails. He seemed to enjoy it.

"I visited him twice at the White House, the first time for only 15 minutes in a small room off the Oval Office. His secretaries didn't so much as blink when they saw me. They showed me in and out as naturally as they would the Secretary of State.

"On my second visit, I met him upstairs in the living quarters. A Secret Service agent ushered me into a dark and somber room filled with heavy wood furniture, and said, 'Make yourself comfortable, he'll be with you shortly.' He motioned to an enormous, intricately carved rosewood bed. 'That's Abraham Lincoln's bed,' he said. 'You mean,' I said, 'I'm to lie down on *that,* on Abraham Lincoln's bed?' 'Lady,' he said, 'it's the best we've got.'

"Soon the door opened and a white-gloved butler brought champagne on a silver tray. Then the President appeared and we spent several hours together. I told him it seemed sacrilegious to violate Abraham Lincoln's bed. He laughed and told me about the White House legend that when you make a wish on the Lincoln bed it always comes true. 'Make a wish,' I said. He closed his eyes and I mounted him. 'See,' he said, 'it never fails.' "

Look magazine feature photographer Stanley Tretick recalled a conversation he once had with Clark R. Mollenhof, a *Look* reporter, concerning Kennedy's womanizing. "Clark used to tell me to document the girls JFK was sneaking into the White House, and I said how the hell are you going to do that? 'Just go to the southwest gate and stand around and watch those delivery vans come and go,' he said. I told him that if they were going in that door they were being smuggled in with the baked goods and floral wreaths and things like that. He implied they were."

Ned Kenworthy, a correspondent with the Washington bureau of *The New York Times,* admitted to editor-reporter Philip Nobile that he had witnessed one of Kennedy's young ladies, a girl no older than twenty, being led up a staircase to JFK's private quarters by Dave Powers. The moment Powers saw Kenworthy, he attempted to camouflage his actions by pointing to a stair-well portrait and proclaiming, "this painting was given to the White House by James Madison."*

Investigating other stories, Nobile uncovered an array of JFK misadventures. During a brief visit to Chicago, Kennedy accidentally walked into a hotel suite where three airline stewardesses were partying with their boyfriends. JFK engaged the awestruck assemblage in idle conversation. One of the boyfriends, a reporter, excused himself and went to the bathroom. When he returned he discovered that Kennedy had absconded with his girlfriend.

The next morning the reporter asked the stewardess what had become of her. "How could you walk out on me like that?" he asked.

"How often will I get to sleep with a President?" she countered.

Then there was the nubile babysitter for a famous newsman's children, who accompanied the family to Camp David one weekend. The newsman was writing an in-depth profile of the President. He learned—but did not report—that Kennedy had instituted a policy of nude bathing in the newly heated Camp David swimming pool. He also discovered that the babysitter was having a hot affair with Kennedy. What he didn't know was that she had become pregnant by him and had to undergo an abortion in Puerto Rico, not the first such procedure JFK had financed.

Despite his lofty position, not all the President's erotic endeavors ended in the bedroom. Shirley MacLaine was

---

*Dave Powers, currently a curator at the JFK Library, was always an obedient and close-mouthed JFK follower, going so far as to write in *Johnny, We Hardly Knew Ye* that whenever Jackie left Washington, Jack and he dined together and then the President said his prayers and went to bed alone. Powers, like other members of JFK's staff, not only bearded for the President but also apparently procured for him. A frequently published story has it that Powers once asked JFK what he wanted for his birthday. The President named a TV actress from California. His wish was granted.

staying at Frank Sinatra's Palm Springs estate early in 1961 when the President decided to visit. As a lark Sinatra sent Shirley in his limousine to meet Jack at the airport. No sooner had JFK closed the door to the limo than his hands were all over her. Startled, she bolted from the car just as it was pulling away. She fell to the tarmac and scraped her knee. The car stopped to retrieve her. She climbed back in and was immediately berated by a Secret Service agent for delaying their departure and endangering the President's life.

Although Shirley and Jack never became lovers, she made a comment that could well have become his epitaph: "I would rather have a President who does it to a woman than a President who does it to his country."

Philip Nobile furnished few names, but the names were readily available to anyone curious enough to ask. "Princess Elizabeth of Yugoslavia was beautiful-beautiful-beautiful," said Doris Lilly, "and always hanging around the White House." Looks, charm, sophistication and royal blood made her enormously appealing. "In contrast to women like Jackie and Pam Turnure, who were cool and impersonal, Elizabeth of Yugoslavia was sweet and warm," said Lem Billings. Her then-husband was Howard Oxenberg, an amicable, well-to-do Seventh Avenue clothing manufacturer who remembered "nothing in particular concerning the Kennedy White House." Aware of the gossip, he added: "Everyone knows about the Washington rumor mill. They love to talk there."

One of JFK's more peculiar encounters during his days in office involved Marlene Dietrich, who told movie director Josh Logan of being invited to the White House and, once there, being pounced on by the President. Dietrich, sixteen years older than Kennedy, managed to deflect the attack without too much difficulty. As he walked her to the elevator on her way out, Kennedy told Dietrich that he had a question for her. "What is it?" she said. "Have you ever slept with my father?" asked Kennedy. "He always claimed you did."

There was conjecture that Jackie's many trips away from Washington were prompted in large degree by disgust with her husband's attentions to other women, particularly Marilyn Monroe, who, disguised in a brunette wig, large sunglasses and an old dress, stayed with Kennedy at the Hotel Carlyle in New York, traveled with him aboard Air Force One (the crew was told that she was Peter Lawford's private secretary) and stayed with him at the Lawford beach house in Santa Monica. Lawford arranged many of their meetings and on at least one occasion took photographs of Marilyn performing fellatio on Kennedy while JFK lounged in a large marble bathtub.

Lawford was friendly with both Marilyn and an intimate friend of hers, Patricia Newcomb, a press agent who probably knew as much about Marilyn as anyone, and was sent abroad for several months by Averell Harriman at the request of the Kennedys following Marilyn's death in 1962. As close in later years to Bobby Kennedy as she had once been to Jack (she worked for Bobby in 1964 when he was a candidate for one of New York's U.S. Senate seats), Pat was purportedly a guest at the White House when Jackie went out of town.

"Only once did I see Jackie lose her composure because of another woman," said Lem Billings. "It was over Odile Rodin, the young French wife of Porfirio Rubirosa, the Dominican playboy-ambassador known for his numerous female conquests and marriages to wealthy heiresses Doris Duke and Barbara Hutton. Jack and Rubi were introduced by Igor Cassini. They had one thing in common: a burning interest in women. They became friends; Jack and Odile became better friends. Rubi, never particularly prone to the vagaries of jealousy, didn't seem to mind; Jackie minded a great deal.

"I couldn't understand what it was about her that infuriated Jackie, unless she simply centered her frustrations on Odile. Jack could be shameless in his sexuality, would simply pull girls' dresses up and so forth. He would corner them at White House dinner parties and ask them to step into the next room away from the noise, where they could hold a 'serious discussion.' Although these women may have been serious, he wasn't. He disappeared with Hjordis Niven, the wife of David Niven, below decks of the presidential yacht for ten minutes or so during his 44th birthday party. One can't draw any hard or fast conclusions from that incident, but it was typical of how he dealt with women."

Purette Spiegler, who worked for Kennedy starting in 1954 when he was Senator and continued in the White House as one of several assistants to Tish Baldridge, stipulated that "it was impossible to work for the Kennedys and not be aware of their marital difficulties. I knew, for instance, that Pam Turnure was involved with JFK when he entered the White House. Pam felt sensitive about it, which is natural. I don't know if it bothered Jackie. I'm not certain if Jackie was aware of her husband's philandering, or to what extent she knew. She would go around asking people if they thought he was seeing Pam, which proves that she wasn't sure.

"Don't forget, Jackie was away a lot. Her place would be taken at White House functions either by Lady Bird Johnson or Ethel Kennedy. Jackie was present only when she wanted to be. She seemed extremely bright, extremely perceptive, so if she didn't know everything about her husband's trysts it was only because she didn't want to know.

"I recollect going to Paris during the Kennedy Administration and meeting a political pollster whose girlfriend, a French businesswoman, had lately visited the White House with a group of European industrialists. There was a reception, and as soon as Kennedy saw her, according to her boyfriend, he asked her to spend the night. In my position I heard such stories day and night. Were they true? I doubt it. Some were possibly true, but if everything said about JFK happened, the man would never have worked."

"If only a tenth of the women rumored to have slept with the President actually slept with him, the number would still be mind-boggling," said journalist Francis Lara. "And the number *was* mind-boggling. Equally surprising was the fact that sexual partners never blew the whistle on him. Nor did they seem to inhibit his ability to function as President.

"They came from everywhere. A *Playboy* centerfold model arrived at the White House bearing a letter to the President from an acquaintance of his in California. Kennedy later wrote to his acquaintance: 'I received your message, both of them.'

"Women would constantly ask Pierre Salinger or Ken O'Donnell if they could meet the President for 'just a minute.' They would be let in. If the minute stretched into several hours—then, so what?

"An attractive Scandinavian model came to the White House one day, marched into Salinger's office and asked if she could 'see' the President. I watched Salinger walk her into JFK's office and come out leaving her alone with Kennedy. This scenario, or a variation thereof, repeated itself often in those days.*

"Americans might be shocked by such behavior, but Europeans take it for granted. A handsome man in the world's most powerful position—a European would expect him to have a mistress or two. When Kennedy met with British Prime Minister Harold Macmillan in Bermuda late in 1961, Kennedy was very obviously having an affair with one of the secretaries he brought along. Macmillan thought that for his own protection Kennedy should perhaps be more private about it, but he didn't have moral or ethical reservations.

"Another example of the European attitude regarding love and marriage can be found in the following anecdote: JFK once received two journalists at the White House, one of whom was Oriana Fallaci, the well-known Italian correspondent, who apparently said to the President: 'I would like to introduce you to my husband's girlfriend. . . .' "

A somewhat conflicting view was provided by Phillipe de Bausset, a Washington bureau chief for *Paris Match,* who found that "the Kennedy regime represented a new kind of Madison Avenue manipulation of political forces. It was geared to the young; it represented hope. But it wasn't based on truth. The press knew for example that Jack and Jackie weren't getting along, though JFK tried to protect the image of a man with a loving wife and beautiful children, everybody contented and smiling. The public expected a dream story, so this is what we gave them. In private I would tell my editor certain things I believed to be true and he would say, 'Just don't write that stuff.'

"We had already run into trouble for publishing a story that Caroline was so unhappy she was seeing a child psychiatrist several times a week. Pierre Salinger ex-

---

*When Gore Vidal wrote *The Best Man,* a play based in part on the Kennedy-Nixon presidential campaign, JFK's womanizing emerged as a sub-theme. The JFK character (William Russell) surmises how he'll be able to sneak women into the White House. After JFK took office, Vidal gave copies of the play to both Jack and Jackie. They read their separate copies in bed together. Jackie said to Jack: "This can't be us, can it?" "No," said JFK. "It's just fiction."

ploded when he saw the piece, called us 'a rag' and threatened to sue because the story wasn't true. Jackie must have ridden him fiercely on that one. Paul Mathias, *Match's* New York correspondent and a personal acquaintance of hers, had to appease her with an assortment of presents he bought for her and charged to *Match's* expense account.

"One evening I attended a formal reception at the National Gallery of Art for André Malraux and the painting of the Mona Lisa. Malraux had arranged to have the Louvre place both the Mona Lisa and Whistler's Mother on direct loan to the Kennedys. The two paintings were exhibited separately at the National Gallery (and later at the Metropolitan Museum of Art in New York). I attended the reception with a photographer. The photographer was taking pictures of President Kennedy mingling with the guests. At one point he began talking in a very intimate manner to an exceptionally beautiful French girl. I said to the photographer, 'Take a picture of them. They make a handsome couple.' The President saw what we were doing, made a beeline for us, put his finger on my chest and said: 'You do not publish that picture, understand?' I said, 'All right, we won't.' He did not want to be seen with that particular person.

"That sort of manipulation was commonplace during the Kennedy years. The JFK administration was one huge public relations show. I used to think how amazed the country would be to find out that Jacqueline Kennedy, supposedly the most desirable and exciting woman on earth, couldn't satisfy her husband. It wasn't entirely her fault. Kennedy was too intent on enjoying himself. It may not have hindered his ability to run the country, but it didn't help either. Had he lived, many of his indiscretions would have become public knowledge. He would not have been reelected. As is, he didn't succeed in carrying out his political agenda. We were prisoners of a myth we helped to create. Professional image makers built an image; journalists bought into the propaganda and were later forced to go along with it."

Despite claims that Kennedy's womanizing had no effect on his Presidential duties, Langdon Marvin recalled two instances which, while humorous, might well have had disastrous results. "Both took place at the Hotel Carlyle in New York," he explained. "In the first, Jack decided to attend a private party being thrown by a female friend of ours in a townhouse across the street from the Carlyle. The hostess, a famous woman in New York society who frequently arranged girls for Jack, had promised a number of attractive young damsels on this occasion, and Jack simply didn't want the Secret Service tagging along. I knew a circuitous route out of the Carlyle through the hotel basement. We managed to elude the Secret Service and reach the party undetected. Within minutes Jack had made his choice of partner for the evening and gone off with her to her apartment. Moments later the Secret Service arrived. Where was the President? Nobody knew. The agent began to pale. On the street in front of the townhouse stood an Army lieutenant with an attaché case handcuffed to his wrist. It suddenly hit me. Jack was off getting laid and the Bagman with the black satchel had been left behind. The Russians could have bombed us to hell and back, and there would have been nothing we could have done about it.

"The second mishap occurred when Jack misplaced his little black telephone book. He had dropped it on the sidewalk somewhere in Arizona during a visit with state officials. Fortunately a former classmate of mine from Harvard, the Governor of Arizona at the time, picked it up, or one of his aides did, and said, 'Send it to the President at the Carlyle.' Until recently Jack had occupied the penthouse apartment at the Carlyle that faced east. The other penthouse apartment, facing west, was one bedroom larger. As soon as it became available, Jack traded apartments and moved in. When the Soviet Foreign Minister visited the United States for a United Nations conference, he was given Jack's old apartment. Unaware of the switch, the elevator operator at the Carlyle placed the parcel containing Jack's little black book on a table in the Soviet Foreign Minister's foyer.

"A day later Jack called me in a panic. 'Where the hell's that damn address book? The elevator boy insists he left it in the foyer, but it's not here.'

"It didn't take long to discern that there had been a terrible mix-up. I envisioned all sorts of headlines about our sex-crazed President in *Pravda* and *The New York Times*. Rushing to the Carlyle, I located the elevator operator, slipped him a couple of $20 bills and told him to find a key to Penthouse East. "The President's apartment?' he asked. 'No,' I said, 'the President's *former* apartment.' He produced a key and we went up there together. The parcel containing the little black book was still sitting on the foyer table where it had been left; to my further relief, it hadn't been touched."

The "other woman" syndrome touched Jackie in different ways on different occasions. At intervals she would retreat and mope for long stretches, very aloof from everyone and glacially cold to the President. It was at these junctures that she went on shopping binges, disbursing thousands of dollars on jewelry, designer clothes, paintings; whatever captured her fancy.

The big payday for Jackie came when the President gave her the money to design and build "Wexford," her own weekend retreat at Atoka, west of Middleburg in the rolling hills of Virginia. The land was sold to the Kennedys for a token payment by Paul and Bunny Mellon. Wexford thus adjoined the vast Mellon estate, and until she built her own stable, Jackie boarded her horses with the Mellons. "I need a place where I can go to be alone," she told friends who wondered why she preferred Wexford to the Kennedy compound at Hyannis Port. It was Jackie's sense of independence, her recognition that she and Jack needed to be apart occasionally, that helped sustain their marriage.

"Jackie had the whip-hand insofar as she cared little what people thought and could therefore walk out of the White House any day if so disposed," observed Peter Lawford. "She also knew that Jack was jealous of her seeing other men because he was convinced that she was doing the same things he was doing. She played on that jealousy in retaliation for his affairs and felt pleased and somewhat reassured when he responded.

"At one particular White House gala, Jackie drank too much champagne, discarded her shoes and danced and flirted with every man in sight. She would throw her head back and laugh, or make eyes at her partner. The ploy evidently worked—Jack took notice: so did the other guests at the White House that night."

Jack and Jackie renewed their hostilities during an Easter pilgrimage to Palm Beach. One Sunday morning when the President balked at the prospect of attending church, the First Lady was overheard saying to him,

"Come on now, you son of a bitch. You got yourself into this and you know your public demands it. So get your damn tie and coat and let's go."

On Good Friday, following another domestic squabble, Jackie went to Mass in a bandana, a short sleeveless dress, sunglasses, and sandals without stockings, scowling at the news photographers as they snapped pictures. To make matters worse, Peter Lawford called for her after church in Bermuda shorts and bare feet.

Benno (Gilbert) Graziani, an Italian journalist who was to grow close to Jackie and even closer to Lee Radziwill, saw still another side of the First Lady. "While Jackie was showing Benno around the White House," reported Francis Lara, "she suddenly opened the door to an office in which two young women were seated. Jackie turned to Benno and said, 'Those two are my husband's lovers."

To the Secret Service, the two in question were known as "Fiddle and Faddle." "They were college roommates who wanted to work on the Kennedy campaign," said Pierre Salinger. "When he was elected, they went on to work in the White House. Priscilla Weir (Fiddle) assisted Evelyn Lincoln; Jill Cowan (Faddle) worked with me. Did Jack play around? Let's say he separated business from pleasure. And he was a human being with human frailties."

The degree to which Jackie reacted to Jack's marital byplay shifted according to her moods. But as time passed she became increasingly philosophic. There were occasions when she would actually tease him about his need for other women. During one vacation in Palm Beach when she and the Lawfords had gone swimming, she returned to the house and said to Jack, "You'd better get down there fast. I saw two of them you'd really go for." Another time, at a White House dinner party, she seated him between two of his latest conquests—just to watch him squirm.

According to Truman Capote, Jackie's only extramarital relationship took place inside her head: "There was a lot of whispering about Jackie but little scandal. Most of her supposed flings were escapades of the imagination. She kept a running log of mind fucks, at the top of which like a colossus loomed André Malraux, followed by Dr. Christiaan Barnard, Henry Kissinger, Alistair Cooke, Cary

Grant,* Robert McNamara, General Maxwell Taylor and
Rudi Nureyev, until she saw photographs of men cavorting nude in Rudi's guest room. Then she decided she
only 'admired' Rudi. She also mentioned Prince Philip,
John Glenn, and Eugene R. Black, President of the
World Bank. There were constant rumors linking her
with Washingtonians like Clark Clifford and Franklin
Roosevelt, Jr. Gianni Agnelli, head of the Fiat automobile empire, was another frequently mentioned possibility. It was all make-believe. Jackie wasn't really flirtatious,
and there was nothing seductive or sensual about her."

There were those who disagreed with Capote. A number of Jackie's friends and acquaintances considered her
a great flirt and coquette, a woman with a wonderful
teasing way about her. She was ultra-feminine. She adored
men as much as her husband adored women. One gossipy tidbit had it that Jackie had become involved with
one of her Secret Service agents. The truth was that the
agent had taken a fancy to Jackie and made the mistake
of letting his feelings be known. Jackie responded by
insisting the agent be transferred to another unit. In
general she claimed to be bewildered by such rumors.
"What can I do?" she asked Toni Bradlee. "I have
dinner with someone, dance with someone for more than
one dance, take a walk with someone, get photographed
with someone without Jack—and immediately people say,
'My God, they must be having an affair.' How do you
respond to something like that?"

"I don't believe Jackie ever cheated on Jack," said
Peter Lawford. "On the other hand, she wasn't completely honest about herself. She doctored up her family
background. She told social fibs to avoid having to make
appearances at certain official functions. She would tell
the press practically anything to get them off her back.
Meanwhile, she obviously knew about Jack's affairs. She
told me she knew. She said once she caught him in the
act. I'm sure she wanted me to know she was aware of
my role in Jack's love life. Taking all this into consideration, it's possible Jackie could have opted to have an
affair of her own. I rather doubt it, but it's possible. She
loved hearing about other people's indiscretions; so did

*Cary Grant also appealed to JFK. The President would call the
actor from time to time "just to hear that impeccable voice."

Jack for that matter But Jackie never talked about herself, whereas if you prodded Jack he would occasionally open up. She felt there was a difference between being curious and candid. I remember something she once said: 'Some day, maybe everything about me will be known, but not with my cooperation.' "

Joe Acquaotta, a driver with the Esplanade Limousine Service in Palm Beach, recalled an incident involving Jackie that took place during one of her many visits to the area. "One day at about 3:30 in the morning, I get a call to pick somebody up at the Biltmore Hotel in my limo. I get there and see a man and a woman looking very sweet, holding hands, misty eyed. The woman breaks away and climbs into the car. It's Jackie Kennedy. I'd driven her maybe fifty times in Palm Beach, so I sure as hell knew what she looked like. I say, 'Hi, Jackie. How're you tonight?' 'I'm not Jackie,' she says. I look at her again in the rearview mirror. It's Jackie, all right. She looks back at me and says nothing. Finally she gives me an address and I drive her there. It's the oceanfront home of Colonel C. Michael Paul, which, as everyone knows, is where she and the President are staying on this visit. As she gets out, I say, 'Good night, Jackie.' She gives me a dirty look and marches off. I have no idea what in hell she was doing holding hands with some fellow in front of the Biltmore Hotel at 3:30 in the morning, but I'm sure it was her. I'd stake my life on it."

19

The most pervasive cover-up perpetrated by the Kennedy administration involved Jack and Jackie's relationship with Dr. Max Jacobson, a New York physician also known as "Dr. Feelgood" and "Miracle Max," a German refugee whose amphetamine-laced injections of multi-vitamins, steroids, hormones, enzymes and animal organ cells eventually led to a license revocation hearing with the New York State Attorney General's office. Max had been pumping amphetamine—the powerful stimulant the drug culture calls "speed"—into the veins of dozens of the country's most famous artists, writers, politicians and jet-setters for well over a decade. Although replete with the names of celebrities, Jacobson's practice catered to people from all walks of life, including some 400 multiple sclerosis sufferers, a number of whom continued to consult with him long after his medical license was revoked.

Many of Max's patients swore by the potions he concocted in his 155 East 72nd Street office and insisted—without always knowing what was in the injections—that he had helped them to attain good health and great success. Most claimed his shots gave them boundless energy, more productive and pleasurable lives, and the ability to work long hours without fatigue.

But at least a few of the doctor's patients quit the treatments, complaining of bad reactions and enslaving dependency on amphetamines. Used over a long period, in medium-to-large doses, the drug has been known to produce memory loss, hallucinations, depression, anxiety, weight loss, paranoia, schizophrenia and hypertension. In later years, the New York City Medical Examiner's office would claim that one of Max's patients died of "acute amphetamine poisoning."

For all his treatments' risks, Dr. Jacobson's list of followers reads like a "Who's Who" of the rich and

famous.* Their ailments ran a long gamut, but the doctor's technique was always the same. Dark-haired, brown-
eyed, red-cheeked, vital, always pacing, Jacobson played
the role of guru and physician. He did not believe in
extensive tests or conventional medications. He was
brusque, forceful, dogmatic and humorous, a compulsive
diagnostician who depended on his intuition rather than
on the complex charts, graphs and reports used by the
majority of his colleagues. A nonconformist and icono-
clast, he frequently worked eighteen hours or more per
day, seven days a week; he would inject himself before
injecting a patient with any new substance in his vast
arsenal. Max's patients often waited for hours to be admitted to one of several rooms in his office. He appeared
suddenly, often in baggy trousers and bloodstained surgical coat, gave an injection, exchanged a few words, then
rushed away to his next patient. When a patient pursued
him with questions, he found himself addressing the doctor's back. Max Jacobson maintained a balance in flight,
something approaching perpetual motion.

John Kennedy's first contact with Max came in the fall
of 1960, one week after addressing a group of Protestant
clergymen in Houston (his dramatic separation-of-church-
and-state address) and a week before his first televised
debate with Nixon. Kennedy had set a grueling campaign
pace, and the long hours and endless travel had finally
taken their toll. Chuck Spalding commented on how tired
his friend looked. He said he knew a doctor, Max

*In addition to Jack and Jackie Kennedy, his best-known patients
included Winston Churchill, Cecil B. DeMille, Judy Garland, Mar-
lene Dietrich, Peter Lorre, Alan Jay Lerner, Van Cliburn, Otto
Preminger, Emilio Pucci, Edward G. Robison, Tennessee Williams,
Truman Capote, Billy Wilder, Hermione Gingold, Eddie Fisher,
Margaret Leighton, Anaïs Nin, Henry Miller, Anthony Quinn, Yul
Brynner, Arlene Francis, Martin Gabel, Franchot Tone, Senator
Claude Pepper, Burgess Meredith, Chita Rivera, Rita Moreno, Chita Rivera,
Hedy Lamarr, Kurt Baum, Leontyne Price, Franco Zeffirelli, Serge
Stavitsky, Maynard Ferguson, Andy Williams, Eddie Albert, Mel
Allen, Mickey Mantle, Roscoe Lee Browne, Tony Franciosa, Roddy
McDowall, Mabel Mercer, Stavros Niarchos, Rebekah Harkness
and Pat Suzuki. Suzuki claimed that visiting Max's office "was like
walking into the William Morris Agency. And of course all these
celebrities turned around and betrayed him when things got a little
tough for him. They disavowed him. They didn't want the publicity."

Jacobson, who had cured him of a nasty case of mononu-
cleosis.

It wasn't the first time Kennedy had heard the name.
Mark Shaw, another of Jacobson's patients, was a staff
photographer for *Life,* at that moment on special assignment to photograph Kennedy and his family. Shaw and
his wife, actress Pat Suzuki, star of the Broadway musical
Flower Drum Song, occasionally socialized with the Kennedys. Mark, who often shot fashion layouts for *Life,*
would later bring back pre-publication photos of London
and Paris fashion openings for Jackie so she could study
the latest designs, then send a friend to pick up this or
that selection. "As First Lady, Jackie was supposed to
buy only American clothes and claimed she did, but
actually she used a lot of European designers," said Pat
Suzuki. "She used European designers and probably just
tore out the labels."

Mark Shaw spoke so highly of Jacobson that Kennedy
gave Chuck Spalding the go-ahead to make an appointment for him. Spalding's only request was that Max clear
his office of other patients and all but essential staff. For
obvious reasons, explained Spalding, the consultation
would have to remain private and confidential.

Max agreed, and the Democratic presidential nominee
arrived at the office alone, having successfully "lost" his
Secret Service escort. He told Max that Mark and Chuck
had each recommended him, and spoken of how he had
helped them withstand the strain of professional activity.

Kennedy said that the demands of his political campaign had been both physically and mentally draining;
that he had difficulty concentrating for long stretches and
often felt tense and weak.

Dr. Jacobson took a brief case history, asked several
questions concerning Kennedy's condition, informed him
he was suffering from stress, and assured him that the
treatment of stress was one of his specialties.

To prove it he gave JFK an injection. The future
President felt a rush of warmth spread through his body.
"After his treatment, he told me his muscle weakness
had disappeared," Jacobson would write in an unpublished autobiography. "He felt . . .calm and very alert. I
gave him a bottle of vitamin drops to be taken orally,
after which he left."

Jacobson treated Kennedy a second time soon after he

became President-elect, visiting him at Hyannis Port with Mark Shaw and Pat Suzuki. Afterwards he attended the inauguration as the guest of still another patient, Florida Senator Claude Pepper and his wife,* but did not hear from Kennedy again until just before the President and Mrs. Kennedy left for Canada on what was to be their first State visit to a foreign country. At that time, Jacobson received a telephone call from Dr. Janet Travell, the President's personal physician, who asked him detailed questions on his treatment of stress.

"Is this in reference to the President?" Jacobson inquired.

"It is," said Travell.

Max gave the White House physician a complete run-down on his treatment of stress, but when he offered to send her the same information in writing and a sample material for tests, she declined.

On May 12, 1961, four days before the Canada trip, Max received a telephone call from the White House. Would he be willing to fly to Palm Beach to see the President?

"When?" asked Max.

"Right now."

On his arrival, he was met by a car and driven to the Charles and Jayne Wrightsman residence, where the Kennedys were staying. He sat and waited on a back porch for several minutes until the President appeared. Kennedy came right to the point. He was concerned with Jackie's overall health. Since the delivery of John Jr., she had suffered periodic depression and severe headaches. He wanted to know whether she could endure the strain of their forthcoming trip to Canada, but more important, whether she would be able to accompany him to Paris, Vienna and London in early June for a Summit conference with Soviet Premier Nikita Khrushchev. Max told Kennedy that to answer the question accurately he would have to meet the patient.

---

*Claude Pepper and his wife became Max's patients in the late 1940s. They remained stalwart supporters long after his medical license was revoked. "For more than 30 years," said Pepper, "I suffered from intense eczema on my hands and scrotum. I had been to Walter Reed Hospital, various military hospitals, skin specialists, the Harvard Medical School. None of them did me any good. Then Max came along, gave me some shots and the itching disappeared."

Jackie was resting in Jayne Wrightsman's bedroom. "She seemed unhappy and complained of a sharp migraine," writes Max. "After a brief discussion I said, 'The least I can do for you is stop your migraine.' I did. I gave her a shot. Within minutes the headache had gone. This broke the ice. Her mood changed completely."

Despite several minor disagreements between Prime Minister John Diefenbaker and President Kennedy, the Canadian conference went well except for a misfortune that had nothing to do with diplomacy. During a tree-planting ceremony on the grounds of Government House in Ottawa, Kennedy bent over to break ground with a shovel and sprained his back. He returned to Washington in acute pain, barely able to hobble.

Several days later, Max's receptionist received an urgent telephone call from Mrs. Dunn in Washington. "Dunn" was the code name he had been assigned by the Secret Service to alert him to calls from the White House. He took the call and was asked if he could fly to Washington. The commercial airlines were fully booked but Mark Shaw, a pilot during World War II, co-owned a twin-engine Cessna aircraft and agreed to fly him to D.C.

"Reservations had been made for me at the Washington Sheraton," writes Max. "The next morning a car took me to the White House. In order not to attract the attention of tourists and press . . . I carried my medical supplies in an attaché case rather than a medical bag. From the entrance I was led to the Secret Service desk guarding the elevator. . . .I was accompanied upstairs where I was seated in the vestibule. After a short time, Providencia Parades appeared and offered me breakfast in the family dining room. Afterwards, she showed me into the sitting room and announced me to Mrs. Kennedy. I was surprised to find her in comparatively good spirits. She was apprehensive about the pending European trip and its strenuous schedule. After her treatment, she said, 'Jack wants to see you.'

"George Thomas . . . appeared at the door and led me through a corridor connecting the two bedrooms to the President. President Kennedy greeted me cordially and asked me to be seated.

"He confirmed the recent press reports of his having aggravated his back condition while planting a tree in Canada. He faced a very tight schedule and was afraid his back might give him trouble during his forthcoming European trip where he would be required to stand or sit for hours on end. Dr. Travell had alleviated his pain by spraying his back with ethyl chloride, which numbs the skin on contact. This method had once been used and then abandoned in Russia . . . because of its lack of therapeutic value. . . .

"I demonstrated an exercise to strengthen the back muscles. I then administered his first [back] treatment, not only to relieve his local discomfort but to provide him with additional strength to cope with stress. Immediately after his treatment was over, he stood up and walked back and forth several times. He said, 'I feel much better.' I replied, jokingly, 'I'm sorry to hear that.'

"He laughed and said, 'I would like you to come with me to Europe next week. I hope you can arrange your schedule.' My answer was, It goes without saying that I consider it a small service not only to you but to the office that made it possible [for me] to escape the persecution of Hitler and establish myself as an American citizen.' "

According to Jacobson's autobiography and corroborating Secret Service files, Max spent four successive days in Washington treating the President and First Lady before returning to New York. On his second day at the White House, he was confronted by an agitated Jackie Kennedy. She had discovered a vial of Demerol in the President's bathroom. Further investigation revealed that a Secret Service man had supplied her husband with the unauthorized drug. The agent was quickly dismissed.

"This was not enough," writes Jacobson, who opposed the use of alcohol and all opiates in conjunction with his amphetamine treatments. "During my next meeting with President Kennedy, I brought up the events of the preceding day with the discovery of the Demerol. In no uncertain terms I emphasized that, contrary to popular belief, Demerol was not only highly addictive, but it would interfere with his function. And furthermore, if he continued to use it, I would no longer see him."

Truman Capote described the common effect of the Jacobson amphetamine treatment as one of "instant euphoria. You feel like Superman. You're flying. Ideas come at the speed of light. You go 72 hours straight without so much as a coffee break. You don't need sleep,

you don't need nourishment. If it's sex you're after, you
go all night. Then you crash—it's like falling down a well,
like parachuting without a parachute. You want to hold
onto something and there's nothing out there but air.
You go running back to East 72nd Street. You're looking
for the German mosquito, the insect with the magic
pinprick. He stings you, and all at once you're soaring
again."

The Kennedys were already mildly addicted by May
31, their departure date for Paris. The President insisted
that Max inject him aboard Air Force One while they
were still on the ground at Idlewild. Max then disem-
barked and with his wife Nina, who also made the trip,
boarded an Air France airliner. It was "the strangest
flight I have ever experienced. Nina and I were the only
passengers on the plane. The pursers and hostesses had a
marvelous time and we received the lousiest service."

The astronomical cost of chartering a transatlantic airliner for two passengers—in order to masquerade their
presence as part of the presidential entourage—would be
absorbed by the American taxpayer, as were their lavish
hotel accommodations. In Paris, the Jacobsons were assigned a huge suite at L'Hôtel Napoleon, then still one of
the more expensive hotels in the city.

Parisians took delight in *la belle Zha-kee's* beaming
presence and her "Gothic Madonna" look. From the
moment Charles de Gaulle greeted the Kennedys at Orly
Airport with a 101-gun salute, all eyes were on Jacqueline, whose major political role in Paris was that of good-
will ambassador, a go-between in what JFK described as
"my difficult talks with Charles de Gaulle."

"I do not think it entirely inappropriate for me to
introduce myself," said JFK. "I am the man who accompanied Jacqueline Kennedy to Paris—and I have enjoyed
it." President Kennedy, the man behind the woman, was
voicing his pride over the tumultuous reception Europeans accorded his wife.

It was Jackie's moment of triumph. She felt like an
empress. She stayed on Quai d'Orsay at the Palais des
Affaires Étrangeres, a large chàteau fronting the Seine,
slept in the *Chambre de la Reine* in a bed last occupied by
Belgium's Queen Fabiola, bathed in a silver mosaic tub
in a mother-of-pearl bathroom, was driven around in a
black bubbletop Citroën limousine with an escort of plumed

horsemen riding alongside. Alexandre, hairdresser of Greta Garbo and Elizabeth Taylor was called in to style Jackie's hair. Hubert de Givenchy designed the gown she would wear to the state supper at Versailles. Her face for that function would be made up by the world-famous Nathalie.

Her fashions and hairstyle became the talk of the town. Although the overall reaction was highly positive, Jackie had her detractors. Countess Consuelo Crespi, fashion consultant to *Vogue,* found the Givenchy look "stunning" but Alexandre's work "not becoming at all. It was not Jackie Kennedy. She wore her hair down for a formal luncheon with De Gaulle at the Elysée Palace, but European women don't wear their hair down on formal occasions. Then for the first evening gala she wore a sweeping fourteenth-century hairdo with a topknot; on the second night—a candlelit supper for 150 guests in the Hall of Mirrors at the Palace of Versailles followed by a command ballet performance in the Palace's Louis XV theater and an outdoor fireworks display—she wore a big chignon topped by a fragile diamond tiara. It was the first time she had changed her hairdo since becoming First Lady. It was a mistake. It didn't work."

Jackie evidently thought otherwise. She asked Alexandre to accompany her to Vienna and London. Later she invited him to visit the White House and continued to use him on occasion years later after she became Mrs. Onassis. General de Gaulle called her "a charming and ravishing woman with extraordinary hair and eyes." He measured every word she said, at one point leaning over and whispering into President Kennedy's ear: "Your wife knows more French history than most French women." "And men," observed Kennedy. It was Jackie who presented De Gaulle with her country's official present: an original letter from the Washington-Lafayette correspondence, which had been purchased for the occasion by Charles and Jayne Wrightsman, at a cost of $90,000.

Following the first luncheon, Jackie hurried off to a child-care and training center. Enormous crowds gathered on every street corner for a look at Jackie and her well-guarded entourage, a group that included Rose Kennedy, Eunice Shriver, Lee Radziwill, Miche Bouvier (then living in Paris and working for Grumman Aircraft) and Tish Baldridge, who attempted to explain Jackie's popularity to the foreign press. "John Kennedy is our President, but she's our movie star."

Although Janet Travell accompanied the Kennedys as White House physician, it was Max Jacobson who provided their medical treatment. Michael J. Samek, a friend and patient, had rigged a special leather carrying-case for Max with built-in pockets for vials and medications. Medical case in hand, Max arrived at the Palais des Affairs Étrangeres immediately following the opening night dinner.

"It was most unusual to find Jackie so loquacious in contrast to her usual reserved attitude toward me," writes Max. "I looked around her room and spotted in a corner an irregularity of the otherwise perfect detail work in the molding. I suspected a microphone. I called her attention to it by pointing in its direction, and put my other hand to my lips. She quickly understood. After our meeting I proceeded to the President's room . . .

"The President was very composed. . . . He asked whether we had a comfortable flight and told me he wanted to see me early the following morning. With the change in time plus a strenuous day, I noted it was important that he spend a restful night."

The next morning, after being treated by Jacobson, Kennedy rejoined De Gaulle for another round of talks, while Jackie, led by Madame de Gaulle and André Malraux, toured the Impressionist paintings exhibit at the Jeu de Paume Museum, journeyed to Malmaison (Empress Josephine's country retreat) and ate a gourmet lunch at La Celle St. Cloud, the long-ago hideaway of Mme. de Pompadour.*

In the late afternoon, with but a single Secret Service agent in tow, Jackie used an unmarked car to visit some of her old Left Bank haunts. For the first time since her arrival she was not recognized. She was still talking about her little excursion that evening when the presidential party arrived at the Palace of Versailles.

More than once that night Jackie was called upon to act as interpreter for her husband and the imposingly tall French President. At the Versailles Theatre after supper,

---

*"Jackie is unique for the wife of an American President," André Malraux told De Gaulle after the Kennedys departed France "Yes, she's unique," agreed de Gaulle. "I can see her in about ten years on the yacht of a Greek petrol millionaire."

she and De Gaulle discussed French literature and poetry. The following day she told Max Jacobson she couldn't remember a time when she had felt better or more confident.

Nina Jacobson remained behind in Paris while Max joined the President, the First Lady and her thirty-five trunks aboard Air Force One for the flight to Vienna. They landed in a heavy rainstorm and quickly divided into two motorcades. One followed Jacqueline to her engagement with Mrs. Nina Khrushchev. The other followed the President to the private residence of the American Ambassador in the Semmering Mountains outside Vienna, where the first meeting with Khrushchev was scheduled to take place.

"No sooner had we arrived than I was hurried up to the living quarters and into the President's room," writes Jacobson. 'Khrushchev is supposedly on his way,' he said. 'You'd better give me something for my back.'

"During the meeting I waited in the vestibule, where I sat on a wide windowsill admiring the view of the mountains. . . . I hadn't eaten since breakfast on the plane, and I was very happy to see Provi [Parades] and George [Thomas] approach me with a platter of Viennese boiled ham sandwiches. As the hours passed I wondered how everything was going. I became increasingly apprehensive. Then the President appeared at the door. I asked, 'How are you feeling, Mr. President?' 'May I be permitted to take a leak before I respond,' he said. When he returned he said that the meeting was nearly over and he was fine. I could retire to my hotel."

Despite the psychological bolstering provided by the amphetamine injections, the President's meetings with Khrushchev did not go well. Secretary of Labor Arthur Goldberg and Secretary of State Dean Rusk had counseled Kennedy to delay the Summit—not enough time had elapsed since the invasion of Cuba debacle—but in an effort to reduce Cold War tension, JFK decided to forge ahead; the result was a sound verbal thrashing at the hands of an older, wiser, more seasoned in-fighter.

If the Summit represented a tactical failure for JFK, it provided another triumph for Jacqueline. As in Paris she dazzled the crowds, the foreign dignitaries and the international press. She even impressed Nikita Khrushchev.

The state banquet took place at Schönbrunn Palace,

Vienna's answer to Versailles. During most of the dinner an enormous crowd stood outside the baroque palace chanting the First Lady's name: "Jah-kee! Jah-kee!" The chanting grew so loud that palace guards had to disperse the crowd.

"They seem to appreciate you," Khrushchev said to Jackie. She beamed. He told her how "exquisite" he found her pink-beaded floor-length white gown. The 250 dinner guests couldn't help but notice that he had drawn his chair closer to hers. They talked about horses and Ukranian folk dances. When he informed her that the Soviet Ukraine had more teachers than the czarist Ukraine, she said, "Oh, Mr. Chairman, don't bore me with statistics." He laughed. When she asked about the Russian dogs that were being sent into outer space, he promised to send her one and did. A photographer for a British newspaper asked Khrushchev if he would pose for a picture with President Kennedy. "I would rather pose with his wife," said the Soviet leader.

Godfrey McHugh, who made the trip as JFK's Air Force aide, recalled how "down" everyone felt on the flight to London. "It was like riding with the losing baseball team after the World Series. Nobody said very much. The President had been intimidated by Khrushchev, particularly on the issue of Berlin—the existing Berlin border would be legalized, East Berlin to be under the complete control of East Germany while West Berlin would be designated an international city. If America attempted to interfere with these plans, said Khrushchev, there would be war. JFK observed that if there were ever a nuclear war between the two great nations, more than seventy million people would perish within the first ten minutes. Khrushchev looked him in the eye and said, 'So be it!'

"Jackie also seemed depressed. While aboard the plane, she wrote a long letter to General de Gaulle commenting on the Summit and expressing her gratitude to him for making her stay in Paris so memorable. It was in French and she asked me to proof it. 'It's a wonderful letter, Jackie,' I said, 'but as a lady, it is inappropriate to address De Gaulle as *"mon général."'* I explained that *mon général* is strictly a male form of address. 'The French are very ticklish when it comes to proper etiquette. He might take offense.'

" 'In that case, the State Department can write its own goddamn letter,' she said, stomping back to her seat."

Air Force One was met at Heathrow Airport by British Prime Minister Harold Macmillan, American Ambassador David Bruce and a cheering throng of Britons. While the President's car proceeded to the Radziwill residence, a three-story Georgian townhouse at 4 Buckingham Place, around the corner from Buckingham Palace, Max Jacobson rejoined his wife at Claridge's. They had barely checked into their hotel room when the telephone rang. It was the President's Secret Service agent. The President's back had begun to hurt again; would Dr. Jacobson mind coming over?

"The car took me to the back entrance," writes Jacobson. "The driver escorted me through the garden to the back door, which was not immediately opened, the reason being that it led into a servants' bathroom which appeared to be temporarily occupied.

"From there we ascended a steep staircase to a large foyer containing nineteenth-century Victorian sculptures on marble pedestals. We climbed another staircase to the second floor. . . . I walked into Lee Radziwill's bedroom where Lee, the President and Jackie were . . . chatting. The President and I retired to an anteroom where I attended to him. After also attending to Mrs. Kennedy, I descended the stairs back to the foyer. . . . Suddenly a handsome man emerged dressed in tails, shook my hand and smiling, introduced himself as 'Stas.' This was the prince. I left and returned to Claridge's."

Max would soon add the Radziwills to his stable of devoted patients. He would go on safari with Stas and visit the Radziwills both in London and at their Queen Anne country estate near Henley-on-Thames. Because Max loved swimming as a form of exercise, the Radziwills installed a huge indoor pool on their Henley property. They also saw Max whenever they turned up in New York, where they owned a twelve-room Fifth Avenue duplex.

The main reason for the London stopover was the christening of Anna Christina Radziwill, the infant daughter of Prince and Princess Radziwill. The ceremony took place at Westminster Cathedral on June 5 and was capped by a reception at the Radziwill residence, where guests included the Duke and Duchess of Devonshire, Ran-

dolph Churchill, Lady Elizabeth Cavendish, Sir Hugh
and Lady Antonia Fraser and Douglas Fairbanks, Jr. The
Kennedys later attended a dinner given by Queen Elizabeth and Prince Philip at Buckingham Palace. Fellow
guests included Harold Macmillan, Louis Earl Mountbat-
ten, David Ormsby-Gore (British Ambassador to the
U.S. and an old friend of the Kennedy family) and other
British dignitaries.

Following the dinner, at 11:45 p.m., the President
again boarded Air Force One for the return flight to
Washington. Jackie remained behind in anticipation of a
week-long trip to Greece that she planned on making
with her sister and brother-in-law.

Two days after his arrival and a televised report to the
nation, President Kennedy flew to Palm Beach where he
agreed to an exclusive interview with Hugh Sidey of
Time-Life. Sidey had dinner with Kennedy and Chuck
Spalding "and a couple of the secretaries" at the Wrightsmans' home. Although he said nothing about it in his
Life article, Sidey was apparently struck by the ostentatious manner in which JFK flaunted his playboy life-style.

While her husband dallied in Palm Beach, Jackie and
the Radziwills made the most of their Greek stay. The
Greek government had provided a commodious villa and
a 125-foot yacht for a tour of the Cyclades Islands. They
visited the artists' colony on Hydra, the small harbor of
Poros, the ruins of the Temple of Poseidon at Sounion.
Jackie went swimming, water-skied, danced the chacha
to "Never on Sunday" at an Athens nightclub, saw the
Acropolis, visited Delos, the birthplace of Apollo (the
island was closed to tourists the day of Jackie's visit), and
strolled the cobblestone streets of Mykonos while hundreds of reporters, photographers and local citizens trailed
after her.

On Jackie's return to Washington, the Kennedys began
using the services of Jacobson on a regular basis, at least
once a week and occasionally as often as three and four
times weekly. By the summer of 1961, they had both
developed a strong dependence on amphetamines. Like
many of Max's patients, they found that they functioned
more efficiently, felt more energetic and required less
sleep than they had in years.

"On the 18th and 19th of September 1961," writes
Jacobson, "I was in the White House when we learned

that Dag Hammarskjöld,* Secretary-General of the United Nations, had died in an airplane crash in Africa. There was great excitement because the Russians would put up a struggle in the naming of a successor to Hammarskjöld. There were rumors (later confirmed) that the crash had not been accidental. Kennedy wanted to appear before the General Assembly and convince them to reject the Russians' 'Troika' (triumvirate) proposal rather than continue with a single Secretary-General. In Kennedy's opinion, this would result in a paralysis of the United Nations' function in the event of a nuclear (or any other) catastrophe.

"Early on the morning of the 25th of September. . . I was called to the phone. I was told to [come] immediately to the Carlyle. I arrived an hour and a half before Kennedy's scheduled speech before the General Assembly. I went directly to his penthouse apartment where David Powers opened the door. Meetings had apparently gone on all night judging from the empty and half-empty glasses and full ashtrays strewn about the room. Powers led me to the President's bedroom. President Kennedy was still in night clothes, and he greeted me with a whisper so hoarse that I could barely understand him. He challenged me, saying, 'What are you going to do about this?' It was imperative that he deliver his U.N. address in person. His presence was necessary to defeat the Russian proposal. I told the President that I would restore his voice. . . . I said I would give him a subcutaneous injection slightly below the larynx. . . . I can still see the surprised expression on Kennedy's face when he could speak again with a normal voice."

"Amphetamines were not illegal in those days, and they represented only one ingredient of many in Max's shots," stressed Michael Samek. "He had a lab in his office where he experimented with his medications. I sometimes helped him prepare the injections. He was influenced by Dr. Paul Niehans, founder of 'La Prairie,' the famous Swiss clinic. Niehans specialized in the injection of animal cells—mainly sheep—into the human blood-

*Hammarskjöld once expressed irritation at Jackie's publicity, and scoffed at her beauty, telling Adlai Stevenson, "I don't know what all the fuss is about. She doesn't even bother attending the parties thrown in her honor by the Congressional wives. Yet for all her disdain, it's impossible to pick up a paper without reading about her."

stream. Like Niehans, Max believed that although he could not prolong life, he could improve its quality. His philosophy was 'Why suffer if you don't have to?' Max used a lot of placenta and bone in his injections. He used calcium, which gave the patient a warm flush the moment it entered the system. He used liver cells quite a bit. He used liver cells to invigorate Jackie. At one point he began experimenting with electric eels. He thought it significant that eels had no kidney. I volunteered for an electric eel injection. His son, Tommy, who was then an intern, marveled at my confidence. I did trust Max. I believed in him more than in any other physician before or since.

"The Kennedys also apparently believed in Max.* They never asked what the injections contained, and he never told them. If he had a shortcoming it was his impatience in answering medical questions from patients. In addition he was disorganized. Once a week or so, I used to put his medical bag in order, clean it up, clean the bottles and so on. That way he at least looked professional, especially when he went to see the Kennedys. In general Max didn't care much about appearances. He was an improviser. His office didn't conform to the standard doctor's office. I was his greatest critic. I used to say, 'Max, you've got to straighten this office out and keep your records straight.' So straightening his bag became my responsibility. I also went out and ordered some waiting-room furniture. Max was very impatient. He didn't have time for such nonsense. I say 'nonsense' because that's how he might have thought of it.

"Another thing about Max—he wasn't associated with any conventional hospitals or medical organizations. He wasn't a member of the American Medical Association. He considered most doctors purely businessmen, money-makers. His disdain for the medical establishment coupled with his success in treating so many well-known patients gave rise to a good deal of professional animos-

---

*In 1962, America delivered medical supplies, farm equipment and foodstuffs to Cuba as ransom for prisoners taken captive during the Bay of Pigs invasion. The main "rescue ship," privately owned by a multi-millionaire named Piero Johnson, was renamed the S.S. Maximus, in honor of Max Jacobson. The name was suggested by JFK.

ity against him. The American Medical Association was out to get him. Max was a medical anarchist, a futurist. He wanted more rationality in medicine. Other doctors were looking to 'cure' MS patients, while Max only wanted to make their lives a little more bearable. Max hated hospitals, hated sickness, hated death and funerals, and so did John Kennedy, for that matter. Kennedy was the ideal patient for Max because he loved life so much. There's that anecdote about how Caroline once showed her father a dead bird she had found on the White House lawn, and how he cringed and said, 'Get that thing out of here, get it away from me.' That's something Max might have done.

"I once went up to Hyannis Port with Max when he treated Jack and Jackie. Mark Shaw was also there. I met Jackie for the first time. He treated her, and then we waited for the President. As we sat in the living room, Max said, 'Isn't this something? Here I am, the son of a kosher butcher from Berlin, and I'm waiting to see the President of the United States.'

"Max treated Jackie at the Carlyle whenever she came to New York and at the White House whenever he treated her husband. When they went on vacation he would fly to wherever they happened to be. Mark Shaw used to fly Max to see Jackie at Glen Ora and Wexford, using a private landing strip that belonged to the Mellons. One day they were forced to land in a cow pasture, narrowly missing a stand of trees. But Max enjoyed the intrigue and adventure associated with these travels. Another day when I was along and we went to the White House, Max was allowed upstairs but I wasn't. I had to wait downstairs. And even Max was hurried along on this particular day. The reason was that Mr. and Mrs. Alexei Adzhubei, Nikita Khrushchev's son-in-law and daughter, had been invited by the Kennedys for a private luncheon. Alexei was a journalist and there was concern that he might report the presence of a physician. The last thing Kennedy wanted the Russians to know was that he was in anything but the best of health."

There were less complimentary reports on Max's practice, one from Ruth Mosse, a nurse who worked for him during part of the JFK administration: "When Jackie visited New York, the Secret Service would telephone the office and say they were sending a car for Max. Then we'd clean him up. He'd leave the office with them and later they'd bring him back. Jackie never came to the office. He went to the Carlyle. Nor did President Kennedy come to the office during this period. Max always went to him.

"It amazed me they saw him at all. Max was absolutely a quack. I know he was. I was there. I saw what was done and what wasn't done. He used bone marrow and cooked it and injected people with it. Some people came down with infections. Others conked out and we had to make sure they could walk again. Yet everybody who was anybody was there. They believed in him the way fanatics believe in religion.

"Max was totally off the wall. When he gave an injection he would just spill the contents of his medical bag on the table and rummage around amid a jumble of unmarked bottles and nameless chemicals until he found what he was looking for. His fingernails were perpetually black from his chemicals. If a patient asked what kind of injection he was being given, Max said, 'If I tell you, will you know?' His attitude was, Do you question God? Max was out of his mind. He would see 30 patients or more a day. He worked 24 hours a day, sometimes for days on end. He was a butcher. Blood was splattered all over his whites. That's why when they came to pick him up for Jackie, we would make him change. And because he was injecting himself with the stuff, his speech often became slurred. It was difficult to understand him at times. My father, who was a psychiatrist, made me quit the job because he feared that Max might begin to inject me."

Ruth Mosse's apprehensions were shared by several Kennedy intimates. Pierre Salinger couldn't understand why the President would consult with somebody as unprofessional in appearance and demeanor as Max Jacobson, and worried that their association might become known to the press. Dr. Janet Travell tried to discuss the matter of amphetamine addiction with the President. He ignored her just as he ignored his brother Bobby's frequent warnings. FBI records indicate that in 1961 Bobby sent five vials of medications Jacobson had left at the White House to FBI laboratories for chemical analysis. The subsequent FBI report showed the presence of amphetamines and steroids at high concentrated levels in each of the five vials.

Chuck Spalding also had a confrontation with Max. Their break took place in a car driven by Max on the way to LaGuardia Airport where Max, Chuck and Ken McKnight (another of Max's cronies and an administrator with the Department of Commerce) were about to board the next shuttle for Washington. Max had an appointment to see Kennedy. They were driving along Sutton Place in Manhattan when Spalding, in the middle of a conversation, said to Max: "Stop the car. I'm getting out right here."

"He didn't just 'get' out of the car," recalled Ken McKnight. "He jumped out, and then he started running. I turned around and watched him tear up the street, his shirt tail flapping in the breeze."

"I just thought Max was behaving irrationally and it was time to leave him," maintained Spalding. "I'm not ashamed I went to him as a patient, but Max's medical miracles shouldn't be overrated. It had reached the point where, though initially intrigued by the guy, I felt I'd had enough. There was too much mumbo-jumbo associated with what he was doing. At first, he gave me a big lift but later he seemed to become increasingly erratic. I knew he was using amphetamines and that most of his patients, people like Alan Jay Lerner and Eddie Fisher, members of the show business crowd, needed to stay on top of themselves and at their highest point, and that this was the basis of his high-visibility practice. But beyond that I quickly saw that the guy was vastly different. He came up with all these fantastic stories about how he'd gotten, oh, a freshly killed elephant, taken out its heart and injected the cells into somebody's chest. Then he'd go through this whole thing about how he could go with practically no sleep, how he would revolutionize the entire human life-cycle. People at the White House began asking questions about him. After a while it just got to me."

"The moment came when Max wanted to stop treating JFK," recalled Michael Samek. "I stayed up half the night with him trying to compose a letter to the President, stipulating his reasons for not wanting to treat him or Jackie any longer. Max was upset because he felt certain members of JFK's inner circle, such as Robert Kennedy and Chuck Spalding, were mistreating him, snubbing him. As for Janet Travell, I can't imagine she was overjoyed with having Max around all the time."

Max recorded the occasion in his memoir:

"At home, after thinking things over, I prepared a letter to the President which I gave him at the beginning of our next session.

"He opened it and read that I had been happy to have rendered my services in the past, that in order to avoid a controversy that might involve me, I asked his permission to discontinue my activities at the White House. He laughed, tore up the letter and said, 'That's out of the question.'"

Although Jacobson continued to treat Jack and Jackie, Robert Kennedy kept up a steady campaign to discredit him. Bobby's newest gambit was to suggest to Jack that all medications he took be submitted first for analysis by the Food and Drug Administration. The President, after much pressure and with apparent embarrassment, asked Max if he would mind complying with this suggestion. Max agreed and forwarded to the Attorney General's office fifteen vials of medication. A week later the FDA confirmed the findings of the FBI laboratories: the medication contained amphetamines and steroids. "I don't care if it's horse piss," the President replied. "It works."

"The combination of steroids and amphetamines no doubt increased Kennedy's sexual drive," said Tom Jacobson, Max's son, who on several occasions substituted for his father. "I treated Jackie once when my father went to London with Alan Jay Lerner to visit the Radziwills. Jackie had a cold. I went to the Carlyle with Ken McKnight. He waited outside the apartment with two Secret Service agents, one of whom was Clint Hill. I spent maybe an hour with Jackie and gave her an injection."

Moments of glamour intermingled with moments of crisis at the White House, insuring a need for Max's continuing involvement. The more tension Kennedy experienced the more amphetamine treatments he demanded. "I remember distinctly one afternoon when there was a very important White House reception," writes Max Jacobson. "At this time the nation was suffering from the impact of the steel [strike] crisis. Kennedy was tense and apprehensive. After his treatment, he smiled and said, 'Now I can go downstairs and shake hands with several hundred intimate friends.'"

In September 1962, when James Meredith became the

first black American to enroll at the University of Mississippi and Kennedy called in federal troops to forestall race riots, Max Jacobson gave the President a series of injections. He did the same during the early days of the Cuban missile crisis, and remained on call whenever the country sent one of its astronauts into space.

"Max was fascinated by NASA and the Space Program," said Michael Samek. "He would discuss the subject for hours with Kennedy. He was convinced it would usher in a new age of medical discoveries."

Another subject they often discussed was the President's physical fitness program. When the topic of the recommended 50-mile hike came up, Kennedy told him he had bet Stas Radziwill that Stas could never match Bobby Kennedy's latest feat—covering the distance in 18 hours or less. They bet $1,000, the loser's check to be made out to the Constructive Research Foundation, an institution started by Max Jacobson to further his work with multiple sclerosis patients. When Eunice Shriver heard about the friendly wager, she bet another $1000, against Stas.

"I decided to join the hikers who now included Chuck Spalding,* Stas and Mark Shaw," Max writes in his memoir. "I barely caught the last plane out of New York to Palm Beach the night before the scheduled day. When we arrived at the hotel, Mark and I didn't bother to undress, as only an hour remained before our predawn start. I must have dozed off when I suddenly heard the telephone. The desk informed us that Mrs. Jacqueline Kennedy was at the front entrance with a Secret Service agent and a car. . . .

"We were shoved into the car and I found myself seated in Jackie's lap but too tired to properly appreciate my position. The distance was short to the beginning of the highway that connected West Palm Beach with Miami, which was chosen for the route. Jackie returned to her residence and another car appeared carrying food, oxygen (which I had requested) and a Secret Service man to check our distance and time. . . .

"I had previously discussed with Stas starting out at such an ungodly hour as 4:00 a.m. in order to reduce

*Max and Chuck had already had their falling-out but remained on friendly enough terms to take part in the 50-mile hike together.

exposure to heat and to see if by noon we were able to cover at least half the distance. If we couldn't do it, I suggested he give up because he had a heart condition. As the sun rose, we marched bravely along the highway. After about sixteen miles a truck appeared . . . and sent us sprawling in all directions. I stepped into nothingness and rolled down a steep embankment. When I regained my composure, I found my left ankle swollen and painful. I decided to ride along in the car, where I could look after my injury. Shortly before noon we achieved our goal in having covered the first twenty-five miles. We settled down for a well-deserved rest. While we rested, Mark Shaw continued his photographic documentation of the trip. When the President arrived, accompanied by Jackie, Lee and Arkadi Gerney, a friend of the Radziwills, Mark . . . shot a full roll of film of the President. After he replaced the film, he asked Jackie to shoot some pictures of us, including himself. Before returning the camera to Mark, the former Inquiring Photographer accidently opened the magazine, exposing the film. . . .

"We arrived at the finish line at 9:45 p.m., with fifteen minutes to spare. Exhausted, we collapsed in the limousine, which turned around to drive us back to Palm Beach. The return trip never seemed to end, and we couldn't believe that any human being could have walked this distance.

"JFK was standing at the entrance to the Wrightsman house and congratulated each of us, jokingly pinning paper medals to our perspiration-soaked shirts. A buffet had been prepared and a jukebox played '*Bei Mir Bist Du Schoën*,' as recorded by the Andrews Sisters."

Ken McKnight recalled a visit Max Jacobson paid to the White House in early 1962 which coincided with the breakup of the Eddie Fisher-Elizabeth Taylor marriage. "Elizabeth Taylor had dumped Eddie for Richard Burton, and Eddie suffered a complete collapse," said McKnight. "He had just returned from Rome. Max was looking after him, shooting him up to keep him calm. He was afraid Eddie might jump out a window. The press was everywhere, and we had to keep moving Eddie around, ending up with him in a suite on the 38th floor of the Hotel Pierre. The telephone rang constantly, and Eddie wouldn't talk to anybody, certainly not to reporters. He wouldn't even talk to old friends like Jack

Benny or Eddie Cantor. He was desolate, totally distraught. He was deeply in love with Elizabeth Taylor, and she had just simply emasculated him in public.

"He would talk about her for hours, describe her in the most intimate detail. He told about how hot she became when making love, how she would crawl around the floor on hands and knees purring like a sex kitten, and how he would mount her from the rear, and the hotter she became the louder she purred.

" 'Why don't you stop torturing yourself, Eddie?' I said. But he wouldn't stop. Then Max called up. He had to go to Washington to see the Kennedys, but he didn't want to leave Eddie behind. Eddie was more than a patient to Max; he was like a son. 'We,re going to have to take Eddie along,' he said.

"So we went to the airport. Also with us was Milton Blackstone, Eddie's manager and a longtime patient of Max. We had Eddie hidden in an old overcoat pulled up all round so nobody would recognize him. In Washington we checked into the Hilton. Max left for the White House. A half hour later the telephone rang. It was Max. He had left a vial of medication on the dresser and he had to have it right away. He wanted me to catch a taxicab and bring it to the White House. Eddie wanted to come along, but Max nixed the request. Although the Kennedys wanted to meet Eddie, he was a bit too hot for them to handle at the moment. I left him with Milt.

"I made the delivery and returned to the hotel. Eddie Fisher was nervously pacing the floor. Somehow the press had learned he was staying there and had tried interviewing him over the telephone. The hotel manager called up several minutes later to report that there were some 50 reporters in the hotel lobby and parking lot. Other guests were complaining and the switchboard was flooded. Max had returned and Eddie was beside himself. The airport had just shut down because of a bad electrical storm. The question was how to sneak Eddie Fisher out of the hotel and get him back to New York.

"I called the manager of the hotel and said we were leaving but there was something I wanted him to do. I told him, 'We can't go out there and have them follow us.' I remembered that when Franklin D. Roosevelt was first elected President, they had the Inaugural Ball at the Hilton, and to hide the fact that he couldn't walk they built a special elevator that transported his car to the ballroom on the second floor. I asked the manager if the elevator still worked, and he said he didn't know but he'd have his engineer check it out. He called back and said, Yes, they had it working and we could use it.

"Next I telephoned Hertz to see if they had a limousine we could rent and they assured me they did, and I asked if they had a chauffeur's hat and they said, Yes, and I told them I'd be right over. I exited the hotel through the delivery entrance and walked two blocks in the pouring rain to the Hertz rental office, where they provided me with a Cadillac limousine and a chauffeur's hat. I drove back to the hotel and onto this elevator and took it up to the second floor and drove the limo into the ballroom. Max, Milt and Eddie came down the elevator that had been blocked off so there would be nobody else on it. We took off. Eddie was in the back seat and we'd shove him down whenever we reached a toll booth. I drove and wore the chauffeur's hat. It was a wild ride."

Later that year, Ken McKnight received a telephone call from Evelyn Lincoln, President Kennedy's private secretary.* She said she had a message she wanted to convey in person. 'We're arriving in New York tomorrow night and the President and his staff will be staying at the Carlyle,' she said. She wanted to know if I would be willing to meet her at the hotel for breakfast. I told her I would. 'Very good,' she said, 'I'll call you tomorrow night when we get in.'

"She called again the following evening and invited me for breakfast at a quarter of eight the next morning.

"I said I would be there. She didn't indicate what she had in mind, but I suspected it had to do with Max. I told Max what had happened. He said, 'That's very interesting. I think I know what it's about. I'll drive you down there first thing in the morning.'

"He dropped me off at 76th Street and Park Avenue. The entire area was roped off. They had barricades ev-

*In an interview with the author, Evelyn Lincoln claimed she had no recollection of anybody named Ken McKnight, the same response she gave the press when first asked about Judith Campbell Exner. Although the name McKnight may no longer ring a bell, Evelyn Lincoln did in fact know him. Ken McKnight provided the author with cards and notes he had received from Mrs. Lincoln.

erywhere. The place was literally crawling with cops, detectives, state troopers and Secret Service. There must have been three hundred men on that block alone, and they increased in number as I approached Madison Avenue. Nobody made any effort to stop me. The lobby of the Carlyle was full of people, mostly Secret Service. I went over to one who was sitting at a card table set up next to the elevator. I knew him from Washington. 'How're you doing, Ken?' he said. 'I'm fine,' I said. 'I'm here to see Evelyn Lincoln.' 'We know that, but you're three minutes early,' he said, pointing to his watch. 'You mean, you were expecting me?' I asked. 'Of course,' he responded. 'We've been monitoring you since the moment you stepped out of Dr. Jacobson's car. Mrs. Lincoln knows you're in the lobby. She'll be sending for you momentarily.'

"Shortly there was a crackling sound on his walkie-talkie. The agent told me to go up to room so-and-so. So I rode the elevator to the designated floor and found Mrs. Lincoln standing in front of her door. She asked me what I wanted for breakfast. She ordered scrambled eggs for herself, and that's what I had—scrambled eggs, toast, bacon, a slice of melon and a cup of coffee.

"We sat there chatting over breakfast. What she told me was that every time Dr. Jacobson traveled to Washington, we were risking exposure in the press. The press covered the railroad stations, the airports, the bus terminals. They watched Dr. Jacobson like a hawk. The President and his staff were concerned. The only solution would be for Dr. Jacobson to move into the White House so that whenever the President or First Lady needed him, he could treat them without the intrusion of the press. She went on to say that they had already mentioned the possibility to Max but that he had balked at the prospect. So they had decided to enlist the help of one of his close friends.

"I said I would be glad to help but that I had previously broached the subject with Max and had been told that he couldn't possibly forsake his four hundred multiple sclerosis patients. Moving into the White House meant he would have to do just that. While he would do anything for the President, fly anywhere at any hour, he just couldn't abandon his practice.

" 'But you will try to convince him anyway, won't

you?' said Mrs. Lincoln. I said I would try and that I would let her know the outcome. Just then the telephone rang. 'I have to go,' she said. 'The President wants me.' She stepped into the elevator and went up, while I went down. Afterwards I returned to Max's office. He chuckled when I related the gist of the conversation. He had suspected as much. He thanked me for going to see Mrs. Lincoln, and reiterated what he had said before—he couldn't just give up his private practice for the sake of the White House. He had too many patients whose very lives depended on him. He would continue to serve the First Family in any way he could, but his base of operation had to remain in New York."

Max Jacobson continued to medicate the Kennedys for the duration of Camelot, never once requesting (or receiving) a single penny above or beyond immediate expenses. On November 15, 1963, he flew to Palm Beach, where he ministered to the President for the last time. "He was in the midst of preparations for his trip to Texas," writes Jacobson. "The atmosphere was tense, although the President seemed relaxed and in good spirits. Rumor had it that the upcoming trip could be risky. I expressed my concern over his welfare. He brushed it laughingly aside and said he was looking forward to it. I remember my disappointment in not being invited along for the trip."

20

Max Jacobson's amphetamine injections provided Jackie Kennedy with the fuel that enabled her to survive the White House Restoration Project. She was determined to make the President's House the most magnificent museum attraction in the world. Her plan indirectly involved the renovation and restoration of Blair House—the President's official guest residence—as well as Lafayette Square, a block-long lot of federal-style office buildings and historic homes facing the White House across Pennsylvania Avenue.*

Jackie began by systematically sorting through some 26,500 items which were stored in the attic and basement of the Executive Mansion, and gradually substituted articles of antiquity for those of modern manufacture. After exhausting the White House storage rooms (and overcoming some resistance on the part of her husband for persisting in what he perceived to be a futile endeavor), she convinced J. B. West to take her to the cavernous Fort Washington warehouse, located on the Maryland side of the Potomac, a repository for White House furniture and furnishings no longer deemed usable. Jackie subsequently rescued dozens of "found" objects and pieces

*Chief of Protocol Angier Biddle Duke and his wife Robin were placed in charge of the Blair House project. Architect John Carl Warnecke, a friend of the Kennedy family, worked on the Lafayette Square project. "No one, but absolutely no one in Washington, gave a damn what happened to Lafayette Square," said Warnecke. "Jackie was the only one. With their giant egos, the rest of them just wanted to tear the old structures down and build new ones. Jackie felt that because of the proximity of Lafayette Square to the White House, this would be criminal. The thing to do was to save the structures and restore them. The job cost $30 million, two thirds of it for the two main office buildings (including the Executive Office Building), the remainder for the smaller houses."

of furniture, had them repaired and refinished, and put to use.

Within six months, Jackie had formed several committees and subcommittees of advisers and experts to help with the work and fund-raising, including a White House Historical Association, a Special Committee for White House Paintings and a Fine Arts Committee, whose first backers had been suggested by Sister Parish but which Jackie quickly expanded.* She spent a weekend at Winterthur, a palatial estate and museum in Greenville, Delaware, belonging to Henry Francis du Pont, a distinguished authority on American furnishings and a member of the wealthy chemicals family. Du Pont agreed to serve as chairman of the Fine Arts Committee. The purpose of the group, according to one of its many public relations bulletins, was "to locate authentic furnishings reflecting the history of the Presidency of the United States, furnishings that are both historically accurate and of museum or gallery quality."

Another innovation by Jackie was the creation of a new White House position, a permanent curator, somebody to catalogue the various acquisitions, prepare reports, edit and write books and oversee an ever-expanding collection. The job went to 26-year-old Lorraine Pearce who, having studied and trained at Winterthur under Henry du Pont, came highly recommended.

In attempting to imbue the White House with a national identity, Jackie decided to reflect the era of President James Monroe (1817–1825), when the mansion was furnished "in the then-fashionable French Empire style." To recreate a French atmosphere Jackie turned to a French decorator, Stephane Boudin, who had contributed to the decor of several of Jackie's other homes, and whose clientele included Jayne Wrightsman and the Duchess of Windsor. Jackie neglected to inform Henry Francis

---

*Other members of the Fine Arts Committee were: Charles Francis Adams, Leroy Davis, Mrs. Douglas Dillon, Mrs. Charles Engelhard, David Finley, Mrs. Henry Ford II, Mrs. Albert Lasker, John L. Loeb, Mrs. Paul Mellon, Mrs. Henry Parish II, Gerald Shea, John Walker, Mrs. George Henry Warren and Mrs. Charles Wrightsman. In addition the Committee was aided by a large number of art and antique experts, who on occasion also met at the White House. Jackie referred to the Fine Arts Committee as "my Politburo."

du Pont of the newest addition to the team, though he soon found out for himself.

Du Pont and Boudin, both in their sixties and both highly opinionated, each convinced that he knew best, agreed on almost nothing. J. B. West discusses them at considerable length in his memoir, *Upstairs at the White House,* recalling that "from the first day the two men met, it was apparent they'd never see eye to eye on anything. Mr. Du Pont, a dignified Eastern millionaire, was interested only in authenticity, and didn't care about arrangement or proportion or compatibility. Monsieur Boudin, a bubbly, dramatic little Frenchman, cared only about pleasing the eye.

"Mrs. Kennedy and I gave them a tour of the White House early in 1961.

"Mr. du Pont, who was slightly deaf, spoke rapidly, walked slowly, and mumbled. Monsieur Boudin was also hard of hearing, spoke halting English, and bounced energetically around the room. They tried desperately to be polite to each other. There were so many 'beg pardons' and 'so sorrys' and 'I'm afraid I don'ts' and 'but don't you means . . .' Mrs. Kennedy and I both had to interpret. We wove in and out of the State rooms, dumbfounded by their total lack of communication."

The reverberations of ensuing arguments between this incompatible duo would be felt in the White House for years to come. Clement E. Conger, White House curator from 1970 to 1986, remarked that Jackie "was quite correct to engage Henry F. du Pont as Chairman of the Committee. He was certainly the greatest authority on Americana during his lifetime. Mrs. Kennedy, however, with a French heritage and love for French things, also engaged Stephane Boudin of Paris who was the rage of Paris as a decorator. She didn't consult or inform Mr. du Pont. Mr. du Pont, we were later told, was very upset by it because Boudin, while a great decorator in Paris, was not really qualified to be the interior designer for the American White House. So some things went too French. Fortunately, by the Nixon-Ford era some of these items, draperies, upholsteries, fabrics, were worn out. The rooms were redone strictly as American rooms."

Of Jackie's many restoration advisers, only Jayne Wrightsman remained devotedly pro-Boudin. The rest were unanimously in favor of dismissing the Frenchman.

James Fosburgh, director of the Special Committee for Whte House Paintings, wrote to Jackie soon after meeting Boudin:

> I hope you will not mind if I speak completely frankly to you. The meeting last Monday with Boudin, when it finally took place, put me in an impossible position. Let me try to explain why. If he is to decide what pictures are to be hung and where, since he knows nothing about American painting or, for that matter, American furniture, there is not the slightest use in my trying to acquire anything further for the White House as there is no reason to suppose that it will not be discarded or relegated to the attic as soon as he sees it. . . .
>
> I am not complaining about Boudin, per se, although some of his crudeness can only be explained by the supposition that he thought . . . I did not understand French, in which he was in error. But every waking moment since October has been devoted to this cause and as a result I would be most unhappy to see our high hopes for this project, which I hold most dear, come to nothing. . . .

The greatest conflict between Boudin and du Pont involved the Blue Room, whose walls the French decorator insisted on painting white, and the Green Room, whose walls were to be done in chartreuse.

"They're too *French*," du Pont gasped when he first saw them. President Kennedy was equally distressed. "The Blue Room should be blue," he insisted, "and the Green Room should be green. Have them redone."

Jackie refused, insisting that the new colors were more historically accurate than the old. Besides, it would cost too much to redecorate.

Kennedy laughed. Money had never been an issue for his wife before. Every time he entered her bedroom the walls were a different color—why should the Blue, Green or Red Rooms be exceptions?

Lorraine Pearce, Jackie's newly appointed curator, fully supported her former mentor. She told James Biddle, assistant curator of the American Wing at the Metropolitan Museum of Art in New York and an adviser to the Fine Arts Committee, that she found herself in a most difficult position. She felt, and Biddle agreed, that she had to approach her work from the curatorial point of view and not merely serve as a coordinator of various decorating whims, which she thought Boudin more or less represented. Biddle transmitted Pearce's statement to du Pont. A few days later Lorraine Pearce attended a seminar at Winterthur and spoke to du Pont personally.

"I must carry out my duties as established by the Fine Arts Committee with you as its Chairman," she insisted. "Mr. Boudin has nothing to do with the Committee and I will certainly not carry out *his* orders to destroy the State rooms."

A few weeks later, Mrs. Pearce reported to du Pont that Jackie had found out about their conversation and had confronted her. "She was very angry that I spoke to you," said Lorraine. "I'm not certain how she learned about our talk, but I told her exactly what I told you."

The First Lady also spoke to du Pont, who had apprised her of his conversation with Lorraine in the first place. Jackie felt Mrs. Pearce had been extremely "disloyal," speaking to him behind her back. "She might have remembered that it was my idea to have a curator," said Jackie. "It was also my idea to ask you to help in the project. I realize Lorraine is dedicated to the White House and to you as well, but it's not for her to accuse me of 'betraying' you. I asked Monsieur Boudin to become part of the team because I felt he could help, and I still feel that way."

Jackie reiterated her position during du Pont's next visit to the White House, emphasizing how invaluable his expertise continued to be in guiding the Fine Arts Committee. She used more or less the same approach when addressing Stephane Boudin, and in this fashion managed to keep both men at bay.

When informed by J. B. West that the renovation project could possibly cost the government several million dollars and thereby create a national furor, Jackie on her own devised a novel plan to raise the necessary funds. To determine the validity of her idea, she telephoned attorney Clark Clifford and invited him to the White House for lunch.

"Clark," she asked, "how many people go through the White House every year?"

"I don't know," said Clifford. "A lot. Maybe one or

two million. I think I could find out. But why do you want to know?"

"Before I answer your questions," said Jackie, "you answer mine. Do any of these people leave money at the White House?"

"No. The White House is public property. People don't pay to go on the tour. Why should they?"

"They shouldn't," responded Jackie. "But we should make available something tangible that they can buy at the White House and take away with them as a memento. We could use the money because, in effect, my goal is to make the White House 'the First House in the Land.'"

"Well, that's certainly a laudable goal. I've read about your renovation project, Jackie, and I'm all for it. I'll continue to think about it."

"Don't let's think about it," said Jackie. "Let's do something about it. I have several ideas. One of them is to sell post cards, not the usual kind but painting post cards of the various State rooms, something the children can take home and paint over. If that's not possible, I want to put together a White House Guidebook, a book with eloquent words and beautiful pictures, the kind of publication the *National Geographic* puts out for its members, but not as corny. We'll sell it for a dollar. People who go through this place in fifteen minutes can't possibly tell you what they've seen. This will remind them, and it will help pay for the renovation project. In fact it can be reprinted every time there's a new administration with material included on the ongoing administration."

Clark Clifford returned to his law office and discussed Jackie's fund-raising plan with Carson Glass, his associate in the firm. Glass thought the guidebook idea a good one and discussed it with David Finley. Jackie, meanwhile, contacted Melville Grosvenor, President of *National Geographic*. "She decided that since the *Geographic* produced such handsome books, they might be appropriate for hers," said Glass. "I took it from there. I was told by Clifford that we would have to incorporate the White House Historical Association. That's the only way it could be made legal. The problem was that nobody owned the White House. There wasn't any authority for setting up a corporation. We had to go to the Department of Justice and try to get some sort of official designation. Nicholas

Katzenbach, the Deputy Attorney General, helped draft proposals. Finally a bill was passed making the White House part of the National Park Service. After that we were able to incorporate.

"There were additional problems. One was obtaining a copyright on the guidebook, the text of which was to be written by Lorraine Pearce, with a foreword by Jackie. The law stipulates that you can't copyright anything written by a federal employee during working hours. We had to say she wrote the book in her offhours, which by and large was true.

"At one point Jackie decided she wanted to have a film made of the White House. She called me along with everybody else involved with the guidebook: Nash Castro of the National Park Service; Robert L. Breeden, Franc Shor and Donald J. Crump of the *Geographic;* two dozen others. We met in the motion picture theater at the White House, where President Kennedy used to like to watch movies after dinner. Jackie was there with her mother, Mrs. Auchincloss. She was trying to decide what film outfit she wanted. Several producers were asked to show samples of their work. We watched the film snippets. Then the lights went on and Jackie stood up and made a little speech.

"The thing I remember most about her was the way she approached us. I can't quote her exactly, but in her little whispery voice she more or less said, 'I don't know anything about these things. This is something that I never learned anything about. I have to leave it to you smart men. You have to do these things for me, but if I can make a small recommendation I would do it the following way.' Then she reeled off a long list of precise instructions, telling us exactly what had to be done. Boy, was she smart. She knew how to get people moving. She coated her instructions with sugar, but we all understood that we were to make certain Jackie got what she wanted.

"The film idea was a prelude to the televised tour of the White House that she eventually conducted for CBS. I received a constant stream of long and detailed letters from Jackie. She also used to write verbose instructions to Clark Clifford, full of items on which she wanted his advice, but he destroyed all of these. I could have killed him. The historical content alone would have been invaluable, but he didn't want to keep the letters because they discussed friends. I always thought he should have kept all of that. I subsequently learned that she apparently suffered from insomnia. In the middle of the night she would get up and write down all her ideas. She made absolutely certain that those in charge knew all her wishes."

Robert L. Breeden, vice-president of the *National Geographic,* confirmed Jackie's high degree of involvement: "She was in on every decision from titles to typeface. She was very exact in what she wanted. She was also very convincing. After she talked to Melville Grosvenor, he agreed to underwrite not only the editorial and photographic costs but to provide an additional public service grant.

"The chief photographer on the guidebook was *Geographic* staffer George F. Mobley. Late one night he was in the Red Room taking pictures for the book. He had to work when the public rooms weren't in use. He complained that every time he finished shooting a room Jackie would change all the furniture and furnishings in it. This meant he had to shoot the room all over again. I think he said he did the Green Room on four separate occasions. They wound up using the third series of photographs. They took the fourth set because Jackie decided she didn't like the room and removed the rug. But the rug they finally settled on after numerous changes was the same rug they had used during the third shooting.

"At any rate, George was taking photographs in the Red Room one night. He was using one of those big, old-fashioned standing cameras for detail work. He had this black cloth over his head and he sensed someone in the room. He took the cloth off his head and he looked around and there was Jackie. They had never been formally introduced. 'Who are you?' she asked. 'I'm George Mobley,' he replied. 'I've been working here for more than a year.' She was very cordial and said, 'Can I have a look?' She put her head under the black cloth and looked and said, 'Oh, it's upside down.' She was looking at the ground glass lens which always projects an upside down image. George thought her comment hilarious because she had once been a photographer. That's the thing about Jackie—you never knew if she was putting you on.

"I recall that one of the photographs we had chosen for the book was of the children, John-John and Caroline, in the little boy's bedroom. Mr. Grosvenor was very insistent that this was just the type of material he wanted to see in the book. Jackie kept removing it from the stack of pictures marked for inclusion. But Grosvenor kept bringing up this photo to her, telling her how cute and charming he found it. We were in a meeting with Jackie to decide on a final choice of photographs. Mr. Grosvenor finally pulled out the picture and said, 'Well, Jackie. This is a great photo—can we use it?' Jackie looked at the photograph and then at us. 'Gentlemen,' she said, 'even at the age of two one's bedroom should be private.' She didn't want a picture of John-John in his bedroom to appear in the book, and that's how it was going to be.*

"There were a number of conflicts with Lorraine Pearce, who wrote the text for the guidebook. One sticky debate we had with her involved the use of captions under the photographs in the book. Lorraine wanted us to use reference numbers and then have the captions appear elsewhere. When it was pointed out to her that this wasn't journalistically the correct way to go about it, she became very obstinate. 'This isn't journalism,' she said, 'this is history.' It was that type of attitude that created log jams.

"Following one particularly difficult meeting with Lorraine, Franc Shor and I took her to lunch at the Mayflower. She was acting very adamant and not very realistic about a number of issues. Franc told her during this luncheon that she was the most arrogant person he had ever met. At that point she broke down in tears. But the arguing didn't cease until July 4, 1962, the day *The White House: An Historic Guide* went on sale.

"Jackie's guidebook was an immediate success. The initial printing of 250,000 was exhausted in three months. The book went to print twice more in 1962. To date it has sold millions of copies and gone through many revisions. President Kennedy had originally warned his wife that she would be assailed for commercializing the White House, but in the end she received high grades for her efforts. *The New York Times* celebrated her 'creative method of raising still more money for the work of reno-

---

*Jackie insisted that the family's private quarters at the White House remain truly private. A staff member who had taken friends on a tour of the upstairs, even though the Kennedys were absent, was severely reprimanded by Jackie.

vation, removing the burden from the shoulders of the already overburdened taxpayer.' "

If Jackie was a tightwad with the taxpayers' money she showed a reckless disregard for the feelings of the rich. "She went at them with gleeful malice," said Truman Capote. "She loaded her various committees and sub-committees with as many wealthy bluebloods as she could find. Then she milked them for all they were worth.

"A member of her Special Committee for White House Paintings told me about being invited to the White House for tea along with a half-dozen other members of the same Committee. When they arrived they found all these paintings propped up about the room. Jackie had selected them from several leading New York art galleries. The guests were told in a somewhat unsubtle manner that if they saw any paintings they liked enough to give to the White House, there would be a quick and easy way to handle matters. By the end of the afternoon there wasn't a picture left unpledged."

Although a master of the "soft sell," Jackie knew when and how to apply pressure. When she heard that a Dr. Ray C. Franklin of Mt. Kisco, New York, owned a Hepplewhite mirror that had once belonged to George Washington, she invited the physician to the White House. She talked to him for hours, explained the project, took him on a personal tour of the State rooms but never asked him for anything. But as he was about to leave she popped the question, and Dr. Franklin found himself offering her the $20,000 antique mirror.

Walter H. Annenberg, political conservative, newspaper and magazine publisher and future Ambassador to the Court of St. James's, was another Jackie victim. Clark Clifford told the story of how Jackie telephoned the wealthy Philadelphian one evening and related her plans for making the White House a national monument. While talking, she alluded to Annenberg's priceless art collection.

"I've been told that you have a magnificent portrait of Ben Franklin by David Martin," said Jackie.

As he listened, Annenberg began to sense the reason behind Jackie's telephone call. "You, Mr. Annenberg, are the first citizen of Philadelphia. And in his day, Benjamin Franklin was the first citizen of Philadelphia. And that's why, Mr. Annenberg, I thought of you. Do you think a great Philadelphia citizen would give the

White House a portrait of another great Philadelphia citizen?"

"It was done so smoothly, so cunningly, that Annenberg never knew what hit him," remarked Clark Clifford. "He said it was one of his favorite portraits and that he would like several days to think it over. He didn't tell her that the painting had cost him $250,000, although he felt certain she already knew. He considered it for all of thirty minutes, called her back and told her she could have the painting for the White House. He shipped it off the following day.*

"She would sometimes invite groups to the White House and ask me to be present to help answer questions. I would reassure them that gifts of money or property, including furniture and *objets d'art,* to the United States for use in the White House are deductible from gross income under the regulations governing charitable contributions. Donations to the United States for use in the White House which were made through Mrs. Kennedy's Fine Arts Committee would be treated as charitable donations for tax purposes after the donation had been formally accepted on behalf of the United States by the government's authorized representative, the Director of the National Park Service.

"But the key to renovating the White House was Jackie's charm and graciousness, and also her genius for getting people to do things—often against their will. She would hold these gatherings at which she would say she needed a certain rug for the Red Room, or curtains for the East Room, and they had to be woven in some obscure town in France or Belgium. They had to be just right. She'd pick out just the kind of Governor Winthrop desk or mantelpiece she wanted, and tell them about that. She'd invite the Colonial Dames or the Washington Historical

*Jackie could be just as persuasive by letter, as when she wrote to Bernard Baruch (Feb. 24, 1962): "Perhaps you know that we are trying to bring things of past Presidents back to the White House. Someone said that you had an Orpen portrait of Woodrow Wilson. The portrait of him there now is really not all it should be—and I thought it would be the most touching and historic thing if there could be a superb portrait of Wilson—given by you. . . . It is unpleasant to write to friends and to people I admire asking them to part with things they love. If you can't spare the picture I will understand . . ."

Society or some other group and put the bite on them.
She would work on Douglas Dillon, Bernard Baruch,
Charles Wrightsman, Paul Mellon, or anybody else she
felt had money or furnishings or both.

"Jackie also did a good deal of verbal lobbying in
places like *Life* and *Look*—'singing for my supper,' she
called it—to let people know about the project and to
solicit funds from the general public. Then, in 1962,
Maxine Cheshire wrote a series of scathing articles on the
renovation project for the *Washington Post,* and Jackie
became incensed."

The seven-article series listed the age, origin, donor
and sometimes dubious value of each piece (Cheshire's
sleuthing revealed that there were several fakes among
the newly acquired antiques, including a Green Room
desk said to have cost $20,000). Cheshire's prying brought
a call from Jackie's husband to then-*Washington Post*
publisher Philip Graham, whose friendship with JFK was
based in part on their occasional bartering of mistresses
and girlfriends. "Maxine Cheshire has reduced my wife
to tears," said the President. "Listen to her." Sure enough,
there in the background was the First Lady, sobbing
audibly.

Jackie's anguish quickly turned to anger. When asked
by Henry Francis du Pont if she had authorized the
Cheshire series, she responded in writing. (September
20, 1962) that she hadn't and that the articles had appalled her. Maxine Cheshire also appalled her. She was
one of the "cleverer and more malicious" of the female
press corps who did so much to make her life and her
children's lives miserable.

Although Jackie stated in the same letter that she was
not "interested in finding a culprit," she managed to
single out two or three, including Lorraine Pearce and
Franco Scalamandré. Scalamandré, responsible for weaving many of the silk fabrics and draperies used in the
renovated White House, had given Cheshire an interview
and had even posed for photographs to be used in conjunction with the Cheshire series.

Adriana Scalamandré Bitter, daughter of Franco Scalamandré, recalled the controversy: "At the time Jacqueline wanted to announce the completion of the restoration
herself, and had planned a program to that effect. There
was a misunderstanding because the *Washington Post*

came to New York and requested an interview and no one had said, 'Don't speak to anybody.' And my father simply answered some questions. And the fact is we had been making silk fabrics for the White House since Herbert Hoover's day. Most of the silk we make is produced right here in New York, which is unusual because nobody else in the United States has a mill like ours. My father brought the process over from Italy.

"So my father gave Maxine Cheshire an interview and when Jackie heard about it, she became enraged. She demanded that my father make a public statement saying that the details he had given Cheshire weren't true. He said, 'I can't do that, Mrs. Kennedy. I can't say they're not true. They have photographs of me with the fabrics on my lap. Besides, they are true. I can't lie, even for the sake of the White House.' "

By letter and over the telephone the First Lady again poured out her anger and frustrations to Henry Francis du Pont, who had become her chief consultant in such affairs. She complained that Scalamendré had "used" the White House in a recent series of newspaper advertisements without telling her first and without obtaining her permission. Scalamendré's worst sin, however, had been to talk with Maxine Cheshire, also without Jackie's authorization. He had gone so far as to discuss her White House bedroom with Cheshire, though he had never even seen it.

Jackie was determined to put Scalamendré "in his place" and planned never again to use him in the White House.

The attack on Lorraine Pearce, who had already been "released" from her curatorial post, was equally fierce. Jackie excoriated the former curator for having the temerity to arrange a "heavy schedule of speaking engagements," again without seeking Jackie's permission in advance, though Jackie had allowed her to join the Fine Arts Advisory Committee. "She can leave the Committee if she persists in these engagements," said the First Lady. It seemed to her that Lorraine was only interested in publicity. Jackie mistrusted and loathed publicity—and anyone who didn't feel the same way couldn't work for her.

Jackie's personal staff was frankly astonished by her uncompromising drive for perfection, the degree to which she became consumed by the renovation project. She spent her days and nights supervising every aspect of the job. Every lampshade, every vase, every andiron came under her scrutiny. Even the chandeliers were moved about from room to room. Walls were constantly repainted, furniture and paintings forever rearranged. She became perturbed when members of her various committees didn't live up to expectations. Mrs. George Henry Warren of Newport was the subject of more than one angry note to a mutual friend: "I hope that if you ever see Mrs. Warren, you will light a fire under her—as there she is sitting in Newport—with so many houses filled with pretty things and she hasn't even produced one tiny thing. That rather annoys me." It annoyed Jackie when certain antique and rug dealers attempted to overcharge the White House, her dismay spilling over in memos to J. B. West: "I so like the rug, but we are short of dollars and I am ENRAGED at everyone trying to gyp the White House. Tell him if he gives it to us he can get a tax deduction and a photo in our book—if not, goodbye."

She exhibited the same force of will and powers of persuasion in exhorting Bernard Boutin and the General Services Administration to provide additional funds for the Blair House and Lafayette Square projects. "I really am not pleased with the two buildings behind the Square— the windows are awful," she wrote to Boutin. Boutin agreed to change the windows, promising that "all work will be performed on an around-the-clock basis with as large a labor force as is feasible." Jackie responded with gratitude and also by requesting a new outlay of monies:

> Dear Bernie: When I was tramping through Blair House the other day with Mrs. Duke and the most charming man from GSA, he told me that there just weren't funds available yet to fix up that corner house next to Blair . . . He said that it would have to wait until after that enormous office building was built, and I am sure we will probably all be dead by then.
>
> I was just thinking—now that Blair House is all fresh and done over, wouldn't it be nice to make that next-door house available soon. . . .

The renovation project with all its obstacles and dilemmas proved convenient for Jackie as a means of avoiding the more mundane duties associated with her position. She was contemptuous of the traditional role of First Lady and opposed to playing the part. "Why should I traipse around to hospitals playing Lady Bountiful when I have so much to do around here?" she said to a member of the Fine Arts Committee. She used the venture as an excuse when it came to attending certain meetings. She bypassed a Congressional wives prayer breakfast, sending Tish Baldridge in her stead, so she could attend a pre-auction exhibition of early American furniture at Parke-Bernet in New York. She used the same excuse for not attending a luncheon of the National Council of Negro Women to which she had been invited as guest speaker.

Harris Wofford, a civil rights adviser to President Kennedy, recollected Jackie's unintentional snub of Martin Luther King in favor of her renovtion project: "It was a troublesome time for King. The President had asked me to bring him over to his residential quarters in the White House to discuss the latest civil rights crisis. We stepped on the elevator but instead of going up, it went down to the basement, and Jacqueline Kennedy entered. She was dressed in jeans and had soot all over her face; her hair was tied in a knot on top of her head. When I introduced them, she said, in that peculiar voice of hers, 'Oh, Dr. King, you would be so thrilled if you could just have been with me in the basement this morning. I discovered a chair straight out of the Andrew Jackson era—a wonderful, beautiful chair.' King responded, 'Yes—yes—is that so?'

"When the elevator reached its destination, Mrs. Kennedy said, 'I've just got to tell Jack about that chair.' Then she stopped and said, 'But I guess the two of you have other things to discuss.' "After she left, King said, 'Well, well—wasn't that something.' "

Jackie partially redeemed herself by agreeing to tape an hour-long tour of the White House with Charles Collingwood for CBS-TV to show the nation the results of her restoration project. The original idea for the program belonged to Blair Clark, who worked for CBS.

"I first talked to Jack about Jackie doing a tour of the White House for television," said Clark. "Our conversation took place early in 1962. I had spoken to Jack at an earlier time about how to use television, a subject on which his father was also well versed. And so was Jack, for that matter. But Jack wanted to know more, so in December 1960, at which time I was vice-president and general manager of CBS News, I brought Fred Friendly to see him at the Carlyle. Fred was a senior news producer at CBS. He and Jack and I talked about what was a whole new concept then. No President had ever really used television before. Past Presidents had been afraid to take chances with it. In the past they'd always concentrated on the press.

"That early contact had been helpful for Jack. His wit and grace and charm were well-suited to television. So I began with him about the White House tour and he said, 'Well, you'll have to persuade her.' So I met with Jackie. She was at first a little apprehensive. She didn't want to give the impression of being an interior decorator. But anyway we had our conversation and then a second conversation, after which I brought down Perry Wolff, a pioneer documentary producer for television, and the three of us chatted, and then I brought down Charles Collingwood, whom I assigned to be the correspondent on this program. Charles knew the Kennedys somewhat, having once been their neighbor in Georgetown. At one point she suggested I conduct the tour instead of her. I said, 'Television executives don't do that.' I meant Jackie was the show, not me. So she finally agreed to do it. Perry Wolff wrote and produced the program, and Charles Collingwood conducted the interview as Jackie strolled through the White House covering the Reception Room, State Dining Room, Red Room, Blue Room, Green Room and the Lincoln Room, examining such items as wallpaper, silverware, china, sofas, desks, lamps, clocks and portraits. Before we were done I had to convince Jackie to persuade JFK to make a brief appearance at the end of the show, which he did."

"Based on information provided by Pam Turnure and Lorraine Pearce, I wrote four drafts of the script," said Perry Wolff. "We taped it in January 1962 in one or two days, including close-ups of the objects Jackie discussed in the course of the show. She did a good deal of ad-libbing and consequently a number of errors crept in concerning the names, dates and so forth. I had to return to the White House and do a voice-over with Jackie to correct some of these.* She had that strange voice and I couldn't hear her at all, although I was standing only four feet away. 'You'll have to speak up,' I told her. 'I am speaking up,' she said. 'But I can't hear you,' I responded. 'I don't talk any louder than this,' she said. She was anxious to get out of there and go fox hunting, and for some reason she seemed particularly peeved that day at Pam Turnure who stood on the periphery watching the recording of the show. I couldn't figure out if it had anything to do with Pam's affair with the President, which the whole world seemed to know about.

"Later that year, Doubleday threw a lot of money at me to produce a book based on the show. Jackie objected at first because she had wanted to do her own book on the renovation project with photo-journalist David Douglas Duncan. Duncan insisted that to do his end of the manuscript he would have to close down the White House for two days. President Kennedy said, 'The last time we closed the White House was 1812, when the British burned it down. We don't plan a repeat performance.' So they allowed me to go ahead with the book, which like the television program was titled *A Tour of the White House with Mrs. John F. Kennedy.*"

"A Tour" was broadcast on Valentine's Day 1962 to an American viewing audience of more that 46 million. Jackie taped introductions in French as well as Spanish, and the show was eventually distributed to 106 countries on every continent. Seen as a major public relations coup for Jackie, the event's only notable detractor was Norman Mailer, whose wordy "review" appeared in *Esquire:* "The voice was a quiet parody of the sort of voice one hears on the radio late at night, dropped softly into the ear by girls who sell soft mattresses, depilatories or creams to brighten the skin." Jackie, he continued, moved like a wooden horse and looked like "a starlet who will never learn to act." He concluded by lambasting the show as

---

*Even after careful editing, a number of errors apparently made it into the televised version. Chris Preuty Rosenfeld, who researched the project for CBS, subsequently wrote to David Finley (Feb. 15, 1962): "How I regret the errors that did creep into the finished broadcast. . . . Of course some of the errors were due to the improvisation of Mrs. Kennedy. The CBS people were too anxious about not troubling her—and in this did her a disservice."

"silly, ill-advised, pointless, empty, dull and obsequious to the most slavish tastes in American life."

Commenting on his assessment of Jackie, Mailer acknowledged that it won him "few friends. It wasn't that I didn't admire Jackie. I had a high opinion of her when I wrote the piece, and I have a high opinion of her now. I just felt that the White House tour badly misused her."

In addition to the White House renovation project, Jackie became involved in a plan to enlarge and restructure the existing White House library, to fill it with "significant American writings that have influenced American thinking—books by presidents, great writers, etc." To help with the project, Jackie approached James T. Babb, who was chief librarian at the Yale University libraries, and in a series of letters explained what she wanted: "I NEVER thought or would let it be a reference library for W.H. staff—it could never be big enough, and all the books would have to have those awful numbers on the back and no one would ever return them.

"I want old books in their [original] bindings wherever possible. The only place I disagree with you is that I don't think it necessary to search for rare, rare first editions. They cost even more than furniture and it was a backbreaking job, and we are still in debt, to get the furniture we wanted. Just what a gentleman's library should look like—some fine books, others not so rare. . . ."

Despite Babb's involvement, the library plans were never completed. Jackie's other arts-related project, the National Cultural Center in Washington, D.C.—which later became the John F. Kennedy Center for the Performing Arts—met with greater success. It was actually President Eisenhower (not Kennedy) who signed into law legislation to authorize creation of the National Cultural Center. Because of Eisenhower's role in the project, President Kennedy invited Mrs. Eisenhower to serve as co-chairperson of the Center's fund-raising drive along with Mrs. Kennedy.

Mamie Eisenhower had reservations. She agreed to serve only on the condition that "all former First Ladies be listed as honorary co-chairwomen." However, if such were not contemplated, she would serve, provided that there were no persons of any other category included, i.e., no sisters of President Kennedy or Mrs. Kennedy and no wives of Cabinet members, etc. She also specified

that the status of the honorary co-chairwomen be absolutely equal. She would "not care to serve in an honorary
capacity subordinate to Mrs. Kennedy. . . ." Mrs. Eisenhower finally lent her name to the fund drive but little
else, appearing in Washington only once to help raise
funds (at a tea also attended by Janet Auchincloss),
afterwards expressing the conviction that it was impossible to work with Mrs. Kennedy in anything but a subordinate role.

An archaeological project that engaged Jackie's interest during her White House tenure was the preservation
of the Pharaonic monuments in Egypt (then still the
United Arab Republic), in particular at Abu Simbel,
during the construction of the Aswan Dam. The process,
which involved the relocation of entire ancient temples,
cost far more than Egypt was prepared to pay. In the
interest of art and history, Jackie decided to become
involved.

JFK speechwriter Richard Goodwin recalled Jackie "as
somebody who chose her areas of concern carefully and
then really went at it. One of her first memos to the
President involved the Aswan Dam matter. She saved
those Egyptian monuments from destruction by getting
Congress to appropriate funds and also by raising funds
privately. To arouse public interest in the venture she
arranged an exhibition of Tut-ankh-Amen treasures at
the National Gallery and then opened the exhibition by
announcing that some $50 million were needed 'to pre-
serve our heritage.' I'll be damned if she didn't raise
most of it."

In 1975, as a demonstration of Egypt's gratitude, the
temple of Dendur was shipped to New York stone by
stone and placed on exhibit at the Metropolitan Museum
of Art. Other museums across the country also featured
their Egyptian acquisitions in a year-long national celebration of Middle Eastern antiquity. For Jackie's part in
the Aswan Dam preservation project, President Gamal
Abdel Nasser presented her in 1961 with a recently exca-
vated limestone statue of a noble of the fifth dynasty, and
a pair of damascened contemporary vases. The vases,
worth less than a thousand dollars apiece, were listed as
"official White House gifts," whereas the statue, valued
in excess of $250,000, remained (and remains today) in
Jackie's personal possession.

21

Jacqueline Kennedy, short-skirted legs tucked beneath her, leaned against a leather cushion in the private compartment of the presidential plane winging from Bogota to San Juan on what had been another highly successful state visit for the Kennedys, this one to Puerto Rico, Venezuela and Colombia. Jackie, according to White House advance man Jerry Bruno, often generated more excitement on the four-day, mid-December 1961 journey than the President. "It's unbelievable," said Bruno. "It's hard to describe. And it wasn't just because she gave several speeches in Spanish. It was because she was the mother of two very exposed children and was Catholic and glamorous and American. I was there two weeks before the presidential party arrived and most of the questions posed by Venezuelan and Colombian government and church officials concerned Jackie rather than JFK. What would she be wearing? What would she do while the President attended meetings? What was she like in private? There was incredible interest in her."

Now, on the return flight, the First Lady had agreed to discuss her first year in the White House with a reporter from *Newsweek*. "The way we spend our evenings," she said. "Before we left Washington we had dinner alone and discussed Ed Gullion, our Ambassador to the Congo, and agreed on what a wonderful man he is . . . and how he was put in the deep-freeze for eight years . . . and Jack said Africa's the greatest challenge for a brilliant man now. He was saying, 'That's the place.'

"Then we had Mr. and Mrs. Franklin D. Roosevelt, Jr., and Ambassador and Mrs. David Ormsby-Gore to dinner, and once again it was fascinating to hear those three men talk. And the women listen, and break in with something occasionally, and it serves a purpose to those three men. . . . And we had the state dinner at Mount

Vernon for Mohammed Ayub Khan, President of Pakistan, and we hope to have a dinner for all extant Nobel Prize winners in the Western Hemisphere. . . .

"I know so much more about everything now than I did a year ago. Think of this time we're living through. Jack and I are both young, with health, and two wonderful children. It was difficult on them at first, especially the first three months when we barely saw them. It almost broke my heart. And you could see it in Caroline. This sad little face. And to have to live in an office building. You left your desk for five minutes and returned to find it piled to the ceiling again. And Jack wasn't used to living and working in the same house. A friend told him to walk around the driveway twice in the morning, so he can pretend he's walking to work."

To the average *Newsweek* reader Jackie's laments surely sounded peevish and spoiled. Caroline's "sad little" face, for instance, must have been brightened by the presence of the large personal staff employed by the Kennedys (and provided by the White House) to look after the children. They had more stuffed animals, dolls, toys, books and games than they knew what to do with. To go to school they had merely to step on an elevator and ride it to the top floor of the White House where Jackie had established a kindergarten and first grade to accommodate them and two dozen of their privileged little playmates.

"I remember reading about what a great mother Jackie was while First Lady, and how difficult it must have been for her to raise her children," said Esther Van Wagoner Tufty. "This is part of the whole, elaborate Kennedy image which the family, from patriarch Joseph Kennedy on down to Jackie Kennedy herself, have spent so much time and money creating. People would tell me that Jackie was snobbish and selfish and spoiled rotten, but she did a marvelous job raising her kids. I, for one, don't see it. I don't see what distinguishes her as a mother from 50 million other American moms, except that she had more cash, employees and elitist tendencies than any of them.

"As for Caroline and John-John, how many children are fortunate enough to grow up in the White House, ride an elevator to school, have their own ponies galloping about on their front lawn, own large enough wardrobes to clothe half the children of Harlem, never have to sit in a doctor's or dentist's waiting room, never have to ride a public bus or subway, know that they can have anything, go anywhere, do practically whatever they want in life? Those kids were treated like royalty. They wanted to meet Bozo the Clown, they met Bozo the Clown. They wanted to pet Lassie, they got to pet Lassie. Am I supposed to feel sorry for them? Must I regard Jackie as Mother-of-the-Year because she read them an occasional bedtime story or once in a while watched their nanny give them a bath?*

"We were all supposed to feel sorry for Jackie. I mean all that drudgery as First Lady, having to meet Heads of State such as Konrad Adenauer and Harold Macmillan, Haile Selassie and Golda Meir, Ben Bella and Jawaharlal Nehru. Incidentally, she used to do these outrageous and hilarious burlesques of some of the heads of state she encountered in the course of her duties. She would adopt the thick Prussian accent of Adenauer, the lisp of the Shah of Iran, the affected lilt of Queen Frederika of Greece. She had a repertoire of maybe fifty world leaders. It was cruel but amusing, the type of lampoon Noël Coward performed so brilliantly.

"She did a fabulous take-off on Achmed Sukarno. Sukarno, the President of Indonesia, visited Washington in the spring of 1961 and wanted to discuss only the sexual proclivities of his favorite movie stars, especially Marilyn Monroe and Gina Lollobrigida. He demanded that the U.S. State Department provide call girls for himself and other members of his party. He did a real 'lech' number on Jackie at a White House reception, inviting her to visit Indonesia—without her husband. She declined the offer. She had a way with men. Ché Guevara once said she was the only American he wanted to meet— and he didn't want to meet her at the conference table.

"I've said it before—Jackie had her good and bad

_____

*Despite all the "help" Jackie had in raising her children, there were moments of distress. At a swimming pool party for children July 1961 Caroline toppled into the deep end of the pool and was in danger of drowning. To rescue her, Mrs. William L. Saltonstall (daughter-in-law of Senator Leverett Saltonstall of Massachusetts) had to dive into the pool. Such incidents made Jackie wary of the reliability of the Secret Service.

points. Too much has been made of both. Like her husband she grew into her role and learned to exercise the powers and responsibilities that went with it. She once bragged to Nancy Tuckerman, 'People told me ninety-nine things that I had to do as First Lady, and I haven't done one of them.' She received plenty of advice from people in the White House about changing her image. She should be more frugal like Mrs. Taft, or more politically outgoing like Mrs. Roosevelt, or let the politics go and look more homespun like Mrs. Truman. She should give up her fancy hairdos. She shouldn't go fox hunting or dress so expensively. But Jackie went right on doing what she wanted to do.

"And not all of it was bad. When she heard that the ladies of the Daughters of the American Revolution objected to her buying UNICEF Christmas cards because the money supposedly went to Communist-controlled countries, she ordered an additional hundred boxes of cards and made certain that the press wrote about it. Every housewife in America bought UNICEF Christmas cards that year.

"When Jackie campaigned with her husband in West Virginia in 1960, she was shocked by the poverty she encountered in the coal-mining areas. As First Lady she decided to do something to improve the situation. She began buying White House crystal from the Morgantown Glassware Guild, an important West Virginia industry. The following year a well-known manufacturer of costly glassware offered to donate a complete set of glassware to the White House, but Jackie demurred. She wanted to continue purchasing glassware in West Virginia 'until they aren't poor there anymore.' After she returned from a trip to India in 1962, she said: 'The poverty in West Virginia hit me more than the poverty in India, maybe because I just didn't realize it existed in the United States.' She insisted she would 'break all the glasses in the White House and order new ones each week, if that's the only way I have of helping them.' "

"I think Jackie felt she was finally doing something worthwhile," said Oleg Cassini. "In the beginning she had been forced to make an adjustment. Then she went to Europe and created a bigger stir than the President. That's when she began to enjoy her position. Before that she saw herself as nothing more than 'the President's wife.' But this was something new to her. She had stolen the show, stolen her husband's thunder."

Igor Cassini took it a step further: "Jackie had always been in love with the world of power and money. And as they say, 'Power corrupts.' In a way it corrupted her. Once she became First Lady she changed—and not for the better."

Whatever its benefits, Jackie's "power trip" caused dissension in the family. "You had to feel sorry for Lee," said Edie Beale. "Playing second fiddle to Jackie couldn't have been easy. Whenever Lee visited the White House or accompanied Jackie on a trip, she had to be reminded that Jackie was Queen of the Circus."

If Lee happened to forget, Jackie made certain she remembered. When the First Lady read that her sister was supposedly more elegantly dressed, she wrote to one of her fashion spies in Paris: "What I really appreciate most of all is your letting me know before Lee about the treasures. Please always do that—now that she knows you are my 'scout,' she is slipping in there before me. So this fall, do let me know about the prettiest things first."

Jackie's greatest problems came from members of the Kennedy family, starting with Ethel Kennedy. "Ethel Kennedy has the mind-set of a vulture," said Truman Capote. "She's the most highly competitive and insanely jealous human being I've ever met. Jackie would give a party at the White House and a week later Ethel felt obligated to throw a shindig at Hickory Hill. She was obsessed by Jackie. Anything Jackie did, she could do better. Jackie referred to her as 'the baby-making machine—wind her up and she becomes pregnant.' "

Then there were Jackie's ongoing differences with Rose Kennedy, a relationship that had never been easy for either one. Capote attributed their problems to the fact that "they were both strong personalities. Jackie was First Lady but Rose was the family matriarch. She called the shots. And in this sense she was like any other mother-in-law, always telling her children, Jackie included, what to eat, where to vacation, how to dress. Jackie wouldn't tolerate directives from her own mother and wasn't about to take advice from Rose.

"They also had differences of opinion on how to raise children. When they didn't want the children to understand what they were saying they would speak French.

Rose was concerned that Caroline and John Jr. should receive proper religious training and would test them to see if they knew their prayers."

J. B. West found that Rose "came to the White House more often when her daughter-in-law was away than when she was in residence. She acted as hostess for her son at official functions during those times, and she was definitely in charge when her son visited *her*."

The President's mother sent frequent letters to various White House staff members criticizing Jackie. When the First Lady sent Air Force One to Palm Beach to retrieve several record albums she had left behind, Rose Kennedy wrote to Ken O'Donnell: "That kind of waste is simply unacceptable."

Following one of Jack and Jackie's visits to Palm Beach, J. B. West received the following letter from Rose:

> When the President used the house in Palm Beach late last spring, after we had gone, a lot of dirty dishes, pots and pans, and linens were left strewn around the kitchen. I would appreciate it if you would tell the staff to leave everything clean in the future, as we have had trouble with rodents.
> Please use your own judgment when you speak with them because I do not want them to think that our help are complaining. . . .

More distressing for Jackie than her mother-in-law's letters were the intrusive antics of Eunice Shriver, which became more intense following Joe Kennedy's stroke. Eunice and Jackie never enjoyed the warmth and closeness that marked the bond, for example, between Eunice and Ethel Kennedy. On a weekend that Jack and Jackie paid a state visit to Mexico, journalist Ruth Montgomery and her husband were invited to the Shrivers' for a quiet Sunday brunch. Eunice and Ruth were sunning themselves beside the swimming pool when the radio brought news of the President's warm reception below the Rio Grande, and Eunice exclaimed, "Isn't it wonderful that Brother is getting the attention this time, instead of Jackie. Honestly, when I think how she has never lifted a finger to help Jack politically and then reaped all that attention in Europe."

American Ambassador to Honduras Charles R. Bur-

rows was witness to an altercation between Eunice and
Jackie that took place in mid-1962 when Mrs. Villeda
Morales, wife of the Honduran president, visited the
United States. "Because she was not here officially, Mrs.
Kennedy was not interested in seeing her," said Burrows.
"Eunice Shriver heard about this, was distressed that
Mrs. Villeda Morales wasn't able to see Mrs. Kennedy,
and said to Mrs. Morales, 'Look, I'll get you in the White
House—you know, the back door, sort of—and we'll see
Mrs. Kennedy.' Mrs. Morales said, 'I'm the wife of a
president and I'm not going to go in by the back door,'
and she went back home—not too happy about it, really.
She felt that she'd been shown the back-of-the-hand by
Jackie Kennedy."

Eunice Shriver was furious with Jackie. One of the first
groups of Peace Corp volunteers—Sargent Shriver's
project—had gone to Honduras. Eunice felt the necessity
of promoting a good-neighbor policy with all of Latin
America, but particularly in Honduras.

The situation was exacerbated, reported Burrows, when
the President of Colombia visited Washington and was
likewise rebuffed by Jackie: "It was an official visit, and
there was a dinner party . . . given by the President. But
Mrs. Kennedy was not there, she was unavailable. It was
during the period when she wasn't doing these things.
The word was that Mrs. Kennedy was not well, and that
the President's mother, Rose Kennedy, would officiate,
which she did. But the day that the dinner party was
reported in the press, there was also a press report and
picture of Mrs. Kennedy water-skiing with John Glenn,
up in Massachusetts or someplace."

The only Kennedy with whom Jackie maintained strong
ties was Joe Kennedy. Lem Billings visited Palm Beach a
few weeks after Joe's stroke at the end of 1961. "It was
the most frustrating day I ever spent," he reminisced.
"The old man couldn't talk. Instead of making words, he
would groan and gurgle. Jack and Jackie were there, and
they were very upset. Especially Jackie. The old man was
used to giving orders, barking at people, yelling. Now he
was reduced to two words. The words were 'no' and
'shit.' Those were the only words he could say. But
Jackie was very devoted to him. Whenever they brought
him to the White House, it was Jackie who looked after
him, wiped his mouth when he would drool at dinner.

The rest of the family seemed squeamish about his paralysis, but Jackie went out of her way to touch and kiss him on his paralyzed right side."

Always dependent on his father's political advice, the President now turned to other family members for the same kind of help. He had always trusted Bobby and looked to Bobby increasingly as time went on. Eunice gradually became an important source, Teddy less so, although after Teddy became Senator from Massachusetts in 1962, his brother consulted with him more often. Most surprisingly, he turned to Jackie for enlightenment.

"Jack developed enormous respect for his wife's political judgment," confirmed George Smathers. "His pride in her achievements grew stronger the longer he remained in office. He used her as a kind of unofficial observer in foreign countries. She went to India, Pakistan, Greece, Italy and other places, and people thought she was merely vacationing. But she was doing far more than that. She was spending time with government officials, buttering them up. She was taking mental notes. I'm told her letters to Jack while she was away in foreign ports were full of subtle political observation. Her sharp eye for detail made her an excellent trouble-shooter for the administration. Her letters, reports might be a better word, held back nothing by way of praise or criticism.

"She also developed into a first-rate public speaker. It was Jackie who spoke to the Bay of Pigs veterans in Spanish after they returned to Miami. She had the ability to handle difficult situations as well as difficult persons. She would have made a splendid Chief of Protocol. Jack often used her as a go-between, a political buffer with people like John Kenneth Galbraith, Chester Bowles and Adlai Stevenson, men he didn't particularly favor."

President Kennedy's dealings with Adlai Stevenson had always been problematic. After the Cuban missile crisis, JFK spread the rumor that Stevenson had recommended a policy of capitulation to the Soviets. The UN Ambassador took issue with the President's characterization of events, and countered by claiming that he had not been kept abreast of late-breaking developments during the missile crisis. He felt that the White House had not properly supported him against accusations of softness toward Cuba, and had indicated disrespect in other ways, hence he was in a mood of smoldering indignation when the President sent Jackie to meet him in New York.

Stevenson and Jackie had shared an interest in literature and the arts, and had always enjoyed being in each other's company. Whereas Stevenson had often felt uncomfortable with JFK, Jackie seemed much easier to talk to. Their New York meeting went well. Jackie followed it by sending Stevenson a watercolor she had done of a sphinx bearing a lady's face; the face strongly resembled her own. An accompanying note read: "A sphinx is rather what I feel like when I go out with you—as it all seems so responsible—and it is really the most marvelous 'cover.'"

The banter inspired Stevenson to invite the First Lady and her sister for lunch at the United Nations. The sisters went and apparently enjoyed themselves. The First Lady wrote again, noting that "the whole atmosphere of that place is so charged with undercurrents and tension and excitement—to work there must make every other place seem about as exciting as a post office. . . .

"You showed Lee and me the most exhilarating side of it—we dream of intrigues in the Delegates' Lounge. Lee, that fickle creature, came there adoring the Greek Ambassador and left in love with Dr. [Ralph] Bunche!

"I was so lucky to have the chance to meet U Thant—and I loved him, but I'm not fickle. . . ."

"By late 1961 and for the duration of Camelot," said author Ralph G. Martin, "Jackie wasn't simply a young woman who had married a famous man; she was a famous woman married to the President of the United States."

The President continued to encourage Jackie to involve herself in the complex world of international diplomacy. Kathy Tollerton, an administrative assistant at the White House during the Kennedy Administration, found Jackie acting as a buffer between Prime Minister Nehru of India and her husband:

"During the Indian leader's visit to the United States in November 1961, the President and Mrs. Kennedy held a small official dinner in Washington for Nehru and his daughter, Mrs. Indira Gandhi, later also to become Prime Minister. Nehru and his daughter had spent the weekend with the Kennedys at Hammersmith Farm, the Auchincloss residence at Newport. As a private joke, Kennedy took

Nehru past the great marble mansions of Newport's millionaires and told him, 'I wanted you to see how the average American lives.'

"The joke didn't go over very well. Previously Kennedy had made several speeches praising India, stating how much we ought to do for that country, how important India was to the West. But evidently Kennedy and Nehru, when they met, didn't get along at all. On Monday morning, the visitors landed on the White House lawn by helicopter, having flown with the President and Mrs. Kennedy from Newport. Many of us had congregated on the lawn to see Nehru and the Kennedys as they returned.

"My first impression was that JFK looked terrible. I had never seen him look worse. He usually looked great, as if he'd had eight hours of sleep. But this time he had wide circles around his eyes and he seemed dreadfully morose. Walking arm-in-arm about ten or fifteen paces behind him were Jackie and Nehru, obviously enjoying a very animated chat together. I had heard that in 1951 during a trip to India, JFK had found Nehru to be self-satisfied, rude, and stuffy. Evidently nothing had changed. But it was just as clear that Jackie and Nehru had hit it off. Jackie later visited India without her husband, which didn't surprise anybody who worked at the White House and happened to see the arrival scene that morning."

Arthur Schlesinger suggested that "President Kennedy relied on his wife for political purposes more than is generally supposed." As early as the 1960 presidential campaign, Schlesinger was instructed (together with John Kenneth Galbraith) to communicate with JFK through Jackie. Kennedy established this hierarchy of communication "because he did not want to upset Ted Sorensen and Richard Goodwin, who were writing speeches and working under intense pressure and who regarded interlopers with great suspicion, not then knowing Galbraith and me as well as we all got to know each other later. . . .

"My general impression is that Jackie rather enjoyed the spectacle of politics, that she was quite willing to play a political role when necessary and that she had (still has) keen reactions to issues of public policy."

Whereas Jackie's noninvolvement policy had long been regarded as part of her charm, her gradual emergence on official trips abroad and in Latin America gave her the self-assurance and status that made her role in her husband's administration increasingly effective. Although relatively few people knew of her burgeoning interest in the actual governing process—and fewer still were willing to acknowledge it—her influence had by 1962 been felt in both the executive and social wings of the White House.

"There was nothing surprising about it," said Charles Bartlett. "I mean it's possible to love a politician without loving politics but it is impossible to marry one without becoming part of his career. It was certainly impossible to be around Jack Kennedy without it having a certain osmotic effect in terms of politics. That's basically all he talked about. Jackie obviously knew exactly what was going on and was effective in carrying out whatever assignments Jack handed her. Jackie maintained a fidelity to her own individuality, but she played an increasingly large role as a behind-the-scenes power broker, a forceful figure within the administration who helped devise a number of its policies, domestic as well as foreign."

Discussing Jackie's role as a political figure, Charlotte Curtis noted, "In those days nobody wanted to admit just how much power Jackie wielded around the White House. You get power in several ways, but two of them are access and leverage, and Jackie certainly had access. Putting aside the question of how or whether she used her access, bear in mind that in Washington the appearance of power is as good as the real thing. In fact, appearance and reality are often inseparable. Power flows to the person who appears to possess it already. The various players in the so-called power-game see to that. They fear that if they offend or somehow disappoint someone who seems to have more power than they do, they will be hit by a retaliatory strike or be put on a permanent blacklist. Of course permanence in Washington is measured in four-year stretches. There is no such thing as 'permanent.' Be that as it may, these other players invest the player they fear, or whose patronage they want to solicit, with more power than that player might actually have. Thus appearance once again becomes reality. Unless you understand this concept, you don't understand Washington. It explains how someone like Jackie gets to play a vital role in political affairs without being very blatant about it."

Sir David Ormsby-Gore also conceded that Jackie exercised greater political clout than has been previously admitted. "The First Lady," he pointed out, "has no constitutional or statutory duties at all, but she's almost constantly on display, and held to the ephemeral ideals of the moment. She's expected to be well-groomed, well-dressed and to make bland statements on behalf of unexceptional causes. With minor exceptions, that's what every First Lady since Jackie has done. Jackie began her term that way but then changed course.

"She took a growing interest in the problems that beset the presidency. Almost every day she sent to the Library of Congress for new material, reference books, historical tomes, documents and newspaper clippings to acquaint herself with the background of political events and soon came up with ideas and suggestions that she passed on to her husband. It was her way of encouraging him to share his thoughts and troubles with her; indeed, he had more troubles than he had bargained for. Jackie would discuss certain topics with the President and beat him down. On the theory that it was too restrictive, she convinced the President to relax the McCarran Immigration Act. And she pushed him to join the Test Ban Treaty with Great Britain and the Soviet Union. A few of his people were against it because they felt he would have to make too many concessions. But Jackie prevailed.

"Because she invariably sided with the moderates over the hardliners, they used to call her 'the White House liberal.' She was all for normalizing relations between the United States and the Soviet Union. In 1963, for example, there was opposition among the President's brain trust to the proposed sale of 150 million bushels of wheat to the Soviets. Jackie wanted the sale to go through. Being a shrewd judge of character and having a real sort of bloodhound's instinct for hidden agendas, she knew which people to push and how far to push them. The sale took place just six weeks before the President's assassination.

"What we're beginning to realize, I think, is that First Ladies know Presidents better, and often influence them more, than most people think. As pressures build and critics carp, the President and his wife tend to grow closer. The intriguing thing is that their personal chemistry is virtually unknown to others. A First Lady's warm embrace or cold stare or furrowed brow can affect her husband's mind and mood, and maybe even ultimately shake nations.

"No First Lady, particularly Jacqueline Kennedy, would ever brag of those moments when her intervention altered the course of events. If anything, Jackie made light of her influence. I recall a small dinner party at the White House when Jack started grumbling about air pollution. 'What the hell am I going to do about air pollution?' he said. Jackie, who never liked mixing shoptalk with social doings, responded, 'Why don't you just order the navy to spray our industrial centers with Chanel Number Five?'

"There was another reason why so few people were aware of Jackie's involvement, the fact for instance that she often observed meetings of the National Security Council. The Kennedys weren't the kind of family to admit that behind every strong man there's a stronger woman. They were too machismo. They wanted the public to perceive the menfolk as operating the controls, the women as mere cheerleaders. Jackie was anything but a cheerleader."*

"JFK bounced a lot of ideas off Jackie," said speech writer Richard Goodwin. "One of those ideas was a trip to India and Pakistan with a stop in Rome to meet the Pope. She thought he wanted her to accompany him; what he meant was: would she be willing to go by herself?"

Jackie agreed to make the good-will expedition provided she be allowed to take along her sister Lee. She also asked her friend Joan Braden, who had been helping her raise funds for the National Cultural Center, to make the trip.

"When I accompanied Jackie to India, I was invited

---

*Others who mentioned Jackie's role as an adviser to JFK included Robert S. McNamara and Major General Chester V. Clifton. Former Secretary of Defense McNamara said: "Jackie is one of the most underrated women in the country. She is extraordinarily acute politically. The President consulted her on any number of issues. I don't mean in the sense of long anguished discussions, but certainly she was informed of what was going on and expressed her views on almost everything." General Clifton, Military Aide to the President, said, "JFK turned to his wife for advice whenever a crisis arose: the Berlin Wall, the Cuban Missiles, the Bay of Pigs. He would talk to her about it and she would talk with him. She wouldn't advise his staff, she would advise him—that's why nobody knew about it."

along as a friend and then I did a piece for *The Saturday Evening Post,"* said Braden. "First it was going to be an official visit and then they downgraded it to semi-official, which meant that all members of the press would have to pay their own way. But my husband Tom had just bought a newspaper, and we didn't have any money. So Jackie deputized me. I fielded many of the questions she was asked in India and Pakistan and answered them for her. In return, I went gratis."

The journey started on March 8, 1962, when a hundred reporters and a three-man film crew from the United States Information Agency—which was dispatched to film Jackie's expedition—joined the First Lady aboard her plane in New York. After two days of receptions and ceremonial teas in and around Rome, Jacqueline visited the Vatican for a private audience with Pope John XXIII, which she subsequently described as "simple and natural." They spoke in French, and she presented the Pontiff with a book of her husband's speeches.

As they landed in New Delhi, Jackie confessed to Joan Braden that she was "scared to death." It was one thing to stand by her husband's side when they visited foreign lands, it was another to represent her country by herself. She seemed a bit stiff as she shook hands with the airport reception party, spoke a few sentences of greeting, responded briefly to the crowd, then drove off in a Cadillac limousine with Prime Minister Nehru, the rest of her entourage following behind.

That evening over dinner, Indira Gandhi taught Jackie the *namaste,* the traditional Indian greeting performed with palms placed together as if in prayer. The first time Jackie used the *namaste* standing in the back seat of an open car at Udaipur, the crowds erupted in a roar. *"Jackie Ki Jai! Ameriki Rani!"* ("Hail Jackie! Queen of America!")

The Indian press rejoiced in her presence, reporting that many more people had turned out to see Mrs. Kennedy than had greeted Queen Elizabeth.

An editorial in one New Delhi newspaper referred to Jackie as "Durga, Goddess of Power." Prew Bhatia, editor of *The Times of India,* wrote: "Nothing else happened in India while Mrs. Kennedy was here. Her presence completely dominated the Indian scene."

Wherever she went, there were presents: a rare Indian carpet, a miniature painting, a silver dagger, an Indian spinning wheel, a golden woven sari of raw silk and cotton. She was given ceremonial attire for her children, a handmade saddle, a baby elephant and a pair of tiger cubs (the elephant and tiger cubs eventually went to zoos in the United States). The governor of Rajasthan presented her with a gold-enameled necklace studded with diamonds and pearls. The gifts she kept, however, were those given to her by Pakistan President Mohammed Ayub Khan—a thoroughbred bay gelding ("Sardar"), flown to the U.S. at government expense aboard a Military Air Transport Service plane, and a second necklace containing diamonds, rubies and emeralds.

Escorted by Ambassador John Kenneth Galbraith, Jackie marveled at the Taj Mahal, sailed down the Ganges River, took a boat trip across the flower-strewn waters of Lake Pichola, lunched on wild boar (she brought along her own supply of bottled water from Washington), rode an eight-foot-high elephant named Bibi and went for a spin on a camel.

When the international press criticized her for wearing high fashion in a country overrun with poverty, Jackie instructed her press attaché to refrain from volunteering any further fashion information. "If you say anything, tell them it's second-hand and that I bought everything at the Ritz Thrift Shop."

Newsweek suggested that Jackie was perhaps socializing with too many Indian princes and visiting too many palaces instead of seeing "the real India."

The barb angered the President, who told Ben Bradlee that the Indian government decided what Jackie should see or not see. "When the French invite you to Paris, they don't show you the sewers," he said. "They take you to Versailles."

JFK nevertheless put Galbraith on notice, instructing him to include more hospital visits and fewer stops in the ornate palaces of India.

The new orders created all sorts of complications. Visiting the Maharajah and Maharani of Jaipur, the Americans informed their hosts that they would have to cut short their stay. When the Maharajah offered to take Jackie on a tour of the City Palace at Jaipur, Galbraith declined.

In her autobiography, *A Princess Remembers,* the Maharani of Jaipur writes: "Mr. Galbraith seemed to think, somewhat absurdly, that we were trying to reap some kind of political advantage from [Jackie's] stay. Mr. Galbraith even wrote to President Kennedy advising him to ask his wife not to come to Jaipur. The President replied that he never interfered with his wife's private arrangements.'"*

Galbraith later defended himself by pointing out that "At the time there was some considerable friction between the Indian government and the old princely houses. . . . My practical obligation was to the Indian government, with whom both the United States government and I had to do business. It was thus that I was led to guide Mrs. Kennedy into the hands of the state authority. But eventually a compromise was achieved by which she went on . . . to visit the Jaipurs . . . at the City Palace."

The City Palace visit took place late at night when the streets of Jaipur were deserted.

Another exchange between the President and the American Ambassador occurred when Jackie insisted on seeing the erotic carvings of the Black Pagoda of Konarac, including—as Galbraith described it—"one accomplished woman making love to two violently tumescent men at the same time."

Galbraith, concerned that a photographer might take a picture, again contacted the President. "What's wrong?" asked Kennedy. "Don't you think she's old enough?"

In the course of the trip there were recurring moments of tension between Jackie and Lee. At odd moments it seemed as if the two sisters wouldn't have minded switching places—Lee would have relished the attention and privilege that came with being First Lady, while Jackie longed for the freedom from etiquette and restraint that governed Lee's existence.

Joan Braden noted that throughout the trip "Lee would be brought up by some car at the rear of the motorcade. By the time she arrived at a given monument or site, the tour would be all but over. That happened at Fatehpur Sikri, Pakistan, where we watched young men dive 200 feet into a tiny pool of water. Lee arrived after the divers were done, so Jackie asked them to perform again."

*Gayatri Devi and Santha Rama Rau, *A Princess Remembers*, p. 278.

On March 26, Jacqueline and her group departed Pakistan and arrived in London for a two-day respite. Awaiting her was an invitation for lunch at Buckingham Palace. When she emerged from the Palace, she was quick to forestall embarrassing comparisons. "I thought the Queen's clothes looked lovely," she told the press. But within the week she had added the prim and matronly British monarch to her growing repertoire of burlesques.

On her return to Washington, the First Lady looked weary. Her mood was not improved by public complaints about her trip. Congressman Walter L. McVey, Republican of Kansas, told *The New York Times* that he had been unable to procure passage on a military service flight from Pakistan to Greece because the plane had been reserved for Jackie's new horse. It was revealed that the USIA-sponsored film of Jacqueline Kennedy's India-Pakistan trip had cost the government more than one hundred thousand dollars. Yet Jackie rarely revealed her feelings about public criticism and Jack's occasional reproaches. Discussing the trip, she said only, "I've missed the family. If people were kind to me in India and Pakistan, it was because I was the wife of the President."

Actually, Jackie's popularity had never been higher than it was now. She was more adept at manipulating opinion polls than any of the Kennedys, and she appeared to be just as influential. On May 8, 1962, she traveled to New London, Connecticut, to christen the *Lafayette*, a 7,000-ton nuclear-powered submarine. Endicott "Chubb" Peabody, a member of one of Massachusetts's most distinguished families and a future Massachusetts governor, attended the same ceremony and remembered the clamor made over the First Lady.

"I knew her before she was Mrs. Kennedy," said Peabody. "I didn't know her well, but I knew her. Her shyness had always been apparent. She was very shy and very pretty. I didn't know her well enough where she could relax and be herself, just well enough to exchange smiles and greetings.

"I also knew Jack. I'd been active in his senatorial campaigns and then in the 1960 presidential campaign. I went to the *Lafayette* christening because I'd been in the subs during World War II and also because I was running for governor.

"But not yet holding office, I couldn't get near Jackie.

Obviously everyone wanted their picture taken with her. She was surrounded by Navy brass, politicians, Secret Service agents, newspaper people. I stood outside a door about 200 yards from where the ceremony was taking place. Jackie christened the vessel and a few minutes later emerged through the door, at which point I merged with her. I took her hand and a horde of photographers descended upon us. She was obviously startled by my forwardness. But I went on shaking her hand while the photographers snapped away. That small gesture with its resultant coverage proved invaluable to my campaign."

Noël Coward had a similar reaction when Jackie attended the opening of one of his plays on Martha's Vineyard. She had intended to arrive at the playhouse anonymously, and she wore a Leon Buchheit wig to disguise herself. But as Coward writes in his published *Diaries:* "The secret got out and the theater was a howling inferno of press photographers and reporters. I felt extremely embarrassed about all this. . . . The whole business hit the headlines in both the Boston and the New York papers; in fact, the press of the world has been plastered with photographs of Mrs. Kennedy and me, all of which, despite the fact that I had nothing to do with it, is marvelous publicity for the show."

Whatever the origin of Jackie's magical draw, it was bound to keep her a full-time prisoner. The smallest activity invariably attracted attention. Henry C. Lindner, a former golf professional at the Newport Country Club, gave Jackie golf lessons during each of her first two summers in the White House and remembered some of the problems she encountered.

"I first met Jackie through Oleg Cassini," said Lindner. "Oleg had taken lessons from me, as had his brother—at Newport and in Palm Beach. One day Oleg said, 'I've got a new customer for you.' A few hours later Jackie Kennedy showed up in the clubhouse.

"She'd taken lessons before at Hyannis Port and didn't have a bad swing. She had a poor grip, but as soon as I changed it her game improved. I gave her lessons every day for a month in the summer of '61 and again the next year. We'd go to the practice tee in the morning and then play nine holes together, and I'd also teach her then.

"I presume she wanted to learn to play better golf because her husband enjoyed the sport. Whether she enjoyed it as much, I don't know. She was concerned about newspaper photographers. They would hide in the rough or behind the trees and follow us from hole to hole. Jackie would order her Secret Service agents after them. She'd be about to address the ball or line up a putt and you'd hear this little clicking sound—like a cricket—emanating from the woods. Suddenly two Secret Service agents would appear and go streaking after the intruder. If they caught up with him, they'd grab his camera and either smash it or expose the film.

"I recall another time I was walking around the Newport course with Jackie and two women spotted her. Usually if people recognized her they would gawk. But these two old biddies started pointing and coming toward us. They walked up to Jackie and one of them said, 'Oh, Jackie, we love you so much. Please give us a smile.' Jackie nodded at them and kept walking. Later I said to her, 'That kind of thing must get pretty boring.' 'Well, it's difficult,' she said. 'It happens every day and while you don't want to be rude, there's sometimes no other choice.'"

Italian photographers—*paparazzi*—were much on Jackie's mind in August 1962 when she decided to join Lee and Stas Radziwill at their rented summer home in southern Italy, Villa Episcopio, a 900-year-old, twelve-room palazzo in Ravello, a thousand feet above Amalfi and the Bay of Salerno. Besides Jacqueline, who brought along her daughter Caroline, house guests included Gianni Agnelli and his wife Mariella (Agnelli, one of the wealthiest men in Italy, had given Jackie funds and equipment for her Aswan Dam project), journalist Benno Graziani and his wife Nicole (Benno had accompanied Jackie and Lee on their recent trip to India and Pakistan) and C.L. Sulzberger of *The New York Times*. Also in the group were three Secret Service agents, who kept in touch with one another by transistor walkie-talkie, as well as an Italian-speaking T-man from the Treasury anti-narcotics service who had been placed on loan. Dozens of Italian security agents were posted outside the house.

Cheering crowds lined the roads every day. *Paparazzi* were out in force. The security operation was complex. To go swimming, Jackie had to board a van, and the security people communicated to those below to clear the entire road to Amalfi. The van drove down and Jackie would board a boat. The police launches kept everyone away and Jackie would be taken to a private beach across the bay where the Radziwills had leased another small house to be used as a cabana.

One day, Jackie and the others joined Agnelli and a five-man mandolin band aboard his yacht. Trailed by police motor launches, the yacht sailed to Paestum. Local authorities closed a section of the beach in Paestum, so Jackie and her companions could swim without hindrance. When Jackie expressed an interest in visiting a certain museum in Paestum, the authorities closed the building to everyone but employees.

Sensing a challenge, *paparazzi* assigned to the First Lady persisted, and soon pictures of a smiling Jackie and a suntanned Lee began appearing in the world press. The President took notice, and on at least two occasions telephoned his wife. When photographs of Jackie swimming with Gianni Agnelli appeared in print, JFK sent her a telegram: "A LITTLE MORE CAROLINE AND LESS AGNELLI."

Jackie took pleasure in Jack's growing jealousy. She asked Agnelli to take her scuba diving. She was fascinated by the sport, though she had engaged in it only once, after hours of instruction in Charles Wrightsman's swimming pool. In the sea, it was a different matter. To her horror, she was approached by a shark and two barracuda. But she followed an instructor's advice and didn't move; the fish ignored her and finally swam away.

C. L. Sulzberger, whose diary accounts of these days later became the basis of a book (*The Last of the Giants*, 1970), found Jackie "a strange girl and also strange looking, but quite lovely despite the fact her eyes are too far apart. She is a good athlete, swims, water-skis, and dances well, has a fine figure. She has an odd habit of halting constantly as she talks, a kind of pause rather than a stutter, so sometimes you think she's through saying something when she isn't.

"I didn't have the impression that she was particularly brilliant, despite her reputation for so being, or unusually cultivated. Speaks good French . . . and some Italian. A rather typical society girl but sweet, exceptionally fond of Caroline and somehow on the whole unspoiled."

What struck Sulzberger about her, however, were Jackie's finely tuned political instincts. She made a number of telling points about her husband's administration and seemed to have a sound psychological understanding of the process.

Among her statements to Sulzberger:

"John Glenn . . . is the most controlled person on earth. . . . He would be a fine Ambassador to Moscow."

"Bobby Kennedy is immensely ambitious and will never feel that he has succeeded in life until he has been elected to something, even Mayor of Hyannis Port. Being appointed to office isn't enough."

Oleg Cassini conjectured: "I think JFK, so to say, 'fell in love' with his wife a second time after they reached the White House and she was able to demonstrate her gifts and abilities. Jackie was not political in the traditional sense and disliked politics at first, resented them. This was not her world. But she found her own world-within-the-world of politics. She became political in her own sense. The presidency is such an awe-inspiring position. The power of Power itself is what is so corruptive.

"There is a lot of the little girl in Jackie and this is undoubtedly part of her charm. There's a lost quality at times. If you look carefully, you can see that her problems appear suddenly on her face and she looks bewildered at these times. Other times she looks completely confident. She's a powerhouse. She's at the top of her form and knows it. She's authoritative, witty and decisive. The one difficulty is that you never know which of the two Jackies to expect. She was as unpredictable as she was changeable."

This dualistic view of Jackie was shared by many who knew her during her White House years. August Heckscher, Special Consultant to the President on the Arts, considered her "an ambivalent figure. . . . In the first place she was devoted to the private life that she could keep for herself and her children and yet, on the other hand, she found that she was becoming more and more the representative of a bright flame of cultural interests in this country. Sometimes she seemed to draw back as if she didn't want to get too much involved in all this. The public had the impression that Mrs. Kennedy was doing an enormous amount for the arts, was busy every moment promoting the arts. She would do one thing with superb taste and it would have a tremendous impact. [But] we were always—I say 'we' in this case, for I was working very closely with Tish Baldrige—trying to get

Six-year-old Jacqueline Bouvier with the family Great Dane. *(Bert & Richard Morgan)*

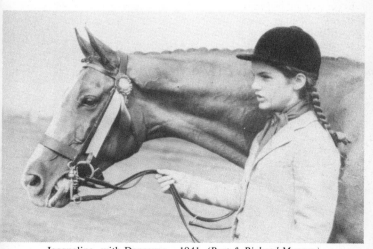

Jacqueline, with Danseuse—1941. *(Bert & Richard Morgan)*

The photograph that ended a marriage: Black Jack Bouvier and Virginia Kernochan holding hands, while Janet Bouvier looks the other way. *(UPI/Bettmann Newsphotos)*

Jackie with her father, John (Black Jack) Vernou Bouvier III, and her grandfather, John Vernou Bouvier, Jr., East Hampton, 1943. *(Courtesy: John F. Kennedy Library)*

Mrs. John Vernou Bouvier III and her two daughters Lee and Jackie, 1941. *(Bert & Richard Morgan)*

Jackie (far left) and friends ham it up at Miss Porter's, 1946. *(Peter Brennan)*

The Inquiring Photographer, 1953. *(UPI/Bettmann Newsphotos)*

"The wedding of the Year." *(UPI/Bettmann Newsphotos)*

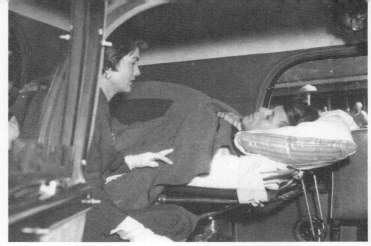

Accompanied by his wife, Jacqueline, Sen. John Kennedy is taken by ambulance to his father's residence at Palm Beach following back surgery in New York. *(UPI/Bettmann Newsphotos)*

Despite her pregnancy, Jackie joins her husband for a busy day of campaigning in and around New York. *(UPI/Bettmann Newsphotos)*

John F. Kennedy surrounded by members of the Kennedy family. Standing, l. to r., Ethel Kennedy, Stephen Smith, Jean Kennedy Smith, JFK, Robert F. Kennedy, Patricia Kennedy Lawford, Sargent Shriver, Joan Kennedy and Peter Lawford. Seated, l. to r., Eunice Kennedy Shriver, Rose Kennedy, Joseph P. Kennedy, Jacqueline Kennedy and Edward M. Kennedy. *(AP/Wide World)*

The John F. Kennedys lounging in Hyannis Port. *(Courtesy: John F. Kennedy Library)*

Angie Dickinson has long hinted of her special friendship with JFK.

Marilyn.

Judith Campbell Exner met JFK in 1960. Their relationship continued for more than two years. *(AP/Wide World)*

"I do not think it entirely inappropriate to introduce myself," said JFK.
"I am the man who accompanied Jacqueline Kennedy to Paris."
(AGIP/Robert Cohen)

"La belle Zha-kee" visits Paris and "feels like a queen."
(AGIP/Robert Cohen)

Dr. Max Jacobson regularly treated Jack and Jackie with amphetamine injections, accompanying them to Vienna for the Summit with Khrushchev.
(Courtesy: Ruth Jacobson)

Master cellist Pablo Casals entertains at the White House.
(Courtesy: John F. Kennedy Library)

"How could this have happened?" Jackie wanted to know months after
the assassination of the President. *(Courtesy: John F. Kennedy Library)*

"To visit Seville and not ride horseback is equal to not coming at all," said Jackie while visiting Spain in 1966. *(AP/WideWorld)*

Jackie and her companion, Roswell Gilpatric, traveled to Mexico together in 1968. *(UPI/Bettmann Newsphotos)*

Jackie supported Bobby's run for the presidency. *(Ron Galella)*

Financial wizard André Meyer advised her against marrying Aristotle Onassis. *(Ron Galella)*

Their 1968 marriage on Skorpios shocked the world. Greek shipping magnate Aristotle Onassis paid $3 million in advance, more later. *(AP/Wide World)*

Jackie on a buying spree. *(Ron Galella)*

Ari's 325-foot *Christina* was one of the world's largest privately owned yachts. *(AP/Wide World)*

Ari's daughter, Christina, loathed Jackie. *(Ron Galella)*

Jackie and Ari take a stroll, 1970. *(Ron Galella)*

Lee Radziwill and Jackie Onassis shopping on Capri, in Italy. *(Ron Galella)*

Jackie Onassis, Caroline and John Kennedy, Jr. enjoy ice cream cones walking on Broadway after Jackie picked up John at school. *(Ron Galella)*

"Jackie was *de trop* [too much]," said her first cousin, Edie Beale, posing near poster advertising the film *Grey Gardens* about her and her mother Edith Bouvier Beale. *(AP/Wide World)*

Andy Warhol: "You could hear her name in the air—'Jackie . . . Jackie . . . Jackie.' " *(AP/Wide World)*

Truman Capote loved to hate Jackie. *(AP/Wide World)*

After Ari's death in 1975, Jackie fought for a $26 million share in his estate. *(Ron Galella)*

"My wonderful little house," is how Jackie describes her $3.5 million estate on Martha's Vineyard, here seen from an aerial view. *(Ron Galella)*

Out on the town with her current beau, diamond dealer Maurice Tempelsman. *(AP/Wide World)*

The 1986 wedding ceremony of 28-year-old Caroline Kennedy to 41-year-old Ed Schlossberg had all the earmarks of any Kennedy extravaganza. *(AP/Wide World)*

Jackie's first grandchild, Rose, was born June 25, 1988. She was named after Caroline's grandmother, the matriarch of the Kennedy family.
(New York Post—Paul Adao)

John F. Kennedy, Jr., has the Bouvier dark eyes and hair.
(AP/Wide World)

A Woman Named Jackie. *(Ron Galella)*

Mrs. Kennedy to do things which she wouldn't do; to receive people at the White House or to ask certain people for dinner, and she would plead that she was busy or that she wasn't having any State dinners at that time, or one thing or another. I remember being disappointed, for example, when I finally did persuade Mrs. Kennedy to invite some poets, who were gathering in Washington for a convocation at the Library of Congress, to come to the White House for sherry . . . and then she cancelled it. I always regretted that because I think it would have been a glorious thing. . . .

"Mrs. Kennedy . . . said, 'Mr. Heckscher, I will do anything for the arts you want. . . .' Then she would go on, as I remember, 'But, of course, I can't be away too much from the children and I can't be present at too many cultural events.' Then, with sort of a smile, she said, 'After all, I'm *not* Mrs. Roosevelt.' "

On the positive side Jackie's greatest assets were her intelligence, insight and curiosity, enhanced by her position and connections. She was a good listener, receptive and seemingly sensitive, although given to excess and a life-style reserved for the very rich and marked by an attraction to material objects such as horses, antiques, clothes, homes and furnishings. She enjoyed parties, travel and people, but only when what she considered the "best" people were involved. She had no tolerance for second- or third-raters, as evidenced by her White House guest lists.

Finances had always been a problem area for Jacqueline, probably because she had never had the kind of money at her disposal she would have liked. Each Christmas at the White House she had Tish Baldridge send out lists of the presents she wanted from each member of the staff. Tish's 1961 letter to Evelyn Lincoln was representative of the lot:

> In case anybody wants to know what Mrs. Kennedy wants for Christmas and they ask you for ideas, she wants:
> "Fruit-of-the-Month" for the [White] House
> She wants art books, and she wants a little sterling coffee pot with a wooden handle—George I—holding only two cups (Tiffany, of course).

Jackie could be equally mercenary when it came to gifts from foreigners (statesmen as well as private citizens), instructing her social secretary to direct the following memo to Angier Biddle Duke:

> People who wish to leave gifts . . .—i.e., hand-made objects, portraits, and other mementos for the President and Mrs. Kennedy or for their children, can leave them at the Embassy chancellery. The donor's name and address should be clearly marked, and the Embassy official who receives the package should make it clear that an acknowledgment will be forthcoming when time will permit, from a member of the President's or Mrs. Kennedy's staff. . . .
>
> Do not ship all these presents back to the White House. Rather, the Embassy officer in charge should make a selection of the very fine handcrafted objects and items which will have a proper place in the Kennedy Museum some day. . . . The gifts which are not shipped should be held for six months (in case the donor should ask for money for his present, in which case the present should be sent back immediately). At the end of six months, the gifts being held in the Embassy should be destroyed, making sure that the local employees do not know. This should be handled with great discretion.

It somehow never occurred to anybody that even the "junk" gifts—as Tish Baldrige labeled the presents earmarked for destruction—would have been of great value to orphanages, hospitals, agencies for the poor, and similar organizations. The same hardened attitude found its way into other Jacqueline-inspired memos, such as one from Tish Baldrige to Angier Biddle Duke demanding repayment from the State Department for gifts from the Kennedys to foreign dignitaries:

> . . . . Mme. Ikeda and the [Japanese] Foreign Minister's wife both showered Mrs. Kennedy and her family with gifts, and she gave an engraved vermeil hand mirror (approximately $90) to Mme. Ikeda. The Pakistanis are bringing personal gifts to Mrs. Kennedy, so she has to give presents to both the Begum at home, and the General's daugh-

ter who is accompanying him. This will add up to about $120 for the two items.

We request reimbursement from the State Department on these items, on the basis that they are not "personal gifts" in any sense of the word. They are obligatory presents made to visiting officials. . . .

Jackie's personal secretary, Mary Gallagher, found that the First Lady's financial problems extended to her personal accounts and were causing JFK concern. Kennedy's worries over his wife's spending reached a high point after they entered the White House. During the second quarter of 1961, for example, Jackie's expenditures on clothing alone exceeded $35,000—and this account was not linked to her "official" White House clothing account, which was being footed by Jackie's father-in-law. A Givenchy bill came to more than $4,000. Embarrassingly high bills came from such select New York boutiques as Chez Ninon and Tiger, a shop owned by Tiger Morse, who was also a patient of Dr. Max Jacobson.

"Tiger Morse was a very talented zany lady with a strange sensibility," said Pat Suzuki. "She owned a boutique on Madison Avenue. She was bright, funny, neurotic and had an incredible eye for color. Jackie discovered her when my husband Mark Shaw did a layout on Tiger for *Life*. Mark once brought to the White House some clothes that Tiger designed. Jackie wore them and then sent them back. But she kept other clothes that Tiger put together for her and wore them privately."

Wearing clothes before returning them was one of Jackie's less admirable traits. Chez Ninon and Bergdorf's, as well as Tiger Morse, complained of the practice. There were others. But unfortunately it did little to lessen the whopping bills that came in monthly, and Mary Gallagher found herself taking "the long way around" in the White House halls to avoid seeing the President. She couldn't take the "reproachful look" on his face.

Like most husbands, Jack complained to others about his wife's spending. He and Jackie argued figures while in company with Ben and Toni Bradlee. One item on his wife's books was "Department stores . . . $40,000," and nobody had an explanation, much less Jackie. She couldn't remember where the money had gone. The President announced he was bringing in Carmine Bellino, an accounting expert and family friend who had worked on various Senate subcommittees deciphering the financial records of the "Mafiosi." Robert Kennedy had used Bellino to control Ethel's spending, though Ethel couldn't compete with Jackie in terms of extravagance, and was even quoted as complaining to Jacqueline: "You're hurting this family's reputation with all that reckless spending."

Various procedures for the regulation of Jackie's personal expenses were put into effect. The First Lady's clothing budget was cut in half, as were "Food and Liquor" and "Miscellaneous"—that great catch-all for whatever item happened to tickle Jackie's fancy. The First Lady took her own stand on Food and Liquor, especially liquor. In her opinion, too much alcohol was being consumed at both official and private functions. She cited as prime example a private White House party held in November 1961 for Lee Radziwill to which she invited their distant relation Gore Vidal.

As the evening passed, according to Arthur Schlesinger, Vidal "gave the strong impression of having drunk far too much." Gore apparently had a conversation with Janet Auchincloss, Jackie's mother, before engaging in several angry exchanges, first with Lem Billings, then with Bobby Kennedy. Bobby found Gore crouching by Jackie while steadying himself by putting his arm on her shoulder. Bobby stepped up and quietly removed the arm. Vidal then went over to Bobby and said, "Never do anything like that to me again." Bobby started to leave when Vidal added, "I have always thought that you were a goddamned impertinent son-of-a-bitch." At that, Bobby said, "Why don't you go fuck yourself?" Vidal replied, "If that is your level of dialogue, I can only respond by saying: 'Drop dead!' At this Bobby turned his back and walked away.

"I know that Lem Billings was threatening to knock Gore's block off, and vice versa," said Blair Clark, also present at the dinner party. "I was near the dance floor when Gore came up to me and said, 'I'm going to take a swing at that bastard.' I didn't prevent Gore by grabbing him or anything that dramatic, but my memory was that Billings was not far away, maybe on the dance floor or on the other side of the dance floor. I said, 'Gore, for God's sake, don't do that. That's just stupid.' He was quite drunk, I think. Some people were aware of the incident, but not everyone by any means. It wasn't a big thing with everyone standing around getting ready to hold coats. My impression is simply that Gore had had an awful lot to drink. So had Billings. So had a lot of people. The altercation with Bobby Kennedy, as I understand it, went back a few years and seemed to be related to several vitriolic statements Gore had made about Bobby in an essay or two he'd written."

Gore Vidal's version of that "famous night" went as follows: "An ancient row with Bobby flared briefly before dinner—no witnesses. I left at 1:30 a.m. with Arthur Schlesinger, Jr., John Kenneth Galbraith, George Plimpton. No one was asked to leave. I was even invited to Hyannis Port a month or so later."

Arthur Schlesinger had it that "Someone, I forget who, perhaps Jacqueline Kennedy, asked me whether I would get him out of there. I enlisted Kenneth Galbraith and George Plimpton. We took Vidal back to his hotel."

Plimpton's account: "Arthur Schlesinger and Ken Galbraith and I gave him a lift. I was staying with the Averell Harrimans. We drove Gore back to the Hay-Adams, I think it was. Only Gore can say whether or not he was smashed. But I think he had a lot of unfortunate things happen to him that night. I didn't see or hear the argument, but I did follow Vidal's subsequent feud with Truman Capote regarding the night in question. Capote in a magazine interview embellished the story, among other things insisting that Vidal had been forcibly ejected from the White House, which wasn't the case. Jackie, however, wasn't happy with Gore's behavior and resolved never to have him in the White House again. So literally he wasn't thrown out but figuratively, of course he was."*

---

*The Vidal-Capote feud didn't erupt until September 1975 when *Playgirl* magazine published the offending interview with Capote as conducted by journalist Richard Zoerink. Through attorney Peter Morrison, Vidal sued Capote for libel. "I must remind you that when I sued TC for libel [Vidal writes the current author], I asked the Court for summary judgment and got it. He was found guilty of libel *per se.* Capote appealed, and, out of money, asked if I would accept a letter confirming the fact that he had lied, etc. I did. He wrote the letter." The letter, dated Oct. 31, 1983, says in part: "I apologize for any distress, inconvenience or expense which may

Jackie blamed herself as much as she blamed anybody else for the failed evening, convinced she had let events get out of hand. From now on, she later told her staff, it would be one-drink-per-guest-per-night, a restriction calculated to preserve sobriety as well as money. The one-drink-per-guest guideline did not work well, however, when smaller parties were held at the White House and guests tended to wander off to look around. On such occasions the guests would often put their half-consumed drinks down and walk about, only to discover that a White House butler had confiscated the unfinished drinks. The guest would invariably have to be supplied with a fresh drink. The First Lady's solution was duly noted by Mary Gallagher:

> She [Jacqueline] instructed Anne [Lincoln, the new housekeeper] to tell the butlers to refill the glasses that looked relatively unfinished and didn't have lipstick marks on the edge. Jackie said to pass them around again—even if a few people get hepatitis.

Gallagher also recorded a conversation in which Jackie seems to have heard about trading stamps for the first time:

> "Oh, Mary, do you know what I've just learned from Anne Lincoln? . . . You know all the food we buy here at the White House? Well, she told me that with the stamps the stores give us, we can trade them in for marvelous gifts!"

When she heard those two anecdotes, journalist Angele Gingras attributed them to Jackie's acute comic sensibility: "Jackie had a Swiftian sense of humor. She was too sophisticated for those around her. Half her memos and statements contained jokes that flew above everyone's head. Can anyone imagine the White House refilling

---

have been caused you as a result of the interview with me published in the September 1975 issue of *Playgirl*. As you know, I was not present at the event about which I was quoted in that interview, and I understand . . . that what I am reported as saying does not accurately set forth what occurred."

half-empty cocktail glasses and then passing them among the guests?

Less humorous were the First Lady's personal expenditures during her husband's first two years in office. The figure for 1961 totaled $105,446.14. In 1962 she spent $121,461.61.

22

By the beginning of 1962, both the FBI and the Secret Service were aware of John Kennedy's involvement with Marilyn Monroe. Both agencies also knew that Marilyn had on several occasions been in and out of New York's Payne Whitney Psychiatric Clinic in a futile effort to break her dependency on sleeping pills and alcohol. Yet despite her addictions and personal problems, Marilyn's relationship with the President continued to thrive.

"She was crazy about Jack," said Peter Lawford. "She devised all sorts of madcap fantasies with herself in the starring role. She would have his children. She would take Jackie's place as First Lady. The fact that he was President allowed her to attach a lot of symbolic meaning to the affair. It was only a lark for him, but she really fell for the guy, for what he represented. In her depressive and doped-out state, she began to fall in love with him—or she convinced herself she was in love, which is basically the same thing.

"Besides telephoning Jack at the White House, she used to send him copies of her love poetry, most of it written early in her career. Then one day she told me she had telephoned Jackie at the White House. For all her romanticism and masochism, Marilyn could also be a mean little bitch. Everybody wrote her up as being the poor, helpless victim, but that wasn't always the case.

"According to Marilyn, Jackie wasn't shaken by the call. Not outwardly. She agreed to step aside. She would divorce Jack and Marilyn could marry him, but she would have to move into the White House. If Marilyn wasn't prepared to live openly in the White House, she might as well forget about it.

"Actually Jackie was infuriated by the call, and for some reason blamed Frank Sinatra for it. She couldn't easily blame me because I was family, so she took it out

374

on him. She and Sinatra had always been on decent terms. He visited the White House, Hyannis Port, Palm Beach. The Kennedys hosted him aboard [their yacht] the *Honey Fitz*. But this was the end of it for Jackie. Sinatra was no longer welcome at the White House, or in any of the other Kennedy bastions.

"The break with Jackie occurred at the same time that Sinatra began to have problems with Bobby Kennedy. Bobby, who at 35 thought of himself as another Wyatt Earp, had been cracking down on many of Sinatra's buddies. He had launched all-out investigations of Sam Giancana, John Roselli, Mickey Cohen, Carlos Marcello, Santo Trafficante and, of course, Jimmy Hoffa. Some of these guys looked to Sinatra for help, and Sinatra turned to Bobby. I went with him. In so many words the Attorney General told us to stuff it, and he told his brother, the President, to steer clear of Sinatra. 'We're going after the bosses of organized crime in this country, and you're socializing with the guy who's pals with half of them,' he said to Jack.

"Jack had planned on spending March 24th to the 26th, 1962, at Sinatra's Palm Springs home. Jackie would be away on her trip to India and Pakistan. It was an ideal time for Jack to relax. In anticipation of the President's visit, Sinatra had added several rooms to his house, two or three cottages for the Secret Service, a heliport to accommodate the President's chopper, even a flagpole. At the last minute, Bobby called me and said I should advise Sinatra that the President couldn't accept his hospitality. I asked him to reconsider, told him how much the visit meant to Sinatra. 'Sinatra's connections to organized crime could possibly embarrass the President,' Bobby responded.

"I telephoned the President. He was sympathetic but adamant. 'I can't stay there as long as Bobby's conducting the Giancana operation. Maybe you can find me another place to stay.'

"So I finally rang up Sinatra and laid it out. I blamed it on security, said that the Secret Service felt his place would be difficult to secure. Sinatra knew bullshit when he heard it. He telephoned Bobby Kennedy and called him every name in the book. He told him what a hypocrite he was, that the Mafia could help Jack get elected but couldn't sit with him in the front of the bus.

"Jack, meanwhile, had made arrangements to spend the weekend at Bing Crosby's Palm Springs home. This blew Sinatra's mind. The other singer wasn't even a goddamn Democrat. Sinatra unfairly blamed the whole thing on me. It ended our friendship. I heard later that he grabbed a sledgehammer and tore apart the concrete heliport he'd built for Kennedy."

Marilyn Monroe spent the weekend with the President at Crosby's home and then saw him again on May 19, two days before his forty-fifth birthday, at a gala celebration and fund-raising affair before 15,000 Democrats at New York's Madison Square Garden. Other celebrities who paid tribute to the President included Ella Fitzgerald, Peggy Lee, Jimmy Durante and Maria Callas. But it was Marilyn in "skin and beads" (to quote Adlai Stevenson) who stole the show with her slithering, throaty renditions of "Thanks for the Memory" and "The Happy Birthday Song." The President followed her performance by addressing the audience: "I can now retire from politics after having had 'Happy Birthday' sung to me in such a sweet, wholesome way."

Peter Lawford had arranged Marilyn's appearance at the Garden that evening but only after ascertaining that Jackie planned on being elsewhere. Playing the role of Master of Ceremonies, Lawford introduced his star attraction as "the 'late' Marilyn Monroe."

"I was commenting on her tardiness," he explained. "Obviously I had no idea she had only months to live. On the other hand, she wasn't herself. I remember Arthur Schlesinger writing that 'talking to Marilyn was like talking to someone under water.'"

Later that evening, following her appearance at a party given by Arthur Krim, President of United Artists, Marilyn spent several hours alone with John Kennedy in his duplex atop the Carlyle. It was to be their last rendezvous. Warned by Robert Kennedy and J. Edgar Hoover that Peter Lawford's Santa Monica beach house had very likely been bugged by the Mafia and at least one of his illicit meetings with Marilyn taped, he decided to end the relationship.

"Marilyn realized the affair was over but couldn't accept it," said Lawford. "She began writing these rather pathetic letters to Jack and continued calling. She threatened to go to the press. He finally sent Bobby Kennedy out to California to cool her off.

"Bobby already knew Marilyn. They had met at a dinner party at my house when he brought Ethel, and again briefly in New York following her appearance at Jack's birthday celebration. He tried to explain to her that the President was an extremely busy man, that running the country was an imposing task, that while Jack cared a great deal for her, he was already married and couldn't very well simply sneak off and see a divorce lawyer. Although it probably wasn't easy for her, she would have to accept this decision and stop calling the President.

"She took it pretty hard. Bobby felt for her. They met again the following day and passed the afternoon walking along the beach. It wasn't Bobby's intention, but that evening they became lovers and spent the night in our guest bedroom.

"Almost immediately the affair got very heavy, and they began seeing a lot of each other. Now Marilyn was calling the Department of Justice instead of the White House. Angie Novello, Bobby's personal secretary, had long conversations with her whenever Bobby wasn't around. Pretty soon Marilyn announced that she was in love with Bobby and that *he* had promised to marry her. It was as if she could no longer tell the difference between Bobby and Jack.

"It was at this point that Twentieth Century-Fox fired her from the big-budgeted CinemaScope motion picture that was never completed, *Something's Got to Give*. She was so zonked most of the time that she slurred her lines. And she couldn't sleep nights. She looked awful. I told her to get the hell off whatever she was taking and screw her head on straight, or her entire career would go down the tubes.

"Marilyn couldn't step on the brakes. Bobby was gradually retreating from her the same way Jack had retreated. She went up the wall. 'They treat everybody like that,' she said. 'They use you and then they dispose of you like so much rubbish.'

"On several occasions when Marilyn came over for dinner or a party, she stayed overnight, especially when she had too much to drink. One time I woke up very early in the morning and discovered her in a robe perched

on the balcony staring at the swimming pool below. I
went out and said, 'Are you all right?' Tears were rolling
down her face. I led her in and made breakfast, and [my
wife] Pat and I consoled her for hours. She was completely down on herself, talked about how ugly she felt,
how worthless, how used and abused.

"During July, Pat and I took her along on two junkets
to Cal-Neva Lodge at Lake Tahoe. On the first we were
all drinking pretty heavily, but Marilyn was also taking
sleeping pills, which none of us realized until it was
almost too late. She became so violently ill she had to be
taken to Reno and from there flown back to Los Angeles
aboard Frank Sinatra's private plane.

"The second visit ended just as abruptly when Joe
DiMaggio suddenly showed up. Somebody evidently told
him that Marilyn had been kidnapped and was being held
at Cal-Neva against her will. There were always call girls
around the lodge and sex and drugs and parties. But
Marilyn certainly wasn't there against her will. DiMaggio
wanted her to go home with him. They argued. She
became upset and once again she had to leave early and
return to Los Angeles aboard Sinatra's plane."

Events peaked the weekend of August 3, 1962, two
days before Marilyn Monroe's apparent suicide. Marilyn
heard that Bobby Kennedy and his family were staying
near San Francisco. She called Peter Lawford and asked
if he had a number for Bobby. He didn't but he thought
Pat might. Pat was visiting her family at Hyannis Port.
He gave Marilyn the telephone number there. Marilyn
called Pat, and Pat eventually located a number for Bobby.

Although Bobby hesitated at first, he ultimately agreed
to see Marilyn. The following day he flew to Los Angeles, took a helicopter from the airport to the Twentieth
Century-Fox lot and was met there by Peter Lawford,
who drove him to Marilyn's home in Brentwood.

They arrived at about two in the afternoon. In anticipation of their visit Marilyn had set out a buffet of
Mexican food—guacamole, stuffed mushrooms, spicy
meatballs—which she had ordered from a nearby restaurant, and a chilled magnum of champagne. It was apparent to her visitors that Marilyn had already downed quite
a bit of champagne on her own. Lawford poured himself
a glass and went out to the swimming pool so Marilyn
and Bobby could talk. Within minutes he heard shouting.

Bobby was saying he was going back to Peter's house. Marilyn insisted that he had promised to spend the afternoon alone with her. Bobby said he was going to leave with or without her.

"They argued back and forth for maybe ten minutes, Marilyn becoming more and more hysterical," said Lawford. "At the height of her anger she allowed how first thing Monday morning she was going to call a press conference and tell the world about the treatment she had suffered at the hands of the Kennedy brothers. Now Bobby became livid. In no uncertain terms he told her she was going to have to leave both Jack and him alone—no more telephone calls, no letters, nothing. They didn't want to hear from her any more.

"Marilyn lost it at this point, screaming obscenities and flailing wildly away at Bobby with her fists. In her fury she picked up a small kitchen knife and lunged at him. I was with them at this point, so I tried to grab Marilyn's arm. We finally knocked her down and managed to wrestle the knife away. Bobby thought we ought to call Dr. Ralph Greenson, her Beverly Hills psychiatrist, and tell him to come over. Dr. Greenson arrived at Marilyn's home within the hour."

What happened next is a matter of conjecture. Authors as diverse as Norman Mailer, Anthony Summers and Earl Wilson have offered detailed, logical, yet often-conflicting published accounts of the events that led to Marilyn Monroe's death the night of August 4. Ironically, the most seemingly logical written version of those events, *My Secret Life with Marilyn Monroe*, a personal memoir by Ted H. Jordan, has to date not been published.

Jordan, a Hollywood supporting actor once married to statuesque striptease artist Lily St. Cyr, had known Marilyn since 1942. "Marilyn," he ventured, "was prone to exaggeration. She had a vivid imagination, the ability to blow events greatly out of proportion. But when she telephoned me about 5:00 p.m. on the last night of her life, she had no possible reason to lie. She told me about her fight with Bobby. She said that Dr. Greenson, who was still there, had given her a shot to quiet her down, and that Lawford and Bobby Kennedy had already gone.

"Marilyn called me a second time that evening. She sounded a thousand miles away. She said Lawford had phoned her around 7:00 and invited her over for some

Chinese dinner and a little poker with friends. Bobby
wanted her to come. But Marilyn suspected that once the
poker game ended, Lawford would invite a couple of
hookers over for Bobby and himself, and they would
expect Marilyn to participate. 'And I've had enough of
that stuff,' she said. 'Bobby promised to stay here, and
that's how it is.'

"She mentioned she had taken sleeping pills earlier in
the evening, which in addition to Greenson's shot and
the alcohol would surely have done her in. After calling
me a second time, she apparently called Lawford and
said her farewell: 'Say good-bye to Pat, say good-bye to
the President, say good-bye to yourself because you've
been a good guy.' Did she know she was dying? Had she
just downed some more pills? Did she mean to kill herself? Did somebody else kill her? I doubt we'll ever know
the answers to these questions.

"I know one thing. Sensing that something wasn't right,
I called Marilyn back that night. Peter Lawford answered
the telephone. So there's no question that after her death
he went over there, presumably to tidy up, to make
certain there was nothing to tie Marilyn to the President
or Attorney General."

Over the next few days while headlines of Marilyn
Monroe's death swept and startled the nation, Bobby
Kennedy carried on as though nothing had happened. On
Monday, he spoke before an American Bar Association
meeting in San Francisco and then traveled to Seattle
with his family to attend the World's Fair. He and his
children spent another week camping out in the North-
west with Supreme Court Justice William O. Douglas.

Approached by the press for a comment on Marilyn's
death, Jacqueline Kennedy said only: "She will go on
eternally."

At an Old Timer's baseball game at Yankee Stadium
three years after Marilyn's death, Robert Kennedy was
introduced to Joe DiMaggio. Kennedy extended his hand;
DiMaggio turned and walked away without shaking it.

More than twenty-three years after her death, in October 1985, ABC-TV's *20/20* had planned to air a segment
exploring the relations between Bobby Kennedy, Jack
Kennedy and Marilyn Monroe. At the last minute Roone
Arledge, president of ABC News and Sports, cancelled
the segment, insisting that it was nothing more than

"gossip column material." Arledge, it developed, had been a loyal and longtime friend of the Kennedys.

India Edwards spoke for many women when she said of JFK: "Kennedy never thought of a woman as anything but a sex object."

Malcolm "Mac" Kilduff, Deputy Press Secretary to the President, suggested that Kennedy objectified all sexual types, not just women: "I recall when the Bolshoi Ballet came to Washington and performed at the old Capitol Theater on F Street. This was during the Cuban missile crisis, but Jackie insisted on attending opening night. The President wanted to see the Bolshoi Ballet as much as I wanted to see a flea circus. When it was over and they went backstage, he whispered in my ear, 'I don't want my picture taken shaking hands with all those Russian fairies.' "

The number of women on Kennedy's horizon seemed to be forever on the rise. Similar to "Fiddle" and "Faddle," the two secretaries on his staff, was the case of the young woman who had known Kennedy intimately when he was a Senator and had fallen in love with him. Assigned a job on the National Security Council staff when he became President, she was always available. Kennedy's nonchalant attitude toward such encounters—as well as his agility in keeping his outside pursuits from interfering with his official duties—was shown one summer afternoon when the two were interrupted by a knock on the President's bedroom door. Angered, Kennedy threw the door open. There stood two top foreign affairs advisers with a batch of secret cables—and a clear view of Kennedy's nude companion. Never bothering to close the door, the President sat down, read the dispatches, and made his decisions before returning to his friend.

The Secret Service files for this period abound with background checks on various women, mostly models and airline stewardesses. Under presidential orders, Secret Service agents would admit such casual women; even more casual were the women admitted to presidential chambers on the strength of a telephone call or a written introduction from a trusted friend; in certain cases it took far less.

"It never occurred to Jack that some of these women might be considered dangerous," said Lem Billings. "They were never searched, never questioned in depth. I remember hearing about an 18-year-old girl visiting from Ireland who wanted to meet the President, so he insisted they usher her straight into the Oval Office. It turned out she had a 14-inch butcher knife in her shoulder bag and had just been released from a mental hospital in Dublin."

The girl was deported to Ireland. Another Camelot deportee was Ellen Rometsch, a sultry, 27-year-old East German model (and suspected agent) who operated a hostess service through the Quorum Club, a private retreat on Capitol Hill patronized by lobbyists, congressional employees and members of the House and Senate. The club's founder and director was Bobby Baker, an influence peddler and former senatorial assistant to Lyndon Johnson, who later went to prison for income tax evasion, theft and conspiracy to defraud the government.

Baker used Ellen Rometsch and other party girls for political and business purposes. Although President Kennedy's name did not appear on a roster of Quorum Club members, eyewitnesses indicate that he occasionally availed himself of both Ellen Rometsch and the club's services, as did Vice-President Lyndon Johnson.

The most widely publicized sex scandal of the early 1960s was the Profumo case in which Britain's War Minister John Profomo—privy to the West's most sensitive defense secrets—had become entangled with Christine Keeler, a call girl kept by London osteopath Stephen Ward. Among Keeler's other clients was a Soviet spy. The possibility existed that Profumo might have accidentally leaked military information to Keeler and that she in turn passed it along to the Russian. Profumo resigned. The British government came within a whit of falling.

The scandal seemed at first to have no American connections. But on June 28, 1963, with President Kennedy traveling abroad, the *New York Journal-American* ran an article that began: "One of the biggest names in American politics—a man who holds 'a very high' elective office—has been injected into Britain's vice-security scandal." Robert Kennedy summoned to Washington the two journalists responsible for the teaser, and determined that the elected official was President Kennedy. Kennedy had supposedly been involved with not one, but two of the call girls in Stephen Ward's exclusive stable: Suzy Chang and Maria Novotny.

Robert Kennedy's first course of action was to deny

the allegations and to threaten legal action against the *Journal-American* if it named names or published any further installments of the story. Lacking adeqate documentation, the newspaper elected to drop the matter. The FBI, however, with the help of Scotland Yard, launched an all-out investigation.

John Kennedy's endless womanizing was slowly catching up with him. The FBI probe revealed that Suzy Chang, 28, born in China and living in London, entered the U.S. at regular intervals to see her ailing mother. Fashionable and exotic, she had been sighted more than once in the company of Dr. Stephen Ward. She had also been seen several times with President Kennedy, on one occasion dining with him at New York's posh "21."

The Maria Novotny story was somewhat more sinister. Blond and bubbly, she had started out as Mariella Capes, a striptease dancer in English nightclubs. In 1960, she had married Horace Dibben, a wealthy British antique dealer and nightclub owner, nearly forty years her senior. Six months later she left Dibben and moved to New York. Within weeks she was living with a television producer, Harry Alan Towers, and running the New York branch of an international girl cartel.

In 1962, Novotny returned to England. Questioned by Scotland Yard in connection with the Profumo case, she admitted to being 19 when she first met John F. Kennedy in December 1960, at a party hosted by singer Vic Damone in a New York hotel. Introduced by Peter Lawford, she and the President-elect wandered off to one of the bedrooms in the suite and engaged in sexual relations. Following the inauguration, Lawford recruited her again, requesting that she set up "something a bit more interesting for the President." The second encounter took place at a Manhattan apartment which Novotny shared with Towers on West 55th Street, and involved two other prostitutes who were dressed as doctor and nurse; in the ensuing sex game, Kennedy played the role of the patient.

What was most alarming to the FBI about this episode was that Harry Towers turned out to be a Soviet agent who had been paid to provide information which might be used to compromise prominent American political figures, including Kennedy. When Novotny returned to

Britain in 1962, Towers fled the United States and reportedly emigrated to Czechoslovakia.*

Such encounters, as even Jackie might have attested if asked, had nothing to do with love and marriage. But John Kennedy, as we know, also had longer-lasting and more serious affairs. His last, with Jackie's friend, Mary Pinchot Meyer, lasted from January 1962 to November 1963, when he was assassinated. A descendant of the Pennsylvania Pinchot family, which produced a two-term governor, Gifford Pinchot, Mary Meyer was the sister of Toni Bradlee and the sister-in-law of Ben Bradlee.

"I honestly had no idea that Mary was involved with Jack," said Toni Bradlee. "And I'm almost positive Ben knew nothing about it. It came as a shock, though of course my sister had known Jack since his student days at Choate, and later when she attended Vassar and he went to Harvard."

In 1945, Mary married Cord Meyer, Jr., a young World War II veteran who lost an eye at Guam in the South Pacific and had gone on to become a top CIA official and founder of the United World Federalist Organization. When they divorced in 1959, Mary inherited a share in her family's multi-million-dollar dry-goods business and used it to establish a modest career as an artist. An old garage adjacent to her brother-in-law's house became her studio.

Mary was a proponent of what was then known as "the Washington Color School," exhibiting brightly colored geometrical designs at the Jefferson Place Gallery. "She was both Bohemian and glamorous, a Brett Ashley type," said CIA Director James Angleton. "She was a free spirit, way ahead of her time," her sister confirmed. James Truitt, a *Washington Post* executive and a confidant of Mary's (it was Truitt who first broke the story of JFK's romance with Mary), recalled that Mary, while vacationing in Italy, spotted a dashing Italian nobleman on his yacht, swam out to meet him and discarded her bikini in the water before climbing aboard.

"I'd known Mary for quite a while," said Blair Clark. "I didn't know her at all intimately, but I had known her

---

*The FBI was still investigating JFK's involvement in the Profumo case at the time of his assassination. The case might well have become an issue in the '64 election had Kennedy lived to run.

for years. She was intelligent, charming and beautiful, with blond hair and pert features. But I didn't know she was seeing Jack. In fact, I had heard a story about her that would seem to indicate just the opposite. I believe it took place at a dinner party at the home of *New York Times* newspaper columnist Arthur Krock. After dinner the men were all seated in the dining room smoking cigars and drinking cognac, and the women had gathered in the living room. Mary refused to join the ladies. She sat on the stairs talking to another woman. Within earshot of the men she said that every woman there wanted to sleep with Jack Kennedy. She was referring to the wives of all those men in the dining room. She said it disdainfully, as if she felt the women were being rather foolish.

"So I didn't know anything and I don't think the Bradlees did either. I was an old friend of Ben Bradlee and of his then-wife Toni, and one night we were all invited to a party at the White House. Mary was going to go as well, and Ben Bradlee suggested we all go together and I escort Mary. So I did. There was nothing in the atmosphere that night to indicate that we were going to a tryst. It was one of those dancing parties for about 125 people, mostly friends. It was a purely social gathering. Yet at a given point during the dancing, Jack and Mary disappeared. They were gone for about half an hour. Inadvertently I'd served as Jack's 'beard.' "

The degree of closeness attained by John Kennedy and Mary Meyer can be gauged by several factors, including a 1963 trip the President made with Mary and Toni to Milford, Pennsylvania, to meet their mother, Ruth Pinchot, an arch-conservative and supporter of Barry Goldwater. Another sign of their closeness was Kennedy's willingness to experiment with drugs in Mary's presence—not just marijuana, as has been widely reported, but also LSD.

James Angleton recalled the details: "Mary kept an art diary in which she began making notations concerning their meetings, of which there were between thirty and forty during their affair—in the White House, at her studio, in the homes of friends. One of Mary's friends was Timothy Leary, the famous 'acid head' guru of the 1960s. Mary apparently told Leary that she and a number of other Washington women had concocted a plot to

'turn on' the world's political leaders with pot and acid in
order to make them less militaristic and more peace-
loving. Leary helped her obtain certain drugs and chemical agents with precisely that end in mind. Later she
developed her own source for drugs.

"In July 1962 while visiting the White House, Mary
took Kennedy into one of the White House bedrooms
and she produced a small box with six joints in it. They
shared one and Kennedy laughingly told her they were
having a White House conference on narcotics in a couple of weeks.

"They smoked two more joints and Kennedy drew his
head back and closed his eyes. He refused a fourth joint.
'Suppose the Russians drop a bomb,' he said. He admitted to having done cocaine and hashish, thanks to Peter
Lawford. Mary claimed they smoked pot on two other
occasions, and on still another occasion they took a mild
acid trip together, during which they made love."

A macabre and tragic aftermath: Mary Meyer, 43, was
shot to death at 12:45 in the afternoon of October 12,
1964, nearly eleven months after the death of President
Kennedy, as she strolled along the Chesapeake and Ohio
Canal towpath in Georgetown, not far from her studio, a
spot where she and Jackie Kennedy had often gone walking together. A 26-year-old black laborer, apprehended
near the scene of the crime, was placed on trial for
Mary's murder. He was acquitted.

Rummaging through her sister's belongings, Toni
Bradlee found her diary, read it and turned it over to
James Angleton who destroyed it at CIA headquarters in
Langley, Virginia. "In my opinion there was nothing to
be gained by keeping it around," said Angleton. "I acted
as a private citizen and a friend of the deceased. The
Meyers had two sons, and that was one consideration. It
was in no way meant to protect Kennedy. I had little
sympathy for the President. The Bay of Pigs fiasco, which
he tried to hang on the CIA and which led to the resignation of CIA Director Allen Dulles, was his own doing. I
think the decision to withdraw air support of the invasion
colored Kennedy's entire career and impacted on everything that followed."

23

Early in 1963, Jackie Kennedy confided to Lee Radziwill that she was expecting another baby later in the year and would soon be cutting back on all official duties. She was determined, however, to be present at as many State dinners as she thought it advisable to attend. In March, when King Hassan II of Morocco visited, he was treated to a performance by the New York City Light Opera Company and a guest list that included Samuel Barber, Sol Hurok, Myrna Loy, Agnes de Mille and Alan Jay Lerner. The young monarch was evidently pleased by his reception.*

In April, the month she announced her pregnancy to the world, Jackie made preparations for the arrival in Washington of Grand Duchess Charlotte of Luxembourg by contacting Basil Rathbone and asking him to present a reading at the White House of selections from Marlowe, Johnson, Donne, Shakespeare's sonnets and the St. Crispin's Day speech from *Henry V*. Rathbone expressed reservations over her latter choice, pointing out that it was a monologue all about doing away with kings, and therefore probably inappropriate for a Grand Duchess. After considering the actor's position, Jackie wrote to Rathbone and explained her reasons for requesting the St. Crispin's speech:

> . . . It is just one of his [JFK's] favorites for whatever lovely dreams of leading or being led on to victory lurk in his soul. He also knows it by heart and I suppose wanted it for the same selfish reasons

---

*He invited Jackie to spend time in Morocco and several years later offered her the deed to her own Moorish palace in a fashionable section of Marrakesh. At first accepting the gift, Jackie reconsidered and later declined it.

I asked for so much Donne and other things I love.
He also knows *Henry V* (and he reminds me of
him—though I don't think he knows that!) . . .

A day later she wrote again, reconfirming her position:

> . . . Shall I tell you why I think it is so appropri-
> ate? . . . Of all the speeches that make you care
> and want to make the extra effort—sacrifice, fight
> or die—for whatever cause—that is the one. The
> only person I would not wish you to say it in front
> of was Khrushchev, as we are not united in purpose
> —but tiny Luxembourg . . . we are all striving for
> the same brave things today.

Basil Rathbone recited the St. Crispin passage and was
joined in the program by an enthusiastic ensemble of
Elizabethan musicians and singers. The performance and
State dinner were memorable. The Grand Duchess, like
King Hassan II before her, went away full of praise for
her hosts, particularly for Jackie, referring to her in the
press as "America's most potent weapon, Madame la
Presidente."

Although she attended a State dinner in July for President Radhakrishnan of India, Jackie was content now to
limit her participation and to administer the mansion
from behind the scenes. She communicated with her staff
primarily through the use of memos. She directed Tish
Baldridge to send a memo asking the various staff members to file her directives and to return them at the end of
the year so they could serve as a record of Jackie's role in
the White House.

Years later Jackie would say: "So many people hit the
White House with their dictaphones running. I never
even kept a journal. I never really wanted to, but it's
such a shame. I thought I wanted to live my life, not
record it. And I'm still glad I did that. But I think there
are so many things that I've forgotten."

Eilene Slocum recalled visiting the White House during Jackie's pregnancy only to find that the tea party she
had been invited to attend was being hosted by Jackie's
mother. "Jackie was out walking the dogs," said Mrs.
Slocum. "I had a feeling she found life difficult at the
White House and loved getting out."

New York socialite Kay Lepercq attended a small dinner party at about this time with her then-husband, Paul Lepercq, at the Washington home of Arthur Schlesinger. Jackie was there and so was Bobby Kennedy. "Neither the President nor Ethel Kennedy were present," said Mrs. Lepercq. "Bobby kept talking about how as Attorney General he laid down the law and so forth. It wasn't very charming, particularly as I suspected that President Kennedy owed his election in large measure to the intervention of the Mafia.

"But Jackie was the true prize. My husband, who happened to be French, also happened to be tall and blond. Jackie went up to him, batted her eyes, and in that insidious whisper said, 'I didn't know Frenchmen were so tall and blond.' "

If Kay Lepercq seemed disenchanted with Jackie, others were even more disillusioned. Frances Parkinson Keyes, a member of the Ladies of the Senate, was in a state of disbelief when she heard that Lady Bird Johnson would be substituting for Jackie at the May 1963 meeting of this group, particularly as Jackie was only a few months pregnant. In turning down her invitation, Mrs. Keyes wrote to Lady Bird: "A party at the White House in the absence of the President's wife would be a little bit like *Hamlet* without the Prince of Denmark, wouldn't it? At least, it would seem that way to me, and I would prefer to continue dwelling on the many times, for many, many years, that I have enjoyed being there in the past."

More deprecating was a letter from Washington socialite Virginia Livingston Hunt to columnist Betty Beale in reaction to a column by Beale complaining of sudden restrictions placed on all social reporters by Mrs. Kennedy. Miss Hunt wrote: "Don't you know that Mrs. Kennedy is the rudest, most self-conscious First Lady since I came here to live; probably before you were born? . . . I happen to be the person who finally got her to go to Junior Village at Christmas, yet neither Tish nor Pam, both of whom I know, took the trouble to tell me she was going. . . . Do not expect any civility from Jackie unless it suits her."

Betty Beale had her own complaints about Jackie, calling her "a cold drink of water—aloof and basically unfriendly. She couldn't take criticism at all. I was the one who broke the story about her doing the Twist at the

White House with Defense Secretary Robert McNamara. For this I was banished by Jackie from all future White House functions. Fortunately, the President overruled her and I was reinstated.

"By 1963, Jackie's relations to the press corps had reached an all-time low. In a way I suppose I can understand why she didn't want us around. She didn't want anybody probing her marriage to the President, which was obviously one of convenience. They were perfectly cast for the role, one behind the other, both of them with a lot of appeal. She was beautiful. He was an attractive, sexy guy. But he never put her first. His love affairs came first. I mean he was egotistical. He would always walk ahead of Jackie into a room. That hadn't been done since the days of Woodrow Wilson. Jackie brought up the rear.

"He certainly didn't behave as if he was very much in love with her. He seemed to care so little about being with her. He wasn't the least bit subtle. And it had been that way from the first. The minute they got engaged he went off on a cruise with his buddies and I've never heard of any man do something like that when he was supposed to be in love. I saw Jackie soon after that, and she didn't say a thing about it."

Jackie's attitude toward the press had finally begun to rub off on her young daughter. Purette Spiegler recalled Caroline Kennedy entering a room one day and having photographers descend upon her, taking pictures of her. She put up her little hand, like her mother would, and said, "No pictures, please."

Jackie was far more brash about it. Barbara Coleman, who worked in the press office for Pierre Salinger, too often saw Jackie storm into the office to berate Salinger. "She was emphatic," said Coleman. "She didn't want any picture appearing anywhere without her approval. At first it was only photographs of the children that concerned her. But by '63, it was any photograph emanating from the White House.

"Pierre's attitude, I thought, was one of absolute kindness toward Jackie. Deferential might be another word to use. He never spoke unfavorably about her to any of us. He told her he would do what he could, realizing he could do only so much.

"The strange thing is that the more she protested, the more popular she became. The media explosion encompassed daily newspaper reports, magazine cover stories, television specials, Broadway plays and musicals, Barbie dolls, record albums and several dozen other commercial tools and ventures. My job in the press office entailed answering telephone inquiries, predominantly from foreign and domestic news services and reporters or editors but also from the public. There were five of us. It was an incredibly busy office. The phones never stopped ringing, and ninety percent of the questions had to do with Jackie. At least ten times a day I would be asked what size shoe she wore.

"Frankly, I couldn't see her in Washington. She gave me the impression of inhabiting a totally different world, of enjoying well-off people and the kinds of things they liked to do; she may have engaged in politics to some extent, but I can't imagine her being comfortable in that domain."

Jackie's pregnancy and her unresolved feelings both toward the White House and her husband's hyperactive libido made her more difficult than ever to be around. Increasingly intolerant of lapses on the part of her staff, Jackie frequently lost her temper, stamping her foot with impatience, her slow, deliberate whisper all too readily hardening into a sneer. She directed the brunt of her annoyance at Tish Baldrige, whose independence and popularity nettled the First Lady.

"Tish had problems with Jackie because Tish, like Jackie, is a very strong-willed person," said Purette Spiegler. "They both had their own ideas about how matters should be handled. Many times she and Jackie didn't see eye-to-eye. But Jackie was the boss. You didn't tell her whom to invite to the White House and whom not to invite. Nor did you tell her which functions to attend and which not. Yet at a certain point Tish began to overstep her bounds."

In an effort to convince Jackie to meet with the United Nations Ambassadors' wives, Tish sent her the following memo:

The United Nations Ambassadors' wives have been complaining for never having met you, and they have been pressuring the life out of us for two and a half years. Every time you go to New York, they give me a hard time about how now is the time to be received by you. Since it is a question of face in their own home countries, we have devised a little plan which will not cause you any extra inconvenience. On Monday, April 22nd, the day of the Kentucky Youth Concert, Mrs. [Dean] Rusk will have all of the U.N. wives down for a big luncheon. Then, it will be announced that you heard they were coming, wanted to see them, and asked if they wouldn't join you for the concert on the lawn. We will have them seated in a special section, and all you will have to do is smile at them and not shake each hand—unless you want to. . . .

Is that okay with you?

Jackie responded in writing: "No, definitely don't ask them to a wild hillbilly concert. I'll do it impromptu either before or after concert—or next day—(But let's still keep it secret and I'll learn of it when they are here.)"

Aware that she had put the First Lady on the spot, Tish adopted a more conciliatory tone in future communiques. On May 1 when Jackie attended the ballet in New York, Tish's memorandum made clear that she would be seated in Rudolf Bing's box and that Bing had been told that it would be impossible for Jackie to go backstage: "Perhaps he can arrange to have Nureyev and Fonteyn brought to your box during an intermission. Please let me know if you don't like this idea. . . . Also, this will be kept from the press, he swears, until you actually arrive. He is likewise keeping this a big secret from Sol Hurok, who would absolutely have the pathway to the box lined with American flags and blaring trumpets. (And a few Russian ones thrown in for good measure!)"

But Jackie had already decided to replace Tish, and on her return to the White House she made Tish's office her first stop.

"Everyone in Washington assumed that Tish had been 'bounced' by Jackie, although on the surface it was kept amiable," said Betty Beale. "Jackie even gave 'dear Tish' a farewell party, a Marine combo singing 'Arrivederci Tish,' words and music by Jackie Kennedy. Tish had very strong ideas on what the correct thing to do was. If

Jackie didn't want to do something, she didn't want somebody telling her what to do or criticizing her for not doing it."

Jackie's new social secretary was Nancy Tuckerman, her old friend and former roommate who had been working as a travel consultant in New York.

"Nancy Tuckerman was much more subservient than Tish, which made it easier on Jackie," said Purette Spiegler. "I think Jackie realized that Tish was a fantastic social secretary but there were personality clashes between them. Nancy Tuckerman seemed shy and retiring, the perfect lady."

Jackie went out of her way to make "Tucky" feel welcome, throwing her a surprise birthday party at which White House personnel filled key roles in a comic skit by Jackie depicting student days at Miss Porter's. The school song was sung to open the performance. J. B. West donned dress and wig to portray Miss Ward, a spinsterish Farmington housemother. Nancy Hough of the Curator's office dressed up like Jackie and imitated her voice perfectly. The real Jackie and Tucky squealed with delight at the snappy progression of "inside" jokes.

Tish Baldrige wasn't the only Kennedy family victim. Another hapless target was Igor Cassini, who made the mistake of reporting in one of his Cholly Knickerbocker columns that the President had attended a private party and danced the night away with Cassini's young daughter, Marina. A tension developed which soon broadened into open aggression on the part of Bobby Kennedy. Never one to take a family slight lightly, the Attorney General launched an intensive investigation into Igor Cassini's dealings with Generalissimo Rafael Trujillo and the Dominican Republic. Cassini had apparently been paid by the Dominican dictator to do some minor public relations work for that country in the United States but had failed to register as a foreign agent. Unaware that Cassini was on Trujillo's payroll and knowing only that the columnist was on good terms with the Latin American leader, President Kennedy sent Cassini and veteran diplomat Robert Murphy to the Dominican Republic for a private meeting with the dictator. Six months later, Trujillo was assassinated and news of Cassini's financial involvement began to leak.

Cassini's sin, as far as Bobby Kennedy was concerned,

was that by not divulging these details he had "been not only playing with his own future, but with the integrity of the government—the integrity of the President."

An indictment was brought in against Cassini for failure to register as a foreign agent. Igor resigned his position as Cholly Knickerbocker. His wife, Charlene Wrightsman, the daughter of Charles and Jayne Wrightsman, wrote an impassioned letter to the President asking his intervention: "I cannot tell you how surprised and shocked I have been by Bobby's harsh and punitive attitude. We always considered ourselves good friends of the Kennedys, and Ghighi still cannot understand why the son of a man whom he considered one of his oldest friends of seventeen years . . . should now be determined to bring him down to total ruin. . . ."

The President showed the letter to Jackie, but neither he nor she seemed to take Charlene Wrightsman very seriously, until she committed suicide several weeks after sending the letter, by taking an overdose of pain killers and sleeping pills. Her death, said Robert Kennedy, made it an "unpleasant case." In the end, Igor Cassini pleaded nolo contendere, and was fined $10,000 and placed on six months' probation.

Jackie's indifference to the troubles of those once close to her extended to her own family. By the time Jackie entered the White House, Edith and Edie Beale were destitute. Doris Francisco, an old friend of the Beales, noted that "by then they had become the talk of East Hampton. Their house was cat-infested, the roof eaten away by raccoons, the garden wild and overgrown. They had no heat, no gas, no electricity. The cats defecated in every room of the house. Jackie Kennedy's aunt and cousin were surviving on garbage pickings and cat food.

"Lois Wright, a painter friend of Edith's, sent a wire to Jackie at the White House saying that Edith and Edie were in trouble. They had no money to pay their utility bills, and they had little or nothing to eat. She feared for their health and wondered if Jackie could help. But Jackie couldn't help. She responded that she didn't have ten cents to give them. Those were more or less her words."

"Jackie did not have the humanity or nobility to help my mother in her hour of need," said Edie Beale. "She helped only after marrying Aristotle Onassis and then mainly because our story was all over the front page and an embarrassment to her. Anyway, it was Onassis who helped. My mother starved and had no heat or working toilet in her house for years. She was in terrific pain because there was no food or heat.

"And what did John F. Kennedy do for us? He put the FBI on our tail. From the beginning of 1962 until the end of the Kennedy Administration, we were under constant FBI surveillance—our house was wired, our mail opened, our telephone bugged. They followed us, interviewed our neighbors about us, parked their car on our front lawn. I think Kennedy thought we were Communists or Soviet agents, maybe visitors from Mars."

On June 26, 1963, four weeks after celebrating his forty-sixth birthday with a dinner cruise around the Potomac aboard the presidential yacht *Sequoia,* President Kennedy visited the Berlin Wall and in a rousing speech declared his support for efforts to defend West Berlin against the Soviets and to reunite Germany. He proclaimed himself a stalwart friend by informing the cheering crowds, *"Ich bin ein Berliner"*—"I am a Berliner" is what he intended to say. His German, unfortunately, was not on a level with Jackie's French. What he actually said was, "I am a jelly donut," referring to an indigenous pastry known as a *"berliner."* The more correct phrase, as Max Jacobson informed him upon his return to the States, would have been *"Ich bin Berliner."*

The President later told Barry Goldwater, with whom he remained friendly despite their opposing political values, that since Jackie had remained at their summer rental on Squaw Island, a mile from the Kennedy compound, he had spent his nights in Germany chasing women, particularly Ursula, a German secretary at the American Embassy in Bonn.

On June 26, JFK began a four-day tour of his ancestral Ireland, ending his European stay in Italy by meeting with the newly elected Pope, Paul VI, for over half an hour at the Vatican and then attending a session at NATO headquarters in Naples where he spoke on the need for Western unity.

While in Italy, Kennedy asked Secretary of State Dean Rusk to make arrangements for him to spend the night in some beautiful spot, presumably for purposes of relaxation —or so Rusk imagined. A former president of the Rockefeller Foundation, Rusk obtained the use of the Foundation's Villa Serbelloni overlooking Lake Como in the Italian Alps. Kennedy made it clear that he wanted the place entirely to himself—no aides, no staff, no servants, no security. He was transported by military helicopter. When Rusk arrived the next morning to pick him up, Kennedy was beaming. He couldn't remember a more wonderful night, he told Rusk. It was painfully obvious to the Secretary of State that the President hadn't spent the night alone.

On the morning of August 7, Jackie took Caroline to her horseback riding lesson in Hyannis. On her return Jackie was overcome by acute stomach and back pains. She had planned to have her baby at Walter Reed Army Hospital in Washington but instead was brought by helicopter to the military hospital at nearby Otis Air Base where a whole ten-room wing had been redecorated and specially equipped for just such an emergency.

The President was called from a conference at the White House and informed that his wife had been taken to Otis. Twenty minutes later, accompanied by several members of the White House press corps, he was on his way to Cape Cod. Since neither of the presidential planes was available, he boarded an eight-seater Lockheed JetStar, the first time the Chief Executive had flown in an aircraft not equipped with the elaborate communications installations with which he always traveled. While JFK was in the air, Dr. John Walsh at Otis, aided by a military medical team of ten, performed a Caesarean section on Jackie and, five weeks early, delivered her of a 4 lb. 1 oz. boy. So frail and tiny was the infant that the Base Chaplain baptised him immediately. Jackie's third child was named Patrick Bouvier Kennedy.

By the time the President arrived, the baby had been placed in an incubator. Early that evening the incubator was wheeled briefly into Jackie's hospital room. As the infant was suffering from hyaline membrane disease, it was decided the following morning to transfer him to the more modern and better equipped Children's Medical Center in Boston. But at 5:00 a.m. on his third day of life, Patrick Bouvier Kennedy died.

The President had spent the previous night with Bobby Kennedy at the hospital in Boston and flew back now to Otis to be with Jackie. He spent an hour alone with her behind closed doors. She told him that great as this loss had been, "the one blow I could not bear would be to lose you." The words would come back to haunt her after her husband's assassination.

The funeral Mass led by Cardinal Cushing was attended by John Kennedy, Lee Radziwill and Jackie's half-brother and half-sister, Jamie and Janet Auchincloss. Jackie was too sick to attend. President Kennedy placed a St. Christopher's medal, fashioned as a money clip—a wedding present from his wife—into the tiny casket before it was buried at the Kennedy family plot (no other Kennedys had yet been buried there) at Holyhood Cemetery in West Roxbury, Massachusetts.

John White, who had seen little of Jackie in recent years, sent her a condolence letter "containing a quotation from Aeschylus about sorrow 'Which falls drop by drop upon the heart.' And she wrote back. She was touched. But then to my amazement I saw the same quotation pop up in one of Bobby Kennedy's speeches after JFK's assassination. I assume she passed the quotation along to him."

On September 12, Jack and Jackie celebrated their tenth wedding anniversary at Hammersmith Farm in Newport—"the scene of the crime," Kennedy quipped to nobody in particular. Among their guests were the Ben Bradlees and Jackie's old friend Sylvia Blake. Yusha Auchincloss, acting as toastmaster, raised his glass and said, "We wish to thank Jackie for bringing the President here on this occasion, and also for arranging it so he could be in the White House."

"I thought she had done a good deal more to get him into office than anybody had ever cared to admit," remarked Yusha.

Sylvia Blake recalled the dinner: "As an anniversary present, Jack gave Jackie a catalogue from J. J. Klejman, the New York antiquities dealer, and told her to select whatever she wanted. He read the items aloud, and though he didn't read the prices, whenever he came to an expensive item he would stage whisper, 'Got to steer her away from that one.' It was humorous. She finally selected a simple coiled serpent bracelet. Her gift to him consisted of a gold St. Christopher's medal to replace the one he had placed in little Patrick's coffin and a red-and-gold leather scrapbook containing before-and-after photographs of the White House rose gardens. Each photograph was accompanied by a quotation from *Bartlett's Quotations* which Jackie had written out by hand."

The following day they went sailing in Narragansett Bay. Afterwards, the President met briefly with Rhode Island's Senator Claiborne Pell, who had been trying to arrange a Newport summer rental for the Kennedys for August and September in 1964. "Jack didn't care for Virginia during the summer months—too hot," said Pell. "For several years he had been contemplating buying the house of Barclay Douglas, called Annadale Farm, located almost next door to Hammersmith Farm and making it the summer White House. It even looked like the White House, which gave me the idea. But Barclay Douglas wanted too much money for it, and we were now talking about renting. Jack didn't want Jackie to find out about it until the deal went through because she preferred Virginia."

While Jack met with Pell, Jackie visited with Sylvia Blake. "I was surprised to find Jackie in such jovial spirits that weekend," said Sylvia. "On the other hand, it was impossible to read Jackie's mind. The thing about her—and everyone says this—is that although she has always been extremely cozy and sweet, she has never been very confiding. Never—not even as a teenager. Some girls spill it out all the time, but she was always very private. You never just asked her questions about herself. You didn't dare intrude beyond a certain point. She wouldn't stand for it, and still won't."

Jackie was in less jovial spirits than she was willing to admit to even an old girlhood companion. Her sister Lee, presently in Europe, sensed as much whenever she and Jackie spoke by telephone. Having developed a close friendship and sometime-romance with Greek shipping tycoon Aristotle Onassis, Lee told Ari of her sister's plight. Jackie, she said, was an extremely introverted person who did not share her thoughts with others but was very vulnerable and evidently suffering greatly.

Onassis suggested that Jackie and Lee visit Greece and cruise the islands. He would put his yacht *Christina* and its crew at their disposal. They could bring friends and travel wherever their hearts desired. They would be his guests but he would remain ashore or out of sight, whichever they preferred. Lee thought the cruise would help revitalize Jackie after her traumatic experience. She telephoned her sister and made the suggestion, adding that Ari would remain ashore if need be.

Jackie accepted the invitation without a moment's hesitation, calling it, "the dream of my life." Yet she also insisted that Ari accompany them on the cruise—"I can't possibly accept this man's hospitality and then not let him come along. It would be too cruel."*

Jack and Bobby Kennedy were somewhat less enthused by the idea. They were concerned with the kind of press that such a venture might engender and its possible effect on the 1964 presidential election, already a major factor in JFK's thinking. Aristotle Onassis, "the Golden Greek," was not only a foreigner but a jet-setter, the worst possible combination from the point of view of the average American. In addition he had been the target of any number of criminal probes and investigations by the Justice Department and the defendant in several legal skirmishes with the U.S. Maritime Commission. The most publicized of these involved the purchase by Onassis of fourteen ships from the Commission with the understanding that they would sail under the American flag. Onassis had made more than $20 million by transferring them to foreign registry. He was indicted, and forced to pay seven million dollars to avoid criminal prosecution.

"Jackie, do you know what you're doing?" asked the President. "Are you aware of this fellow's reputation? It's enough that your sister's involved with him."

The President knew of Lee's long-range plan to have her present marriage to Stas Radziwill annulled and then to marry Aristotle Onassis; there were rumors afloat that Onassis would like nothing better than to become brother-in-law to the President of the United States.

Bobby Kennedy made it clear to Jackie that any such maneuver on Lee's part would have to wait until after the next presidential election.

The President also laid down the law: if Jackie insisted on taking the cruise, Stas Radziwill would have to be

---

*By coincidence, Jackie had recently invited Maria Callas, Ari's steady companion, to perform at the White House in October for Emperor Haile Selassie of Ethiopia. Callas had declined, but she had sent a telegram to the Kennedys commiserating with them on the death of their newborn son.

included, as well as an additional chaperone—for the sake of appearance, if for no other reason. Onassis had been divorced from his wife Tina since the advent of Maria Callas. It would hardly do for the First Lady and her married sister to be seen in close company with a divorced man renowned as a connoisseur of beautiful women.

Jackie agreed, and the President asked his friends, Franklin D. Roosevelt, Jr., and Franklin's then-wife Suzanne if they would be willing to act as chaperones.

"I'm not certain 'asked' is the correct term," said Roosevelt. "I went on the cruise really at the command of the President, who said he wanted someone who was his friend and whom he could trust to go along. We had a very good time, but I didn't really want to babysit for Jackie. I was Undersecretary of Commerce at the time and I didn't think the trip would add much luster to my political image, aside from the fact that I had a lot to do at that particular point.

"Although I was a very old and personal friend of both the President and Mrs. Kennedy, I didn't feel it was the right place for a government official to be, away from his public duties in Washington, floating around . . . in the Eastern Mediterranean. I was concerned that this might be called sort of a playboy cruise, even with my wife there, and I didn't need anything like that.

"It had nothing to do with Jackie, whom I admired tremendously. In fact, I was somewhat responsible for getting her and Jack together. They had already met through the Bartletts, but I was the one who then encouraged Jack Kennedy to continue dating her. I remember telling him one day that there was a lady in Washington who I thought was his equal at conversation and repartee and was intellectually his equal and was one of the most beautiful girls in America, 'Who's that?' he asked. 'Her name is Jacqueline Bouvier,' I said. 'I know her,' he responded. 'We've dated a few times.' 'Well keep dating her,' I told him. 'She's hot stuff.'

"I also knew Onassis. I first met him on Long Island in March or April of 1942. We met again after the war at which time he attempted to retain my services to represent him in one of his myriad legal cases. I didn't bite but we maintained a friendship, which I imagine also played a role in Kennedy's wanting me to go along on this cruise.

"On the way, before I joined Jackie in Piraeus, which is the harbor of Athens, Greece, I had gone to Egypt to meet with President Nasser on some very hush-hush matters that President Kennedy wanted me to discuss. And then I met with the President of Somalia about why he was buying his arms from the Russians instead of perhaps being closer to the United States diplomatically and buying them from us. It was after this, on October 4, that we joined Onassis aboard his yacht."

The *Christina,* as Jackie already knew, was more than just the world's most luxurious pleasure craft; at 325 feet and named for Ari's daughter, it was the floating home of one of the most vital men Jackie had ever met.

On their first night aboard ship, Onassis—who had invited his sister Artemis along—gave a dinner party in Jackie's honor followed by a midnight dance on the mosaic dance floor-cum-swimming pool located on deck. In the morning, the *Christina,* decorated with red roses and pink gladioli, carrying a crew of sixty including a band, a masseuse and two hair-stylists, lifted anchor and powered into the Aegean en route to Istanbul.

"Onassis was wonderful," said Roosevelt, "very educated (though not formally), very well-read, very well-informed on all sorts of world affairs details, and a very brilliant man as well as a most charming man. He was not a good-looking, handsome man by any manner or means, but he was a most engaging and witty person.

"Our first port was Lesbos, the island of Sappho, which we explored while Onassis stayed discreetly aboard. He was sensitive to causing embarrassment to anybody who was in the group. He wasn't particularly sensitive about showing his wealth. There was an almost garish quality to the luxury aboard the *Christina*—barstools upholstered with the scrotums of whales, a bar handrail of whale ivory, lapis lazuli fireplaces, gold-plated bathroom fixtures. There were 42 telephones, a doctor's office, beauty salon, movie theater, nine staterooms—each named after a different Greek island. Jackie occupied Chios, whose previous occupants included Sir Winston Churchill and Greta Garbo.

"At any rate, our next port was Crete. Jackie asked me to speak to Onassis and tell him that he didn't have to hide out, that she would like it if he would come ashore with us. So he did, and he obviously enjoyed playing tour guide to his wide-eyed guests."

Jackie described her days in ten-page letters to "My dearest, dearest Jack," ending one letter with "Wish you could enjoy the Mediterranean calm with me." The President called her several times late at night. Onassis, meanwhile, smothered his guests with comfort and luxury. Two chefs—one French, one Greek—prepared caviar-filled eggs, foie gras, steamed lobsters, jumbo shrimps. Ari entertained the First Lady with his rich lode of anecdotes and stories of life in ancient Smyrna, the city of his birth (which they also visited during the cruise), and of grandmother Gethsemane who had imparted much of her native wisdom to him. In a way she reminded Jackie of her own Bouvier grandfather. Ari talked of his early struggles, of how he had once been a telephone operator in Argentina for twenty-five cents an hour, had married the daughter of a powerful Greek shipping magnate and slowly risen to his present station. Often Ari and Jackie sat together on the poop deck under a wildly starlit sky long after the others had gone to bed. They became friends, attending small dinner parties in port and midnight bouzouki dances. They visited Ithaca and then stopped at Ari's private paradise of Skorpios—an island of cypress trees and rocky hillsides. It was there, walking together along the water's edge, that Jackie told her host she wished her Greek idyll would never end.

"Onassis was charming, interesting, humorous," said Suzanne Roosevelt (today Mrs. Suzanne Kloman). "But there was nothing going on between him and Jackie. Jackie may have flirted a little, but that was how she related to men. She loved to have her admirers around, including FDR Jr. She used to tease Franklin. She was horrid. She was so dreamy that he'd be floating on air. I didn't realize it myself at the time, but that was simply Jackie's style. Franklin loved to sit and talk to her; so did Onassis, I imagine.

"If there was anything going on it was between Ari and Lee. Maria Callas wasn't there for the first time in four years. Jackie's sister brought Stas Radziwill along, but Stas left during the trip. We began to look like a boat full of jet-setters, and President Kennedy didn't want that image."

Franklin Jr. confirmed the arrangement: "It was no secret that Jackie's sister was a great friend of Ari's—and I think probably everybody knows by now that there was very definitely a relationship between Lee and Ari. But while that was going on, Jackie was there simply for the rest.

"Jackie and I did rib each other a lot. I did it to her and she did it to me. It was a good-natured, humorous give-and-take. I must say in retrospect perhaps I missed something, but Jackie and I never had an affair."

A photographer in a motor boat took a snapshot of Jackie sunbathing in her bikini on the deck of the *Christina,* and the picture appeared on front pages around the world. When he saw the photograph, Jack Kennedy sent his wife a complaining telegram urging her to return to Washington. She ignored the wire. The press described several of the parties Onassis threw aboard his yacht, loud, cacophonic soirées often lasting until dawn. "Does this sort of behavior seem fitting for a woman in mourning?" asked an editorial in the *Boston Globe.* Rep. Oliver Bolton of Ohio said in Congress that the First Lady demonstrated "poor judgment and perhaps impropriety in accepting the lavish hospitality of a man who has defrauded the American public." The congressman raised several pertinent questions, chief among them: "Why doesn't the lady see more of her own country instead of gallivanting all over Europe?"

After the *Christina* docked in Istanbul, Jackie toured the city and received a diamond and ruby necklace from Ari then easily worth in excess of fifty thousand dollars. He gave his other female guests lesser baubles. Lee complained to JFK that Onassis "showered" Jackie with gifts. "I can't stand it," she wrote. "He gave me three dinky little bracelets that Caroline wouldn't even wear to her own birthday party." The gesture served as a message: Aristotle Onassis had no intention of marrying Lee Radziwill, then or ever.

Jackie returned to Washington after spending several more days in Morocco as the guest of King Hassan II. If she felt at all contrite about her convincing demonstration of independence, she didn't show it. She remained only briefly at the White House, long enough to argue with her husband, before heading off to her new weekend home at Atoka.

"Jack and Jackie were both strong-willed and independent people." said Janet Auchincloss. "They argued, just like every married couple, but they always patched up their differences."

Friends noticed that the President seemed more willing to make sacrifices to his wife's happiness than he had previously. The same applied to Jackie.

"Will you join us in Texas next month?" JFK asked Jackie.

"I'll campaign with you wherever you want," she promised.

She changed her mind several times before making her decision final, but so did he. "He really didn't want to go," said Lem Billings. " 'Why can't [Lyndon] Johnson wash his goddamn own laundry?' he said. Maybe he had a premonition. But then at the end he seemed pretty gung ho. 'Jackie will show those Texas broads a thing or two about fashion,' he said. He was all fired up."

"Jack made Jackie go to Texas, insisted she go," said George Smathers. "She went as peacemaker. There was that squabble between Governor John Connally and Senator Ralph Yarborough which threatened to divide the Democratic Party in Texas. Jackie would have to brown up the person JFK wasn't talking to at the moment—the old political buffer routine."

Larry O'Brien held himself to blame for the fatal journey to Texas. "Unfortunately, I was responsible for the trip to Texas. I've reflected on it on and off many times over the years because this is something that will be deeply embedded in my consciousness for the rest of my life. The trip really came about because of the friendly senior Congressman from Texas, Albert Thomas, who was basically responsible for the Houston Space Center.

"He came to visit me one day and said they were going to have a testimonial dinner for him down there and allowed how it would be a great honor if the President could attend. Well, that led me to talk to the President about it and at that time the feeling was that politically, at least, Kennedy wasn't in such great shape in Texas, that he could be in better shape. Certain little disturbing things had occurred and maybe it wasn't a bad time to take a run-through, and the Al Thomas dinner could be the handle, though you wouldn't go down there just for the dinner. So that was the start of putting together the trip. And from Houston we moved into Fort Worth and Dallas, and would have moved on to Austin, ultimately."

Dallas came up at a small dinner party at the White House on October 23. Hervé Alphand was there with his wife Nicole, Franklin and Suzanne Roosevelt and Princess Irene Galitzine, the prominent Italian fashion designer and socialite who had also been aboard the *Christina* during Jackie's recent cruise.

"We ate in the family dining room that evening and spoke of the forthcoming presidential trip to Dallas," said Hervé Alphand. FDR Jr. mentioned that Adlai Stevenson had recently been attacked in Dallas and spat upon and pelted with rotten eggs by an angry mob. Stevenson had warned Jackie against going, and Senator William Fulbright and Bobby Kennedy voiced the same opinion. Despite these warnings, Jackie wanted to be with her husband—if he went, she would go with him.

"I told her to give the trip another thought, then changed the subject to Charles de Gaulle's pending 1964 visit to the United States. The White House would surely be his first stop. Jackie remarked she would also like to have him come to Hyannis Port, so there could be a less-formal exchange between Kennedy and De Gaulle. 'I thought of Palm Beach,' she said, 'but I detest that place.'

"I then said that France had designed several articles of jewelry which we had planned to present to Mrs. Kennedy to celebrate Patrick's birth. I wondered whether De Gaulle might still bring these articles along. Mention of Patrick's name startled Jackie. She caught her breath and slowly resumed. She already knew about the jewelry and said she would be pleased to receive it, but she would prefer that it be given to her by André Malraux.

"I didn't realize of course that De Gaulle would be coming to Washington sooner than expected, and that this would be the last time I would ever see my good friend, President John F. Kennedy."

On November 13, the Black Watch (the Royal Highland Regiment) presented a special performance on the South Lawn. Guests that afternoon were 1700 children between the ages of six and thirteen from child-care agencies served by the United Givers Fund in the Greater Washington area. The President, Mrs. Kennedy, Caroline and John watched the drills and highland dancing from the balcony of the White House.

The last White House reception under President Kennedy took place on November 20, the night before his ill-fated departure for Texas. The evening marked Mrs. Kennedy's first official White House appearance at a social function since the death of Patrick. The event was the annual reception for the Supreme Court Justices, their wives, and other judicial officials, spouses and guests. As always, there was interest in how Mrs. Kennedy would look, how she would dress, how she had arranged the details of the reception that she always supervised personally.

White House correspondent Jessie Stearns recalled how elated the press corps were that day: "We had been invited to cover the reception, to take pictures and make written impressions to share with our readers. Such openness on the part of Jackie Kennedy was uncharacteristic. She had been nasty to us from the very beginning.

"I remember the details so clearly because the reception took place only a few days before the assassination. It was a period when JFK, though reportedly 'settling down' with Jackie, was still playing around with other women. There was ample evidence to support this notion, including actual sightings by some very reliable sources. That nobody reported these activities in the press was due to the fact that a President's personal sex life was then considered 'off-limits.'

"At this particular reception I was standing near the foot of the grand stairway down which marched the honor guard carrying the presidential flag and the Stars and Stripes, followed by the President, First Lady and guests of honor. They emerged to the Marine Band's playing of 'Hail to the Chief.'

"All of a sudden I heard this scuffling on the staircase, a kind of pushing and pulling. People were straining to look. But a moment later they came into sight. President Kennedy's hair was standing up on one side as though somebody had taken a clump and yanked it. He appeared momentarily ruffled and flustered. Jackie seemed quite upset. JFK began to pat down his hair, smoothing it back in place. As I recall, they then quickly moved us out of there. For obvious reasons they didn't want the press corps standing around and asking questions.

"What I imagine happened is that Jackie returned from her weekend home at Atoka, where she had been horseback riding, and either heard or saw something that irritated her. She arrived about 1:30 in the afternoon, and the reception started at 6:30. I can fathom her just seething with anger for those five hours, and then he came over and she flew at him with words and whatever else. And I'm still willing to bet they had it out again in their private quarters after the reception."

"I don't know if the Kennedys argued the night before we left," said Larry O'Brien. "That's not the kind of information he would have shared with me. It's possible they had a Mr. and Mrs. quarrel. I do know that in the helicopter on the White House lawn the President asked General McHugh about the weather conditions in Texas and McHugh gave him some kind of weather report and the President said, 'Oh gosh, I don't know whether Mrs. Kennedy will have the right clothes for those weather conditions.' We had been waiting for her for several minutes to emerge from the White House and join us in the helicopter. His concern indicated that he was enthused that she was coming along. And pleased, because it was basically a political trip. A split in the Democratic Party in Texas could have hurt him in the next election. It had become a fence-mending operation, and Jackie was a pretty good carpenter. It also indicated that she planned on playing a larger role in '64."

Godfrey McHugh revealed that the trip to Texas "wasn't so much for votes as it was for money, because Texas was where the money is, and if you have a serious squabble in the Democratic Party in Texas, you're not going to get the financial support you need to orchestrate a presidential campaign.

"It was also a question of being perceived to be interested in the problems of the Southwest. I don't think the President had to go. He had other problems on his agenda, such as Vietnam and Cambodia. But since he had already committed himself he figured he might as well go all out. There had been a discussion, for example, as to whether he should use the bubbletop on his car during the Dallas motorcade. Jackie wanted the bubbletop because she worried about her hair blowing all over the place. In Washington somebody had driven one of the White House secretaries up and down Pennsylvania Avenue for half an hour in an open convertible to see how her hair would stand up. The Secret Service wanted the bubbletop in place for security reasons. But JFK wanted the open car, and he also wanted his Dallas motorcade route published. 'If you want people to turn out,' he said, 'they have to know where to find you.' "

Jackie's nervousness on the flight was evident from the urgency with which she smoked a full pack of Salems, while working with State Department interpreter Donald F. Barnes on a short speech she would give in Spanish that evening before the League of United Latin American Citizens. She and Pam Turnure then went over the itinerary, which called for the Kennedys to visit the state's five major cities, ending the tour with a stop at the LBJ Ranch, where the Vice-President had planned a huge, home-style barbecue and a horseback ride on the range.

At San Antonio, their first stop that day, Jackie remained close to her husband as he presented a dedication speech honoring the completion of a new research facility as part of the Aerospace Medical Center at Brooks Air Force Base. They then flew to Houston for Jackie's little presentation and the testimonial dinner in honor of Al Thomas at the Houston Coliseum. Afterwards, they flew to Fort Worth, arriving at the Texas Hotel at nearly one o'clock in the morning, Friday, November 22.

Jackie would later recall jagged bits and pieces of her last night with Jack, providing some of them to William Manchester for use in his book, *Death of a President*, later insisting that her revelations be either entirely eliminated or severely edited. Jackie told her husband, for instance, that she couldn't stand John Connally. "That petulant, self-indulgent mouth," she remarked. "He's just one of those men—oh, I don't know. If a man's good-looking enough, it seems to be something ruinous; they almost get soft. I just can't bear his weak mouth and his sitting there saying all these great things about himself." She concluded by saying that she "hated" Connally, a term diluted in *Death of a President* to "disliked."

They occupied a three-room suite and slept in separate bedrooms that night. The President had injured his groin earlier in the month and also had stomach cramps on this particular night, the result of nervous exhaustion, a condition he frequently suffered but managed to hide from the American public. He and Jackie embraced in the middle of his bedroom, their arms draped around each other. They were both so weary, she later said, that it seemed they were holding each other up.

Larry O'Brien was first into the President's suite in the morning. "I was distressed," said O'Brien. "The Texas newspapers had as a lead story the trouble between Lyndon Johnson and Ralph Yarborough. Yarborough accused Johnson of siding with Connally, and Ralph was refusing to ride in the same car as Lyndon. So the breach between Yarborough and Connally had widened, and we now also had Johnson to worry about.

"The President was going to speak at a breakfast and then address an outdoor audience that morning before returning to the plane and going on to Dallas. I decided I had to do something with regard to the Yarborough-Johnson-Connally affair. It bothered me because we were down there and the emphasis should have been on the President, but it was being diverted to some extent by this. I told the President I was going downstairs to see if I could locate Yarborough before the motorcade left the hotel and have a talk with him. I found him standing in front of the hotel. It was about ten minutes before departure time, and all the busloads of press were lined up and waiting to go. So I said to him, 'Gee, Ralph, this situation is so awkward, you and Johnson not riding in the same car. Just look at those buses. The entire press is now focused on the two of us standing here. You're really responsible for creating a situation that's hurting the President. I know you think very highly of the President, so why would you want to do that?' Ralph said something like, 'Well, maybe you've got a point.' And I said, 'Why don't you just get in the car with the Vice-President and we can get this thing over with.' He agreed to do it. 'I understand what you're saying,' he said, 'and I'll join Johnson.' So that was agreed to and then maybe a minute or two later Johnson came out of the hotel and I grabbed him and told him Yarborough was going to ride with him. Johnson didn't comment particularly. The two of them just climbed into the car, and that was that.

"When we landed at Dallas's Love Field I wanted to be sure that the situation continued in that motorcade, so while Jack and Jackie worked the crowd, after we stepped off Air Force One and before the motorcade was formed, I hung back to see to it that Yarborough and Johnson got into the same car together again, which they did. It caused me to be almost late in joining the motorcade, so I just jumped into a car which had four or five Texas congressmen in it. I just jumped in and off we went in the motorcade."

The motorcade departed Love Field at 12:55 p.m. First, as usual, came the police motorcycle escort, then the big Lincoln carrying the President and Mrs. Kennedy and Governor John Connally and his wife. On the back seat between the President and First Lady there was a large bouquet of long-stemmed red roses, a pleasant contrast to the strawberry pink wool suit and matching pillbox hat she had decided to wear for the Dallas procession. When she received the flowers at Love Field, Jackie noted that since arriving in Texas she had been presented only with bouquets of the state's more famous yellow rose. The red roses reminded her of the *Christina* and her trip to Greece. For more than thirty minutes they drove along, smiling and waving at the large, friendly crowds. Having reached the downtown section of Dallas, the motorcade made a sharp left turn at the corner of Elm and Houston Streets, where the road heads down an incline toward an underpass. The crowds were thinner at this point, but just as warm and exuberant. At 1:30, their car passed the Texas School Book Depository. From a sixth-floor window of the building an assassin, presumably a social misfit named Lee Harvey Oswald, aiming his rifle, tracked the presidential car in the cross hairs of his telescopic sight. Then the shots rang out, echoing through the Dealey Plaza below.

The number of rounds and the number of assassins involved in the plot to kill Kennedy, assuming there was one, remain as much a mystery today, twenty-five years after the event, as they were then. Within a period of less than six seconds at least three shots were fired. The first bullet hit the President in the back of his neck, brushed his right lung, severed his windpipe, exited his throat. Another shot, believed to be the second of three, severely wounded Governor John Connally, who was sitting on a jump seat directly in front of the President. The third shot struck the President in the back of his head, blowing away the right rear quadrant of his skull, creating a viscous cloud of blood and brain tissue.

All the difficult and costly training that had gone into

the shaping of what had often been touted as the world's most efficient enforcement agency—the United States Secret Service—slid by the wayside.

Secret Service agents and crack Dallas police officers stared at one another in mute disbelief, each waiting for the others to act. Like many, Jackie's first thought was that a motorcycle had backfired several times. On closer scrutiny she saw in disbelief that a substantial portion of her husband's skull was missing. Blood and gore gushed from the cavernous wound. The President's brain matter, gray and sticky, seemed to cover everything.

Jackie screamed: "My God, what are they doing? My God, they've killed Jack, they've killed my husband . . . Jack, Jack!"

Explaining her reaction, she told the Warren Commission investigators that she was "trying to hold his hair on. But from the front there was nothing. I suppose there must have been. But from the back you could see, you know, you were trying to hold his hair on, and his skull on."

Governor Connally's wife, Nellie, acting on her own good judgment, pulled her wounded husband into her lap and out of the line of fire, bending over him with her own body.

"I was looking this way, to the left," Jackie told the Warren Commission, trying to make them understand why she hadn't done the same for the President. "I used to think if I only had been looking to the right, I would have seen the first shot hit him, then I could have pulled him down, and then the second shot would not have hit him."

The only problem with Jackie's explanation was the existence of the Zapruder film,* which showed plainly that within an instant of the first shot Jackie was looking to the right, directly at her husband, and, riveted to her seat, continued to stare at Jack for the next seven seconds without moving to his aid.

When Jackie did move it was in an unexpected direction. She jumped up, scrambled out of her seat and onto

---

*Abraham Zapruder, a Dallas manufacturer of woman's garments, happened to shoot a home movie of the motorcade at the precise moment of the assassination and thus captured it on film. He subsequently sold it to Time-Life for $50,000.

the trunk of the car, accidentally kicking what was left of
her husband's head in the process, and began inching her
way to the right rear of the vehicle. Her destination: a
large mounted rubber handgrip at the very rear of the
trunk, which if reached, could serve as a means of egress
from the suddenly accelerating car. She had reacted not
only to the finality of her husband's wounds but to Governor Connally's anguished cry of grief: "God, they are
going to kill us all!" Jackie panicked. In her moment of
truth her instinct was self-preservation. The excuses she
later tendered for her abortive flight seemed to change
with the seasons. She told the Warren Commission she
had no recollection of ever having climbed onto the trunk
of the car. She told William Manchester that she had
crawled out to try and retrieve a portion of her husband's
head. *Life* had it that she was on the trunk of the automobile seeking help for her fatally wounded mate.

Help arrived in the person of Secret Service agent
Clint Hill. Seeing the First Lady floundering precariously
on the slippery sloping chassis and beginning to lose her
balance, Hill bounded from the follow-up car and within
seconds was on the trunk of the presidential car, pushing
Jackie back onto her blood-soaked seat.

Her momentary loss of courage was not featured by
the media. At the last instant, realizing she could not
attain the hand grip, she extended her hand in the direction of oncoming Clint Hill. To some viewers of the
Zapruder film it appeared as if she had pulled him to
safety rather than the other way round. Faithful to the
Secret Service code of silence, Hill said little to dispel
this idea. And while Jackie did not exaggerate her own
role, she also never confessed or discussed her moment
of horror. If anything, she blamed others for her misfortune—the driver of the presidential limousine for not
pulling out and speeding up sooner; John Connally for
surviving the ambush while the President perished; Lyndon
and Lady Bird Johnson for daring to shatter her kaleido-
scopic dream.

24

Within six minutes of the gunfire, the President's car lurched to a halt in front of the emergency entrance to Parkland Memorial Hospital. Cradling him in her arms, Jackie refused to surrender the President until Clint Hill wrapped the gaping head wound in his own suit jacket. The back seat was a wasteland of blood and gore, the bouquet of crushed roses afloat in a musty pool of body fluids and brain fragments.

Jackie's clothes were so heavily caked with blood that the first medic she encountered thought she had been wounded along with her husband. Lady Bird Johnson, arriving at Parkland shortly after Jackie, saw her standing by herself in the narrow corridor outside the trauma room where they had taken Jack and observed that she looked more alone and vulnerable at that moment than anyone she had ever seen. She embraced Jackie and asked if she needed a change of clothing. Jackie didn't. She wanted the world to see what "they"—the elusive "they"—had done to Jack. Her blood-splattered outfit represented a badge of courage—the President's courage—and she had no intention of taking it off.

In the limousine, as bullets fell upon them from above, Jackie had made her attempted escape. Now with her husband close to death, she wanted more than anything to be with him. After trying to push aside the head nurse, she turned to Dr. George Burkley, JFK's personal physician, whose first impulse was to offer her a sedative. "I don't want a sedative, I want to be with my husband when he dies," she said. It was her prerogative, and though the doctors in the trauma room objected, Dr. Burkley insisted she be allowed to enter.

The trauma room was filled with doctors and nurses attempting to accomplish the impossible. The hopelessness of the situation had been clear to Jackie when they were still at Dealey Plaza, site of the slaughter. Once in the room she dropped to a knee to pray, then rose slowly. A tall Texas doctor stood before her. "Mrs. Kennedy, your husband has sustained a fatal wound," he said. "I know," she whispered. Dr. Burkley felt for the President's pulse: there was none.

It was over. They pulled a sheet up to cover his body. It was too short and his foot stuck out, whiter than the sheet. Jackie took his foot and kissed it. Then she pulled back the sheet. She kissed his lips. His eyes were open and she kissed them. She kissed his hands and his fingers. Then she held his hand and refused to let go.

Mac Kilduff, acting press secretary on the Texas trip, made the official announcement at 2:31 p.m., following the administration of the last sacraments of the Church by two priests.

"I went to Ken O'Donnell who was with Jackie in the trauma room, because Ken was Chief of Staff," said Kilduff. "I told him I was going to have to make some sort of announcement. There were too many reporters running around who already knew, including Bob Pierpoint and Dan Rather. At least they had deep suspicions. It was only a matter of time. Ken said, 'Don't ask me. Ask the President.'

"So I went and found Johnson. They had him tucked away in another trauma room and he was sitting there with Lady Bird and Secret Service agent Rufus Youngblood. I didn't know what to call him. I wasn't going to call him Lyndon. I called him Mr. President and Lady Bird kind of yelled or let out an audible gasp. I said, 'I have to announce President Kennedy's death.' He said, 'We don't know what kind of a Communist conspiracy this might be.' It always struck me as kind of strange that he said 'Communist' conspiracy, because given the political climate of Texas it could just as easily have been a John Birch Society uprising.

"You could almost see Johnson's mind clicking. 'We don't know if they could be after me, the Speaker, the Secretary of State. I think I better get out of here and I'll wait for you after you make your announcement.' I went out to the car with him. They took him back to Air Force One. Some people complained that it was crass of him to use Air Force One instead of Air Force Two, but that decision was made by the Secret Service, not LBJ."

A new problem had arisen. Dr. Earl Rose, the Dallas County Medical Examiner, whose offices were located at Parkland, had decreed that the President's body would have to remain in Dallas until an autopsy could be performed. A murder had been committed and state law dictated the procedure. It didn't matter that the murder victim was the President of the United States: the law was the law.

Kennedy's people assured Rose that an autopsy would be performed as soon as they got the President's body back to Washington. But the medical examiner, having enlisted the support of a local magistrate, insisted that since JFK had been killed in Dallas it was in Dallas that the autopsy had to take place.

"We're taking him back to Washington," said Ken O'Donnell.

A van delivered a bronze casket for the dead President. Jackie placed her bloodstained wedding band on her husband's finger just before they lifted the body into the casket and wheeled it past the two irate public officials to a waiting white hearse. She then insisted on riding in the back of the hearse with her husband. To her immense relief, they were going home.

Or were they? Lyndon Johnson seemed to have other ideas in mind. While the casket was carried aboard Air Force One and relegated to the tail section of the aircraft, Johnson had put in a call to Federal District Judge Sarah T. Hughes, a local Kennedy appointee, asking her to come and administer the Oath of Office. As soon as the Kennedy camp realized there would be a delay, they began to struggle with the Johnson brigade.

"The problem," observed Air Force General Godfrey McHugh, "was that Lyndon Johnson had taken over the aircraft. When we arrived, Ken O'Donnell, who was the 'start man,' the person in charge of the plane's departure, told me to speak to the captain and tell him to get going. I was the ranking Air Force officer on the flight and therefore the logical person to transmit this order. Also, I knew the captain extremely well. His name was James Swindal, and I'd picked him for the job. So I went forward to the cockpit and said, 'Come on, let's go. Get the damn airplane off the ground.' 'I need clearance from the President,' Swindal replied. 'Well,' I said, 'the President is in the back in his coffin.' And Swindal said, 'No, I mean Johnson.' All at once it dawned on me: Lyndon Baines Johnson was the President of the United States.

" 'Where the hell is Johnson?' I asked. Swindal shrugged and said, 'Midship, I suppose.' So I turned back and started to search for him. I looked high and low but couldn't find him. I now noticed that the shades were drawn throughout the plane. Many people were crying, including a number of Secret Service agents. Pam Turnure's face was streaked with mascara. Evelyn Lincoln was sobbing. Others were trying to hide their tears. My mission was to find Johnson, and I finally located him—in a closet off the bathroom in the President's bedroom. He was scared to death, screaming, 'They're going to kill us, they're going to shoot down the plane, they're going to kill us all.' He had gone berserk. I slapped him, a quick one, and went to the rear compartment of the plane and stayed there with Jackie and the casket.'"*

General Chester V. Clifton, JFK's other military aide on the trip, recalled that as soon as Jackie and her party reached the plane, "the contest about whether to go or not became very tense. The Kennedy group wanted to get out of there as quickly as possible. We had been warned against removing the President's mortal remains from the hospital before the autopsy could be performed. So we had, you might say, spirited the casket away and taken some cars and a hearse and driven off. The last thing we wanted was the medical examiner showing up at the airport with a court order forcing us to surrender the body.

"We didn't know what to think. Were the assassins

---

*In fairness to LBJ, there were those who testified that Godfrey McHugh was the one acting in a strange manner. Jack Valenti, who later joined LBJ's staff, found himself aboard Air Force One on the flight from Dallas to Washington. He said in his LBJ Library oral history: "A man later identified as General McHugh kept darting back and forth and going from the rear of the plane to the forward part of the plane. I learned later he was the Air Force aide to the President. I must say he was in a state of near hysteria, his hair flying wildly. He was darting back and forth with his hair awry and in a general state of confusion."

Others, however, including speechwriter Richard N. Goodwin, thought LBJ a raving paranoid. According to Goodwin's recent book, *Remembering America: A Voice from the Sixties,* both Goodwin and Bill Moyers sought advice from psychiatrists about LBJ.

American or did they represent a foreign power? Could we be shot down if we took off? We were totally in the dark, so much so that American troops around the world had been placed on military alert.

"Everybody was on edge that day, including Lyndon Johnson. I did not witness the supposed head-on collision between McHugh and Johnson, but I do know that Johnson was certainly not in complete control of what he was thinking and doing for a while, which admittedly alarmed me.

"My own impression was that it would have been best to leave Dallas as soon as possible rather than sit around waiting for Judge Hughes to appear. Ken O'Donnell and I went up to the cockpit after McHugh returned, and we had a talk with Swindal, who didn't know what to do. 'Look, Jim,' I said, 'I'll tell you when we're going, and I don't care who tells you otherwise.' He said, 'That suits me; you're the highest ranking military officer on this plane. I'll take your orders.' He turned over two of his engines and a minute later Mac Kilduff came running up. 'President Johnson wants you to kill the engines.' O'Donnell gave Kilduff a strange look. Kilduff countered by saying, 'You're no longer in charge here, Ken. There's a new President. And the new President insists on being sworn in before we leave the ground.' So Ken and I went looking for Johnson. I thought we could work it out with him, don't you know, but Johnson was intransigent.

"He said he had spoken to Bobby Kennedy and Bobby told him to take the Oath in Texas. Bobby Kennedy later denied he said any such thing. Nevertheless I suppose Johnson had his personal reasons. My guess is that he was concerned that if anything happened to him before we reached Washington, the country would be in a hell of a dilemma; there wouldn't be a President, and a situation like that could be contested for years to come.

"By the time we finished fussing about whether to go or not, Johnson seemed a lot calmer and began making telephone calls to Washington, setting up Cabinet meetings and giving instructions. But there was a period there when he was not entirely coherent about what he wanted and what would have been best for everyone concerned."

Cecil Stoughton, White House photographer, recorded the swearing-in ceremony with his camera. "The woman judge arrived with a police escort and as she stepped into the plane Mac Kilduff caught sight of me and said, 'Thank God you're here. The President's going to take the Oath and you're going to have to take the pictures and give them to the press.'

"I couldn't fathom the necessity of taking the Oath, because once the President is dead, the Vice-President automatically becomes Chief Executive. Be that as it may, the entire ceremony took no more than two minutes, though it seemed an eternity. When we were ready to go, Ken O'Donnell went back to get Jackie. I understand O'Donnell told her she didn't have to do it, if she didn't want; she said she felt she owed the country that much. So she came along and stood to Johnson's left, Lady Bird to his right. Twenty-seven persons—all that could crowd into the President's gold-carpeted private quarters in the midsection of the jet—witnessed that solemn ceremony. Though dry-eyed, Jackie seemed out of it. She was in a state of shock. In most of the photos you can see the dried blotches of blood on her clothing. There were traces of blood on Dr. Burkley's shirt.

"I felt for Jackie. I felt for myself because I knew what working with Johnson would be like. So did everyone there. I remember a Secret Service agent telling me—this was in '62—'We've got to keep Kennedy healthy,' by which he meant they didn't need Johnson as President. They knew it was going to be terrible if he ever got to be Numero Uno. And he did, and it was.

"In my case he couldn't get enough pictures taken of himself. Johnson had me taking pictures when he went to the bathroom. All the Johnsons had big mouths and big teeth. The corners of their lips were tied to the edge of my camera and when I raised my camera it pulled strings and their mouths flew open. It was automatic. They went into smile."

Following the brief ceremony Jackie returned to her seat next to her husband's casket, where she was presently joined by Ken O'Donnell, Dave Powers and Larry O'Brien. Twice during the flight Lyndon Johnson sent Bill Moyers, soon to become his assistant, to the rear of the plane to ask O'Donnell and O'Brien to join him, and on both occasions JFK's lieutenants refused.

"We wanted to be with Jackie," said Larry O'Brien. "We needed her and she needed us. Ken was quite bitter about Lyndon Johnson. I didn't feel Jackie was necessarily bitter toward anyone in particular, just in general.

"On the plane we had a long discussion about the relationship of the Irish Mafia to Jack and what it meant to him and what it meant to her and all the rest. Jack was very close to the Irish Mafia. Ken, Dave and I didn't always attend the soirées—the social events—in the White House but our relationship with the President was an extensive one and a close one over a long period of time. It was a professional rather than a social relationship, especially in my case. Nevertheless he had a close affinity to all of us. He was proud of his Irish heritage. We went with him on his trip to Ireland. He was very emotionally involved on that trip. And we had a lot in common because we'd always tell a lot of stories, and we had the Massachusetts background. And Jackie, when I'd chat with her from time to time, would kid around about it. But she recognized—and she discussed this at some length on the plane coming back from Dallas—the unique, if you will, relationship between Jack and the so-called Irish Mafia. She recognized how close we were to him and how deeply he felt about us.

"In the middle of all this talk, Ken O'Donnell broke out a bottle of Scotch. 'I don't know about you guys,' he said, 'but I can sure use a stiff drink.' So we all joined him, including Jackie, who had never tasted Scotch before. She didn't care for it particularly, but on this occasion she took a second shot and I imagine felt a bit better for it.

"All in all, I don't think I have ever experienced the kind of courage she demonstrated, first at the hospital in Dallas and on that plane to Washington, and then during the funeral. We had a number of conversations during that period and in the months that followed and there were times when she would say, 'How could this have happened?' and: 'Life has no meaning for me anymore.' But on the whole she acquitted herself magnificently and became a symbol for all of us, of great nobility and character in an age of general impoverishment of soul.' "

As the plane approached Washington, Godfrey McHugh noticed that Jackie still had particles of the President's brain on her hat and suit. "It wasn't just the dried splotches of blood," he remarked. "That wasn't so bad. It was the gray brain matter. I pointed it out to her. She gave me the hat and I cleaned it off, fixed it up and handed it back. But she wouldn't let me touch the suit, 'Let them see what they've done,' she said. 'I want them to see.' "

Air Force One landed and Bobby Kennedy clambered aboard. He was in the same sort of absolute, numb shock that Jackie seemed to be experiencing. People would speak to him, and it was as though he didn't hear them. He was absolutely numb and moving about almost mechanically. He couldn't be penetrated, although he managed to communicate to Jackie that a lone suspect had been apprehended, a small-time Communist named Oswald. The notion that such a "silly little" character could assassinate the President saddened Jackie further; it robbed the act of moral significance. In Jackie's eyes it trivialized her husband's death. "If it had at least been for his civil rights stand," she said.

The breach between the Kennedy and Johnson camps widened when Kennedy's staff blocked the aisle of the airplane preventing the new President from disembarking with the casket. Instead of accompanying the body to Bethesda Naval Hospital for the required autopsy, Johnson immediately headed for the White House, where he penned individual letters to Caroline and John Jr., telling them how "proud" they should be of their father.

En route to Bethesda, Jackie asked Bobby about Lyndon Johnson's claim that the Attorney General had advised him to take the Oath of Office while still in Dallas. When Bobby denied the story, Jackie said, "The last thing Jack told me about Lyndon is that he's incapable of telling the truth."

Jackie had asked Ken O'Donnell and Larry O'Brien to remain with her during the autopsy and then to stay at the White House for several days as her personal guests. Larry O'Brien called his wife after their arrival and told her he was back but that he wouldn't be coming home. He remained at the White House with Jackie throughout the four-day funeral proceedings and then joined her to view the grave site at Arlington National Cemetery the day before Thanksgiving.

While still at Bethesda, Jackie was joined by Dr. John Walsh, who recommended that she rest for an hour or two while the autopsy continued. To help her relax he injected her with 100 milligrams of Visatril, which under normal circumstances would have enabled her to sleep for 12 hours without any trouble. Under the present circumstances, the shot seemed only to stimulate Jackie.

Robert McNamara rushed to Bethesda to console Bobby and Jackie and wound up listening to Jackie for hours as she recounted every detail of the assassination. "From the moment they reached Parkland, she remembered everything," said McNamara. "Talking it all out over and over became a kind of purgation for her. Her real problem now was the future. She knew she couldn't stay in the White House, but she didn't know where to go. She and Jack had sold their house in Georgetown. She had friends there and she enjoyed it. She wanted to do all the things she had always done with Jack."

As the night wore on, others began to arrive, including the Bradlees and the Bartletts. Janet and Hugh Auchincloss, recently back from a trip to the Middle East, had met Jackie at the airport and followed her to Bethesda. "As terrible as this is," said Janet, "think how much worse it would have been had Jack lived and been maimed." Jackie urged her mother and stepfather to stay at the White House and gave them Jack's room for a night.

Janet, in an effort to spare her daughter any more pain than necessary, asked White House nanny Maud Shaw to apprise Caroline of her father's death. Caroline cried so violently at the news that the nanny feared she might choke. The following morning the child saw a copy of *The New York Times* a maid had left behind. She asked her grandmother Janet why her father's picture was outlined in black. John Jr., too young to comprehend, was told nothing.

While leaving the mechanics and logistics of the funeral to Sargent Shriver, Jackie (who was consulted by Shriver on every move) had already contacted Angier Biddle Duke requesting from the Chief of Protocol details of the funeral that had been held nearly a century earlier for Abraham Lincoln. Duke forwarded the request to Rutherford Rogers, Acting Librarian of Congress, who sent information not only of President Lincoln's funeral but on those of George Washington, Woodrow Wilson, Ulysses S. Grant and even Edward VII. Duke was able to get this material into Mrs. Kennedy's hands within twenty-four hours.

The autopsy completed (though not very satisfactorily,

according to future inquiries and commissions),* Kennedy's corpse was returned to the White House and borne to a specially constructed catafalque in the East Room. Godfrey McHugh, who had been placed in charge of the Honor Guard assigned to stand over the coffin in which Kennedy was to be buried (as opposed to the casket in which he had been transported from Dallas to Washington), recalled Jackie saying, "But we can't leave him like that, we have to have flowers." Flowers were brought and McHugh arranged them to one side of the coffin.

"She had another concern," said McHugh. "It bothered her that the Honor Guard, consisting of one man from each branch of the armed services, looked away from the coffin when they stood at attention. 'But Jackie,' I said, 'they *always* look away. They always have, for years and years. That's what they're supposed to do. It's military protocol.' 'I don't care,' she said. 'If they're guarding the coffin, let them look at it. They look absurd staring into space. Starting with the next shift, order them to look at the President.'

"Well, I couldn't figure that one out. But it seemed like a small matter compared to the enormity of the assassination. So when the next shift arrived, I told the navy officer in charge to have his men stare at the coffin. 'But we never do that, sir,' he said. 'I don't care, those are your orders,' I snapped.

"On the next shift the Honor Guard stared at the

---

*The autopsy of JFK was at best a whitewash, at worst a mockery. Orchestrated by Robert Kennedy and some other members of the family, it was performed without benefit of a forensic pathologist. Following the autopsy a number of bodily materials mysteriously disappeared, including JFK's brain, tissue sections, blood smears and organ samples. In 1979, the Select Committee on Assassinations determined that in all probability Robert Kennedy disposed of these and other materials out of concern that they "would be placed on public display in future years in an institution such as the Smithsonian." How much of a role, if any, Jacqueline Kennedy played in the disappearance of those materials is open to question. Former Attorney General Ramsey Clark told this writer, "After JFK's assassination, when I was Attorney General, I was approached by Jackie and asked to suppress all of the autopsy x-rays and documentation from the public. She didn't want this material to be splashed all over the media—newspapers and television—during the lifetime of her children. I found this a reasonable request."

coffin. But when the shift ended, the officer said, 'We can't do it that way again, sir. I'm afraid some of my men may faint.' 'Why should they faint?' I inquired. 'They tend to faint if they stare at the same spot for an hour at a time. If they stare into space they can at least look at a number of different images.' 'Well,' I responded, 'I regret that very, very much, but then you will simply have to cut them down to half-hour shifts, or whatever it takes to prevent their passing out. But they will have to look at the coffin.' ''

At 10:00 a.m. on the morning of the 23rd, Father John Cavanaugh, an old friend of the Kennedys, conducted a Low Mass for family and intimates of the slain President in the East Room. Prior to the Mass, he met privately with Jackie. He had come early, he explained, to hear her confession.

"What am I supposed to confess, Father?" she said angrily. "That I neglected to watch the calendar and ate meat some Friday three months ago?" Thus began a five-minute diatribe that ended with the widow's demand that the clergyman explain her husband's murder: "Why, why? How could God do something like that?"

That evening, overtired and full of drugs (her physician had given her two injections of Amytal), Jackie thrashed around in bed, crying and keening, calling out her husband's name, talking to him, rolling from her own mattress to the one he used when he stayed with her, burrowing into his pillow and weeping until she fell into a troubled sleep. After several hours she awoke. Unable to fall back to sleep she found some blue White House stationery and began writing her husband a letter. Starting "My Darling Jack," she wrote about sleeping in his bed, about Caroline and John-John, about Patrick, about their marriage, about their plans and promises. She began to cry, the tears welling up and rolling down her cheek, staining the page and smudging the words. She wrote on. After she finished she folded the letter and placed it in an envelope.

During the autopsy the night before, Dr. Burkley had retrieved her wedding band and returned it to her. She intended to replace it with a few of Jack's favorite articles: samples of scrimshaw, a bracelet he had given her, a set of gold cuff links she had given him. She would include her letter and letters from the children. She went

to the playroom the next morning and asked them to
write to their father. John-John, not old enough to write,
merely scribbled and doodled on a blank sheet of paper,
his older sister helping to guide his hand. Then Caroline,
in blue ballpoint, printed her message: "Dear Daddy,
We're all going to miss you. Daddy I love you very
much. Caroline."

She had thought also to include in the package a plain
gold ring with emerald chips she had received from Jack
after Patrick's death, but she decided at the last moment
not to part with it.

Jackie asked Bobby Kennedy to accompany her to the
East Room. Waiting for them there was Godfrey McHugh,
who helped them open the coffin. Bobby added a *PT-109*
tiepin and an engraved silver rosary to the articles Jackie
had brought along. The two men watched as she arranged the items the way she wanted them. She gazed at
her husband's face. She began to stroke his hair and
continued to caress it as the minutes ticked by. Sensing
what she wanted, McHugh left the room and quickly
returned with a pair of scissors. Jackie bent forward and
carefully cut a lock of the President's hair. Bobby slowly
lowered the lid of the coffin. Jackie turned and left the
room.

Sometime earlier that morning, Jackie had been seen
by Dr. Max Jacobson, who had flown in to attend the
funeral. Jacobson's elixir had finally settled Jackie's nerves.
Nothing, however, could adequately prepare her for the
latest outflow of news. Two days after his arrest, Lee
Harvey Oswald, while being escorted by two Dallas police officers, was shot at point blank range and killed by
one Jack Ruby, a character in his own way as "far out"
and bizarre as Oswald himself. "One more awful thing,"
Jackie remarked on hearing the announcement. She was
neither impressed nor moved by Ruby's statement to the
FBI that he had killed Oswald to spare Mrs. Kennedy the
unenviable task of having to return to Dallas for the trial.
Only the day before, she had written a letter to console
the widow of Dallas Patrolman J.D. Tippit, Oswald's
other murder victim. Now Oswald was also dead, murdered before television cameras, the assault viewed "live"
over network television.

The drama of the President's funeral also played itself
out over the airwaves. Millions watched as Jackie, a child

in each hand, left the North Portico of the White House and accompanied the coffin as it was taken to the Capitol Rotunda, where the President would lie in state. Viewers saw Jacqueline and Caroline kneel at the President's flag-draped coffin. Then the first of 250,000 mourners went filing by.

Later in the day Lee Radziwill and her husband arrived from London to relieve the Auchinclosses. "Lee will be sleeping with me in my bedroom," Jackie announced and directed Stas Radziwill to Jack's bedroom. Another White House guest, though the press knew nothing of his presence, was Aristotle Onassis, who flew to Washington from Hamburg, West Germany, when he heard the news. Jackie's twin Bouvier aunts and their husbands were also in attendance, although they did not stay overnight in the White House.

Jackie continued to worry about where she and the children would live after the White House. President Johnson had told her to take as much time as needed, but she realized she couldn't take forever. John Kenneth Galbraith, home from India, discussed the situation with Mr. and Mrs. Averell Harriman, and they offered her their home in Georgetown at 3038 N Street, a three-story, 11-room colonial-style brick residence only three blocks from where Jack and Jackie once lived. The Harrimans arranged to move into the Georgetown Inn, and told Jackie to stay until she found a permanent home of her own.

Relieved of this burden, Jacqueline would now focus on the final and most important phase of the funeral. She insisted that the Mass be held at the modest-sized St. Matthew's Cathedral and approved of her husband's burial site at Arlington National Cemetery. Once his final resting place was ready, his coffin would be joined by the bodies of the Kennedys' unnamed baby girl, stillborn in 1956, and Patrick Bouvier Kennedy, dead only since August. A fitting memorial would be designed at the site by architect John Warnecke.

Rising above her grief, Jackie resolved to impress her husband's place in history on the American consciousness, to remind Americans what had been taken from them. The funeral provided a means of demonstrating JFK's importance as a global leader, his historic links with Abraham Lincoln, Andrew Jackson and Franklin

Roosevelt. A procession of international dignitaries would march to St. Matthew's behind Jackie and other members of the immediate family. The coffin would be drawn by the same gun caisson that had carried Franklin D. Roosevelt to his grave in 1945. A riderless horse (ironically named "Black Jack") with boots reversed in their stirrups, would follow the coffin, while muffled drum rolls marked the way. At the entrance to St. Matthew's, Jackie and her children would be received by Cardinal Cushing. She would kiss the Cardinal's ring before entering the cathedral. She and the children would emerge after the service to the strains of "Hail to the Chief." And at her gentle prodding, John-John would salute the American flag atop his father's coffin.

Though majestic and grand, the ceremony was not without its simple moments. Before the morning service, Sargent Shriver handed out Mass cards with Jackie's inscription: "Dear God, please take care of your servant John Fitzgerald Kennedy." In any other country the funeral memento would have been a medallion or something else of value. "But these were just little pieces of paper, and we were handing them out to all the big shots," Shriver informed the press. "Suddenly there I was in front of French President Charles de Gaulle, and I can remember him taking the card. He looked at it and then handed it to his aide. The card was so simple, the gesture so regal."

Burial at Arlington followed the Mass, and afterwards Jackie met privately at the White House with De Gaulle, Emperor Haile Selassie of Ethiopia, Ireland's President Eamon de Valera and Prince Philip, who suggested that a receiving line would be a more efficient way of greeting the other foreign dignitaries than simple mingling. The queue—220 representatives from 102 nations, including eight chiefs of state and 11 heads of government—stretched from the Red Room back through the Blue Room and the State Dining Room. John Davis, having flown from Italy to pay his respects, found his cousin in "an elevated mood. Finally she was running the White House. She loved being the center of attraction with all the world's dignitaries coming to pay homage to her. It was only later that the true horror of what had happened hit her.

"What seemed astounding was the complete recklessness with which the Kennedys led their lives. The family
took big risks, and that meant suffering big losses. The
plots, for example, to eliminate Fidel Castro with the
help of the Mob were simply preposterous. The Kennedys knew of two such plots, but eight were planned in
all—one on the day that Kennedy was shot.

"JFK would sleep with anyone regardless of the circumstances. He had real charisma and great potential,
but he was young and thought he was above harm. His
personal recklessness is why the Kennedys never pushed
the assassination investigation. The family didn't want to
uncover the connection among the CIA, the Mafia and
the President.

"It seemed apparent to almost everybody except the
Kennedys that the assassination of JFK was not a one-
man operation. Surely, as Attorney General, Robert Kennedy was privy to all sorts of information which must
have raised questions in his mind. Yet he seemed perfectly satisfied with the simple-minded conclusions reached
by the Warren Commission.

"I remember asking Janet, Jackie's mother, why *she*
didn't get Jackie to investigate. Janet said, 'Will it bring
Jack back?' 'No, it won't,' I said, 'but maybe we can
bring the murderers to justice.' Janet shrugged. In 1974,
I talked to Jackie about it. She very quickly changed the
subject. That's characteristically how she dealt with anything unpleasant—she dismissed it by switching channels.
By the time we discussed the assassination she had gotten
over it. She didn't want to be reminded of that period.
She wasn't interested in historical truth." George de
Mohrenschildt, an old friend of Jackie's father, was a
known associate of Lee Harvey Oswald. After JFK's
assassination, de Mohrenschildt contacted Janet Auchincloss, whom he also knew, and requested a meeting with
Jackie. Jackie refused. Such avenues might well have
been explored.

"At the time he died I too was idealistic about JFK.
Now whenever I see those old films of Kennedy on
television, I have to stop myself from heaving. It's hard
to believe that here was this absolute fake, this womanizer and opportunist, coming off like Euripides. All our
dreams invested in that! What a disappointment!"

Cecil Stoughton, who took the official photographs of

Jackie on the receiving line greeting the visiting government officials, remembered thinking, "How can she stand to do this?" But on this particular day Jackie transcended rank, outdid herself. She remained serene, embracing some, reassuring others. To Soviet Deputy Premier Anastas I. Mikoyan she said, "Please tell Mr. Chairman President [Khrushchev] that I know he and my husband worked together for a peaceful world, and now he and you must carry on my husband's work." Mikoyan listened to the translation and then buried his face in his hands.

Later that evening, Jackie and other family members celebrated John-John's third birthday with a small party in the family dining room. The Bradlees attended, and Toni noticed the redness in and around Jackie's eyes—the result of tears and exhaustion. A larger birthday party for both children (Caroline and John Jr. were born the same week, three years apart) would be held a few days later. At midnight Jackie and Bobby visited the President's gravesite at Arlington. The eternal flame flickered blue in the cool night. They prayed, and Jackie left a bouquet of lilies of the valley next to the President's grave.

The following day, Tuesday, November 26, Jackie wrote to Lyndon Johnson: "Dear Mr. President: Thank you for walking yesterday—behind Jack. You did not have to do that. I am sure many people forbade you to take such a risk, but you did it anyway. . . ."

On December first, she received a response from the new President: "Jackie, You have been magnificent and have won a warm place in the heart of history. I only wish things could be different—that I didn't have to be here. But the Almighty has willed differently, and now Lady Bird and I need your help. . . ."

Although Jackie gained tremendous public acclaim for her deportment during and after the funeral, she was criticized in some quarters for having overplayed her role. Angier Biddle Duke recalled seeing her do "a little bob, a curtsy, to Prince Philip, the husband of Queen Elizabeth, when she encountered him in a corridor of the White House. The Prince took it as a courtesy. But when I reminded her that wives of heads of state don't curtsy to other heads of state, she said, 'But I am no longer the wife of a head of state.' It was a drop-dead line and it upset me."

Author John Hersey received a 1964 letter from Jackie which he found more than slightly embarrassing: "Actually, it was a formal letter that had been prepared for a number of people. Jackie was putting together a private memorial volume of writings on JFK and wanted the rights to reprint my *PT-109* story. But there was a postscript in her hand speaking about how moved she had been by the article and how she read it over again night after night. This, of course, was a gross exaggeration. I think she wanted to tell me how much the piece meant but she overstated the case. It was a very strange little note."

Charles de Gaulle admired Jackie (more, apparently, than he admired her husband, whom he ultimately described as "a President with the style of a hairdresser's assistant—he combed his way through problems"), but found the funeral an over-produced, over-dramatized spectacle. When he returned to France he wrote precise instructions for his own funeral: he wanted the very simplest of functions, a plain carpenter's coffin in his own private plot, with only his family and the townspeople attending. He requested that no heads of state or public officials accompany his body to the cemetery.

Finally, there were Jackie's dealings with journalist Teddy White. "A week after the assassination, I received a telephone call from Jackie inviting me up to Hyannis Port, where she had gone to spend Thanksgiving," said White. "She knew I was writing a summation of the assassination for *Life,* and would I be willing to come up to have a talk with her?

"It was storming so I rented a car and driver to take me from New York. Looking pale and drained, Jackie indicated she had left Washington to escape prying eyes, understandable considering that for four days, as never before in history, an entire nation had entered the sorrow and private suffering of the widow of this fallen leader.

"She said she had also come to Hyannis Port to see Joe Kennedy, to be alone with him and tell him how his son lost his life. She had barged past Rose Kennedy and Ann Gargan into his room and told him everything.

"She and I spoke for nearly four hours. She mentioned Patrick's death as prelude to the assassination. The baby's passing had been a very emotional event for both parents, and I think in a way the President reached out for her as he hadn't done before. There weren't too many of these moments in their lives. That they had attained a new intimacy so soon before the end only intensified the degree of Jackie's loss.

"She regurgitated many of the details of the assassination. She remembered the pink-rose rings on the inside of the President's skull after the top had been blown off. 'The inside of his head was so beautiful,' she said. 'I tried to hold the top of his head down, so more brains wouldn't spill out. But I knew he was dead.' Aboard Air Force One, prior to Lyndon Johnson's swearing-in, she had taken a Kleenex and wiped splotches of blood and matted clumps of her husband's hair from her face. Later she deeply regretted this. From the moment of the assassination, people were trying to get her to change her clothes, eradicate all signs of the crime. She didn't want them to forget. Her only solace was that he hadn't suffered. He had this 'very neat' expression on his face after being hit. He had made a special point of telling her on a number of occasions that he never wanted to end up like his father; he preferred death to permanent disability. He said this to her the first time when he underwent back surgery early in their marriage.

"We spoke a bit about the political climate that had led to the assassination—the idea of a plot or even of government involvement in the event. Jackie couldn't have cared less about the myriad theories as to who might be behind her husband's murder. What difference did it make whether he was killed by the CIA, the FBI, the Mafia, or simply by some half-crazed misanthrope? He was gone, and what counted for her was that his death be placed in some kind of social context.

" 'Only bitter old men write history,' she said. 'Jack's life had more to do with myth, magic, legend, saga, and story than with political theory or political science.' That's when she came out with her Camelot theory. She believed, and John Kennedy shared the belief, that history belongs to heroes, and heroes must not be forgotten. She didn't want Jack to be forgotten, or have his accomplishments cast in an unfavorable light. She wanted him to be remembered as a hero. She reported how at night he would often listen to *Camelot* on their phonograph, and how he personally identified with the words of the last song: 'Don't let it be forgot, that once there was a spot, for one brief shining moment that was known as Camelot.'

"She put it so passionately that, seen in a certain light, it almost made sense. I realized it was a misreading of history, but I was taken with Jackie's ability to frame the tragedy in such human and romantic terms. Also, there was something extremely compelling about her. At that moment she could have sold me anything from an Edsel to the Brooklyn Bridge.

"Yet all she wanted was for me to hang this *Life* epilogue on the Camelot conceit. It didn't seem like a hell of a lot to ask. So I said to myself, why not? If that's all she wants, let her have it. So the epitaph of the Kennedy administration became Camelot—a magic moment in American history when gallant men danced with beautiful women, when great deeds were done and when the White House became the center of the universe."

25

On November 26, the day after John Kennedy's funeral, Jackie invited Lady Bird Johnson for tea at the White House. "Don't be frightened of this house," Jackie told her. "Some of the happiest years of my marriage have been spent here. You will be happy here."

Afterwards, they wandered from room to room, Jackie pointing out various features and introducing the new First Lady to the staff members she would need to know. Before Lady Bird left, Jackie asked her for a favor: she didn't want to disrupt Caroline's classes until semester's end, and she wondered if the White House school could remain open until then, at which time the school would be moved to the British Embassy. Lady Bird assured Jackie that she agreed.

Jackie also asked Lyndon Johnson for several favors. "I remember going over to the Oval Office to ask him for two things," she said in her oral history for the LBJ Library. "One was to name the Space Center in Florida 'Cape Kennedy.' Now that I think back on it, that was so wrong. If I'd known Cape Canaveral was the name from the time of Columbus, it would be the last thing Jack would have wanted . . .*

"And the other one, which is so trivial, was: there were plans for the renovation of Washington and there was this commission, and I thought it might come to an end. I asked President Johnson if he'd be nice enough to receive the commission and sort of give approval to the work they were doing, and he did. It was one of the first things he did."

*On Nov. 29, 1963, President Johnson issued Executive Order 11129 changing the name of Cape Canaveral Auxiliary Air Force Station and the Launch Operations Center of the National Aeronautics and Space Administration to the John F. Kennedy Space Center.

Johnson did more than that—he suggested that Lady Bird make the beautification of Washington her own special project (a project that was also recommended to Lady Bird by her press secretary, Liz Carpenter) and at the same time establish a permanent "Committee for the Preservation of the White House," of which Jackie would become a member. Although Jackie joined the committee, she refused to attend meetings at the White House, stating that "to return to that place is too painful to even contemplate."

The Washington renovation project that Jackie suggested to President Johnson eventually fell under the partial sponsorship of the National Trust, a fund-raising organization for the preservation of buildings and structures around the country, including Washington. Judy White, an employee with the Trust, noted that "Jackie once made a $1,000 contribution, but that was years ago—nothing since then, despite a lot of talk on her part about the importance of conservation and preservation."

Before leaving the White House, Jackie sent Lady Bird an eleven-page handwritten memo in that Eastern finishing school backhand of hers, on foolscap, reviewing all aspects of her work on the White House renovation project during the thousand days of Camelot, including the art works she had helped accumulate for the Executive Mansion.

Liz Carpenter said of Jackie's lengthy memo: "I had a strange feeling when this was delivered that it was pretty grim—rather ghoulish—that Jackie sat up late at night in the White House and put so much emphasis on furniture when she must be in dreadful shock and sorrow over her husband's death. But those were material things that meant something to her, and she wanted Mrs. Johnson to know the background."

Jackie went around handing out mementos to Jack's friends and members of the White House staff—the President's ties to the Irish Mafia, his Navy dog tags to Cardinal Cushing—and bidding her farewells. (To J. B. West: "Will you be my friend for life?" To Godfrey McHugh: "First I didn't want in, now I can't seem to leave.")

It is customary for departing Presidents to add one painting to the White House's permanent collection. Jackie and the rest of the Kennedy clan chose a view of the

Seine in Paris by Claude Monet and mounted it in the Green Room. On December 6, her final day at the White House, the former First Lady wrote to Nikita Khrushchev, reiterating more or less what she had told Mikoyan at JFK's funeral, that it was now up to the Russians to carry on the mission of peace they and her husband had undertaken.

When Lady Bird arrived at the White House, she was handed a brief note left by Jackie: "I wish you a happy arrival in your new house, Lady Bird. Remember—you will be happy here. Love, Jackie." The former First Lady left another calling card, a brass wall plaque over the mantel, in Lady Bird's bedroom, which read: "IN THIS ROOM LIVED JOHN FITZGERALD KENNEDY WITH HIS WIFE JACQUELINE—DURING THE TWO YEARS, TEN MONTHS AND TWO DAYS HE WAS PRESIDENT OF THE UNITED STATES—JANUARY 20, 1961—NOVEMBER 22, 1963."

The memento didn't appeal to Lyndon Johnson, who pointed out that Jackie had mounted it beneath a similar plaque attesting to the fact that Abraham Lincoln had also on occasion slept there.

On the evening of Jackie's first day on N Street, two antique lanterns beside the front door were lit, and a small squadron of Secret Service agents surrounded the property. (Jackie and her children were initially provided with Secret Service protection for a period of two years, later increased to four. In 1968, Secret Service protection for all Presidents' widows was extended until death or remarriage, and for Presidents' children until the age of sixteen.)

Neighbors and curiosity seekers jammed the street in front of the Harriman house to watch a procession of movers transport the family's possessions and personal effects—a long rack containing Jackie's fur coats, Caroline's two-wheeler bicycle, a series of large boxes marked "John Jr.'s toys," and identical cages housing the children's pet parakeets. The onlookers saw a sad reminder—a bulging, ten-year-old briefcase with the initials, "JFK," Jackie's wedding present to her husband.

At Jackie's request, two Navy stewards were provided by President Johnson to help her move from the White House and to assist her in her transition to private life. When Jackie asked that the two stewards be permitted to remain with her for several months, the President as-sented. Anticipating the possibility of political backlash, Tazewell Shepard, JFK's former naval aide, recommended in a memo that Mrs. Kennedy be declared "a Government agency." President Johnson dismissed this suggestion, while approving the long-term loan of an 18-foot Coast Guard boat for Jackie's use and enjoyment.

Cognizant of the political benefits of remaining on solid terms with the former First Lady, Lyndon Johnson did everything he could to make her transition easy. On December 11, 1963, with Johnson's sanction, Congress voted Mrs. Kennedy office space for one year (later extended) and a staff of her own choice (she chose Pam Turnure and Nancy Tuckerman) at a combined salary for that period not to exceed $50,000, as well as $15,000 to defray funeral expenses. In addition, she was entitled to receive the yearly pension of $10,000 granted to widows of Presidents for life or until they remarried, and free mailing privileges for life. When Jackie's office operating expenses for 1964 exceeded the allowance by $120,000, the President sent her to Bernard Boutin at GSA. "Surprisingly" said Boutin, who helped complete the paper work, "Congress acted very quickly and passed a supplemental appropriation to take care of these expenses. It was done quickly and without controversy. Jackie received the full amount."

Johnson did more. He asked Congress to rename the National Cultural Center the John F. Kennedy Center for the Performing Arts, and he sent a bill to Congress for $17.5 million to help finance the enterprise. He and Lady Bird made a substantial personal contribution to the John F. Kennedy Memorial Library Fund, a project riddled by problems and setbacks. It was not completed until 1979, when a structure of ultra-modern design was rendered by architect I. M. Pei along a desolate if picturesque stretch at Columbia Point, adjacent to the Boston campus of the University of Massachusetts.

Although Jackie apparently admired Lady Bird, she remained ambivalent toward the President. Arthur Krock observed that "The various Mrs. Kennedys didn't like Johnson at all and resented some of . . . his personal mannerisms, his personal manners."

Franklin D. Roosevelt, Jr., recalled some of the difficulties between Jackie and LBJ: "During the first three or four months after the assassination, a number of us—

Charles Bartlett was one; McGeorge Bundy was one; Averell Harriman was one; I was one; people in the State Department who were close friends of Jack Kennedy's—made it a point to stop in and see Jackie, usually for tea in the late afternoon to just buoy up her spirits. Sometimes there would be as many as a half-dozen old friends. This little group paid attention to Jackie in her hour of terrible loneliness.

"She was reasonably open with us, not to the extent of discussing her most intimate thoughts, but she did keep us apprised of how she fared from day to day. She mentioned she felt a good deal of pressure coming from Lyndon Johnson. He kept inviting her back to the White House, but she refused to go. Every function, every State dinner, she received a written invitation followed by a telephone call. Johnson didn't accept defeat gracefully. He recognized that Jackie was the supreme prize, the most sought-after woman in the world, and that gaining her support could constitute a vital coup. He tried every ploy imaginable. At Christmas, just before Jackie left for Palm Beach, he dispatched his daughter, Luci, with gifts for the children. He and Lady Bird sent flowers every few weeks. He offered her a number of positions in his administration—ambassadorships, chief of protocol, directorships of various governmental agencies devoted to the arts.

"I happened to be there one afternoon when he telephoned. Jackie took it in the other room. When she returned, she was fuming. 'It was Lyndon,' she said. 'He said to me, "Sweetheart, listen, Lady Bird and I want to see you over here at our next White House dinner party. Jack was a great man, but you've got to start living again." ' She was furious, and not just about his condescending attitude toward Jack. 'How dare that oversize, cowpunching oaf call me sweetheart,' she said. 'Who the hell does he think he is?'

"The next time I saw the President I told him he had hurt Jackie's feelings. 'How do you figure that?' he asked. 'Well, Mr. President, I don't think she appreciates being called sweetheart.' Johnson drew himself up to his full height and said, 'I'm tired as hell of this bullshit. Where I come from, we call the ladies sweetheart, and the ladies call their gentlemen honey. I've bent over backwards for that woman. I've done cartwheels and deep knee squats, and all I get is criticism.'

"Although they maintained contact, the relationship between Jackie and President Johnson continued to deteriorate. There was a cocktail party for Jackie at the F Street Club in Washington. Friends and associates of JFK were present in force. With the exception of a surprise party Bobby and Ethel Kennedy organized for Jackie at the Harriman house, this was the first social function Jackie had attended since the assassination. President Johnson promised to come, and he kept his promise. But I don't think anybody even spoke to him. He stood there with a drink in hand and nobody went near him.

"To the majority of these people he was still Vice-President. They resented him, and so did Jackie. She and Bobby were the focus of attention, and Lyndon Johnson was odd man out.

"I suppose Bobby was primarily to blame for the strained relations between Jackie and LBJ. The animosity that existed between Bobby and Lyndon has been widely chronicled. Their mutual distrust and distaste only increased after the assassination. Bobby had been no less devastated by the tragedy than Jackie. He couldn't sleep, couldn't work, couldn't eat. He saw Jackie nearly every day. They were bound by a common sense of loss.

"In mid-December, Jackie asked me to have a look at a house she eventually bought, a 14-room, three-story, fawn-colored brick Colonial at 3017 N Street, across the street from the Harriman residence. The asking price was $195,000. The only problem was that the house was raised high off the street by several flights of steps; it was easy to see into the windows, which meant the draperies had to be kept drawn. Jackie had become Washington's number one tourist attraction. Morning, noon and night the street was clogged with people peering in at her and the children. They would line up on both sides of the street. As Jackie walked down the block, they just stood watching, almost reverently. The local police and Secret Service had to clear a path through the crowd so she could move. Women were always breaking through police lines trying to grab and hug the children as they went in and out. Not only were the sidewalks packed with people, there was also bumper-to-bumper traffic in front of the house. The tour buses added Jackie's house to their sightseeing itinerary. Huge buses with hundreds of tourists hanging out the windows would rumble down her street. It had become a nightmare."

In January, Jackie thanked the American people over national television for their outpouring of condolences. The former First Lady made the tape of her first public statement since the assassination in Robert F. Kennedy's Justice Department office. "All the bright light [has] gone from the world," she told the cameras.

She met with Billy Baldwin to discuss the decoration of her new house. She had already begun to put away her books in the living room bookcases and mount her beautiful collection of drawings of all schools and periods.

"Look," she said to Baldwin, "I have some beautiful things to show you." She produced, one after another, small pieces of Greek sculpture and Roman fragments, each one a rare treasure. "These are the beginnings of a collection Jack started," she added. She began placing the lovely objects around the room. Then she said: "It's so sad to be doing this. Like a young married couple fixing up their first house together. I could never make the White House personal . . ." She choked back tears. "Oh, Mr. Baldwin, I'm afraid I'm going to embarrass you. I just can't hold it in any longer." Sinking into a chair, she buried her face in her hands and wept. Although he wanted to comfort her, Baldwin didn't know what to say; he remained seated and said nothing.

Finally, she looked up, drying her eyes with a handkerchief.

"I know from my very brief acquaintance with you that you are a sympathetic man," she said. "Do you mind if I tell you something? I know my husband was devoted to me. I know he was proud of me. It took a very long time for us to work everything out, but we did, and we were about to have a real life together. I was going to campaign with him. I know I held a very special place for him—a unique place. . . ."

Jackie talked on and on about Jack Kennedy, about their life together, about what could have been and should have been.

"Can anyone understand how it is to have lived in the White House and then, suddenly, to be living alone as the President's widow? There's something so final about it. And the children. The world is pouring terrible adoration at the feet of my children and I fear for them, for this awful exposure. How can I bring them up normally? We would never even have named John after his father if we had known. . . ."

They eventually discussed the decoration of Jackie's new home. She wanted the children's bedrooms to look exactly like their rooms at the White House, and she gave Billy photographs to help guide him. They discussed her bedroom as well, and Billy came away with a long list of notations and ideas. He also left thoroughly depressed and shaken by his meeting with Jackie.

Others came away with the self-same feeling. She spoke increasingly now of the fact that her husband's "special grace" had been replaced by the "crude folksiness" of the Johnsons, more than once referring to them as "Colonel Cornpone and his little Porkchop." She had clearly come to think of Bobby Kennedy as the heir presumptive of her husband's position, herself as the dowager queen, and the palace guard of Harvard academics and Irish "Mafiosi" (she called them "the Murph-iosi") that had surrounded John Kennedy, as a sort of government-in-exile.

But it was only on better days that she was at all able to think of politics. Usually she was too haunted by her loss to think of anything or anyone but Jack. John Davis remarked that "When the realization of her situation hit home, it was almost too much for her. Miche Bouvier visited her in Washington a month after the funeral and found her in a terrible way. She couldn't stop crying. She later told my mother that her own life was dominated by Jack's death and that everything she did and everywhere she went reminded her of him. She couldn't escape him. She would take a walk or a drive in Washington, see a sight that she associated with her husband and immediately fall apart.

"Frankly, it was difficult to think of Jackie as 'falling apart.' She seemed so basically unemotional and without feeling or sensitivity that I couldn't imagine her shedding tears. Not that she was a happy person. She had never been happy. But she wasn't the type to sit around and mope. I began to think that perhaps I had somehow underestimated my cousin."

Robert McNamara was one of those who saw a great deal of Jackie during this period. "It was terribly sad," he said. "Here she had been elevated to the position of

mythical folk heroine, yet she remained practically a
prisoner in her own home. She couldn't go out for a walk
or a bite to eat without being mobbed. I once took her to
a restaurant in Georgetown for lunch. People at neighboring tables stared; waiters and waitresses stared. I kept
praying that nobody approached her for an autograph."

At her worst, Jackie was inconsolable. She remained
in bed for long hours, taking sedatives and anti-depres-
sants by day and sleeping pills by night, unable to be
with anyone but also unable to be by herself. Left alone
with her bereavement, she became obsessed with the
thought that she had somehow failed her husband, obsessed by the assassination itself, confessing to her Aunt
Michelle that she had replayed the event a thousand
times, analyzing it from every conceivable angle and
perspective.

At other points Jackie couldn't bring herself to admit
that her husband was dead. She spoke about him in the
present and future tense ("Jack says . . ." "Jack wants . . ."
"Jack will be . . .") as though he had merely stepped
to the corner for a newspaper.

Wallowing in self-pity, Jackie sometimes lashed out at
her staff, accusing them of not working hard enough,
refusing to pay them overtime, firing them for the smallest infraction and then, remorseful, rehiring them. When
President Kennedy's secretary, Evelyn Lincoln, complained
about the volume of work, Jackie said to her, "Oh, Mrs.
Lincoln, all this shouldn't be so hard for you, because
you still have your husband. What do I have now? Just
the library." On another occasion, she asked Mrs. Lincoln why she needed so much office space in the Executive Office Building. Mrs. Lincoln explained that she
needed the space for all the presidential files and paperwork.
"But those things all belong to me!" Jackie exploded.

"She was in bad shape," confirmed Lem Billings. "She
couldn't help herself, sometimes treating Jack's old friends
the same way she treated the servants, making luncheon
appointments she didn't keep, throwing small get-togethers
she didn't attend. Yet in the middle of all this she was
capable of the most thoughtful acts. At a certain moment
when Bobby Kennedy, reaching the depths of his depression, expressed doubts about remaining in Washington
and continuing in public service, Jackie sat down and
wrote him a letter—a most feeling letter, in which she

implored him not to give up, not to quit. She told him she needed him and that the children, especially John Jr., needed him as a surrogate father, as somebody they could turn to, now that their own father was gone. And another thing—and this the most vital in the long run—was how much the country still needed him. It was time, she wrote, to honor Jack's memory—not continue to mourn it. They would both, herself included, be negligent in their responsibilities to that memory if they collapsed. Jack would want them both to carry on what he had stood for, and died for—she through the children, Bobby through public service.''

Toward the beginning of 1964, Jackie began attending small dinners at the homes of friends like Franklin D. Roosevelt, Jr., Bill Walton, Douglas Dillon, Robert McNamara and Michael Forrestal, who had served as an adviser to Kennedy and was a close associate of Averell Harriman. "No matter who gave the party," said Roosevelt, "the guest list was always the same. And at the end of the evening I would drive her home. And that's when I would worry because there would always be strangers in front of Jackie's house. They sat on the steps of the new house, ate candy and threw the wrappers on the ground. The more brazen ones would actually climb the stairs and peep into Jackie's dining-room window on the ground floor, and although there were net curtains drawn across it, at night they could see inside. 'I can't take it anymore,' Jackie used to say. 'They're like locusts, they're everywhere. I can't even change my clothes in private because they can look into my bedroom window.' "

The press was just as merciless, posting photographers and reporters outside her door on a round-the-clock basis in the event she or the children went anywhere. They would pop their flashbulbs in Caroline's face, and she would ask her mother why "those silly people" were taking her picture.

Jacqueline Hirsh, who taught French at Caroline's White House school (and had been giving President Kennedy private tutorials in that language at the time of his death), recalled the effect that the assassination had on Caroline: "I used to see her privately every Monday on N Street. For a while there it was very rough. The child just looked ghastly, so pale and unhappy. I used to take her and her cousin, Sydney Lawford, out for a walk or a drive. Caroline comprehended fully what had happened. If a reporter or photographer approached her in the car and said, 'Hi, Caroline,' she would crouch on the floor so she couldn't be seen. 'Please tell me when nobody's looking,' she would say. You could see that it was always on her mind. But she never complained, not once."

Washington attorney William Joyce, who later became outside counsel to Aristotle Onassis's Olympic Airways and whose daughter had been a classmate of Caroline's at the White House school, met Jackie at another child's birthday party when "the former First Lady was still in mourning. Caroline was there. Jackie was wearing lavender sandals and what looked like a track suit. I felt sorry for Caroline. She was one of the wannest looking children I've ever seen. Even before her father died she looked lost. She always seemed lonely, more so now than ever. Later, when Jackie married Aristotle Onassis, I had more to do with her, albeit only in an indirect sense. In fact, this was the only time I met her in person."

Toward the end of January 1964, Jackie joined Lee Radziwill, actor Marlon Brando and Brando's business manager, George Englund, for a three-hour luncheon at Washington's Jockey Club. "The sisters were enchanted by Brando," said Franklin D. Roosevelt, Jr. "Jackie found him extremely attractive. Primarily they spoke of India. Jackie told Brando that Nehru had taught her how to stand on her head and meditate. The only damper was Jackie's indignation at the press for following her to the restaurant and taking photographs as she emerged with Lee.

In an effort to "get away from it all," Jackie spent a February weekend at the Hotel Carlyle in New York and, for the first time in months, felt "like a human being—I can walk the streets and not be singled out." She began to feel that perhaps she had found her Mecca, or rediscovered it, since New York was her hometown. She came for another weekend, extended her stay, had breakfast with Irwin Shaw, lunch with Truman Capote, dinner with Pamela Hayward (Mrs. Leland Hayward was the former Mrs. Randolph Churchill and the future Mrs. Averell Harriman). She ended her stay by accompanying Bobby Kennedy to the Waldorf Towers for a visit with an ailing ex-President Herbert Hoover. According to the nurse attending Mr. Hoover, "Bobby bossed his sister-in-law around and said, 'Jackie, sit there,' 'Jackie, do this,' 'Jackie, do that.' " Despite the tension created by Bobby during the Hoover visit, Jackie felt infinitely more comfortable and relaxed in New York than she did in Washington, a town that would forever remind her of Jack and the mournful days that followed his death.

At Easter, she took the children skiing to Stowe, Vermont, where she caught up with Bobby, Ted and their families. Leaving Caroline and John Jr. with their little cousins, Jackie set out on a Caribbean holiday at Bunny Mellon's house overlooking Half-Moon Bay in Antigua. Bobby Kennedy, Lee Radziwill and Chuck Spalding also went along on the trip. When Bobby became depressed, Jackie gave him a copy of Edith Hamilton's *The Greek Way,* which he spent the remainder of the vacation reading. Bobby was still full of grief. It was "almost as if he were on the rack," said his friend John Siegenthaler.

Back in Washington, Jackie went to dinner at a French restaurant with the McNamaras and the Ormsby-Gores. David and Sissie Ormsby-Gore (Lord and Lady Harlech-to-be) had been a great comfort to Jackie in recent months, but now Jackie learned that they were to leave Washington soon and return to London. The same applied to Hervé and Nicole Alphand with regard to Paris. Jackie's crowd was slowly dispersing, and the former First Lady continued to wonder whether she too might not be better off in another city, namely New York.

Bobby Kennedy had also chosen to make his stand in New York. Richard Goodwin remarked that the "bad blood between RFK and LBJ existed on both sides. Bobby thought Johnson had tried to bull his way into the Oval Office after Jack's death, without waiting a decent amount of time. Johnson wanted to give the State of the Union message on Tuesday, which was the day after the funeral. They engaged in several bitter, mean conversations. Later, Bobby felt that Johnson was taking credit for a lot of things Jack had done, and not saying enough about the fact that President Kennedy was responsible. Bobby became enraged at anybody who had once been close to Jack showing allegiance of any kind to Johnson, including Sargent Shriver, Robert McNamara, and McGeorge Bundy.

"I stayed on through 1965, writing Civil Rights speeches mostly. It became apparent that the schism between the

two camps—Johnson versus Kennedy—would never heal.
Bobby asked if I thought Johnson might consider endorsing him for the vice-presidential spot in '64. This was before Johnson announced his intention to bypass members
of his Cabinet for the position. I said to him, 'If Johnson
had to choose between you and Ho Chi Minh as a running mate, he'd go with Ho Chi Minh.' "

Jackie's friend Joan Braden experienced another facet
of Bobby's ongoing depressions. Preparing a proposal for
a 1987 autobiography (never published), Braden depicts
Bobby as baring his grief to her over his brother's death.

"My heart wrenched from complicated tugs of emotion," the proposal reads. "He had never seemed more
vulnerable. When he asked me to go upstairs, I went. On
the bed, we kissed. Then he got up to take off his tie.
But I could not go through with it. He was hurt, silent
and angry. I watched his straight back under the street-
lights as he walked toward his car. Why hadn't I done it?
. . . Tom [Braden] would have understood, even if Ethel
would not have."

On May 29, 1964, the occasion of JFK's forty-seventh
birthday commemoration, Jackie took the children to
Arlington National Cemetery and placed flowers on their
father's grave, attended a memorial Mass at St. Matthew's and went to Hyannis Port, where she talked via
television satellite to viewers throughout Europe and the
United States, using the opportunity to transmit a message calling for world peace. When it was over she collapsed with sadness, aware that she could not remain in
Washington if she hoped to fully regain her strength.

Lee Radziwill agreed that New York would be the
better place to live. Jackie put up for sale not only her
new home on N Street, but Wexford in Virginia.

On the advice of French-born financier André Meyer,
director of Lazard Frères, she spent $200,000 on an ele-
gant fifteen-room (five bedroom/five bath) cooperative
apartment at 1040 Fifth Avenue, corner of 85th Street,
fourteen of its twenty-three windows overlooking Central
Park, the Metropolitan Museum of Art and the Central
Park reservoir, around which she was soon seen fast-
walking for exercise, trailed at a discreet distance by her
Secret Service man. Her maintenance on the apartment
amounted to $14,000 a year, a figure which has since
multiplied. In addition, she spent approximately $125,000

to have the apartment refurbished and redecorated. To temporarily replace Wexford, she rented a ten-room summer residence in Glen Cove, Long Island, five minutes from a house leased for the summer by Robert Kennedy.

Though the *Washington Post* regretted that Georgetown was losing a long-time resident, adding that she, Jackie, "came among us like some wildly unexpected fairy queen—and with her goes the heart of everyone who lived in this place when she did," her announced departure was not well received by most Washingtonians, who accused her of deserting the world of John F. Kennedy. It was a quixotic reaction, for while claiming her as national property, people were at the same time highly critical of her, the general unspoken assumption being that "mourning did not become Jacqueline Kennedy."

Jackie's resettlement held a number of personal advantages. Her friends, the McGeorge Bundys, lived at the same address. Her sister lived just down the street at 969 Fifth Avenue. Her stepbrother, Yusha Auchincloss, was a few blocks away at 1105 Park Avenue. Also in the neighborhood at 990 Fifth Avenue were Peter and Pat Lawford, while Stephen and Jean Smith resided at 950 Fifth Avenue. After Bobby Kennedy took up residence in New York, he lived at 40 United Nations Plaza.

While painters, plasterers and plumbers worked on Jackie's apartment, she moved into an eighteenth-floor suite at the Hotel Carlyle and spent her days organizing efforts on behalf of the John F. Kennedy Memorial Library, gathering together a sampling of presidential memorabilia, including Kennedy's desk and rocking chair, to be sent on a cross-country exhibition. She flew to Boston to inspect a proposed two-acre library site adjacent to Harvard. (The university, under pressure from community leaders opposed to the construction of still another high-rise structure in so congested an area, later reneged on their offer, forcing the library trustees to build in out-of-the-way Columbia Point.) While in Boston, she saw Samuel H. Beer, Eaton Professor of the Science of Government at Harvard and a member of the executive committee of the JFK Library, who remembered her from a previous meeting as being "still in a state of shock, heavily sedated, with an almost ghostly appearance. But now she looked like the Mrs. Kennedy of old—vibrant and lovely."

To raise funds for the library, she organized a mammoth assault on rich and poor at home and abroad. She mounted a one-woman telephone campaign that rivaled her efforts on behalf of the White House renovation project. Without her direct solicitation, the French government would never have given a $100,000 contribution. Jackie's old standby, Gianni Agnelli, likewise donated $100,000, and André Meyer gave $250,000. Although he would have contributed, Jackie curiously refrained from asking Aristotle Onassis.

She attended a luncheon at the Pan American Union, where it was announced that Puerto Rico had decided to join Venezuela in giving $100,000 each to the library fund, and she was guest of honor at a dinner thrown by the Stephen Smiths and the trustees of the library at the St. Regis Hotel in New York. In her black sleeveless dress and elbow-length white gloves, Jackie looked wistful and waif-like but very beautiful. Among the 300 guests were President and Mrs. Lyndon Johnson. A selection of JFK's favorite poetry was read aloud after dinner by actor Fredric March. In the margins Jackie had made notes explaining why JFK had liked each particular poem. Her comments were also read aloud.

Jackie traveled widely, interviewing well-known architects for the library. These included Louis Kahn, Mies Van Der Rohe, Philip Johnson and I. M. Pei, who eventually won the assignment. Philip Johnson recalled meeting Jackie in the sculpture garden at the Museum of Modern Art to discuss the project. "I had just finished making some alterations to the garden, which is the reason I asked her to meet me there," he said. "She seemed unaware of my involvement with the garden, and I didn't say anything. In fact it wasn't clear why we were meeting at all. She didn't speak very directly about the JFK Library, more generally about city planning, that sort of thing.

"I had the feeling when we met at MOMA that she had a long list of architects she wanted to see but that she had already made up her mind about Pei for the library. She had this list which I imagine somebody had given her and she wanted to go through the formalities. I gathered there were many problems concerning the project—a strict budget, the Kennedy family, an uncertain site. But having to deal with the entire Kennedy clan was the biggest problem. Whenever you have a group with whom to contend, you're in trouble.

"I always thought of Jackie as a kind of world planner. She's a dilettante but in the best sense of that word—she's interested in the arts and in artists, writers, architects and so forth. Although I've never been particularly Kennedyish in approach, I would have loved to do the library. My impression of the Pei product is not very positive, though I've only seen it in pictures."

On June 19, a small plane carrying Teddy Kennedy and four fellow passengers to a Massachusetts Democratic Convention at Springfield crashed outside Northampton, killing two and injuring the others. Teddy suffered cracked vertebrae and a punctured lung, but when Jackie arrived at Northampton's Cooley-Dickinson Hospital two days later, she found him sitting up in bed loudly humming an Irish ballad.

Jackie went on a two-week cruise of the Adriatic with Charles and Jayne Wrightsman, visiting Yugoslavia and spending several days with Lee and Stas Radziwill in Italy before returning to the United States for the Democratic National Convention in Atlantic City. "Now there are only five or six of us left," Bobby Kennedy told the convention, introducing a 20-minute film on his slain brother. He then quoted five lines from Shakespeare's *Romeo and Juliet,* which Jackie had suggested. The film—and Bobby's moving introduction—set the elegaic tone that would sweep the Democrats back into office. Yet Lyndon Johnson, having seen too many leftover *PT 109* tieclips on the proud chests of his Secret Service detail, fretted over Jackie's presence at the convention. Only Jacqueline Kennedy could upset LBJ's carefully laid victory plans.

"I was doing advance work for Johnson at the time," said Jerry Bruno. "Marvin Watson was the convention coordinator for the President. He was in charge. His big concern was Jackie Kennedy. He was afraid she would hit the floor, steal the convention and turn it over to Bobby. Watson asked me two or three times to keep an eye on Jackie, let him know exactly what she was doing. 'Don't let her out of your sight,' he told me. She caused more concern for the Johnson people at the '64 convention than anybody else did. As a matter of fact, they rearranged the agenda because of her. They didn't want her anywhere near the Convention Center until after the balloting. Averell Harriman enraged Johnson by organizing a reception for Jackie so she could meet all the delegates and alternates. The crush was incredible. I mean glass doors were kicked down. People were fighting to get in. She stood there for three hours smiling and shaking hands. It's fair to say that she *was* the Democratic Convention."

The convention over, Jackie lent herself here and there to Bobby's senatorial bid against Republican Kenneth Keating of New York. She even allowed Bobby to be photographed with the late President's son on several occasions and was loudly criticized for it. She attended a celebrity-studded party (guests included Paddy Chayefsky, Leonard Bernstein, Gloria Vanderbilt, Lillian Hellman, Lauren Bacall, John Kenneth Galbraith and Arthur Schlesinger) hosted by attorney William vanden Heuvel in his apartment at the Dakota.*

Having fulfilled her familial responsibilities, Jackie informed Bobby that she had no intention of voting in the forthcoming election. "I'm not going to vote for any other person, because this vote would have been his."

Back at the Carlyle, she called Billy Baldwin and asked him to do for her Fifth Avenue apartment what he hadn't finished doing to her N Street home. So that Billy could come and go at will, she placed one of her four Secret Service agents at his disposal. The tiny, slim decorator and the large, lumbering agent were soon spotted all over town together, the agent carrying Billy's roll of swatches and samples.

In September, Caroline was enrolled in the second grade at the Convent of the Sacred Heart, a prestigious Catholic school on East 91st Street; two of her cousins, Sydney and Victoria Lawford, also went there. The following fall, St. David's School welcomed a new boy in the person of John F. Kennedy, Jr. Jackie took the children to the New York World's Fair, to the circus, and rowing in Central Park. She supervised her son's riding lessons. Well-to-do matrons eavesdropped to catch the gist of her last-minute instructions to the lad: "Keep your

---

*Jackie also supported Pierre Salinger, who ran for Senator in California—and lost. Salinger's slogan was: "Let the man who spoke for two Presidents speak for you."

heels down," she whispered. On a more advanced level, Caroline rode Macaroni at a club show in West Barnstable, placing sixth out of twelve young competitors. She lacked her mother's poise and confidence on a horse but proved a far better loser.

Taking note of all the glitz and glamour, a querulous writer in the "Voice of the People" column of the *Daily News* wanted to know "What part of Harlem will Mrs. Kennedy live in as a symbol of her husband's Civil Rights bill?"

Dorothy Schiff, owner of the *New York Post,* spent two afternoons at the Carlyle with Jackie, the first in early October. They spoke at length of Robert Kennedy's campaign for New York Senator. Jackie said, "He must win. He will win. He must win. Or maybe it is just because one wants it so much that one thinks that."

They also spoke of men. Jackie felt that men over sixty were often more attractive than their younger counterparts; for instance, General Maxwell Taylor was marvelous and lean, while classmates of Jack's had let themselves go and looked awful.

Schiff finally got around to the real reason for her visit—she wanted Jackie to write a column for the *Post*.

"You could just write about places you go to and anything you like."

"Oh, I can't write," Jackie snickered. "I've had a number of requests from magazines—they all want me to write about gracious living or fashion. But I am interested in the same things Jack was interested in."

A month later, on the weekend before the first anniversary of JFK's death, Dorothy returned to Jackie's apartment at the Carlyle, this time for lunch. Jackie didn't look well. She had lost weight. Her skin, having been exposed the week before to the Palm Beach sun, appeared tanned but leathery. There were white circles under her brown eyes. Her eyes were dull. Her hair looked dusty, with no gleam to it. She said she felt disorganized.

"It was hard talking to her," Schiff noted in her diaries. "She let silences go on. She is odd and different, very much less the queen than she was."

The advent of the first anniversary of JFK's death rekindled Jackie's darkest emotions. Her sense of loss was well expressed in a passage she wrote for a memorial issue of *Look:* "Now I think that I should have known that he was magic all along. I did know it—but I should have guessed it could not last. I should have known that it was asking too much to dream that I might have grown old with him and see our children grow up together. So now he is a legend when he would have preferred to be a man."

Orville Freeman, Secretary of Agriculture under JFK, remembered that a year after the assassination, his wife Jane sent Jackie "a little note and some flowers, and she called us back and said that we were the only ones who remembered that date or that fact and said or did anything about it. She said she had just gone into Central Park and sat and had a good cry."

Rosemary Sorrentino, who still worked for hairstylist Kenneth, recalled the first anniversary "because Jackie came in to have her hair done about that time. I hadn't seen her in quite a while, but I was conscious of the date and hadn't made any other appointments for that afternoon. Provi, her maid, had told me about all the nights that Jackie stayed in her room crying her eyes out. So I wasn't totally unprepared.

"She came into my room at Kenneth's and didn't say much. I started working on her hair. She had some gray hair and said that she had tried to have it colored in Italy. I was about to dye it when she went on a crying jag, and of course I tried to comfort her. I said that one day she would realize that everything happens for a reason. I didn't know what to say. I didn't want to pry or bring up the past. I wanted to shield her as much as I could. So I just fastened on this single theme and kept repeating myself. Finally she stopped crying, and I asked if she wanted me to continue with her hair—and she did."

Jackie's renewed grief manifested itself in a number of ways, the most prevalent being anger. While always susceptible to fits of temper, Jackie's latest tantrums occurred with greater frequency and were generally more intense. Early in 1964, she had asked author William Manchester, a great admirer of President Kennedy, to write the definitive story of the assassination. In exchange for her cooperation, Manchester agreed to give Jacqueline and Bobby Kennedy editorial control over the completed manuscript and to donate a large percentage of the royalties to the JFK Library.

A motivating factor in Jackie's decision to contact Manchester was the disclosure that author Jim Bishop was also writing a book on the assassination. Bishop had written a previous book, *A Day in the Life of President Kennedy*, which had recently been published by Random House; the same publisher planned to bring out his assassination tome. Infuriated, Jacqueline wrote to Bennett Cerf, the director of Random House and an acquaintance, objecting to Bishop's proposed work and asking Cerf to dissuade the author. "I believe people know that the Manchester book will be the historically accurate account of those days," she wrote, "and I intend to see that they continue to realize that."

A few weeks later, she telephoned Cerf and restated her case. She defined Bishop as "a hack, a writer of third-rate clichés" and complained that when he came to the White House to do his *Day in the Life* volume, he took advantage of the President's invitation to "wander at will through the White House." Jackie came in one day and discovered the author counting the dresses in her private closet. Another time when little Caroline was in the bathtub, being bathed by the nurse, Jackie found Bishop sitting in the bathroom. Jackie told Cerf that her husband hadn't finished reading the galleys of *Day in the Life*. He had brought them along on that fateful trip to Texas with the intention of reading them there. She, on the other hand, had read the book and didn't like it. She was sorry they ever gave Bishop access to the White House—he had proven himself a "confounded nuisance." She considered him arrogant and she didn't like him. And now he was planning to write a book on her husband's assassination.

"Please say you won't publish the book," said Jackie, and she started to cry.

"I can't stop him from writing this book," responded Cerf. "We have a contract with him. I can refuse to publish it, true, but you know that the day I refuse to publish it, fifty other publishers will jump for it. This is a sure best-seller."

"Bennett, I'm asking you as a personal favor not to publish this book."

"The person you must talk to is Jim Bishop," said

Cerf. "I'm sure that if you ask him personally he won't do it."

Cerf gave Jackie Jim Bishop's private telephone number in Florida and she called him up. Bishop did not respond sympathetically. He didn't see why there couldn't be two books on the assassination.

"Because there can't," said Jackie.

"Well, then have the other fellow cease and desist. I am going to write my account, and that's all there is to it."

"Nobody will speak to you, nobody will interview with you," said Jackie, hanging up the phone.

Jim Bishop's *The Day Kennedy Was Shot* appeared in 1968, a year after William Manchester's *The Death of a President;* although the Bishop book sold fewer copies than the Manchester, it nevertheless had a long run on the best-seller lists, receiving excellent reviews, as did the Manchester volume. But it was published by Funk and Wagnalls, not Random House. Long before it emerged, Jackie had forgotten about Jim Bishop and turned her fury upon William Manchester, nearly destroying him in the process.

Following Jackie's appearance in black crepe and white ermine at a United Nations Christmas concert, she, Caroline and John Jr. joined the Bradens and a number of Kennedys on a skiing vacation at Aspen, Colorado. One evening Jackie told Joan Braden how much she missed Jack. "There'll never be another Jack," she said. "I now understand why he lived so intensely and on the brink. And I'm glad he did."

They had moved into their Fifth Avenue apartment, and by early 1965 Jackie was receiving visitors. Lyndon Johnson, Hubert Humphrey, Adlai Stevenson, Haile Selassie and King Hassan II all beat a path to her door. Randolph Churchill, Winston's son, sent a housewarming present in John Jr.'s name: a painted tin trunk containing a specially bound set of his father's collected works, all 49 volumes. The books were kept in the dining room and at supper the children invented a guessing game—"Which of Winston Churchill's books are we thinking of?" Bunny Mellon gave Jackie a $17,000 Louis XV bed, then cried when told she didn't care for it. Rudolf Nureyev visited, and a Secret Service agent posted outside the apartment heard strange sounds emerging from within—furniture being moved, thumps and thuds, giggling and applause: apparently the ballet star had performed a solo for Jackie in her living room. One evening, she accompanied director Harold Clurman to a production of *Tartuffe* at the Washington Square Theatre in Greenwich Village. Norman Podhoretz gave a party and invited her to meet the glittering literati; she agreed to attend only if Norman Mailer didn't. "I wasn't invited," said Mailer, "and therefore didn't have to be uninvited. But it didn't help my dying friendship with Podhoretz." Jackie still harbored resentment against Mailer for his critical attack on her television tour of the White House. Midge Decter, the wife of Norman Podhoretz, later termed Jackie "the world's oldest 16-year-old."

In mink and diamonds, Jackie attended a gala performance of *Tosca* at the Met. At her request, Met director Rudolf Bing took her backstage and introduced her to the female lead. Maria Callas hadn't performed at the Met in nearly seven years. "You were magnificent," said Jackie. "You are magnificent, too," responded the prima donna. They exchanged smiles and shook hands. They were soon to come out swinging.

Jackie went skiing at Whiteface Mountain in upstate New York, stayed several days with the Radziwills in Acapulco (she became depressed again because it reminded her of her honeymoon with Jack), then returned to New York to catch Maurice Chevalier's one-man Broadway show. Author Philip Roth escorted her to small dinner parties in Manhattan. Bill Walton, who eventually moved to Manhattan, took her to museums and art galleries. *New Yorker* cartoonist Charles Addams squired her to the movies and to New York's finest restaurants.

Kay Lepercq, a close friend of Addams's, remembered conversations she had with him about Jackie: "Ever since Jackie flirted with my former husband at that dinner party in Washington, I remained curious about her. 'What is she like?' I asked. 'I wish I knew,' he [Addams] said. He admitted he was so befuddled by her he sent one of her letters to a handwriting analyst without identifying Jackie as its author. He received an extremely negative report on the handwriting. It was the script of an egomaniac.

"When they went out, she constantly complained that

she couldn't go anywhere without people staring at her. They would be in the lobby of a movie theater and people would start jostling each other so they could get a closer look. She told Charlie she wanted nothing more than a peaceful evening at the movies. So I said to him, 'Well, perhaps she should consider letting down her hair— she used to wear her hair in a huge bouffant—and stop wearing sunglasses indoors. Then, maybe, she won't be instantly identifiable.'

"On occasion, you had to feel sorry for Jackie. I knew a woman who lived in the same building and whose maid was friendly with Jackie's cook. I went over there once and met the cook and she was telling me what a horrible and mean and nasty person Jackie could be. I said, 'How do you know that?' And she said, 'Oh, through the keyhole, over the telephone and from the wastebasket.' I have to believe that half her employees were snitching on her to the press and the other half were writing books about her."

Tobacco heiress Doris Duke, whom Jackie visited at her estates in both Newport and Somerville, New Jersey, prescribed a stricter code in dealing with servants than that which Jackie followed. Phil Strider, Miss Duke's butler, overheard Doris's directives. "When I hire somebody," she said, "I give him or her a printed sheet of rules, and keep a copy posted on the bulletin board. The first rule is that the employee will be dismissed if he discusses his employment or employer—with anyone at any time. You must be firm with them, or they will step all over you."

Doris Duke's Victorian regulations didn't quite fit Jackie's nouveau sensibility, but the former First Lady did eventually agree to serve as a member of Doris Duke's Newport Restoration Foundation, a project designed to restore and rehabilitate many of the area's Colonial structures and homes. "With Doris Duke's money and Jackie's taste, how can the project fail?" asked the *New York Post.* "Jackie lent her name to the foundation but didn't do a thing for it," said Dick Banks. "Doris never said anything about it because they're friends, but she was dismayed. As for publicity, Jackie loved it, couldn't get enough of it. It's the old saw: she protesteth too much."

The late Flora Whitney Miller, former chairwoman of

the Whitney Museum of Art, agreed that Jackie's mind wasn't on philanthropic causes at this point: "She had been a member of our Board since 1962 but didn't do very much of anything. I suppose she was too involved with her own projects—the JFK Library and so forth. We even gave her a title—chairwoman of the museum's National Committee—and she did attend the ribbon-cutting for the dedication of the new site on Madison Avenue. She brought along André Meyer and posed for photographers. It was all show. I never felt she took a great interest in what we were trying to do. In 1968, we happily honored her request that she not be reappointed to the Board. I recognize that she had other concerns and priorities, but she never struck me as anything other than a publicity maven who had been elevated to an impossible position by virtue of having been the slain President's widow. If she hadn't married John Kennedy, she would have turned out just like her sister—a dull, self-centered, spoiled jet-setter with no abiding interests outside her own small packet of concerns, mostly of a personal nature."

In April when the Johnsons dedicated the East Garden to her, Jackie dispatched her mother to the White House festivities in her stead, thereby offending the Johnsons. Instead of revisiting the White House, she chose later in the year to attend a $150-per-head benefit for the Boston Symphony Orchestra, as well as a benefit in New York for Asia House. She tried to appease the President by sending him three crayon drawings by John-John, and an accompanying letter: "You must have left that art phase when Luci left the 3rd grade."

"No matter what Jackie did she was lambasted for it," lamented Franklin D. Roosevelt, Jr. "She felt self-conscious and afraid. She was in therapy in New York, but the kinds of problems she had don't disappear in a day."

Jackie's behavior was erratic. There were times when she seemed to withdraw from everyone. Liza Minnelli, having her hair done at Kenneth's one day, saw Jackie as the former First Lady was about to leave. She walked up to her and said, "Hello, Mrs. Kennedy. I'm Liza Minnelli. Do you remember me?" Jackie practically ignored her. She smiled coldly and turned her head away. The slight, while perhaps not intentional, had become a common gesture on Jackie's part. Her oldest friends were often afraid to approach her for fear of being similarly ignored or even reproached.

One reason for her mounting reserve was the constantly escalating onslaught of attention heaped upon her by the media. Reporters and photographers were everywhere, and the more she barricaded herself behind elaborate screens of privacy, the greater seemed her allure, her mystery, and the more heated and sophisticated became the attempts to invade her privacy. She nevertheless sought refuge behind a series of masks, her favorite being the large oval sunglasses and the forced frothy smile, which while no disguise must have provided a sense of security. The big smile led one acquaintance to dub her the "Manhattan Mona Lisa."

According to most accounts she became increasingly paranoid. It began to seem to her that the same "they" who had murdered her husband were now bent on commercializing and degrading her. Every doorman, delivery boy, neighbor, waiter, taxi driver, anyone who had ever attended her in a store or smiled at her on the street, was a potential enemy. She seemed suspicious of everyone. She refused to step into a taxicab until her Secret Service agent had inspected it thoroughly. Her friends were instructed not to talk to reporters under threat of banishment from her circle. Pam Turnure and Nancy Tuckerman, who were now working for Jackie out of a crowded four-room suite at 400 Park Avenue, were told not to reveal even what books they were reading. A young woman who was giving piano lessons to Caroline Kennedy, and who disclosed that fact to a journalist, was summarily dismissed. Doris Duke's sobering advice began finally to make sense to Jackie. When a cook (the one who spied on her) let it be known that Jackie had gone from a size 12 to a size 8 and back to a size 10, she was fired. A second cook, Annemarie Huste, was dismissed because she announced her intention to publish a cookbook. A private limousine service that Jackie used occasionally was advised that no individual driver could be dispatched for Jackie more than twice, so that no chauffeur would have intimate knowledge of her more frequent destinations.

Her apparent paranoia wasn't helped by a series of ghoulish incidents involving Caroline and John-John. As Caroline returned home one day, a middle-aged woman approached her on the street and told her that she had evidence that her father, the late President, was still alive; the woman then began shouting epithets at the frightened child.

Caroline's Secret Service escort whisked her into the lobby of her building and police took the distraught woman to Bellevue Hospital for psychiatric observation. The woman was apparently well known at Bellevue, boasting a long history of mental disturbance.

It was Jackie herself who had to cope with the gaggle of boys who followed her and John Jr. after school one afternoon, shouting: "Your father is dead! Your father is dead!" "He squeezed my hand as if to reassure me," Jackie told friends. The boy's teacher at St. David's told her that John Jr. made enemies as easily as friends, and only the other day had punched a classmate in the nose.

"Jackie wasn't upset about the nose-punching incident," said Peter Lawford. "If anything, she was proud. She was worried that without a father, he might grow up to be a hairdresser."

Photographer Stanley Tretick gave Jackie a photo album of pictures he had taken for *Look* of John Jr. with the President. "She hadn't wanted me to take the pictures," said Tretick. "But now she was very appreciative and talked about how the kids would run to the President when he stepped off the helicopter, how he hugged them, things like that. It seemed the memories were kind of tough and she just needed to hash them over from time to time. It was therapeutic for her, like talking to a psychiatrist."

Princess Lee Radziwill threw a bash which she called "a teeny tiny dance for less than 100—just a little thing we're giving to brighten Jackie's day." Lee might have gotten away with this offhand attempt to downgrade her party, were it not for her impressive guest list, headed by her sister. Flashbulbs went off as Jacqueline Bouvier Kennedy arrived in a white silk Yves Saint Laurent evening gown and white mink jacket, escorted by Averell Harriman. Others at the party included Leopold Stokowski, Sam Spiegel, Leonard Bernstein, Sammy Davis, Jr., Maurice Chevalier, Arlene Francis, Bunny Mellon, Pierre Salinger, Adlai Stevenson, Franklin D. Roosevelt, Jr., Pat Lawford, Stephen Smith and Bobby Kennedy. Another guest at the party was Mike Nichols who quickly emerged as Jackie's leading admirer. Several years younger, Nichols pursued her (though simultaneously dating Gloria Steinem), and as a friend of his cryptically reported, "wound up having something more than a friendship and less than a romance with Jackie.".

The soirée marked the onset of a hectic period in Jackie's life. In May 1965, Great Britain invited her to attend the ceremonial inauguration of a monument to John F. Kennedy at Runnymede where King John had signed the Magna Carta. There the British government had set aside a corner of an English field which would be forever the property of America. Traveling with Jackie in an aircraft made available by President Johnson were Bobby and Ted Kennedy, Secretary of State Dean Rusk, six American Secret Service agents, two agents of the British Special Branch, Jackie's children and retainers. At the ceremony, Queen Elizabeth saw Jacqueline Kennedy shed a discreet tear as speaker after speaker extolled her husband's deeds. Writing to President Johnson after the ceremony, Jackie noted, "It was such an emotional and difficult day for me—so many thoughts of all my loss surged in me again."

While still in London, Caroline and John Jr. sat for artist Cecil Beaton. Their mother felt Beaton successfully captured Caroline's sensitivity tinged by sadness, and marveled at the resemblance between John Jr. and the late President at the same age, though the boy would grow up to look much more like his mother. As much as she appreciated the artwork, Jacqueline would not have cared for Beaton's description of her in his *Diaries:* "She is very much an over-lifesize caricature of herself. Huge baseball players' shoulders and haunches, big boyish hands and feet; very dark, beautiful receptive eyes looking roguish or sad—sometimes they pop too much—mouth very large and generous, with a smile turning down at the corners in an inverted laugh; a somewhat negroid appearance; the suspicion of a mustache, and very dark hair."*

In June, Jackie hired a new governess for the children. (Maud Shaw had retired during their trip to England, annoying Jackie by announcing her intention to write a

*See Cecil Beaton, *Self-Portrait with Friends: The Selected Diaries of Cecil Beaton, 1926–1974,* p. 341; also Hugo Vickers, *Cecil Beaton: A Biography,* p. 491.

book on her experiences with the Kennedys.) Later in the month she toured Canada, visited Boston, attended the New York premier of *Leonard Bernstein's Theater Songs* and went house-hunting in New Jersey.

In July, she celebrated her 36th birthday with the Kennedys at Hyannis Port, where she had inherited her husband's house. Then she flew to Virginia to see Bunny Mellon and turned up at Hammersmith Farm to help her mother plan the construction of a new windmill residence on the property, their old windmill having burned to the ground.

In August, she went to Boston to attend Cardinal Cushing's birthday party and returned to Newport for a party given by Senator and Mrs. Claiborne Pell. Toward the end of August, Jackie and author George Plimpton, who had grown very close to Jackie's children, gave a party at Hammersmith Farm for Caroline Kennedy and all her playmates. "It was an end-of-summer deal for all the children, and there were maybe seventy kids there that day," said Plimpton. "It was a sort of treasure hunt. I wrote a pirate's log and Jackie read it to the children, all collected around her, and then there were various clues around the estate. A group of us were dressed up as pirates. It was quite elaborate, I must say. We went to the Coast Guard station and they gave us a long boat. In the boat were Senator Claiborne Pell, Anthony B. Akers, John Barry Ryan III, a fellow named 'Bev' Bogert—who was dressed in an admiral's outfit—and myself. There must have been seven of us in there, as I recall, all dressed up as pirates and armed to the teeth. Jackie made us up. Then the kids, after running around Hammersmith Farm and picking up all these clues, finally came down to the water where the treasure could be found—it was a chest full of fake pearls and other gemstones, and there was a brown rubber snake on top of the lid. According to the log I had written, as soon as the first shovel hit the earth near the treasure the pirates were supposed to come to reclaim the chest. As soon as the kids reached the treasure, there was a terrible yell from the sea and around the bend came this long boat with all of these pirates. Half the children turned and ran, the other half jumped up and down and cheered. I remember I stepped off the boat and plunged into about fifteen feet of cold water. Aside from that little mishap, it was a great deal of fun."

In September, Jackie attended a birthday party at Hyannis Port for Joan Kennedy, accompanied Rose Kennedy to Boston and was guest of honor at a dinner party in New York given by Charles and Jane Engelhard.

In October, she attended a United Nations reception for Pope Paul VI. Then she rented the Sign of the Dove restaurant and "Killer Joe" Piro's discotheque band for a midnight buffet and early morning dance party that she and William vanden Heuvel gave in honor of John Kenneth Galbraith. She leased a small farm from Mr. and Mrs. W. Douglas Barden of Bernardsville, New Jersey, in the middle of fashionable Essex Fox Hounds Club country. A few years later she purchased a renovated barn on ten acres down the road from her Bernardsville friends and neighbors, the Murray McDonnells, an Irish Catholic clan as large and as wealthy as the Kennedys. Jackie boarded her horses and ponies with the McDonnells.

In November, she became exceedingly depressed, and in her sadness turned to Truman Capote. Bennett Cerf, Truman's publisher, having been told the story, recounted it in his unpublished oral history at Columbia University:

"Truman arrived home* and there was a girl waiting for him in his house, a girl who had a key to his apartment, and was upstairs painting when he arrived, waiting for him to come home. That girl was Jacqueline Kennedy. It was just about the anniversary of the assassination— two years . . . after the assassination. She was very low. Who did she turn to? Her great friend Truman Capote. As Phyllis [Cerf's wife] said, 'That was one place where she knew she was safe alone.' The Secret Service were in the car below. Truman went to the refrigerator and found two bottles of the best champagne on ice. The two of them together killed these two great big bottles of champagne and sat up practically all night talking. At about five in the morning, Jackie went down to her car and went home with the Secret Service people."

---

*Capote, a neighbor of Robert F. Kennedy, lived at the United Nations Plaza in Manhattan.

26

"After Jackie left Washington we saw very little of her," recalled Charles Bartlett. "We accompanied her on a trip to Cambodia in 1967, but otherwise we saw her only in the Far Hills-Peapack-Bernardsville [New Jersey] area, where she had her weekend house and my in-laws had theirs. I had the feeling she didn't want to be reminded of the past."

Toni Bradlee also gradually lost contact with Jackie. "There was a kind of disconnectedness on her part as to what a best friend is supposed to be," she said. "I don't think she probably ever had a very close friend. There are people who have best friends and there are people who don't. Some people prefer to have many acquaintances and no close personal friends. That seemed to be Jackie's mode. I'm not sure she ever really experienced the need for an intimate friend. She had social friends—Bunny Mellon, Jayne Wrightsman, Nancy Tuckerman—but there are friendships and then there are friendships.

"My former husband [Ben Bradlee] wrote a book called *Conversations With Kennedy,* which didn't please Jackie, but I don't think that would have had much to do with how she felt about me, really. I can't explain it. Neither one of us made an overture. We saw each other occasionally, briefly. It wasn't unfriendly, but it was painful. I think it brought back bad memories for Jackie."

A number of former friends felt slighted by Jackie. Photographer Richard Avedon was discarded for supposedly issuing a negative statement about JFK's political policies. Charles Addams, although he didn't remember it, apparently made an indiscreet comment to a reporter and received similar treatment. John B. White, who hadn't seen Jackie in some time, was walking on the street in D.C. to Bill Walton's house, "and there she was at his [Walton's] front door. It had been such a long time, and

461

she was by then a widow. She was living in New York. It was about three years after the assassination. She seemed uncomfortable on seeing me again. There was nothing left between us. She had a whole new world of friends. She acted as if there was no need for me to even appear. And I have never heard from her since."

Jackie had entered a bright new universe. She had left politics behind and in its place had adopted international society. Her broad smile could be discerned flashing across any of two dozen varied landscapes. She would turn up for lunch with Vivi Stokes Crespi at the Colony in Manhattan, in her Chez Ninon navy blue Balenciaga coat, wearing a crisp camelia on one shoulder, a Coco Chanel handbag dangling from the other, though Chanel herself proclaimed Jackie "the worst dresser on any continent." La Côte Basque diners looked up dazzled to see her enter with Cecil Beaton (after falling out with Jackie and her sister Lee, Truman Capote lampooned them both in the "La Côte Basque" section of his unfinished novel, *Answered Prayers*).

One evening she appeared at the Russian Tea Room with Arthur Schlesinger, then on to the Copa. Another night she dined with Mike Nichols at Sardi's, then went with him to Arthur's, Sybil Burton's popular discotheque. They danced and held hands. She and Nichols, together with actor Alan Arkin and his wife, turned up at Nathan's hot dog stand in Coney Island for franks, fried clams and french fries. There were other meals—at Le Mistral, La Grenouille, La Caravelle, Orsini (where she gave a small dinner party for Nureyev), and again, on a cold day, she was at the Colony with Baron and Baroness Fabrizio Serena and Allessandro di Montezemolo. The topic of discussion was the recent floods in Florence that were destroying that city's most treasured works of art.

Jackie immediately became involved, telephoning Bobby Kennedy and Robert McNamara to see what funds could be mobilized through official channels. She was also named Honorary Chairman of C.R.I.A., the Committee for the Rescue of Italian Art, an organization that launched public appeals and private fund-raising affairs. Art historian Paul Oskar Kristeller, a member of the same group, remembered attending a meeting at the Institute of Fine Arts at New York University. "It was attended by most of the Committee, and was presided over by Mrs. Kennedy. I spoke up and said I hoped that a decent share of the funds would be allotted to the preservation and the restoration of art books and manuscripts and documents.

"Mrs. Kennedy responded in a rather sarcastic way: 'You will not convince the general public and our donors that this is as important as the works of art themselves.'

"I spoke back at her and said, 'I don't care what the donors say—this is a necessary expenditure.'

"I am happy to report that I was backed by the other art historians present, because they realized the importance of manuscripts and books, since many of them use such materials for their own research. So the Committee supported me in standing up to Mrs. Kennedy. She was a charming lady, but she didn't understand the point. She was opposed, and she was voted down. The libraries and the archives received their funds, not only from this country but also from other countries, and from the Italian government, and there was a strong effort to repair the damage."

She also served on a committee to try and save the 83-year-old New York Metropolitan Opera House from demolition and eventually crossed swords with another authority in the field, Metropolitan Opera House manager Rudolf Bing, who told the press that Mrs. Kennedy had attended the opera "only rarely," knew nothing about it, wasn't the least bit interested in it and had no knowledge of the rundown condition of the building. "I regret," he went on, "that such a distinguished lady allows herself to comment on something about which she is so ill-informed."

Although she had regained her natural vigor, Jackie continued to visit Dr. Max Jacobson from time to time. "I saw her at the office after the assassination," said Ken McKnight. "She was with Clint Hill. I suspect the terrible events of those years had drawn them close. He was often the only human being who could probably understand her terror and anguish. From what I understand, he felt as awful about the assassination as she did. He once broke down on the TV show '60 Minutes.' He began to cry, saying over and over he wished he had been killed instead of Kennedy, which is a terrible burden to carry around."

Ruth Jacobson, Max's third wife, also encountered Jackie in the office. "The day I saw her," said Ruth, "she was with Lee Radziwill. They were both giggling and acting silly. I can't say they were drunk, but they were acting very giddy."

In mid-1966, Jackie wrote to Lady Bird Johnson in response to a letter seeking advice on the continuation of the White House restoration project. Among other things, Lady Bird was eager to acquire a new set of china for the White House. "Just a word of warning," wrote Jackie. "Don't let the American china companies do it—I had them trying to copy plates of the Monroe period . . . from our first days in the White House. The results always looked more like hotel china than the Truman & Eisenhower plates do now . . . Jansen (in Paris) is the one to do it. . . . Luckily they have a New York office—so one avoids the buying-it-abroad problem. . . .

"The only other thing I can think of is trying to keep the public rooms—ground and first floor—as 18th and 19th century as possible—so no one in the future will ever change it—and it will remain always a glimpse for Americans back into the days of our country's beginning."

She had one other suggestion to offer. Concerning a donor who had lent the White House several valuable portraits, she wrote: "The Fine Arts Committee should threaten, persuade, seduce, coerce him to leave them permanently to the White House, even in his will."

She had David Webb, whom she now privately addressed as "Cellini," mount a piece of coral that JFK had picked up off one of the Solomon Islands during World War II and make a necklace of it for her. She wore it for the first time with a bright pink jumpsuit while entertaining Diana Vreeland. She was invited by New York socialites John and Didi Ryan to their apartment to play "Camouflage," a sort of Easter egg hunt for everyday objects half-hidden in a drawing room. She took John Jr. to Serendipity for hamburgers and slush sundaes. Dining at Le Pavillon with the visiting Hervé Alphands, she switched the conversation from French to English when Bobby Kennedy joined the party and was overheard saying, "Oh Bobby, you're so-o-o-o reckless." She then told her dinner companions that the most important thing to her about a man "is that he must weigh more and have bigger feet than I do." When approached for an autograph by another diner, she replied with a smiling, breathy "No—thank you."

There were other doings. She and her sister Lee emerged from the Lafayette Restaurant in matching mini-skirts that fell five inches above the knee. Standing outside Bergdorf Goodman with her, Mike Nichols said, "Taking you any place is like going out with a national monument." "Yes," she responded, "but isn't it fun?" Asked by Bunny Mellon whether she had seen Billy Baldwin recently, Jackie replied, "Why, yes, I almost stepped on him in the elevator yesterday."

After visiting Lasata, her grandfather's former estate at East Hampton, she told the wealthy Fifi Fell that it was both "smaller and less luxurious" than her childhood memory. Soviet poet Yevgeny Yevtushenko came away from Jackie's Fifth Avenue apartment amazed by her knowledge of Russian literature. She would sit with George Plimpton while he read Caroline to sleep at night with selections from Robert Louis Stevenson's *Treasure Island*. ("I learned it's very difficult to read Robert Louis Stevenson to a young girl," he said. "I always thought *Treasure Island* would knock her dead, but I don't think we ever got through the first two pages of the book before she fell asleep.")

Jackie was a regular at Nicholas Kounovsky's fashionable and exclusive gym on West 57th Street. Ivo Lupis, one of her instructors, said: "It was the 'in' place in those days. Only people with 'means' were members and there were only a few places like it where women could go. Physical conditioning and jogging hadn't yet become a craze. In order to attend Kounovsky's, one was interviewed. Although some people regarded this as a screening device, in fact it was instituted only as a means of evaluating the individual's physical ability. But it did contribute to the gym's elite aura. So did Jackie."

A pattern had emerged. The former First Lady spent Mondays through Fridays in New York, weekends and holidays in New Jersey, vacations in faraway resorts. She particularly enjoyed her Bernardsville horsey-set weekends. Because of her high visibility there were some initial reservations to her joining the Essex Fox Hounds Hunt Club, but these were quickly overcome when influential members such as C. Douglas Dillon and Murray McDonnell spoke up in her behalf.

"I helped Jackie get into the club and I helped her socially when she first came to Bernardsville," said Dillon. "I suppose some of the club members were wary of having reporters chase them around. These are people who insist on maintaining a low profile. I told them that Jackie felt the same way."

Lewis C. Murdock, retired banker and Master of the Hunt, observed that members didn't want publicity "for the simple reason that we're located so close to New York. It makes people want to come out here to see what's going on and to hunt fox. We haven't enough country to accommodate all those people. It also bothers the members to have strangers snooping about; it creates opposition to the hunt. Fox hunting requires space and tolerant neighbors, which is why we're selective about who joins."

The quaint, moneyed reaches of Somerset County, with its English village flavor, became the place Jackie went "to get away from it all." She opened charge accounts at all the local stores, including Beval, where she went to have her riding needs attended to. Beverly L. Walter, the proprietor, had known Jackie since her early Kennedy days "when she first rode to hounds in Virginia. Now that she had a nearby home, she became a steady customer."

When not riding to hounds, she could be found on a "hack," more often than not on some unsuspecting neighbor's property. "She would hack, or ride informally through the woods, usually on my land," said Patricia Shea of Bedminster. "She would bring her horse in a van, park on our dirt road and ride through the pine trees. She loved it. Because of who she was I never said anything, but it did irk me that she never asked permission."

If Bernardsville offered privacy, Jackie's frequent travels provided diversity. She and the children started 1966 with a ski vacation with Bobby Kennedy and his family at Sun Valley, Idaho, then headed for the Alpine ski slopes of Gstaad, Switzerland, where they were the guests of John Kenneth Galbraith, staying in a neighboring chalet vacated by the owners for the occasion.

After Gstaad, Jackie went to Rome and, despite assurances to friends that she wanted to spend "a quiet few days," the Roman aristocracy went into high gear. Everywhere she went, the adoring crowds cheered and applauded her. Princess Irene Galitzine threw a small dinner in her behalf and made her an ankle-length black gown for her return visit with the Pope. She dined with sculptor Pericle Fasine at George's, a smart English restaurant. She went on a fox hunt with her husband's former schoolmate, Count Dino Pecci-Blunt, and was entertained by Prince Aspreno Colonna at an elegant private dinner party for thirty at the 15th-century ocher-colored Palazzo Colonna. She also visited the villa of Gianni Agnelli at the exclusive beach resort of Forte Del Marmi.

But most of her time in Rome was spent with Valentino, then a little-known couturier outside his native Italy, whose understated, fluffy creations she had discovered several years earlier in New York. After she moved into her Fifth Avenue apartment, Valentino went to see her with his entire collection, a fitter, an assistant and a model. She decided to adopt him as her dressmaker-in-chief and over the next five years he designed scores of dresses for her. As in the White House, she continued to have the bills sent to the attention of Joe Kennedy.

Over Easter vacation, Jackie took the children to Cordoba, Argentina, to stay on the cattle ranch of Miguel A. Carcano, whose daughters had been friends of Joe Kennedy's sons. While there, John-John placed a stone on a stone monument laid years earlier by his father. Jackie was photographed by some professional lensmen hidden in the bushes while she changed into a bathing suit on a private beach. The rear views appeared in the Argentine magazine *Gente,* but newspapers in the United States refused to reproduce them. Unfazed by the incident, Jackie returned to New York, dropped off the children and two days later departed on a trip to Spain organized by the Duke and Duchess of Alba, as well as Angier Biddle Duke, America's new Ambassador to Spain.

Jay Rutherford, Duke's assistant in the Office of Protocol during the Kennedy administration and currently the representative in Madrid for Hearst Headlines and the Mutual Broadcasting System Corporation, flew to New York to accompany Jackie back to Spain: "I had been asked by *Constanza* magazine to write an article on Jackie's visit to Spain. Since I already knew her, I thought I might get an insider's view. I spent several days going over the ground rules with Nancy Tuckerman. Every quote, I was told, had to be cleared with her first, which precluded the possibility of turning out a fresh, newsy kind of story.

"There was still a tremendous amount of interest in Jackie and all kinds of sidebar speculations in the European press on her relationship with Antonio Garrigues, Spain's Ambassador to the Vatican. Garrigues, 62, a widower with eight children, had been a great friend of the Kennedy family. He and Jackie had last seen each other during her recent visit to Rome, and journalists immediately elevated this into a Cinderella story.

"She became annoyed when we landed in Madrid and were greeted by hundreds of reporters all yelling questions at her at once. She said something to me about feeling as if we were back at Madison Square Garden. Of course she knew how to handle the media. She had lots of practice. We spent a night in Madrid and the following day left for Seville."

With typical Spanish hospitality, the Duke and Duchess of Alba warmly greeted Jackie upon her arrival in Seville, installing her in the Palacio de las Duenas. Mrs. Robin Duke had made her own hairdresser available to Jackie, flying her from Madrid for the duration of Jackie's stay. While having her hair done, she glanced at the latest issue of *Womens Wear Daily,* which reported that she had become one of the "REALGIRLS—honest, natural, open, decontrived, de-kooked, delicious, subtle, feminine, young, modern, in love with life, knows how to have fun." Her first major invitation in Seville was the International Red Cross Ball, a glamorous charity debutante party for 2,500 guests hosted by the Duke of Medinaceli in the courtyard of his Casa de Pilatos. There Jackie ran full-face into the 250 photographers who were to crowd and jostle the guests and each other throughout the visit. She also encountered a frosty Princess Grace of Monaco, accompanied by the Prince, both piqued at being upstaged by Jackie. When Mrs. Kennedy arrived at the ball, Princess Grace disappeared into the nearest powder room and remained hidden for the next hour, while Prince Rainier stepped outside to nervously smoke a cigarette.

Several days into her vacation, Jackie seemed ready to fly back to Madrid. Adding to her annoyance were the continuing rumors linking her and Garrigues. As the rumors mounted, Ambassador Duke called an impromptu press conference, saying, "I want to make it crystal-clear and completely understood that there is no basis in fact in rumors of an engagement."

She chose to stay, and almost immediately her vacation began to improve. In Seville's magnificent bullring, Spain's three leading *toreros,* El Cordobés, Paco Camino and El Viti, all bypassed Princess Grace, offering their hats and first bulls to Jackie. In response, she hastily dispatched a U.S. Embassy aide to the nearest American airbase for three Kennedy half-dollars, which she slipped inside the hats before returning them. Though she turned away when the *picadors* lanced the bulls, she watched each pass of the bulls with fascination, proclaiming the fights "exciting and beautiful."

Cleveland Amory, speaking for the Humane Society of America, had already chastised her love of fox hunting. He now responded to Jackie's ruminations on bullfighting by writing: "It is a sad and singularly ironic footnote to our modern age of violence that Mrs. Jacqueline Kennedy, of all people, who has seen the barbarism of the present era at such tragic firsthand, should now see fit to condone and even compliment . . . one of the last relics of the barbarism of the past era."

Jackie's response to Amory was a return to the bullfights. She also decided to ride in the fair. "To visit Seville and not ride horseback is equal to not coming at all," she declared. Whereupon donning the traditional *traje corio* (black-trimmed red jacket, flowing chaps, flat broad-brimmed hat), she mounted a white stallion and made a leisurely *paseo* of the fair grounds. The press attacked her for extravagance.

"Jackie was aware that donning the Andalusian riding habit would rile critics, but she thought it a matter of good taste to do what she did since the Duke of Alba made it all available, and he was her host," said Jay Rutherford. "To do otherwise would have been rude. She was anxious to avail herself of pleasure and privilege and wasn't taking into account the consequences of public evaluation."

Just as pleasurable was the final night's American Embassy dinner given for her in Madrid, where she was seated between Prince Juan Carlos de Bourbon, today the King of Spain, then the 28-year-old heir to the throne, and Spain's Minister of Industry, Gregorio Lopez Bravo,

42, a rising star on the political scene whose vibrancy and charisma reminded her of JFK.

In early June, she took the children to Hawaii. They first flew to San Francisco and were joined there by Peter Lawford and two of his children, Christopher, 11, and Sydney, 9. With them went Lawford's long-time friend, John Spierling, a handsome Honolulu bachelor and businessman. Only Lawford's and Spierling's cars had access to the secluded Japanese-style three-bedroom beachfront house Jackie had leased in Kahala at $3,000 per month from Republican Senator Peter Dominick of Colorado.

However, she was also seen with architect John Carl Warnecke. An eligible divorced man, Warnecke joined Jackie and her children on several outings. On one of them, an overnight camping trip, John Jr. toppled backward into a campfire but was quickly pulled out by Secret Service agent John Walsh. Sustaining second-degree burns on arms, hands and buttocks, the boy was rushed to the nearest hospital, where he was treated and released. The blisters were later cut away and certain burned areas of skin removed.

After seven weeks in Hawaii, Jackie returned to celebrate her thirty-seventh birthday at a party thrown by Paul and Bunny Mellon. She then flew to Hammersmith Farm to attend the wedding of her half-sister Janet Jennings Auchincloss and Lewis Rutherford, a Princeton graduate (and direct descendant of Peter Stuyvesant), who had been teaching in Hong Kong. Dick Banks believed that Jackie's appearance at the wedding "made a three-ring circus of it, which is why Janet's friends didn't want her to be there. She came anyway, as did thousands of tourists and hundreds of news photographers. Newport was in total gridlock that day. They were there to see Jackie and John-John, who as a page was dressed like Little Lord Fauntleroy. The bride was so completely upstaged at her own wedding that she broke down in tears."

That fall, Jackie attended another wedding, this one for Pam Turnure and Robert N. Timmins, a wealthy Canadian tin magnate, at St. Ignatius Loyola Church in New York. Jackie threw a reception for the couple in her apartment. In subsequent years she both visited them and sent her children to stay with them at their home in

Montreal, an indication of just how close she had grown to her late husband's ex-lover.

"I can't imagine what drew Jackie to Kennedy's former mistress," said Truman Capote. "She was impossible to outguess. She had a tendency to overdo friendships at first, with the result that she became quickly bored or disillusioned by her enthusiasm. She developed crushes on people, but they rarely lasted. The only friendships that endure with Jackie are those where she calls the shots. Bunny Mellon has lasted because she's terrified of Jackie. Nancy Tuckerman lingers because she's Jackie's front man, her indentured slave.

"The others come and go. Robin Douglas-Home was dropped because he had the temerity to write an article on Jackie. She dropped me for a couple of reasons. First, I told the world that I sat and chatted with her in her bedroom while she dressed for dinner. Secondly, I grew too friendly with Lee. Never mind that when Jackie moved back to New York, I took care of her. I talked endlessly with her about her sorrows. I gave her a porcelain rose on the first anniversary of Kennedy's assassination. I introduced her to all my friends. Oliver Smith, former co-director of American Ballet Theater and a set designer, wanted to meet her so I arranged a luncheon at his Willow Street home in Brooklyn Heights. They became fast friends. He escorted her here and there, invited her to dinner parties, attended hers. She used to go to his home to sketch. Never a word of thanks from her for that or any other favor. She mistreated people, bounced them around like rubber balls. Look at what happened to poor William Manchester."

"Poor William Manchester" was about to be put through the wringer by both Bobby and Jackie Kennedy. She had been difficult with regard to other Kennedy books. When Maud Shaw wrote *White House Nannie,* Jackie enlisted the help of Sol M. Linowitz, then Chairman of the Board of Xerox Corporation, and threatened to sue the publisher. When Red Fay penned *The Pleasure of His Company,* she insisted on a number of changes and deletions. Although Fay complied with her requests, when he sent her his first royalty check in the amount of $3,000 as a donation to the JFK Library, she returned it. She had also been very upset with Arthur Schlesinger when *A Thousand Days* was first serialized in *Life,* but when his

book began winning literary prizes, she made up with
him. The fact remains that neither Fay nor Schlesinger
had written authorized books, whereas Manchester had
been personally approached by Jackie to write his account. In light of this, her ultimate objections to the
publication of *The Death of a President* seemed even
more unreasonable.

"When I undertook the assassination book, I was already deep into a book on the Krupps," said Manchester. "I also had a college teaching post. Jackie called and
said that Jim Bishop, whom she couldn't abide, was
about to do a book on the events of November 22.
Would I be willing to write the official account of the
assassination? I said to my secretary, 'How can I refuse
Jacqueline Kennedy?' But after nearly three years of
back-breaking research and writing, after postponing all
my other responsibilities, after the manuscript had been
edited and approved, she decided she didn't want it to
appear, or wanted it to appear in some unrecognizable
form."

Jackie's rationale, as expressed in her oral history for
the Lyndon Baines Johnson Library, was that she had
been locked "in a shell of grief . . . and it's rather hard to
stop when the floodgates open. I just talked about the
private things. Then the man went away, and I think he
was very upset during the writing of the book. I know
that afterwards there were so many things . . . which
were mostly expressions of grief of mine and Caroline's
that I wanted to take out of the book. And whether or
not they got out they were all printed around. Now it
doesn't seem to matter so much, but then I had such a
feeling.

"I know that everybody else wanted the political things
unfair to President Johnson out. And the way that book
was done—now, in hindsight—it seems wrong to have
ever done that book at that time. Don't forget, these
were people in shock. Before we moved out of the White
House, Jim Bishop was saying he was going to write a
book. . . . All these people were going to do these things,
and you thought maybe to just not have this coming up,
coming up, getting more and more sensational. Choose
one person, ask everybody to just speak to him, maybe
that would be the right thing to do. Well, it turned out
not to be."

What Jackie didn't say in her oral history was that while doing her own interviews with Manchester, she had been drinking—heavily and continually. It was the only way she could get through her reminiscences; and it helped account for the highly personal nature and tone in parts of the book. "The political things," as Jackie referred to them, had to do with Manchester's supposedly shabby depiction of President Johnson, an editorial prerogative that Robert Kennedy's advisers, including Ed Guthman, Burke Marshall, John Seigenthaler, Frank Mankiewicz, Arthur Schlesinger and Dick Goodwin (all of whom had read the manuscript and become involved in the case), felt could become a liability should Bobby eventually decide to seek national office. Incredibly, Jackie's main reader for many months was Pam Turnure, who at Jackie's instigation made written suggestions for emendations. Manchester's position was that he refused to allow a secretary to Mrs. Kennedy tell him how to write history.

The situation was further aggravated when first-serial rights were sold to *Look* magazine for $665,000, a sum slated to go not to the JFK Library but to Manchester. Because of the nature of his financial agreement with the Kennedys, these monies represented a large share of his earnings on the project. When Jackie learned of *Look*'s plans to serialize the volume, she became totally irrational. In so many words she insisted that while she had no desire to suppress the work, which was to be published in hardcover by Harper & Row (Bobby Kennedy had made this decision), she objected to its exploitation by a national magazine and was prepared to do whatever she had to do to protect her own privacy and the privacy of her children.

She was prepared to fight, she told Manchester, and she was going to win: "Anybody who is against me will look like a rat, unless I run off with Eddie Fisher."

There were two sides to the issue and both were correct. *The New York Times* ran a lead editorial summing up one side: "History belongs to everyone, not just to participants. . . . Having made her original decision [asking that the book be written], Mrs. Kennedy cannot now escape its consequences."

The other side was expressed by Richard Goodwin, who lived in William Manchester's hometown (Middletown, Connecticut) and was asked by the Kennedys to help mediate the controversy: "The Manchester controversy was a matter of law. The memorandum of understanding or contract he made with Bobby and Jackie wasn't unusual. He needed their permission to use certain quotes and ultimately to publish. Jackie felt betrayed. She was right both from a legal and ethical point of view. Manchester pure and simple broke the contract."*

In the struggle over *The Death of a President*, Harper & Row was represented by Cass Canfield and Evan W. Thomas, the men responsible for publishing John Kennedy's *Profiles in Courage* and Robert Kennedy's *The Enemy Within*, a book about the Mob. Because of their ties to the Kennedy family, the publisher took a more conciliatory view of events than the magazine. *Look*, represented by Chairman of the Board Mike Cowles and Editor-in-Chief William Attwood, who had been a diplomat under President Kennedy, demonstrated more backbone, and, in turn, incurred greater wrath.

When Mike Cowles went up to Hyannis Port to try to settle his publication's differences with Jackie Kennedy and pave the way for the book's serialization, he was figuratively mugged. "Mrs. Kennedy became very abusive," said William Attwood in an oral history he did for Columbia University. "She called Mike a son-of-a-bitch and a bastard . . . and she became quite hysterical and violent, verbally violent, to the point that Mike came back a little amazed . . . that the great lady of the funeral and all that could talk just that way.

"Mrs. Kennedy . . . had by this time . . . become really out of control so far as the rest of the family was concerned. . . . She'd become an embarrassment, certainly to Bob Kennedy, who . . . still had his political future in mind, and this kind of little sordid battle over the memoirs was not something he wanted to be involved in, nor did he want to get involved in a battle with the

*The key clause in the memorandum of understanding, signed by William Manchester on March 28, 1964, read: "The final text shall not be published unless and until approved [by Jacqueline and Robert Kennedy]." Manchester later argued that the telegram did not constitute a final statement of approval.

press, because on the whole . . . the other newspapers and magazines were instinctively on our side.''

Although Manchester felt that Evan Thomas had bent over backwards to appease the Kennedys, the Harper & Row editor defended his actions on the grounds that he wanted to work out a peaceful settlement and if possible avoid litigation. ''I think it was a mistake on Manchester's part to sign a contract with the Kennedys giving them the final editorial discretion over the contents of the book,'' said Thomas. ''But I also felt that Jackie was acting poorly. There seemed to be considerable confusion because I had sent the manuscript to her before setting it in type, and my understanding was that she, or at least the family, liked it at first, then became less than friendly about the book as time went on. I never fully understood what she objected to in specific, because she hadn't said much about it. I think an injustice was done in delaying publication. Jackie had the manuscript early on and could have resolved it then. But later on she took a hostile view of it for some reason. It upset Manchester a great deal, and me too. What upset me most was that I never understood the basis for her objection. It seems she had originally wanted a book and then, when it became reality, decided she didn't.''

Manchester shared his editor's bewilderment over Jackie's sudden about-face. From the day he turned in the completed manuscript, he had been making changes and alterations to suit the various readers of the work. ''Every time I made one concession, the Kennedys presented a whole new list of demands,'' said Manchester. ''This went on for months. Finally I said, 'no more'— and that's when all hell broke loose.''

On November 28, 1966, while Manchester was in London trying to escape a steady barrage of newspaper hype, Jackie wrote to him insisting that he make further changes: ''The changes I am talking about . . . all touch upon things of a personal nature that I cannot bear to be made public. There are many other matters, I know, but these are all of that sort, and they are absolutely necessary to me and my children. I cannot believe that you will not do this much.''

Nobody seemed to be exempt from the fracas. On December 16 of the same year, Jackie received a handwritten note from President Lyndon Johnson:

Dear Jackie:

> Lady Bird and I have been distressed to read the
> press accounts of your unhappiness about the Man-
> chester book. Some of these accounts attribute your
> concern to passages in the book which are critical
> or defamatory of us. If this is so, I want you to
> know while we deeply appreciate your characteris-
> tic kindness and sensitivity, we hope you will not
> subject yourself to any discomfort or distress on
> our account. One never becomes inured to slander
> but we have learned to live with it. In any event,
> your own tranquility is important to both of us, and
> we would not want you to endure any unpleasantness
> on our account.

Spurred on, Jackie continued to attack Manchester,
releasing a statement to the press (which had been written by Ted Sorensen) condemning the author and his
publisher. By now she had also turned against Harper &
Row for ignoring "accepted standards of propriety and
good faith," for violating "the dignity and privacy my
children and I have striven with difficulty to retain" and
for penning "a premature account of the events of November 1963 that is in part both tasteless and distorted."

Prepared to press her case in a court of law, she
ordered her attorney, Simon H. Rifkind, a former judge
and senior partner of Paul Weiss Rifkind Wharton and
Garrison, to seek an injunction preventing publication of
the book or any part thereof, and at the same time to sue
all parties involved in the proposed publication of the
book.

"Why she cooperated with the venture, read the manuscript, apparently liked it and then told the press I had
written a tasteless and terrible book I will never know,"
said William Manchester. "I spoke with that woman for
many hours, shared some of her deepest, darkest thoughts,
wrote the authorized account of President Kennedy's assassination, but I don't have the faintest idea what Jackie
Kennedy Onassis is really like. That's a question I will
take to my grave."

Legal action did not prevent behind-the-scenes negotiations. *Look*, Harper & Row and the author all finally
agreed to another round of excisions. "And when we

agreed to make the changes," noted William Attwood, "we then suggested our lawyers meet with their lawyers and with her . . . and that's when I went up to the room [at *Look*'s office] with Dick Goodwin and with her to go over the first installment, which was the one to which she most objected, which described the actual assassination.

"I recall, before I went up, Mike Cowles, whose last experience with her had been so unsettling, said, 'Whatever you do, whatever she says, however she screams, and whatever name she calls you, keep your cool.'

"I said, 'Don't worry, Mike. I've been four years in the government in Africa, and I've had a lot of people yelling at me, I've had demonstrations outside the Embassy, and she doesn't faze me.'

"Well, to my surprise, she was very quiet and agreeable and pleasant and cooperative, and we went over the areas in that long first installment to which she objected . . . and a good deal of it she had no objection to at all. . . . It was interesting because she was so agreeable during the meeting. We talked about old times and our previous meetings [in the White House], and she left with a smile. And yet, somehow or other, by the time she got to the door, she saw the press waiting for her, she managed to burst into tears, and so the headlines in the afternoon papers were, 'Jackie Leaves Meeting in Tears.' It had become a . . . public relations battle, so we had to be cast in the role of the villains who were trying to embarrass the poor widow. That caused a little bad feeling too, because it was clearly an act. If she'd done any crying it would have been upstairs with me looking at the words, and as she read the words of the shooting and the blood on her dress and brains all over the car. She read them with perfect equanimity . . . and the tears and the emotion didn't come until she faced the press."

There was an odd footnote to the Manchester case. To the dismay of many of those who felt that William Manchester had been trampled upon by the Kennedys, the author came out for Bobby Kennedy when he ran for President in 1968, calling him "Genuinely humane . . . the least understood man in the presidential arena." Jacqueline Kennedy called Manchester, and later wrote him a letter: "When I read this spring that you were giving your support to Robert Kennedy, I was absolutely startled—then so touched—and much more than that. . . .

I want you to know that the last time I saw Bobby alive we spoke of that. And it meant the same to him. . . . You gave him what he was pleading for from others—a wiping off of the blackboard of the past—a faith in now—and a generosity of such magnitude and sacrifice."

Once a Kennedy, always a Kennedy. Everything Jackie did or said in public was measured by members of the Kennedy family as being either advantageous or damaging to the clan's political image. The Manchester imbroglio hadn't helped, nor did Jackie's apparent life of luxury. She had started the new year with a return trip to Antigua. Bunny Mellon offered to buy or build her a home on this small, idyllic island, but Bobby Kennedy insisted she turn it down. Bobby and Teddy Kennedy together forced her to terminate the grant she had received from the government to keep open her Park Avenue office.

"Jackie had her problems with the Kennedys," said French journalist Paul Mathias. "JFK left behind an estate worth $15 million, but most of it was locked up in trusts for the children. The will hadn't been updated since 1954 and didn't contain adequate provisions for Jackie's welfare. She purchased her Fifth Avenue apartment with the money from the sale of her house in Georgetown, and she purchased that house with monies left to her children. There was a trust in Jackie's name which yielded $150,000 per year; if she remarried, this trust reverted to the children. She had money from the sale of the house at Atoka and she owned the house at Hyannis Port, which after JFK's death included a trailer in back of the house. She had it installed for the Secret Service because she didn't want them hanging around inside her house. She found them intrusive. There were some incidental sums, the widow's stipend that she received from the government as well as Kennedy's personal possessions: books, artifacts, furniture. All told she had about $200,000 a year on which to live. Bobby supplemented her income with a $50,000 annual allowance. But even this didn't take her very far. Here was somebody who loved beautiful objects, who would spend $100,000 on a snuff box or a flower pot that had once belonged to Catherine the Great.

"The Kennedys didn't care a whit about snuff boxes or Fabergé eggs or Persian rugs. All their homes looked like a Howard Johnson. They didn't go in for great art or furniture or porcelain. They're interested in power, in politics. They spent their money on buying votes. Andy Warhol could have been elected President for the amount Joe Kennedy spent to get JFK into office. But they didn't spend on anything else. They never tipped. They paid their help as little as possible. After Joe Kennedy suffered his stroke, they began importing their help—gardeners, cooks, maids—from Costa Rica and the Dominican Republic, because they were the only ones who would work for those kind of wages. They never had money with them. They charged everything. They went to Stop & Shop and they charged. Ethel Kennedy would drive into a local gas station and say 'Fill'er up,' and the gas station attendant would say, 'Do you have any cash with you today, Mrs. Kennedy?' They were the joke of Hyannis Port. And Bobby was as cheap as his father. Jackie couldn't go to him and say, 'Look here, I just stopped by A La Vieille Russie and I saw this darling little 18th-century decanter for only $60,000.' He would have laughed in her face. Even convincing him to spring for day-to-day essentials wasn't easy. Jackie needed a new car. To get it she practically had to bribe him by promising to go on the stump if and when he ran for President.

"There were rumors that after the assassination Jackie and Bobby became involved in a sexual relationship. Jackie, as we know from her marriage to JFK, had a history of going after unobtainable men. And Bobby, while nothing like JFK, enjoyed his share of flings. I would be amazed, however, to learn that the relationship between Jackie and Bobby had ever been consummated. I won't rule out the possibility of a flirtation, the possibility that something might in time have developed. Under the circumstances, there is nothing terribly far-fetched about that."

Mary DeGrace, who worked for Ethel Kennedy at Hyannis Port for seventeen years, was well aware of the rumors concerning Bobby and Jackie. "It was back-room gossip at the compound," she said. "There were reports all the time in the tabloids about this supposed romance between Jackie and Robert Kennedy. The staff at the compound were all abuzz about these rumors. There was more a feeling in the air than anything that anybody actually saw. On weekends the family would congregate for dinner at Bobby's house. One time, Jackie walked in for dinner and Ethel just rose from the table and went to her room. There was a strain between the two women. It had to do with Bobby. Whether it was sexual or not between Jackie and Bobby I don't know, but something was going on. I would say it reached a peak during the summer of 1967, the year before Bobby got killed. Ethel felt threatened by Jackie. It seemed as though Bobby and Jackie were working up to something and while nothing happened, Ethel worried that something might happen.

"I heard one story that sounded rather revealing. Katherine, an elderly maid who worked for Ethel, was present one day when Teddy Kennedy came into the house, went over to Ethel and bent over to kiss her. She pushed him away and told him, 'There will be no situation here like Bobby and Jackie.' Ethel evidently was very sensitive to what might be going on between Bobby and Jackie, or what she thought could go on if things got out of hand."

Mary DeGrace had no great affection for Ethel: "I did laundry for the family from 7:30 a.m. to 5:00 p.m., five days a week, every week of summer for all those years. It took them four or five years before they realized I had a name. I received minimum wage during my entire period of employment and received a gift only once—a picture of Bobby Kennedy after his death. Because they paid so little, the help was always leaving. During one ten-week stretch we had thirteen cooks. In later years, as the children grew up, I used to find pot in the laundry, in the pants pockets, especially with young David, the one who later overdosed. I would chuck it and tell Ena, Ethel's nursemaid for many years. Ena, who was Costa Rican, had seen Ethel through most of her eleven children. You couldn't tell Ethel. You couldn't even tell Ena. If I turned it over to Ena, she would hide it from Ethel.

"The one thing that was nice about Ethel, and this was true of Jackie as well, was that if the family ate steak for dinner, so did the help. In Rose Kennedy's household, if she ate steak, you ate hamburger; if she ate hamburger, you ate hot dogs. And you weren't allowed a dessert in Rose's house. Those were the Kennedys. They divided the world into us and them.

"For all Ethel Kennedy's compulsiveness, her house was a pigsty. They went to morning Mass every day, but they never cleaned up after themselves. Jackie's house seemed much more in order. Of course there weren't as many kids. I remember opening up Jackie's house one summer before anybody got there. She had a canopied bed in a very Cape Cod setting. Nothing that would suggest ostentatious wealth except for her wardrobe closet. It was a double closet and it was crammed with clothes. And there were maybe thirty pairs of shoes. This was a place she stayed only one month each year, so it seemed an overabundance of clothing.

"I found Jackie to be very pleasant. Other maids didn't like her. Whenever she saw me, she had a smile for me and 'Hello, how are you?'

"After seventeen years, Ethel and I had words over her laundry bill. She thought I was sending out too many things to be cleaned. I washed and ironed shirts, towels, underpants, pillow cases, even dungarees. Who irons dungarees these days, especially with a crease down the middle of the pants leg? The washing machine ran from the minute I arrived until after I left, when one of the other maids took over. But we sent out larger items—sheets, blankets, draperies. One day, Ethel came into the laundry room and told me, 'You must be in cahoots with the laundry man. My laundry bill so far this year comes to $700, and you're going to pay for it!' So I told her she could wish with one hand and shit in the other and see which one got filled up first. Then I threw down the iron and walked out the door.

"In 1982, I interviewed for a maid's job with Jackie. This was a year after I had quit Ethel Kennedy. I thought she might mention the incident. But she didn't. In fact she didn't even recognize me. She had seen and greeted me a thousand times over the past two decades but when I appeared at her house in street clothes she didn't know me from a hole in the wall. I didn't take the job."

In March 1967, Jackie, John Jr. and Caroline flew to Acapulco to spend several weeks with Lee Radziwill and her children, who were then attending the Lycée Français in London. Although Jackie no longer felt the intense sense of loss she had experienced on her previous visit to Acapulco, she was plagued by other problems. At one point a powerboat carrying a half-dozen Mexican photographers caused her sailboat to capsize. The press was rampant and its presence gave the Secret Service headaches. There was also a strain in the relationship between Jackie and Lee. The cause of their differences was Truman Capote, who in recent months had grown closer to Lee than to Jackie. Sensing in Lee a vulnerability and sensitivity he claimed he could never find in her sister, Truman had accompanied Lee to Morocco, and there apparently encouraged her to embark on an acting career.

"We were very tight," said Truman. "We even talked about marriage, though not the kind you read about in *Good Housekeeping*. I called her 'Princess dearest,' she called me her best friend. I fancied myself another Dr. Doolittle. I thought, 'This poor child has lived her entire life in her older sister's shadow, watching her climb from peak to peak. Why not give her a boost?'

"She told me her deepest regret was that she wasn't brought up or educated to have a *métier*. 'I'm mainly interested in the arts,' she said, 'but because of my kind of education, my interests were never channeled in any particular area.' So I introduced her to Milton Goldman, a theatrical agent who handled such talents as Laurence Olivier and John Gielgud, and he set her up with a role in Chicago. Madame Queen Kennedy [Jackie] didn't like it. The two sisters were very jealous of each other. They even competed in the gift-giving department. Madame Queen gave me a lavender porcelain jar that said OPIUM in big black letters. Princess dearest sent me a gold-lined Schlumberger cigarette box, inscribed: 'To my Answered Prayer, with love, Lee.' "

Although Lee later complained that she would have preferred to play Chekhov or appear with Maureen Stapleton in a dinner theater showcase in Phoenix, her first role was Tracy Lord, the wealthy, egocentric heroine of Philip Barry's frothy comedy *The Philadelphia Story*, which opened the 1967 summer season at Chicago's Ivanhoe Theater. Gerald Clarke, Capote's biographer,* reveals that while Kenneth flew from New York to do Lee's hair, George Masters, a Hollywood makeup artist, flew in from California to prepare her face. Stas Radziwill and Capote were there to hold her hand. The humor, according to Clarke, was provided mainly by Masters, who insisted on calling Stas "Princie" and "complained that the colors of Lee's Saint Laurent dresses—shocking pink, purple and chartreuse—were all wrong. One of

*Gerald Clarke, *Capote*, pp. 387–390.

them, he said, looked like 'a dog's lunch—the Supremes wouldn't even *think* of wearing something like that.' "

"Lee lays golden egg," said one reviewer of her performance; "Pathetic, lamentable and sad," mourned another. Even Capote winced to see his creation make a fool of herself on stage. "If Lee hadn't existed, somebody would have had to create her," he said, long after their ultimate falling out. "I couldn't believe my eyes. I thought there must be some mistake. She deserves another chance."

The late David Susskind, independent producer and television talk show host, recalled "bumping into Truman at a party in New York and hearing him carry on about Lee Radziwill, what a great actress she could be if only cast in the right role. He started badgering me, telephoning at all hours, appearing in my office. He carried around a portfolio of pictures of Lee as Tracy Lord. The reviews were terrible, but Truman insisted she had talent. Besides, he said, look at all the publicity she had reaped in *The Philadelphia Story*. 'Television is her medium,' he said. So we went to ABC and sold them on the idea of casting Lee in Truman's adaptation of John Van Druten's comedy *The Voice of the Turtle*. They agreed to pay her fifty thousand dollars to play the lead.

"After sitting on it a few weeks, I called Truman and said, 'What would you say to a non-comedic role for Lee? I'd like to do a remake of the 1944 Otto Preminger movie *Laura*. Lee will take over Gene Tierney's role, and we'll get George Sanders to fill Clifton Webb's shoes. And you'll write the final script.' Truman spoke to Lee and she had no objections provided we tape in London, so she could be close to home. 'Fine,' I said. 'I'll arrange it.' In addition to George Sanders we signed Robert Stack, Arlene Francis and Farley Granger.

"We held our first rehearsal in London in the fall of '67, and it became clear the moment our leading lady read that I had made a colossal mistake. To put it bluntly, Lee Radziwill or Bouvier, the name she used professionally, couldn't act. Not only couldn't she get a line across, she couldn't move. And no amount of coaching could possibly unlock her talent, because she had none.

"I telephoned Truman in New York and leveled with him. He agreed to have it out with Lee, and apparently tried to convince her that she *was* Laura. All she had to do was pretend she was hostessing one of her cocktail parties. 'Be charming the way you are when you have fifty for dinner,' he said. It didn't work. If anything, her acting became even more mechanical. And the amazing part of it was that she never acknowledged any insecurity at all. No matter how terrible her acting, she felt she was doing fine. Our rehearsal schedule progressed. As the shooting date approached, I began to panic. I tried ringing Truman again, only to learn that he had departed for the Bahamas without leaving a forwarding address or telephone number.

"What truly angered me was Lee's attitude. She was constantly late for rehearsal because of late-night doings at her home. Into the final week of rehearsals, she didn't know her lines, didn't know her cues, didn't know where to enter or exit. An ABC executive who braved two days of rehearsal said to me, 'She's got to go.' I agreed.

"But how do you fire the sister-in-law of the former President of the United States, and the sister of probably the most formidable woman in the world? Answer: You don't; you make her quit. I devised a plan. I instructed the director to attack her acting so mercilessly and so often that she would drop out rather than go on. The plan, while well-conceived, was opposed by the other members of the cast who insisted that no matter how inadequate her performance she must not be humiliated. We decided instead to use the last week of rehearsal as a crash-course in acting for our unfortunate star.

"The ill-fated production went forward. We had to do as many as thirty takes in some instances, and the only way to get it done was to focus the camera on anything but Lee. The taped version aired in the States in December 1970 and in England in January, netting uniformly disastrous reviews in both countries. It ended Lee's theatrical career and it nearly ended mine."

While Lee cavorted on stage and in company with Truman Capote, Jackie went to Newport News, Virginia, where her daughter christened the *USS John F. Kennedy,* a giant $200,000,000 aircraft carrier, in a major media event. The Navy spent $300,000 on the opening ceremonies alone. "The brass wasn't overly pleased by that figure," said Admiral Thomas Moorer, former commander of the Seventh Fleet. "But this was a big boat and a big show. President Johnson flew in for it. The dignitaries were being brought over from the airport by helicopter. Robert McNamara, who had arrived with Mrs. Kennedy to give the dedication address, was out there telling the helicopter pilots where to land. We had sailors on hand who were in charge of that operation, but that didn't seem to deter McNamara.

"Mrs. Kennedy was standing there watching all this. She said to me,'I know you gentlemen get nervous when you have a large ceremony like this.' I told her that I never get nervous, but that the Secretary of Defense looked pretty nervous. And this fellow was in charge of everything, including Vietnam."

On May 30, 1967, news arrived that Lady Harlech, wife of David Ormsby-Gore, had been killed in an automobile accident in North Wales. Jackie and Robert Kennedy flew to England for the funeral service. Two weeks later, Jackie returned to London with Caroline and John Jr. en route to a six-week "sentimental journey" to Ireland, which included horseback riding in Waterford, a meeting with President Eamon de Valera, the Irish Sweepstakes, and a visit to the Kennedy ancestral home at Duganstown.

Jackie spent most of her time with the Murray McDonnells, her Bernardsville neighbors, and their eight offspring, at Woodstown House, a 53-room mansion at Waterford. On one occasion Caroline and a half-dozen McDonnell children were splashing in a nearby pond when some 50 press photographers descended upon them. Caroline's Secret Service escort rounded up the children and drove them back to the McDonnell estate. Upset by the incident, Jackie telephoned Ireland's Department of External Affairs and asked them to issue a statement that neither she nor the children wanted anything more than to be left in peace.

Another incident took place approximately two weeks later that was potentially much more hazardous, and could have ended tragically for Jackie. The circumstances surrounding this incident are described in a letter, dated August 7, 1967, only recently unearthed, which Jackie wrote to Thomas T. Hendrick, Special Assistant to the Secretary, Department of the Treasury, Secret Service Detail:

"After we had been in Ireland for two weeks, I started

to slip away in the evening to swim. With ten children in the house, one needed a bit of solitude. I drove myself, and told no one where I was going.

"One day Mr. [John] Walsh found out I had left, and guessing I had gone to the cove, followed me. He watched me swimming for three days and I never knew it. The place I swam was dangerous, but I didn't know that, as the tide was fairly low in the evening. The fourth day we were all on a picnic at high tide. Mr. Walsh was with the McDonnells and all the little children on a huge safe sandbar. I escaped from the group, unnoticed I thought, walked half-a-mile up the beach behind the dunes to the channel I always swam across and back.

"In mid-channel I found myself in a terrible current. The tide was rushing in with such force [that] if I did not make the end spit of land opposite, I would be swept into a bay twelve miles long. The water was so cold that one could not hold one's fingers together. I am a very good swimmer and can swim for miles and hours, but the combination of current and cold were something I had never known. There was no one in sight to yell to.

"I was becoming exhausted, swallowing water and slipping past the spit of land, when I felt a great porpoise at my side. It was Mr. Walsh. He set his shoulder against mine and together we made the spit. Then I sat on the beach coughing up sea water for half an hour while he found a poor itinerant and borrowed a blanket for me. Then we walked a mile until we came to a dirt road, and the McDonnells, noticing we had gone, eventually arrived there, followed by the car with Irish detectives."

Jackie recommended that Walsh receive the Agency's highest honors: "He saved my son from a campfire in Hawaii last year, and me this year . . . [He] has twice averted disaster, and brought honor to the tradition of the Seret Service."

In April 1968, at Jackie's request, Walsh became head of her Secret Service detail, leading her to comment to Hendrick in a letter that her entire escort was now Irish, as were many of her staff. "I never imagined that I would become the chatelaine of a band of Irishmen and women! —but they are the only ones who stay—I suppose it is because the Kennedys are Irish and all Irishmen stick together so much. In my house, everyone has been with me since I moved to New York, except for cooks who wander in and out—and the last one [Annemarie Huste] is now writing a book about working for me and Billy Rose!

"So it is a quality I am particularly grateful for, as I can't have everyone who comes in the door writing a book, the children's English nurse Maud Shaw already did so—and the Irish are loyal enough never to do that—and they get on well together . . . I know their bad qualities are being too clannish and pugnacious—and I imagine maybe [that's] why . . . they drive everyone who isn't Irish right up the wall."

"Jackie Kennedy was the tease, the temptress of her age," said Paul Mathias. "She perfected the art, she invented it. She was Miss Narcissist, perpetually searching mirrors for worry wrinkles and strands of prematurely gray hair. She didn't worry about growing old; she worried about looking old. Within 18 months of JFK's assassination she had two dozen of the world's most brilliant and important men dangling like marionettes, dancing at her fingertips, most of them very married, very old, or very queer."

Mathias's outspoken assessment contained barbs of truth. In the years immediately following the President's death, a number of renowned gentlemen pursued Jackie. Even Adlai Stevenson, in his own self-deprecating fashion, demonstrated more than a passing interest. When Jackie was still living in Georgetown in 1964, he wrote to her: "Please be merciful and indulge an old man and let me know when you are in New York." After she moved to New York, he again wrote: "Welcome to New York! I hope you can find some peace here, I haven't! And I will give you none—until you set aside an evening for me—alone, small group, medium, large—whatever and whomever you wish." The more he saw of her, the more intrigued he became. He began inviting her on trips. To Washington: "Would you like to go on a little junket with me to Washington on Sunday—fly down in a special plane in the afternoon and fly back . . . in the evening?" To Spain (the year before Jackie went by herself): "Would you like to be 'the crowning jewel' of an otherwise fantastic Feria? If so, your jewel box is at hand, although presently imprisoned by Southeast Asia, the Middle East, Article 19, and sundry alarms. But, after all, how can you see the world save in the tender care of a safe, old chaperone like me!"

Jackie kept Stevenson at arm's length with playful, suggestive notes, never fully committing herself yet never totally rejecting him either. She had a more difficult time with poet Robert Lowell, with whom she had formed a distant friendship in 1964 when he sent her copies of his books, as well as a copy of Plutarch's *Lives*, which she subsequently gave to Bobby Kennedy. Lowell and Jackie had met only once during her years in Washington, at a 1962 White House dinner for André Malraux. During 1965 and 1966, they saw each other occasionally, brought together by mutual friend Blair Clark. In a letter to Lowell, Jackie remarked how pleased she was to have a "friend across Central Park," and the line became the title of a new Lowell poem, appearing in *Notebook 1967–8*. Their friendship was consecrated as an official piece of gossip when a picture of the couple appeared on the front page of *Womens Wear Daily* on December 1, 1965. They had been photographed at the opening night of *Hogan's Goat,* a play by William Alfred. Within days, Lowell was telling friends he intended to divorce his then-wife, literary critic Elizabeth Hardwick, in order to marry Jackie Kennedy.

"For a while Lowell had a rather big obsession about Jackie," said Blair Clark. "She didn't realize, I don't think, that he was a manic-depressive, that he took lithium and was in and out of hospitals on a regular basis. When I realized how obsessed he had become with her, I told her that in my opinion he was going into another of his manic spins. I said that his obsessions with women often brought on these episodes, and that she ought to be careful. The obsessions acted as a triggering device. I was close to him, and was brought in whenever he had an episode. I recognized the signs. He was certainly very interested in her. He had a fixation on her. He was charmed by her. And she was interested in him, but only as a personality, somebody to converse with now and again."

Lowell did, in fact, suffer a manic-depressive episode and over Christmas of 1965 wound up at McLean Hospital in Boston. There Jackie wrote him, thanking him for a recent book he had sent on Alexander the Great and telling him that at his suggestion she had read Juvenal and Cato. Unwilling to deal directly with the subject of his illness, she remarked that he was wise to "go away" over the holidays—as if he had gone on vacation rather than into a mental hospital.

After his release he continued to see her and continued to recommend books. Jackie introduced "Cal"—as everyone called him—to Bobby Kennedy. "Jackie was more refined and cultivated than the Kennedys," said Blair Clark, "and I think she wanted to educate Bobby by exposing him to somebody like Lowell, much as she had educated Jack. Perhaps she wanted to plane down the rough edges before he ran for president. Lowell and Bobby Kennedy had several lengthy conversations during this period, not about politics so much as literature."

In the few months after his wife's death, Lord Harlech had been prominently mentioned as a possible future husband for Jackie. She had seen him during her trip to Ireland; he had visited her on a trip to the United States. For his part Harlech issued a stern denial ("We are simply good friends") which, unhappily, coincided with an announcement that Jackie was going on a private trip to the Far East, and would be accompanied by none other than Lord Harlech.

It looked as if something was afoot after all. The press pictured the November 1967 trip to Cambodia and Thailand as a premarital honeymoon or, if nothing else, a prelude to marriage. Why else would they be traveling together? When it was pointed out that Michael V. Forrestal and Mr. and Mrs. Charles Bartlett were accompanying them, the press reasoned that Jackie had decided to transport her own witnesses, and possibly planned to marry Lord Harlech in Cambodia.

Few journalists seemed aware of the true significance of the expedition. What they thought was an erotic jaunt by two lovers was actually a carefully orchestrated semi-political mission, discreetly sponsored by the U.S. State Department and camouflaged as private enterprise. Washington had some notion that Jackie might be able to stem the growing anti-American tide in Cambodia, a by-product of the war in Vietnam, and perhaps work her magic on Prince Sihanouk, Cambodia's chief of state, in a manner comparable to her dealings with Charles de Gaulle. Cambodia had broken off formal relations with the United States; Defense Secretary Robert McNamara devised the idea of sending Jackie, and Averell Harriman worked out the details of the visit. Before assenting to it, Jackie checked with Bobby Kennedy who agreed that the mission was "worth trying."

To help guide her, Jackie had decided to take Lord Harlech, a skilled and experienced British diplomat, while Forrestal was both a trusted friend and an expert in Southeast Asian affairs. Leaving from New York, Jackie stopped over in Rome for three days, then boarded a commercial jetliner whose first-class compartment had been turned into a bedroom for Jackie for the twelve-hour flight.

Prince Sihanouk's welcome at Phnom Penh airport presented Jackie's advisers with their first obstacle. Scrutinizing an advance copy of the speech, Lord Harlech came across a comment bound to give offense. What the Prince proposed to say was that had President Kennedy lived, there would now be no war in Vietnam. Uttered as part of a welcoming speech for Mrs. Kennedy, the remark would have the same effect as some of William Manchester's anti-Johnson statements in *Death of a President*. Lord Harlech advised Jackie to appeal to Sihanouk to eliminate the passage. The request was made from the airplane by two-way radio. The Prince consented. In return, Jackie agreed to add a line to her arrival address, affirming that "President Kennedy would have loved to visit Cambodia."

The highlight of the trip for Jackie were the temples of Angkor Wat, intriguing remnants of Asia's great past. For three days, she and Lord Harlech wandered among the historic ruins taking photographs and gathering souvenirs. She diplomatically ignored Sihanouk's occasional anti-American rhetoric. In Sihanoukville, Cambodia, she dedicated a boulevard to her late husband. She ate lunch at the Prince's villa and fed the royal elephants. An American Air Force C-45 then flew the group—sans Lord Harlech, who returned to England—to the more congenial country of Thailand, where they were received by King Bhumibol and the beautiful and fashionable Queen Sirikit, often called the "Jackie of the East."

At Bangkok, Jackie and her friends were installed in the royal palace, entertained at a royal reception and treated to a gala performance of the Royal Ballet. In honor of her visit, the Temple of the Emerald Buddha was lit up in all its glory. For Jackie, Thailand and her visit to Angkor made the long and tiresome journey worthwhile. As for Lord Harlech, the trip was in effect the last act of a non-existent romantic drama.

Her most important relationships during this phase were with the still-married Roswell Gilpatric and André Meyer. The Gilpatric affair had been kept so low-key that not even Jackie's "closest" companions suspected it, that is until the couple traveled together in March 1968 to see the Mayan ruins of Mexico. Born in New York in 1906, Gilpatric holds a law degree from Yale University, served as a former Under Secretary of the Air Force and as Deputy Secretary of Defense during the Kennedy Administration.

"I had known Jack Kennedy since he was a Congressman," said Gilpatric. "I met Jackie when she became First Lady. They had many informal dinners and social occasions, which seemed to be the style they both preferred. I also spoke with Jackie at several of the Hickory Hill seminars given by Robert Kennedy and had a number of one-on-ones with JFK at the White House. Then Jackie came down to my place on the eastern shore of Maryland during the White House years. We were only friends at that point. The relationship evolved slowly after the assassination.

"The strange thing about the Yucatan trip is that by then I realized we weren't going to work out. While we were on the trip, Jackie alluded several times to Onassis, and told me her intentions. I found her very straightforward. She hadn't entirely decided [to pursue Onassis] but seemed to be leaning that way."

Angus Ash, covering the Mexican trip for *Womens Wear Daily*, recalled that "there was a lot of public smooching and hand-holding between Jackie and Gilpatric. It took place in full view of the press. Jackie was all over the place, at one point jumping into a stream, fully dressed. John Walsh, her Secret Service agent, had to go in after her. Another time she climbed one of the Mayan pyramids and posed like the Queen of England opening Ascot.

"Jackie didn't mind the Mexican press because they wrote glowing reports about her. But she was angry about the American papers whom she felt were insulting to her. Since I was the only American reporter on this trip, I received the brunt of her anger. She was especially down on *Womens Wear Daily* because we reported how much she spent on her clothes and went into great detail on her social doings.

"Gilpatric talked to me and was at least civil, but Jackie refused and did her best to have me banned from the group. From time to time her Secret Service detail gave me trouble. I have no idea why they were on this trip, since presumably it wasn't government sponsored, but they were there and looking out for Jackie. I remember reporting that John Walsh, who was about 6'5", had been forced to ride a small donkey while everybody else rode horseback. Jackie didn't appreciate my comments. The next day, an agent took me aside and told me that if I didn't watch myself, I might end up in a Mexican jail. At another point, as we were boarding the press plane, Jackie had one of her henchmen announce that only photographers—not reporters—would be allowed aboard. Fortunately, I had several friends among the Mexican photographers and two of them kept detailed notes for me. Then when I was filing my final report from Mexico, the telephone went mysteriously dead. It took forty-eight hours to get through again.

"But that's not the end. Somehow Rose Kennedy got her hands on an advance copy of the final series. This is the one that had all the juicy business about Jackie and Gilpatric flirting with each other. Rose telephoned John Fairchild, editorial director of *WWD*, and urged him to cancel the piece—it would have an adverse effect on the children, which was a strange excuse since Jackie's children were far too young to read the publication. To his everlasting credit, John ran the piece intact."

Though on the verge of a separation, Roswell Gilpatric was still married when he squired Jackie to Mexico. His wife Madelin knew about the affair. "It had nothing to do with me," she said, "since our marriage was essentially over."

While Jackie's relationship with Roswell Gilpatric was clearly defined, her friendship with André Meyer was a highly complex arrangement. It was complicated by several factors, not least of which was that Meyer had become Jackie's financial adviser. "Jackie wanted somebody outside the family circle to handle her money," said Truman Capote. "She trusted Meyer. She would consult him for this, that and the other. He was her confidant, her lay analyst, her investment counselor. He not only made money for her, he gave her advice on raising the children, on travel, on real estate. In return, Meyer had a girl who, if not in love with him, at least wanted to please him, to make him happy."

Roswell Gilpatric maintained that he frequently saw André at Jackie's apartment: "He was evidently advising her on all sorts of matters. I knew him apart from her. She valued his guidance—in business and in personal affairs. She also frequently visited him. He lived at the Carlyle with Bella, his wife."

A contributing factor to the complexity of their relationship was André's deep affection for Jackie. While not prepared to divorce his wife, he was completely taken with Jackie. According to Cary Reich, André Meyer's biographer,* many of the financier's friends and relations felt that Jackie was toying with him. What drove those around him to distraction, writes Reich, was "Jackie's manner, particularly the breathless, little-girl-lost way in which she would implore Meyer, 'André, what should I do? I don't know what to *do*.' " Marianne Gerschel, Meyer's granddaughter, is quoted as saying, "This little-girl voice coming across the room would be enough to drive you absolutely out of your mind. I suppose I was fourteen at the time, and I remember thinking, 'My God, you know, he can't be taken in by this garbage.' But it was something my grandfather just couldn't see."

Another witness is Madeleine Malraux, the former wife of André Malraux and a member of what Reich calls the "Carlyle retinue," a group of women who were friends and often lovers of the financier. Jackie, as Madeleine Malraux portrays her in the Reich biography, "is a very intelligent woman, but also very superficial—and Malraux was certain [writes Reich] that Meyer agreed with this assessment. But, she says, 'André did not want it pointed out to him.' Searching for a word to describe Jackie, Malraux came up with the term *allumeuse*. 'It's someone who gives you hope, someone *qui craque l'allumette*— who lights the match, you know? Jacqueline Kennedy . . . is a coquette.' "

Jackie's natural flirtatiousness, often carried out in front

*Cary Reich, *Financier: The Biography of André Meyer*, p. 261.

of André's wife and family, was bound to create animosity. Helene Gaillet, a professional photographer and for many years the live-in companion of Felix Rohatyn, Meyer's partner at Lazard, spoke of Jackie's friendship with André.

"I was a friend of Jackie's in New York at that time," she began. "I was seeing Felix Rohatyn. Felix was like André's adopted son—they were the closest of friends as well as business associates. Jackie was with André. Felix and I would join them for lunch or dinner at the Carlyle practically every Sunday. The meals were always in André's apartment, so I developed a very clear picture of the mechanics of their relationship. I can safely say that André's grandchildren did not like Jackie. The only one who liked her was the son, Philippe, who lived in France. The grandchildren didn't care for her at all.

"As far as women like Madeleine Malraux go, you have to place her commentary in context with the situation. Most of the women who came up to his apartment were intent on having André Meyer's complete attention. He was famous and powerful, and that's one of the reasons they were there. These women would compete and vie with each other. But what was evident when these other women were there, and Jackie was present at the same time, was that there was always a degree of jealousy on the part of these women toward Jackie. The reason was obvious: Jackie received all of André's attention and the other women got none. She received his attention because of who she was. The others, including Madeleine Malraux, all fell a bit below Jackie in terms of rank. I've seen this happen not only in this particular circumstance but in a hundred others. Having lived for ten years in the power circuit, I've seen it happen over and over with Jackie.

"Being an unattached and single woman once again, Jackie also represented a tremendous threat to all the married women in her social circle. With her personality and fame and beauty, she only had to enter a room full of couples and conversation came to a dead halt. Forget it. She had that electrifying aura that made the room stop, and four men would immediately dash over to speak to her. Or they didn't because they were intrigued. Or intimidated. She intimidated men. It took a certain type of man to become romantically involved with somebody as famous as Jackie. She intimidated men and set off a jealousy factor in women. The only woman who wasn't jealous was André's wife. Bella was really incredibly fabulous in being able to support this entire situation. She was incredible because she was such a gentlewoman. She never uttered a word of complaint, ever.

"I always thought highly of Jackie. She seemed wise, even concerning the smallest details. She had it all figured out. She taught me something quite wonderful: never take a second helping at any meal. It's good advice first of all in a dietary sense, and second of all if you take a second helping and half the people don't then you're behind on the eating part of the meal. It was a totally new concept for me as far as the social aspect of things was concerned. It made sense, but I just never thought about it until I heard it from Jackie.

"I think Jackie is afraid of women. She's afraid of being used. That's what happened between us. She won't allow herself to get too close to another woman. She refuses to become chummy. And probably that's more true for her with women than men. She and André were extremely close."

27

In 1962, while First Lady, Jackie went to New York to see a new doctor named Henry Lax, a distinguished Hungarian-born internist whose patients and friends included Doris Duke, the Duke of Windsor, Adlai Stevenson, Merle Oberon, Igor Stravinsky, Zsa Zsa Gabor and Greta Garbo. Associated with Lenox Hill Hospital, Henry Lax exuded the kind of confidence and gentle compassion that Jackie admired in a man. His office at 160 East 72nd Street was conveniently located, and he gave her all the special considerations she had come to expect as First Lady. After moving to New York, she began to consult regularly with the physician, relating to him as she related to André Meyer, adopting a little-girl pose and turning to him for personal as well as medical advice. What she didn't realize until she became a regular patient was that Meyer was a patient in the same office, in fact saw Dr. Lax on a daily basis. At 11:00 a.m. each day, the doctor would appear in André's Carlyle apartment to listen to the financier's chest and take his blood pressure: André Meyer had a chronic heart condition.

To her amazement, Jackie learned that another of Lax's patients was Aristotle Onassis. "The Greek," as Bobby Kennedy called him, saw Dr. Lax whenever he came to New York. It was Lax who first introduced Ari to André. Onassis had always wanted to meet Meyer. When he heard that they shared the same physician, he asked the doctor to effect an introduction.

Jackie's ties to Aristotle Onassis had grown stronger in recent months. She had visited him not only at Skorpios but also at his Avenue Foch apartment in Paris. In New York they went to El Morocco and "21" with Rudolf Nureyev and Margot Fonteyn, and to Dionysius and Mykonos, two plain but authentic Greek restaurants, with Christina Onassis, Ari's daughter. On several occasions they were trailed by an American photographer named Ron Galella, whose candid snapshots of Jackie—in restaurants, at nightclubs, walking along the street—created a brisk market. But even the photographs of Onassis and Jackie together did little to arouse public curiosity. The prospect of a union between them seemed too remote to be taken seriously.

In March 1968, several days after Robert Kennedy announced his candidacy for President, Onassis was interviewed at a cocktail party at the George V Hotel in Paris. Asked his opinion of Jacqueline Kennedy, he said: "She is a totally misunderstood woman. Perhaps she even misunderstands herself. She's being held up as a model of propriety, constancy and of so many of those boring American female virtues. She's now utterly devoid of mystery. She needs a small scandal to bring her alive. A peccadillo, an indiscretion. Something should happen to her to win our fresh compassion. The world loves to pity fallen grandeur."

Bobby Kennedy found the statement disconcerting. Confronting his sister-in-law, he was told that she and Onassis had discussed marriage but had reached no decisions. "He's a family weakness," said Bobby. "First your sister and now you." Several days later Jackie received a visit at home from Ethel and Joan Kennedy. They stood on the vast oriental rug in Jackie's superb living room and begged her not to marry Onassis; such an action with all the negative publicity attached to it would irrevocably damage the family name and Bobby's chances for the presidency.

Bobby was the next visitor. He entreated Jackie to wait, at least until the presidential election was over. He wanted to avoid damage to his image. "There's nothing wrong with Onassis," he told her. "I'm sure he's the sweetest fellow on earth. But it might be taken the wrong way. And I won't get a second chance."

Jackie agreed to compromise, to go along with the Kennedys, for the moment at any rate. After the election she would decide. Bobby said he hoped she would decide against it.

It was also Bobby who convinced her to attend the funeral of Martin Luther King, Jr., in Atlanta in April 1968. Jackie would have preferred to visit the family after the funeral, but she again acceded to her brother-in-law's

request. Bernard Fensterwald, Jr., the attorney for James
Earl Ray, the man convicted of King's assassination,
later observed that Jackie Kennedy and Coretta Scott
King "were in the same boat. Coretta resented her husband for all his womanizing but modeled herself instantly
after Jackie. Her performance at the funeral was right on
cue. Both women played the martyr role to perfection. In
both cases their performance served a national purpose.
In my humble opinion, neither one of them was as distraught as they appeared. The only difference is that
Mrs. King didn't turn around and get married to Aristotle Onassis."

Several weeks after the King funeral, Jackie attended a
New York dinner party where she encountered Arthur
Schlesinger. Drawing him aside, she told him, "Do you
know what I think will happen to Bobby? The same thing
that happened to Jack. There is too much hatred in this
country, and more people hate Bobby than hated Jack."

That Easter, Jackie and her children flew to Palm
Beach with Aristotle Onassis aboard an Olympic Airways
jet; Olympus was one of a number of companies owned
by the Onassis family. Tipped off to their arrival, local
photographer Bob Davidoff drove to the West Palm Beach
Airport to meet the plane. "I drove my car right onto the
tarmac and sat waiting for them," explained Davidoff.
"The plane landed and Jackie stepped off with the kids.
She allowed me to take a few photographs before they
drove off in a waiting limousine. But there was no sign of
Onassis. I knew he was on the plane, and I knew he was
waiting for me to disappear so he could disembark and
join Jackie. I had brought along my son Ken, and we
were prepared to sit there all night if necessary. Finally a
stewardess emerged from the plane and approached me.
'I hope you took some nice photographs of Mrs. Kennedy,' she said. 'We're just going to clean things up
here.'

"I smiled and told her that I wanted very much to take
a picture of Mr. Onassis. 'He's not on the plane,' she
said. 'He's not here.' 'Well,' I said, 'I'll just kind of hang
around and wait.' She repeated that Onassis wasn't on
the flight. I shrugged and said, 'That's all right, I have
nothing else to do.' She told me to wait a minute. She
returned to the plane and quickly came out again. She

said that a very good friend of Mr. Onassis was on the plane, but that it wasn't him.

"A few minutes passed and finally Aristotle Onassis apeared. I went over to him and, while we were talking, my son was taking photographs. 'You know, quite a few people mistake me for Ari—we're very good friends,' he said. 'We might even be cousins, I'm not sure.'

" 'That's strange,' I told him, 'because I photographed him once before with Maria Callas, and you're a dead ringer for him.' 'Yes, many people tell me that,' he said. After a while he grew weary of the game and left. He and Jackie spent their vacation together at the Wrightsmans' but made no public appearances. Our pictures were the only ones that proved he had been to Palm Beach with Jackie."

In May, after Onassis made a substantial contribution to Robert Kennedy's campaign fund, Jackie joined the *Christina* in the Virgin Islands on a secret four-day cruise. She then returned to New York and was seen out on the town with actor Kevin McCarthy, and by herself at a Park Avenue party given by Arlene Francis and her husband, Martin Gabel. She went to the Colony with Roswell Gilpatric. It was Gilpatric who, a week later, accompanied her to JFK Airport and placed her aboard a private jet leased by IBM president Thomas Watson to fly to Los Angeles and the bedside of Bobby Kennedy, who had been mortally wounded only minutes after his California Democratic primary victory. Gilpatric remained behind, but Jackie and Watson were soon joined by Stas Radziwill, who had flown all night from London.

They were met at Los Angeles International Airport by Chuck Spalding. The moment she saw him, Jackie said, "Chuck, what's the story? I want it straight from the shoulder."

Chuck replied, "Jackie, he's dying."

It was something she had almost come to expect, this terrifying carbon copy of her husband's tragic fate, but the expectation did not lessen the blow. At Good Samaritan Hospital, Jackie took a sedative to calm herself. She then listened as Ethel described the sequence of events that had led Bobby and his entourage through the swinging doors of the Ambassador Hotel's pantry into the hands of a young Palestinian Arab, Sirhan Sirhan, bent on revenge for the Arab defeat in the recent Six-Day War.*

At the hospital Jackie told Frank Mankiewicz: "The Church . . . is at its best only at the time of death. The rest of the time it's often rather silly little men running around in their black suits. But the Catholic Church understands death. I'll tell you who else understands death are the Black churches. I remember at the funeral of Martin Luther King, I was looking at those faces, and I realized that they knew death. They see it all the time and they're ready for it . . . in the way in which a good Catholic is. We know death. . . . As a matter of fact, if it weren't for the children, we'd welcome it."

Robert F. Kennedy died at 1:44 a.m., June 6, 1968. His body was flown to New York aboard Air Force One. Jackie, in telephone contact with Leonard Bernstein, first from California and then while airborne, helped select appropriate music for the funeral.

After the funeral on June 8 at St. Patrick's Cathedral, she managed to snub Lady Bird Johnson. Lady Bird's *White House Diary* recalls the encounter: "Then I found myself in front of Mrs. Jacqueline Kennedy. I called her name and put out my hand. She looked at me as if from a great distance, as though I were an apparition. I murmured some word of sorrow and walked on. . . ."

Columnist Pete Hamill rode the 21-car funeral train that carried the coffin from New York to Washington, D.C., where it was taken to Arlington National Cemetery for burial near the grave of John Kennedy. He remembered seeing Jackie as she passed through the train "looking sort of icy." Hamill's companion, actress Shirley MacLaine, said, "The two women, Mrs. Ethel

---

*As with the assassination of JFK, myriad theories surrounded the death of his younger brother. The most convincing theory was recently suggested by former CIA contract man Robert Morrow in *The Senator Must Die: The Murder of Robert F. Kennedy,* which argues that RFK was killed by two members of SAVAK, the CIA-trained Iranian secret police, to prevent his becoming president and cutting off support to the Shah of Iran (who was secretly supporting Nixon for president). Sirhan Shihan, argues Morrow, was predominantly a diversion whose shots were not fatal. The real assassin, standing behind Kennedy, shot him at point-blank range with a specially equipped camera gun and then escaped with the famous "girl in the polka-dot dress."

Kennedy and Mrs. Jackie Kennedy, came through, Jackie first, very regal, as only she can be, with this marvelous sense of sort of anticipatory dignity. She was always able, somehow, to anticipate when the train was going to lurch or when it would bump, and queenlike, take hold of something so that when the bump came, she wasn't disturbed or dislodged. . . ."

Despite her frosty regality, Jackie was overcome by fear, by panic, the same emotions and impulses that had motivated her to try to escape from the back seat of a blood-stained limousine in Dallas, Texas. Panic quickly turned to anger, to bitterness. If America ever had a claim on Jacqueline after JFK's death, that claim was now forfeited. If she had felt any doubt or obligation to consider the impact of her actions on the political prospects of the remaining Kennedys, they were resolved by the shots that ended Bobby's life. Once again, did it matter who had pulled the trigger, or for what twisted reason?

"I hate this country," she bitterly lamented the day after Bobby's burial. "I despise America and I don't want my children to live here any more. If they're killing Kennedys, my kids are number-one targets. . . . I want to get out of this country."

Her intention could not have been more blatant had she placed a marriage announcement on the front page of *The New York Times*. In a sense, her decision to marry Onassis most probably was made at the grave of Robert F. Kennedy.

Jackie spent the summer shuttling between Newport and Hyannis Port, where she was soon joined by Aristotle Onassis. She wanted the children to become better acquainted with him and, at the same time, hoped to introduce him to members of the Auchincloss and Kennedy families. He made a promising start with Caroline and John Jr., arriving at the compound weighted down with presents.

Larry Newman, Jackie's neighbor on the Cape, saw her and Onassis "go up the street together, holding hands, dancing, doing ballet steps, playing like kids. I would see them eating their lunch—hot fish and cold champagne— and they seemed extremely happy. I said to myself, 'Isn't it tremendous that at last she has found someone to be with?' We've all heard so much about the money she received for marrying Onassis, but it looked to me as though they were very much in love. He seemed like an attractive fellow, a guy who knew how to handle the romance question.''

Rose Kennedy played a distinct if unwitting role in Jackie's decision to remarry, continually telling Jackie's mother that her daughter was going to have to cut back on her expenditures, including her personal staff. "This cannot go on," Rose said to Janet Auchincloss. "Now that Jack isn't here to provide for her, Jackie's going to have to learn to survive on less. My husband's office cannot continue to finance every whim of hers."

Onassis represented a means of escape for Jackie as well as the financial independence she had so long craved. She needed security, and she adored luxury, and Onassis offered both. She wanted a strong male figure in her young son's life, and she wanted to evade what she described as America's "oppressive obsession" with her and her children.

"I can't very well marry a dentist from New Jersey," she once told Truman Capote while dining with him at Elaine's. In many ways, Onassis reminded Jackie of Joseph P. Kennedy—both were self-made, accomplished, resourceful men who believed in themselves and lived life to the fullest.

Although Rose Kennedy voiced concern over the religious question (Onassis was both divorced and a member of the Greek Orthodox Church), she found their guest charming and entertaining. He was twenty-three years Jacqueline's senior (he was 62,* she 39), but judging by her attraction to older men this might well have been considered an advantage.

Rose's feeling was not shared by Jackie's mother. Jonathan Tapper, major-domo for Janet Auchincloss, reported that Janet "didn't particularly care for Aristotle Onassis. She considered him vulgar, both in appearance and manner. She would talk negatively about him. He didn't have the air of elegance Jackie deserved."

---

*Biographers of Aristotle Onassis seem evenly divided as to whether he was born in 1900 or 1906. The current author uses 1906 as the date since it was provided by Costa Gratsos, a close associate of Onassis.

Janet had her reasons to resent Onassis. For one thing, she knew that before Jackie he had been involved with Lee; for another, she had read accounts of his affairs with women like Veronica Lake, Evita Peron, Gloria Swanson and Maria Callas, his "friendships" with Greta Garbo and Elizabeth Taylor, his physical abuse of the rich and sophisticated Ingebord Dedichen, as well as the dissolution of his marriage to Athina "Tina" Livanos, the younger daughter of Greek shipowner Stavros Livanos. When they married in 1946, Ari was 40, Tina 17, the same difference in years as Ari and Jackie. Giovanni Meneghini, the husband of Maria Callas and the person most responsible for her successful career, branded Onassis a "moral leper." Janet Auchincloss, the perfect social climber, would have far preferred somebody of Lord Harlech's station for her daughter than the short, swarthy Greek she now proposed to marry.

André Meyer, whose judgment Jackie generally trusted, had similar reservations. "André may have advised Jackie not to marry Ari, but not because he was emotionally involved with her," said Helene Gaillet. "I think he was against the marriage because, although Ari wasn't vulgar, he did come from a lower rank of society. I became friendly with him and found him to be very down-to-earth. He didn't have the *savoir faire* and the refinement which the Meyers had. And I believe André thought that Ari wouldn't be the gentlemen's gentleman who would help Jackie become the number one woman of the world, although I'm not sure that was ever a desire of hers."

In August, Jackie and Teddy Kennedy traveled to Skorpios as Ari's guests. Jackie had met 18-year-old Christina before, but not Alexander, her 20-year-old brother, both of whom had the misfortune of resembling Ari, their father, rather than Tina, their slender mother. Both were attached to their mother and, since their parents had parted in 1959, had been irreconcilably hostile to the women with whom their father associated, particularly Maria Callas, whom they blamed for breaking up their parents' marriage. They were equally hostile to the men in their mother's life. Within a year after she divorced Ari, Tina was married to the Marquess of Blandford for a relatively short time; she divorced him, and, after her sister Eugenie died, Tina stepped into her shoes by marrying Eugenie's husband, Greek shipping magnate Stavros

Niarchos, Ari's lifelong nemesis and archrival. The word in Athens was that Onassis wanted to marry Jackie simply to impress Niarchos, who several years earlier had been briefly married to Charlotte Ford, daughter of Henry Ford II.

Alexander and Christina were no more accepting of Jacqueline Kennedy than of Maria Callas. Nothing short of a reconciliation between their actual mother and father would satisfy them. Although distantly polite, neither of them warmed up to Jackie, or gave the slightest indication that they ever would.

While Jackie went off on a two-day shopping tour of Athens, Teddy Kennedy remained behind to discuss the pending marriage. "I did not expect a dowry, and I did not get one," Onassis laughingly told his friends.

Teddy had come to Greece to negotiate the terms of a prenuptial contract with arguably the world's toughest negotiator. He felt as uneasy as Onassis felt comfortable and began by mentioning his late brother, the former President of the United States. After several minutes, he said, "We love Jackie and want her to have a happy and secure future."

"So do I," Onassis replied.

"If she remarries she will lose her income from the Kennedy Trust," warned the Senator.

"How much?"

"Approximately $175,000 a year," said Kennedy.

Onassis, having previously explored the matter with Jackie, knew of her situation and thought it odd that one of America's wealthiest families would place her on such a limited budget. Her total income, both from the trust and subsidiary funds, was paltry for a person of supposed means. Although he said nothing about it to Teddy, he told Jackie that she was being kept a political prisoner by the Kennedys. He assured Teddy he would replenish any and all funds she might forfeit as a result of their marriage. He also promised a sizable monthly allowance but did not specify the exact amount, nor did Teddy press for one. The Senator did point out that, by remarrying, Jackie would lose her $10,000 annual widow's pension and the protection afforded by the Secret Service Division.

Neither consideration fazed Onassis. He agreed to assume full responsibility for the lost pension and declared his intention to expand his present security forces to insure Jackie's safety. He was in the process of building a kennel on Skorpios to house a pack of well-trained German shepherd police dogs.

"She will get whatever she wants or needs," said Onassis. "My attorneys will prepare a letter of agreement and send it to you and we can then review it point by point."

The prospective bride returned to Skorpios with a dozen new pairs of shoes and matching handbags. (Shoes, she had heard, were also Maria Callas's fetish.) A day after her return, Onassis gave a party for his guests aboard the brightly lit *Christina.* Aware of Teddy's weakness for wine and women, the Greek tycoon had an abundance of both on hand. Nicos Mastorakis, a member of the Greek press, came aboard as a moonlighting guitarist together with a band from Athens. Nobody minded particularly when he brandished a camera and took photographs of Jackie in a long peasant skirt and scarlet silk blouse or of Ari dancing the *surtaki,* but then he pointed the lens in Teddy's direction. Flushed with *ouzo* and holding a young blonde, the Senator demanded that Mastorakis surrender the roll of film. "If you report any of this, have one comma out of place, run one photo, I'll have your ass," Kennedy told the reporter. Onassis intervened and pulled the pair apart. The party continued as if nothing had happened, though Kennedy's attitude did not exactly endear him to his host.

The prenuptial agreement reached Ted Kennedy, who made a copy and sent it to André Meyer, Jackie's financial adviser. Meyer found the agreement inadequate in a number of respects. He telephoned Onassis and they made an appointment to meet on September 25 in Meyer's apartment at the Carlyle.

Although they were friends, André and Ari had words over the terms of the agreement. By the time Onassis returned to his offices at 647 Fifth Avenue, he was visibly upset. Constantine (Costa) Gratsos, director of Ari's New York operations, had gone home for the night. Costa's executive secretary, Lynn Alpha Smith, was still there. Lynn served as Ari's secretary whenever he visited New York.

"When he was in this country, Onassis worked out of Gratsos's office," she said. "He didn't spend much time in New York because he didn't want to pay taxes here. That's also why he never owned residential property in the U.S., preferring to rent a suite at the Hotel Pierre. It wasn't unusual for him to work nights. He was a workaholic and like most workaholics he was an insomniac who slept maybe four or five hours a night.

"He was subject to abrupt mood shifts. He would yell in business meetings when things didn't go his way. I remember him once screaming and shouting and cursing, and in the middle of all this he suddenly turned toward me and in his sweetest voice said: 'Would you mind getting me a glass of water, Miss Alpha. My throat is a little dry.' I did. He drank it. He thanked me and then turned back to the business at hand and started screaming again.

"On this particular night he arrived with an angry scowl on his face. He said, 'Where's that bottle we keep around here?' I went into the outer office and brought back a bottle of Johnnie Walker Black Label. Knowing that he rarely drank straight liquor, I poured a single shot into a glass; he told me to double it.

"While he sipped his drink, he dictated a memo for André Meyer, summarizing their session. I typed it and he read it, making a number of changes by hand. I retyped it. He then asked me to take a taxi and deliver it to the Carlyle."

The memorandum, which never refers to Jackie by name but rather as "the person-in-question," indicates the vast difference between what André Meyer wanted Onassis to pay ($20 million), and what he finally paid ($3 million), for the privilege of marrying the former First Lady. The figure Meyer managed to extricate from Onassis was nearly twice what Ted Kennedy had worked out at Skorpios. More than a prenuptial contract, the memorandum reads like a deed of sale, as if by paying out an agreed-upon sum Onassis was acquiring a commercial property:

"With reference to a meeting held last night September 25th, 1968, between Mr. A. M. and Mr. A. O. at the Carlyle Hotel.

"The following is being suggested by Mr. A. O.

1. To replace at their present value by the equivalent amount in cash of all and any assets that the person-in-question will have to surrender to the benefit of the children under the existing present provisions as a consequence of a marriage.

"Alternatively, to provide in cash the necessary capital to produce such income which the person-in-question might be enjoying at present and will have to surrender to the children as a consequence of a marriage.

2. Such capital, which will be provided in cash immediately, will have no restrictions or any terms or conditions whatsoever, thus making the person-in-question sole and absolute deponent. It is hoped that it will be appreciated that by such arrangements an improvement and a far-reaching advantage is being achieved to the benefit of the person-in-question. Among other things, contrary to the existing provisions, the person-in-question will be free to remarry, not only in the event of death of her husband, but also in the event of a divorce. On the other hand, the children will immediately, by the surrender of the person-in-question's share, derive the benefit of such surrender immediately.

Bearing in mind that the present income of the person-in-question as it was mentioned at the meeting (by Mr. A. M.) is in the range of $250/300,000 net after taxes, this could be amply taken care of by the purchase of the necessary tax-free bonds.

"It is certain that there will be no problem for Mr. A. M. and Mr. A. O. to work out reasonable arrangements to safeguard the person-in-question from inflationary risks.

"It is expected that in all fairness this suggestion will not only protect the future of the person-in-question but very substantially improve immediately the situation of the children.

"Anything over and above these provisions must remain a discretion and a privilege of the husband of the person-in-question and it would be unfair to deprive such husband of the legitimate aspirations that he may entertain, if any. . . .

"The sum of twenty [million] indicated in the meeting, as a capital, apart from the fact that in the final analysis would be futile, due to gift, income, and other taxes that it necessarily would entail, apart from being detrimental to the feelings of either party, it might easily lead to the thought of an acquisition instead of a marriage.''*

---

*Despite claims to the contrary, there were no other prenuptial contracts. Christian Cafarakis, a former steward aboard the *Christina*, wrote a book, *The Fabulous Onassis* (1972), claiming the existence

The following day, September 26, Onassis and Meyer modified the terms of Ari's awkwardly phrased memorandum still further. Onassis agreed to pay her $3 million outright, which could either be deposited in her bank account or used to buy non-taxable bonds, plus the annual interest on a $1 million trust for each of her children until they reached the age of 21. In the event of a divorce or (his) death, Jackie would receive an additional $200,000 per year for life. In return she would relinquish her hereditary rights, which under Greek law meant she surrendered her claim to a maximum of one-fourth of her husband's estate. Two of Jackie's many lawyers, Eliot Bailan and Ben O'Sullivan, finalized the agreement.

"Onassis felt he had made a pretty decent deal for Jackie," said Lynn Alpha Smith. " 'Do you think $3 million is too much?' he asked me. 'Hell no,' I said. 'You can buy a supertanker on that, but then you have to pay fuel, maintenance, insurance and a lot of extras.'

"We used to call Jackie 'supertanker' around the office. Onassis didn't mind. It made him laugh. 'It's supertanker on the line,' I'd announce whenever she called.

"In my eyes—and in the eyes of many people—Jackie was an acquisition, nothing more or less. The dowry system was acceptable in Greece, only in this case it was Onassis who had to provide the dowry."

Doris Litty, a close friend of Onassis, felt Ari's reason for marrying Jackie was that "he wanted to show the world, as well as Stavros Niarchos, that he could buy anything or anybody. Jackie and Ari didn't fit together very well. But it wasn't the old 'Beauty and the Beast' syndrome, which is how most people chose to view it. On

---

of a prenuptial contract containing 170 separate clauses, including clauses on sleeping arrangements, conjugal visits, etc. The book was co-authored by artist-writer Jacques Harvey, who admitted to this author: "The prenuptial contract in that book is all bullshit. My publisher gave me a difficult time because there weren't enough sensational items in the manuscript. I knew Onassis so I telephoned him and asked if he minded if we put in some stuff about a prenuptial agreement. 'That's okay, that's good,' he said. He even conspired in the hoax by calling Roy Cohn, his attorney in New York, and telling him to play along if anybody called from the press. He loved publicity. He became rich from publicity. He once said to me, 'The more the newspapers write about me, the more confidence my bankers have in me.' "

the surface it might have looked that way. To the world at large, Jackie was an exquisitely handsome woman and Onassis a not very good-looking man. He looked more like a toad. But the image people have of beauty doesn't always apply. John Kennedy was a good-looking man, no question about that. But Onassis was more appealing and more handsome after you got to know him. It's peculiar, but looks don't really have that much to do with it. Onassis was a magnetic man who had power and a way of talking. Carlo Ponti is another example. Sophia Loren had a choice between Cary Grant and Carlo Ponti. She married Ponti. There are many men who marry beautiful women and everybody wonders how. These men are often magnetic and strong. I found Onassis very magnetic. His charm wasn't like movie star charm or drawing room charm. There's an attraction some men have and Onassis had it.''

Jackie and Ari saw little of each other that fall. Onassis returned to Athens for endless rounds of business negotiations with the Greek junta leader, Premier George Papadopoulos. Jackie stayed in New York to help her son make the adjustment that came with entrance to a new school. The teachers at St. David's had recommended that John-John repeat the first grade, stating that he lacked the maturity or skills to move ahead with his classmates. Jackie enrolled him in the second grade at the elite Collegiate School. She also hired a new governess for the children, Martha, who was to become a permanent member of the household, later serving as Jackie's major-domo.

Onassis had already begun the slow process of distancing himself from Maria Callas, never quite finding the courage to tell her the complete truth. Over the years he had made her wealthy with presents of jewelry, furs, an interest in a tanker, and outright gifts of cash. He now told her that she had been named in his will (after his death, she would receive 10 million francs) and as a token of appreciation wrote her an immediate check for $50,000. Yet for all his generosity he couldn't bring himself to tell her about his marriage plans.

Jackie, meanwhile, had lunch at "21" with Washington attorney Edward Bennett Williams, the main purpose of which presumably was to discuss some of the legal ramifications of the marriage. (Williams once represented a

client in a libel suit against Onassis and wasn't particularly keen on Ari.) She also conferred with Boston's
Cardinal Cushing in an effort to enlist his support in what
she realized would be a publicly unpopular action. In the
course of their two-hour meeting, Cushing admitted that
certain members of the Kennedy clan had tried to convince him to dissuade her from going ahead with her
plans. He had considered it and decided Jackie was right
to remarry, even if the Vatican refused to recognize it.
She was alone—a widow with two children—and she was
entitled to the same freedom and happiness as anybody
else. Because of his support of the marriage, critics accused him of accepting a huge donation for the Cathoic
Church from Onassis, though no proof of this allegation
ever came to light.

On October 15, 1968, the *Boston Herald-Traveler* published a front-page report confirming that Jacqueline Kennedy would soon marry Greek shipping billionaire Aristotle
Socrates Onassis. As soon as Jackie read the report, she
telephoned Onassis at his Glyfada villa outside Athens,
to tell him that their little secret was beyond the rumor
stage. She felt they should marry quickly.

Onassis, for his part, was somewhat taken aback by the
haste with which Jackie now felt they should move. Lilly
Lawrence, the daughter of Dr. Reza Fallah, head of the
Iranian Oil Syndicate, herself extremely close to Onassis,
was privy to some of the negotiations that preceded the
marriage: "Ari told me that he had begun to have second
thoughts. He wanted to reconsider. He wanted more
time. Jackie couldn't afford to let him off the hook. A
reversal on his part would have permanently besmirched
her reputation. Now that she had spoken to Cardinal
Cusing, now that it had been in the press, she insisted he
go through with it."

Lynn Alpha Smith recalled that Onassis telephoned
Gratsos early on October 17 and confirmed their plans.
"We immediately scrambled around getting a plane ready,"
she said. "We needed a plane so that Jackie and her
wedding party could fly to Greece and then be taken to
Skorpios, which is where they were going to marry. The
plane had to be cleaned up. Tourist-class passengers aboard
Olympic flights were unlike passengers on most other
airlines. At least half were Greek peasants visiting their
relatives in America. They would sneak their broiled

chickens and feta cheeses aboard, and the planes would reek for days. The sanitation was poor. At first Jackie refused to fly Olympic. So we got the plane cleaned up, and after she married Onassis we cleaned up the whole fleet so Jackie would fly on them."

Ninety passengers were "bounced" from a scheduled Olympic Airways flight on the night of the 17th to make room for Jackie and her entourage (including Caroline, John Jr., Pat Lawford, Jean Smith, and Hugh and Janet Auchincloss). Stas and Lee Radziwill and their two children flew to Greece from Paris.

Earlier in the day, Onassis visited Zolotas, his favorite jewelry store in Athens where the week before he had picked up a $1.25 million heart-shaped ruby and diamond engagement ring for Jackie. Now he bought a diamond clip for Janet Auchincloss and assorted pins and trinkets as party favors for their wedding guests. He also bought Jackie diamond earrings and a ruby-encrusted gold bracelet, a small sampling of the more than $5 million worth of jewelry he would drop in her lap over the term of their marriage.

The following morning, Ari went to the remote airport of Andravida, 192 miles west of Athens, to await Jackie's flight. He had company: 300 reporters had gathered at the airfield to greet him. When would the big event take place? they asked. "Within the next three days," he responded. Where? "Skorpios." Where would they honeymoon? "We will either stay on Skorpios or cruise the Mediterranean." He brought the informal question-and-answer period to an abrupt halt. "I have so many family problems to settle before the wedding. Please leave me be and give me your blessing."

By "family problems" Onassis meant his children, Alexander and Christina, who were appalled by their father's marital plans. Both considered Jacqueline an interloper, an adventuress whose primary interest in their father was monetary gain. Alexander, whose influence over his younger, very impressionable sister seemed profound, was particularly opposed to the idea of his father's remarriage. He had read commentaries in the international press on the coming event and found them distressing. Truman Capote had called Jacqueline an "American geisha," a term that Alexander soon adopted as his own, also calling her "the widow." Gore Vidal was equally concise. Asked what he thought of the match, Jackie's distant relation said: "I can only give you two words: highly suitable."

On the day Onassis told them of his plans to marry Jackie Kennedy, Christina threw a tantrum; Alexander left the house and spent the afternoon speeding aimlessly around Athens in his Alfa Romeo. At first both children refused to attend the wedding and it took considerable delicacy on the part of Ari's immediate family to change their minds.

Nothing, not even his children, could divert Onassis from what he had come to believe was his manifest destiny. "He should have married Maria Callas," said society photographer Jerome Zerbe. "He told his friends that his greatest folly was that ego trip of marrying that silly Jackie Kennedy. It was the most expensive, ridiculous mistake he ever made. It was indicative of a greater failing on his part. He believed money was a more powerful force than morality. The person Onassis wanted to marry he couldn't. We all know who that was—Queen Elizabeth. She would have been the top. But he couldn't have her. So he settled for Jackie."

Collecting his $3-million bride at Andravida, Onassis placed her aboard his own DC-6B, and flew her and her children north to the Aktion Air Base, then on to Skorpios by helicopter.

An army of journalists followed, many of them heading for the tiny fishing village of Nidri on the island of Lefkas, less than two nautical miles from Skorpios. Hiring a fleet of caïques, they surrounded Onassis's 500-acre island. On October 19, the day before the wedding, Jackie made a personal plea to the press: "We wish our wedding to be a private moment in the little chapel among the cypresses of Skorpios, with only members of the family and their children. Understand that even though people may be well-known, they still hold in their hearts the emotion of a simple person for the moments that are the most important we know on earth—birth, marriage and death."

Unfortunately, these reporters were not being paid to ignore what many considered the outstanding human interest story of the decade. When it became clear that the press was not about to retreat, the Greek government sent in the navy with orders to "shoot out of the water" any vessel (from aircraft carrier to rowboat) that came within 1,000 meters of Skorpios. It was agreed that four newsmen would be permitted to attend the wedding as a kind of "champagne pool," their reports to be distributed to all.

The wedding took place at 5:15 p.m. on October 20, 1968, in the tiny whitewashed chapel of Panayitsa ("Holy Virgin"), which stood on Skorpios amid bougainvillaea and jasmine. Jackie, according to a press report, "looked drawn and concerned" in a long-sleeved, two-piece dress designed by Valentino. Her hair was secured with an ivory ribbon. The groom wore a dark blue double-breasted business suit, and even in black elevator shoes only reached to Jackie's nose. Caroline appeared dazzled and wan; John Jr. kept his head down throughout the ceremony. Jackie kept glancing anxiously towards them. Ari's children both looked nervous and grim. Not even the weather cooperated: a cold, driving rain buffeted Skorpios and the surrounding sea.

The wet air was perfumed with incense as the couple came, hand-in-hand, before the heavily bearded and robed priest. They each held a flickering, symbolic candle. Hymns and prayers were chanted, first in Greek and then in English. The priest slowly intoned the words that made them man and wife. Wedding bands were exchanged and a pair of leather wreaths covered with twigs and blossoms were held over their heads. They then took three sips of red wine from a silver chalice and were led three times around the altar. As they emerged from the tiny chapel, not once having exchanged a kiss, they were pelted with rice and sugared almonds—sugar for happiness, rice for fertility. They held their reception aboard the *Christina*, which is where they spent their wedding night.

The public outcry was deafening. The day after their wedding a British tabloid ran the headline: "Jackie Weds Blank Check." "The Reaction Here Is Anger, Shock and Dismay," said *The New York Times*. "America Has Lost a Saint," headlined the West German *Bild-Zeitung*. "Jack Kennedy Dies Today for a Second Time," observed Rome's *Il Messagero*. *Le Monde* wrote: "The second Mrs. Onassis will cause to be forgotten the radiant Snow White who contributed so much to the popularity of her first husband." "This woman now lives in a state of spiritual degradation, a public sinner," barked *L'Observatore della Domenica*.

Criticism of the marriage came in a variety of forms and from a wide spectrum of sources:

Monsignor Fausto Vellaine (Chief, Vatican Press Office): "It is clear that when a Catholic marries a divorced man, she knowingly violates the law of the Church."

Alexander Onassis: "My father needs a wife, but I don't need a stepmother.

Maria Callas: "Jackie did well to give a grandfather to her children."

Lady Bird Johnson: "I feel strangely freer. No shadow walks beside me down the hall of the White House. . . . I wonder what it would have been like if we had entered this [White House] life unaccompanied by that shadow."

Coco Chanel: "Everyone knew she was not cut out for dignity. You mustn't ask a woman with a touch of vulgarity to spend the rest of her life over a corpse."

Joan Rivers: "Come on, tell the truth. Would you sleep with Onassis? Do you believe she does? Well, she had to do something—you can't stay at Bergdorf's shopping all day."

Jackie had been forewarned. An acquaintance anticipated public reaction by telling her, "But, Jackie, you're going to fall off your pedestal if you marry him." Jackie replied, "That's better than freezing there."

The friend was correct. Each day her children's Secret Service agents sifted through bundles of hate mail that arrived at her Fifth Avenue apartment. Television commentators condemned her for her greed. Editorials appeared describing the former First Lady as a traitor to her country.

What went unsaid irked her more than what was said and printed. Her friends talked among themselves and for the most part were as perplexed by the marriage as anybody in the public sector.

"What was distressing about it," said Charlotte Curtis, "was that while the marriage seemed precipitous, it wasn't. It had been carefully planned and orchestrated, but it was presented as if in a moment of weakness following Bobby Kennedy's death, Jackie went off and did this strange, unaccountable act. Both parties obviously had something the other wanted. Onassis wanted a social showpiece, and Jackie wanted financial security.

A Woman Named Jackie 515

"I'm not saying Bobby's death didn't come as a shock. I'm sure it touched Jackie deeply to see his agony and his misery and his torment after Jack died and then to see him pull himself out of it, and become the person that he was when he died. That surge of idealism, the sense that they would get another crack at it, died hard with Bobby's assassination. I'm certain all of that played a part in Jackie's decision to remarry. But to marry Onassis is something else again. After Jack Kennedy, no less.

"Of course it's easy to idealize and make a god out of JFK and his wife and everything else. In truth, his administration accomplished very little of note. And we all know that the president walked around with his fly unzipped. Still, it seemed a far cry from Aristotle Onassis and his floating circus. All those jaded jet-setters and cynical industrialists. Onassis's main interest was making money, and for a time at least it seemed that Jackie shared his enthusiasm."

Lucky Roosevelt happened to believe that Jackie married Onassis in a moment of weakness: "It was so out of character for her, it was mind-boggling. I will never understand it. She was an exquisite creature. There might have been inner toughness. She must have had it—look at the way she handled Jack's death. But after Bobby's death she disintegrated. And if the truth is ever known, I'm sure she must have had some kind of what we used to call in the old days a 'breakdown,' a nervous breakdown. Something had to have happened after Bobby's death to have triggered her marriage.

"I think it was just so awful. Furthermore, I think her behavior was so uncharacteristic of her. She's a woman of great dignity. Even as a young girl she had dignity. And there was something to me so undignified about the marriage to Onassis. It was such an aberration. I was working for the *Washington Post* at the time. I will never forget that particular moment as long as I live. I went in for something and I saw Philip Geyelin. He came screaming through the newsroom and he blurted out this incredible bit of news. Somehow I didn't know all the gossip. Everybody else had heard about it. I didn't. I sat back. I said, 'Don't be ridiculous. It's not true.' 'You just wait,' he said. 'We're going with the story.' It was just incongruous. It made no sense."

It made no sense to Sylvia Blake either. "I have no

idea why she married him," said Sylvia. "I can't imagine. Isn't it interesting? It's a mystery because she never talked about it. I met them together just once, when she came with him to dinner at the Shrivers' in Paris. My husband was the Minister of Foreign Affairs at the American Embassy in Paris when Sargent Shriver was the Ambassador. And I must say, I was speechless. I guess everybody else was, too. I mean, to me, he was so unattractive—about five feet tall—and I thought he was just not very pleasant. He didn't seem to have a lot of charm. She introduced me to him. He was the kind of man who looked just one inch above your head, as if absolutely bored to tears."

Not all the reviews were negative. Jackie had her defenders. Lee Radziwill, who may well have been inwardly jealous, nevertheless told the press: "If Jackie's new husband had been blond, rich, young and Anglo-Saxon, most Americans would have been much happier."

Elizabeth Taylor: "I find Ari charming, kind and considerate. I think that Jackie made an excellent choice."

Roswell Gilpatric: "She once told me that she felt she could count on Onassis. It was an attribute she looked for in all her friends. One of the things she is looking for . . . is a private life—not being in the public eye all the time—and he can afford to give her that privacy and protection."

"When she announced the marriage," said Pierre Salinger, "I wrote her a long letter. I said she wasn't hurting anyone; she could do anything she wanted."

But the words of support that apparently meant most to Jackie came in the form of a twelve-page letter from Edie Beale, of all people. "I told her she had done the right thing," said Edie. "I invited her to Grey Gardens and told her to bring her new husband. We were all very curious to meet him."

28

The pealing of the wedding bells had barely faded when Aristotle Onassis flew off to attend to business, leaving Jackie and her children on Skorpios. On the afternoon of October 24, Ari and Premier Papadopoulos were riding in the back seat of the dictator's limousine as it drove through the streets of Athens flanked by a police escort. The two men discussed a ten-year, $400-million investment project called "Omega" involving the construction of an oil refinery, an aluminum plant, shipyards and air terminals. Although Stavros Niarchos eventually took over the project, for the moment Onassis was to be its chief financial backer. This alliance between Onassis and the Greek military government made Jackie's marriage a matter of ever greater controversy in the United States.

During Ari's absence, Jackie bade a tearful farewell to her children and sent them off with her mother and stepfather. They spent the night in Athens, and the following morning flew back to New York and school. The other wedding guests had all dispersed by the time Onassis returned.

Jackie and Ari were finally alone. For three weeks they swam, sunbathed, took long walks and went fishing together. They made two brief trips to Athens (one on business, one for pleasure) and sailed to the island of Rhodes aboard the *Christina*.

Onassis amused himself from time to time by boasting to his business associates (as well as to friends of his wife) about his sex life with Jackie. Over the telephone he told Gratsos one morning that he had performed five times the night before, and twice again that morning.

("Onassis could be a bit gamey," said Lynn Alpha Smith. "I remember once when some woman he was seeing—this was before Jackie—called me up to say she could not come to dinner that night because she had a sore throat. She asked me to explain this to Onassis. I went in to tell him. He laughed. 'That's not all that's sore,' he said.")

Afternoons, while Ari transacted business, Jackie read or attended to her correspondence. Secrecy had been so important that many of her friends first knew of the wedding when they read about it in the newspapers. She had a good deal of explaining to do. One of those to receive a hand-written letter from Skorpios was Roswell Gilpatric: "I would have told you before I left," she wrote, "but then everything happened so much more quickly than I'd planned. I saw somewhere what you had said, and I was very touched—dear Ross, I hope you know all you were and are and will ever be to me. With my love, J."

The letter and four earlier notes addressed to Gilpatric, purportedly removed from an office file by an employee in Gilpatric's law firm (the employee claimed and evidently proved he had found them in a wastebasket), later turned up in the possession of Charles Hamilton, a New York autograph dealer. Although the letters were retrieved by Gilpatric, they were quoted at length in the press.

"Jackie understood," remarked Gilpatric. "Onassis felt otherwise. According to sources, he became exercised, probably because she wrote one letter while on her honeymoon and it pertained to a relationship that ended shortly before their marriage. I don't think he minded except that it became public knowledge, and this proved slightly embarrassing. Still, he was always very polite whenever we met, which happened now and again at parties and restaurants."

Although incensed by the Gilpatric disclosure, Ari had his own problems with past paramours. Baroness Marie-Hélène Rothschild, whose mother, Maggie van Zuylen, was a great friend of Maria Callas, commented on how distraught the opera singer became over losing Onassis: "Maria was madly in love with Ari, sincerely in love with him. She had a mad passion for him. They were like two wild beasts together. They got along well, but in the end she wasn't glamorous enough for him. Jackie Kennedy was glamorous. Maria learned of the marriage not from Onassis but by reading about it in the newspapers, like everybody else. She was totally devastated. It was dreadful, awful. She was so frightfully broken up, so disappointed, so profoundly hurt.

"People perpetually claimed that Maria and Ari were too much alike. Every biographer who has written of them has said as much. In reality nothing could be further from the truth. Maria wasn't at all the flamboyant, highly charged personage she evoked on stage. She was a great actress, a magnificent opera singer, but off-stage she was shy, humorless, always earnest. I think the word is 'heavy.' Ari was the antithesis. He was like a Greek pirate, full of intelligence and a Mediterranean humor. Truly ugly, but he made up for it with his vibrant energy and force of will. He wasn't happy unless he had twenty people around him at all times, whereas Maria only wanted to be alone with him. Ari was flirtatious, Maria wasn't. He refused to go on long sea voyages alone with her. He always took my mother along. Ari would say he should marry the two of them because my mother was very witty and gay, and Maria was so serious. She was too much in love with Ari for her own good. She couldn't relax with him. She was clumsy, always dropping things or saying the wrong thing.

"After she divorced Meneghini for Ari, he began to lose interest in her. He became further disenchanted when she temporarily gave up her career. My mother and I would constantly tell her what to do, how to behave if she wanted to win him back. A short time after his marriage to Jackie, he began to see Maria again. My mother acted as intermediary. We told Maria that if she wanted to conquer Ari she had to be more elusive. She was always there for him, always at his disposal. I once made her hide out at my country house so he wouldn't find her. This agitated him, made him edgy. But the effect quickly wore off because within a week she was again groveling at his feet."

During her honeymoon, Jackie contacted Billy Baldwin and invited him to Athens. She booked his passage aboard Olympic Airways and sent a car to meet him at the airport. When he arrived at the Glyfada house, he was treated to his first Greek lunch. "I will kill you if you pretend to like it," Jackie warned him. She then led him on a tour of the residence, pointing out rooms that demanded his attention. She wanted Glyfada refurbished primarily because the previous tenant, Maria Callas, had conceived most of the original decorations.

A day later Jackie took Baldwin along to Skorpios. The decorator found the *Christina* appalling—its pink marble bathrooms, elaborate sitting rooms and salons, plus a dining room whose walls were covered with murals of naked little girls depicting the four seasons (which Jackie soon eliminated). The sole exception was Ari's book-lined study—"One of the greatest rooms I had ever been in," effused Baldwin—with its El Greco and priceless jade Buddha. He was similarly inspired by the island and the villa that was being constructed on it for Jackie and Ari. Because her children were scheduled to visit over Christmas, Jackie wanted Baldwin to complete his work on the unfinished villa even before he turned his attention to Glyfada.

After three days in Greece, Baldwin submitted a bill to Onassis's New York office for $25,000 "For services rendered." Onassis paid it, though he thought it outrageous. But this was only the beginning. One evening while in Paris, Ari received a telephone call from his sister, Mrs. Artemis Garoufalidis, at Glyfada. Shippers were in the process of delivering tens of thousands of dollars' worth of chairs, tables and sofas from David Barrett and Thomas d'Angelis, a pair of classic furniture dealers in New York. What should she do? "Sign for them," said Ari. "Jackie ordered them." The only bills Onassis refused to pay were for two television sets Baldwin had ordered for the house on Skorpios: the island had no TV reception.

Jacques Harvey, a French-born artist and author who first met Onassis at Maxim's, received an invitation for cocktails at the Greek tycoon's Avenue Foch home in Paris: "This was perhaps nine months after his marriage to Jackie. I had been to the apartment once or twice before. It was one of the costliest in Paris. It had a spacious drawing room and living room, nicely furnished with Persian rugs and antiques—nothing out of this world but certainly quite charming. I also remembered a large portrait of Tina, Ari's first wife. When I arrived I noticed that the interior had been substantially altered. Jackie had taken a designer—I don't know who—and turned everything upside down. She had swept out the rugs and the portrait and replaced most of the furniture and fabrics. The results can only be described as 'California pastel,' with lots of beads and bangles and unattractive wall hangings, the kind of decor you might find in a Palm Springs beauty salon: everything pink, lavender, light green, awful. It was nauseating. Onassis thought so as well. 'This woman has no taste,' he said. His three sisters—Merope, Calirrhoë and Artemis—were equally outraged.

"I assume Onassis and Jackie married each other for business purposes. She had found a benefactor in Ari, and he had located somebody to improve his sagging image. He had been blacklisted in the United States since World War II. He was the subject of numerous international investigations by the CIA, the KGB, Interpol, Scotland Yard, British and French intelligence services. He was having problems getting loans from U.S. banks. He married her partially to clean up his act in America, and to a certain extent she helped in that regard.

"I don't know what else she had to offer. I had dinner twice with Jackie—once in Rome at Alfredo's, once in Paris at Maxim's with Christina and a few others. Jackie is one of the dullest women I've ever met. When she was First Lady and nobody knew her except from afar, she made a dazzling impression in Europe, especially in France because of her French heritage. But when she married Onassis and spent more time in Paris and attended some social functions, people couldn't understand what was so special about her. Europeans, who are generally much more chic and sophisticated than Americans, laughed at her. She was nothing; an ordinary American woman with average tastes and some money. She was a creation of the American imagination, Madison Avenue, *Womens Wear Daily, Vogue*. She was sharp enough to know that the more she exposed herself, the less impressive she would be. She had nothing to say, so she said nothing.

"In Europe today she's seen for what she is—a big zero. The trouble with America is that when talking about Jackie everyone becomes so sentimental. She has built a protective wall around herself. People are afraid that if they say anything derogatory about her they'll be removed from the 'A-line' party list.

"She's very manipulative, self-serving, a real bone-crusher, and very adept at it. The whole Kennedy clan has constructed a litany of lies about itself and now, finally, they're beginning to emerge. Most of the fabrications are built around JFK, and Jackie has created many of them herself."

A much closer friend of Onassis than Jacques Harvey was Maia Calligas, a Greek yachtswoman now living in Athens. "Ari and I met through André Embiricos," she said. "Embiricos and Onassis anchored their yachts side-by-side at Monte Carlo in the 1950s. Every morning, Onassis appeared on the neighboring boat while André, an old man compared to Ari, ate his breakfast. They used to talk about Dow Jones, IBM, GM, things like that. Onassis respected the old man's opinions.

"Two things about Onassis stood out. First, he was a financial genius. He kept ledger books for business purposes but actually everything was in his head. He knew the whereabouts of every boat he owned at any given moment, and he never gambled, not even in business. He once told me at the Casino in Monte Carlo that I was a fool to play. 'Even if you win you lose, because the Casino takes a high percentage. Never gamble on anything unless it's a sure thing.'

"The second thing one noticed was his essential loneliness. Onassis was the loneliest person in the world. It wasn't that he didn't have any friends, acquaintances or family. He did, but he was usually by himself. I remember seeing him at Monte Carlo sitting near the boats, staring out to sea, sad and lonely. I think all that money made him lonely. Every tycoon I've ever known, especially the self-made ones, has been like that. They are alone because money builds walls.

"He might have been less lonely had he married Maria Callas instead of Jackie. For me and for his other friends, Maria Callas was the real wife. Callas and Onassis were a couple. They had a true love affair. His relationship with Jackie was not a love affair; it was a business deal."

For all their differences, the first year of Jackie's marriage to Ari seemed satisfying enough. Onassis began to see Maria Callas again but only sporadically and as a friend. His first impulse was to try to make a success of his new marriage. When the honeymoon ended, he accompanied Jackie to London to visit her sister, then back to the United States, staying with her at 1040 Fifth Avenue. They attended several dinner parties together, including one at the home of Henry Ford II, which was also attended by David Rockefeller, a man Onassis had long wanted to meet. Ari in turn introduced Jackie to J. Paul Getty.

While in New York, she had her hair dyed and straightened by Rosemary Sorrentino: "There was so much clamor about the marriage that Nancy Tuckerman asked me to meet Jackie at her apartment and do her hair there. They sent a limo for me and I entered her building through the back entrance on Madison Avenue. I was disguised as a maid. Ron Galella, the pesky photographer, was parked in front of her house. When I saw Jackie she seemed very happy, a far cry from that day in 1964 when she broke down in my room at Kenneth's."

Over Christmas, Jackie and Ari returned to Greece, accompanied by her children. After the children went back to New York and Ari flew to Rome on business, Jackie went in search of Greek antiques with Alexis Miotis, Director of the Greek National Theater. "I'd known Onassis since 1922 and Jackie and I met at a party in New York in 1952–3 when she was an inquiring photographer with the *Washington Times-Herald*," said Miotis. "I had been aboard the *Christina* in 1963 when Jackie and Lee cruised with Onassis, while she was First Lady. I was also largely responsible for getting Ari together with Maria Callas. I staged two of Maria's operas— *Norma* and *Medea*—at La Scala and Covent Garden. I directed them. I was at Covent Garden in '58 when Onassis showed up in London and called me. I told him I was too busy with the Callas opera to get together. 'Oh, I know her,' he said. 'I met her through Elsa Maxwell on the Lido.' When the opera closed I threw a bash for 400 at the Dorchester and that's when Onassis and Maria got together again, and started their relationship.

"After Ari married Jackie, I accompanied them on several excursions aboard the *Christina,* once to Delphi. Then Jackie came twice to see me at Epidaurus, the ancient Greek stage dating to the 4th century B.C., about three hours from Athens. In the beginning, Jackie and Ari seemed harmonious. Jackie is a sweet person, very noble. Her behavior sets a standard for those around her. Obviously many people thought the marriage a sham, but I saw nothing wrong with it. Ari had a sense of glory about everything. He paid a good deal of attention to the 'glorious' people. He admired Jackie because she was

First Lady, not only in the White House but First Lady of the land. Ari wanted to be Emperor of the Seas and wanted a Cleopatra to sit by his side. For Jackie, it was his charm combined with his money. He had money, yes, but he also had charisma. He was a domineering personality. He was the one man she could marry who would never become Mr. Jackie Kennedy.''

William Joyce, legal counsel for Olympic, found Jackie's attitude something less than noble. Over Easter vacation, 1969, she brought her children to Greece, boarding an Olympic transatlantic flight with John Jr.'s pet rabbit. "Despite airline regulations," said Joyce, "she refused to allow the animal to ride in the baggage compartment with other household pets. 'My husband owns this airline,' she kept repeating. She wanted to keep the rabbit in First Class. It finally rode up front with the crew.

"Then she used to appear at the Olympic reservations desk minutes before a flight, without a reservation, and demand a [First Class] seat. Not just one seat, four seats—she didn't want to sit near anybody. If the plane happened to be booked, she would tell them to 'bounce' a few passengers. And she never paid. 'Charge it to my husband,' she ordered. Nobody ever informed her that technically he didn't own the airline; his sisters did. So when she didn't pay, they would receive the bills.''

Angelo Katapodis, operator of a travel agency on the island of Ithaca, nine nautical miles from Skorpios, remembered a visit Ari and Jackie paid that spring: "The party included Mr. and Mrs. Onassis, Christina, Caroline, John Jr. and Martin Luther King III, the 10-year-old son of the late civil rights leader. The boy was a guest of Jackie and her son.

"Onassis had a great feeling for Ithaca. Many of his department heads, including Costa Gratsos, hailed from the island. My father owned a dry goods shop and had sold Onassis material for his various homes. This time they purchased printed cotton fabric out of which Jackie hoped to fashion curtains for the villa at Skorpios.

"My impression of Jackie was not favorable. She had that silly grin permanently affixed to her face. She wasn't very nice to her husband, who wore white slacks, white deck shoes and was otherwise bare chested. She kept telling him to put on his shirt. She was pushy. At a certain point when things weren't moving quickly enough, she put a hand on her hip and began to tap a foot.

"You could see she didn't get along with Christina. Christina and Alexander already had strained relations with their father, who treated them like appendages. They were both frightened of him. It might not have been so very difficult for Jackie to win them over, especially Christina, who warmed to the least affection. It was a huge mistake on Jackie's part that she didn't. Maria Callas made the same mistake. Both women were resented. Ultimately, this did more to shatter the marriage than all the money she apparently spent.

After sailing to Nice, Monte Carlo, Villefranche, San Remo and Capri with Jackie, her husband celebrated her fortieth birthday by hosting a dawn-to-dusk bash at the Neraida nightclub on the Seronis Gulf, ten miles from Athens. When Jackie arrived, she startled those present by displaying a whole new array of jewels, her birthday presents from Ari, among them a 40.42 carat Cartier diamond ring (one carat for each year) estimated at $1 million. She also received a solid gold belt adorned with a lion's head (her astrological sign) and a pair of "Apollo II" emerald, sapphire, diamond and ruby earrings to celebrate man's walk on the moon.

At the party, Katina Paxinou, the Greek actress, sat alongside Mrs. Onassis, and when she complimented Jackie on her new earrings, which dangled from her ears like chandeliers (two spheres representing earth and the moon were joined by what was supposed to be a miniature spaceship), the birthday girl giggled and said, "Ari was actually apologetic about them. He felt they were such trifles. But he promised me that, if I'm good, next year he'll give me the moon itself."

"The first gift Jackie gave Ari was at Christmas 1968," said Costa Gratsos. "It was a pen-and-ink sketch of the *Christina* in the form of a bookplate, with Ari's name underneath, to be used in his collection of books. He gave her the *Christina,* she gave him the bookplate."

Yvette Bertin, an employee of Olympic Airways in Paris, noted that "while Maria Callas frequently came into the office with Mr. Onassis, Jackie never did. She was once spotted waiting for him in the limousine outside the office. She had very strange eyes—very round. She looked either like she was drugged or had experienced some tremendous shock. There was something rather frightening about her."

Mrs. J. Boyer, director of public relations for Maxim's, observed that "even when Onassis was married to Jackie, he usually came in by himself or sometimes with Maria Callas when Jackie was in the States. Jackie occasionally came to Maxim's with Mrs. Nicole Alphand or with her sister, Lee Radziwill. But I do recall several meals she took with Ari. She was really nothing compared to Callas. Jackie was so proud of being half French. She told everyone her name was Bouvier. But Jackie was a typical American. I used to hear what a stylish woman she was, but I've rarely seen somebody with such shabby taste. It astonished me. She wasn't at all elegant in the French sense.

"Jackie disappointed the French, who felt she should never have married after Kennedy. She was the widow of an American hero. To have taken lovers would have been acceptable, but to remarry, especially a man as public and controversial as Onassis, seemed unwise. It was obviously for money. The French, who love love stories, thought: 'This woman has a bank vault for a heart.' "*

In the fall of 1969 while in Paris, Jackie dropped in on Countess Guyot de Renty, her landlady during her year at the Sorbonne. "We had kept in touch and she visited me every few years," said the Countess. "This was the first I'd seen of her since her marriage to Onassis. She was very simply dressed. I even said to her, 'Jackie, I think your pullover is backwards.' She said, 'Yes, I'm still the same.'

"But I wondered. I thought her marriage to Onassis very strange. I would never have expected it. On the other hand, so many things had happened over the years. The assassination of her husband must have been a great trauma, followed by the trauma of his brother's assassi-

---

*Roger Viard, former maître d' at Maxim's, offered a similar assessment: "Maria Callas was a large, elegant, theatrical personality. She and Onassis were the couple. Jackie was very American. She didn't have the same elegance. She was ordinary. If it weren't for the Kennedy name, nobody would have looked at her. In terms of Maxim's, Jackie, so to speak, passed through without leaving a trace."

nation. She wanted to change her life afterward and try to forget."

Onassis did business in Switzerland each year and always stayed at the five-star Hôtel des Bergues in Geneva. On one occasion he took Jackie along, though usually she opted to stay behind and go shopping in Athens or Paris on the $30,000 per month allowance he gave her. John Rigas, a journalist for UPI in Athens, acknowledged that "Jackie would helicopter into town from Skorpios, especially when Onassis was away on business, and we would get tips on where to find her. She traveled around with a security guard named George Sinos and a woman companion, an employee of Onassis who was there to help orient Jackie and translate for her from Greek to English and vice versa. There were rumors that she was actually spying on Jackie for Onassis, telling him how much money she had spent, that sort of thing. Knowing Onassis, that's entirely possible.

"Everybody recognized Jackie in Athens. They would stop and stare or say something. She would smile and keep walking. She was neither beautiful nor interesting, but she seemed appealing and if she and Onassis weren't deeply in love, they appeared to enjoy each other's company. There was talk at various times that he would divorce Jackie and remarry his first wife or marry Maria Callas. It seemed implausible. Had he wanted to marry Callas he could have done so long before Jackie came along. I suppose he told Callas his marriage to Jackie was a business arrangement, something he needed for his personal image. And although this was probably true, I doubt she bought it or ever trusted him again."

The mixed apprehensions that people had of Jackie—good, bad and indifferent—indicated that she was both better and worse than her public image suggested. The same can be said of Onassis, who at least made an effort to fulfill his end of the bargain. "He was very generous with Jackie's children," said Costa Gratsos. "He bought John-John a speedboat and Caroline a sailboat for use at Skorpios. He bought John-John a jukebox and a mini-jeep to ride around the island. He gave them Shetland ponies. But beyond presents, he tried to give of himself, to be with them. He attended their school plays in New York and went out to Jackie's place in New Jersey to watch them ride. And the truth is, Ari hated it there. He didn't care for horses at all. But he'd go out anyway, when he was in New York, and most of the time he'd just stand around. He was always complaining that the mud and the horse dung ruined his shoes and pants.

"Once when he complained, Jackie told him off. 'You're so badly dressed, what difference does it make?' she said. She was right. He didn't care about clothes. He had an elderly Greek tailor who made his clothes. All his suits were out of style. He was superstitious about his suits. If he closed a good deal in a particular suit or tie or pair of shoes, he wanted to wear the same outfit next time around. He also tended to wear the same suit for days on end. I would say to him, 'Who do you think you are— Howard Hughes?' Jackie tried to induce him to invest in a new wardrobe. One day she walked into a fancy men's store in Palm Beach and emerged with 365 new silk ties for Ari at $30 a tie. But when he learned she had charged the purchase to him, he became infuriated. In fact, he used to criticize *her* attire because all she wore were slacks and T-shirts. 'What the hell does she do with all the clothes she buys?' he used to ask.

"They were just very different. Ari had money and knew luxury, but was a man of simple tastes. His favorite food was pot roast. He preferred a *taverna* or café for a meal as opposed to a very fancy restaurant. Even when he went to '21,' he ordered knockwurst and a bottle of beer. When he escorted Jackie, he usually went to better places, such as Coq Hardi in Bougival, outside Paris, but even there he ordered the same meal every time—a dry martini with an olive and onions, 'salade de boeuf' [beef salad] and a steak. They would have some Bordeaux with the meal. His only extravagance was a bottle of champagne. He would have it instead of dessert.

"He often went to a *taverna* on Lefkas called Nick the Greek, where he enjoyed eating, drinking, singing and dancing. Or he would go on a crockery-smashing spree at the Neraida, where he hosted Jackie's fortieth birthday party. She wouldn't stand for that kind of exuberance, labelled it uncouth and unsophisticated, so he would go without her. He once took a group there, including Odile Rodin and Italian actress Elsa Martinelli, and they nearly got busted for nudity and disturbing the peace.

"Ari enjoyed nightlife, the international clubs like El Morocco, Privé, Regine's, Raffles. Jackie tolerated them.

Slumming for her consisted of Saturday lunch with Ari at P. J. Clarke's. She once went to the powder room there and attracted a following of a half-dozen curious female patrons. Jackie couldn't tolerate her husband's hours, his no-sleep policy, the fact that he would retire late and rise early, his penchant for making business calls until three o'clock in the morning. Nor did he share her enthusiasm for the ballet, theater (unless it was Greek), opera (unless it featured Callas), museums and art galleries. They started with separate beds in the same bedroom and ended with separate beds on separate continents.

"Mostly, Jackie enjoyed shopping and receiving gifts from Ari. She was a speed shopper. She could be in and out of any store in the world in ten minutes or less, having run through $100,000 or more. She didn't bother with prices, just pointed. She bought anything and everything: music boxes, antique clocks, fur coats, furniture, shoes. She loved hitting the international fashion shows—Valentino, Molyneux, Lanvin—and buying the entire collection. At the beginning Ari encouraged it. In addition to giving her a portfolio of credit cards, he loved leaving little presents for her on her silver breakfast tray—a bracelet, a string of cultured pearls, an antique lace handkerchief. Sometimes only a poem or a letter. He wrote to her because she complained that John Kennedy wrote her only a few letters in the course of their marriage."

"It was the last full year of my friendship with Jackie," said Truman Capote. "I accompanied her on one of those shop-till-you-drop sprees. She would walk into a store, order two dozen silk blouses in different shades, give them an address and walk out. She seemed in a daze, hypnotized. I gave a party and my dog chewed up Lee Radziwill's sable coat. Prince Radziwill was furious, Jackie amused. 'Don't worry,' Jackie told Stas, 'we can buy another sable for Lee tomorrow and charge it to Ari. He won't mind.' "

Robert David Lyon Gardiner, the New York socialite, was at a dinner with Jackie at the Fifth Avenue home of Lady Jean Campbell. "Jackie came without Onassis," said Gardiner. "The yacht was tied up at the 79th Street boat basin. They sat her next to me and my wife. But Jackie stared into space all evening. She seemed to be in the clouds, and I don't know why. She had that vague smile on her face. A striking looking woman, she had those high cheekbones and that certain look with the dark hair she got from her father, Black Jack. But she didn't say a word."

This period was not without its tribulations for Mr. and Mrs. Onassis. In late 1968 an Olympic Airways Boeing 707 from New York to Athens was hijacked to Paris by two men representing a leftist political organization. Simultaneously there was a bomb scare aboard an Olympic Airways flight originating in Athens on which Alexander Onassis was a scheduled passenger. In April 1969 the FBI uncovered a plot by a radical political group to bomb the First National City Bank at 91st Street and Madison Avenue, presumably while Jackie was conducting business there. In July, Greek police learned of a subversive group's plan to kidnap Jackie. The same month, a plane on which she was flying to New York was searched in London for hidden explosives. In August, the Athens office of Olympic Airways was bombed. Police blamed anti-junta elements. An anti-junta pamphlet accused Onassis of being "the main banker for the junta." In October, Jackie allegedly used judo to flip Marvin Finkelstein, a photographer for the New York *Daily News,* when he attempted to photograph her as she emerged from the X-rated movie *I Am Curious (Yellow).* Witnesses to the incident testified that Finkelstein slipped.

There were other distressing episodes. On July 18, 1969, six women who had aided Robert Kennedy in his 1968 presidential campaign and five male friends of Senator Ted Kennedy met for a party at a cottage on Chappaquiddick, a small islet just off Martha's Vineyard. The occasion was the 46th Edgartown Yacht Club Regatta, which Ted entered and lost. One of the six women in the group was Mary Jo Kopechne, a fun-loving, 28-year-old blonde who had been Robert Kennedy's secretary. The women had reservations in a motel several miles from the motor inn where the men were registered.

Mary Jo and Teddy left the party by themselves around 11:15 p.m. to catch the last ferry back to the Vineyard. Instead of taking the road leading to the ferry, Ted turned onto a road leading to a narrow wooden bridge without guard rails. His 1967 Oldsmobile plunged into the water and landed upside down in the murky current. Kennedy managed to climb out; Mary Jo did not. The Senator from Massachusetts did not report the accident to authorities for more than nine hours. Suppressed testimony and other evidence now indicate that Ted Kennedy was more than an innocent participant in a deplorable accident. Leo Damore, author of *Senatorial Privilege: The Chappaquiddick Cover-Up* (1988), a thoroughly researched study of the event, leaves little doubt that a) Kennedy left the party with Mary Jo for a romantic interlude; b) he was inebriated; c) he drove off the bridge at a high rate of speed; and d) he was driving without a valid license. There is also a good deal in the Damore book (and elsewhere) to indicate that Kennedy spent hours (before notifying the police) trying to convince others in the group to take responsibility for the accident.

It is significant that one of the first people Teddy tried to contact was Jacqueline Onassis. Unable to locate her by telephone, he instead called Helga Wagner, an Austrian-born blonde from Palm Beach who has been identified as one of his closest confidantes. But it was Jackie who ultimately provided solace. A short while after his troubles began, Teddy received one of Jackie's typically effusive letters, saying that Caroline Kennedy had been without a godfather since her Uncle Bobby's death the previous year and that she would very much like to have her Uncle Teddy take over as godfather.

The needless tragedy was more than Joseph P. Kennedy could bear. With three sons gone and his fourth the object of a national scandal, the Ambassador did not survive the year. Jackie's ties to the Kennedy clan had been weakened by one more severed strand.

"While it was good, the marriage between Jackie and Ari was very good," said John Karavlas, second captain of the *Christina*. "They made a trip to Corfu that stands out in my memory. Ari's daughter came along. But not Alexander—he was rarely around after Jackie entered the picture. We had spent the afternoon on Corfu and at nightfall the crew met at a *taverna* for dinner. Jackie and Ari were supposed to be there, but they never appeared. Midway through dinner the first captain told me to check the *Christina*—perhaps they were asleep. I walked to the dock and boarded the yacht. I checked every deck, every stateroom—no Jackie, no Ari. I started to leave when I heard sounds coming from a small flat fishing vessel Ari kept tied to the *Christina*. I moved closer in the darkness to have a look. As I peered in I could make out a man's nude posterior rising and falling, rising and falling. The man heard me and looked over his shoulder. It was Onassis. He was on top and Jackie was beneath him. They were making love. 'What do you want?' Onassis asked me. 'I was just looking for you, sir,' I said. 'Well, you found me,' he said, never breaking rhythm.

"Onassis enjoyed making love in unusual locations, often in semi-public places. He was much older than his wife but he still had an active libido. They seemed to argue a lot. They had a tempestuous relationship. But they also made love."

Jackie's sexuality may indeed have blossomed during her second marriage, in part as the result of a conversation she once had with her physician, Dr. Henry Lax, who answered several frank questions she put to him. Renée Luttgen, a companion to the doctor and also his office assistant, revealed certain details of Jackie's relationship with Lax. "Jackie would appear at the office as though stepping on stage. Everything, the smile, the gestures, the words, seemed manufactured and carefully rehearsed. She was completely unnatural. She would wear her sunglasses on top of her head and assume a pose when I opened the door, as if some other patient might see the former First Lady. She and Henry were close, but she always called him 'Dr. Lax.' She was very correct. She would consult him on everything—interfamilial relations, travel, food, sex. She played up to him with that insufferable little girl's voice. She had the rather annoying habit of speaking about herself in the third person. I considered it phony, but he thought highly of her, found her very bright.

"He gave her advice. He taught her how to exercise, told her it was preferable to walk quickly rather than race around the Central Park reservoir. When Onassis died, he advised her to get a job and keep busy. He saw other members of the family, including Rose Kennedy and Lee Radziwill and Ethel Kennedy. After Bobby Kennedy's assassination, Ethel wanted something for the funeral so she wouldn't cry. And Henry said, 'Why shouldn't you cry? It's the most natural and normal thing under the circumstances.' So much for that silly family motto—Kennedys never cry.

"One day Jackie told him she had been brought up a Catholic and didn't know much about the points of sex gratification, so Henry drew the female anatomy on a sheet of paper and then traced it with his finger on the palm of her hand, explaining how everything worked. I imagine it helped because the subject never came up again.

"Jackie was something of a health faddist. She insisted on doing every test as it became fashionable—a sugar tolerance test, a heart stress test, whatever. I can attest to the fact that she was in excellent physical health.

"She worried about Caroline, who as a rebellious teenager ate a pound or two of chocolate every day and put on a lot of weight. It was also bad for her skin. She once yelled at Caroline over the telephone from Henry's office. On two occasions, after much coercion on Jackie's part, Henry agreed to prescribe diet pills for Caroline, though in limited quantities. Each Rx was for 15 pills and renewable three times—120 pills in all.

"Although Onassis was also his patient, I don't know if Henry discussed Ari's health with Jackie. I know he thought Onassis should have had a kidney operation earlier in life and recommended it to him, but Onassis didn't follow through. I'm also not sure what Henry thought of their merger. He respected Onassis and found him amusing. I remember seeing Onassis in a restaurant and not recognizing him. His etiquette—the slurping of soup, the way he tore his bread—led me to the conclusion that this man was either a king or a peasant. And in a way Onassis was a little bit of both."

Fanny Warburg, a distant relative of the wealthy Warburg family, worked for Dr. Lax for more than thirty-five years. "I had many conversations with Jackie," she said. "I drew a lot of blood in the process of taking tests. I did electrocardiograms, X-rays, the usual. I knew her for many years. One thing I can say is that I never got anything from her. I never got a tip, perfume, a Christmas gift. She never brought a thing. Of course, the whole Kennedy family, many of whom were patients of Dr. Lax, were that way. Other patients gave me lovely, lovely gifts.

"Caroline and John Jr. were also occasional patients. They came in when they had the flu, a cold, nothing serious. Jackie came in for advice as well as treatment.

She was moody, snobbish, self-important. I didn't find
her all that intelligent. I thought Lee was more intelligent
and much less snobbish. [In fact] I didn't find Lee snobbish at all. Jackie was also very naive. One time I was
there for an hour explaining what her cholesterol count
meant. After all this, she said, 'Oh, do both men and
women have cholesterol?'

"Jackie did some strange things. She used to leave her
disposable dressing gown on the floor for me to pick up.
She would simply take it off and drop it after an examination, like a queen or princess. Other patients placed
theirs in a bin—not Jackie. She lacked consideration. She
just wasn't a nice person. She also came in with dirty
feet. I couldn't figure it out. She didn't seem to care what
people thought."

Carol Rosenwald, an author and restaurateur, experienced a somewhat similar reaction when she encountered
Jackie at a Collegiate School function: "Our sons both
went to Collegiate at the same time. I saw her at an event
called Field Day. Jackie was there to see John Jr. She
was unkempt. She had unwashed, stringy hair that day.
Her sweater had a run in it. Frankly, she looked like
she'd just gotten out of bed. I was surprised."

The day in question may have been an unusually bad
one for Jackie. Other Collegiate mothers were more complimentary. Sally Bitterman, whose son, Brooks, was a
classmate and friend of John Jr., observed her at a number of parent meetings: "She was always very quiet and
never used her fame to get anything special for her son.
Once after Brooks had a play date at the Kennedy apartment, Jackie called to make sure he had gotten home
safely. Most mothers didn't do that."

Marjorie Housepian Dobkin, an academic dean at Barnard College, had three Collegiate sons and served with
Jackie on the school's Education Committee: "The Committee existed to decide about school expansion and the
construction of a new building. I was asked to be on the
Committee presumably because of my educational involvement, while Jackie was asked presumably because
they needed funds for the expansion and the building of
the new site. There were approximately four meetings. I
don't know whether she gave money, but I tend to doubt
it. At one meeting she asked the group whether it was
okay for her son to do his homework with the stereo

blasting. The question was completely out of place, but people answered it. Some said yes, some no.

"When John Jr. went to Collegiate, the Secret Service used to sit around in the lobby of the school. It must have been a low priority assignment, because it couldn't have been very interesting to sit around school all day. After a while they would doze off. They would wake up and find out that the class had gone off someplace. 'Where's John?' they would ask. 'At the museum,' somebody would say. So they'd race over to the museum and look for him there.

"There were three or four bag ladies who were always around the school, harmless old biddies in sneakers with their hair in curlers, and they would ask people, 'Where's John-John?' They once went up to him. 'Do you know John?' 'Yes,' he said, 'I do.' 'What's he like?' they asked. 'He's a great guy,' he answered."

One of the Secret Service agents newly assigned to the Kennedy children was James Kalafatis. Being of Greek heritage, Kalafatis proved invaluable after Jackie married Onassis. He not only spoke the language but helped her and the children understand the culture. He explained what this meant and what that meant. He enabled her to appreciate Greeks more as people. He taught her about Greek food. He explained the Greek Orthodox Church. He made the transition easier.

One day in the fall of 1969, when Jackie and her son went bicycle riding in Central Park, Ron Galella leaped out at them from behind a clump of bushes with his camera, causing John Jr. to swerve and nearly crash. It was the second incident in less than a week involving Galella and Jackie's children. The other had taken place at the Brearley School to which Caroline had transferred from Convent of the Sacred Heart. Galella had followed the child to a Brearley carnival, taking photographs and embarrassing her in front of her friends. After the second incident Jackie decided that something had to be done. Ordering the Secret Service agents on duty to apprehend the photographer, she demanded that he be placed under arrest and booked at the nearest police precinct. Claiming that his relentless pursuit caused her and her children "grievous mental anguish," she sought a permanent injunction to keep Galella 200 yards from her Fifth Avenue apartment building and 100 yards from her person (or her children) anywhere else. Represented by attorney Alfred Julien, the photographer counter-claimed, seeking $1.3 million in punitive damages for "false arrest, malicious persecution, and interference with my livelihood as a photographer." The affair culminated in two highly publicized trials, one in 1972 and the other in 1981.

By the time Jackie and Ari returned to Skorpios from a February 1970 cruise to Mexico, there were discernible cracks in the marriage. Their visitors that summer included Rose Kennedy and the Radziwills. Stas Radziwill later told Max Jacobson that the union seemed to be turning sour. His own marriage, he added, was also on the rocks: he and Lee were on the verge of a separation leading to a divorce.

Another visitor to Skorpios, this one uninvited, was Ron Galella. The photographer hired a local fisherman to smuggle him ashore. He took photographs of the island and later followed its inhabitants to Capri, trailing Jackie, Lee and their respective children through the crowded narrow streets, snapping pictures as he went.

Aristotle Onassis had his own continuing mix of family irritations, quite apart from his problems with his wife. Christina commuted regularly between London (her mother's home), Lausanne, Switzerland (residence of her maternal grandmother), Paris, Monte Carlo, Athens, Skorpios and New York (actually the city of her and her brother Alexander's birth). Ari's possessiveness towards his children had less to do with geography than with marriage. As in previous Greek generations, he felt he was entitled to choose a suitable mate for his daughter. His choice was Peter Goulandris, a 23-year-old scion of a family that controlled four separate shipping lines, including more than 130 vessels valued at an estimated $2 billion. They owned yachts, islands, race horses and soccer teams. Christina had known Peter her entire life. His mother, Maria Goulandris, was by birth a Lemos, the wealthiest of all Greek shipping families. A marriage between Christina and Peter would unite three of the most powerful families in Greece and create a triumvirate that would rule the seas for centuries to come.*

---

*Jackie was independently friendly with members of the Goulandris family, among them Niki Goulandris, a socialite and vice-president of the Goulandris Natural History Museum, Kifissia, Greece. "So many false things have been said about Jackie," insisted Niki Goulandris. "For example, Jackie would often walk around barefoot. It was ridiculous that the press wrote she had so many pairs of shoes."

Ari's vision held little appeal for his daughter. Onassis turned first to his sister, Artemis, and then to Jackie for help in convincing Christina to become engaged to this willing and wealthy young man. Jackie's intervention was met with great hostility by her stepdaughter, who resented perhaps even more Jackie's attempts to remake her physically.

"Jackie was hypercritical of Christina's appearance," said Costa Gratsos. "She was too fat, too hirsute, not fashionable enough. Jackie encouraged her to go for electrolysis treatments, took her shopping, sent her to a diet doctor, induced her to exercise, escorted her to a make-up salon. After several weeks, Christina rebelled, and angrily told Jackie that she didn't want to look like one more 'vapid' American high-fashion model."

The engagement to Goulandris didn't take place, and in addition, relations between Onassis and his son were more strained than ever. Alexander's hostility over the marriage to Jackie was a constant threat because it weighed on his father's conscience. And now, in the midst of being prepared to one day pick up the family reins, Alexander had romantic problems of his own, having fallen in love with Fiona Campbell Thyssen, the Scottish-born model and ex-wife of one of Europe's most successful industrialists, sixteen years older than Alexander and mother of two teenage children. In light of their age difference, Onassis bitterly opposed Alexander's plan to marry Fiona. Jackie supported her husband's view of the situation. Alexander, reluctantly and angrily, deferred to his father's wish but none of this made him feel better about his stepmother and the "preposterous marriage" that he felt had been imposed on him.

Besides the children—his and hers—there was the matter of the Kennedys, and Jackie's devotion to the legend of her first husband. Although Onassis did not complain that the memory of the late President seemed to obtrude at every step—was not Jackie's past one of the reasons he had married her?—it must have been difficult for a proud Greek husband to live in the shadow of another man. It created an inner conflict which he had not foreseen and which arose whenever his wife observed one of her numerous anniversaries—the anniversary of Jack's birth, the anniversary of their wedding, the anniversary of his death, the anniversary of highlights in his career which Jackie frequently drew to the children's attention.

One such celebration involved the presentation to the White House of the official portraits of John and Jacqueline Kennedy, a tradition generally observed after each new administration. After unsuccessful attempts by several portrait artists to win the commission, Jackie settled on Aaron Shikler, a New York artist, to carry out the assignment. Shikler succeeded in capturing what he called Jackie's "extraordinary, almost spooky, beauty." The portrait of the late President showed Kennedy in a moment of dejection, his head bowed and arms crossed.

Jackie sanctioned both portraits but had little desire to return to the White House. Writing in response to an invitation from Pat Nixon, she said—

> As you know, the thought of returning to the White House is difficult for me. I really do not have the courage to go through an official ceremony, and bring the children back to the only home they both knew with their father under such traumatic conditions. With the press and everything, things I try to avoid in their little lives, I know the experience would be hard on them and not leave them with the memories of the White House I would like them to have.

—and then went on to suggest that a *private* viewing of the portraits might be arranged at a time convenient for the Nixons.

Jackie's return to the White House—her first and last—took place on February 3, 1971. She and her children were flown from LaGuardia Airport aboard Air Force One. It was a return trip she felt compelled to make. After viewing the portraits, Jackie, John Jr. and Caroline joined President and Mrs. Nixon and their two daughters, Tricia and Julie, for a private supper.

They talked in very general terms about all the changes that had taken place in the years since Jackie had occupied the White House. The Nixons were determined to steer the conversation away from anything that might distress their guest or make the visit sad. At one point, Jackie looked at President Nixon and said, "I always lived in a dream world."

The Kennedy portraits were not officially unveiled until March 1971. Shikler had previously agreed to write an article on his work for *McCall's* for the same month, including studies for the portrait of Jackie commissioned by the White House Historical Association. Said Shikler: "The only big screw-up came when somehow Maxine Cheshire got hold of one of the studies before it appeared in the magazine. It ran in the *Washington Post*. Jackie was very upset. She called me up and said, 'What are we going to do now?' It wasn't the White House portrait, just one of the studies, so I wasn't upset. But Jackie was angry. She said, 'Nothing has changed in that town—nothing.' "

With yet another Kennedy event behind her, Jackie joined up with Ari on Martinique, briefly visited the Mellons on Antigua, then sailed via the Canary Islands to Skorpios. Also aboard was Johnny Meyer, an aide and procurer for Onassis who had performed the same services years earlier for Howard Hughes. Onassis once wanted to buy TWA from Hughes and paid Meyer to expedite negotiations. The deal never materialized, but Meyer remained on Ari's payroll.

In a proposal for a book never written, Meyer recalled that it was on this cruise that Jackie asked him if he thought Ari would allow her to plan some of the meals. After all, she organized a few meals at the White House in her day. Meyer broached the simple request with his employer. "Why doesn't she just behave herself and do nothing?" Ari responded. "I think she's bored," said Meyer. Onassis shrugged his shoulders and replied, "Then let her decorate the menus."

Jacques Harvey maintained that Onassis would from time to time humiliate his wife. "I heard him insult her once. In front of Jackie he told his chauffeur to accompany her to Maxim's because he wanted to go and see a particularly attractive young girl who had made several advances to him."

Canadian oil executive Roger F. Bentley, a guest aboard the *Christina* on the voyage from Martinique to Skorpios, recalled that "Jackie and Ari barely spoke to one another. They argued once at dinner. Jackie corrected some factual error on Ari's part—the capital city of an African nation. 'Don't contradict me in front of others,' Ari thundered. She left the table and wasn't seen for the rest of the evening.

"Onassis was beset by personal problems. His former sister-in-law, Eugenie Livanos Niarchos, had been found dead on Spetsopoula, a Greek island belonging to Stavros Niarchos. The circumstances of her death were highly suspicious. The body bore wounds supposedly sustained when Niarchos attempted to revive his wife. An autopsy indicated she had died of barbiturate poisoning. Niarchos was exonerated. What tortured Onassis was the disclosure that his former wife Tina, Eugenie's younger sister, would soon marry Niarchos."

That summer, Onassis experienced an even greater blow. Christina, severely depressed over the death of her aunt and unable to cope with her father's marriage, announced her intention to marry an American she had met at a hotel swimming pool in Monte Carlo. Joseph R. Bolker, 48, short and wiry, was a twice-divorced father of four, a Los Angeles realtor of relatively modest means and probably the first man to care genuinely about Christina as a person.

Ari began telephoning his international network of aides and advisers for explanations and answers. "He called me first," said Costa Gratsos. "He was yelling and screaming. I thought a major deal had collapsed. 'Who's Joe Bolker?' he kept saying. 'Who?' I asked. 'Bolker . . . Bolker . . . B-O-L-K-E-R . . . Bolker.' 'Never heard of him,' I responded. It took him 20 minutes to calm down. He said he was having a bug placed in Christina's London flat. Then he hung up and he called his brother-in-law, Nikos Konialidis, managing director of Olympic Airways. They conversed for no less than four hours, Skorpios to New York. Nikos had a red light outside his office door and a sign that read: WHEN LIGHT IS ON DO NOT UNDER ANY CIRCUMSTANCES ENTER. That light was on the entire morning. Later, I received calls from 'Professor,' Ioannides Georgakis [President of Olympic Airways] in Athens; Thomas Lincoln [attorney for Ari's shipping lines, Victory Carriers], Nigel Neilson [head of public relations for Onassis] in London, and a host of others. Everybody asked the same question: 'Who is Joe Bolker?'

"The last person he called was Christina. He implored her to give up the plan; she refused. He sent Alexander to see her but his approach proved no more successful.

Jackie also failed. Christina described Jackie to Bolker as 'my father's unhappy compulsion.' Christina's mother had nothing to say because she was on the verge of marrying Niarchos. For Ari there was only one thing to do: if he could not dissuade his daughter from getting married, he could at least insure that Bolker didn't touch the Onassis fortune.

Ari's threat to disinherit his daughter only spurred her on. She and Joe Bolker were married in Las Vegas on July 29, 1971. The date was significant: Onassis was on Skorpios celebrating his wife's forty-second birthday at a belated party when word arrived. For the duration of their brief marriage, the Bolkers, residing in Los Angeles, were subjected to extraordinary pressures.

The pressures exerted by Onassis through his intermediaries were always of a legal nature. But after six months, Ari ordered Johnny Meyer to "Get her back, even if you have to kidnap her."

"I finally got through to Christina," writes Meyer. "I was lucky—she wanted to go home, but didn't know what to do about the maid she had brought over to live with her in Los Angeles, and her Mercedes, and the $10,000 she brought with her when she eloped.

"I told her to get dressed as if she was going to the store, and to put her passport and the other things she would need in a shopping bag. And I told her to go to a phone booth near her apartment at Century Towers and call me. When she called, I said, 'Wait there.'

"We had it all set up with Pan American. Christina and I were to go through the airport metal detector first, and our two security men were supposed to walk around it. But George Tzaforos, one of the two guards followed right behind me, and the other one was right behind him. They were each carrying a pair of .45's, one on the left and one on the right. When they hit the metal detector, the bells started ringing. . . . Pan Am wanted to get them through, but it was embarrassing."

Unable and unwilling to withstand the force and will of her father, Christina agreed to divorce Joe Bolker, the first of a procession of failed marriages for a woman often billed as one of the world's richest. In return she was reinstated in her father's will. Onassis, however, wasn't quite finished with Bolker. He told Meyer to get the Mercedes and Christina's $10,000 back from Bolker, and to have him pay the maid's airfare home to Greece. Meyer reminded Onassis that she could fly Olympic and save everybody a lot of trouble and expense. "No," Ari said. "Make him pay.

29

Aristotle Onassis tried until the last moment to discourage his wife from proceeding in her single-minded legal vendetta against Ron Galella. "Publicity is like rain," he told her. "When you're soaking wet, what difference do a few drops more make?" He advised her that if she sued, the public would perceive her as vindictive and mean-spirited. Jackie had no intention of backing down.

Judge Irving Ben Cooper of the U.S. District Court dismissed Galella's countersuit and imposed a permanent injunction prohibiting the aggressive photographer from coming within 150 feet of Jackie, 225 feet of her children and 300 feet of 1040 Fifth Avenue. Galella appealed. A final judgment was handed down whereby he could come within 25 feet of Jackie and 30 feet of her children.

To his immense distress, Onassis received a bill for more than $500,000 from Jackie's law firm—Paul Weiss Rifkind Wharton and Garrison—for their part in the case. Onassis flatly refused to pay. He had already given them a $50,000 retainer; he told Jackie to pay the rest out of her allowance. When the law firm sued Onassis, he hired attorney Roy M. Cohn to negotiate a settlement. The firm agreed to accept an additional $235,000 and to close the matter. Onassis gave his wife a check in that amount to deposit in her account and within an hour she sent her own check to Simon Rifkind.

While the Galella affair was being temporarily laid to rest, a Greek photographer named Nikos Koulouris was taken to court in Lefkas and sentenced to six months' imprisonment on four charges related to his surreptitious attempts to take pictures on Skorpios. "And it didn't cost me a penny," boasted Ari.

"The European paparazzi were much rougher than their American counterparts," said Secret Service agent James Kalafatis. "Galella was mild by comparison. The

Europeans moved in swarms, twenty to thirty to a pack and became very physical—pushing, shoving, screaming, taunting. Being Secret Service in a foreign country, our options were limited. You couldn't just arrest these guys and haul them in. We lacked jurisdiction over there. The most I could do was get the local authorities to take action, but even that was difficult. They weren't crazy about Americans in Greece in those days."

The next photographic coup to appear in print was the now-famous nude pictures of Jackie and Ari sunbathing on Skorpios shot by ten enterprising photographers in diving outfits using underwater cameras and telephoto lenses. The nineteen-page full frontal portfolio of Jackie entitled "The Billion Dollar Bush" appeared first in *Playmen* (an Italian publication). The photos were brought to America and first published in *Screw* and later in the then-new magazine *Hustler*. The photographs eventually appeared in scores of tabloids around the world.

Jackie pretended to shrug it off, telling an American reporter: "It doesn't touch my real life which is with my children and my husband." But, according to Costa Gratsos, Jackie asked her husband to sue those responsible for taking the photographs as well as any newspapers or magazines that published them.

"There are too many," said Onassis.

"Sue them all," Jackie replied.

Asked by one journalist whether he and Jackie were nudists, Onassis responded: "It happens that I sometimes take off my pants to put on my bathing suit. Anything's possible . . ."

Said Jackie's mother, Janet Auchincloss: "It's awful to think what has happened to the human race that they have to go underwater to spy on people. I just try not to think about it."

Rose Kennedy telephoned Jackie the moment she heard. How could Jackie allow such a thing to happen, she asked. If not for herself, had she no concern for the children? And where was that highly touted security team Onassis had promised to provide?

A year before Ari's death, he admitted to Roy Cohn that he and one of the Italian photographers in the group had planned the entire operation. "Jackie did nothing but complain about Ron Galella and all the other media types who conspired to make her life impossible," said

Cohn. "Onassis figured if she appeared in the nude, nothing else they did could ever offend her again. She wanted him to give her the money for a lawsuit against the photographers. When he refused, she went around telling friends he was a tightwad.

"I liked Onassis," Cohn continued. "He had an odd sensibility. I heard an amusing story about him. There was a reporter-photographer in Paris who worked for one of the business weeklies, and this fellow was always after Onassis for an interview. Business was the one subject Onassis would not touch with reporters. He would disclose the names of every woman he had bedded, but he would not discuss financial affairs. And that's exactly what this fellow wanted to write about. One evening he followed Onassis into The Crazy Horse Saloon, still badgering him for an interview. Onassis went to the men's room and the reporter went along. Ari headed for a stall, did his business, came out five minutes later and the guy was standing there waiting for him. 'Look,' said Ari, 'if I agree to give you an exclusive, will you go away?' 'What sort of exclusive?' asked the journalist, suspiciously. 'I'll let you in on the key to my success—social, financial and otherwise. I've never really gone public with any of this. But I will for you, if only for peace of mind.' 'You've got a deal,' said the fellow. And with that Ari lowered his trousers, dropped his drawers, put a hand underneath the family jewels and deftly hoisted the entire mechanism upward and forward. 'Here's my secret,' he said, 'I've got balls.' "

Whether he recognized it yet or not, he also had a rapidly failing marriage on his hands. He had all but given up hope of ever moving into Jackie's apartment on Fifth Avenue. "Jackie always had some excuse as to why Ari couldn't stay," said Costa Gratsos. " 'The decorators are in,' she would say. I never saw an apartment undergo so many decorating changes. It was an upper-class version of the working-class woman's mania with cleaning house, which psychiatrists recognize as an attempt to wash away guilt or atone for forbidden desires, although Ari never attached such meaning to it. 'She likes refurbishing the apartment,' he would claim when asked why he had to stay at the Pierre.

"When he did sleep in Jackie's apartment, it was in a guest room that contained pink floral wallpaper and white wicker furniture. She refused to change it though it was more suitable for a little girl than a shipping magnate. Nor would she empty the adjoining bathroom, which she used for extra storage space.

"She offered other excuses as well. 'Caroline has friends in this weekend.' Caroline Kennedy was by then attending prep school at Concord Academy in Massachusetts and would presumably invite her classmates down to New York for a visit. It was one thing or another. Ari would go over there for dinner, but only when Jackie had dinner parties, and even then he wasn't always invited. He often took his meals alone in restaurants.

"He would go to '21' or El Morocco by himself at night because Jackie preferred to sketch or read at home. He complained he didn't get along with her New York friends, whereas she didn't care for his business associates. 'Half her male friends are fags,' he used to say. These supposedly highly cultivated intercontinentals looked down on him. With those dark glasses that he wore indoors and out, he looked like a gangster. He wore them for medical reasons. He suffered from macular degeneration, an eye disease that destroys the retina, and the dark glasses helped filter out the glare caused by bright light. He saw better at night than during the day, which is one reason he tended to work at night. Nevertheless, Jackie's friends thought the shades made him look like Al Capone."

Lynn Alpha Smith recalled the constant turmoil in Ari's New York office "whenever the boss and his wife were in town. One Monday morning, I came into the office and was told by Gratsos to call Onassis at the Pierre. Gratsos warned me that Ari was in a foul mood because he'd spent the weekend with Jackie and Jackie's mother at Hammersmith Farm. By this point he realized what a total prima donna he had married, which is the one thing he truly detested, and usually saw through.

"Jackie rarely telephoned the office on her own behalf," Smith said. "She had Nancy Tuckerman call for her. Tuckerman was on the Olympic Airways employment rolls, but actually worked for Jackie as a kind of glorified office girl. She would bring in the bills at the end of every month, including Jackie's grocery charges. Sometimes she would show up less than 15 days after the allowance had been received to ask for more money from Onassis's financial man, Creon Broun. Creon would go crazy. The thing is Jackie was receiving an allowance of $30,000 per month, and she would try and get more by presenting bills that were supposed to be covered by her allowance.

"Then there were loads of extras. Jackie wanted a John Singer Sargent drawing she had seen at some gallery. She had Nancy Tuckerman call to ask if Onassis would buy it for her. I told her I'd transmit the question to Onassis, who was then in London. I asked Creon Broun to tell Onassis. The following day, Ari called directly from England. 'You tell her she'll have to pay for it out of her own account,' said Onassis. He didn't sound happy. Creon Broun bitched continually about how much money Jackie used to spend. He'd walk around the office holding the bills. 'Can you believe this?' he'd ask. 'She spent $5,000 this month on slacks alone.' You'd think it was his money the way he carried on.

"I used to live at 220 East 73rd Street. Nancy Tuckerman lived in an adjoining building and I saw her occasionally. One evening, she invited me for tea and started pumping me about some townhouse on Gracie Square that Jackie wanted Onassis to buy her. She wanted to know if Onassis had put any money down on the house, or what he thought of the idea. She had obviously been put up to it by Jackie. I said I didn't know anything about it. I thought to myself, 'What kind of a marriage is this if Jackie doesn't go straight to her husband about such affairs?' But I kept my mouth shut.

"Gratsos told me once that the degree of Jackie's affection for Onassis was in direct proportion to the amount of money she received in return."

"What was incredible," said Costa Gratsos, "is that Jackie couldn't make it on the amount of money she received each month. It started at $30,000, tax-free, disbursed by the New York office. Later, Ari became angry over her prodigal spending and moved her account to his Monte Carlo office where he could presumably watch it more closely. He also scaled down her allowance to about $20,000 a month.

"On the other hand, he was partially to blame for the problem. For a time, he had encouraged her in her buying and shopping and spending. Whenever anybody questioned him about it, he reminded them how much suffering she had endured and how she had been practically excommunicated by the Catholic Church for marrying him. I had the feeling he was merely echoing her line. Yet he was convinced she had class. He once said to me that Maria Callas was more like him—tempestuous, earthy, a bit vulgar—while Jackie was by nature cool and introspective.

"I can't say he didn't admire her at first. He mentioned how he had once sat with her at a sidewalk café in Paris when a group of American tourists clambered off a bus. One of them, a middle-aged woman wearing a flowered straw hat, recognized Jackie, approached and without a word spat in her face. Ari jumped up and tried to find a policeman to arrest the woman, but Jackie stopped him. 'She's not worth arresting,' said Jackie. Ari admired her valor in such situations.

"Eventually Jackie went too far, even for Ari. With the disarming coquetry for which she was famous, she frequently complained about her financial woes. Upon the recommendation of her pal André Meyer, but against Ari's advice, she invested in the stock market and lost some $300,000. This was from the $3 million prenuptial gift he gave her. She pleaded with him, begged him to replenish it. And he kept refusing, saying he had told her to keep it in tax-free bonds. But even here he relented. One morning he impetuously stuffed $1 million in large currency into a leather suitcase and took it up to Meyer's apartment at the Carlyle. Meyer was shocked. 'I would have taken a check, Ari,' he said. The whole point was the shock value of watching André Meyer open a suitcase containing $1 million in cold cash. 'It was almost worth the trip just to see the expression on that old weasel's face,' Onassis said.

"It was a bit sickening. Jackie not only had the interest from her newly replenished $3 million, she had the $20,000 to $30,000 monthly allowance as well as charge privileges in numerous luxury stores around the world. I'm talking compulsive spending. Ari showed me one bill for $5,000 for a private messenger service, a $6,000 bill for the care and feeding of her pets, a $7,000 bill for odds and ends from the local pharmacy. This woman was out to break the bank.

"She had one charming little rule: Ari had to bring back a present from every part of the world he visited. Once, all he brought her was a simple apron from South

Africa. She was livid. I suppose she expected a shoebox of raw diamonds.

"After Ari cracked down on his wife's budget and put her on a short leash, she became highly agitated. The calls became more frequent, the demands more plaintive."

Jackie had a quick way of raising cash which she had practiced since her days in the White House. After wearing her costly garments once or twice, sometimes not at all, she would resell them and squirrel away the money. Her favorite resale house, Encore of New York, on Madison Avenue at 84th Street, did a steady trade on Jackie's slightly used, and sometimes new, clothing. According to Carol Selig, owner of Encore, Jackie "consigned everything from coats, suits and gowns, to pocketbooks, blouses and slacks. The labels were only the best: Yves Saint Laurent, Valentino, Halston, Christian Dior."

That she had engaged in this practice since the White House was first disclosed in 1969 by Mary Gallagher, her former secretary, in her published memoir, *My Life With Jacqueline Kennedy*. In the book, Gallagher claims that Jackie's clothing was resold under "my name and home address." As the various items were sold, Encore's check would come to Mary, and she would deposit it in her personal account, at the same time writing out a check for the same amount to be deposited in Jackie's account.

Once, apparently, Gallagher took a fancy to a blue cloth coat, which Jackie hoped would bring $65.00. Jackie gave her the coat, and Mary gave her the money. On rare occasions, she writes, Jackie would be in a "generous mood" and give her old clothes away. One example was a red maternity dress, which the secretary couldn't use and which the consignment houses wouldn't take.

Jacques Harvey noted that Onassis had on his staff a couple, George and Ellen Ciros, who managed his Avenue Foch apartment in Paris and for whom Jackie had genuine affection: "Ellen was the one who traveled with Jackie as a kind of interpreter-companion when Jackie first married Onassis. Christina was also extremely fond of her. Ellen must have been the best-dressed servant in captivity, because Jackie and Christina both gave her dozens of dresses over the years."

Although Christina Onassis was no clothes horse, she had certain drives and compulsions that were almost humorous in their intensity. "Christina had a Coca-Cola fetish," said Costa Gratsos. "She would consume up to thirty bottles of Coke a day. She was such an aficionado of the product, she could tell by a very slight variance in taste which Coca-Cola bottling plant the bottle came from. This was particularly true in Europe, where the taste and sweetness varied from country to country. This addiction undoubtedly added to her weight problem."

She had a more expensive obsession with jewelry. Beny Aristea, proprietress of Nidri Gold, a classic Greek jewelry store on the island adjacent to Skorpios, confirmed that Christina "splurged on the best gold articles in the store: rings, necklaces, bracelets and crucifixes. She liked gem stones, too, but her main interest was gold. She bought it for herself and her friends. She would come in religiously every other week. She wouldn't say much, just select various items from the display case, dozens of them. She always had a bodyguard along. We would box the items and she would leave quickly. Then we would send the bill. Within days a man would come to pay. It's difficult to say how much she spent. Probably upwards of $1 million a year for over ten years. And we were only one store among many that she frequented."

"Christina was Jackie's spiritual antithesis," said Costa Gratsos. "Christina was spoiled and naive, but she was also generous to a fault. She gave away invaluable possessions, not only to friends and acquaintances but to complete strangers. I remember a party she attended where a certain guest greatly admired a black pearl necklace she happened to be wearing. 'Do you want it?' Christina asked her. 'You must be joking,' said the stranger. 'No, I'm not,' responded Christina. 'I don't even like the necklace. If you want it, its yours.' She unclasped it and placed it around the other woman's neck. This wasn't an isolated incident. If she went into a store and bought several dresses, she also frequently bought one for the saleslady. Perhaps she felt a certain degree of guilt over having so much when others had so little. She was known to be an easy mark.

"Ari possessed the same instinctive generosity. He not only supported an entire sixty-member family, he treated his employees and servants like family. He expected them to work hard, but he rewarded them with gifts and kindness. He took care of them in other ways. If a gardener on Skorpios, for example, had a wife in need of medical attention, he made certain she received it. If the same employee had a bright son who qualified for a college education, he subsidized the boy's schooling. That's why his employees were so loyal. Many of them stayed with him for years and years.

"He was also an extravagant tipper. If he ate a $50 meal in a restaurant, he left a $50 tip. If he took a taxicab, he gave the driver double the meter. If he came across a Greek busboy or waiter in New York or Paris, he always slipped the fellow a $100 bill."

It was Onassis, not Jackie, who came to the aid of Edith and Edie Beale of Grey Gardens on Lily Pond Lane in East Hampton. His first exposure to the Beales was Edie's long and supportive letter after his marriage to Jackie. When he arrived in New York following the honeymoon, he telephoned them at Grey Gardens. Edith said she knew he had "a soft spot" for singers, especially sopranos, and proceeded to sing to him. He then sang a song back to her over the telephone. After that he sent mother and daughter a wardrobe of leather clothing, as well as a dark blue blanket with a white anchor on it from the *Christina*. They called it "the Onassis blanket."

In 1971, irate neighbors called upon the Suffolk County Health Department to declare Grey Gardens a health hazard, to have its tenants (the Beales) evicted and the large, rotting, cat-infested residence razed. When the press learned of the incident and remembered that Big Edie was the sister of Black Jack Bouvier, Jackie Onassis's father, the story gained national prominence. "Something looked askew to the world," said "Little Edie" Beale. "On the one hand, you had a former First Lady and the wife of one of the richest men on earth, and then you had her cousin and aunt who were about to be dispossessed and were totally without funds. It didn't look right. Jackie realized she had a public relations problem on her hands. Instead of paying the price herself, she brought Onassis into the picture."

Bouvier Beale, Edith Beale's lawyer son, objected to Jackie's intervention. "I wanted Edith and Edie out of Grey Gardens because I wanted to get them into more normal surroundings," he said. "I had talked about getting them a place on the west coast of Florida. I realized it would have been difficult getting them out of there, figuratively leading Mother forth in chains in front of the

TV cameras. She was a highly opinionated, very powerful person. She understood how to use the media. Here
were these Republican village fathers in East Hampton
tormenting this poor liberal for her political convictions.
That's how she played it in the press. So I knew it
wouldn't be easy. But I say the raid of Grey Gardens by
the Health Department was a Godsend, a way to get
them out of there and to restore a little normalcy into
their lives.

"Jackie managed to fix up the house over my dead
body. I had a big fight with her about it. She claimed
Edith and Edie would never leave, and she certainly
didn't care for all the publicity that was coming out about
the case, especially the publicity linking her as the wife of
one of the world's richest men to these two poor relatives
of hers. So she took care of it. But I wanted to get them
out and she didn't. The stench was unbearable. There
was raccoon and cat excrement everywhere. The place
had been boarded up. Mother had gotten into a fight
with the sanitation department out there and they had
stopped coming around to pick up the garbage. They
hadn't picked it up in six months."

One of the people whose help Jackie solicited in dealing with the Suffolk County Department of Health was
attorney William J. vanden Heuvel. "When I went into
the house for the first time," he recalled, "it was beyond
belief—a pile of rubbish, cats, raccoons, vermin. I personally helped with others to clean it up. There were
over 1,000 large green plastic garbage bags filled with
stuff removed from Grey Gardens. It had to be done on
an emergency basis. I supervised the rubbish removal. I
had to be there because I was the only interface with
Mrs. Beale she would trust and accept.

"Aristotle Onassis paid for the repair of the house. I
sent the bills to him. I used to talk with him about it. He
was very interested. He frequently chatted with Mrs.
Beale on the telephone and found her quite charming.

"The old roof, which had practically been eaten away,
had to be replaced. The sick cats had to be taken out of
the house. There was a dead cat in Mrs. Beale's bedroom. She was an extraordinary person in many respects,
a beautiful woman with big blue eyes and lots of white
hair—there was an incredible portrait of her as a debutante in her house.

"She still loved to sing. After much of the work was done I went out there again and she came out of the house for the first time in 11 years. She couldn't move well, but she managed to get out, and we had a picnic on the front lawn and the grass was taller than I am, and I'm 6'2". We sat in the sun and on the grass and she sang—it was one of the most remarkable scenes."

Doris Francisco, Edith Beale's friend, recalled a visit to Grey Gardens by Jackie's children. "John Jr. insisted on seeing the attic and rummaging through all the heaps of junk. His Secret Service agent insisted on going up there after him. When they came down, John said it reminded him of a stage. He found a board and an old rusty rollerskate, which Edith let him keep. I suppose he wanted to make a skateboard for himself."

Jackie also visited the Beales. Accompanied by Miche Bouvier, who had returned from France to live on Long Island, Jacqueline spent several hours at Grey Gardens reminiscing about the past.

In late May 1972, Lilly Lawrence and her husband Bunty arranged a nine-day trip to Teheran, Iran, for Jackie, Ari and several companions. The expedition, part business but largely pleasure, was financed by Lilly's father, Dr. Reza Fallah.

"Ari informed me that we would go over on Olympic," recollected Lilly. "He said Nancy Tuckerman would make all the travel arrangements, so I ordered that a Persian rug be sent to her for all her trouble.

"Tuckerman called me a day or two before we were to leave and said I should send a check for $3,000. 'What for?' I asked. 'For two round-trip airplane tickets for yourself and Mr. Lawrence. If you don't send the money, I can't send the tickets.' I was flabbergasted. Here we were hosting Jackie and her party for nine days, putting them up in the best suites at the Teheran Hilton, allowing Jackie to charge everything—clothes, jewelry, gifts—to my father's account, and she didn't have the common decency to provide a pair of complimentary tickets aboard her husband's airline.

"I'll never forget how she tried to do us out of $3,000 on that trip. Bunty advised me to make the check payable to Olympic Airways, not to Jackie. Once in Teheran, her entourage ran up a huge hotel bill, including long-distance telephone calls, round-the-clock room-service requests, open-ended charging of gifts. Jackie purchased Persian rugs, a number of sheepskin jackets for herself and her children, sheepskin boots, necklaces, earrings, gold bracelets, wall hangings, silk ties, objets d'art, lamps, antiques, a brass trunk. She acquired so much jewelry, in fact, that one jeweler gave her a valuable item on the house. Evenings, the group toured the finest restaurants and nightclubs, again charging everything in sight to my father. Jackie hinted that she would like to take home some golden caviar as a souvenir of her trip, so we arranged to have a massive quantity sent to her hotel. Their total bill for the nine-day stay came to more than $650,000.

"Before she left, Jackie announced she would be leaving a $700 check to be distributed among the hotel staff who had served her. But no check was ever found. When we returned to New York, she didn't send me so much as a bouquet of flowers.

"I'm bored with the trip, I'm bored with the woman, but I'm not bored with the fact that she held me up for $3,000 at the outset.

"Jackie is a total actress, a craft she learned as a result of her political experience. The truth is she held John F. Kennedy in disdain. She was aware of his going with other women and never forgave him for it. All this business about Jackie making her peace with the Kennedys is just so much window dressing. She disliked the family and engineered a relationship of convenience with them, one of self-preservation for herself. She didn't care for politicians at all, and was constantly on the lookout for socially acclaimed people like Jayne Wrightsman and Bunny Mellon.

"Part of Jackie's acting technique was demonstrated at the funeral of JFK. Actually it was RFK, not Jackie, who directed it, while Jackie played the female lead with her two little helpers—the children—as supporting cast. The chorus was represented by all the visiting dignitaries from abroad.

"Jackie also treated Ari miserably. Ari was like a father to me. I knew more about him than Christina did. He would come over to my place and weep like a baby over the way Jackie dealt with him. She pulled some incredible maneuvers. She gave up her $10,000 widow's pension when they married and then she went to him and said, 'I feel I'm married to one of the richest men in the world and I don't think I should get a [Presidential widow's] pension. I'm penniless and now I'm in your hands.' Of course, she was just as penniless with the $10,000 per year as without."

"Jackie has pulled some strange moves," agreed gossip columnist Cindy Adams. "I know a carpenter who built some bookshelves for her and afterwards she asked him if he would rather be paid or have an autographed photo of her. He said he would prefer an autographed check."

If Jackie squandered her husband's money, she was always tight with her own. She had to pay out of her own budget, for example, to repaint her Fifth Avenue apartment. Once, she called in a representative of the Union Square Painting Company and asked for estimates. When she found it would cost $5,000 for the paint job, she cancelled the project rather than spend the money. Another painting firm was later offered the same job with the following option: if they waived payment she would recommend them to all her friends, thus generating a great deal of added business. They too opted for payment. This offer became commonplace in Jackie's Fifth Avenue household: to work for nothing and gain her everlasting confidence, or to charge and become the victim of her merciless wrath.

She used the same technique in dealing with department stores. "She used to buy clothes at Bonwit Teller and ask for a reduction," said Cindy Adams. "She claimed that if she was seen wearing an item from a specific store, everyone else would want to buy the same item."

A variation on the theme included returning much of the merchandise she had bought previously on impulse, a tactic she practiced regularly at some of New York's most exclusive emporiums—Hermès, Gucci, Saks, Bloomingdale's (where she bought housewares), Alexanders (phonograph records), Serendipity (novelty items), Hammacher Schlemmer, Henri Bendel, F.A.O. Schwarz, and Art Bag Creations (pocketbooks). "She did a real number in the shoe department at Bergdorf Goodman," said a former Bergdorf salesman. "She'd buy three dozen pairs at a single sitting, then return the entire lot the following day. Her sister Lee pulled the same number. I told them they were going to cost me my job."

Shopping—for almost anything—is a major preoccupation with Jackie. "She has an eye for immediately spotting the most precious and expensive object wherever she goes," Onassis once said. Money, it would seem, was her Achilles' heel. In the heat of the moment, Jackie seemed unaware of exactly how much she had spent; when it finally hit her, she would wonder where it all went. In an effort to keep expenditures in check, even while married to Onassis, she began taking her sister along on shopping sprees, but Lee's philosophy on spending proved to be disquietingly similar. "I'm constantly falling in love with objects, and they follow me around the world," she told *Architectural Digest*. Whenever they went shopping together, the two sisters invariably ended up at the Hotel Carlyle, where, over coffee and cake, they tallied up the calories along with the purchases.

The Onassis marriage was soon mired in a new rut. Husband and wife squabbled over her obligatory appearance at still another Kennedy-sponsored event—the first-anniversary performance of Leonard Bernstein's *Mass* at the John F. Kennedy Center for the Performing Arts. It was her first appearance at the Center she had worked so assiduously to help erect. Ari was equally unhappy when Jackie flew with Frank Sinatra to Providence, Rhode Island, to attend a Sinatra concert, her first reunion with Sinatra since their White House falling out.*

If Ari resented Sinatra, Jackie felt similarly about Elizabeth Taylor. Jackie's friends tell of a quarrel over an incident in Rome involving Onassis and Taylor. The tycoon and the actress were lunching together, along with other friends, when an intruder began annoying Taylor. Gallantly, Onassis splashed a glass of champagne in the intruder's face.

Jackie claimed to be embarrassed. "I'm ashamed of you," she told her husband. She protested that "the children had seen news accounts."

By contrast, Ari's renewed affair with Maria Callas no longer bothered Jackie. Whatever jealousy Onassis had been able to muster from the affair had long been re-

---

*In 1974, Sinatra saw Jackie again, escoring her to the Uris Theatre in New York, where he was to perform with Ella Fitzgerald and Count Basie. Backstage later with bandleader Peter Duchin, a misty-eyed Jackie remarked, "I wish it were all starting again."

placed by indifference on Jackie's part. This hadn't always been the case. Once when Ari and Callas were photographed dining at Maxim's, Jackie saw the photographs, demanded a symbolic replay of her husband's evening out with Callas, and got it. They went to Maxim's, sat at the same table, ordered the same meal, then ended the evening at Regine's.

Another flurry of possessiveness overcame Jackie when a photographer caught Onassis kissing Callas under a beach umbrella, on a private Greek island owned by Ari's friend André Embiricos. Responding like a dalmatian to the fire bell, Jackie flew to Greece, to Onassis, and to the yacht *Christina,* in order to squelch rumors.

In private, Maria Callas referred to Jackie as "the other woman," but in public, whenever asked about her, she was the model of decorum. "The scandal exists because Ari has never brought us together," she told an interviewer. "I don't understand why she doesn't come into my life." But they were empty words on Callas's part. She deeply resented her rival (so much that she once attempted suicide), while Jackie, the victor, showed nothing but disdain for Callas. If she resented Callas, it was not for romantic reasons but rather on materialistic grounds. When she learned that Ari had given Maria a pair of 100-year-old gold earrings and set aside considerable funds for her personal use, she exploded. But the feeling among Ari's friends was that it was the money and the image she cared about, not whether her husband was having an ongoing affair with Callas.

Helene Rochas, the French socialite, felt that "Maria and Ari were the primary couple, while Ari and Jackie were something else. My guess is that Jackie probably didn't have enough feeling to care whom he saw, as long as it didn't embarrass her."

Jackie increasingly complained to her friends about Ari. "He's such a loner," she said. His tastes, she claimed, were vulgar. She told of wearing a large diamond ring he had picked out for her. She was mortified when somebody asked derisively, "What is THAT?" She also complained of being "stuck" on Skorpios for long stretches "with nothing to do and nobody to see."

The wear and tear of their constant differences showed in a variety of ways. Toward the end of 1972 when the *Christina* arrived in Florida, Jackie and Ari were barely communicating with each other. Jackie had brought her children along for their semi-annual visit with Rose Kennedy at Palm Beach. But Jackie's relations with Rose were also lukewarm, and she was spending her nights aboard the *Christina*, then anchored outside Lake Worth. To reach the yacht, Onassis had to run a little motorboat back and forth to the marina for his wife.

One afternoon Jackie asked Rose's personal security guard to drive her to the Sailfish Pub, near the marina, so she could catch the boat.

"I'm sorry, Mrs. Onassis," said the guard, "but Mrs. Kennedy asked me to stick around and run her over to Worth Avenue later in the afternoon."

"Well, this won't take more than a few minutes. You'll be back in plenty of time."

"She distinctly told me not to leave."

"I don't care," said Jackie. "I'm in a hurry, and I want to leave right now."

"I can't do that, Mrs. Onassis. Do you want me to call a taxicab for you instead?"

"You'd better call one for yourself, because you're fired," Jackie snarled.

Rose Kennedy had been standing outside the room and apparently overheard the entire conversation. She barged in and addressed Jackie: "You can't fire him. He's *my* employee. You can either call a taxicab or you can walk."

Jackie called a taxicab.

The atmosphere aboard the *Christina* during Jackie and Ari's stay reflected the burgeoning discord of an imploding marriage. Johnny Meyer recalled one of several episodes in his unpublished memoirs: "Sir John Louden and his wife were invited aboard for a luncheon with about a dozen other guests. Louden is the head of British Petroleum, but he is a very easy-going guy. He goes to Palm Beach every year just to get away from everything. He doesn't want anyone to make a fuss over him. He doesn't even have his number in the telephone book. Anyway, Louden looks like he's in his forties, and his wife, well, she looks about eighty. There were two round tables set up on the deck for the guests, with Jackie at one and Ari at the other. Lady Louden was at Ari's table, and she said she felt cold, and asked if their table could be moved into the cabin. Ari said no, it was his party, but he sent a couple of stewards to get her a blanket. They brought it back to him, and he handed it to Sir John. 'Here,' Ari quipped, 'I've got a blanket to put around your mother.' Jackie told me later, 'I wanted to fall in the swimming pool.

Jackie was so taken aback by her husband's boorish behavior that she vacated the *Christina* that evening, and with her children moved in temporarily with Jayne Wrightsman. But she was soon back. She joined Ari for a short cruise to Lyford Cay, where they were entertained by CBS President William S. Paley, then for a much longer cruise to Sardinia, the Aga Khan's holiday camp for millionaire and royal friends. There were rumors afloat that Jackie was preparing to ditch Onassis in favor of the Aga Khan. Jackie scoffed at the notion. "What will they think of next?" she asked a reporter.

Mark Shaw, the *Life* photographer friend of both Jackie Onassis and Dr. Max Jacobson, died mysteriously in his Kips Bay, New York, apartment on January 26, 1969, at the age of 47. Although family members claimed he had died of a heart attack, the autopsy by New York associate medical examiner Dr. Michael M. Baden revealed other causes. There was no evidence of heart disease, but Shaw's internal organs were laden with methamphetamine residue. (Methamphetamine is a form of amphetamine.) There was heavy scarring and discoloration along the veins in Shaw's arms—the "tracks" of someone who repeatedly injects himself with drugs.

Although even actress Pat Suzuki, Shaw's former wife, claimed that Dr. Jacobson had nothing to do with her husband's death, the Federal Bureau of Narcotics and Dangerous Drugs ordered seizure of all controlled drugs and substances in Jacobson's possession. They then launched an intensive investigation into Jacobson's practice. Three years later, Boyce Renseberger of *The New York Times* wrote a long investigative piece on Jacobson detailing his use of "amphetamines . . . to lift the moods of famous patients."

With Jacobson's long list of professional enemies in the upper echelons of the medical establishment, it was not long before other investigative bodies entered the fray. The New York State Attorney General's Office was one; the New York State Department of Education for Medi-

cal Licensing was another. In anticipation of a possible
license-revocation hearing, Jacobson retained the services
of the Louis Nizer law firm in New York.

The Kennedy family also began to have trepidations.
"Several days after the appearance of the *Times* article,
the Kennedys contacted Max and asked him to a meeting
at the Joseph P. Kennedy Foundation in New York,"
said Ruth Jacobson. "They feared public exposure. They
wanted to ascertain that Max intended to abide by the
medical code of ethics in not talking about specific patients, dead or alive. They were worried that Max might
bring the former President and First Lady into future
discussions.

"Max told them that if they reviewed events following
the assassination of JFK, they would see that almost
everyone associated with the Kennedy White House had
written a book about their experiences. Max hadn't, and
actually should have, because his association had been
purely unofficial. And he received some pretty good offers, I can tell you that—especially from British publishers. But he never took a farthing, and he assured the
Kennedy Foundation he would never betray his confidential and privileged dealings with the late President."

In his unpublished autobiography, Dr. Jacobson traces
the events that daily brought him closer to a showdown
with the all-powerful medical establishment, culminating
in a medical license-revocation hearing as conducted by
prosecutors from the New York State Attorney General's
Office. Once again the Kennedy Foundation became concerned. Even a partial disclosure of Max Jacobson's frequent treatment of President and Mrs. Kennedy with
high and often risky dosages of amphetamine-laced com-
pounds, it was thought, would greatly damage the family's image.

"On May 28, 1973," writes Jacobson, "I received a
phone call from Jackie's friend Chuck Spalding, asking to
see me. My wife [Ruth], who took the call, told him that
on the 30th I was to attend the first of medical panel
hearings and she would prefer that I rest the next day;
therefore, unless it was absolutely pressing, she wanted
to postpone his visit until the following week. Spalding
insisted on the importance of the meeting and said he
would pass by early the following afternoon.

"At about noon the next day, he telephoned and apologized for the fact that he couldn't pick me up but asked whether I could arrange to meet him at his apartment. I arrived there around 3:00 p.m. and, when I rang the bell, Chuck greeted me at the door. He said, 'There's somebody here who wants to see you.' All of a sudden I found myself embraced and kissed by that 'somebody'—it was Jackie. Chuck ushered us into a room and excused himself.*

"She said she was sorry about the unfair publicity in the press. . . . I said, 'You ought to know better than anyone else what I did for Jack.' I reminded her of the Demerol incident when a Secret Service agent had given the President a vial of Demerol and I insisted he not take the medication. She seemed to have forgotten all about it. I also reminded her about when I accompanied them on the Paris-Vienna-London trip, and how well JFK functioned in spite of the enormous pressures of the meetings, and countless other occasions at the United Nations, the Carlyle, Washington, Hyannis Port, Glen Ora and Palm Beach—and never for a fee.

"Insofar as the meeting being called under the pretense of its 'extreme importance,' I soon learned for whom it was so important. Jackie asked me what I would say if the White House came up during the hearings. I reassured her that there was no reason for concern—medical ethics and discretion had been part of my life for the past fifty years. I had no intention of changing now. I said that my conscience was clear and that I had nothing to hide.

*For the record, it should be pointed out that when interviewed by the present author, Chuck Spalding denied any knowledge of such a meeting: "I've got to tell you, I'm not going to lie to you. I've been straight up to you. As far as I know, there's not a shred of truth in that. I never talked to Mrs. Jacobson. You can do what you want with it, but that's that. It's just bullshit. I wasn't there. I never had such a meeting."

In response to Spalding's denial, Mrs. Ruth Jacobson cited telephone logs, diaries, appointment books, calendars and Max Jacobson's autobiography. "You can only lie if there's nobody on the other end to contradict you," said Mrs. Jacobson. "When Chuck telephoned the office [then located on East 87th Street], I happened to be the person he spoke with. I made the notations in the telephone log, in the appointment book and so forth. Max is dead, but I am still here to bear witness to the truth."

"I told her that I was very concerned about the outcome of these panel hearings. I said that, to date, I had paid outright $35,000 in legal fees and that this did not cover any part of the pending hearings. I told her the Constructive Research Foundation [the Foundation established to cover Jacobson's multiple sclerosis research] owed me $12,000. Money had never been my concern and I had accumulated none. . . . But now that I was in a needy position, there was nothing and nobody to fall back on. Jack Kennedy certainly wasn't available. She replied, 'Don't worry, all will be taken care of.'

"I was relieved after the long two-hour meeting, and arrived home elated. The forthcoming assistance, however, never arrived."

On April 25, 1975, after more than two years of hearings and 5,000 pages of testimony, the New York State Board of Regents revoked Max Jacobson's medical license. He was found guilty on 48 counts of unprofessional conduct in 11 specifications, and an additional count of fraud. Among other things, he was charged with and convicted of administering amphetamines without sound medical justification, failure to keep adequate records on his use of controlled substances, as well as inability to account for medical irregularities in the administration of his research foundation. Investigators, according to the 42-page report itemizing the case against Jacobson, were also concerned about lax sterilization standards in Max's office and laboratory. "On October 26, 1970," said the report, "placenta was observed in respondent's refrigerator. . . next to bread, sandwiches, storage batteries and various other types of lunch components." Against this had to be balanced the more than 300 statements and affidavits from patients of all backgrounds and walks of life who supported Dr. Jacobson and his unorthodox medical methodology. "The final judgment of a physician's success," read one such report, "must come from the doctor's patients, not from the American Medical Association or the State Board of Regents. I am a commercial artist and I am a 20-year sufferer of multiple sclerosis. Were it not for the treatments I receive from Dr. Max Jacobson, I would not only be unable to work but I would probably be long dead."

"The loss of his medical license was one disappointment," said Ruth Jacobson, "Jackie Onassis was another. The pledges and promises, but never the delivery. I find it strange that she solicited Max's help, received it, promised to help defray his legal expenses [which cost more than $100,000] and was then never heard from again. The degree to which Max kept his end of the bargain can be gauged by the fact that the White House came up for discussion only once in the two years, only to be quickly dismissed. But where was Jackie during and after all this? Where's the help she promised? I'm still waiting. And so is Max. The hearing all but killed him. He died five years after having his license revoked."

Athens, January 22, 1973: The sound of crockery smashing against a *taverna's* brick fireplace on Alexander Onassis's 24th birthday had only just faded when his father in New York received news of a crash in which his son had been gravely injured. The effect on Ari was shattering. Alexander, heir and successor to the Onassis millions, had gone up in his father's Piaggio (an amphibian airplane) to help train his father's new personal pilot, an American named Donald McCusker; an experienced Canadian co-pilot accompanied them on the flight.

Witnesses at Athens Airport described the crash as taking place seconds after liftoff. The plane banked sharply to the right, hitting the ground with the right float. It spun off the runway onto the right wing tip and cartwheeled in a circle for another 460 feet, smashing the nose, the tail and the other wing before coming to rest. The first rescuers to reach the wreckage were unable to identify Alexander except by the monogram on a blood-soaked handkerchief found in his pocket. Unconscious and suffering from severe head wounds, he was rushed to the Red Cross Hospital in Athens. The two other crew members, though injured, would recover.

Those who saw Aristotle Onassis at Kennedy Airport the following day were struck by his appearance. He seemed to have aged overnight, his skin paling and his hair graying before their eyes. His eyes looked glazed and red. Jackie had arranged for an eminent Boston neurosurgeon to accompany them to Athens. A heart specialist from Dallas was also en route to Athens, and in London, aides had chartered a Trident to transport a British brain specialist to Alexander's side.

By the time Ari, Jackie and the Boston neurosurgeon

arrived in Athens, Alexander's condition had deteriorated still further. At the hospital, Onassis was informed by surgeons that his son was clinically dead, his brain having ceased to function although his heart continued to beat.

The hospital corridor quickly filled with members of the immediate family. Tina, Alexander's mother, arrived from Switzerland with Stavros Niarchos. Christina Onassis came from Brazil where she had been visiting a woman friend. Fiona Thyssen arrived from London. The three Onassis sisters completed the chorus of woe. Only Jackie was composed, as though she could not grieve over the predicament of the young man who had considered her his natural enemy.

"Alexander despised Jackie," said Costa Gratsos. "One night at Maxim's, the three—Ari, Alexander and Jackie—were gossiping about some showgirl who was taking an older man for all he was worth. Alexander turned to his stepmother and said, 'Jackie, surely you don't think there's anything wrong in a girl marrying for money, do you?'

"Two months before the accident Ari had promised Alexander he would investigate the possibility of divorce. He was prepared to sever the tie regardless of the cost or consequences. Then the tragedy occurred. Ari himself may as well have been on the plane. Alexander's death destroyed him. He didn't really want to live any more. He brought Alexander's remains to Skorpios and buried them next to the little chapel. He went through the funeral as if in a deep trance. Ari felt somehow responsible for the crash. He became convinced that the plane had been sabotaged, and offered a million dollar reward to anyone who could prove that Alexander had been murdered. He was convinced his enemies had plotted the devious act. It was impossible to divert him from this idea. When Jackie tried to talk him out of this obsession, it only angered him, and the more readily Christina and his sisters echoed his vague suspicions, the more he resented Jackie's refusal to join him in his campaign.

"I sided with Jackie in this instance, and I told Ari as much. He said to me, 'She refused to associate herself with the view that John Kennedy had been the victim of a conspiracy, and I'm sure he was.' 'No, Ari,' I said. 'She never denied the possibility of a conspiracy. She said only that the knowledge of such a conspiracy would do little good, since it wouldn't restore Kennedy. The woman has her faults, but you can't blame her for being the type of person who refuses to indulge in the hypothetical.' Jackie is very much a 'here-and-now' person. What she can see, touch, hear is what she accepts as truth."

Onassis hired French journalist Jacques Harvey to investigate the crash of his son. "He paid me a lot of money," noted Harvey. "I turned the case inside out, interviewed a thousand unhinged souls full of malicious, half-baked stories. At the end, I told Onassis that in my opinion the crash had been an accident. God was responsible.

"Alexander's death soured his feelings for Olympic Airways and for flying in general, and he soon began negotiations to sell the airline to the Greek government. The government took advantage of his weakened state. The Tarzan of the boardroom had grown as meek as a mouse. Acting on behalf of his family, he surrendered the airline at a fraction of its worth. In the wake of his personal tragedy, he was faced with a number of business problems—a rise in oil prices, reduction of consumption and over-production of tankers, increasing interest rates. He lost a great deal of money when plans for a fleet of supertankers and an oil refinery he wanted to build in New Hampshire fell through.

"In addition he thought he was being taken for every penny by his wife. He felt she didn't share his grief, his despair, over Alexander. His perceptions, whether right or wrong, produced friction and unhappiness. He was a very bitter man. He wasn't feeling well and showed great strain. Obviously that strain affected the marriage."

One observer of Ari's grief was Helene Gaillet, who had gone to dinner with Onassis in New York a week before Alexander's death. "I was then still living with Felix Rohatyn, but Ari and I were close friends. Over dinner he invited me to visit him at Skorpios. I was in Paris a week after the accident, about to fly to Kinshasa to photograph the Muhammad Ali–George Foreman heavyweight championship fight. Foreman sustained a bad cut in training camp and the fight had to be postponed. Since Felix was on a business trip, I saw no reason to return immediately to New York. So I telephoned Ari on Skorpios and asked him if he still wanted company. 'Absolutely,' he said. 'When do you want to come?' 'How about tomorrow?' I asked. The arrangements were made, and a day later I was flown to Glyfada to spend the night with Christina and one of Ari's sisters, before being helicoptered to Skorpios. The landing port there is on top of the mountain. Ari picked me up in his jeep and drove me—slowly, because his eyesight wasn't good—around the island. Over the next week Ari and I had many talks about his son and he took me to the little chapel where he was buried. We spent a lot of time together talking. I think Ari started letting go of his life after his son died. I had that strong feeling. I had a sort of perception of who he was and what he was doing, and that he was no longer going to be satisfied with anything. He seemed heartbroken that he could no longer do anything for his son, because his son was no longer there. He began to lose interest. He began to give up.

"Ari had always been fabulous, brilliant, down-to-earth. While I was there he wasn't at all preoccupied with business. We walked along the beach. We went swimming. He did some gardening. His employees, the people who worked for him at Skorpios, seemed very fond of him.

"After a few days, Jackie arrived. Other guests included British Ambassador to Spain Sir John Russell, his wife and two children. I have to say Ari didn't seem displeased with Jackie at this point. If there was tension—and there might well have been—I didn't see it. But then again, I wasn't looking for it."

Helene Gaillet returned to New York and Jackie turned to one of her Camelot friends, Pierre Salinger, to help elevate Ari's spirits. Salinger had just started working at *L'Express,* a French magazine based in Paris, when Jackie telephoned him. "Please, Pierre, do me a favor," she said. "I'm coming to Paris. Meet me at the airport. Ari is so unhappy about his son's death. I think he should get away on a cruise, and I want you to come along."

"We flew Olympic to Dakar and sailed ten days on the *Christina* across the Atlantic to Trinidad," recalled Salinger. "Ari would rise about noon, go swimming in the pool, eat lunch and then we'd spend the afternoon and evening together. Ari had trouble sleeping. He worked late at night placing dozens of international telephone calls. Frankly, I enjoyed being with him. He was an amazing storyteller. He loathed politicians, especially

Franklin Delano Roosevelt. After dinner, he drank ouzo and sang the nostalgic Greek songs he loved so much. He seemed morose but didn't make a fetish of it, keeping his deepest, darkest thoughts to himself."

"Until his son's death, Ari was one of the all-time greats," observed Peter Beard. "He generated tremendous energy. He was obsessive, interested, constantly working on his own thing, but every now and then he would look you right in the eye and really talk to you. His talk was amazing—real genius-type stuff."

American-born photographer Beard, a frequent visitor to Skorpios, entered Jackie's life as "a kind of playmate-babysitter for her children. Also, we had certain people in common. I knew Truman Capote and I had been married to Minnie Cushing. The Cushings and Auchinclosses were neighbors in Newport. I knew her mother before I knew Jackie. Janet Auchincloss is one of the most boring people alive. But Jackie is really very gutsy, very brave, not at all afraid to take chances. I was doing a book, *Longing for Darkness*, on the author Isak Dinesen, and Jackie agreed to write an afterword. She seemed so interested I convinced her to do her own book, *One Special Summer*, based on the scrapbooks she and Lee Radziwill kept during their student-day sojourn in Europe."

Beard fulfilled other functions. For one thing, he soon became Lee Radziwill's lover. When Lee and Stas Radziwill divorced in 1974, Peter was mentioned as a reason for the breakup. "Obviously such simplifications are always ridiculous," he said. "They had been married for quite a while and had had their differences."

It was Beard who taught Caroline Kennedy how to use a camera. "If teaching someone to hold a piece of technological equipment in the air and squeeze their index finger is teaching them photography, I suppose I taught her," he said. "Basically I spent time with Jackie and Lee and their children at Skorpios, on Long Island and in Kenya, where I own a plantation. In 1974, John Jr. and I climbed Mt. Kenya together, while Caroline stayed with the game warden of Mt. Kenya, a very close friend of mine."

On Skorpios, Beard once bet Aristotle Onassis that he could hold his breath under water for more than four minutes; Beard managed the feat and won $10,000.

The money went into a film project that later evolved

into the underground movie classic *Grey Gardens*, a documentary on the lives of Edith and Edie Beale. "Actually I put up $20,000," said Beard. "The initial concept was quite different from what it eventually became. I conceived it as a study of the erosion of life on Long Island. Long Island would be a metaphor for a community declining in its environmental qualities as it gets near the urban center—the disease center. The Beales were to have played only a small part in it. It was intended to present a picture of Long Island in its heyday, the Long Island of the Bouviers, when Jackie and Lee were children."

Beard brought in filmmaker Jonas Mekas to shoot preliminary footage. Mekas recalled his first meeting with Jackie and Lee, who had compiled names of people to interview on film and places to visit. "The two sisters were very different," he remarked. "Jackie was straight on, whereas Lee was a schemer. She was always scheming. She lacked Jackie's know-how and talent but was always trying to make it. She couldn't find a niche for herself. Jackie also had a better sense of humor. She used to call her Fifth Avenue apartment 'the dump,' after the opening line in *Who's Afraid of Virginia Woolf?*— 'What a dump!'

"We shot a number of sequences on Long Island— Jackie and Caroline waterskiing; Jackie and Lee swimming; John Kennedy, Jr., and Tony Radziwill riding on top of a station wagon; the two boys playing Frisbee together at the beach. There was a fabulous sequence in which John Jr. imitates Mick Jagger, wriggling around the living room and lip-synching to one of Jagger's record albums. We used a number of photographs from Jackie's childhood scrapbooks, and a lot of background music. For example, there would be a still on screen of Black Jack Bouvier, and as accompaniment a recording of 'My Heart Belongs to Daddy.'

"Eventually I gave Lee Radziwill a 15-minute condensed version of the preliminary footage. Jackie saw this version and liked it. Then the money began to run out. Also, while we were making the rough cut, some television producers heard about it and began to pester Jackie and pressure her to do it for one of the major networks. That's when I bowed out."

Peter Beard brought in the Maysles Brothers, best

known for *Gimme Shelter,* a film detailing the Rolling Stones' 1969 U.S. tour. David and Albert Maysles deserve credit for persevering for two years and finishing *Grey Gardens,* but I was the one who pointed them in the right direction," said Beard. "They were interested in Jackie Onassis and her scrapbooks. I kept telling them, 'Don't you understand? Grey Gardens and the Beales is where it's at and this is the whole project, so why don't you get with it and try and come here and film?' The more I saw of the Beales, the more I realized that the film had to be about them. They were just so brilliantly, ingeniously, totally nuts—in the most fabulous way."

David Maysles characterized the difficulty of the project: "The documentary was an artistic but not a commercial success. There were numerous battles along the way. Lee Radziwill was renting a house in Montauk at the time and riding around in a limo, and I had the distinct impression that the Beales, who were barely subsisting, didn't appreciate her very much. After we decided to do more on the Beales and less on the Bouviers, Lee became quite indignant. 'There's too much footage on Edith and Edie,' she yelled. That's when she and Peter abandoned the project, leaving us to raise the funds and make the film.

"The Beales became instant 'celebutantes.' Edie Beale was hired to perform at Reno Sweeney, a Manhattan nightclub, where she danced, sang, signed autographs, and in general ran amok. According to Edie, the eight-day stint proved successful until Jackie put an end to it. Jackie apparently did it by having one of her lawyers call up the club and make trouble. Jackie didn't want the publicity. At intermission, as part of her act, Edie would field questions posed by the audience, usually dealing with Jackie, sometimes with the Kennedys. And of course Edie, in her frank and irrepressible manner, would respond to the questions. And so there was a daily run of press on her act. And Jackie didn't want it. At least that's what Edie contended."

"Edie Beale was an absolute gas," said Andy Warhol, who attended each of her performances at Reno Sweeney. "The whole family—Kennedy-Onassis-Bouvier-Beale-Radziwill-Auchincloss—made more news than any other family around. Something was always happening. Jackie joined the Municipal Arts Society and helped lead the fight to save Grand Central Station from demolition. Lee Radziwill wrote several autobiographical essays for *Ladies' Home Journal,* an outgrowth of the documentary that she and Peter Beard attempted to put on film before the Maysles Brothers arrived on the scene. To the enormous embarrassment of his Secret Service detail, JFK Jr. was the victim in a Central Park mugging that resulted in the theft of his bicycle and tennis racket. Caroline had been taking private flying lessons at Hanscomb Airfield, not far from Concord Academy, until the death of Alexander Onassis, when Jackie put an end to the lessons.

"One day, Lee Radziwill called and asked me to take her and Jackie to the Brooklyn Museum to see a show of Egyptian art. Jackie had just returned from Egypt. We drove out to Brooklyn in an old station wagon I owned. I'd recently appeared in a movie, *The Driver's Seat,* starring Elizabeth Taylor. 'What's Elizabeth Taylor really like?' Jackie kept asking in the car.

"We finally reached the museum. As we wandered through the galleries, every person there seemed to recognize Jackie. They whispered among themselves. You could hear her name in the air: 'Jackie . . . Jackie . . . Jackie.' It was weird. Somehow she managed to concentrate on the exhibition. She commented on almost every artifact—its history, purpose, the name of the Pharaoh associated with it. What surprised me as much as her knowledge was her ability to mentally block out all those intrusive onlookers.

"What I didn't realize until I saw her apartment was that Jackie is a sentimentalist. I remember her library with its comfortable settee, deep-cushioned easy chairs, 18th-century tables, boiserie-covered walls, bookshelves filled with albums of family photographs, books on art and history, knickknacks including Greek worry beads of blue glass, a Cambodian ring, an earthen jug from Mexico, a jade trinket from China. There were baskets of fruit and flowers, the heady scent of lit Rigaud candles, paintings of horses and a large selection of the children's handiwork; there were also some photographs of Skorpios, I think taken by Caroline, including a view of Alexander Onassis's gravestone."

30

Jackie spent part of the summer of 1973 with Ari on Skorpios. According to Costa Gratsos, she did nothing but complain: she felt bored, loathed the food, didn't enjoy the company. She virtually ignored her husband's houseguests (including William P. Tavoulas, President of Mobil Oil Corp.) and entertained herself by showing first-run movies. When she didn't get her way, Jackie pouted. She spoke critically of her husband in front of the children, thus alienating him still further from them. Mostly she maintained a sullen silence, a cold aggressive silence, paying her husband scant attention and doing her best to steer clear of him.

Basically, Jackie couldn't cope with the dark passions that stirred within the Greek family, both because of the intensity of these passions and because she felt like an outsider. She was more a Kennedy than an Onassis, more a Bouvier than a Kennedy. Her instinct was to submerge pain; Ari's was to experience it. Jackie couldn't understand, for example, how her husband in the throes of despair could invite his former wife Tina and her husband, Stavros Niarchos, his antagonist, to visit Skorpios that summer and share his grief. She didn't begin to understand the symbolic relationships that the wealthy Greek families have with one another. And she didn't want to understand.

In November 1973, Jackie became involved in activities commemorating the tenth anniversary of John F. Kennedy's assassination. Preoccupation with this event blinded her to the overt signs of an illness that would soon ravage Ari's health. He had lost weight, felt listless, and developed a drooping left eyelid. In early December 1973, he flew to New York to see a specialist who placed him in Lenox Hill Hospital for observation; he registered as "Philipps" and left after a week without telling anyone that his illness had been diagnosed as myasthenia gravis, a debilitating disease of the muscles about which physicians knew relatively little. He joked about the disease. When he could no longer keep his eye open he taped his eyelid to his forehead with sticking plaster. His photograph in the *New York Post* was topped by the caption, "Onassis suffers stroke." He had not suffered a stroke, although the symptoms were not entirely dissimilar. He told Costa Gratsos: "The doctors keep telling me to have an operation but won't guarantee the results. So what's the point?"

Gratsos and others in Ari's camp were aware of just how unconcerned Jackie was over her husband's condition. On her way from Skorpios to New York that fall, she stopped in Paris and went on an enormous buying spree. In New York, she toured Bloomingdale's, spending thousands of dollars on household items for her New Jersey hideaway.

Susan Panopoulos had replaced Lynn Alpha Smith as private secretary to Costa Gratsos. "I was only an employee, very close to Gratsos, and I'm still close to his family," she said. "But I could see what was going on. Much of the same was happening as took place before I arrived: bills, screaming, a lot of talking around the office. That sort of thing."

Jackie convinced her husband to take her to Acapulco to celebrate the New Year. The sun and pleasant climate, she said, would improve his failing health. They flew down on his private Lear Jet. Once there, they argued. Jackie expressed a wish to own a house in Acapulco. Onassis insisted he didn't want such a house and resented her asking him to buy one—he had been generous enough considering her recent attitude. They were still bickering the day (January 3, 1974) they returned to New York. Jackie lost her temper, called Ari an ingrate and said she didn't want his "goddamn money."

"In that case, you won't be disappointed," he retorted.

It was in this frame of mind, while flying back to Manhattan, that Onassis decided to rewrite his will.

Removing himself to a seat at the rear of the plane, Onassis wrote out by hand (in compliance with Greek law), a document intended to serve as his last will and testament. Christina was to be the prime beneficiary, but the will began with an homage to his dead son through the formation of a cultural foundation in Alexander's name. It was somewhat of an irony considering that young Onassis had flunked his high school graduation exams (from a lycée in Paris) and could not have been less interested in the world of art and literature. His father nevertheless wrote:

> If my death occurs before I proceed with the establishment of a cultural institution in Vaduz, Liechtenstein, or elsewhere under the name of "Alexander Onassis Foundation," its purpose, among others, to operate, maintain, and promote the Nursing, Educational, Literary Works, Religious, Scientific Research, Journalistic and Artistic endeavors, proclaiming International and National Contests, prize awards in money, similar to the plan of the Nobel Institution in Sweden, I entrust and command the undersigned executors of my will to establish such a Cultural Foundation.

The problem of Jackie was quickly resolved: "Having already taken care of my wife Jacqueline Bouvier and having extracted a written agreement through [a] notary in [the] USA, by which she gives up her hereditary rights on my inheritance, I limit [the] share for her and her two children John and Caroline." The limitation he set included a lifetime income for Jackie of $200,000 per year, while the children would each receive $25,000 a year until they turned 21. Onassis also took precautions against the possibility of his wife contesting the will, noting that if this should happen, "I command the executors of my will and the rest of my heirs that they deny her such a right through all legal means, cost and expense charged on my inheritance."

The will adhered to the financial conditions set forth in Ari's prenuptial agreement with Jackie. It constituted the minimum he could possibly leave Jackie, since obviously the courts would uphold the prenuptial agreement. Although the largest part of the estate went to Christina (by way of a complicated set of interlocking trusts), Onassis also set aside $60,000 a year for life for his cousin and business aide Costa Konialidis; $30,000 a year for life to Costa Gratsos, to his lawyer Stelios Papadimitriou and to Nicolas Cokkinis, a managing director long in Onassis's employment; $20,000 a year for life to Costa Vlassapoulos, his director in Monte Carlo; chauffeurs, chefs, maids and butlers were also bequeathed large sums of money.

Onassis was still scribbling when the plane landed in West Palm Beach for refueling. Minutes later, Jackie and Ari were seen in the airport coffee shop eating bacon, lettuce and tomato sandwiches. Their sociable snack was a smoke screen for the benefit of the public. As soon as they returned to the plane, Onassis picked up where he had left off. "My yacht, the *Christina*, if my daughter and wife so wish, they can keep for their personal use," he wrote. If maintenance and operating expenses proved prohibitive, they were instructed to present the vessel to the Greek treasury. A separate clause made the same stipulation with regard to Skorpios, the one condition being that 30 acres of land surrounding his son's tomb had to remain intact. In both cases—the yacht as well as the island—he allotted Jackie one-quarter ownership rights, the remaining 75 percent to his daughter. A final insult to Jackie: he named as chief executrix of his will "Athina née Livanos-Onassis-Blandford-Niarchos, the mother of my son, Alexander."

When they saw him in New York again, Ari's associates were alarmed by his condition. "The pallor of his skin had turned deep gray," said Costa Gratsos. "And when he spoke he slurred his words so badly that he could barely be understood. He told me about the latest altercation with Jackie. 'I've had it with her,' he said. He had given Johnny Meyer instructions to hire a private detective to shadow Jackie. Meyer also borrowed equipment with which to bug her telephone. Ari felt if he could catch her with another man he'd be in a strong position to file for divorce. His banker, George Moore, and two or three lawyers, advised him that without such evidence, a divorce would be a costly proposition. Jackie would try to break the prenuptial agreement, and would very likely succeed.

In April, while on an American opera tour, Maria Callas agreed to be interviewed by Barbara Walters for the "Today" show. Describing Onassis as "the big love of my life," she added that "love is so much better when you are not married." Asked whether she had any harsh feelings towards Mrs. Onassis, Callas replied, "Why should

I? Of course, if she treats Mr. Onassis very badly, I might be very angry."

Onassis meanwhile had embarked on what was to be his last extended cruise. His destination was Monte Carlo, the eastern Mediterranean and the Middle East. His companion on the voyage was Christina, who had begun to familiarize herself with the family business by working for her father in New York. Ari was not only trying to give his daughter a purpose in life, he was easing her into the shoes of her late brother, grooming her as a future partner and eventual successor.

In Monte Carlo, Ari entertained Prince Rainier and Princess Grace with a shipboard dinner. After dinner, while Christina and Grace chatted, Ari became embroiled in an unfortunate argument with his former friend. Weary yet combative, Onassis could not stop talking about the time in the 1950s when the Prince had forced him to sell his shares in the Société des Bains de Mer which controlled the Bank of Monte Carlo. Amends were made before the Prince and Princess left the yacht, but the damage had once again been wrought. Rainer later told the press: "It was all very sad. To have come so far just to end up heartbroken and ill on board this vast yacht with only your daughter for company seemed almost unfair."

Jackie met up with Ari in Madrid. Paul Mathias, who was also in Madrid at the time, encountered the couple at a local nightclub: "Behaving as though she did not have a care in the world, Jackie tried her skill with castanets and even coaxed her reluctant mate on to the dance floor where he performed like a wounded beast. She was the master; he was clearly her slave."

Jackie and Christina were more at odds than ever. The former First Lady lost no opportunity in criticizing her stepdaughter's table manners. "What disturbed Christina even more was that Jackie likewise criticized Ari's table manners," reported Costa Gratsos. "According to Jackie, he slurped his soup, didn't lift his elbow off the table when he ate, downed his food too quickly. It reached the point where Jackie refused to take her meals with him."

Jackie also criticized Christina for flitting from place to place and from playboy to playboy without the formation of any real attachment. Christina's latest love interest, Mick Flick, the young Daimler-Benz heir, was a playboy with his own bankroll. Tall and popular among women of the international set, Flick cared for Christina but in no way was prepared to marry her. In a moment of candor (and cruelty), he told her that he preferred tall slim blondes with long legs. Christina bleached her hair blond, but she could do nothing about her fleshy legs and thick ankles. One day that summer, she was found unconscious in her London apartment, and was rushed to Middlesex Hospital under the name of Miss A. Danoi. Not for the first time she had taken an overdose of sleeping pills.

Ari refused to turn to Jackie for help. Instead, he summoned his former wife. Tina flew from Paris to London to be with her daughter. Christina recovered quickly. She renewed her friendship with Peter Goulandris, which pleased Ari, and several months later announced their intention to wed. The marriage never took place.

If Christina suffered wide fluctuations of mood, her mother had a more serious problem. A pill addict, she took large doses of barbiturates and tranquilizers to combat the insomnia that had plagued her since the death of her son. On the morning of September 10, 1974, Tina was found dead in Niarchos's Paris residence. A doctor attributed her death to edema of the lung. Although her sudden demise seemed as mysterious and unexpected as that of her sister, an official autopsy supported the initial postmortem findings.

In his biography of Jackie Onassis, author Stephen Birmingham* correctly gauges Christina's reaction to the event: "Some superstitious strain out of her Smyrna peasant past suggested to Christina that some sinister force had to be connected with all these deaths—first her aunt, then her brother, now her mother. It must be Jackie who was bringing all the bad luck to the family, 'undermining everything' as her brother had predicted. To Christina it seemed as though Jackie killed every life she touched. She was the Angel of Death. This terrible conviction was all the more powerful because, by then, Christina could see that her father was also dying."

"Christina was highly distraught," confirmed Costa Gratsos. "She felt Jackie was somehow to blame. Death was never very far from 'the Black Widow,' as Christina now called her. Jackie was the world's most inveterate

*Stephen Birmingham, *Jacqueline Bouvier Kennedy Onassis*, p. 195.

bystander to tragedy. Witness John and Robert Kennedy. Christina feared Jackie. She felt she had magical powers. Everybody around her had perished."

Onassis returned to New York's Lenox Hill Hospital for further testing, while Jackie went on a series of grandiose shopping sprees. She finally visited her husband in the hospital and noted that his face had ballooned to twice its normal size, the result of a high cortisone regimen his physicians had prescribed as a means of countering the disease. During one of her hospital visits, Onassis became enraged at his wife. His doctor called it "a cortisone rage."

Jackie kept in touch daily with Caroline who, during this time, was working with a film unit on a documentary about Appalachian miners, and was delighted with her daughter when the mining family with whom Caroline lodged told a television interviewer, "She's just folks!"

Jacqueline became involved in a photographic project of her own. At the invitation of a friend, Karl Katz, one-time director of New York's Jewish Museum and a curator at the Metropolitan Museum of Art, she attended a preview at the newly founded International Center of Photography on Fifth Avenue, and talked to its executive director, Cornell Capa, a top photographer who had once covered Senator John F. Kennedy for *Life*. She stayed for lunch, and took copious notes on everything Capa and Katz told her about the Center's activities, then went home and wrote it up in her smoothest journalistic style.

"Jackie did it on her own initiative," said Capa. "She penned an anonymous piece for the 'Talk of the Town' section of *The New Yorker*, and it remained anonymous for about five minutes until the Associated Press discovered that she wrote it, and it became widely known that she did it.

"She wasn't on the Board the first year, but she was Honorary Chairperson for our first anniversary exhibition, a retrospective featuring Ernst Haas. About two years later, she became a member of the Board. She guest-curated an Atget exhibition and was involved with the publication of a corresponding book. Next came *Allure* by Diana Vreeland. Jackie helped arrange the show and edit the book by the same title. She also gave a dinner at ICP to honor Mrs. Vreeland."

Testimony of just how separated Jackie and Ari's lives had become was provided by Greek publisher Helen Vlachos, who had grown close to Onassis during his years with Maria Callas. "After Jackie came along, I saw less of him," she said. "And I never saw him and Jackie together. She came to Mykonos with her sister Lee. We had a very small party because Jackie didn't want many people present. Another time I had dinner at her apartment in New York, but again, Ari was nowhere in sight. Nor was he mentioned. Jackie was a beautiful woman and always nice to me, but I found her very affected; she wasn't at all natural—she always spoke in that very small polite voice. The marriage to Ari wasn't difficult to understand. She married him for his money. Why else? He was a charmer, but that alone wasn't enough."

Released from Lenox Hill, Onassis decided he wanted to break the Kennedy connection and the marriage, liquidate his emotional commitment. Jackie's reign was at an end. The private detective and the wiretap operation had yielded nothing by way of documentation—Jackie's extramarital meanderings were limited to escorted luncheons, dinners and harmless nights out on the town. Ari realized that for the sake of a successful divorce he would have to adopt another tactic.

In accordance with his plan, he set up a series of meetings with attorney Roy Cohn, first at "21" and then at El Morocco. "Among the things that infuriated Ari was Jackie's habit of sending both her maid and Nancy Tuckerman to his office at the end of each month with shopping bills for such 'vital necessities' as the purchase of 200 pairs of shoes at one sitting for a total of $60,000," said Cohn. "He threw the bill on the table and clutched his throat. 'I've had it up to here with her,' he said. 'I cannot understand her. All she does is spend, spend, spend—and she's never in the same place as I am. If I'm in Paris, she's in New York. If I go to Skorpios, she goes to London.'

"Ari maintained that Jackie's travels and the distances that separated them were the less of his complaints, and that her spending was his bigger beef. 'I am an enormously wealthy man,' he said, 'but still I find it hard to understand why I should receive a bill for 200 pairs of shoes. It isn't as though I don't provide her with a generous expense account—I do. What's more, the shoes are only one item. She orders handbags, dresses, gowns and coats by the dozen—more than enough to stock a Fifth Avenue specialty shop. This woman has no conception of when to stop squandering my money. I'm fed up with her, and I want a divorce.'

"After a pause he came back to what I believed was the real reason behind his wanting a divorce—not her spending, which he could afford, but her coldheartedness. 'She's never with me,' he said sadly. 'We socialize in different circles. Anywhere I am, she is somewhere else. If she goes to Elaine's, Le Cirque or the Persian Room, or Lincoln Center or the Metropolitan Museum of Art, I find myself alone in Paris at Maxim's and Regine's, or in London at the Savoy, the Dorchester, or the Ritz. She wants my money but not me.'

"He discussed in detail his desire to spring the divorce action as a big surprise before Jackie could launch an effective counterattack in an area where it would hurt him most—the pocketbook.

"He didn't want her to get wind of it because he feared she might end up with a larger share of his property than she would through a routine divorce proceeding. He admitted that the year before, while they were cruising off Haiti, he tried to convince her to sign a divorce agreement; he told her they would remarry secretly 24 hours later. A divorce without alimony, he said, would convince the public that she wasn't interested in his money. Of course he had no intention of remarrying. But Jackie didn't fall for it; she was far too intelligent.

" 'This time the center of the action is going to be in Greece, where I can take care of myself,' said Ari. 'But I'm worried what she can do to me in Paris, in London and in New York, where I have major buildings. That's why I need you. I have already retained lawyers in Paris and London, but I want someone like you to protect me here.' "

Washington columnist Jack Anderson remembered the sequence of events that involved him in the divorce drama: "I received a call in D.C. from Onassis to come to New York. Actually he asked when I was coming next and I said I'd be down in about ten days. I gave him a date and a time. He invited me to lunch and since he was a newsworthy figure I accepted. I'd met him once before on some public occasion.

"My associate, Les Whitten, and I took the shuttle to New York. We were met at the airport by a chauffeured limousine which we hadn't expected. The chauffeur had my name. Larry O'Brien, who was then Commissioner of the National Basketball Association, had been on the same plane so I offered him a lift into the city in the limo.

"We were driven to La Caravelle. Onassis was waiting in the restaurant in his dark glasses. Over lunch he accused his wife of all kinds of spending crimes, and this was the first indication I had of why he had wanted to see me. After lunch he took us back to his offices at the recently completed 51-story Olympic Towers, and turned us over to a couple of his associates. These fellows produced a slew of bills that Jackie had charged and put us in touch with a number of people who could verify Jackie's spending, such as Lilly Lawrence. Les Whitten and I spent three days checking sources and going through various documentation.

"The results were dismaying. In addition to a huge monthly allowance, Jackie regularly went out and bought up the fanciest fashions in New York and Paris. She'd walk through town with her husband's credit cards and even without the credit cards, just using his name, charging clothes. But that was only part of the operation. After buying the clothes, she'd go out and sell them at Encore and other stores, and then stash the cash.

"Onassis wanted me to expose his wife. 'Investigate and find out what she's doing with all that extra money,' he said.

"After we checked our facts and finished the interviews, but before we wrote the story, we called Jackie to ask if she wanted to comment. We got as far as Nancy Tuckerman. 'Mrs. Onassis will not dignify those charges with a comment,' she said. So we ran the articles. I never saw Onassis again. He died several months after our meeting."

Soon after setting the divorce proceedings in motion, Onassis returned to Athens to complete the transfer of Olympic Airways to the Greek government. Early in February 1975, a telephone call for Jackie came from Athens saying that Ari had collapsed with excruciating pains in the chest. The disease had begun to affect his heart as well as his lungs and liver. Jackie contacted an

American cardiologist, Dr. Isidor Rosenfeld, and flew with him to Athens where Ari was being attended by his sisters. Christina arrived from Gstaad, Switzerland, where she had gone skiing with Peter Goulandris. None of the family members, including Jackie and Ari, would admit the seriousness of the illness. They became alarmed only when Dr. Rosenfeld insisted that Onassis be flown to Paris and placed in the American Hospital at Neuilly-sur-Seine, where he would receive the best possible care.

Onassis balked at first, convinced that if he went into the American Hospital he would never come out. Dr. Jean Caroli, Ari's longtime Paris-based physician, flew to Athens and convinced him to agree to Rosenfeld's suggestion. Christina, Jackie, Ari's sister Artemis and Dr. Caroli accompanied him on the flight to Paris.

Caroli sat next to Onassis and tried to entertain him with light-hearted banter. But Onassis became extremely somber. According to Jacques Harvey, he turned to Caroli and said he felt close to his dead son, Alexander. "As they prepared to land in Paris," noted Harvey, "Ari said to the physician, 'Professor, do you know the meaning of the Greek word *thanatos*—'death'? You know I will never come out of the hospital alive. Well, you must practice *thanatos* on me. I do not want to suffer. I would rather be dead.'"

Against doctor's orders, Onassis insisted on spending the night at his apartment in the Avenue Foch, transferring to the hospital the following morning. Gray and haggard, 40 pounds underweight, he refused a stretcher and entered the clinic under his own power. On Sunday, February 16, his gall bladder was removed. Although a family spokesperson announced that he was "recuperating nicely," he spent the next five weeks drifting in and out of consciousness, kept alive by a respirator, a kidney machine and massive infusions of antibiotics.

Christina and Artemis took charge at the hospital, giving Jackie little say in the proceedings. Although she visited her husband every day, she insisted on pursuing her social life and dined out with friends most evenings. Her attitude did not endear her to Ari's grief-stricken family. Christina refused to share the Avenue Foch apartment with her stepmother and moved into the Hotel Plaza-Athénée. At the hospital they would barely acknowledge each other's presence. Christina made a point of leaving the room whenever Jackie arrived.

A day after the gall bladder operation, Jackie phoned Dr. Henry Lax at his New York office. She wanted Lax to come to Europe. He said he had spoken to Ari's doctors at the American Hospital and that he couldn't do more for the patient than was being done.

"Tell Ari not to let the ship go down," instructed Dr. Lax.

During the first week in March, she telephoned Dr. Lax a second time to report that there seemed to be some improvement in her husband's condition. Did the doctor think she could leave Ari's bedside for several days and return to New York?

"Jackie," said the physician, "the whole world is watching. Stay put."

Despite Lax's warning, she had made up her mind to fly home for a few days. Onassis made no attempt to dissuade her. Nor did Christina, who thought she planned to return after the weekend.

Johnny Meyer, usually a Jackie detractor, in this case defended her decision. In his book proposal, he writes: "Jackie and I both talked to the doctor. He told us that Ari was going to get better. They wouldn't let me in to see Ari, so I bribed a nurse, who slipped me in at lunch hour when all the guards went together to eat. Onassis had tubes in his arms, and in his nose, and it looked like he had tubes in his head, too. All he could do was give me a little wave with his hand. But the doctor said he was getting better, so Jackie and I got on the plane and flew home."

They left Paris on a Friday. On Monday, Jackie called Ari's sister and was told his condition had not changed. Later in the week, she went skiing in New Hampshire. Ari went into a rapid decline, but Jackie could not be reached by telephone and when they did reach her she seemed not to appreciate the seriousness of his condition. Maria Callas was permitted a tearful last visit with Ari, but his illness was such that he barely recognized her. Jackie was still in New York on Saturday, March 15—the day Onassis died with his daughter by his bedside.

It was left for Johnny Meyer to notify Jackie of her husband's death. Jackie, her mother, Teddy Kennedy and Jackie's children arrived in Paris the day after Ari's death. The cause of death was listed as bronchial pneumonia. Jackie visited the body in the small hospital chapel where it was lying on an open bier, a Greek Orthodox icon on the corpse's chest. Afterwards, when she left the hospital, she broke into a large smile for the photographers.

Journalist James Brady happened to be, just coincidentally, in Paris on the day Onassis died: "As I recall, a day or two after Ari died I saw fashion designer Valentino in the lobby of the Hotel St. Regis. 'What are you doing in Paris?' I asked. 'Jackie Onassis phoned me in Italy and asked me to meet her. She said she needs a new black dress for the funeral and so I brought something along and fitted it on her.'

"I must say I found it hard to believe that Jackie didn't have a few suitable black dresses in her wardrobe already. It struck me as superficial that, in the midst of flying the ocean to view her husband's body for the first time after he was dead, she would think, 'Yes, get the dressmaker here because I have to look right.' I mean when you're notified that your husband just died, you don't usually think to yourself, 'Oh, gee, do I have something to wear?' There's something very frivolous and shallow about somebody who's so concerned with her image that she forgets about the mourning process."

Wearing her new Valentino beneath a black leather coat, Jackie was first off the Olympic Airways 727 after it touched down at the military airfield at Aktion on the rainy afternoon of March 18. The coffin bearing her husband's body was in the aircraft's main hold. Jackie was followed down the ramp by Senator Edward Kennedy and then by Christina Onassis, who had been weeping from the moment the plane left Orly Airfield in Paris. Seeing a throng of photographers, Christina moaned, "Who are all these people?" Guiding her stepdaughter to the waiting limousine, Jackie said to her: "Hang on. Take it easy. It'll soon be over."

Ted Kennedy, Jackie and Christina sat in the back seat of the lead limousine. As the funeral procession pulled out, Teddy turned toward Christina and said, "Now it's time to take care of Jackie."

Christina leaned forward in her seat. "Stop the car," she told the driver. Bursting into tears afresh, she unlocked the door and leaped out of the limousine, joining her aunts in the follow-up limousine. In a brief interview with the current author, she said: "It seemed almost inconceivable that Ted Kennedy would choose that moment to discuss financial matters. But it was Jackie's hyena-like smile that drove me from the car. She was like a hungry vulture waiting to feast on my father's flesh. I wanted to get as far away from her as possible."

The funeral party made its way to Skorpios where Ari's coffin was carried up a winding path to the small chapel where he and Jackie had married six and a half years earlier. Six pallbearers and the priest carrying a cross led a procession of mourners past a half-dozen large wreaths of red, white and pink flowers, including one inscribed "To Ari from Jackie."

In accord with Ari's wishes, the half-hour service was simple and without eulogy. During the ceremony, Jackie knelt to kiss the coffin, but showed no outward emotion. A much more intense emotional reaction came from Christina, who cried and trembled as the coffin was being lowered into the earth only yards from the tomb of Alexander Onassis.

In Athens, following the funeral, Jackie gave the press a short, carefully worded statement. "Aristotle Onassis rescued me at a moment when my life was engulfed in shadows. He brought me into a world where one could find both happiness and love. We lived through many beautiful experiences together which cannot be forgotten, and for which I will be eternally grateful . . . Nothing has changed [in my relationship] with Aristotle's sisters and his daughter. The same love binds us as when he lived." Asked whether she anticipated a legal battle with Christina over the Onassis estate, she replied, "I'll answer with something my husband often told me: 'Throughout the world people love fairy tales and especially those related to the lives of the rich. You must learn to understand this and accept it.'"

Aristotle Onassis left behind an estate worth roughly $1 billion, including his private fleet of tankers. The major share was bequeathed to his daughter, who had already inherited some $270 million from her mother's estate, making her one of the wealthiest women in the world. To protect her inheritance from taxes, Christina Onassis visited the U.S. Embassy in Paris and renounced her American citizenship.

When *The New York Times* ran a story confirming

Ari's intention, prior to his death, to divorce his wife, Jackie became violently upset and called upon Christina to deny the report, threatening to cause trouble if she didn't. Christina subsequently issued a statement, which, while it proved totally false, mollified Jackie:

"Miss Christina Onassis is very much distressed at the distorted stories and speculations which appeared in the international press about her father and Mrs. Jacqueline Onassis. These stories are totally untrue and she repudiates them. In fact, the marriage of the late Mr. Onassis and Mrs. Jacqueline Onassis was a happy marriage and all rumors of intended divorce are untrue. Her relationship with Mrs. Onassis was always and still is based on mutual friendship and respect, and there are no financial or other disputes separating them."

Three days later, Christina and Jackie flew separately to Skorpios for the Greek Orthodox service on the fortieth day after Ari's death. Christina had already seen to it that Jackie's personal belongings on Skorpios and aboard the *Christina* were removed and shipped to her at Ari's apartment in Paris. Jackie visited both for the last time. She boarded the *Christina* to pick up an item that hadn't been forwarded, but which also didn't belong to her: Ari's priceless jade Buddha. Christina allowed her to take it with her.

In an effort to show family unity, Jackie returned to Greece three months later to attend the wedding at Glyfada of Christina and her most recent flame, Alexander Andreadis, heir to a Greek banking and industrial fortune. "I so love that child," Jackie said of Christina. "At last I can see happy days ahead for her."

Jackie and the stepdaughter she claimed to love became involved in a bitter 18-month legal dispute over the Onassis estate. The gist of the battle hinged on an interpretation of the will Onassis had written in anger while flying with Jackie from Acapulco to New York. Simon Rifkind, Jackie's attorney, hoped to overthrow the document on the grounds that it was invalid, Greek law ordaining that a last testament be composed "in a single sitting in a single location." Onassis had violated both stipulations. He had interrupted the composition of the will to have lunch in a Florida coffee shop while the airplane was being refueled; and an airplane while airborne doesn't technically qualify as "a place." Onassis had prepared his will in numerous locations as the plane flew from one country to another. By invalidating the document, Rifkind could try to prove that his client's husband had died intestate, which, again according to Greek law, entitled Jackie to receive 12.5 percent (or $125 million) of Ari's estimated billion-dollar estate.

Anticipating a protracted court fight, and not wanting to further alienate Ted Kennedy (the Onassis empire still needed influential friends in Washington), Christina's advisers offered the widow the flat sum of $20 million, provided Jackie relinquish all further claims to the estate, including her one-quarter share in both Skorpios and the *Christina*. Because of stiff U.S. inheritance taxes, Rifkind demanded—and received—a settlement of $26 million for his famous client: $20 million to be retained by Jackie (less legal fees), the remainder to cover estate taxes. Taking into account the prenuptial payment, monthly allowance, jewelry and other gifts, clothes and travel, Jackie's gross for the period of her marriage came to more than $42 million, or nearly $7 million per year for each year they were married.*

The settlement afforded Jackie security and peace of mind. It gave Christina the assurance she would never need to see her stepmother again. It also left Christina an enormous stake of her own, far more money than she could ever spend in a single lifetime. What it didn't give her was happiness. While still married to Alexander Andreadis, she met, had an affair with and later married Sergei Kauzov, divisional head of a Soviet shipping firm based in Paris and, according to published reports, a possible KGB agent. ("Who is Dostoyevski?" Christina inquired of friends after staying with Kauzov's family in Moscow.) Kauzov, however, soon went the way of his predecessors, Bolker and Andreadis, receiving as part of his alimony settlement a large oil tanker and the funds to keep it afloat.

Despite—or maybe because of—her massive fortune, Christina became an international madcap who danced at Studio 54 in Manhattan, dined at Tour d'Argent in Paris,

---

*The estate settlement carried two additional clauses: 1) all personal letters Jackie had written to Ari over the years had to be returned; 2) neither Christina nor Jackie would be permitted to discuss the terms of their final settlement.

wore Gucci leather and Pucci dresses, had her nose bobbed, her hair streaked and became addicted to all sorts of drugs and medications, especially amphetamines, which she took regularly to combat a weight problem.

"Christina often visited expensive fat farms in Switzerland and Spain and underwent medical treatment for obesity as the dress sizes of her lavish Yves Saint Laurent gowns—some with exorbitant price tags—grew constantly larger," said Truman Capote. "She substituted designer labels for style. I used to see her in all the clubs, always with a bottle of Coca-Cola in hand. Later she switched to diet soda. She had a loud, booming laugh and loved to throw parties, but she was a depressive with sad raccoon eyes. She had a voracious sexual appetite and paid men to take her to bed. She loathed Jackie, could barely tolerate her. She told me she had stripped the house on Skorpios that Jackie shared with her father and turned it over to her staff. After her father's death, she tried to take over the business, but spent too much time dieting, marrying and getting divorced. She never fulfilled the promise her father held out for her."

In 1980, Christina, while visiting New York, attempted to commit suicide by swallowing half a bottle of barbiturates as she had done on a number of other occasions. She was taken to Lenox Hill Hospital. The following day, Jackie, who had been apprised, telephoned Dr. Henry Lax and asked him to speak with Christina. Lax visited her at Lenox Hill and tried to impress upon her his concern for her welfare. Renée Luttgen was present a few weeks later when Dr. Lax over the telephone said to Christina: "Now that you're out of the hospital, you're back to your old agitated self; you lose your temper too easily. You always yell at people. You shouldn't yell at people so much."

She was married for the fourth and last time to suave French businessman and pharmaceuticals heir Thierry Roussel, who fathered her only child, Athina (named after Christina's mother), in 1985. All might have gone well had not Thierry fallen for Gaby Landhage, a gorgeous Swedish model, and sired two children by her, the older about the same age as Athina. Christina and Thierry were divorced after three years and ten days, and he reportedly walked away with $75 million, or nearly $75,000 for each day of their marriage. "Little Tina" became the center of her mother's life. She was given a complete zoo at the age of six months. A nine-man security force was hired to protect her. The child was never left alone. Special alarm systems were installed in every room of every house they occupied to insure against kidnapping. Christina had finally found her *raison d'être*.

"I don't like to talk about Jackie Kennedy," she said not long before the end of her unhappy life. "She is the most mercenary person I've ever met. She thinks, talks and dreams of nothing but money. What she doesn't realize is that I would have given her fifty times what I gave her for the pleasure of never having to see her again. I would have paid any price. What amazes me is that she survives while everybody around her drops. She's dangerous, she's deadly. She has decimated at least two families—the Kennedys and mine. If I never see her again as long as I live it will be too soon."

On November 19, 1988, while staying with her Argentinian friends Alberto and Marina Dodero at their villa outside Buenos Aires, Christina Onassis suffered pulmonary edema and, after being flown by helicopter to a nearby hospital, was pronounced dead. Her remains were returned to Skorpios and laid to rest in the family cemetery plot, next to the little chapel, beside the bodies of her father and brother.

As sole heir of Christina's inherited fortune, her daughter Athina instantly became the world's wealthiest baby. Jackie Onassis had no comment and did not attend the funeral.

31

"People forget that Jackie endured some difficult times," said Franklin D. Roosevelt, Jr. "Jack Kennedy and Aristotle Onassis were both exceptionally powerful men who didn't always treat women with kid gloves. There were times when Jackie was diminished by them, dominated by them, forced to follow in their footsteps. No doubt she enjoyed aspects of that role. She derived a certain amount of independence. But essentially it repeated a pattern that had become familiar in her life—to define herself in terms of a particular man. First she was Black Jack Bouvier's daughter, then Jack Kennedy's wife and, in the end, Jack Kennedy's survivor. Later she became Mrs. Aristotle Onassis, and eventually his [somewhat] disinherited widow.

"After Onassis's death, Jackie's great struggle was the need to forge a new identity for herself. She no longer wanted to be known as the wife of a former President of the United States, or the wife of one of the wealthiest men on earth. Finally, she wanted to be recognized on the strength of her own merits; she wanted to achieve success, but in her own way and on her own terms."

The search for a new identity started when Jackie went to lunch with Dorothy Schiff, whom she hadn't seen in a number of years. The publisher of the *New York Post*, a longtime fund raiser for the Democratic Party, wanted her to enter the race for the U.S. Senate in New York against Senator James Buckley. Jackie declined the offer, but after lunch, when she toured the newspaper's press room and editorial offices, she was reminded of her early, curtailed career as an inquiring photographer.

To friends she expressed a certain tedium with her current lifestyle. Alone again in New York, she seemed somehow less social, spending more evenings at home than she spent out, helping her son with his homework, reading, or watching television while spooning yogurt out of a paper container. She almost never went to cocktail parties and avoided most charity benefits, even those she helped organize. Occasionally, Jackie baked cookies or chocolate cakes for friends. She never gave large dinner parties, preferring small dinners, sometimes black tie, usually not, mostly for eight, for twenty-four at most. Guests were seated at four round tables of six. Her residential staff in New York consisted of a housekeeper, maid, butler and cook. Her New Jersey property was maintained by a year-round caretaker couple.

The flow of Jackie's life had settled into a pattern not unlike that of most other well-to-do Manhattan dowagers. She shopped—though less avariciously than when married to Onassis—at all the best stores, ordered her groceries (usually by telephone) from the East 85th Street Gristede's (she was an erratic tipper, according to one of the delivery boys, giving a dollar one day, nothing the next), went to Miss Grimble's for cheesecake, bought brownies at William Greenberg's, and chocolate truffles at $15 a pound from Kron's. One day, she purchased a pound of asparagus at The Empire Fruit Market, her regular stop for fruits and vegetables. Later she noticed a better price at another neighborhood market, returned the original purchase and thereby saved a quarter by buying the asparagus at the second stand. Her flowers came from "Flowers by Philip" on Madison Avenue. The nearby Larimore Drug Store handled most of her pharmaceutical needs.

Several mornings a week, she donned her well-worn blue and white running shoes, standard-issue sweatsuit, and a pair of soft white cotton gloves for a brisk walk around the Central Park reservoir. For added exercise she rode her bicycle through Central Park and joined an aerobics class at the 15-story Vertical Club on East 61st Street. Otherwise, she occupied herself by rearranging the museum-quality Regency and Louis XV furniture in her apartment, switching rugs, moving around paintings, framed photographs and her rare collection of objets d'art. She visited her dentist, her gynecologist, her allergist, and her psychoanalyst, whom she saw as often as four times a week. She went to Kenneth's to have her hair styled and colored (he came to her only on special occasions, as when she gave or attended a formal dinner). She also regularly received treatments from a shiatsu acupuncturist named Lillian Biko.

"Usually I treated Jackie at her apartment," said Biko, a Malaysian who studied acupuncture in the United States. "How often I see a patient depends on how he or she reacts to the process. I see most people intermittently, when they feel particularly tense or have an injury of some sort. I saw Jackie regularly. She was probably my best patient. She had a high pain threshold, in fact welcomed it because it was part of the process; it helped relieve her tension. She had lots of tension because she was very secretive. But she did things to help herself. She jogged, water-skied, rode horses and practiced yoga."

Jackie's aunt, Michelle Putnam, noted that for all her activity her niece seemed listless. "This wasn't my only observation, but I brought it to her attention. She was mostly puttering around New York. On weekends she drove her own green BMW across the George Washington Bridge to her country house in New Jersey. On the occasional weekends she remained in the city, she usually painted and sketched. She had an easel set up in front of one of her Fifth Avenue windows. Next to the easel was a high-power telescope through which she enjoyed observing people in the park: the most watched woman in the world was at heart a voyeur.

"But none of this seemed very invigorating. The first time I suggested she might enjoy getting a part-time job, her reaction seemed to be one of surprise: 'What, me—work?' But, the more she heard it from people and the more she thought about it, the more she warmed to the idea. Finally, she met with Tish Baldrige, her former social secretary at the White House. Tish suggested that Jackie consider publishing as a possible career, and made luncheon appointments for Jackie with several people she knew, including Thomas H. Guinzburg, publisher of Viking Press and a friend of the Bouviers."

"We had lunch at Le Perigord Park in Manhattan," recalled Guinzburg. "I originally knew Lee, her sister, when she was married to Michael Canfield, Cass's son, and through Lee I met Jackie. This was around 1956. So I had the inside track, since we knew a number of people in common.

"I recognized at once what a boon she could be to a publishing firm. She had access to a wide range of interesting and important figures. She knew literally *everyone*, and in publishing it's not so much what you know but whom you know. I also understood that while they were young, her children would always come first. They were teenagers at this point, but it became apparent that if I wanted Jackie at Viking, I would have to create a schedule for her which was highly flexible."

The first luncheon with Guinzburg was followed by more meetings and then a press conference at which it was announced that Mrs. Jacqueline Onassis would begin work in early September 1975 as a $10,000-a-year, four-days-a-week, consulting editor at Viking. Once again she had done the unexpected; she had decided to become a career woman.

"Viking staffers suddenly began reporting to work in their Guccis and pearls," observed Guinzburg. "There were all sorts of rumors, primarily that we were on the brink of bankruptcy and Jackie had been brought in as a publicity stunt to resuscitate the company. Once she began reporting for work, the media started camping out in the lobby. To get to the elevator you had to climb over pup tents, television cables, lights, and cameramen. The three major networks were there 24 hours a day. Then there were the groupies and crackpots who used to hang out. Every day for weeks the switchboard lit up like a Christmas tree."

Reporters were surprised to learn that, although she had been assigned an assistant, a 26-year-old college graduate named Becky Singleton, her office was small and spartan, containing only a desk, chair, telephone and bulletin board.

Because Jackie had only recently joined the firm, Guinzburg asked a more experienced editor, Barbara Burn, to work with her. "Jackie wasn't quite certain what was expected of her," recalled Burn. "So we discussed the various kinds of projects that she could work on, and what role she might play as an editor. As it turned out, she really liked to work on manuscripts and put books together. She had a flair for it and worked hard at it.

"Before she came, everybody at Viking was reasonably skeptical. After she arrived, we were all pleasantly surprised that she wasn't a stuffed shirt with a funny voice. She was no Marie Antoinette-at-the-farm. It wasn't just playing out. She was really very serious about what she did. The minute everybody got over the idea that she was who she was, and took her seriously, she began to relax a little. She didn't know a lot about how to put a book together at first, but she was willing to roll up her sleeves and learn. Of course, you never did quite get over the fact that there was a magazine cover walking down the corridor—that would hit you every so often.''

Barbara Burn's praise aside, Jackie had her share of problems at Viking. One of the first books she undertook, *"Remember the Ladies": Women of America, 1750–1815*, a celebration of 18th-century American womanhood, became the cause of a mini-scandal. Designed to accompany a Bicentennial exhibit that subsequently traveled to six cities under the auspices of the Pilgrim Society and the Plymouth Historical Society, the book was proposed to Jackie by Muffie Brandon, whose husband, Henry Brandon, was Washington correspondent for *The Sunday Times* of London. Active in the restoration and preservation of historic homes in Plymouth, Muffie met the author of the book, historian and university professor Linda Grant De Pauw, and offered to help her find a publisher.

Three years after the book's publication, an article in the March 1979 issue of *Ms.* by Gloria Steinem made false claims regarding Jackie's participation in the project. According to Steinem, Jackie Onassis had not only acquired the book but had seemingly researched, designed and edited it as well. Steinem further implied that it had been Jackie's idea to integrate black and native American women into the text. A description in the article, attributed to Muffie Brandon, had Jacqueline "crawling around the floor, arranging picture layouts" for the volume, which included some 200 illustrations.

The article infuriated Linda Grant De Pauw. "I wrote a 'letter to the editor' pointing out that I had written the text while Conover Hunt, curator of the exhibit, wrote the captions for the illustrations. The theme, organization and interpretative frameworks of both the exhibition and the book were my creations. Integration of black and native American women was a distinctive feature of my approach, not, as Steinem suggested, something included at Mrs. Onassis's suggestion. The description of Mrs. Onassis crawling around on the floor was pure fantasy. In fact, at no time while writing the book or at any time before or since did I have any communication of any kind, oral or written, direct or indirect, with Jacqueline Onassis. I don't know what she did or does for other authors, but in my case she was non-existent."

Bryan Holme, director of Viking's Studio Books division, the rarefied, expensive, word-and-picture coffee table volumes that became fashionable in the 1960s and '70s, affirmed Jackie's interest in publishing: "She used to come to our office and watch us put together our books. She enjoyed the combination of illustrations and words. She asked loads of questions. I'd answer them and her eyes would light up. 'I didn't know that. That's fascinating,' she would say. That's how she learned about publishing. And gradually she'd do this and do that—write an introduction, provide captions, edit the text.

"Her involvement with Studio Books reached its height with the publication of *In the Russian Style,* an elegant volume depicting the sumptuousness of eighteenth- and nineteenth-century Imperial Russia. Jackie selected the illustrations and wrote the text. The book was published in conjunction with an exhibition arranged by Diana Vreeland at the Costume Institute of the Metropolitan Museum of Art. To gather additional pictorial matter for the book, Jackie arranged a tour of some of the great private collections and museums of the Soviet Union. She went there with Thomas Hoving, Director of the Metropolitan Museum, and returned with all sorts of exciting material."

Candace Fischer, a researcher for the Costume Institute, likewise became involved in the project: "The inspiration for *In the Russian Style* was Diana Vreeland, but once Jackie took over she completely dominated it. She demonstrated the same drive and enthusiasm I imagine she brought to the White House restoration project, an almost schoolgirl attitude. She would rise at six in the morning and start to work on the book. An hour later, she would call me and say, 'Do you remember that photograph we saw yesterday? Shall we go back and get it?' And of course we had seen hundreds of photos the day before. Then she gave me page after page of handwritten notes based on Tolstoy's *War and Peace.* She would copy excerpts that pertained to clothing and lifestyles of the period. 'You've got to read this,' she would write."

For all Jackie's efforts, *In the Russian Style* received decidedly mixed reviews. Nicholas Nabokov in the *New York Review of Books* (March 3, 1977) derided Jackie for producing "an outwardly handsome book" which ultimately lacked content and was prone to misstatement: "The flashy layout, the seeming earnestness of purpose and the ill-conceived pretension to thorough scholarship may readily seduce and even interest an innocent reader or viewer." Nabokov's critique recalled the attacks levied against Jackie's televised tour of the White House during Camelot, and repeated a charge that others had made before—Jackie was all glitter-and-gold, lots of surface but no substance.

In March 1976, Mr. and Mrs. Thomas Guinzburg accompanied Jackie on a two-week vacation to Montego Bay, Jamaica. Others in the party included John Kennedy, Jr., Tim Shriver and Peter and Cheray Duchin. Cheray's mother, Audrey Zauderer (today Audrey del Rosario), owned an estate in Round Hill, the poshest section of Montego Bay. Round Hill was also the name of the nearby luxury resort where the group stayed. Another guest at the same resort was Rod Gibson, a reporter for the *National Enquirer*, who had been sent to do a story on Jackie.

"I suppose you'd call it a stakeout more than an assignment," said Gibson. "I was there with Vince Eckersley, a photographer for the *Enquirer*. On arriving, we sent Jackie a bouquet of orchids. There was no response, but it seemed that when she knew we were around, she began appearing at the beach almost twice as much as she had previously, though never talking to us and feigning distress whenever Eckersley started taking pictures. It was a game of cat and mouse.

"I knew another reporter who'd covered Jackie for the *Enquirer*. His name was Gerry Hunt, and his fix on the lady was that she was totally unpredictable. She had a split personality. One day she started yelling at him to leave her 'and my family alone.' Another day she took a long walk with him through the woods and talked off the record.

"One morning at Round Hill, I took John, Jr., and Tim Shriver snorkling. This was in an effort to gain an interview with Jackie. My partner lent the two boys one of his underwater cameras. The next day, the manager of

Round Hill called us into his office. He returned the camera to Eckersley and said, 'You boys have been great. You're great guests. But Jackie's also a great guest, and she's down here for privacy. So please lay off her. She asked me to return this camera, but respectfully declines a personal interview.'

" 'There goes our last hope,' I told Eckersley. I'd given up on the interview, but thought we might still get close enough so he could take a few snapshots.

"Several days later we were relaxing on the beach. 'Thank God this vacation is coming to an end,' said Eckersley. 'I'm sick and tired of following that woman around.' And right then Jackie appeared. She was alone. It was dusk, the sun was going down and there was no one around. Eckersley saw her and said, 'Goddammit, there she is now.' It was a perfect photo situation, the moment we'd been waiting for. He picked up his camera, I don't think Jackie even saw us at first, but there was something so regal about her and so wondrous about the moment, with her alone like that, that Eckersley couldn't bring himself to take the picture. She walked to the water's edge, doffed her beach jacket and went in for a swim; just sort of glided off like a water bird of exotic origin. She gave no indication of ever having seen us, but she obviously had, because she didn't return to pick up her jacket. She swam off and got out of the water somewhere else, and sent somebody from the hotel to retrieve her jacket."

The Jackie of this period was perceived differently by different people. Andy Warhol went to a Manhattan restaurant one evening with Jackie and Tennessee Williams. "Jackie seemed a bit nervous about being with Tennessee, and Tennessee seemed a bit nervous about being with Jackie," reflected Warhol. "All Jackie kept talking about was household business, beautifying the home, where to buy this and that, and so forth. She sounded like a glorified housewife, although of course she wasn't."

Rosey Grier, the former New York Giants football player who became friendly with Jackie after the assassination of Robert Kennedy, recalled a rather unpleasant occasion: "One day I went to get an ice-cream cone with her near her apartment. When we were in the store, some lady walked up to her and started talking. 'You and

I have something in common,' she announced. 'What's that?' Jackie asked. 'My daughter died the same day your husband was killed,' she responded flatly.

"In 1976, I started 'Giant Step,' a program designed to inspire and encourage young people trapped in the ghetto. Jackie agreed to serve on the Board of Directors, and in 1977, she flew out to Los Angeles, and went into the inner city and visited some of the kids in their homes in Watts. She attended a benefit for the organization and was easily the main attraction.

"In time I grew close to John Jr. I once accompanied him to a carnival at the Collegiate School. We won a silver dollar together in some event, and I placed him in charge of it, the only stipulation being that he couldn't spend it without my permission."

Aileen Mehle, better known as "Suzy" to the readers of her syndicated society column, attended the 1977 opening of the movie *The Turning Point,* with Jackie and Bunny Mellon: "I remember it very well because there was so much hoopla attached to it. Farrah Fawcett was there. This was when she was starring in 'Charlie's Angels' on television. We drove up to the theater and all these photographers clustered around Farrah. The place was thronged. It was one of those Hollywood previews in New York with dozens of big names [attending]. Suddenly somebody yelled, 'Hey, there's Jackie!' and that was it for Farrah. The photographers deserted her like so many rats clambering off a sinking barge. They surrounded Jackie and started shooting away."

Anthony Quinn, a devoted personal admirer, had a falling out with Jackie over his appearance as an Onassis-type character in a third-rate film, *The Greek Tycoon,* for which he reportedly received $1 million. The actor and his wife, Yolanda, were sitting in a restaurant in Cannes when Jackie entered with a friend. Quinn waved at her, but Jackie sailed by without so much as a nod.*

Irving Mansfield, whose late wife Jacqueline Susann wrote a thinly disguised fictional account of Jackie Onassis's life, *Dolores,* found himself in a Doubleday Book Shop

---

*Jacqueline Bisset, starring as a Jackie-like character in the same film, remarked: "Jackie has a strangely unrevealing face. She never says anything that can possibly be quoted. She's very difficult to read."

on Fifth Avenue in Manhattan when Jackie entered the store. "I was there on a promotional tour for the reissue of several of my wife's books," he said. "Jackie Onassis approached the display table, saw what it was all about and made an exaggerated gesture, as if to hold her nose. She did it practically in my face. It was rude and ugly."

Less overt but equally rude was her reaction on stepping into an elevator in London and finding herself face to face with Gore Vidal. Jackie and Gore hadn't seen each other since Vidal's imbroglio at the White House with Robert Kennedy. More than a dozen years had elapsed, but Jackie hadn't forgotten. She turned her back on Vidal and stared into space. Vidal did likewise.

But Jackie did have her better moments. Richie Berlin, daughter of the late Richard Berlin, President of Hearst Publications, had a broken leg and a plaster cast up to her hip, and was trying to hail a taxicab in a driving New York rainstorm. "Along came a cab," she said. "I was on crutches and wondering how to get myself and the crutches into the back seat. The cab pulled right up and out stepped Jackie Onassis. She instantly understood my predicament. She held my crutches and helped me into the cab. She then placed them where they should be for getting out. I realized she knew where to put them, because she had probably done it a thousand times for JFK. In that small gesture she demonstrated both sense and style. She even had an unspoken sense of humor about it. To be helped into a cab by Jackie Onassis: it gave me a rush. It was dramatic. It blew my mind."

Rosamond Bernier, the wife of *New York Times* art critic John Russell, and herself a well-established lecturer on art at the Metropolitan Museum of Art, was "struck by Jackie's exquisite, almost regal politeness. You do a little favor for her—a nothing—and you get the most elegantly couched, handwritten letter of gratitude. She came to a dinner at our home for Princess Margaret, and followed up with the most thoughtful and sensitive letter.

"I invited Jackie to supper one evening along with Stephen Spender, the English poet. Caroline Kennedy was there and so was my husband. Stephen saw that Jackie really could talk seriously, and so he asked her what the thing was that she was proudest of as an accomplishment in her life. She thought a moment and said, very quietly, 'Well, I went through some pretty difficult times, and I kept my sanity.' I thought that very moving. It's also a tremendous tribute. Anyone who went through what she went through, and managed to retain her balance, deserves credit.

"I don't say that she's the perfect human being. Like the rest of us, she has her shortcomings. I think partially because of what she went through she finds it difficult to open up to people. This difficulty is compounded by the fact that she is fundamentally a very private person. She does not like undue familiarity. It's not that she's standoffish—I think she's a genuinely solitary and almost shy person. She's not the kind of woman who is ever extremely intimate with a friend. I would not presume on our friendship."

Gloria Steinem agreed that Jackie was at times "almost overly discreet and delicate." Hoping to convince her to actively support the Equal Rights Amendment and lend her influential voice to the feminist movement, Steinem called her. "She approved the movement and even supported it, but would not march," said Steinem. "She did donate a large sum of money to the *Ms.* Foundation, thereby automatically becoming a lifetime subscriber to the magazine. Basically none of the Kennedy women would come out for Women's Liberation. They were already in the limelight and didn't want to expose themselves any more than they had to. But I suppose ideologically Jackie was behind it, and put her money where her mouth was."

Jackie attended several sessions of the Democratic National Convention in New York, in part to show support for Sargent Shriver, whose bid to capture his party's presidential nomination that year was unsuccessful. After the convention, Harris Wofford encountered her at the Shrivers', and was able to talk with her at length, something he had never done at the White House. "I had known Jackie at the White House only in passing. To my surprise she seemed much more intellectual and well-informed than I realized. She was bold and wanted to talk about a whole body of issues, including lesbianism. I was amazed at how thoughtful, intelligent, interesting and attractive she was."

Author David Halberstam saw Jackie at a party the night Jimmy Carter won the presidency. "We knew each other slightly, and I noticed no one was talking to her very much, as if intimidated by her," he stipulated. "So I went over, spoke what was largely small talk and, among other things, asked what she had been doing on the same night sixteen years earlier—in 1960. She was very pleasant and seemed eager to talk about it."

Gloria Emerson happened to be at the same party. "Most of the people there seemed afraid to talk to Jackie," she said. "Those who did talk to her addressed her in the same reverential tone usually reserved for the Queen of England. David Halberstam broke the ice by asking something like, 'So, Jackie, what was it like being married to Onassis?' She cracked up. It put her at ease."

Hugh Auchincloss died in November 1976. Jackie attended the funeral service for her stepfather in Newport. In repaying recent debts incurred by his brokerage firm as the result of poor real estate investments, Auchincloss had managed to deplete what remained of the family fortune. Merrywood had been sold; Hammersmith Farm had also been sold, with the exception of the twelve-room former servants' house which Janet Auchincloss continued to use. Utilizing her Onassis settlement, Jackie secretly established a million-dollar trust fund for her mother, enabling her to live in relative ease.

In early February 1977, Edith Beale, 81, fell ill and had to be taken to Southampton Hospital. When they placed her in a small, airless room, Doris Francisco telephoned Jackie in New York. "Get Auntie Edith the best room in the house, and send Nancy Tuckerman the bills," ordered Jackie. Edith died three days later.

Jackie's presence at the funeral brought out the press. Services were held at Most Holy Trinity Church in East Hampton. Little Edie borrowed Doris Francisco's mink coat for the occasion. At the end of the service, a recording was played of Edith singing "Together Again."

"Jackie wanted to borrow the record to make a tape for herself, but I wouldn't let her," boasted Little Edie. "My mother was in complete agony the last six years of her life. Onassis fixed up Grey Gardens, but Jackie did nothing for us. She let my mother starve and freeze."

Following a brief grave-site ceremony, family and friends of the deceased congregated for lunch at John Duck's restaurant in Southampton. "Upon arriving, Little Edie and I went to the powder room, and found Jackie gazing intently into a large mirror, studying her reflection," said

Doris Francisco. "She sat there for maybe five minutes, staring at her image."

After her mother's death, Edie Beale put Grey Gardens up for sale. "When Jackie heard about it, she called and begged me to reconsider," said Edie. "She was very upset that I would want to be rid of the place. When I explained that I needed to move to a warmer climate, she offered to send me to Key West provided I didn't sell Grey Gardens. It was that or an apartment in New York.

"Once Jackie learned that Ben Bradlee and Sally Quinn were willing to pay $225,000 for Grey Gardens, she became frantic. She resented Bradlee because of his book on John Kennedy.* This time she had Nancy Tuckerman call. Nancy said that Jackie was *very* upset. At the time, Jackie was sending me $600 per month for living expenses. But I liked Ben Bradlee, and [anyway] my brother, Bouvier Beale, handled the legal aspects of the sale. After I moved to Miami Beach, Jackie reduced my monthly allowance to three hundred dollars. But the money from the sale of the house went into the bank, and I live off the interest."

The same year as Edith Beale's death, Jackie's professional life took a sudden turn. She resigned her position that fall when Viking published Jeffrey Archer's *Shall We Tell the President?*, a novel depicting "President" Edward Kennedy as the target of an assassination attempt. A scathing review in *The New York Times* by John Leonard ended with the statement: "There is a word for such a book. The word is trash. Anybody associated with its publication should be ashamed of herself." It was clearly a poison dart aimed at Jackie. The truth was that she had nothing to do with the book's publication—had not read it, and had been cautioned by Thomas Guinzburg *not* to read it. But when Guinzburg issued a public statement hinting that had Jackie objected, the book would never have been published, she quit.

---

*In 1976, a year after the publication of Bradlee's *Conversations With Kennedy*, he and Sally Quinn saw Jackie walking up Madison Avenue with Peter and Cheray Duchin. Opening his arms to embrace Jackie, Bradlee was met with a baleful stare and was shunted to the side as Jackie pushed by him. She was apparently upset by the highly personal nature and tone of the book. She never resumed their friendship.

Jackie had other contacts in the publishing world. John Sargent, the robust, bearded Chairman of the Board of Doubleday Books, was an old friend and occasional escort. Sensing an opportunity, he met with Jackie and discussed the possibility of her joining Doubleday as an Associate Editor. She was definitely interested.

Sargent went to see Sandy Richardson, who was then Editor in Chief, and informed him that Jackie Onassis might agree to join Doubleday. Neither Richardson nor any of the other Doubleday executives he approached had much say in the matter. Sargent, like Guinzburg before him, realized what an invaluable addition the former First Lady could be.

"My impression was that there was more to her leaving Viking than the Jeffrey Archer novel," said Sandy Richardson. "There had been some nasty business about Lord Snowden's memoirs and other similar books Jackie had wanted to do. Apparently they didn't feel Lord Snowden, the one-time husband of Princess Margaret, was highbrow enough. Jackie invited him for lunch, and they were rude to him. Doubleday was more charitable towards the kind of book Jackie does best. At Doubleday she always has been able to do more or less whatever she wants to do.

"Another advantage for Jackie was that Nancy Tuckerman already worked in publicity at Doubleday. She wasn't instrumental in bringing Jackie into the firm, but it didn't do any harm. Jackie came aboard in the spring of 1978. At first, there was a great deal of twittering and fluttering among employees. She walked into the employee snack bar and the room immediately fell silent. People stared at her in the elevator for at least the first eight or nine months, but then she began to ride up anonymously like everybody else. Whether they became used to her or were just too polite to stare, I don't know. But she seemed to have become more of a workaday person.

"She was basically there to bring in celebrities. She did that and several other things, such as art and photography books, a continuation of her role at Viking. She was supposed to acquire books through her connections with people like Diana Vreeland. She always worked only three days a week—Tuesdays through Thursdays—but she kept in touch by telephone the other two days. I dealt with her at weekly editorial meetings, and at other times when she had questions or problems. She didn't edit much, if at all. She read manuscripts for other people and brought in manuscripts herself which others read. I had the feeling she wasn't getting major stuff done, but she began to do much better later on. I left the company after she'd been there about two years."

While Jackie had her supporters at Doubleday, the majority of her co-workers found her presence at the company alternately laughable and distressing. Stories of her mishaps and daily upsets soon began to spread. An editor who sat next to her at her first Wednesday morning editorial meeting suggested that she looked more "like a frightened chicken than a former First Lady." The main purpose of the meeting was to have various editors make verbal presentations of their proposed books so they could sign them up. At Jackie's first presentation, she turned to the same editor and said, "I'm so nervous about this. What do I say, how do I say it?"

"There were two major divisions at Doubleday," he said. "There was trade, which is where Jackie worked, and there was nonfiction, which included cookbooks, how-to books, health books, and so on. Both groups held their respective editorial meetings at the same time. On one occasion, Jackie went to the wrong room and sat through a non-fiction divisional meeting. She was so oblivious she didn't realize it, and wouldn't have realized it had not someone else in the room spoken up and told her she was at the wrong meeting.

"Many of the editors at Doubleday resented her. We were all handling as many as 15 books at a time—too much work for too little pay. Jackie took on as few books as she pleased. She was paid full-time, but worked part-time. What's more, she had assistants, secretaries, gophers, telephone ladies working for her. They gave her an assistant named Ray Roberts who practically became her guide dog. He won't admit it, but he did everything for her. They gave her a secretary, Kathy Bayer, who did the rest of her drudgery. It cost Doubleday a fortune to keep Jackie on staff, but it provided a constant flow of free publicity. Whenever Jackie's name appeared in the press, Doubleday also received a plug. Most of us believed that the reason they hired her in the first place was the hope that she would one day produce her own memoir. That will probably never happen. Still, she holds that hope out, teases the brass with it, and that's another reason they keep her on."

Another Doubleday editor recalled that "for the first year of her employment, Jackie's followers used to crowd the lobby waiting to catch a glimpse of her. They'd be there even when she didn't report to work. The company would send someone down to tell them that Jackie wasn't coming in that day, but they wouldn't believe the person, and wouldn't leave.

"Jackie supposedly disliked all manner of publicity and wanted to be left alone by the public. That was the story at any rate. But she was once riding the elevator at Doubleday, and Sophia Loren was on the same elevator. Loren was preparing a cookbook for publication by Doubleday. When the other passengers started noticing Loren and ignoring Jackie, Jackie became rattled, and stomped off the elevator at her floor.

"She was never particularly friendly with the other editors. They didn't consider her a Member of the Club, and she preferred to remain outside the realm. I found her rather cold and remote. She seemed to exist on at least two separate planes. She would give you a big warm smile one day, and the next day pretend she didn't know you. I had a friend in her department, an editor, who told me over dinner one evening that she felt [she and Jackie] had established a close working relationship. 'Once you got to know her,' she said, 'Jackie can be quite lovely. I went out on a date with another Doubleday staffer. After dinner we went to the theater and there on line directly behind us stood Jackie with an escort. We smiled at her and said, "Hi." She looked at us as if she had never seen either one of us before. She completely ignored us.' "

Individual authors also expressed their reservations. "I got no requests for line changes," maintained Don Cook, writer of *Ten Men and History*, profiles of Charles de Gaulle, Willy Brandt and other international statesmen. "[But] Jackie sent me lots of flowery, handwritten notes on how much she liked the book. And I got two lunches with her, one at '21' and another in her apartment."

"She was terrific to work with," remarked Sarah Lazin, the former Director of Rolling Stone Press who worked with Jackie on *The Ballad of John and Yoko*, a collection of interviews with the famous pair.

"Editors I know at other houses would say, 'Oh, how's your Jackie book?' as if it didn't really exist. . . .'"

Mimi Kazon, a former political columnist for the now-defunct *East Side Express*, started a conversation with Jackie at a book party ("the room absolutely tilted when she entered"), and ended it by agreeing to send the Doubleday editor a packet of her best material for possible publication. "I'd always been a devout Jackie fan," admitted Kazon. "I used to relish all those stories about her, how she would go into Ungaro's on Madison Avenue during her lunch break and charge $10,000 worth of clothes, and then go to Zitomer's, a pharmacy on East 76th Street, and charge a pack of Dentyne gum. So I was thrilled when she asked me to send her some of my columns. I put them in the mail, and a few months later the telephone rang and a soft voice said, 'This is Jackie Onassis of Doubleday. I received your columns and found them quick and witty. But they were all about power, and frankly I'm not into power.'"

32

"Jackie Onassis deserves credit for the way she brought up Caroline and John Jr. to be well-adjusted, serious, completely out-of-the-limelight people," said Betty McMahon, whose children occasionally played with Jackie's in Palm Beach. "She did it by herself and she did it against all odds. Things might have turned out differently. Look at all the troubles experienced by so many of the other Kennedy young."

Jackie was all too aware of the disturbing events that had befallen various members of the tribe: Peter Lawford's increasing dependence on drugs and alcohol and the gradual erosion of his marriage to Pat Kennedy Lawford; Bobby Kennedy's youngsters tumbling from one catastrophe to the next (reckless driving with nearly fatal accidents, school failings and expulsions, drug busts and suspended sentences); Teddy's daughter, Kara, experimenting with marijuana and hashish, running away from home and ending up in a halfway house; Joan Kennedy's admitted alcoholism; the amputation of Teddy Jr.'s leg following the detection of bone-marrow cancer.

Much against her will and better judgment, Jackie found herself thrust into many of these family situations. When Joan, for instance, learned of her husband's extramarital affairs (most prominently mentioned were New York socialite Amanda Burden, skier Suzy Chaffee and former Canadian Premier Pierre Trudeau's ex-wife, Margaret), she turned to Jackie for advice. If anybody knew about Kennedy infidelity it had to be Jackie Kennedy Onassis. Her summation of the situation demonstrated a nonchalance that nearly took Joan's breath away. "Kennedy men are like that," said Jackie. "They'll go after anything in skirts. It doesn't mean a thing." It apparently meant more to Joan than it did to Jackie; following Ted Kennedy's unsuccessful bid for the 1980 Democratic presidential nomination (in which Joan campaigned with her husband), she filed for divorce.

Joan Kennedy was clearly confused, and had been for some time. She couldn't cope. In terms of competence she was the antithesis of Jackie, and in terms of "love of family" she was the antithesis of Ethel. She wanted to fit in but couldn't; lacking Jackie's strength, she fell by the wayside. Jackie, the original "odd woman out," had the stamina to fight the most dangerous and destructive forces in the Kennedy family, yet she also had the intelligence to embrace those parts of it that could enhance her life.

Harrison Rainie, a Washington correspondent for the New York *Daily News* and a Kennedy family biographer, felt "Jackie tended to resist the enforced togetherness embraced by the rest of the family. She was never one of those relentless buffs, like Bobby and Ethel, continually clamoring for family reunions. She was particularly wary of the Robert Kennedy household, which was more important to the children's generation than any of the others. She didn't want Caroline and John to play second fiddle, and didn't want them to be exposed to an environment that was considered unstructured and untamed."

Caroline Kennedy had grown into adolescence and young womanhood bearing a poignant resemblance to her late father. She possessed a determined sense of personal privacy despite the tragic and dramatic events that had surrounded her. It was her sense of privacy and distaste for formality that convinced her to bypass the ritual of the debutante party. Although her mother objected, Caroline refused to "come out." Iron-willed and self-determined, she also decided to put off college for a year to enroll in a Work of Art program in London conducted by Sotheby's, the prestigious art auctioneers. During her stay in London an incident took place that nearly made her regret her decision. It was October 24, 1975, and Caroline was staying at the home of family friend Sir Hugh Fraser, a Catholic member of Parliament, when a bomb exploded under Fraser's red Jaguar, the one in which he was about to drive his young American houseguest to her course. A neighbor walking his dog was killed in the blast.

Caroline insisted on remaining in London against her mother's wishes, but agreed to enroll in Radcliffe the following September. She kept her promise, arriving at college in her own car, the same model BMW that her mother drove. Like her mother, she performed well academically. She wore the baggy sweaters and formless skirts then popular on campus, dated occasionally but preferred socializing within the confined circle of a group of friends. During the summer following her sophomore year, she took a job as a copygirl with the New York *Daily News*. The newspaper permitted her to accompany other reporters to Memphis to cover the death of Elvis Presley, but then refused to run the article she wrote. Rewritten, it was published in *Rolling Stone* instead.

By the beginning of her junior year Caroline was going steady with Thomas R. Carney, a slick, soft-spoken New York novelist and free-lance writer, ten years her senior. A one-time copywriter at Doubleday, Carney had been introduced to Caroline by her mother. An Irish Catholic and graduate of Yale, Tom seemed to possess all the prerequisites as future husband material for Caroline, including an interest in athletics and the desire to become a screenwriter. Jacqueline was unsuccessful in finding a producer for one of Tom's early scripts, but was quick to invite him along when she and Caroline vacationed together in the Caribbean. Tom invited Caroline to spend a week at his father's horse ranch in Wyoming. "What ended it was the publicity," said Carney. "I couldn't see spending the rest of my life with cameras hovering around my head."

Somewhat ruffled by the break-up of what had been a serious relationship, Caroline graduated from Radcliffe in 1980, returned to New York, moved into a West Side apartment with two friends,* and accepted a job in the Film and Television Development Office of the Metropolitan Museum of Art. Taking full advantage of her presence, the New York press began to cover Caroline, not always in complimentary terms. Among the unpleasant incidents they reported was a confrontation she had

---

*Jackie thought Manhattan's Upper West Side unsafe for an unattached young woman. Her fears were justified when, in 1981, a deranged 35-year-old California law school graduate showed up at Caroline's apartment building and started to harass her. The man was charged with aggravated harassment and criminal trespass. Defending himself at his one-day trial, he was declared mentally unstable and was eventually remanded to a California psychiatric institution for observation.

in a Madison Avenue ice-cream parlor. Caroline strolled in one afternoon and demanded immediate service.

"You'll have to take a number, just like everyone else," insisted the man behind the counter.

"But I'm not like everyone else," she said angrily. "I'm Caroline Kennedy."

"I don't care if you're the Duchess of Windsor, you still have to take a number."

Caroline stormed out.

The tabloids reported that she tried the same tactic with the same lack of success several weeks later in a First National City Bank while trying to avoid a long Friday morning line.

Then there were the Caroline stories that didn't make the press.

Tracey Dewart waited tables part-time at Ruppert's, a trendy restaurant on the Upper East Side of Manhattan, and in the summer of 1979, found herself waiting on Caroline Kennedy: "She was with a guy and she kept taking pieces of cheese out of this fellow's salad. She had her legs up on another chair at the table. She was acting very obnoxious. I asked if she wanted her own salad, and she said she did. She was demanding and bossy, ordering me to get this and get that—another fork, an extra glass of water, the works. I was miffed."

Mimi Kazon tried interviewing Caroline several times for her newspaper column. "She didn't just say 'No,' " reported Kazon. "It was the way she said it. She made a big deal about it. I found her brother much more gracious and outgoing. He understood I was only doing my job and tried to make it easier for me."

Raising John Jr. was more difficult for Jackie than bringing up her daughter. "I'm afraid he's going to grow up to be a fruit," she once lamented to a family employee. Fatherless and substantially without direction, John became the object of a "toughening up" regimen devised and implemented by his task-oriented mother. After the assassination and before they vacated the White House, she made her young son spend a night alone in his father's bed. Five years later, she asked a Secret Service agent to give John boxing lessons. At Collegiate he bloodied a classmate's nose because the boy insisted on calling him John-John.

After school one day, he pelted newspaper photographers with snowballs and hurled empty Pepsi bottles over the heads of pedestrians. Following a surprise birthday party his mother threw for him at Le Club, he became involved in a fist-fight between his pseudo-macho Kennedy cousins and a reporter. His mother thought him undisciplined. At age eleven he was packed off—along with Tony Radziwill—to the Drake Island Adventure Center at Plymouth, England, for what was billed as a "week-long course for young people in sailing, canoeing, climbing and character development." At thirteen he participated in the rugged Outward Bound program to learn survival skills. The 26-day course culminated on Hurricane Island, a craggy, isolated outcrop off the coast of Maine, where he was deposited with no food, a gallon of water, two wooden matches, and a book on outdoor living.

This was preliminary to still another "rite of passage," a 70-day survival course arranged by the National Outdoor Leadership School. Part of this training took John Jr. back to Kenya. There he was put out into the wilds to learn survival technique in the deep African bush. When he and his accompanying band of six—three girls and three boys—disappeared for two days, a Masai warrior had to be dispatched to find them.

More to his liking was the month he spent at Chase Golf and Tennis Camp in Bethlehem, New Hampshire, where at fifteen he acquired his first girlfriend, a popular future debutante, Christina Goodman, who attended the Spence School in New York and continued to see him for about a year after camp.

"He was a good kid," she said. "But it was difficult for him in the sense that he was always being watched, and probably always will be. Also, no matter what he does in his lifetime, he'll [probably] never accomplish what his father did. And I guess he has to live with that."

Not entirely satisfied with his progress, Jackie enrolled him in the tenth grade at Phillips Academy in Andover, Massachusetts. She also placed him in the care of New York psychiatrist Ted Becker. Her concerns were manifold: She worried about his poor academic performance in school; she opposed an expressed wish on his part to become an actor (he started acting in school plays at Andover and continued when he attended Brown University); she thought she detected inherent "softness" in his character; she feared the unhappy and negative influence on him of other young members of the Kennedy clan, such as David Kennedy and Robert F. Kennedy, Jr., both of whom were addicted to hard drugs despite repeated courses of treatment in detoxification centers. Jackie's final solution to what she perceived as her son's "problem"—and Becker may well have given her the idea—was to induce him to go to Guatemala to help in a Peace Corps rebuilding program following a major earthquake.

"The trouble with John," said Robert Kennedy's son David,* "was simply that he matured later than most. I also think the death of Aristotle Onassis hit him harder than people realize. He didn't know his own father and didn't remember him except through the memorabilia he and his sister collected. Onassis and John were fairly close. They would go to ball games together. Onassis took him fishing once, gave him two $100 bills and told him to go buy some worms. So there was that relationship which ended at an inopportune time.

"Then his mother pushed too hard, threatened him with a kind of emotional blackmail. If he behaved himself and did what she said, she held out the carrot. But she was also very quick in turning the cold shoulder. If he did something she didn't like, she would wave the whip. Basically, that's how she related to everyone.

"For example, Jackie went through the ceiling when she heard about John's interest in acting. She told him point-blank that it couldn't be. This was at Brown University when he appeared in several student productions. Producer Robert Stigwood, of *Saturday Night Fever* and *Grease* fame, telephoned John and started talking about the possibility of John's playing the role of his father in a motion picture based on John F. Kennedy's younger years. John was very enthusiastic. But his mother wanted nothing to do with it. She wanted him to get on with his studies, finish college—and *then* do what he wanted with his life, so long as it wasn't acting.

Following his graduation from Brown in 1983, JFK, Jr., attended a work-study program in India, then returned to New York and after several other jobs worked

---

*David had troubles of his own. He died of an overdose of cocaine and Demerol in 1984.

as Acting Deputy Executive Director of the 42nd Street Development Corporation, a non-profit organization co-founded by his mother (with former advertising executive Fred Papert), and which for years had been lobbying for the construction of a national theater center in Times Square. He rented an apartment on West 86th Street, rode his 10-speed bike to and from work, paid $6,000 a year to belong to the Plus One Fitness Club in SoHo, made the disco scene, attended occasional charity affairs and switched girlfriends: Christina Haag, a budding actress, replaced Sally Munro, both were graduates of Brown.

To fulfill his yearning for the stage, he played the male lead in *Winners*, a Brian Friel drama about an Irish-Catholic youth engaged to marry his pregnant girlfriend (played by Christina Haag); at the end of the 90-minute production, the tragic pair is found drowned.

"Jackie did not attend, but other family members did come," said Nye Heron, Executive Director of the Irish Arts Center, where the play was mounted. "There were only six performances and at his mother's request there were no reviews or reviewers. He's one of the finest actors I've seen. He could have a successful acting career, but evidently that's not going to happen."

The rumor mill began to churn the moment Jackie was seen in public with any well-known male figure. Within months of Ari's death, she was linked with men no less celebrated than Adnan Khashoggi, Warren Beatty and Dr. Christiaan Barnard, none of whom she knew beyond one or two meetings for lunch or dinner. Aware of the curiosity and attention her name and presence still generated, she tried to lower her social profile, dating men whose professions and personalities kept them substantially out of the public eye. While vacationing in Jamaica in 1976 with the Guinzburgs and the Duchins, she encountered Carl Killingsworth, a friendly, dignified NBC-TV executive whom she had met once before in Greece.

"I met her in Greece shortly before Onassis died," recalled Killingsworth. "I was visiting Sarah Churchill. Sarah had a house in Greece and I visited her there every year. We spent a day aboard the *Christina*, and the big topic of conversation was whether to lunch on the yacht or on the beach.

"The second meeting took place at the home of Audrey Zauderer, Cheray Duchin's mother. She gave a party and Jackie was there. In talking to her, I was immediately struck by her wit. More important than her looks, she had a terrific sense of humor.

"I began to see her in New York. I found her retiring rather than shy. She wasn't shy about talking to people, but she was not particularly outgoing. In other words, she didn't talk about herself very much. I suppose that's why I remember so vividly the few comments she did make about herself. She told me that Onassis would stay at El Morocco all night and wanted her to stay with him. 'He could party until dawn, but I couldn't,' she said.

"What was unnerving about being with her was the constant stream of photographers. I'm very private myself and I wasn't used to it. 'Just relax and pretend they're not there,' she said to me. But they were there. We mostly went to screenings and art galleries, and the press was perpetually after us.

"On one occasion we went to a screening of *All the President's Men,* then to P. J. Clarke's and Jimmy Weston's, where we bumped into Frank Sinatra. Sinatra sat with us for two or three hours, and I had the feeling that Jackie very much enjoyed his company.

"She wasn't spoiled. I took her to a lot of inexpensive restaurants and she never said anything. She seemed just as happy to go to moderate, out-of-the-way restaurants, the places I like to go, as to the more expensive establishments.

"That's one of the two things that surprised me about her, the other being that she had a photograph of Robert Kennedy on top of her piano. That was the only family photograph I remember seeing displayed in her apartment. Certainly no other photograph was more prominently displayed. I think it probably fueled some of the gossip about herself and Bobby. People would visit her apartment, see the photo, and talk."

Her relationship with Carl Killingsworth gave way to a seemingly incongruous and brief romance with columnist Pete Hamill, then writing for New York's *Daily News.* It was Hamill who helped Caroline Kennedy obtain her summer position with the paper. Hamill, divorced and the father of two, was 42 when he began to date 48-year-old Jackie Onassis. Since 1970, he had been living with actress Shirley MacLaine, an affair that ended when MacLaine refused to marry him.

Hamill soon realized what many others already knew: privacy was a problem when it came to the former First Lady. Photographers dogged the couple's footsteps wherever they went. On November 17, 1977, Jackie attended a publication party for Hamill's new novel, *Flesh and Blood*, at O'Neal's Baloon restaurant near Lincoln Center. Joy Gross, health spa proprietress and author, whose daughter had married Brian Hamill, brother of Pete, was there as well. "It was pathetic," she said. "A roomful of supposedly sophisticated New Yorkers, including members of the press, clawed, kicked and shoved their way forward to get a better look at Jackie. She wasn't permitted to relax or enjoy herself because of the crush of people. Photographers climbed on top of chairs or on each other's shoulders for an unobstructed shot. After a while she stood up to leave. John Hamill, another of Pete's brothers, escorted her out. It was raining. He put her in a cab. When he came back, he made the remark that a date with Jackie was like 'taking out a big bright red fire engine.'

"Following the O'Neal's melee, Pete and some family members and friends gathered at P. J. Clarke's and Jackie snuck in to rejoin us. She sat next to me and I was impressed with the difference in her voice, the way she spoke in private versus how she spoke on television or in public—in other words, as before at O'Neal's. In public she had that little wispy voice, but the voice I heard coming out of her at P. J. Clarke's was crisp and confident. She was discussing literature, and she was obviously well informed. The little girl voice was gone.

"I'm not sure what drew Jackie to Pete. I know he visited her in Hyannis Port. He brought one of his daughters along, and Caroline was also there. Jackie must have respected his literary skills. He's good at what he does. He introduced her to a lot of writers for her publishing career. He was attentive to her children. I think he pursued Jackie because he was a man who at that point was impressed with people who had names. And in addition she was attractive and bright."

Pete Hamill spoke little of Jackie after the relationship dissolved. A contributing factor in the breakup may have been an article Hamill had written for his previous employer, the New York *Post,* roasting Jackie for her marriage to Aristotle Onassis. The *Post* had killed the piece and buried it in its files. But now that Hamill and Jackie were an item and Hamill was with the *Daily News,* owner Rupert Murdoch decided to run bits and pieces on *Page Six,* the *Post*'s gossip section.

"Many marriages are put together the same way as the Jackie-Ari deal," it began, "although the brutally commercial nature of the contract is often disguised with romantic notions about love and time. Some women can be bought with a guarantee of ham and eggs in the morning and a roof over the head; others with a mink coat on the anniversary of the selling of the contract. . . ."

The *Post* attack turned brutal: "It is outrageous to think that someone will spend $120,000 a year on clothing in a world where so few people have more than the clothes on their back. It is obscene that a woman would have more money in a month to use on applying paste to her face and spray to her hair than the average citizen of Latin America could earn in 100 years. . . ."

Hamill reacted by denouncing Murdoch and trying to explain the circumstances surrounding the *Post* article. Although Jackie claimed to understand and even to sympathize, she surely must have had her doubts. Within a matter of months, the relationship with Hamill had cooled and she was being squired by Peter Davis, a writer and documentary filmmaker, eight years her junior.

Richard Meryman, a former correspondent for *Life* and an old friend of Davis's, was unaware of the relationship until the night the Merymans gave a small dinner party at their brownstone in Greenwich Village. "I telephoned Peter to invite him, and he said he wanted to bring a date. So I said fine. And then he brought Jackie Onassis.

"What was interesting about it was that it was quite a glittering party. The people there included a screenwriter named Frank Pierson, who had won an Academy Award, and Calvin Trillin, the writer, and their wives, and me—a journalist who had covered quite a number of famous people—and several others. This was a group of people who had enjoyed plenty of exposure to big names, famous and glamorous names—and Jackie Onassis walked in and everybody's mouth dropped open. Alice Trillin went just absolutely bananas. She just talked and talked and talked and talked. She talked the whole evening. She talked to anyone who would listen. She got fixed on some book she had just read, *the* book of the day, and she just yakked and yakked about this book which nobody else at the table had read.

"Calvin Trillin was just as thunderstruck as his wife. As far as I could tell, he never looked at Jackie the entire evening. He couldn't bring himself to do it. It was a very unnatural evening. Nobody really talked to her. I thought to myself: this must be the effect she has all the time, so she must be used to it. She seemed to have this strange hold on some very sensible, normal, articulate people who were just sort of bowled over by her presence. It's a presence that she brings into a room, an extraordinary aura of all the historic events connected to her.

"As the host, I decided I'd better have a conversation with her. One of the things that interested me about her was that she seemed to be a one-on-one person. I'd expected her, as a result of being First Lady, to be much more group-oriented. She wasn't. But in a person-to-person situation, she became animated. She was really very gossipy. We knew several people in common and she became very chatty about some of them. But she was also somehow much more shy than I had expected. According to Peter, she was a bit put off by the fact that we all seemed to be old friends, which we weren't. The Piersons had never before met the Trillins. But it was a highly verbal group. We were all writers, one way or another, and this may have given the impression that we all knew each other.

"The relationship between Jackie and Peter was serious. Not that either of them thought it would end in matrimony. I think Peter faced reality from the beginning with Jackie. This was an amazing event that comes once in a lifetime—amazing and wonderful. But he didn't have great expectations. He took it as it came, and when it ended he was grateful for the relationship, and for having known her."

As usual, there were a number of platonic relationships in Jackie's life. *The New Yorker* writer Brendan Gill escorted her to occasional dinner-dances. From time to time she saw her old friend John Marquand, Jr.: "People were constantly saying to me, 'Oh John, you know Jackie Onassis. Will you please get her to contribute $100,000 to such-and-such a charity?' I always turned them down. I never even mentioned these requests to Jackie." Karl Katz, presently Director of Special Projects at the Metropolitan Museum of Art, accompanied her on an unannounced May 1978 junket to Israel, primarily to view the recently completed John F. Kennedy Memorial on the outskirts of Jerusalem. She also visited the art galleries and antique dealers on Madison Avenue with Bill Walton. And she attended the ballet with Oliver Smith.

Jackie became concerned when Lee Radziwill informed her in April 1979 of her intention to marry Newton Cope, the millionaire owner of the plush Huntington Hotel in San Francisco, whom she first met two years earlier at a dinner party given by art collector Whitney Warren. Lee's romance with Peter Beard had faded, as had a subsequent relationship with highlife lawyer Peter Tufo. In the interim, Stas Radziwill had suffered a fatal heart attack, and Lee had launched another new career, this one as an interior decorator, which also seemed ill-fated. Newton Cope and California represented a means of escape.

The wedding, set for May 3, was to include a civil ceremony and reception at Whitney Warren's showplace house on Telegraph Hill. Invitations had been sent, flowers ordered, champagne put on ice, caviar and smoked salmon set in place. But five minutes before the appointed hour and one day after *People* magazine went to press reporting the ceremony as having taken place, Lee Radziwill called it off. "The princess is common," complained Whitney Warren. "She never even bothered to call me to apologize."

"It really wasn't Lee's fault," said Newton Cope. "What happened is that we were in New York the week before the ceremony. We had dinner at Jackie's house one night, and we discussed our plans with her. She was very cordial. She didn't accompany us to California for the wedding, but she wished us luck and all that. The minute we returned to San Francisco, I started receiving telephone calls from this lawyer of Jackie's—the latest in a long line— and this fellow became involved and threw a monkeywrench into the works.

"There was a prenuptial agreement which Lee and I thought was the best way to handle the marriage. But

Jackie's attorney wanted to change the terms of the agreement. He called again and asked me, 'Well, what are you going to do?' And I said, 'Hell, that's my business.' So he said, 'I'm not Lee's attorney. I'm just trying to help out.' 'Well, you're not helping,' I told him.

"The prenuptial agreement was cut and dry, but he wanted more guarantees for Lee. He kept saying, 'I don't want to interfere with your marriage or your personal life. I'm not Lee's attorney, but her sister asked me to look in on this thing.' And I said, 'Well, you've looked.' But he just couldn't let it go at that. 'We want something a little more solid,' he explained. So I finally exploded: 'I'm not buying a celebrity the way Onassis did. I'm marrying a wife whom I love.'

"The pieces didn't fit. It was a mutual thing. The lawyer was only part of the problem. There was the question of logistics—Lee lived on the East Coast and I lived on the West Coast. We kept hemming and hawing and in the end it never materialized. I said to her, 'Why don't we wait until the fall and then do it?' And she said, 'Well, do you think you can stop this thing—it's so late?' I said, 'Oh, yeah. I'll just call up the judge and tell him to forget it.' So we agreed to wait until the fall. But we went on our honeymoon anyway without getting married. We figured why not enjoy the two or three weeks that we'd planned. We went to La Samanna on St. Martin in the Caribbean. Then we returned to New York, and eventually I returned to San Francisco by myself."

Just when everyone was wondering whether Lee and Jacqueline were ever going to marry again, their mother—Janet Auchincloss—announced that *she* intended to take the plunge for the third time. For the benefit of the press, the family described her suitor as "a very close childhood friend." Bingham Morris, a retired investment banker from Southampton, L.I., had been married to Mary Rawlins, a bridesmaid at Janet's wedding to Black Jack Bouvier. When Mary died, Bingham Morris telephoned Janet. Several meetings ensued in New York and shortly a small wedding ceremony took place at Newport. By mutual agreement, Janet's husband retained his house in Southampton, and the couple spent only six months of each year together.

Incredibly, it was the fiftieth year of Jackie's life. With her svelte, athletic figure, glossy head of hair and photo-

genic face, she looked considerably younger, save for
some lines around her eyes. The thought of a modified
face-lift had occurred to her ten years earlier. Dr. Lax
convinced her then that such a procedure would be wasted.
Now she broached the subject again and Lax recommended "at most, some cosmetic surgery in the eye
region—a face-lift [at this stage of your life] is too radical
and too apparent."

Lax referred her to noted New York plastic surgeon
John Conley who explained the basically painless procedure. An incision is made in the crease of the upper
eyelids and beneath the eyelash line of the lower lids.
Excess skin, tissue and fat are removed through the incisions. The incisions are then sutured to conceal any evidence of surgery. The operation takes roughly an hour
and a half. The healing process takes up to six weeks.
Until then, the eye area is red and often black and blue.
Swelling and bruising vary., depending on the patient. It
is recommended that patients limit their post-operative
physical activities and avoid exposure to the sun. On the
average the cosmetic benefits of an eye lift last ten to
fifteen years.

Jackie elected to have surgery at St. Vincent's Hospital
in Greenwich Village. She entered the hospital in the
early morning wearing a silk scarf over her head, sunglasses over her eyes and no makeup. She registered
under an assumed name and remained for several days
after the surgery. She continued to heal at home. Dr.
Conley, whose hobby was writing verse, composed a
poem for Jackie and sent it to her. Two months after
surgery, she looked 35 again. What pleased her most was
the knowledge that not a single reporter, photographer
or gossip columnist had uncovered her little secret. Rumors of her cosmetic surgery would circulate for years to
come, but the concrete details of where, when and how
never emerged. On August 16, 1979, Dr. Conley sent
Dr. Lax a brief note confirming that Jackie looked wonderful and seemed happy—"and that pleases both of us."

The first public function she attended following her
eyelift was the long-awaited dedication on October 20,
1979, of the John F. Kennedy Presidential Library in
Boston. Covering the event for ABC News, Capitol Hill
correspondent Sam Donaldson recalled the presence of
Ted Kennedy, Ted's sisters, their spouses, Jackie's children,

Lady Bird Johnson and countless Camelot dignitaries. "Of course Jackie was there, looking spectacular. Jimmy Carter was still President and he made the dedication speech. When he finished, he went over to Jackie and gave her a big kiss. I don't think they had ever met before. I'll never forget the expression on her face. I swear to God, I thought she was going to deck him. She was furious."

Not long after the dedication, Jackie attended a performance by lyricist Sylvia Fine Kaye, the wife of comedian Danny Kaye, at the 92nd Street "Y" in Manhattan. Arthur Kirson, a teacher and former campaign worker for Robert Kennedy, attended the same performance. "I'd always wanted to meet Jackie, and I never had," he said. "But at this performance, not through any choice of hers or mine, we were physically thrown together. Following the recital, there was a reception in an anteroom adjacent to the auditorium, and I happened to find myself standing next to her. I was amazed at how young and vibrant she looked. We chatted for a little bit, very casually. While we were doing this, someone passed by, a nondescript little woman, and, recognizing Jackie, stopped and said to her, 'Why don't you try sharing your money with all of us?' Jackie was mortified. She really was completely agape. She certainly did not expect something like this in those surroundings, and it just left her absolutely speechless. I didn't know what to say, so I just looked at Jackie and said, 'Can I get you a drink?' She said, 'Yes, please.' The woman glared at Jackie for several moments and finally left as I went for the drink. But when it happened Jackie didn't know what to say, where to look, what to do. None of it made any sense to her at all. She was embarrassed. It caught her completely out in left field."

Jackie decided to build for herself a 19-room Cape Cod-style manse consisting of a 13-room main house plus a six-room adjoining guest house, on 375 acres of oceanfront property in the village of Gay Head on Martha's Vineyard. (She would later add another 50-acre plot to her earlier holdings, making her landowner of one of the largest private estates on the island.) To design her vacation home she went straight to the top, approaching I. M. Pei, only to be told that he did not undertake private residences. Finally she retained Hugh Jacobson, a socially connected architect from Washington, D.C., who submitted his plans for the house (complete with shingles, brick chimney, teak sundeck, heated towel racks and hot-water toilet bowls) to the Gay Head Planning Board.

After six months of haggling with one general contractor, Jackie and her attorney, Alexander Forger, in whose name the deeds to the property were registered, hired the contracting team of Harry Garvey and Frank Wangler to carry out Jacobson's design plans. According to Wangler, "Jackie would appear at the construction site on weekends, often with Bunny Mellon, to check on the progress of the house and plan the landscaping. She also brought along Caroline and John. I used to sit and shoot the breeze with John. You couldn't do that with his sister. She was friendly but not sociable. I had the feeling she looked on the construction crew as if we were servants.

"A number of problems arose during the construction of the house. Just to name a few, there was a stainless steel roof underneath the shingles which nobody had bothered to ground. This left the house, which is situated far from any other high buildings, open to the possibility of a disastrous lightning strike. Additionally, the window screen system devised to keep insects out of the house didn't work. They were called pocket screens, and instead of being permanently attached, they dropped down in the sill when you closed the window and came up when you opened the window. Well, one day I received a telephone call from Jackie at seven in the morning. She apologized for the ungodly hour but she said there was a catastrophe out at the house. I drove over there. The walls were covered with bugs. The entire ceiling looked like somebody had sprayed it with green paint. I had to go in there with a vacuum cleaner and vacuum them out. We had to install conventional window screens throughout the house.

"We built an attached barn and silo about 200 feet from the house which served as JFK Jr.'s quarters. The bedroom on the third floor contained a large, heart-shaped bed. The trouble here was that the silo exceeded the maximum height imposed by local building codes. We had to cut three feet out of the structure and lower the whole silo with a crane.

"At another point the blueprints for the house were leaked to the press. Jackie's attorney was quite upset. We suspected one of the fellows on the crew, but the fellow swore he had nothing to do with it. He even said he'd been approached by the *National Enquirer* and was offered $10,000 if he'd provide them 'with a photo of Jackie standing on the front doorstep to the house,' which he refused to do.

"Jackie was informal when it came to security. She had a caretaker, Albert Fisher, and a Greek houseboy, Vasily Terrionios, who had been Aristotle Onassis's houseboy and then worked for Christina Onassis. But Jackie insisted on keeping the front gate unlocked. Once, some strangers came riding up the 2,000-foot driveway to have a look around. She approached their car, said 'Hi,' and chatted with them for ten minutes.

"After the house was essentially finished in the summer of 1981, Jackie wanted a number of changes, some minor, some major. A minor job entailed removing a lot of mirrors that had been installed in her bathroom. She took me in there and said, 'Frank, I know a lot of people must think I'm bizarre and nuts and crazy and a Hollywood actress and all that, and that I like to look at myself, but that's not the case. Take them out!'

"Along major lines, she wanted all the ceilings dropped from ten to eight and a half feet. And since she had set aside a suite of rooms for Bunny Mellon, Bunny also wanted changes made. Bunny owned a DC-10 Whisperjet, very plush inside, which she placed at Jackie's disposal and which she used to transport her new furniture to the Vineyard.

"Jackie owns a boat, a 30-foot SeaCraft, *MS-109,* which she docks at Menemsha Pond and uses primarily for waterskiing. She bought herself a Jeep Wagoneer, the same as mine, and a blue-gray Chevrolet Blazer. She has a VCR in the house and a library of cassettes labeled 'Hyannis,' 'Jack,' 'Rose,' whatever, which she keeps on a shelf in her bedroom. She once said to me, 'I've seen the worst of everything, I've seen the best of everything. But I can't replace my family.'

"After the wrinkles had all been ironed out, she took seven or eight of the people involved with the construction of the house to dinner at the Charlotte Inn in Edgartown. The meal consisted of cold cuts, cheeses, fresh fruits, four or five different kinds of beer and wine. It was pleasant and Jackie seemed delighted with her new abode. 'My little house,' she called it. 'My wonderful little house.' With the land, the house had to cost her roughly $3.5 million to build.''

Among Jacqueline's first and most frequent visitors on Martha's Vineyard was Maurice Tempelsman. A somewhat elusive though politically powerful figure, Tempelsman had known Jackie for years—first as a friend, later as her financial adviser, more recently as a beau and companion. In Maurice it seemed, she had finally found the equilibrium and peace of mind she had so long sought and failed to find in either of her marriages. "I admire Maurice's strength and his success," she told friends. "I truly hope my notoriety doesn't force him out of my life."

At first glance, Tempelsman appeared an unlikely companion for Jackie. Born into an Orthodox Jewish family in Antwerp, Belgium, in 1929 (the same year as Jackie), he, his younger sister and his parents fled Europe in 1940 to escape the Nazi onslaught. After spending two years on the Caribbean island of Jamaica, the family arrived in New York. By age 15, he was taking night courses in Business Administration at New York University, working days for his father, Leon, a diamond broker. It was Maurice, at 21, who imaginatively hitched the family firm, Leon Tempelsman & Son, to the global marketplace by convincing U.S. government officials to buy boart industrial diamonds for its stockpile of strategic materials maintained for national emergencies. He made millions as the middleman in the operation, purchasing the diamonds from African suppliers. He later acted as middleman in a transaction that brought uranium to the United States in exchange for surplus agricultural commodities.

In addition to turning a profit, Tempelsman's deals made him a familiar figure in select Washington circles. He retained Adlai Stevenson as his attorney. (His present attorney is Ted Sorensen.) He became, according to U.S. Department of Justice files, a key representative and associate of Harry Oppenheimer, owner-director of both Anglo-American and DeBeers, the world's largest miners and distributors of gold and diamonds. In the process he befriended a number of African potentates, most notably Zaire's President Mobutu Sese Seko, while expanding his own operations into Zaire, Sierra Leone and Gabon. Tempelsman's current empire includes mining interests, diamond and mineral sales and distribution companies, the world's second largest petroleum drill-bit manufacturing corporation and a sprawling network of related concerns.

Maurice's friendship with Jackie dated to the late 1950s. The Department of Justice files on Tempelsman contain the essential facts: "Tempelsman was the man who arranged the meeting for Harry Oppenheimer with John Kennedy when Kennedy was President-elect. The meeting was held at the Hotel Carlyle." Oppenheimer and Tempelsman had both made generous contributions to Kennedy's campaign fund. Kennedy (and other Chiefs of State) looked to Tempelsman for advice and information when dealing with African leaders. Tempelsman and his wife, Lily, married since 1949, were frequent guests at the White House both during the Kennedy years and in subsequent administrations. They attended the gala dinner for Pakistani President Mohammed Ayub Khan that the Kennedys gave at Mount Vernon in 1961.

For all his considerable accomplishments and wealth, Maurice Tempelsman struck many people as nothing more than a "poor man's Aristotle Onassis." Tempelsman, like Onassis, was short, portly, older looking than his actual years; both men smoked Dunhill cigars and collected rare art. Both were financial wizards. Their other common denominator was a shared love of the sea; both owned boats, though the *Relemar*,* Maurice's moderate-size schooner, was hardly in a class with the *Christina*. Yet in 1980, the year their relationship became serious, Maurice and Jackie navigated the *Relemar* up the eastern seacoast from Savannah, Georgia, to Beaufort, South Carolina. It was the first of many such cruises. They were inseparable and were soon seen in top-of-the-line restaurants, at Broadway plays, on leisurely strolls through Central Park. They were photographed walking arm in arm into a Nantucket art gallery. Maurice even accompanied her when

---

*The Relemar was named for Maurice's three children: Rena, Leon, and Marcee. All are now married and have children of their own. Leon, a graduate of the Harvard Business School, works with his father.

she made a round of political appearances in support of Ted Kennedy's 1980 run for the Democratic Party presidential nomination.

"You can be sure Maurice Tempelsman gives Jackie lots of presents," said Truman Capote. "What's more, not only Jackie but Lee, too, has made money on the basis of Tempelsman's advice on when to buy and when to sell in the volatile silver and gold markets. Girls like Jackie don't change."

But there were those who felt she had changed and that Maurice was the catalyst.

Nancy Bastien, an artist who spends part of each year on Martha's Vineyard, had also always thought of Jackie as a "luxury-laden Cinderella type." That was the impression she derived from reading about Jackie in the press. "So I was surprised," she said, "to see this rather simply dressed, unassuming person up and about the Vineyard. She would go to Aquinnah, a large snack bar near her house, for hamburgers and ice-cream cones. Or she would visit the Martha's Vineyard Agricultural Society fair in West Tisbury and walk from booth to booth with everybody else.

"At other times, especially when Tempelsman was around, she seemed to prefer privacy. My boyfriend and I once came upon Jackie and Tempelsman in an inlet looking at birds. It was a bird preserve, very isolated and remote. They were looking at a majestic blue heron through a shared pair of field glasses. When we came upon them, Jackie quickly pulled down her sunglasses from atop her head. Then she pointed to the blue heron and said, 'There he goes.' And with that they trampled off into the tall grass."

Maurice Tempelsman's cousin Rose Schreiber made the point that if Jackie married her first husband for status and her second for money, then her latest attachment was based on mutual respect and friendship. It was a mature, comfortable, intimate relationship, but one which obviously excited both parties. In many respects, it was a far better, healthier relationship than any Jackie had experienced before.

"Although Maurice appears to be meek and unassuming, he is a charming, worldly figure," observed his cousin. "He dresses well, likes to read, loves to travel and go to the opera. He has *savoir faire*. He also enjoys the simple pleasures that nature has to offer, which is probably something he and Jackie share. At the same time, he can be very effervescent and lively. Women have always been attracted to him. I have seen them chase after him at parties. He practically has to push them away.

"The pity of it is his marriage. His wife, Lily, is also from Belgium, although Maurice met her in the United States. He was 17 when they met and 20 when they married. He married at too young an age. His parents wanted him to marry the daughter of his father's then business partner, but Maurice refused. He and Lily were very close and discussed everything together, including his business affairs.

"A major development in the marriage had to do with religious commitment. Lily is a very observant Jew, strictly Orthodox. As a matter of fact, she told me she didn't enjoy going to the White House with Maurice because he would never ask for kosher meals. His parents kept a kosher home, and so did Lily. At one time or another, their three children all went to Ramaz, a Jewish day school. But after a point Maurice stopped going to synagogue. Lily would go, and he would go boating. This gradual disaffection very much bothered Lily.

"Perhaps she used this issue to rationalize the Jackie business. Lily is a marriage counselor at the Jewish Board of Guardians. When the children were older, she went back to school to earn her master's degree so she could practice. There's a certain irony in her becoming a marriage counselor at the very moment that her own marriage began to crumble.

"It was Lily in November 1982 who took the initiative in asking Maurice to leave. He would have stayed with her. But it had reached the point where every time she opened the newspaper, she would come across another photograph of Maurice with Jackie. They separated on friendly terms, and are still married."

Maurice moved out of their apartment at the Normandy, 86th Street and Riverside Drive, into a comfortable hotel suite on the East Side, spending several nights each week at Jackie's apartment, the number of nights increasing with time. John Kennedy, Jr., worked for Tempelsman in Africa one summer, and Maurice's grown children began visiting Jackie, staying in her guest house on Martha's Vineyard. From all indications, Jacqueline understood that the chances of formalizing her relationship with Maurice were slim at best. "We can't marry because his wife won't grant him a divorce," she informed Dr. Lax. "You don't have to marry to be together," he responded. More than likely she preferred it that way—she had long come to appreciate her independence.

33

Jacqueline Kennedy Onassis managed to get around. New Yorkers encountered her everywhere. Earl Blackwell, who makes his living by cataloguing the intricacies of the rich and famous, writes in his latest (1986) *Celebrity Register,* quoting an anonymous observer: " 'I'd been to the Metropolitan. It was a Tuesday afternoon. I'd taken off early from work to see the Vatican show. . . . I stopped at a coffee shop on Madison. Just a coffee shop, a greasy hamburger joint and, then, she came in. She walked in. To eat! At the counter! With a copy of *New York* magazine. I mean everything just stopped, even the burgers ceased their sizzling. She ate a burger while wearing a tan raincoat and black pants and she had, I think it was, a Gucci shoulder bag and a Cartier tank watch and . . .' "

Yes, Jackie Onassis gets around. Here she was eating a hamburger, there she was prowling among Literary Lions at a benefit for the New York Public Library. There were press shots of her at publishing parties, at public ceremonies, outside restaurants, inside museums. She switched from Valentino to the more sedate fashions of Carolina Herrera. She left Kenneth and emerged at the hair salon of former Kenneth employee Thomas Morrissey. It was a period of personal transition. If the 1970s were years of consolidation and recovery from her perilous loss of reputation as the wife of Aristotle Onassis, then the 1980s signified a decade of progress. Fame and fortune notwithstanding, it was clear that Jackie, in her fifties, had succeeded in casting off at least some measure of her image as an international jet-setter, as a member of the idle rich, and had attained independent status as a fundraiser and career woman.

In many ways she seemed more boisterous, more rambunctious, happier than she had ever been. Rosey Grier recalled the childish glee with which she poured a tepid cup of coffee out her Fifth Avenue living room window at passers-by below.

Dr. Sanford Friedman, a New York cardiologist, sat directly behind her at a performance of the Metropolitan Opera Company on a night she behaved more like a restless teenager than a grown woman. "Maurice Tempelsman sat next to her," recalled the physician. "Jackie couldn't sit still. She kept moving her head, leaning it on his shoulder, whispering in his ear, giggling, talking aloud, fidgeting in her seat. It was distracting, but you couldn't very well tell Jacqueline Onassis to please shut up. What did Norman Mailer say of her? She wasn't merely a celebrity, but a legend; not a legend, but a myth—no, not just a myth, rather a historic archetype, virtually a demiurge. I don't know, do you even address a demiurge?"

Vincent Roppatte, former director of the Enrico Caruso Beauty Salon, encountered a somewhat less demiurgical Jacqueline: "I used to do Lee Radziwill's hair, but I also knew Jackie because she came in to Caruso's for Cyclax facials—it's an English product used by the Queen and the Queen Mother. Jackie loved it. You can still obtain it in London, but it's difficult to find in the States.

"Anyway, she came in for a facial one day, and as she was leaving she passed me at the front desk and stopped to chat. We'd been at the same party the night before. I was there with Liza Minnelli, whose hair I do for magazine layouts. So Jackie said to me, 'Oh, I saw you last night with Liza Minnelli.' 'Oh yeah?' I said, and she said 'Yeah.' And then she noticed I was wearing a black silk shirt, an Italian number low cut in front. 'My God,' she remarked, 'that's quite a décolleté shirt you have on.' She stopped for a moment and then said, 'But of course you have the body to wear it.' "

In 1981, when Nancy Reagan, the new First Lady, experienced an onslaught of negative publicity, Jackie called to offer advice on how to deal with the press. Nancy, who had long taken her fashion cues from Jackie, didn't get to meet her until 1985 when publisher Katharine Graham invited both to a small dinner party at her estate on Martha's Vineyard, not far from Jackie's home. Included in the gathering were *Newsweek* editor Meg Greenfield and White House aide Michael K. Deaver. Deaver, like Vincent Roppatte, soon discovered Jackie's humorous, flirtatious side. As they both dipped into a five-pound box of chocolates Deaver had bought for Kay Graham, Jackie said to him, "How can you eat this candy and stay so thin? You're so svelte. You're like a young Fred Astaire."

While generally more content and relaxed, Jackie soon proved that she was still susceptible to excesses of fury and the need for revenge. On July 21, 1981, emerging from the Hollywood Twin movie theater on Eighth Avenue at 47th Street (where she had gone to see a revival of *Death in Venice*), she ran into her old enemy Ron Galella. In their first courtroom clash nine years earlier, Galella had been issued a court order prohibiting him from going within 25 feet of Mrs. Onassis. Presently, Galella was standing directly in her path, camera aimed and ready.

"He was at least as close as a foot," Jackie told the court in December 1981, having sued Galella a second time, "I tried to hail a taxi . . . in the middle of Eighth Avenue with traffic all around me. He was jumping all around me, in front and in back, and very close at times, so no taxi could see me. Every time I raised my arm he'd be in front of me.

"I was frightened and confused. I was frightened on two accounts. One was being hit by a car coming from one direction or another; the other was a lot of rather weird people were coming out of the buildings along Eighth Avenue . . . and they were all pointing, yelling, 'Oh, look, it's Jackie O. Hey, Jackie,' and some of them were coming up to me.

"I was beginning to be rather sort of teased or followed by them. And so my reactions were confusion and fright and desperation."

Jackie's next encounter with the photographer, according to her courtroom testimony, took place on Martha's Vineyard over Labor Day weekend. On that occasion, she and Maurice Tempelsman went boating, only to find that Galella had not only followed them to the Vineyard but had taken out a boat.

"We rowed out from the shore of Menemsha Pond in a dinghy to my boat, which is a sort of fishing boat with an outboard motor on the back," she testified. "We were trying to board it. We saw this smaller motorboat with a roof, further away, with people. They came by. As they saw us trying to board from the dinghy to the big boat, they came zooming by, making a wake, frightening us.

The engine of our boat stalled. We couldn't start it. I recognized one of them as Galella."

Several weeks later on the evening of September 23, Harry Garvey (the contractor responsible for Jackie's house on Martha's Vineyard), his wife Twanette, with Jackie, and Maurice Tempelsman watched the Twyla Tharp Dance Company perform at the Winter Garden Theater in midtown Manhattan. Twanette and Twyla were sisters, and the Garveys had four complimentary tickets. Ron Galella and two other photographers awaited the party as Tempelsman's limousine pulled up to the theater. Galella and his companions brushed past ticket-holders and entered the theater in an effort to position themselves in front of Jackie. When she and her party left the theater after the performance, Galella followed and hopped into a car to follow her limousine. The chase ended with Jackie and Maurice, having dropped off the Garveys, driving to the stationhouse on East 60th Street and registering an official complaint with the police.

At the second trial, held before the same Irving Ben Cooper who presided over the first trial, Galella admitted he had transgressed the 1972 injunction, but that he had done so because he believed it violated his First Amendment rights. "The entire case was a violation of my rights," he said at a later date. "I realized my defense wasn't going to be deemed adequate, not in that court. But it's how I felt then and it's how I feel today.

"Jackie is both manipulative and hypocritical. I'm certain she enjoyed the publicity I gave her. She pretended not to, but she did. A maid I know and once dated in order to obtain information on Jackie told me she kept scrapbooks—one set for herself, two for the children, and she would sit on her bed for hours and go through all the European magazines, clipping photographs of herself.

"I believe it was Maurice Tempelsman who encouraged Jackie to take action against me the second time around. And for valid reason—he had a wife, and at that time was still living with her. He didn't need me hanging around taking pictures. My wife, Betty, and I were standing in front of Jackie's apartment building early one morning when who should appear but Maurice Tempelsman. He came out of her building wearing what looked like pajama bottoms under his suit. He saw us and took off like a bat out of hell.

"My lawyer Marvin Mitchelson, of palimony fame, saved me from going to jail for seven years. Instead, I was ordered to pay $10,000 in damages directly to Jackie and prohibited from ever taking another photograph of her. That's justice, me giving Jackie Onassis money. Betty made out the check, 'She'll have to endorse it; at least we'll have her autograph,' Betty told me. But she didn't even give us that satisfaction—she had Nancy Tuckerman sign it for her."

Having trounced Ron Galella, Jackie was soon back in court. Her latest opponents were Christian Dior, Inc., Landsdowne Advertising Inc., photographer Richard Avedon, part-time model Barbara Reynolds and Ron Smith Celebrity Look-Alikes. The basis of her complaint was that Barbara Reynolds, a Jackie look-alike, had posed for a Christian Dior advertisement making it appear that Mrs. Onassis herself was acting as a photographic model for Dior, endorsing its products and participating in a Dior publicity campaign. In seeking an injunction against further use of the ad—which had already appeared in *Harper's Bazaar, Womens Wear Daily, The New York Times Magazine* and *The New Yorker*—and a permanent injunction against the creation of any new ads along similar lines, Jackie complained that the advertisement was embarrassing and disturbing to her and injurious to her reputation. "I have never permitted the publicity value of my name, likeness or picture to be used in connection with any commercial products," read her complaint.

Richard A. Kurnit, attorney for Barbara Reynolds and Ron Smith, took the pretrial deposition directly from Jackie. "Lawyers tend to be more deferential toward Jackie than with others," he remarked. "So do judges. Obviously it's because of who she is. She's impressive. She didn't testify at the actual 'look-alike' trial but she was there, seated right in front of the judge's nose.

"We lost the case as well as the appeal, and I'm still mystified by it. If an advertisement is misleading, if a false message is imparted, I have no qualms with a decision that might go against it. But in this case there was no question that the person in the ad was impersonating Jackie and was standing next to Charles de Gaulle, who is dead, and that it was an actor impersonating De Gaulle. Jackie claimed that her friends thought it was her. But

Barbara Reynolds, the model in the ad, was clearly dressed to impersonate a Jackie Kennedy of some 25 years ago, when she was First Lady."

Richard de Combray, an American writer with male-model good looks and homes in New York and Paris, had an experience with Jackie that demonstrates the necessity of her self-protective mechanism. "What happened was very simple," explained De Combray. "Jacqueline Onassis was my editor at Doubleday, and as with most editors and writers, we developed not a friendship, but a pleasant acquaintanceship. We were introduced by Mike Nichols, the director. Originally we planned on doing a book on the famous French writer Colette. The first time we had lunch, her assistant editor came along. The Colette book didn't work out, but we wound up working on a novel [*Goodbye Europe*, 1983] instead.

"One evening, I had Jackie, Maurice Tempelsman, Claudette Colbert, Mike Nichols and Alan Pryce-Jones over to my apartment in New York for dinner. The apartment opens on a garden and we ate alfresco. For Jackie's sake, I made certain we sat in an area of the garden well protected from the neighbors' view.

"I soon discovered that she possessed the secret of charm, which is to make the other person feel charming and terrific. It's not an actress's charm where you put it on, and you are tra-la-la wonderful; it's a charm that communicates to the person you're with, and they feel they're being charming. That's a precious gift, and very few people have it. I found it before only in Noël Coward. He had it, and so does Jackie.

"What happened next is that she and I again went out to lunch, this time alone. Just as we exited the restaurant, a photographer approached and started taking pictures. I realized for the first time you can get terribly upset at a photographer. 'Get away from here, stop taking our picture,' I said. We ducked into a stationery store and the photographer finally went away. But our photograph appeared on the front page of the *New York Post*.

"At this point, I left town and went to California to visit Lillian Hellman. A reporter tracked me down and interviewed me over the telephone. I assumed from what she said she was interviewing me about *Goodbye Europe*, which had just been published. In the guise of an interest in my book, what was really on her mind was Jacqueline

Onassis—how I felt about her and what was going on between us that we were photographed together. The problem inherent in any kind of friendship with Jacqueline Onassis is that it's held up to such intense scrutiny, unlike any ordinary friendship. It puts tremendous pressure on everyone. A reporter or photographer will see two people sitting together, one being Jackie, and will immediately presume that this is more than a simple editor-author relationship.

"So in the course of this telephone interview, I said I thought Jackie was wonderful, which I do think. And the reporter said something like, 'Well, is it a romance or a marriage?' I mean it was a joke, the idea of a romance or marriage. 'It's absolutely not on our minds,' I said. When it was printed, the quote read: 'It's not on our minds at this time.' That's when the trouble started. Things got blown completely out of proportion. The press started calling. They called friends of mine. I realized, since all this was new to me, that what happens when you are considered even a potential liaison with Jacqueline Onassis, you are grilled in this relentless way; they put an X-ray over everything about you and they go through the archives. It was a very painful experience for me. It was painful to pick up the telephone and find reporters at the other end, or have friends call and ask questions. I became totally paranoid, thinking maybe that my phone was tapped. Why was the press bothering me? It got very ugly. Jackie was disturbed as well because, I guess, part of her always lives in fear of something like this happening. It injured our working friendship. Both of us became gun-shy after that, afraid to go out and have lunch together. Jackie did everything to avoid publicity. She wants nothing to do with the press. It's an interesting phenomenon—she has become *too* famous. I was so naive. I hadn't understood the lethal quality of the press. They will really go after anything if it's going to net exciting news. And if necessary, they will even misquote you."

Given her recognition factor, Jackie could appreciate an incident that took place at a 1984 fund-raiser. Approaching famed author Isaac Bashevis Singer, she said to him, "I am also a writer." She failed to introduce herself, and the venerable old novelist did not know her at first glance. He peered at her through thick spectacles and said, "That's very nice, girlie. Keep working and I'm sure you'll get somewhere."

Jackie did get somewhere, not as a writer but in terms of her publishing career. She continued to produce the oversize coffee-table book that generated little income, but also concentrated on acquiring more commercial properties. Thus while she undertook a lavish picture book on Versailles with British fashion photographer Deborah Turbeville and a text on French history by her cousin-by-marriage Louis Auchincloss, she also went after a series of "kiss-and-tell" autobiographies by celebrities like Gelsey Kirkland and Michael Jackson. But her major breakthrough came in the area of fiction, and began over lunch one day late in 1978, with literary agent Roslyn Targ.

"We were eating and I was pitching book ideas," said Targ. "I mentioned a biography of Leonardo da Vinci, which made little impact on Jackie. Then I mentioned *Call the Darkness Light,* by Nancy Zaroulis, the saga of one woman's fight for liberation from the slavery of the 19th-century New England textile mills. The book seemed appropriate for Jackie; she had endured great tragedy and emerged triumphant. She is a survivor. She has grown through her experiences, and so did the main character in this work of fiction. It was the first novel she acquired for Doubleday, and it became a major success."

Jackie acquired the novel for Doubleday but did little work on it; that responsibility was delegated to another editor. Yet Jackie's involvement in the project aided in its promotion. The publisher gave a reception for the author in a room above the Doubleday Book Shop on 53rd Street and Fifth Avenue, followed by a banquet for 14 guests in a private suite at the St. Regis Hotel. Seventy-five photographers forced their way into the reception and consented to leave only if granted five minutes to snap pictures of Jackie. "What about Nancy Zaroulis, the author of the book?" shouted a Doubleday executive. The press agreed to take Nancy's picture, but only if Jackie posed with her. She did, and the novel was launched.

Although many Doubleday employees continued to regard Jackie as "part-time, three-days-a-week help," the firm promoted her in 1982 to full editor, the highest editorial rank in her department. She received an accompanying pay raise and was moved into a larger office. She responded by commissioning Gelsey Kirkland and Gelsey's husband, Greg Lawrence, to write *Dancing on My Grave,* an account of the ballerina's sexual escapades and personal experiences with drugs.

Jackie's biggest commercial triumph came when she and her assistant, Shaye Areheart, traveled to Los Angeles in the fall of 1983 in an effort to convince Michael Jackson to write his memoirs. Their first meeting, scheduled for a posh Hollywood restaurant, never came about. Jackson, noted for his shyness as much as for his one white glove, stood Jackie up. It proved an embarrassment, but it also provided her with an opportunity to demonstrate her zeal. Another appointment was arranged, this one at Jackson's mansion in Encino. "It played like 'Tea for Two,' " claimed a witness to the historical encounter, "both of them cooing like lovebirds in those fragile, whispery voices of theirs." The ensuing book contract, carrying an advance of $400,000, proved the publishing coup of the season. Jackie's colleagues sent her a large bouquet of flowers. Jackson sealed the contract by taking Jackie on a personal guided tour of Disneyland.

Moonwalk, ghostwritten for Jackson by Stephen Davis, appeared in 1988 and streaked to the top of the charts. In a brief introduction to the book, Jacqueline Onassis asks a rhetorical question: "What can one say about Michael Jackson?" Not much apparently. Although a great financial success, the book had little to offer by way of content.

Bertelsmann A.G., the West German publishing conglomerate that purchased Doubleday in 1986, saw fit to reward Jackie by again raising her salary. According to company insiders, she was now earning $45,000 per year and was generally regarded as the firm's most aggressive celebrity chaser. Among those she approached for autobiographies were Elizabeth Taylor, Brigitte Bardot, Greta Garbo, Ted Turner, Prince, Barbara Walters and Rudolf Nureyev. Carly Simon, a neighbor of hers on Martha's Vineyard, agreed to write her life story for Jackie. And late in 1988, Jackie arranged for Doubleday to be the American publisher of the novels of Egyptian author Naguib Nahfouz, winner of the 1988 Nobel Prize for literature.

*   *   *

Budding screenwriter Tom Carney ultimately broke off his relationship with Caroline Kennedy because he didn't want to become known as "Mr. Caroline Kennedy." That designation would belong to a later suitor, an author-artist, self-styled Renaissance man named Edwin Arthur Schlossberg who, like Maurice Tempelsman, came from an Orthodox Jewish background. Schlossberg's father, founder of Alfred Schlossberg, Inc., a Manhattan textile company, was president of Congregation Rodeph Sholom and a contributor of substantial sums to Jewish and Zionist causes.

Like other newly rich Jewish families, the Alfred Schlossbergs bought a vacation home in Palm Beach and socialized with the upwardly mobile, sending their son Edwin to the progressive Birch Wathen School in New York, then on to Columbia University. He returned to Columbia as a graduate student and, in 1971, earned a Ph.D. in science and literature. Although often praised for his intelligence and resourcefulness, Schlossberg also had his share of detractors. If Maurice Tempelsman was a minister without portfolio, Ed Schlossberg gave the impression to some of being a climber without a rope.

His Ph.D. dissertation—an imaginary conversation in several sections between Albert Einstein and Samuel Beckett—was a pedantic, pretentious, often bewildering polemic that neither elucidated nor enlightened. Following graduation and a short-lived college teaching stint at Southern Illinois University, Schlossberg began producing novelty and instruction books such as *The Kids' Pocket Calculator Game Book* and *The Home Computer Handbook*. He wrote sophomoric avant-garde poetry, designed high-tech T-shirts, experimented by painting on aluminum and Plexiglass. The art world did not roll over. Nor did the world of architecture when he billed himself as a design specialist of museum and educational exhibits and environments. His main undertaking—the Brooklyn Children's Museum—was eventually taken over by another designer, Brent Saville, who described Schlossberg as a pompous, self-centered individual with more moxie than understanding, more luck than insight. Others found him opportunistic, shallow and insincere.

Whatever Schlossberg's drawbacks, he appealed to Caroline Kennedy. She met him at a dinner party late in 1981 and invited him to her mother's Christmas party.

Tall, husky and prematurely gray, Schlossberg made a fine impression on Jacqueline; she took him by the hand and introduced him to her guests as "my daughter's new friend, Ed Schlossberg." Ed was 13 years older than Caroline. After the party Jackie asked her daughter whether she didn't find him *too* old; Caroline teasingly reminded her mother that both her husbands had been a good deal older than she.

Although Caroline now occupied her own small flat on East 78th Street, she began to spend most of her time in Ed's expensively furnished Wooster Street loft in SoHo. Weekends they often drove to Chester, Massachusetts, where his parents owned a renovated barn with a splendid view of the surrounding Berkshires. A friend of Caroline's insisted that although quiet, "Ed has a great sense of humor. He and Caroline never argue. In that sense they're quite a bit like Jackie and Maurice Tempelsman. I remember a party at which Tempelsman held forth on ancient Egyptian art, while Ed Schlossberg gave somebody a quick brush-up on conceptual art. It made for an amusing juxtaposition."

Ed Schlossberg represented a new direction for Caroline. To her, he appeared loyal, witty, bright, warm and supportive. In April 1984, when David Kennedy, 28, was found dead from an overdose of drugs in his room at the Brazilian Court Motel in Palm Beach, it was Schlossberg who helped Caroline through her subsequent depression.

"On the other side," said journalist Harrison Rainie, "being with an almost middle-aged man meant having to give up some longstanding friends of her own age and background. It was one more little rebellion on Caroline's part, a way of getting out from under the family boot. One reason Caroline undoubtedly liked Schlossberg is that he was so different from her Kennedy cousins—unathletic, intellectual, artistic. That's probably why Jackie appreciated him as well."

Schlossberg's attentions and her own growing maturity were factors in Caroline's desire to finally upgrade her overall appearance. She began to dress with the same elegant taste as her mother, and for the first time, spent substantial sums on jewelry, paying $6,000 for a new watch. She went on a rigid diet and used professionals to style her hair. At her 27th birthday party, she wore a filmy black and yellow silk pajama suit chosen for her by

Ed. She told admirers of the outfit that he seleced most of her clothing. She had gained new responsibilities, including appointment to the Board of Trustees at the John F. Kennedy Library. She became manager and coordinating producer in her division at the Metropolitan Museum of Art. Then, in 1985, she surprised people by resigning her position to enroll at the Columbia University School of Law. A year later, her brother enrolled at New York University Law School. Their usually unflappable mother was ecstatic that both her children had opted for legal careers.

Rumors of an Ed-and-Caroline marriage began to surface as early as January 1984, at which time it was also rumored that there was interfamilial opposition to such a union. The reasons most often cited had to do with Schlossberg's apparent refusal to sign a prenuptial agreement drawn up by Kennedy family lawyers to protect Caroline's inheritance; there was also the sticky religious issue. The Kennedys were regarded as one of the leading Irish-Catholic clans in America, and the fact that Schlossberg was Jewish had to raise questions in the minds of certain family members.

A parallel situation arose with regard to Maria Shriver's long-term romance with bodybuilder-turned-actor Arnold Schwarzenegger. While not Jewish, Schwarzenegger was an outspoken celebrity, a rabid Republican and a foreigner with a strong, sometimes embarrassing German accent. It wasn't so much how he spoke but rather what he said. Arnold tended to sound too much like the warmongering mechanical men he so often impersonated on the silver screen.

The impediments and obstacles to both relationships were gradually overcome. Maria Shriver's marriage to an actor seemed less objectionable when she, herself, became a television news commentator and thus a public personality. And if the Kennedys were about to embrace Arnold Schwarzenegger, could Ed Schlossberg be far behind?

In a quiet statement in *The New York Times* in March 1986, Jacqueline Onassis announced her daughter's engagement to Schlossberg and plans for a July 19th Hyannis Port wedding, thereby upstaging the April nuptials of Shriver-Schwarzenegger. The date might have been more carefully chosen: it happened to be the 17th anniversary

of Chappaquiddick, the day Caroline's uncle Ted drove a
car off the road and passenger Mary Jo Kopechne to her
death.

The wedding ceremony of 28-year-old Caroline to
41-year-old Ed Schlossberg had all the earmarks of any
Kennedy extravaganza: clambakes, sailboat races, touch
football games. But while the broad outlines were similar, the fine details of this wedding were somewhat different. The informal invitations (Jackie loathed them)
featured a pastel-shaded watercolor rendering of the Kennedy Compound topped by the essential fact that the
ceremony would take place at 3:00 p.m. at the Church of
Our Lady of Victory, Centerville, Massachusetts. White-
and-gold Cadillac limousines delivered the principals to
the newly painted, flower-studded country church. Fashion designer Willi Smith had bedecked the ushers in
violet linen jackets and white slacks, the bridesmaids in
two-piece, ankle length, lavender-and-white floral pat-
terned dresses, the groom in a baggy blue suit and silver
tie. Carolina Herrera created a white satin organza gown
for Caroline with a 25-foot train, the bodice and short
sleeves appliquéd with clovers (or shamrocks—nobody
could tell which they were supposed to be). There were
425 guests (21 of them Ed's, the others were the Kennedys'), 2,500 spectators, hundreds of press photographers,
and a security force of more than a hundred.

Mary Tierney, covering the ceremony for the *Chicago
Tribune*, remarked "Ed Schlossberg looked funny in this
oversized suit. He looked like a ragbag. Caroline coming
out of the church looked ungainly. Her train was too
long. The dresses for the bridesmaids were unappealing
and unflattering. Jackie looked damn good, but as somebody there said to me, 'If a masseuse pounded on you so
many hours a day, you'd look good too.' She exited the
church arm in arm with Teddy Kennedy. She was teary-
eyed—tears of happiness. She's more attractive than her
daughter, though her son is an Adonis. He was best man,
Maria Shriver was maid of honor. Mae Schlossberg, Ed's
mother, tripped as she came out of the church. Her ankle
swelled and she had to leave the reception early.

"But there was something drastically wrong with the
wedding ceremony. No rabbi was present. Why wouldn't
they have a rabbi there? The groom's faith should have
been represented. There was no formal wedding Mass,

but that was the only concession the Kennedys made. In this day and age, one would look for some recognizable sign that this was not simply one Catholic marrying another Catholic.

"I suppose this was a concession to Rose Kennedy, but Rose didn't attend the ceremony. At 96, she was 'out to lunch.' She's convinced that Jack and Bobby Kennedy are still alive. She has been ga-ga for years."

Attorney Eugene Girden, a friend of Alfred and Mae Schlossberg, confirmed that they were upset by the marital arrangements: "Ed's father had nice words about Jackie. He likes her. But there was initial disappointment about the marriage to Caroline because of the religious problem, especially in having a Catholic wedding. It bothered him a great deal."

Two huge tents had been pitched on the lawns of the Kennedy Compound. One long white tent was for the post-ceremony reception line; the other completely round marquee was where guests were seated for the champagne dinner. Between the tents, under white beach umbrellas, were white wicker chairs and tables where guests could sit and socialize.

The lighting in the dinner tent was provided by flickering Japanese lanterns suspended from long bamboo poles. Fragrant baskets and arrangements of flowers stood everywhere. Ted Kennedy offered the toasts: first to Rose Kennedy (who watched part of the reception from a wheelchair on the porch of her house); second to the elder Schlossbergs; third to the bride and groom; and fourth to Jackie, "that extraordinary gallant woman, Jack's only love. He would have been so proud of you today."

After the dinner, the dancing, the music, the singing (provided by Carly Simon), the tears and the toasts, the guests repaired to the manicured Compound lawn to watch George Plimpton's special nighttime treat: an ornate fireworks display.

"The first part of it," explained Plimpton, "consisted of tributes to some of the relatives and guests. There were about 15 of them: a Chinese rose for Rose Kennedy, a sailboat for Ted Kennedy, a long column for lanky John Kenneth Galbraith, a bow tie for sartorial Arthur Schlesinger. I wanted the fireworks to suggest the essence of each individual. And then there was the main body of the show which I called 'What Ed Schlossberg

Does.' There was a problem here because by the time
this part of the show took place, a fog bank had rolled in
off the ocean. I tried to get the show moved up to beat
these clouds that were obviously coming in off the sea,
but Carly Simon's manager wouldn't let her sing earlier
than scheduled. So she sang, and then the fog rolled in.
And that's the one thing that kills fireworks. When fireworks go off in a cloud, they sort of fizzle. It's like
summer lightning. You just see the colors and they are
usually diffused by the fog. I was very disappointed, but
as it turned out everyone loved it because they felt it
typified the theme. It faithfully represented 'What Ed
Schlossberg Does.' What he does in life seems to be a
mystery to everyone. He's a sort of conceptual theorist or
whatever. So the obscuring effect in this case worked to
the show's advantage."

The moment the last firework fizzled in the sky, Ed
Schlossberg and his bride were off in their white-and-gold
limousine for Boston's Ritz-Carlton Hotel and the start
of a month-long honeymoon in Hawaii and Japan. They
then returned to New York and moved into a co-op not
far from Jackie's apartment; later, with the announcement
of Caroline's pregnancy, they moved into another co-op,
plunking down $2.65 million for an eleventh floor, 12-room
apartment on Park Avenue at 78th Street. True to form,
Schlossberg placed himself in charge of interior decoration; Caroline concentrated on the more immediate task
of completing law school. She succeeded, graduating in
June 1988, posing for the press in cap and gown next to
her proud husband, beaming mother, handsome brother
and contemplative uncle, Senator Edward M. Kennedy.
Nancy Tuckerman and housekeeper Martha also attended
the graduation ceremonies which were held under a tent
set up in Ancell Plaza on the Columbia University campus. The final family guest was Maurice Tempelsman,
who sat several rows behind the others and did not join
them until the press photographers had finished taking
pictures and disappeared from sight.

"We have a little joke in the family," said Jackie's
cousin Bouvier Beale, "which goes something like this: If
Jackie hadn't married the Irishman, we all could have
sunk into shabby gentility, and nobody would have been
the wiser. I mean it's very upsetting to have the focus of

publicity placed upon a very average situation, and just because of the act of marriage."

Very likely there were periods, particularly in later years, when Jackie would have concurred with this assessment. To her immense displeasure, her personal existence continued to be an area of endless fascination to members of the press. Although Maurice Tempelsman had become a permanent fixture in her life, the press insisted on inventing new partners for her. A mere luncheon at Le Cirque with widower William Paley had gossip columnists buzzing for weeks.

In 1982, when she went to China for several days as the guest of I. M. Pei to attend the opening of a hotel he had designed at a resort 25 miles from Peking, it was automatically assumed she would soon become an architect's wife. After the death of Princess Grace, a popular French publication, *Ici Paris,* predicted that "Prince Rainier will probably marry Jackie Onassis. . . ." Jackie and Prince Rainier had been seen together in Paris, but what the publication neglected to mention was that the purpose of their meeting had been to discuss the possibility of Rainier writing his autobiography for Doubleday.

The most preposterous of Jackie's "newspaper romances" had to be the one linking her and Ted Kennedy, largely the result of their meeting in London in January 1985 to attend the funeral in North Wales of Lord Harlech, the former David Ormsby-Gore. What disturbed Jackie most about the rumor was that she and Joan Kennedy had become good friends. When Joan realized the full extent of her alcohol problem, it was to Jackie she turned for help. She looked to Jackie again following the sudden death of investment banker John J. McNamara, a man she strongly considered marrying after her divorce from Ted.

She called Jackie after McNamara's funeral and poured out her heart. Jackie invited Joan to visit her in New York—and after a week or so Joan did. Joan fell apart the moment she saw Jackie. "When does the heartache end?" she said. "I finally meet a decent man, and he's taken from me. It's just not fair."

"Joan, do you really expect life to be fair after everything we've gone through?" asked Jackie. "It's up to you to take what happiness you can find. And you have to soldier on, whether you like it or not."

"You're the only one in this family who understands," said Joan.

Jackies greatest moment of understanding came in March 1985 with the death of her half-sister, 39-year-old Janet Auchincloss Rutherford.

"Jackie was very close to Janet Jr.," said Yusha Auchincloss. "They shared the same interests in art and literature. Janet stayed with Jackie whenever she came back from Hong Kong for a visit. Caroline Kennedy was godmother to one of Janet Jr.'s children. Janet Jr. returned for a visit in September 1984 and complained of a backache. It didn't seem serious. I suggested she see a chiropractor, thinking she'd hurt it while playing with the kids. It turned out to be cancer. She had bone marrow transplant treatments. She used to be at Boston's Peter Bent Brigham Hospital, where I would drive her when she became an outpatient. Jackie spent a great deal of time with her. Janet did well. I think she went into remission but then she developed acute pneumonia. Jackie was there with her when she died at Beth Israel Hospital in Boston."

"When Janet Jr. was ill in the hospital," said Eilene Slocum, "Jackie rallied around. She was with her every single moment in the last days of her illness. She was simply superb. Those were her finest hours."

Jackie's friend Sylvia Blake agreed. "It was a high point in Jackie's life the way she took care of Janet Rutherford when she was dying of cancer. She stayed with Janet day and night. Jackie has this quality of standing strong at difficult moments. You don't hear from her for long periods, but then something happens and she's there for you. When my mother died early in 1986, I saw a lot of Jackie. She couldn't have been more kind and thoughtful, loving and sweet."

Janet Jr. was cremated, her ashes strewn in New York, Newport and Hong Kong. A catered, private memorial was held for Janet at Hammersmith Farm. Newport portrait artist Dick Banks complained that Janet Jr.'s friends weren't permitted to attend the memorial. "That was Jackie's decision," he said. "She [claimed she] didn't want to create a 'carnival atmosphere.' So we were excluded from the ceremony.

"After Janet Jr.'s death, her mother developed the first symptoms of Alzheimer's disease. I have to admit that when this happened, Jackie began to take care of her mother. She would visit her frequently, get out with her as much as possible. Any animosity that existed between them disappeared."

Janet Auchincloss had good and bad days. "The manifestations of the illness seem to come and go," said Dorothy Desjardins, spokesperson for the new owners of Hammersmith Farm. "The present owners allowed her to use the main house for Janet Jr.'s memorial. After that, Janet would occasionally wander up to the house and start straightening the furniture. If the books weren't pushed back on the bookshelf, they looked 'naughty' to her and she would push them back. On better days, I've seen her ride a horse. On worse days, it can be quite awful apparently."

Jackie's mother could remember details from her dim past: the name of a dog she owned as a child, the date she and Black Jack Bouvier were divorced; more recent names and events often escaped her entirely. Asked a question about John F. Kennedy, she looked at her interlocutor and said, "Who's John F. Kennedy?"

Alan Pryce-Jones felt Jackie could have done better in terms of her mother: "She may have set up a million-dollar trust for Janet, but she didn't do much to save Hammersmith Farm. People approached Jackie and said, 'If you invest $800,000 or so you'll have a property worth six or seven times as much.' She would simply shrug them off. She didn't want to be bothered with it. She didn't seem to care whether it went or not, or for what amount or to whom. So it sold for far less than it's worth and it became a commercial enterprise, and is now shown to tourists as 'the house where Jackie O. grew up as an adolescent.'

"I always felt that Janet didn't care much that Jackie was First Lady, and if anything, that it was an imposition on Janet's privacy. She was pretty hard on both Jackie and Lee, nicer to her second grouping of kids. You'd ask her about Jackie or Lee and she'd just wave her hand and say, 'Oh Jackie. She's okay, she's all right.' With the other kids she'd go into much greater detail on what they were doing. She gave the impression that she had been hurt by Jackie and Lee over many years and never fully forgave them for the way they treated her. When asked why she didn't bail out Hammersmith Farm, Jackie once said, 'I don't want to talk about it.' That must also have left harsh feelings on Janet's part. For somebody as interested in money as Jackie seems to be, you'd have thought Hammersmith Farm would have made a wise investment.

"Once Janet became ill and the fight went out of her, Jackie paid her more heed. I have to believe that the death of Janet Jr. at such a young age devastated her mother and softened Jackie. It's a guess, because neither of them ever spoke about it."

If Jacqueline's days seemed more tranquil, if she managed to attain a self-confidence and softness she had previously lacked, she also continued to deal harshly with anyone she felt had betrayed her, including members of her own family. Her half-brother Jamie Auchincloss was never forgiven for having talked to Kitty Kelley when Kelley wrote her version of Jackie's life. "It's impossible to be related to somebody as famous as Jacqueline Onassis," said Jamie in his own defense. "The disclosure that truly annoyed her was that her wedding dress had been placed in a box with the date of her wedding on it, and her pink assassination suit had been placed in another box with its date on it, and the two boxes had been stored in mother's attic in Georgetown, one on top of the other.

"After that, we didn't talk very much anymore. There weren't many reasons for us to talk to each other or get together anyway, so it didn't seem too obvious that two people in the family weren't talking. Still I could have done without the break, particularly since I felt a fondness and friendship for Jackie. I ended up writing her a letter of apology that must have gone down as one of the silliest pieces of garble and gibberish ever, because I just did not know what to say.

"It's strange but I believe I got to know Caroline and John Jr. and even Jack Kennedy better than I know Jackie. I think she can establish friendships but I think everybody feels, without exception, that there's also a loner quality and a remoteness there."

Jackie's cousin John Davis, whose family portraits of the Bouviers and the Kennedys annoyed Jackie immensely, received similar treatment. "That didn't bother me at all," said Davis. "What did disturb me was that she also punished my mother."

Jackie's treatment of Maude Davis and Michelle Putnam, her father's twin sisters, was blatantly cruel. Demonstrating her hostility toward John, she failed to show up in Connecticut at the eightieth birthday party of her aunts, an affair attended by all other members of the family. She then compounded the insult by inviting neither aunt to Caroline's wedding. When Michelle Putnam died in September 1987, Jackie attended the funeral at St. Vincent Ferrer in New York, but barely spoke to Maude Davis and not at all to John.

"She not only didn't speak to John, she refused to shake his hand," said Marianne Strong, who also attended the funeral. "I don't think I've ever seen anything like it before. She shook everybody else's hand. She looked through John; around him, behind him, but not at him. In her eyes he didn't exist."

Jackie's fickleness emerged in other instances as well. She donated money to Channel 13, New York's public television station, but refused to give to the Jewish Opera in Tel Aviv when solicited by Maurice Tempelsman's cousin, Rose Schreiber. She went to Albany to protest a bill removing landmark status from religious properties (a case centered on whether St. Bartholomew's Church in New York should be permitted to erect a residential tower atop its main office). She refused, however, to take part in a symposium on Women and the Constitution sponsored by four other former First Ladies at the Jimmy Carter Presidential Center in Atlanta, Georgia. She campaigned vociferously against Mort Zuckerman's plans to construct 58- and 68-story skyscrapers at Columbus Circle (they would "cast a long shadow over Central Park"), but she said not a word when the Kennedy family announced its intention to build a Merchandise Mart hi-rise at Times Square, putting dozens of small merchants out of business. She attended Marietta Tree's dinner for art dealer Harriet Crawley and the Opening Night Gala of the Martha Graham Dance Company's 61st season, while declining invitations to scores of other dinners and opening night galas. She traveled to Cambridge, Massachusetts, for the dedication of a park to John F. Kennedy on what would have been the late President's 70th birthday, but she refused to allow the JFK Center for the Performing Arts in conjunction with ABC Television to present a filmed retrospective as a remembrance of the 25th year since the assassination of

Jack Kennedy and the 20th since the assassination of his brother Robert. The Kennedy family was otherwise eager to participate, but Jackie's voice carried more weight than theirs. When Norman Mailer asked her to help publicize the 1986 PEN International Celebration in New York, she agreed; the results, according to Jane Yeoman, coordinator of the event, were less dramatic than expected: "Jackie lent her name to the benefit committee and donated $1,000, but she didn't attend the meetings and we didn't hear from her further."

People wondered whether Jackie had actually changed or whether they had simply imagined a change. In 1986, she reduced her work load at Doubleday to three half-days a week. She spent nearly as much time at the beauty parlor on facials and comb-outs as she did at the office. She remained in psychotherapy once a week, having switched to a new $150-per-session Park Avenue practitioner. Still an active equestrienne, she continued to ride to hounds at the Essex Hunt Club in New Jersey. (In 1985, she won her second straight Lady Ardmore Challenge trophy for vaulting fences.) Several times each year, she rode with Charles S. Whitehouse, Sylvia Blake's brother, at the Piedmont Hunt's weekend point-to-point races in Middleburg, Virginia, staying either with Bunny Mellon or occasionally by herself at the Red Fox Inn.

Exceedingly wary of the press, she nevertheless attended the Senatorial Campaign Committee's annual black-tie dinner-dance in November 1985, organized that year at the Metropolitan Club by Louette Samuels, and gladly posed with every businessman who had donated $1,000 to be at the affair. Covering the event for her newspaper, Mimi Kazon described Jackie as "a dream in a high-necked, long-sleeved red dress just to her knees. Sheer black stockings, plain black patent pumps and a small black clutch handbag picked up the black of the midriff of her dress. Huge round diamonds circled in black were at her ears. She wore a plain gold wedding band, her only other jewelry.

"Most amusing were these little men in monkey suits with drinks in their hand who lined up and then posed with Jackie one after the other, the tops of their bald pates reaching her shoulder line. The more daring ones would try to wrap themselves around her, take her arm, put their arm around her waistline. It was like the kissing booth at a small-town carnival, where the fellows paid a dollar each to buss the local beauty queen. Jackie was amazingly good-natured about it all. She smiled the whole way through what must have been quite an ordeal. Presumably these business executives had their pictures with Jackie blown up to lifesize for the walls of their office."

Charlotte Curtis found Jackie "a bit smug and sanctimonious on these public occasions. I remember her carrying forth in front of one of those cocktail crowds on how nobody at these functions really did anything. Coming from somebody whose workload didn't exactly represent slave labor, it sounded somewhat strange. When somebody at the party pointed out that most of the people there were gainfully employed, Jackie said, 'But they're so dull.'

"Then she was co-chairperson of a Municipal Art Society dinner for the famous Japanese-American sculptor Isamu Noguchi. The party took place in a tent set up in a parking lot across from the Isamu Noguchi Garden Museum in Long Island City, Queens. Those at Jackie's table included Philip Johnson, Elizabeth de Cuevas, William Walton, Martha Graham and Isamu Noguchi. Jackie spoke so quietly nobody could hear her. She ate so little, it seemed impolite for anybody to request seconds. She kept putting on and taking off her reading glasses. One of her earrings fell off and a dozen men scurried around on the floor to retrieve it. Noguchi took her on a personal tour of his sculpture garden. As she followed him around she kept saying, 'How nice' and 'How beautiful.' I have rarely seen greater lack of inspiration."

Newspaper chitchat had it that Jackie flew into a rage at a maid who put her new $10,000 Christian Lacroix gown in a stack of dresses to be donated to a Manhattan charity thrift shop. When the error was discovered, Nancy Tuckerman frantically telephoned the thrift shop, but it was too late. The gown had been snapped up for $100 by an eagle-eyed customer. Jackie had better luck when a dozen of her Indian miniatures, temporarily removed from their frames, were accidentally carted off with the garbage. An astute Department of Sanitation employee set the valuable paintings aside and this time when Nancy Tuckerman called she was able to retrieve them.

Each year from 1982 through 1985, Jackie visited India. In 1985, she went with S. Cary Welsh, curator of Islamic and Later Indian Art at the Fogg Museum, Harvard University. "The trip was in connection with the India Festival then taking place across the United States," explained Welsh. "The Metropolitan Museum of Art had scheduled an exhibition as had the Costume Institute. Doubleday, in association with the Museum, published a book, *A Second Paradise: Indian Courtly Life 1590—1947*, written by Naveen Paitnaik and edited by Jacqueline Onassis. I wrote the introduction. My wife and I accompanied her to India. We went to Delhi, Baroda, Jaipur, Jodhpur, Hyderabad and several other districts. We traveled mostly by plane and car, and we stayed at the palaces.

"Jackie's very popular in India. She was successful at getting the princely families to lend their costumes for use at the Costume Institute exhibition. Although she's recognized on the street, we were not troubled by the press. For the most part we were able to wander around as though Jackie was just a plain old garden variety type of person, something she can't often do in the States. I suspect that's one reason she enjoys India so much. Nobody bothers her."

Jackie attended a number of social events connected with the India Festival and gave one party herself. The guest list included S. Cary Welsh, poet Mark Strand, Prince Michael and Princess Marina of Greece, Jayne Wrightsman and the Maharani of Jaipur. The food, according to Welsh, was impeccable, the conversation equally enticing. "To the great excitement of the girls," reported *Vanity Fair*, "John Kennedy, Jr., arrived to drop off his backpack. To the great disappointment of the girls, he left after ten minutes."

The hostess enjoyed the large party sufficiently to throw another mass gathering the following year, this one at her house on Martha's Vineyard for two dozen of her Kennedy nieces and nephews and two dozen of their friends. The affair enhanced Jackie's popularity among the younger generation, but had no effect on the way the older Kennedys perceived her.

Richard Zoerink, an acquaintance of Pat Kennedy Lawford, said: "There are two things I was told never to mention around Pat: the assassinations and Jacqueline Kennedy Onassis. Those two subjects are *verboten*. I've played Trivial Pursuit with Pat and she was constantly landing on yellow, which is history, I believe. And practically every other question in history is about the Kennedys. And if it had anything to do with Jacqueline Onassis or the assassinations you didn't ask the question. I was instructed to say, 'Oh, I got the cards mixed up.' And she'd pull out another card.

"One day we were playing and she landed on yellow and it was something about Jackie Onassis. A question about her maiden name—Bouvier. And I said, 'Oh, I got the cards mixed up.' And she said, 'You know, I think I should get that.' And I laughed and said, 'Okay,' and gave it to her. And she answered the question. But in general you knew this was just something you didn't ask her.

"This doesn't mean Pat would ever speak negatively of Jackie, at least not in public. She cares too much for Jackie's children. Family is important to Pat. They're very protective of one another. Anything that Pat would say that might hurt Jacqueline Kennedy Onassis is something that would also hurt her niece and nephew. My impression is that though Pat doesn't like Jackie too much, she would never do or say anything that might harm Caroline or John Jr."

Following Caroline's marriage to Ed Schlossberg, there was considerable conjecture as to what kind of grandmother Jackie might make. The answer would come soon enough. By the spring of 1988, Caroline had ordered her baby's layette at Cerutti on Madison Avenue, the same shop where she herself had been outfitted as an infant. While taking Lamaze lessons with her husband and completing requirements for her law degree, Caroline flew to Boston on several occasions to oversee the design of a statue of her father that will stand in front of the gold-domed State House on Beacon Street. Unlike her mother, she enjoyed an easy pregnancy. She also visited Rose Kennedy at Hyannis Port and her mother on Martha's Vineyard.

During the beginning of June, Jackie's common refrain to friends became, "I'm going to be a grandmother—imagine that."

When Caroline's labor began on Friday, June 24, she telephoned her physician, Dr. Frederick W. Martens, Jr., and was told to start timing her contractions. When the contractions reached three-minute intervals, Maurice Tempelsman's limousine picked up the expectant parents and took them to New York Hospital-Cornell Medical Center. To protect her privacy, Caroline was listed as "Mrs. Sylva" on the seventh floor of the hospital. A pair of security guards stood outside her $720-a-day private room. She was prepped for the delivery in a private birthing room.

Caroline's labor lasted less than 24 hours. At 3:30 a.m. on Saturday, June 25th, she gave birth to a 7-lb., 12-oz. baby named Rose after Caroline's grandmother, the matriarch of the Kennedy family, one month short of her 98th birthday.

According to published sources, Jackie was a nervous wreck during the final hours of Caroline's delivery as she kept vigil at the hospital with John. She paced and chewed her nails to distraction, and to John's distraction as well. He kept telling his mother to "cool out."

The birth of his niece, for which he had armed himself with quality cigars, marked the start of a promising period for John. He was currently working as a $1,100-a-week summer associate with the Los Angeles law firm of Manatt, Phelps, Rothenberg & Phillips. His sister held the same job the summer before at Paul Weiss Rifkind Wharton and Garrison in Manhattan.

John entered national politics by introducing Senator Ted Kennedy at the 1988 Democratic National Convention in Atlanta, and while what he said was forgettable, he made a striking appearance, so much so that *People* magazine named him "The Sexiest Man Alive." As he neared completion of his third and last year in law school, he announced his intention to begin his career as an assistant prosecutor in Manhattan District Attorney Robert Morgenthau's office.

Having hired a full-time, sleep-in nurse, Caroline Kennedy planned to divide the year between passing the New York State law boards and preparing a book on a law-related issue for William Morrow. Yielding to family pressure to raise her child as a Catholic, she insisted that Rose Kennedy Schlossberg be baptized at St. Thomas More Church in Manhattan. Maude Davis, now the sole remaining Bouvier from Black Jack's generation, was not invited.

And what of Lee Radziwill? Having ended still another

romance—with New York architect Richard Meier—and having launched still another career—director of special events for fashion designer Giorgio Armani—Lee announced her intention to marry Hollywood director Herbert Ross, also of Jewish heritage. For once, Lee saw a plan to completion. A small, private affair, the wedding took place in Lee's Manhattan apartment and was followed by a reception in Jackie's dining room. Guests included Rudolf Nureyev, Bernadette Peters, Steve Martin, Daryl Hannah and decorator Mark Hampton.

As for "Granny O," Jackie's new press moniker, she commemorated the twenty-fifth anniversary of JFK's assassination by attending an 8:30 a.m. private Mass at St. Thomas More, accompanied by Caroline and John Jr. Jackie attended no public ceremony and issued no public statement in connection with the occasion.

As of her sixtieth birthday (July 28, 1989), Jacqueline Bouvier Kennedy Onassis remains an everlasting mystery. "I am happiest when I am alone," she was once quoted as saying. In her highly individualistic way, she is as elegant and regal as ever. She continues to hate publicity—or at least pretends to. Yet when it comes to celebrity, she is our reigning star, albeit one whose reputation seems to rise and fall according to the temper of the times. She is still the target of more gossip and innuendo than any ten Hollywood movie legends combined, but she has gradually learned to deal with the clamor, to circumvent it. One question remains: What is Jackie really like? And the answer is: We may never truly know.

Chapter Notes

When and where possible the author has provided source notes within the body of the text. The following chapter notes are included to supplement the textual references. And while the following is not necessarily a complete list of sources, it provides the interested reader with some idea of the author's methodology. Also included are occasional comments of an extraneous but informative nature.

CHAPTER 1

Jackie's Bouvier grandfather, The Major, was a guest speaker at the 1931 dedication ceremony of the George Washington Bridge. "I was in school that day," recalls Miche Bouvier, "but other members of the family were in attendance, including Jackie's father. The Major was a magnificent orator. Every July Fourth, he delivered the Independence Day speech at East Hampton. He was a well-known and highly respected local figure."

After she became First Lady, Jackie wrote to *The Nutley Sun* explaining her family's early connection to Nutley, New Jersey: "The Bouviers left Nutley when my father was a boy. However, I remember my grandfather and father constantly talking about it, and I had a very clear picture of it in my imagination as the place where my adored father grew up. I have never lived there, just driven through the town as a little girl, with my father pointing out things to me—a pond where he went ice skating is what I remember most—but then I was only about six years old."

Black Jack Bouvier's letter "to a friend" during World War I was written to Tom Collier, July 12, 1918.

Details of Black Jack's $80,000 loan in 1922 were provided by Herman Darvick. The loan agreement itself was sold at auction by Mr. Darvick: Herman Darvick Autograph Auctions, Sale No. 4, Sept. 4, 1986, The Sheraton City Squire Hotel, New York City.

Before marrying Emma Louise Stone, Bud Bouvier had

been involved with Edna Woolworth Hutton, mother of five-and-dime heiress Barbara Hutton, at a time when Edna was married to stockbroker Franklyn Laws Hutton. Edna committed suicide not long after the disintegration of her romance with Bud by taking poison while staying at the Plaza Hotel in New York.

In 1962, St. Philomena Church in East Hampton, where Jackie's parents were married, changed its name to Most Holy Trinity. The Church Board changed the name because an investigation by the Vatican revealed questions as to the textual authenticity of Philomena. Old-time East Hamptonites, however, still refer to the church by its original name.

The two volumes that proved most valuable as sources for background data on the Bouvier family were: Kathleen Bouvier, *To Jack With Love—Black Jack Bouvier: A Remembrance,* New York: Zebra Books, 1979; John H. Davis, *The Bouviers: Portrait of an American Family,* New York: Farrar, Straus & Giroux, 1969. It is noteworthy that both authors are members of the Bouvier family.

Background information on East Hampton and the Bouvier and Lee families comes from many sources, including the Long Island Room of the East Hampton Free Library, the archives of *The East Hampton Star,* and such privately printed volumes as Jeannette Edwards Rattray, *Fifty Years of the Maidstone Club, 1891-1941,* issued in 1941 to members of the club. Personal interviews for this chapter were conducted with the following: Janet Auchincloss, John H. Davis, Miche Bouvier, Michelle Putnam, Marianne Strong, Tom Collier, Herman Darvick, John Ficke, Louis Ehret, Edie Beale, Truman Capote, Peter Bloom, Jim Divine.

CHAPTER 2

Two volumes particularly helpful on Jackie's early youth are: John H. Davis, *The Kennedys: Dynasty and Disaster, 1848-1983,* New York: McGraw-Hill, 1984; Mary Van Rensselaer Thayer, *Jacqueline Bouvier Kennedy,* Garden City, N.Y.: Doubleday, 1961. Also useful have been the newspaper morgues of *The New York Times,* New York *Daily News, Wall Street Journal* and *The East Hampton Star.* The John F. Kennedy Library, Columbia Point, Boston, Massachusetts, provided additional newspaper and magazine material on the early life of Jacqueline Bouvier Kennedy Onassis.

Richard Newton, Esq., MFH (Master of Fox Hounds) for the Suffolk Hunt, was, according to Queenie Simmonds-

Nielsen, "a great favorite of Janet Bouvier's. A gentleman to his fingertips, until someone should accidentally ride past one of his hounds, Newton would then pull the rider over and berate him (or her) in language that would put a sailor to shame. Newton always rode to the hunt in his four-in-hand pulled by four horses with docked tails, even though you were not allowed to dock horses' tails in those days."

One of Jackie's early poems, often reprinted after she became First Lady, was entitled "Sea Joy"—

> When I go down to the sandy shore
> I can think of nothing I want more
> Than to live by the booming blue sea
> As the seagulls flutter round about me
>
> I can run about when the tide is out
> With the wind and the sand and the sea all about
> And the seagulls are swirling and diving for fish
> Oh—to live by the sea is my only wish.

The charge concerning Black Jack Bouvier's bisexuality has been leveled from several quarters. See Charles Schwartz, *Cole Porter: A Biography*, p. 176: "Some of Cole's most intense affairs were with men from distinguished families. . . . Cole, for instance, was reported to have been very much taken at one time with 'Black-Jack' Bouvier. Flamboyant and handsome, John Vernou Bouvier III was, like Cole, a Yale man of the class of 1914, and later the father of Jacqueline Kennedy Onassis. 'I'm just mad about Jack,' Cole is supposed to have enthused about him to his very close friends at the height of his relationship with Bouvier." An interview with Schwartz by the present author yielded no additional information. Schwartz contended he could no longer remember his source for this charge. Further investigation on the part of the present author, however, reveals that several members of the Bouvier family were aware of a sexual relationship between Black Jack and Cole Porter. One family member contends: "Jack was *very* 'bi.' He joined, from time to time, Cole and [actor] Monty Woolley on their hunts for working class MALES. And not for bridge purposes!"

Personal interviews for this chapter were conducted with Louis Ehret, Edie Beale, Miche Bouvier, Michelle Putnam, Peter Bloom, Janet Auchincloss, Martin Simmonds, Queenie Simmonds-Nielsen, Samuel Lester, John H. Davis, Marianne Strong, Judith Frame, Anthony Cangiolosi, Franklyn Ives, Alexandra Webb.

CHAPTER 3

Black Jack Bouvier's financial woes at the time of his separation from Janet are discussed at length in John H. Davis, *The Bouviers*. Further details were provided the author by Peter Bloom, a former employee of James T. Lee, and John Ficke, Black Jack's one-time bookkeeper.

A copy of the 1937 letter from Jack Bouvier to James T. Lee was provided by Herman Darvick who sold same at auction on Sept. 4, 1986, as part of lot #203, Herman Darvick Autograph Auction (see notes, chapter 1).

Details of immediate events leading to the divorce of Jack and Janet Bouvier can be found in the newspaper morgue of the New York *Daily Mirror*. Further information concerning the divorce hearing and resulting agreements is located in courtroom files: Case #65098, Bouvier vs. Bouvier, July 22, 1940. Washoe County Clerk's Office, Second Judicial District Court, County Courthouse, Reno, Nevada. The built-in hypocrisy of the typical Reno divorce case with its six-week residency requirement is evident from the following testimony as offered by Janet Bouvier during the direct examination phase of her divorce hearing:

Q. Where do you reside in Washoe County, Nevada?

A. At the Lazy A Bar Ranch.

Q. When you came to Nevada, was it with the purpose of making Nevada your permanent residence?

A: It was.

Q: And such intention has abided with you ever since?

A. Yes.

Q: And such is still your intention?

A: Yes.

Just as hypocritical was covenant #9 of the divorce agreement between Jack and Janet Bouvier, which provided as follows:

Inasmuch as the parties hereto believe that the love and respect of each child for both parents should be maintained and strengthened, each of the parties hereto agrees not to do, say or permit to be done or said, directly or indirectly, anything which might tend to diminish the love and respect of

either child toward either parent; and each party
will refrain wholly from discussing with either child,
and from commenting upon to either child, the
character or conduct of the other party, save and
except, if at all, to speak in words of praise calculated to increase the love and respect of the child
toward the parent mentioned.

Personal interviews for this chapter were conducted with
Peter Bloom, John Ficke, Judith Frame, Martin Simmonds,
Elisabeth Draper, Fanny Gardiner, Earl E. T. Smith, Herman
Darvick, Franklin d'Olier, Jr., Winifred d'Olier, Edie Beale,
Bouvier Beale.

CHAPTER 4

Background and historical information on the Auchincloss
family comes from the archives of the *Washington Post* and
the *Washington Times Herald*, as well as the New York
Genealogical and Biographical Society. The latter contained
a number of family documents, including: Charles C.
Auchincloss, *Family Chart and Notes*, 1934; Joanna Russell
Auchincloss and Caroline Auchincloss Fowler, *The Auchincloss Family*, Freeport, ME: The Dingley Press, 1957.

The following published interviews with author Gore Vidal
proved valuable as sources of information on Hugh D.
Auchincloss: Stephen Schiff, "Gore's Wars," *Vanity Fair*,
June 1987; Rudy Maxa, "Gore Vidal's Washington," *Washing-
tonian*, July 1987.

Concerning Hugh Auchincloss's penchant for pornography, Jamie Auchincloss told the author: "The first time I
met Gore Vidal, he told me that Daddy had the world's
largest collection of pornography. Later he said that Daddy
was the dullest man in the world. I told Vidal that he was
lying. Daddy couldn't have the world's largest collection of
pornography and also be the dullest man in the world."
Asked about this exchange, Vidal responded: "I'm amazed
that Jamie thinks a liking for porno precludes dullness—*vide*
Marquis de Sade." Jamie Auchincloss confirmed that his
father owned a large collection of pornographic material.

The author was taken on a personal tour of Hammersmith
Farm, Newport, R.I., by Dorothy Desjardins, representative of Hammersmith's present owners, Camelot Gardens,
Inc. The house and property have remained substantially
intact. The author's Washington researcher, Tony Mazzaschi,
was taken on a tour of Merrywood in McLean, VA, by

Michael Kay, son of the present owners of that estate. Jamie Auchincloss, who grew up at Merrywood, accompanied Mazzaschi on the tour and provided useful reminiscences.

The Holton-Arms School, once situated on Hillyer Place, N.W., in Washington, D.C., is today located on the 88-acre wooded Granger campus in Bethesda, MD.

Historical information on Miss Porter's School was found at the Hartford Public Library, Hartford, CT, and the Farmington Public Library, Farmington, CT. In addition, the author consulted back issues of *Salmagundy*, the student newspaper on whose staff Jackie worked, provided courtesy of Rachel Phillips Belash, Head of School. Jackie's regular cartoon series in *Salmagundy* was entitled "Frenzied Frieda," a kind of take-off on *The Perils of Pauline*. Typical of Jackie's poetry contributions to the newspaper is "Song of the Night Watchman," which begins:

> I walk the city in the rain
> Up and down my lonesome beat.
> The street lamps make the
> puddles shine
> And I hear echoes of my feet.
>
> Through the mist the buildings
> blur,
> Strung on strands of neon light,
> I smell the Cohans' Irish Stew
> But cannot stop to have a bite. . . .

The letter to Jackie (at Miss Porter's) from her Bouvier grandfather appears in Mary Van Rensselaer Thayer, *Jacqueline Bouvier Kennedy,* pp. 64-65.

Jackie's complete Yearbook legend at Miss Porter's reads as follows:

JACQUELINE LEE BOUVIER
"MERRYWOOD"
MC LEAN, VIRGINIA
"Jackie"

Favorite Song: "Lime House Blues"
Always Saying: "Play a Rhumba next"
Most Known For: Wit
Aversion: People who ask if her horse is still alive
Where Found: Laughing with Tucky
Ambition: Not to be a housewife

Personal interviews for this chapter were conducted with Jamie Auchincloss, Fanny Gardiner, Yusha Auchincloss, Dick Banks, Gore Vidal, Winifred d'Olier, Edie Beale, John H. Davis, Michael Kay, Nancy Dickerson, Wyatt Dickerson, Nina Auchincloss Steers Straight, Dorothy Desjardins, Louis Ehret, Miche Bouvier, Elisabeth Draper, Lily Pulitzer, Eilene Slocum, Noreen Drexel.

CHAPTER 5

John H. Davis's family histories on the Bouviers and the Kennedys proved useful for this chapter, as did Kathleen Bouvier's *To Jack With Love* and Mary Thayer's *Jacqueline Bouvier Kennedy*.

Igor Cassini's written assessment of Jackie as "Deb of the Year" appeared originally in the *New York Journal-American*.

Letter from Black Jack Bouvier to Jackie ("I suppose it won't be long . . .") can be found in Thayer, *JBK*, p. 74.

"A woman can have wealth . . .": Passage quoted verbatim by Edie Beale. Similar missives can be found in Davis, *The Kennedys*, p. 197-199.

Letter from Jackie to Yusha Auchincloss ("They are the most wonderful . . ."): Thayer, *JBK*, p. 80.

Personal interviews conducted with Janet Auchincloss, George Gardner, Jerome Zerbe, Sylvia Whitehouse Blake, Igor Cassini, Charlotte Curtis, Selwa "Lucky" Roosevelt, John H. Davis, Yusha Auchincloss, Jonathan Isham, Peter Reed, Chris O'Donnell, Nuala Pell, Edie Beale, Bouvier Beale, John Ficke.

CHAPTER 6

Personal interviews for this chapter were conducted with John Sterling, Elaine Lorillard, Frank Waldrop, John G. W. Husted, Jr., Mary deLimur Weinmann, Cecilia Parker Geyelin, Betty Fretz, Estelle Gaines, Jack Kassowitz, Selwa "Lucky" Roosevelt, John B. White, Godfrey McHugh, Charles Bartlett, Lewis Buck, John Sherman Cooper, Lem Billings.

CHAPTER 7

Family friend Dinah Bridge's statement about Jackie is from an interview in the oral history collection at the John F. Kennedy Library, Boston, Mass.

The lives of Joe Kennedy, Jr., Kathleen Kennedy and

Rosemary Kennedy have been fully documented in numerous books and articles. Joe Jr., Jack Kennedy's older brother, lost his life in August 1944 when he volunteered to fly a Navy Liberator bomber loaded with explosives from England to within a few miles of a German V-bomb base where he would eject and the plane would be guided the rest of the way by remote control. A malfunction caused the plane to explode long before it reached its destination.

Equally devastating for the family was the death four years later of Kathleen. Raised a dutiful Catholic, Jack's sister rebelled against her family and religion by marrying a Protestant nobleman outside the church (the Marquess of Harrington), and later as a young widow by commencing an affair with a married man (Peter Fitzwilliam). In many ways Kick's life had been as romantic as any film heroine's but it ended unhappily and much too soon.

If Kick was the most rebellious, daring and doomed of the Kennedy sisters, Rosemary was the most beautiful and perhaps the most tragic member of the clan. Diagnosed as a "problem child" and a "slow learner," she was later deemed mentally retarded, dangerous not only to others but to herself. In 1941, Joe Kennedy, without his wife's knowledge, ordered a prefrontal lobotomy performed on Rosemary. The operation proved a dismal failure. No longer able to function independently, she was placed in a remote convent, where she became a woeful reminder to the psychiatric community of a barbaric medical procedure long since abandoned.

Personal interviews for this chapter were conducted with John H. Davis, Ralph G. Martin, Frank Waldrop, Estelle Gaines, Lem Billings, David Horowitz, Louis Ehret, James Rousmaniere, Cass Canfield, Jr., Aileen Bowdoin Train, John P. Marquand, Jr.

CHAPTER 8

Concerning the Kennedy family touch football games: Before quitting the sport, Jackie once asked Ted Sorensen, "When I get the ball, which way do I run?"

Jack Kennedy was aware that he didn't meet Janet Auchincloss's social expectations for Jackie. Arriving at Hammersmith Farm by car with a group of boisterous acquaintances at 3:00 a.m., he reminded them that he was still courting Jackie, then added, "Let's cut it down, fellows. I'm not too solid with the family, and they might throw me out."

Accounts of the JFK-Jackie nuptials appeared in numerous newspapers, including *The New York Times*, *Washington Post*, *Boston Globe* and *Miami Herald*. The clipping files of these and other periodicals were consulted throughout the writing of this book. See also John H. Davis, *The Kennedys*, pp. 211-222.

"The pressures of public life . . .": Red Fay's statements appear in his book, *The Pleasure of His Company*, p. 163.

Interviews for this chapter were conducted with Larry O'Brien, Janet Auchincloss, Estelle Gaines, Lois K. Alexander, Red Fay, Mary deLimur Weinmann, John H. Davis, Marianne Strong, Michelle Putnam, John B. White, Sylvia Blake, George Smathers, Evelyn Lincoln, Yusha Auchincloss, Eilene Slocum.

CHAPTER 9

A slightly different version of the Kennedy painting story appears in Collier and Horowitz, *The Kennedys: An American Drama*, p. 195.

Interviews for this chapter were conducted with Selwa "Lucky" Roosevelt, Jeanne Murray Vanderbilt, Lem Billings, Judge James Knott, George Vigouroux, Marianne Strong, Doris Lilly, Oleg Cassini, Slim Aarons, Langdon Marvin.

CHAPTER 10

Truman Capote, fond of repeating stories, described the 1955 New York dinner party not only to the present author but to Lawrence Grobel who used it in his book, *Conversations with Capote*, pp. 180-181.

The Inga Arvad affair is described at length in documents contained in the FBI files, released to the author under the Freedom of Information Act. The case is also described at length in Joan and Clay Blair, Jr., *The Search for JFK*, which proved useful in tracing a number of JFK's amorous adventures, including his unsuccessful pursuit of Olivia de Havilland, which is also described in this chapter. Other books consulted for the purposes of this chapter are: Kitty Kelley, *Jackie Oh!*; Gene Tierney with Mickey Herskowitz, *Self-Portrait*; Ralph G. Martin, *A Hero for Our Time*; Nancy Dickerson, *Among Those Present*.

The FBI files on Joseph F. Kennedy, many of them made available here for the first time, also proved useful. Among other telling facts, the files reveal that Joe Kennedy was far more than a Special Service Contact for the FBI. In 1956,

President Eisenhower asked him to serve on a special commission to review the government's foreign intelligence activities, a position that brought him into close contact with the CIA, then headed by Allen Dulles. FBI files indicate that Joe Kennedy met regularly with J. Edgar Hoover during this period "to discuss" CIA activities. In effect, he was acting the part of Hoover's personal mole, gathering highly sensitive data from the CIA and passing it along to the FBI.

The full title of the genealogy that describes the supposed JFK-Durie Malcolm marriage is: *The Blauvelt Family Genealogy, a Comprehensive Compilation of the Descendants of Gerritt Hendricksen (Blauvelt), 1620-1687, who came to America in 1638.* It was written by Louis Blauvelt and published by the Association of Blauvelt Descendants in East Orange, NJ.

The Alicja Purdom Clark case as documented in FBI files (revealed to the current author in full for the first time) indicates that in July 1963, a man identified as Robert Garden approached then-Senator John G. Tower with material from the supposedly sealed court record of Purdom's "lawsuit" against JFK. Garden, who identified himself as a private detective, evidently wanted to sell this material to Tower and told Tower's representative that he wanted to sell it to Teamster boss Jimmy Hoffa as well. Hoffa was a known target of the Kennedys and could presumably have used the material for blackmail purposes.

The interview with Mrs. Alicja Corning Clark was conducted by journalist Sharon Churcher of *Penthouse* magazine for her column ("USA Confidential").

The John Sharon statements are from his oral history at the JFK Library. The interview was conducted on Nov. 7, 1967.

Personal interviews for this chapter were conducted with: Truman Capote, George Smathers, James Rousmaniere, Langdon Marvin, Susan Imhoff, Edward Folger, Frank Waldrop, John Hersey, Lucio Manisco, Nancy Dickerson, Margaret Louise Coit, Lem Billings, Earl E.T. Smith.

CHAPTER 11

The two most helpful volumes for this chapter were Ralph G. Martin, *A Hero for Our Times,* and Hugh Sidey, *John F. Kennedy, President.*

Letter from Jackie to Bernard Baruch, November 9, 1954: Bernard M. Baruch Papers, Princeton University Library, Princeton, NJ.

Letter from Jackie to President Dwight Eisenhower, November 17, 1954: Dwight D. Eisenhower Presidential Library, Abilene, KS.

The fullest account of the *Profiles in Courage*-Pulitzer Prize controversy can be found in Herbert S. Parmet, *Jack: The Struggles of John F. Kennedy*, pp. 320-333. In addition to the sources and interview subjects mentioned in the text of *A Woman Named Jackie*, the current author used the Cass Canfield transcripts in the Oral History Collection, Columbia University Libraries, New York, NY.

Tempest Storm describes her affair with JFK in her autobiography, *Tempest Storm: The Lady Is a Vamp*, pp. 157-160.

Jackie letter to Lady Bird Johnson: This letter and approximately 150 other letters from Jackie Kennedy Onassis to Lyndon and/or Lady Bird Johnson (and from the Johnsons to Jacqueline) were released for the first time. The correspondence is housed at the Lyndon Baines Johnson Library, Austin, Texas. Eleven of the letters are still unavailable. The others were released to the author by the late James E. O'Neill, Director, Office of Presidential Libraries, National Archives, Washington, D.C.

Jackie to Bess Furman, November 24, 1952: Bess Furman Armstrong correspondence file, Library of Congress, Washington, D.C.

Interviews for this chapter were conducted with Ralph G. Martin, Helen McCauley, Langdon Marvin, Charles Bartlett, George Smathers, Herbert S. Parmet, Margaret Louise Coit, Blair Clark, Tom Hailey, Jules Davids, Angele Gingras, Evan W. Thomas, Clark Clifford, Janet Travell, Truman Capote, Cleveland Amory, Philip Nobile, James E. O'Neill, Emile de Antonio, Ormande de Kay.

CHAPTER 12

Accounts of JFK's womanizing during this period appear in Ralph G. Martin, *A Hero*, p. 113; V. De Foggia (Philip Nobile), "JFK and the Teenager," *Forum*, July 1985.

After Bobby and Ethel Kennedy moved into Hickory Hill, Jackie painted as a housewarming present a picture of the RFK household at Hyannis Port. The painting shows children running wild, hanging off the roof and sliding down bannisters, as well as an exhausted cook leaving by the back door while a new cook enters from the front.

Igor Cassini's description of the party was presented during an interview with the current author; a similar description appears in his book, *I'd Do It All Over Again*, p. 174.

Full descriptions of Black Jack Bouvier's death and funeral can be found in John H. Davis, *The Bouviers*, pp. 313-317; Kathleen Bouvier, *To Jack With Love*, pp. 275-280.

Interviews for this chapter were conducted with George Smathers, Elaine Lorillard, Charles Bartlett, Janet Auchincloss, Peter Lawford, Lem Billings, Igor Cassini, Lyle Stuart, Elisabeth Draper, Yusha Auchincloss, John H. Davis, Edie Beale.

CHAPTER 13

Bruce Gould's testimony is from his oral history transcript at the Columbia University Libraries.

The Jackie-Dean Acheson encounter is based on material from several sources, including Acheson's oral history transcript at the JFK Library. See also Walter Isaacson and Evan Thomas, *The Wise Men*, pp. 589-590. The "how one capable" letter from Jackie to Acheson, March 7, 1958, is housed in the Dean Acheson papers at Yale University Library (Rare Book and Manuscript Collection), New Haven, CT. The remainder of their correspondence is from the same source. The letter from Acheson to Harry S Truman (asterisked footnote) is from the Harry S Truman Library, Independence, MO.

Jackie on Mrs. John Sherman Cooper: Interview with Jacqueline Bouvier Kennedy Onassis, May 13, 1981. Senator John Sherman Cooper Collection, University of Kentucky Library, Lexington, KY.

Interviews for this chapter were conducted with George Smathers, Larry O'Brien, Lem Billings, Jacob K. Javits, Yusha Auchincloss, Mary Tierney, Joseph Cerrell, Nancy Dickerson, James Rousmaniere.

CHAPTER 14

The attributions to Joe Alsop are paraphrases from his oral history transcript, a copy of which is located among his papers in the manuscript division, Library of Congress, Washington, D.C. Joe Alsop gave the current author access to these papers.

Elizabeth Gatov's comments: oral history interview, John F. Kennedy Library.

Clara Shirpser's comments: *One Woman's Role in Democratic Party Politics: National, State and Local, 1950-1973*, an oral history interview conducted 1972-1973, Regional Oral History Office, The Bancroft Library.

Peter Lisagor's comments: oral history interview, JFK Library.

Valentine's Day Card: Arthur Krock papers, Princeton University Library.

Personal interviews for this chapter were conducted with Nancy Tenney Coleman, George Smathers, Peter Lawford, Dorothy Desjardins, Langdon Marvin, Slim Aarons, Larry O'Brien, Jerry Bruno, Charles Peters, Francis Lara.

CHAPTER 15

Much of the material in this chapter is of an original nature and was made available to the author by the FBI, Dept. of Justice, Washington, D.C.

The Sophia Loren anecdote can be found in Maxine Cheshire, *Maxine Cheshire, Reporter,* pp. 71-72.

The section on Janet DesRosiers is based partially on an interview with the subject, partially on a published article— Lloyd Grove, "Candidate JFK: Scribbles From the Trail," *Washington Post,* May 29, 1987.

Judith Exner's flaws and inconsistencies: On pp. 263-265 of *My Story,* Exner's book on her affair with JFK, she claims to have been treated with a series of amphetamine injections by the late Dr. Max Jacobson of New York. Dr. Jacobson's widow, Ruth Jacobson, disputes this claim, maintaining that Exner was never a patient of her husband and that there is no patient record or chart for her. Says Ruth Jacobson: "Exner knew Tommy Jacobson, Max's son, but she was never treated by my husband. She apparently heard of his treatments from other patients and then conveniently placed herself in his practice. After her book appeared, my husband, then still alive, was amazed to read that he supposedly treated her, that she was a regular patient. He absolutely denied it."

A vast discrepancy between Exner's book and the *People* magazine article exists with respect to her description of the events that ensued on April 6, 1960, when she claims to have visited JFK at his Georgetown home while Jackie was in Florida. In the 1977 book, she writes: "As we came into the living room, a large man stood up and Jack introduced us, but I have never remembered his name. . . . I gathered he was a railroad lobbyist." Eleven years later (and 28 years after the event) she has a miraculous rekindling of memory; the *People* article reads: "A third person, a lobbyist named Bill, was at dinner that night."

In both the book and article we learn that JFK and "Bill"

discussed the forthcoming West Virginia primary that evening. In the book, she describes their conversation (pp. 129-130) as follows: "There was no question in Jack's mind that he would win in West Virginia, regardless of the religious issue. The Kennedy spirit was indomitable." Yet in *People* she is quoted as saying: "[Bill] and Jack spent the evening discussing strategy for the West Virginia primary. . . . That was the one he really worried about because he was a Catholic and running against Hubert Humphrey, a Protestant, in a state that was 95 percent Protestant." The two appraisals couldn't be more contradictory.

Exner's various versions don't add up. Ovid Demaris, who helped her write *My Story,* told the present author: "Exner called me one day after the book was published and said, 'You know, I'm sorry that I didn't tell you the *whole* truth because I didn't want to hurt Jack any more than he'd been hurt, but Jack did know that I was having an affair with Giancana.' In the book, JFK supposedly wasn't aware of the affair with Giancana." Apparently having forgotten her conversation with Demaris, Exner went on to spell out a different story for Kelley. In the *People* article we read: "Only when she was no longer sleeping with Kennedy, she says, did she allow herself to drift into an affair with Giancana, who was a widower. The affair lasted just a few months, during the fall of 1962."

Although one must be highly skeptical of Exner's claims, an interesting subplot is suggested by investigative reporter Anthony Summers in *Goddess,* his 1985 biography of Marilyn Monroe. In early 1961, writes Summers (p. 237), JFK was about to be named by Peter Fairchild as one of several co-respondents in a divorce action against his Hollywood starlet wife, a woman named Judy Meredith. Others to be named included Dean Martin, Jerry Lewis and Frank Sinatra. Jerry Lewis, writes Summers, asked Judith Exner, who had worked for him at Paramount Studios, to induce Sam Giancana to intervene with this private detective, a well-known Hollywood gumshoe named Fred Otash, who was handling the divorce investigation. Giancana obliged, according to Summers, and the evidence linking JFK to Judy Meredith was destroyed. Although Otash apparently confirmed the story for Summers, Judy Meredith did not. Interviewed by Summers, she denied ever having slept with JFK.

A more recent twist on the JFK-Exner affair came to light in July 1988, when the tabloids reported that one Richard Crummitt (with the help of author Frances Leighton) was trying to get a book published claiming that he is the "love child" of JFK and Exner. The major problem is that Crummit was born in the spring of 1964, two years after Exner stopped seeing JFK.

Prince Stanislas Radziwill was first married to the present Baroness de Challot, wife of a Swiss banker. They were divorced and the marriage eventually annulled. His second wife, shipping heiress Grace Kolin, is now the Countess of Dudley. This marriage was a civil ceremony, not recognized by the church, and took place before the first was annulled.

Lee Radziwill's marriage to Michael Canfield was annulled on February 15, 1964, on the grounds that "Canfield, a non-Catholic, had no intention of having children when he married her."

President Dwight Eisenhower was as critical of the Kennedys as they were of him. In a 1965 interview for the Herbert Hoover Presidential Library oral history collection, he said: "Every day you'll find one of the Kennedys somewhere in the papers. It's Robert or Teddy or Jackie and, if they can't get anybody else, well, they get young John or somebody."

In her oral history at the JFK Library, Janet Travell discusses the precautions she took following the attempted burglary of JFK's medical records: "Regarding his records, I went around where he had been a patient in New York Hospital, in Boston and Palm Beach, wherever he had been, approached the superintendent or somebody on the staff whom I knew. All of his records were put under safekeeping and under lock and key instead of in an open office file. I tracked down almost everything that was available."

Betty Cason Hickman's comments: oral history interview, LBJ Library.

Concerning Jackie's reluctance to talk to the press, she did agree to a written interview with Fletcher Knebel, author of *Seven Days in May*, for a magazine article. Her responses were humorous. Asked if JFK remembered the birthdays of members of his immediate family, she wrote: "What a dreary question."

Tip O'Neill's expression of acute disappointment can be found in the memoir he wrote with the help of William Novak, *The Life and Political Memoirs of Speaker Tip O'Neill*, p. 101.

JFK's victory over Richard Nixon in the 1960 presidential race was by no means a clear mandate. JFK received 303 Electoral votes to Nixon's 219. He received 34,227,096 popular votes to Nixon's 34,108,546.

Jack Conway's comments: See Arthur Schlesinger, Jr., *Robert Kennedy and His Times,* p. 220.

Jackie letter to Oleg Cassini, December 30, 1960. See Oleg Cassini, *In My Own Fashion,* pp. 309-310.

Information on the Richard P. Pavlick case is taken from FBI, Secret Service and Department of Health files which were released to the author under the Freedom of Information Act.

The following were interview subjects for this chapter: Bob Phillips, Toni Bradlee, Deirdre Henderson, Herbert Parmet, Russell Hemenway, Janet DesRosiers, David Blair McCloskey, Langdon Marvin, Blair Clark, Ovid Demaris, Peter Lawford, Joseph Cerrell, George Smathers, Larry Newman, Truman Capote, Lem Billings, Norman Mailer, Harris Wofford, Joan Braden, Mary Tierney, Betty Beale, Newton Steers, Yusha Auchincloss, Robert Green, Marty Venker, Ida Large, Gregg Dodge, Gladys Dise, Earl E. T. Smith, Irving Mansfield, Slim Aarons, Mary Bass Gibson, Thomas L. Souder, Oleg Cassini, Igor Cassini, Tish Baldrige.

CHAPTER 16

The poem Robert Frost wrote for the Inauguration was "Dedication." Blinded by the bright sun, he recited "The Gift Outright."

The Mayflower Hotel luncheon and ensuing activites are described at length in John H. Davis, *The Kennedys,* pp. 260-263.

The following interviews were conducted for this chapter: Sister Parish, Oleg Cassini, Halston, Rosemary Sorrentino, John H. Davis, Miche Bouvier, Edie Beale, Peter Lawford, Ken McKnight.

CHAPTER 17

The two most useful sources for this chapter were the memoirs of J. B. West (written with Mary Lynn Kotz), *Upstairs at the White House: My Life With the First Ladies,* pp. 204-282, and the White House social files, John F. Kennedy Library, which are used here for the first time. These files were opened and made available to the author after appeal to the Director of Presidential Libraries, Washington, D.C. Encompassing thousands of cubic feet of correspondence, memos, reports and clippings, the social files provide "backstage" insight into Jackie's management of this aspect of the White House. Many of the memos and much of the information in this chapter are taken from these files. Also valuable were the files and records of the General Services Administration, 1961-1963, JFK Library, as they related to certain projects initiated by the First Lady.

Herbert H. S. Feldman comments: Herbert H. S. Feldman Diaries, vol. 7, William R. Perkins Library, Duke University Archives, manuscript division, Durham, N.C.

Pablo Casals White House concert: See White House social files.

"I would have died for President Kennedy": René Verdon to author (letter), January 22, 1986. Liz Carpenter's comments on Verdon: Elizabeth Carpenter oral history interview, LBJ Library.

Jackie and Pierre Salinger: Aside from an interview with Salinger, the former press secretary made available the manuscript of an article he had written for publication in a German magazine; all except the first note in this section are from that article. The first note (". . . I thought you had made an arrangement") appeared in an article by Salinger, "Kennedy Remembered," *McCall's*, June 1988.

Interviews for this chapter were conducted with Sister Parish, Leonard Bernstein, Franklin D. Roosevelt, Jr., Lem Billings, Sandy Fox, May Lynn Kotz, John Walker, Bernard L. Boutin, Rusty Young, Mary Gallagher, Tish Baldrige, Charlotte Curtis, Jean-Paul Ansellem, Zella West, Gladys Tartiere, Hebe Dorsey, José Ferrer, Roger Fessaguet, Craig Claiborne, Jamie Auchincloss, Pierre Salinger, Cecil Stoughton, Garnett Stackleberg, Hope Ridings Miller, Esther Van Wagoner Tufty.

CHAPTER 18

A major source for the material in this chapter was the Secret Service, Department of the Treasury, Washington, D.C., which released previously undisclosed files to the author documenting JFK's hour-by-hour movements, including records of his until-now rumored extramarital affairs.

The frequently reported story concerning Dave Powers and the Hollywood actress first appeared in Traphes Bryant and Frances Spitz Leighton, *Dog Days at the White House: The Outrageous Memoirs of the Presidential Kennel Keeper*, p. 37.

Philip Nobile: See V. De Foggia, "JFK and the Teenager," *Forum*, July 1985.

Interviews for this chapter were conducted with Marty Venker, Mrs. Barnard Lamotte, Doris Lilly, Peter Lawford,

Leslie Devereux, Stanley Tretick, Howard Oxenberg, Lem Billings, Liz Smith, Marianne Strong, Purette Spiegler, Francis Lara, Philippe de Bausset, John Walker, Langdon Marvin, Pierre Salinger, Truman Capote, Toni Bradlee, Joe Acquaotta.

CHAPTER 19

This chapter is based largely on the personal archives of the late Dr. Max Jacobson, released to the author by his widow, Ruth Jacobson, containing medical records, appointment books, tapes, photographs, courtroom documents, travel logs, as well as a lengthy unpublished memoir by Dr. Jacobson completed shortly before his death in 1980.

The "space" dog sent by Khrushchev to the White House was named Pushinka. He become Caroline's pet, in addition to her ponies, Macaroni and Tex, and a pair of parakeets, Maybelle and Bluebelle.

When the Cuban Missile Crisis began, Jackie, who had been staying at Glen Ora, returned to the White House. "I want to be with my husband," she announced, though she could have opted for the relative safety of Peanut Island, the presidential bomb shelter off Palm Beach. His wife's presence didn't stop JFK from lusting after other women. In *Tell It to the King*, author Larry King relates an anecdote involving an attractive secretary who had been sent to the White House from the Department of Commerce to work for Robert McNamara. The secretary was present the day JFK and his advisors waited to see whether Khrushchev intended to comply with America's ultimatum or whether World War III was about to begin. Suddenly JFK noticed the new secretary. "Who's that?" he asked. "She's filling in," responded McNamara. JFK leaned closer to McNamara. "Bob, I want her name and her number," he said. "We may avert war here tonight."

Interviews for this chapter were conducted with Tom Jacobson, Ruth Jacobson, Ken McKnight, Michael Samek, Pat Suzuki, Chuck Spalding, Claude Pepper, Truman Capote, Alexandre, Hubert de Givenchy, Consuelo Crespi, Arthur Goldberg, Godfrey McHugh, Ruth Mosse, John H. Davis.

CHAPTER 20

Files, papers, correspondence, memos and other materials concerning the White House restoration project have been secured from a number of sources, including the National

Gallery of Art (Washington, D.C.); Smithsonian Institution (Washington, D.C.); the White House social files (JFK Library); Angier Biddle Duke Papers (Duke University Library, Durham, NC); National Geographic Society (Washington, D.C.); General Services Administration files (JFK Library); the Franco Scalamandré Collection (New York); the Henry Francis du Pont Collection, Winterthur Museum and Gardens (Greenville, DE); Bernard M. Baruch Papers, Princeton University Library, as well as Milton Lunin and Truman Capote who provided the author with copies of several pertinent letters. Many of these documents appear in print here for the first time.

Other valuable sources include J. B. West's *Upstairs at the White House* and Maxine Cheshire's six-part series on the restoration project which appeared in the *Washington Post* (August-September 1962.).

"To locate authentic furnishings . . .": White House social files.

"I hope you . . .": James Fosburgh to Jackie, n.d., James Fosburgh Papers, Library of Congress.

The Walter Annenberg anecdote appears in a slightly different form in John Cooney, *The Annenbergs,* pp. 265-266.

"Perhaps you know . . .": Jackie to Bernard Baruch, Bernard M. Baruch Papers, Princeton University Libraries.

"I so like the rug . . .": Jackie to J. B. West, *Upstairs at the White House.*

"I really am not pleased . . .": Jackie to Bernard Boutin, April 7, 1963, GSA files, JFK Library.

"Dear Bernie . . .": Jackie to Bernard Boutin, November 8, 1963, GSA files.

"How I regret . . .": Chris Preuty Rosenfeld to David Finley, David Finley correspondence file, White House Historical Association, Library of Congress.

"Significant American writings" and other excerpts: Jackie to James T. Babb, April 30, 1963, Yale University Library, New Haven, CT.

"All former first ladies . . .": Memorandum for the Record, John S. D. Eisenhower, March 7, 1962, Dwight D. Eisenhower Library, Abilene, Kansas.

Personal interviews for this chapter were conducted with John Carl Warnecke, Angier Biddle Duke, Clement E. Conger, Lorraine Pearce, Truman Capote, Clark Clifford, Carson Glass, Conrad Wirth, Nash Castro, Robert L. Breeden, Donald J. Crump, Adriana Scalamandré Bitter, Harris Wofford, Blair Clark, Perry Wolff, Norman Mailer, Richard Goodwin.

CHAPTER 21

"The way we spend our evenings . . .": See *Newsweek* January 1, 1962.

The references to J. B. West are from his book, *Upstairs at the White House,* p. 234.

"Because she was not . . .": Charles R. Burrows Oral History, JFK Library.

"A Sphinx is . . .": Jackie to Adlai Stevenson, February 4, 1963, Adlai E. Stevenson Papers, Princeton University Libraries.

"The whole atmosphere . . .": Jackie to Stevenson, February 9, 1963, Stevenson Papers, Princeton.

"President Kennedy relied . . .": Arthur Schlesinger, Jr., letter to author, July 7, 1986.

Galbraith defended himself: John Kenneth Galbraith letter to author, March 23, 1987.

Erotic carvings: See Ralph G. Martin, *A Hero for Our Times,* p. 337.

Diaries: See Noël Coward, *The Noël Coward Diaries,* p. 476.

C. L. Sulzberger: See C. L. Sulzberger, *The Last of the Giants,* pp. 914-916.

August Heckscher: August Heckscher Oral History, JFK Library.

"In case anybody wants to know . . .": Letitia Baldrige to Evelyn Lincoln, October 27, 1961, White House social files, JFK Library.

"People who wish to leave gifts . . .": Baldrige to Angier Biddle Duke, May 22, 1963, White House social files.

"Mme Ikeda . . .": Tish Baldrige memo to Angier Biddle Duke, June 30, 1961, White House social files.

Jackie's excessive spending is dealt with in some depth by Mary Gallagher, *My Life With Jacqueline Kennedy,* and by Ben Bradlee, *Conversations With Kennedy.*

Arthur Schlesinger: See Arthur M. Schlesinger, Jr., *Robert Kennedy and His Times,* pp. 594-596.

Gore Vidal's version: Vidal letter to author, May 10, 1986.

Interviews for this chapter were conducted with Jerry Bruno, Esther Van Wagoner Tufty, Jane Suydam, Alice Gaither, Mrs. Anthony Hass, Oleg Cassini, Igor Cassini, Edie Beale, Truman Capote, Lem Billings, Ruth Montgomery, George Smathers, Ralph G. Martin, Kathy Tollerton, Charles Bartlett, Charlotte Curtis, David Ormsby-Gore (Lord Harlech), Robert McNamara, Chester V. Clifton, Richard Goodwin,

Joan Braden, Endicott "Chubb" Peabody, Henry C. Lindner, Pat Suzuki, Jamie Auchincloss, Blair Clark, George Plimpton, Peter Morrison, Richard Zoerink.

CHAPTER 22

In addition to the JFK affairs mentioned in this book, there were apparently others. Ralph G. Martin, *A Hero for Our Time,* p. 444, quotes CBS correspondent Robert Pierpoint as having seen JFK emerge from a Palm Beach cottage one morning with a young woman. They embraced and then stepped into JFK's limo, where "the woman disappeared into the President's arms." Pierpoint next saw one of JFK's sisters drive up in a convertible, cruise over to her brother's car, and call out, "Come on, Mildred!" Mildred gave the President a last lingering kiss before leaving him and joining his sister.

"Kennedy never thought . . .": India Edwards oral history, November 10, 1975. Harry S. Truman Library.

Ellen Rometsch: Fearful that Rometsch would "name names," including that of his brother, the President, Attorney General Robert Kennedy sent La Vern Duffy, a close friend and Senate investigator, to Germany (following Rometsch's deportation) to speak to her and "calm her down." J. Edgar Hoover used Rometsch and other sexual scandals to "blackmail" JFK into giving him free reign in such instances as his one-man assault on Martin Luther King.

The Profumo case: The author had access to FBI files; in addition the following books were consulted: Stephen Dorril, *Honeytrap,* 1987; Phillip Knightley and Caroline Kennedy, *An Affair of State,* 1987.

Interviews were conducted with Peter Lawford, Stanley Tretick, Ted H. Jordan, Tory Pryor, Mac Kilduff, Lem Billings, Toni Bradlee, James Angleton, Cord Meyer, Jr., Blair Clark.

CHAPTER 23

"It is just one . . .": Jackie to Basil Rathbone, April 1, 1963. Text of this letter appears in 1970 catalogue—Paul Richards Auction House, Boston, MA.

"Shall I tell . . .": Jackie to Rathbone, April 2, 1963, Richards Auction House catalogue.

" 'So many people . . .' ": Jackie interview, University of Kentucky oral history collection.

Frances Parkinson Keyes to Lady Bird, May 1, 1963, White House social files.

Virginia Livingston Hunt to Betty Beale, March 30, 1963, White House social files.

Memo from Tish Baldridge to Jackie, March 4, 1963, White House social files.

Memo from Tish Baldridge to Jackie, April 12, 1963, White House social files.

"been not only playing . . .": RFK oral history, JFK Library.

"I cannot tell you . . .": The complete text of this letter can be found in Louis Nizer, *Reflections Without Mirrors*, pp. 414-416. Nizer represented Igor Cassini in his legal case.

"Ich bin ein Berliner . . .": See Joel Makower, *Boom! Talkin' About Our Generation*, 1985.

Barry Goldwater: See Larry King with Peter Occhiogrosso, *Tell It to the King*, 1988.

Villa Serbelloni: See Thomas J. Schoenbaum, *Waging Peace & War: Dean Rusk in the Truman, Kennedy and Johnson Years*, p. 282.

"That petulant, self-indulgent mouth . . .": Jackie's candid reaction to Gov. John Connally is one of many fragments she later forced William Manchester to remove from his book, *Death of a President*. Many of these fragments were later published in the press during the lengthy legal skirmish over the book's contents.

Interviews for this chapter were conducted with Eilene Slocum, Kay Lepercq, Betty Beale, Purette Spiegler, Barbara Coleman, Oleg Cassini, Igor Cassini, Doris Francisco, Lois Wright, Edie Beale, John B. White, Yusha Auchincloss, Sylvia Blake, Claiborne Pell, Nuala Pell, Franklin D. Roosevelt, Jr., Suzanne Perrin Kloman, Geroge Smathers, Larry O'Brien, Hervé Alphand, Sarah McClendon, Jessie Stearns, Godfrey McHugh, George-Michael Evica.

CHAPTER 24

In an FBI report filed on August 3, 1964 by Special Agent M. C. Clements, Jack Ruby is quoted as saying that he killed Lee Harvery Oswald "to save Mrs. Kennedy the ordeal of coming back to the trial of Oswald in Dallas." Ruby later denied ever having made such a comment to an FBI agent.

Letter (November 26, 1963) from Jackie to LBJ, and from LBJ to Jackie (December 1, 1963): LBJ Library.

De Gaulle's comments on JFK: *Time,* November 23, 1970.

Interviews for this chapter were conducted with Mac Kilduff, Godfrey McHugh, Chester V. Clffton, Jack Valenti, Cecil

Stoughton, Larry O'Brien, Robert McNamara, Janet Auchincloss, Angier Biddle Duke, Ramsey Clark, John H. Davis, Edward Jay Epstein, John Hersey, Teddy White, George-Michael Evica.

CHAPTER 25

"Don't be frightened. . . .": Lady Bird Johnson, *A White House Diary*, p. 11.

"I remember going over. . . .": Jacqueline Kennedy Onassis oral history interview, January 11, 1974, LBJ Library.

"I had a strange feeling. . . .": Liz Carpenter oral history, LBJ Library.

"The various Mrs. Kennedys . . .": Arthur Krock oral history, LBJ Library.

"It was Lyndon. . . .": A somewhat altered version of this story appears in Robert Parker, *Capitol Hill in Black and White*, p. 133.

Billy Baldwin: See Billy Baldwin, *Billy Baldwin Remembers*, pp. 109-113.

Evelyn Lincoln: This anecdote appears in several books, including John H. Davis, *The Kennedys*, p. 509.

Bobby "bossed his sister-in-law around. . . .": Neil Mac-Neil oral history, Herbert Hoover Presidential Library, West Branch, Iowa.

Joan Braden and RFK: See "The Braden Proposal," *Washington Post*, September 8, 1987.

Dorothy Schiff and Jackie: See David Porter, *Men, Money and Magic: The Story of Dorothy Schiff*, pp. 290-298.

"I believe people know. . . .": Jackie to Bennett Cerf, October 1, 1964, Bennett Cerf Papers, Columbia University Libraries, New York.

She telephoned Cerf: Bennett Cerf oral history, Columbia University Libraries.

"You must have left. . . .": Jackie to LBJ, November 30, 1965, LBJ Library.

"It was such an emotional . . .": Jackie to LBJ, May 16, 1965, LBJ Library.

Interviews for this chapter were conducted with Judy White, Bernard Boutin, Franklin D. Roosevelt, Jr., John H. Davis, Robert McNamara, Michelle Putnam, Lem Billings, Jacqueline Hirsch, William Joyce, Richard Goodwin, Samuel H. Beer, Philip Johnson, Jerry Bruno, Pierre Salinger, Orville Freeman, Rosemary Sorrentino, Phyllis Cerf Wagner, Joan Braden, Marty Venker, Charles Addams, Norman Mailer, Kay Lepercq, Phil Strider, Dick Banks, Flora Whitney Miller,

Peter Lawford, Stanley Tretick, George Plimpton, Claiborne Pell, Nuala Pell, Bev Bogert, C. Douglas Dillon.

CHAPTER 26

"Just a word of warning. . . .": Jackie to Lady Bird, April 1966, LBJ Library.

JFK, Jr., burns: Secret Service files report, July 6, 1966.

"The changes I am talking about. . . .": Jackie letter to William Manchester, November 28, 1966, courtesy: Harold Matson.

"Dear Jackie. . . .": LBJ to Jackie, December 16, 1966, LBJ Library.

"And when we agreed. . . .": William Attwood oral history, Columbia University Libraries. Numerous additional sources were consulted regarding the Manchester book controversy, including *Time, Newsweek, The New York Times* and *Chicago Tribune.* Also useful was William Manchester, *Controversy and Other Essays in Journalism, 1950-1975,* 1976.

Odd footnote: See Arthur M. Schlesinger, Jr., *Robert Kennedy and His Times,* p. 898.

"After we had been in Ireland. . . .": Jackie to Thomas T. Hendrick, August 7, 1967, Harry S Truman Library, Independence, MO.

"I never imagined. . . .": Jackie to Hendrick, April 19, 1968, Truman Library.

"Please be merciful. . . .": Adlai Stevenson to Jackie, May 30, 1984, Princeton University Libraries.

"Welcome to New York. . . .": Stevenson to Jackie, September 16, 1964, Princeton.

"Would you like to go . . . .": Stevenson to Jackie, December 17, 1964.

"Would you like to be . . . .": Stevenson to Jackie, March 3, 1965.

Robert Lowell and Jackie: See C. David Heymann, *American Aristocracy: The Lives and Times of James Russell, Amy and Robert Lowell,* as well as Ian Hamilton, *Robert Lowell: A Biography.* Lowell's correspondence with Jackie is housed at the Houghton Library, Harvard University, Cambridge, MA.

Personal interviews for this chapter were conducted with Charles Bartlett, Toni Bradlee, Charles Addams, John B. White, Monique Van Vooren, Paul Oskar Kristeller, Ken McKnight, Ruth Jacobson, George Plimpton, Ivo Lupis, C. Douglas Dillon, Lewis Murdock, Sharon Churcher, Bev Walter, Patricia Shea, Scott Shea, Jay Rutherford, Angier

Biddle Duke, Cleveland Amory, Dick Banks, Truman Capote, William Manchester, Richard Goodwin, Evan W. Thomas, Harold Matson, Paul Mathias, Mary DeGrace, David Susskind, Thomas Moorer, Thomas T. Hendrick, Blair Clark, Roswell Gilpatric, Agnes Ash, Madelin Gilpatric, Marianne Strong, Helene Gaillet.

CHAPTER 27

Renee Luttgen, a former employee and companion of Dr. Henry Lax, supplied the author with copies of correspondence, diaries, photographs and other memorabilia pertaining to Lax.

Pete Hamill and Shirley MacLaine: See Jean Stein and George Plimpton, *American Journey: The Times of Robert Kennedy,* pp. 158-159.

Interviews for this chapter were conducted with Renee Luttgen, Bernard Fensterwald, Roswell Gilpatric, Larry Newman, Truman Capote, Jonathan Tapper, Helene Gaillet, Lynn Alpha Smith, Doris Lilly, Lilly Lawrence, Maria Papastamou, Jerome Zerbe, Charlotte Curtis, Selwa "Lucky" Roosevelt, Sylvia Blake, Pierre Salinger, Edie Beale.

CHAPTER 28

Portrait artist Aaron Shikler recently completed the official White House portraits of Ronald and Nancy Reagan.

"As you know, the thought . . .": Jackie to Pat Nixon, first published in Julie Nixon Eisenhower, *Pat Nixon: The Untold Story,* p. 309.

In a proposal for a book never written: The Johnny Meyer book proposal was prepared by Meyer with the help of the late George Clifford. It was made available to the current author by Mrs. Gerry Clifford.

Johnny Meyer's role in the Christina Onassis-Joe Bolker marriage is described in detail in the Meyer-Clifford book proposal.

Interviews for this chapter were conducted with Costa Gratsos, Lynn Alpha Smith, Roswell Gilpatric, Marie-Helene Rothschild, Jacques Harvey, Maia Calligas, Rosemary Sorrentino, Alexis Miotis, William Joyce, Doris Ford, Angelo Katopodis, Yvette Bertin, Mrs. J. Boyer, Guyot de Renty, John Rigas, Roger Viard, Truman Capote, Robert David Lyon Gardiner, Helga Wagner, John Karavlas, Renee Luttgen, Fanny Warburg, Carol Rosenwald, Sally Bitterman, Marjorie Housepian Dobkin, Marty Venker, James

Kalafatis, Ruth Jacobson, Ron Galella, Niki Goulandris, Aaron Shikler, Roger Bentley.

CHAPTER 29

A version of Andy Warhol's Brooklyn Museum visit with Jackie and Lee appeared in his book, *Andy Warhol's Exposures*, 1978.

Interviews for this chapter were conducted with Ron Galella, Betty Galella, James Kalafatis, Costa Gratsos, Roy Cohn, Lynn Alpha Smith, Carol Selig, Jacques Harvey, Beny Aristea, Edie Beale, Bouvier Beale, William J. vanden Heuvel, Doris Francisco, Lilly Lawrence, Cindy Adams, Helene Rochas, Pat Suzuki, Ruth Jacobson, Chuck Spalding, Helene Gaillet, Pierre Salinger, Peter Beard, Jonas Mekas, David Maysles, Andy Warhol.

CHAPTER 30

"Goddam money": See L. J. Davis, *Onassis, Aristotle and Christina*, p. 182.

The corresponding book on Atget was *Atget's Gardens* authored by William Howard Adams, published by Doubleday in 1979. Jackie wrote an introduction to the book.

Maria Callas was permitted a tearful last visit: Callas's last years were lonely and meaningless. She had more or less abandoned her singing career, and she rejected her husband Meneghini's offer of a reconciliation after Ari's death. Callas died of a heart attack in September 1977, two years after Ari.

Personal interviews were conducted with Costa Gratsos, Susan Panopoulos, Paul Mathias, Cornell Capa, Helen Vlachos, Roy Cohn, Jack Anderson, Les Whitten, Jacques Harvey, Renee Luttgen, Ezio Petersen, James Brady, Christina Onassis, Truman Capote.

CHAPTER 31

R. Sargent Schriver, Jr., ran in two political campaigns. In 1972, he succeeded Senator Thomas Eagleton as George McGovern's running mate during the presidential election. Eagleton had withdrawn from the Democratic ticket after it was disclosed that he had undergone recent psychiatric treatment, including electroshock therapy. In 1976 Shriver announced his candidacy for the presidency, performed poorly in four primaries (New Hampshire, Vermont, Massachusetts and Illinois), and withdrew. Jackie donated $25,000 to his 1976 campaign.

The Don Cook and Sarah Lazin interviews originally appeared in a *People* magazine profile of Jackie: Giola Dillberto, "A Working Woman," *People,* June 18, 1984.

Interviews for this chapter were conducted with Franklin D. Roosevelt, Jr., Lillian Biko, Michelle Putnam, Thomas H. Guinzburg, Barbara Burn, Linda Grant De Pauw, Muffie Brandon, Bryan Holme, Candace Fischer, Audrey del Rosario, Rod Gibson, Andy Warhol, Rosey Grier, Aileen Mehle, Irving Mansfield, Richie Berlin, Rosamond Bernier, Gloria Steinem, Gloria Emerson, Doris Francisco, Edie Beale, Sandy Richardson, Mimi Kazon.

CHAPTER 32

"I'm afraid he's going to grow up to be a fruit. . . .": See Bill Adler, *The Kennedy Children,* pp. 83-114. Adler's book also contains information on the night JFK Jr. was forced to sleep in his late father's White House bed.

"A number of problems arose during the construction of the house": Regarding his decision not to ground Jackie's stainless steel roof, architect Hugh Jacobson said: "This is insane, childish—as though I had invented stainless steel. Steel is superior to copper. Copper is a better conductor of electricity. I've never had any of my buildings hit by lightning." Regarding the pocket screen system, he said: "That's not an architectural error. That's called nature. If you put in an insect screen that will keep them out, you will not be able to look out the window because it's so dense. It's a thing I've designed that I've used on about 20 houses." Concerning the silo, he said: "If a farmer built a silo higher than the ridge of the barn and the good city Fathers came up and said, 'Take it down,' do you think the farmer would do it? Not on your life."

Maurice Tempelsman: Among the published sources consulted by the author are the following: Edward Jay Epstein, *The Rise and Fall of Diamonds. The Shattering of a Brilliant Illusion;* Jonathan Kwitny, *Endless Enemies: The Making of an Unfriendly World;* Maxine Cheshire, "VlP: Jackie Onassis' American Tycoon," *Washington Post,* June 25, 1980; Paul Gibson, "De Beers: Can a Cartel Be Forever?" *Forbes,* May 28, 1979; Louis Kraar, "Maurice Tempelsman's African Connections," *Fortune,* November 15, 1982.

The Department of Justice file on Tempelsman: The Maurice Tempelsman file (#60-143-13), September 12, 1974, was compiled as part of a 1974 Dept. of Justice antitrust investigation of international diamond operations with particular attention paid to De Beers.

Interviews for this chapter were conducted with Betty McMahon, Harrison Rainie, Tom Carney, Tracey Dewart, Mimi Kazon, Christina Goodman, David Kennedy, Nye Heron, Carl Killingsworth, Joy Gross, Richard Meryman, John Marquand, Jr., Newton Cope, Renee Luttgen, Sam Donaldson, Arthur Kirson, Bill Adler, Frank Wangler, Hugh Jacobson, George Goulart, Jon Klingensmith, Mike Rotando, Steven DeFelice, Steven Gramkowski, Rose Schreiber, Nancy Bastien, Jonathan Kwitny, Edward Jay Epstein, Truman Capote, Renee Vago.

CHAPTER 33

Nancy Reagan and Jackie at Katherine Graham's home on Martha's Vineyard: See Michael K. Deaver with Mickey Herskowitz, *Behind the Scenes*, pp. 118-119.

Ron Galella: Courtroom testimony is from a transcript of the trial which took place December 13-16, 1981, at U.S. District Court, Southern District of New York (Case #70 civ. 4348).

"To the great excitement . . .": "Parties," *Vanity Fair*, December 1985.

Personal interviews for this chapter were conducted with Earl Blackwell, Philip Johnson, Rosey Grier, Sanford Friedman, Vincent Roppate, Ron Galella, Betty Galella, Barbara Reynolds, Ron Smith, Richard A. Kurnit, Richard de Combray, Roslyn Targ, John H. Davis, Marianne Strong, Eugene Girden, Tom Carney, Ronald Feldman, Brent Saville, Harrison Rainie, Sharon Churcher, Mary Tierney, George Plimpton, Bouvier Beale, Yusha Auchincloss, Eilene Slocum, Sylvia Blake, Dick Banks, Dorothy Desjardins, Alan Pryce-Jones, Jamie Auchincloss, Michelle Putnam, Rose Schreiber, Casey Hughes, Fletcher Hodges, Norman Mailer, Jane Yeoman, Mimi Kazon, Charlotte Curtis, S. Cary Welch, Richard Zoerink, Peter Evans.

Bibliography

Aarons, Slim. *A Wonderful Time: An Intimate Portrait of the Good Life*. New York: Harper & Row, 1974.

Abbe, Kathryn McLaughlin, and Frances McLaughlin Gill. *Twins on Twins*. New York: Clarkson N. Potter, 1980.

Acheson, Dean. *Power and Diplomacy*. Cambridge, Mass.: Harvard University Press, 1958.

Adams, William Howard. *Atget's Gardens*. Garden City, N.Y.: Doubleday, 1979.

Adler, Bill. *The Kennedy Children*. New York: Franklin Watts, 1980.

Agel, Jerome and Eugene Boe. *22 Fires*. New York: Bantam, 1977.

Alexander, Lois K. *Blacks in the History of Fashion*. New York: Harlem Institute of Fashion, 1982.

Alphand, Hervé. *L'étonnement d'etre: Journal 1939-1973*. Paris: Fayard, 1977.

Alsop, Susan Mary. *To Marietta From Paris 1945-1960*. Garden City, N.Y.: Doubleday, 1975.

Amory, Cleveland. *Who Killed Society?* New York: Harper & Brothers, 1960.

Anderson, Jack. *Washington Exposé*. Washington, D.C.: Public Affairs Press, 1967.

Angeli, Daniel and Jean-Paul Dousset. *Private Pictures*. New York: Viking, 1980.

Anger, Kenneth. *Hollywood Babylon*. San Francisco: Straight Arrow, 1975.

————. *Hollywood Babylon II*. New York: Dutton, 1984.

Anson, Robert Sam. *"They've Killed the President!": The Search for the Murderers of John F. Kennedy*. New York: Bantam, 1975.

Ardoin, John and Gerald Fitzgerald. *Callas*. London: Thames & Hudson, 1974.

Aronson, Steven M.L. *Hype*. New York: William Morrow, 1983.

Astor, Brook. *Footprints: An Autobiography*. New York: Doubleday, 1980.

Auchincloss, Joanna Russell and Caroline Auchincloss Fowler. *The Auchincloss Family*. Freeport, ME: The Dingley Press, 1957.

Bacall, Lauren. *By Myself*. New York: Knopf, 1978.

Bacon, James. *Made in Hollywood*. Chicago: Contemporary Books, 1977.

Bair, Marjorie, ed. *Jacqueline Kennedy in the White House*. New York: Paperback Library, 1963.

Baker, Bobby. *Wheeling and Dealing, Confessions of a Capitol Hill Operator*. New York: Norton, 1978.

Baker, Carlos. *Ernest Hemingway. A Life Story*. New York: Charles Scribner's Sons, 1969.

Baldridge, Letitia. *Letitia Baldridge's Complete Guide to Executive Manners*. New York: Rawson, 1985.

—————. *Of Diamonds and Diplomats*. Boston: Houghton Mifflin, 1968.

Baldwin, Billy. *Billy Baldwin Remembers*. New York: Harcourt Brace Jovanovich, 1974.

Barrow, Andrew. *Gossip: A History of High Society From 1920 to 1970*. New York: Coward, McCann & Geoghegan, 1978.

Bayh, Marvella. *Marvella, A Personal Journey*. New York: Harcourt Brace Jovanovich, 1979.

Beaton, Cecil. *Self Portrait With Friends: The Selected Diaries of Cecil Beaton 1926-1974*, edited by Richard Buckle. New York: Times Books, 1979.

Beschloss, Micael R. *Kennedy and Roosevelt: The Uneasy Alliance*. New York: Norton, 1980.

Bevington, Helen. *Along Came the Witch: A Journal in the 1960's*. New York: Harcourt Brace Jovanovich, 1976.

Birmingham, Stephen. *Jacqueline Bouvier Kennedy Onassis*. New York: Grosset & Dunlap, 1978.

—————. *Real Lace: America's Irish Rich*. New York: Harper & Row, 1973.

—————. *"The Rest of Us": The Rise of America's Eastern European Jews*. Boston: Little, Brown, 1984.

—————. *The Right People: A Portrait of the American Social Establishment*. Boston: Little, Brown, 1968.

Bishop, Jim. *A Day in the Life of President Kennedy*. New York: Random House, 1964.

—————. *The Day Kennedy Was Shot*. New York: Funk & Wagnalls, 1968.

Blackwell, Earl. *Earl Blackwell's Celebrity Register*. Towson, Mass.: Times Publishing Group, 1986.

Blair, Joan and Clay, Jr. *The Search for JFK*. New York: Berkley, 1976.

Blakey, G. Robert and Richard N. Billings. *The Plot to Kill the President*. New York: Times Books, 1981.

Boller, Paul F., Jr. *Presidential Anecdotes*. New York; Oxford: Oxford University Press, 1958.

Bouvier, Jacqueline and Lee. *One Special Summer*. New York: Delacorte Press, 1974.

Bouvier, John Vernou, Jr. *Our Forebears*. Privately printed, 1931, 1942, 1944, 1947.

Bouvier, Kathleen. *To Jack With Love, Black Jack Bouvier: A Remembrance*. New York: Kensington, 1979.

Bradlee, Benjamin C. *Conversations With Kennedy*. New York: Norton, 1975.

Brady, Frank. *Onassis, An Extravagant Life*. Englewood Cliffs, N.J.: Prentice-Hall, 1977.

Branch, Taylor. *Parting the Waters: America in the King Years*. New York: Simon & Schuster, 1988.

Brauer, Carl M. *John F. Kennedy and the Second Reconstruction*. New York: Columbia University Press.

Bray, Howard. *The Pillars of the Post: The Making of a News Empire in Washington*. New York: W.W. Norton, 1980.

Brolin, Brent C. *The Battle of St. Bart's: A Tale of Heroism, Connivance and Bumbling*. New York: William Morrow, 1988.

Bruno, Jerry and Jeff Greenfield. *The Advance Man*. New York: William Morrow, 1971.

Bryan, J., III, and Charles J. V. Murphy. *The Windsor Story*. New York: William Morrow, 1979.

Bryant, Traphes and Frances Spatz Leighton. *Dog Days at the White House: The Outrageous Memoirs of the Presidential Kennel Keeper*. New York: Macmillan, 1975.

Buchwald, Art. *The Establishment Is Alive and Well in Washington*. New York: Putnam, 1968.

Buck, Pearl S. *The Kennedy Women*. New York: Cowles, 1970.

Burns, James MacGregor. *Edward Kennedy and the Camelot Legacy*. New York: Norton, 1976.

_____. *John Kennedy: A Political Profile*. New York: Harcourt Brace Jovanovich, 1960.

Butler, Paul F., Jr. *Presidential Wives*. Oxford: Oxford University Press, 1988.

Cafarakis, Christian, with Jacques Harvey, *The Fabulous Onassis: His Life and Loves*. New York: William Morrow, 1972.

Cameron, Gail. *Rose, A Biography of Rose Fitzgerald Kennedy*. New York: Putnam, 1971.

Canfield, Michael and Alan Weberman. *Coup d'Etat in America: The CIA and the Assassination of John F. Kennedy.* New York: Third Press, 1975.

Capote, Truman. *Answered Prayers, The Unfinished Novel.* New York: Random House, 1987.

————. *A Capote Reader.* New York: Random House, 1987.

————. *Music for Chameleons.* New York: Random House, 1975.

Caroli, Betty Boyd. *First Ladies.* New York; Oxford: Oxford University Press, 1987.

Carpozi, George, Jr. *The Hidden Side of Jacqueline Kennedy.* New York: Pyramid, 1967.

Carter, Ernestine. *Magic Names of Fashion.* Englewood Cliffs, N.J.: Prentice-Hall, 1980.

Carter, Rosalynn. *First Lady From Plains.* Boston: Houghton Mifflin, 1984.

Cassini, Igor. *I'd Do It All Over Again.* New York, Putnam, 1977.

Cassini, Oleg. *In My Own Fashion, An Autobiography.* New York: Simon & Schuster, 1987.

Cerf, Bennett. *At Random: The Reminiscences of Bennett Cerf,* New York: Random House, 1977.

Chellis, Joan. *Living With the Kennedys: The Joan Kennedy Story.* New York: Simon & Schuster, 1985.

Cheshire, Maxine. *Maxine Cheshire, Reporter.* Boston: Houghton Mifflin, 1978.

Childs, Marquis. *Witness to Power.* New York: McGraw-Hill, 1975.

Churcher, Sharon. *New York Confidential.* New York: Crown, 1986.

Churchill, Sarah. *Keep on Dancing: An Autobiography.* New York: Coward, McCann & Geoghegan, 1981.

Clinch, Nancy Gager. *The Kennedy Neurosis.* New York: Grosset & Dunlap, 1973.

Colby, Gerard. *DuPont Dynasty.* Secaucus, N.J.: Lyle Stuart, 1984.

Collier, Peter and David Horowitz. *The Kennedys: An American Drama.* New York: Summit, 1984.

A Concise Compendium of The Warren Commission Report on the Assassination of John F. Kennedy. New York: Popular Library, 1964.

Cooper, Diana. *The Rainbow Comes and Goes.* Boston: Houghton Mifflin, 1958.

Cooney, John. *The American Pope: The Life and Times of Francis Cardinal Spellman.* New York: Times Books, 1984.

————. *The Annenbergs*. New York: Simon & Schuster, 1982.

Cormier, Frank. *Presidents Are People Too*. Washington, D.C.: Public Affairs Press, 1966.

Coward, Noël. *The Noël Coward Diaries*. Edited by Graham Payn and Sheridan Morley. Boston: Little; Brown, 1982.

Cowles, Virginia. *The Astors*. New York: Knopf, 1979.

Curtis, Charlotte. *First Lady*. New York: Pyramid, 1962.

————. *The Rich and Other Atrocities*. New York: Harper & Row, 1976.

Cutler, John Henry. *Cardinal Cushing of Boston*. New York: Hawthorn Books, 1970.

Dallas, Rita and Jeanina Ratcliffe. *The Kennedy Case*. New York: Putnam, 1975.

Damore, Leo. *The Cape Cod Years of John Fitzgerald Kennedy*. Englewood Cliffs, N.J.: Prentice-Hall, 1967.

————. *Senatorial Privilege: The Chappaquidick Cover-Up*. Washington, D.C.: Regnery-Gateway, 1988.

Dareff, Hal. *Jacqueline Kennedy: A Portrait in Courage*. New York: Parents' Magazine Press, 1966.

David, Lester. *Joan—The Reluctant Kennedy, A Biographical Profile*. New York: Funk & Wagnalls, 1974.

David, Lester and Irene. *Bobby Kennedy.: The Making of a Folk Hero*. New York: Dodd, Mead, 1986.

Davis, Deborah. *Katherine the Great: Katherine Graham and the Washington Post*. New York: Harcourt Brace Jovanovich, 1979.

Davis, John H. *The Bouviers, Portrait of an American Family:* New York: Farrar, Strauss & Giroux, 1969.

————. *The Kennedys: Dynasty and Disaster 1848-1983*. New York: McGraw-Hill, 1984.

Davis, L.J. *Onassis, Aristotle and Christina*. New York: St. Martin's, 1986.

Davis, William and Christina Tree. *The Kennedy Library*. Exton, Pa.: Schiffer, 1980.

Davison, Jean. *Oswald's Game*. New York: Norton, 1983.

Deaver, Michael K., with Mickey Herskowitz. *Behind the Scenes*. New York: William Morrow, 1988.

de Combray, Richard. *Goodbye Europe, A Novel in Six Parts*. Garden City, N.Y.: Doubleday, 1983.

de Gaulle, Charles. *Lettres, Notes et Carnets, Janvier 1964-Juin 1966*. Paris: PLON, 1987.

Demaris, Ovid. *The Last Mafioso: The Treacherous World of Jimmy Fratianno*. New York: Times Books, 1981.

De Pauw, Linda Grant. *Remember the Ladies: Women of America, 1750-1815*. New York: Viking 1976.

de Toledano, Ralph. *R.F.K.: The Man Who Would Be President*. New York: Putnam, 1967.

Devi, Gayatri and Santha Rama Rau. *A Princess Remembers*. Garden City, N.Y.: Anchor, 1985.

Dickerson, Nancy. *Among Those Present: A Reporter's View of Twenty-five Years in Washington*. New York: Random House, 1976.

Donovan, Robert J. *PT 109: John F. Kennedy in World War II*. New York: McGraw-Hill, 1961.

Drosnin, Michael. *Citizen Hughes*. New York: Holt, Rinehart and Winston, 1985.

Dorril, Stephen. *Honeytrap*. London: Weidenfeld and Nicholson, 1987.

Eban, Abba. *Abba Eban: An Autobiography*. New York: Random House, 1977.

Eisenhower, Julie Nixon. *Pat Nixon: The Untold Story*. New York: Simon & Schuster, 1986.

Englund, Steven. *Grace of Monaco*. Garden City, N.Y.: Doubleday, 1984.

Epstein, Edward Jay. *Inquest: The Warren Commission and the Establishment of the Truth*. New York: Viking, 1966.
————. *The Rise and Fall of Diamonds, The Shattering of a Brilliant Illusion*. New York: Simon & Schuster, 1982.

Evans, Peter. *Ari: The Life and Times of Aristotle Onassis*. New York: Summit Books, 1986.

Evans, Rowland and Robert Novak. *Lyndon B. Johnson: The Exercise of Power*. New York: New American Library, 1966.

Evica, George-Michael. *And We Are All Mortal: New Evidence and Analysis in the John F. Kennedy Assassination*. Hartford, Conn.: University of Hartford Press, 1978.

Exner, Judith, as told to Ovid Demaris: *My Story*. New York: Grove Press, 1977.

Fairlie, Henry. *The Kennedy Promise: The Politics of Expectation*. New York: Doubleday, 1972.

Fay, Paul B., Jr. *The Pleasure of His Company*. New York: Harper & Row, 1966.

Finsterwald, Bernard J. *Coincidence or Conspiracy*. New York: Kensington, 1977.

Fisher, Eddie. *Eddie: My Life, My Loves*. New York: Harper & Row, 1981.

Folsom, Merrill. *More Great American Mansions and Their Stories*. New York: Hastings House, 1967.

Fontaine, Joan. *No Bed of Roses: An Autobiography*. New York: William Morrow, 1978.

Four days: The Historical Record of the Death of President Kennedy. Compiled by United Press International and American Heritage Magazine. New York: American Heritage, 1964.

Frank, Gerold. *Zsa Zsa Gabor, My Story*. New York: World, 1960.

Frank, Sid and Arden Davis Melick. *The Presidents: Tidbits and Trivia*. Maplewood, N.J.: Hammond, 1986.

Fraser, Nicholas, Philip Jacobson, Mark Ottaway and Lewis Chester. *Aristotle Onassis*. Philadelphia: Lippincott, 1977.

Frischauer, Willi. *Onassis*. New York: Meredith Press, 1968.

Gadney, Reg. *Kennedy*. New York: Holt, Rinehart and Winston, 1983.

Galbraith, John Kenneth. *Ambassador's Journal: A Personal Account of the Kennedy Years*. Boston: Houghton Mifflin, 1969.

Galella, Ron. *Jacqueline*. New York: Sheed and Ward, 1974.
————. *Off-guard: Beautiful People Unveiled Before the Camera Lens*. New York: McGraw-Hill, 1976.

Gallagher, Mary Barelli. *My Life With Jacqueline Kennedy*. New York: David McKay, 1969.

Gardine, Michael. *Billy Baldwin: An Autobiography*. Boston: Little, Brown, 1985.

Gardner, Ralph, Jr. *Young, Gifted, and Rich: The Secrets of America's Most Successful Entrepreneurs*. New York: Simon & Schuster, 1984.

Getty, J. Paul. *As I See It: The Autobiography of J. Paul Getty*. New York: Berkley, 1976.

Giancana, Antoinette and Thomas C. Renner. *Mafia Princess: Growing Up in Sam Giancana's Family*. New York: William Morrow, 1984.

Gibson, Barbara. *Life With Rose Kennedy*. New York: Warner, 1986.

Gingras, Angele de T. *"From Bussing to Bugging": The Best in Congressional Humor*. Washington, D.C.: Acropolis Books, 1973.

Gold, Arthur and Robert Fizdale. *The Life of Misia Sert*. New York: Knopf, 1980.

Goldman, Eric F. *The Tragedy of Lyndon Johnson*. New York: Knopf, 1969.

Goodwin, Doris Kearns. *The Fitzgeralds and the Kennedys: An American Saga*. New York: Simon & Schuster, 1987.

Goodwin, Richard N. *Remembering America: A Voice From the Sixties*. Boston: Little, Brown, 1988.

Granger, Stewart. *Sparks Fly Upward*. New York: Putnam, 1981.

Gray, Earle. *Wildcats: The Story of Pacific Petroleum and Westcoast Transmission.* Toronto: McClelland and Stewart, 1982.

Grier, Roosevelt. *"Rosey": The Gentle Giant.* Tulsa, Oklahoma. Honor Books, 1986.

Grobel, Lawrence. *Conversations with Capote.* New York: New American Library, 1985.

Guiles, Fred Lawrence. *Legend: The Life and Death of Marilyn Monroe.* New York: Stein and Day, 1984.

Gulley, Bill and Mary Ellen Reese. *Breaking Cover.* New York: Simon & Schuster, 1980.

Guthman, Edwin. *We Band of Brothers: A Memoir of Robert F. Kennedy.* New York: Harper & Row, 1971.

Guthrie, Lee. *Jackie, the Price of the Pedestal.* New York: Drake, 1978.

Halberstam, David. *The Best and the Brightest.* New York: Random House, 1969.

Hall, Gordon Langley and Ann Pinchot. *Jacqueline Kennedy, A Biography.* New York: Frederick Fell, 1964.

Halle, Kay. *The Grand Original: Portraits of Randolph Churchill by His Friends.* Boston: Houghton Mifflin, 1971.

Hamilton, Ian. *Robert Lowell, A Biography.* New York: Random House, 1982.

Harris, Bill. *John Fitzgerald Kennedy, A Photographic Tribute.* New York: Crescent, 1983.

Harris, Fred R. *Potomac Fever.* New York: Norton, 1977.

Harris, Kenneth. *Conversations.* London: Hodder and Stoughton, 1967.

Harris, Warren G. *Cary Grant: A Touch of Elegance.* Garden City, N.Y.: Doubleday, 1987.

Healy, Diana Dixon. *America's First Ladies: Private Lives of the Presidential Wives, 1789-1989.* New York: Atheneum, 1988.

Heller, Deane and David. *Jacqueline Kennedy: The Complete Story of America's First Lady.* Derby, Conn.: Monarch Books, 1961.

————. *Jacqueline Kennedy: The Warmly Human Story of the Woman All Americans Have Taken to Their Heart.* New York: Monarch Books, 1961.

Hemingway, Mary Walsh. *How It Was.* New York: Knopf, 1976.

Herbert, David. *Second Son: An Autobiography.* London: Peter Owen, 1972.

Hersh, Burton. *The Education of Edward Kennedy: A Family Biography.* New York: William Morrow, 1972.

Heymann, C. David. *American Aristocracy: The Lives and Times of James Russell, Amy and Robert Lowell*. New York: Dodd, Mead, 1980.

_____. *Poor Little Rich Girl: The Life and Legend of Barbara Hutton*. Secaucus, N.J.: Lyle Stuart, 1984.

Hibbert, Christopher. *The Royal Victorians: King Edward VII, His Family and Friends*. Philadelphia: Lippincott, 1976.

Higham, Charles. *The Life of Marlene Dietrich*. New York: Norton, 1977.

_____. *Sisters: The Story of Olivia de Havilland and Joan Fontaine*. New York: Putnam, 1984.

Hofstadter, Richard, ed. *Great Issues in American History From Reconstruction to the Present Day, 1864-1969*. New York: Knopf, 1958.

Hohenberg, John. *The Pulitzer Prizes: A History of the Awards in Books, Drama, Music and Journalism, Based on the Private Files Over Six Decades*. New York: Columbia University Press, 1974.

Honan, William H. *Ted Kennedy: Profile of a Survivor*. New York: Quadrangle Books, 1972.

Hosmer, Charles B., Jr. *Preservation Comes of Age: From Williamsburg to the National Trust, 1926-1949*. Vol. II. Charlottesville, Va.: University Press of Virginia, 1981.

Hurt, Henry. *Reasonable Doubt: An Investigation into the Assassination of John F. Kennedy*. New York: Holt, Rinehart and Winston, 1985.

Huste, Annemarie. *Annemarie's Personal Cook Book*. London: Bartholomew House, 1968.

In the Russian Style. Edited by Jacqueline Onassis. New York: Viking, 1976.

Isaacson, Walter and Evan Thomas. *The Wise Men—Six Friends and the World They Made: Acheson, Bohlen, Harriman, Kennan, Lovett, McCloy*. New York: Simon & Schuster, 1986.

Jackson, Michael. *Moonwalk*. New York: Doubleday, 1988.

Jamieson, Katherine Hall. *Packaging the Presidency: A History and Criticism of Presidential Campaign Advertising*. Oxford: Oxford University Press, 1984.

Joesten, Joachim. *Onassis*. New York: Tower, 1973.

Johnson, Lady Bird. *A White House Diary*. New York: Holt, Rinehart & Winston, 1970.

Johnson, Lyndon Baines. *The Vantage Point: Perspectives of the Presidency 1963-1969*. New York: Holt, Rhinehart and Winston, 1971.

Johnson, Sam Houston. *My Brother Lyndon*. New York: Cowles, 1969.

Josephson, Matthew. *The Money Lords: The Great Finance Capitalists 1925-1950*. New York: Weybright & Talley, 1972.

Kantor, Seth. *The Ruby Cover-up*. New York: Kensington, 1978.

Kearns, Doris. *Lyndon Johnson and the American Dream*. New York: Harper & Row, 1976.

Keenan, Brigid. *The Women We Wanted to Look Like*. New York: St. Martin's, 1977.

Kellerman, Barbara. *All the President's Kin*. London: Robson, 1981.

Kelley, Kitty. *Elizabeth Taylor: The Last Star*. New York: Simon & Schuster, 1981.

_____. *His Way: The Unauthorized Biography of Frank Sinatra*. New York: Bantam, 1986.

_____. *Jackie Oh!* Secaucus, N.J.: Lyle Stuart, 1979.

Kelly, Tom. *The Imperial Post: The Meyers, The Grahams and The Paper That Rules Washington*. New York: William Morrow, 1983.

Kennedy, Edward M., ed. *The Fruitful Bough. Reminiscences of Joseph P. Kennedy*. Privately printed, 1970.

Kennedy, John F. *As We Remember Joe*. Privately printed, 1945.

_____. *Profiles in Courage*. New York: Harper & Row, 1965.

_____. *Public Papers of the President, 1961, 1962, 1963*. 3 vols. U.S. Government Printing Office, 1962, 1963, 1964.

_____. *Why England Slept*. New York: Wilfred Funk, 1940:

Kennedy, Robert F. *The Enemy Within*. New York: Harper & Row, 1960.

_____. *In His Own Words: The Unpublished Recollections of the Kennedy Years,* eds. Edwin O. Guthman and Jeffrey Schulman. New York: Bantam, 1988.

_____. *Thirteen Days: A Memoir of the Cuban Missile Crisis*. New York: Norton, 1969.

_____. *To Seek a New World*. Garden City, N.Y.: Doubleday, 1967.

Kennedy, Rose Fitzgerald. *Times to Remember*. New York: Doubleday, 1974.

The Kennedys: A New York Times Profile. Edited by Gene Brown. New York: Arno Press, 1980.

Kern, Montague, Patricia W. Levering, Ralph B. Levering. *The Kennedy Crises: The Press, The Presidency, and Foreign Policy*. Chapel Hill, N.C.: University of North Carolina Press, 1983.

King, Coretta Scott. *My Life With Martin Luther King, Jr*. New York: Holt, Rinehart & Winston, 1969.

King, Larry, with Peter Occhiogrosso. *Tell It to the King*. New York: G. P. Putnam's Sons, 1988.

Klapthor, Margaret Brown. *The First Ladies*. Washington, D.C.: The White House Historical Association, 1975.

Knightley, Phillip and Caroline Kennedy. *An Affair of State: The Profumo Case and the Framing of Stephen Ward*. New York: Atheneum, 1987.

Konolige, Kit. *The Richest Women in the World*. New York: Macmillan, 1985.

Koskoff, David E. *Joseph P. Kennedy, A Life and Times*. Englewood Cliffs, N.J.: Prentice-Hall, 1974.

Kramer, Frieda. *Jackie. A Truly Intimate Biography*. New York: Gosset & Dunlap, 1979.

Krock, Arthur. *In the Nation 1932-1966*. New York: McGraw-Hill, 1966.

_____. *Memoirs: Sixty Years on the Firing Line*. New York: Funk & Wagnalls, 1968.

Kwitny, Jonathan. *Endless Enemies: The Making of an Unfriendly World*. New York: Congdon & Weed, 1984.

Lamarr, Hedy. *Ecstasy and Me: My Life as a Woman*. New York: Fawcett, 1967.

Lambro, Donald. *Washington—City of Scandals: Investigating Congress and Other Big Spenders*. Boston: Little, Brown, 1984.

Lane, Mark. *Rush to Judgement: A Critique of the Warren Commission's Inquiry into the Murders of President John F. Kennedy, Officer J.D. Tippit and Lee Harvey Oswald*. New York: Holt, Rinehart & Winston, 1966.

Lash, Joseph P. *Eleanor: The Years Alone*. New York: Norton, 1972.

Lasky, Victor. *J.F.K., The Man and The Myth*. New York: Macmillan, 1963.

Lawford, Lady Mary (May) Sommerville, as told to Buddy Galon. *"Bitch!": The Autobiography of Lady Lawford*. Brookline, Mass.: Brandon, 1986.

Lax, Henry. *Sidelights From the Surgery*. London: Pallas, 1929.

Leamer, Laurence. *Make-Believe: The Story of Nancy and Ronald Reagan*. New York: Harper & Row, 1983.

Leary, Timothy. *Changing My Mind, Among Others: Life-time Writings, Selected and Introduced by the Author.* Englewood Cliffs, N.J.: Prentice-Hall, 1982.

—————: *Flashbacks: An Autobiography.* Los Angeles: J.P. Tarcher, 1983.

Lee, Martin A. and Bruce Shalain. *Acid Dreams: The CIA, LSD, and the Sixties Rebellion.* New York: Grove, 1985.

Lerner, Max. *Ted and the Kennedy Legend: A Study in Character and Destiny.* New York: St. Martin's, 1980.

Lieberson, Goddard, ed. *John Fitzgerald Kennedy . . . As We Remember Him.* New York: Atheneum, 1965.

Lifton, David S. *Best Evidence: Disguise and Deception in the Assassination of John F. Kennedy.* New York: Macmillan, 1980.

Lilienthal, David E. *The Journals of David E. Lilienthal, Volume V, The Harvest Years 1959-1963.* New York: Harper & Row, 1972.

Lilly, Doris. *Those Fabulous Greeks: Onassis, Niarchos, and Livanos.* London: W.H. Allen, 1971.

Lincoln, Anne H. *The Kennedy White House Parties.* New York: Viking, 1967.

Lincoln, Evelyn. *My Twelve Years With John F. Kennedy.* New York: David McKay, 1965.

Logan, Joshua. *Movie Stars, Real People, and Me.* New York: Delacorte Press, 1978.

Louchheim, Kate. *By the Political Sea.* Garden City, N.Y.: Doubleday, 1970.

Lowe, Jacques. *Kennedy, A Time Remembered.* London: Quartet Books, 1983.

Lowell, Robert. *History.* New York: Farrar, Straus & Giroux, 1973.

MacMahon, Edward B. and Leonard Curry. *Medical Cover-Ups in the White House.* Washington, D.C.: Farragut, 1987.

Macmillan, Harold. *At the End of the Day, 1961-1963.* New York: Harper & Row, 1973.

MacPherson, Myra. *The Power Lovers: An Intimate Look at Politics and Marriage.* New York: Putnam, 1975.

Mailer, Norman. *Marilyn.* New York: Grosset & Dunlap, 1973.

—————: *Of Women and Their Elegance.* New York: Simon & Schuster, 1980.

—————. *The Presidential Papers.* New York: Dell, 1963.

Makower, Joel. *Boom! Talkin' About Our Generation.* New York: Contemporary Books, 1985.

Manchester, William. *Controversy and Other Essays in Journalism, 1950-1975.* Boston: Little, Brown, 1976.

_____. *The Death of a President: November 20-November 25, 1963*. New York: Harper & Row, 1967.

_____. *One Brief Shining Moment: Remembering Kennedy*. Boston: Little, Brown, 1983.

_____. *Portrait of a President: John F. Kennedy in Profile*. Boston: Little, Brown, 1962.

Manso, Peter. *Mailer, His Life and Times*. New York: Simon & Schuster, 1985.

Martin, John Bartlow. *Adlai Stevenson and the World: The Life of Adlai Stevenson*. Garden City, N.Y.: Doubleday, 1977.

Martin, Ralph G. *A Hero for Our Time: An Intimate Story of the Kennedy Years*. New York: Ballantine Books, 1983.

_____. *Cissy: The Extraordinary Life of Eleanor Medill Patterson*. New York: Simon & Schuster, 1979.

Massy, Christian de, Baron. *Palace: My Life in the Royal Family of Monaco*. New York: Atheneum, 1986.

Maxwell, Elsa. *The Celebrity Circus*. New York: Appleton-Century, 1963.

_____. *R.S.V.P: Elsa Maxwell's Own Story*. Boston: Little, Brown, 1954.

McCarthy, Dennis V.N. *Protecting the President: The Inside Story of a Secret Service Agent*. New York: William Morrow, 1985.

McCarthy, Joe. *The Remarkable Kennedys*. New York: Dial Press, 1960.

McConnell, Brian. *The History of Assassination*. Nashville: Aurora, 1970.

McMillan, Priscilla Johnson. *Marina and Lee*. New York: Harper & Row, 1977.

McTaggart, Lynne. *Kathleen Kennedy, Her Life and Times*. New York: Holt, Rinehart & Winston, 1983.

Means, Marianne. *The Woman in the White House*. New York: Random House, 1963.

Meneghini, Giovanni Battista. *My Wife Maria Callas*. New York: Farrar, Straus & Giroux, 1982.

Michaelis, David. *The Best of Friends*. New York: William Morrow, 1983.

Miers, Earl Schenck. *America and Its Presidents*. New York: Grosset & Dunlap, 1964.

Miller, Alice P., compiler. *A Kennedy Chronology*. New York: Birthdate Research, 1968.

Miller, Arthur. *Timebends: A Life*. New York: Grove Press, 1987.

Miller, Hope Ridings. *Embassy Row: The Life & Times of Diplomatic Washington*. New York: Holt, Rinehart and Winston, 1969.

――――. *Scandals in the Highest Office: Facts and Fictions in the Private Lives of our Presidents*. New York: Random House, 1973.

Miller, Merle. *Lyndon, An Oral Biography*. New York: Putnam, 1980.

――――. *Plain Speaking: An Oral Biography of Harry S Truman*. New York: Berkley, 1973.

Miller, William "Fishbait." *Fishbait*. Englewood Cliffs, N.J.: Prentice-Hall, 1977.

Montgomery, Ruth. *Flowers at the White House: An Informal Tour of the Home of the Presidents of the United States*. New York: M. Barrows, 1967.

――――. *Hail to the Chiefs: My Life and Times with Six Presidents*. New York: Coward-McCann, 1970.

Mooney, Booth. *LBJ, An Irreverent Chronicle*. New York: Crowell, 1976.

Morrow, Lance. *The Chief: A Memoir of Fathers and Sons*. New York: Random House, 1984.

Morrow, Robert. *The Senator Must Die: The Murder of Robert Kennedy*. Santa Monica, CA: Roundtable, 1988.

Nicholas, William. *The Bobby Kennedy Nobody Knows*. New York: Fawcett, 1967.

Nin, Anaïs: *The Diary of Anaïs Nin, 1947-1955*. Volume 5. New York: Harcourt, Brace, Jovanovich, 1974.

Niven, David. *The Moon's a Balloon*. New York: Putnam, 1972.

Nixon, Richard. *RN*. New York: Grosset & Dunlap, 1978.

Nizer, Louis. *Reflections Without Mirrors: An Autobiography of the Mind*. New York: Doubleday, 1978.

Noguchi, Thomas T. with Joseph Dimona. *Coroner to the Stars*. London: Corgi Books, 1983.

Nowakowski, Tadeusz. *The Radziwills: The Social History of a Great European Family*. New York: Delacorte, 1974.

Nunnerley, David. *President Kennedy & Britain*. New York: St. Martin's, 1972.

Oates, Stephen B. *Let the Trumpet Sound: The Life of Martin Luther King, Jr*. New York: Harper & Row, 1982.

――――. *William Faulkner: The Man & the Artist*. New York: Harper & Row, 1987.

O'Brien, Lawrence F. *No Final Victories: A Life in Politics—from John F. Kennedy to Watergate*. New York: Doubleday, 1974.

O'Donnell, Kenneth P. and David F. Powers with Joe Mc-Carthy. *"Johnny We Hardly Knew Ye."* Boston: Little, Brown, 1970.

O'Neill, Tip with William Novak. *Man of the House: The Life and Political Memoirs of Speaker Tip O'Neill.* New York: Random House, 1987.

Osmond, Humphrey. *Predicting the Past: Memos on the Enticing Universe of Possibility,* produced by Jerome Agel. New York: Macmillan, 1951.

Paper, Lewis J. *The Promise and the Performance: The Leadership of John F. Kennedy.* New York: Crown, 1975.

Parker, Robert. *Capitol Hill in Black and White.* New York: Dodd, Mead, 1987.

Parmet, Herbert S. *Jack: The Struggles of John F. Kennedy.* New York: Dial Press, 1980.

Persico, Joseph L. *The Imperial Rockefeller: A Biography of Nelson A. Rockefeller.* New York: Simon & Schuster, 1982.

Peters, Charles. *Tilting at Windmills: An Autobiography.* Reading, Mass.: Addison-Wesley, 1988.

Peyser, Joan. *Bernstein, A Biography.* New York: William Morrow, 1987.

Phillips, John. *Papa John, An Autobiography of John Phillips.* Garden City, N.Y.: Doubleday, 1986.

Political Profiles: The Kennedy Years. New York: Facts on File, 1976.

Political Profiles: The Johnson Years. New York: Facts on File, 1976.

Potter, Jeffrey. *Men, Money & Magic: The Story of Dorothy Schiff.* New York: Coward, McCann & Geoghegan, 1976.

Powers, Thomas. *The Man Who Kept the Secrets; Richard Helms and the CIA.* New York: Knopf, 1979.

The President's Commission on the Assassination of President Kennedy. (The Warren Commission) *Hearings and Exhibits.* Vols. I-XXXVI: U.S. Government Printing Office, September, 1964.

Rachlin, Harvey. *The Kennedys: A Chronological History 1823-Present.* New York: World Almanac, 1986.

Rainie, Harrison and John Quinn. *Growing Up Kennedy: The Third Wave Comes of Age.* New York: Putnam, 1983.

Randall, Monica. *The Mansions of Long Island's Gold Coast.* New York: Hastings House, 1979.

Rapaport, Roger. *The Super-Doctors.* Chicago: Playboy Press, 1975.

Rather, Dan and Gary Paul Gates. *The Palace Guard*. New York: Harper & Row, 1974.

Rather, Dan with Mickey Herskowitz. *The Camera Never Blinks: Adventures of a TV Journalist*. New York: William Morrow, 1977.

Rattray, Jeannette Edwards. *Fifty Years of the Maidstone Club, 1891-1941*. Souvenir publication privately printed for members of the club (1941).

Reich, Cary. *Financier: The Biography of André Meyer, A Story of Money, Power, and the Reshaping of American Business*. New York: William Morrow, 1983.

Rense, Paige, ed. *Celebrity Homes;* Architectural Digest Presents the Private Worlds of Thirty International Personalities. Middlesex, England: Penguin, 1979.

Report of the Warren Commission on the Assassination of President Kennedy. New York: Bantam, 1964.

Rhea, Mini. *I Was Jacqueline Kennedy's Dressmaker*. New York: Fleet, 1962.

Riese, Randall and Neal Hitchens. *The Unabridged Marilyn: Her Life From A to Z*. New York: Congdon & Weed, 1987.

Romero, Gerry. *Sinatra's Women*. New York: Manor Books, 1976.

Roosevelt, Felicia Warburg. *Doers and Dowagers*. Garden City, N.Y.; Doubleday, 1975.

Rowe, Robert. *The Bobby Baker Story*. New York: Parallax, 1967.

Rush, George. *Confessions of an Ex-Secret Service Agent*. New York: Donald I. Fine, 1988.

Rust, Zad. *Teddy Bare, The Last of the Kennedy Clan*. Boston; Los Angeles: Western Islands, 1971.

Salinger, Pierre. *With Kennedy*. Garden City, N.Y.: Doubleday, 1966.

Saunders, Frank, with James Southwood. *Torn Lace Curtain*. New York: Holt, Rinehart & Winston, 1982.

Scheim, David E. *Contract On America: The Mafia Murder of President John F. Kennedy*. New York: Shapolsky, 1988.

Schlesinger, Arthur M., Jr. *The Cycles of American History*. Boston: Houghton Mifflin, 1986.

————. *The Imperial Presidency*. New York, Boston: Atlantic Monthly, 1973.

————. *Robert Kennedy and His Times*. Boston: Houghton Mifflin, 1978.

————. *A Thousand Days, John F. Kennedy in the White House*. Boston: Houghton Mifflin, 1965.

Sciacca, Tony. *Kennedy and His Women*. New York: Manor, 1976.

Schoenbaum, Thomas J. *Waging Peace & War: Dean Rusk in the Truman, Kennedy & Johnson Years*. New York: Simon & Schuster, 1988.

Schoor, Gene. *Young John Kennedy*. New York: Harcourt, Brace & World, 1963.

Schwartz, Charles. *Cole Porter, A Biography*. New York: Dial, 1977.

Sealy, Shirley. *The Celebrity Sex Register*. New York: Simon & Schuster, 1982.

Seaman, Barbara. *Lovely Me: The Life of Jacqueline Susann*. New York: William Morrow, 1987.

Searls, Hank. *The Lost Prince: Young Joe, The Forgotten Kennedy*. New York: New American Library, 1969.

Shannon, William V. *The Heir Apparent: Robert Kennedy and the Struggle for Power*. New York: Macmillan, 1967.

Shaw, Mark. *The John F. Kennedys: A Family Album*. New York: Farrar, Straus & Giroux, 1964.

Shaw, Maud. *White House Nannie: My Years With Caroline and John Kennedy, Jr.* New York: New American Library, 1965.

Shepard, Tazewell, Jr. *John F. Kennedy, Man of the Sea*. New York: William Morrow, 1965.

Shulman, Irving. *"Jackie!": The Exploitation of a First Lady*. New York: Trident, 1970.

Sidey, Hugh. *John F. Kennedy, President*. New York: Atheneum, 1964.

Sills, Beverly and Lawrence Linderman. *Beverly: An Autobiography*. New York: Bantam, 1987.

Silverman, Debora. *Selling Culture: Bloomingdale's, Diana Vreeland, and the New Aristocracy of Taste in America*. New York: Pantheon, 1986.

Slatzer, Robert. *The Life and Curious Death of Marilyn Monroe*. New York: Pinnacle, 1974.

Smith, Jane S. *Elsie De Wolfe: A Life in the High Style*. New York: Atheneum, 1982.

Smith, Malcolm E. *John F. Kennedy's 13 Great Mistakes in the White House*. Smithtown, N.Y.: Suffolk House, 1980.

Smith, Marie. *Entertaining in the White House*. Washington, D.C.: Acropolis Books, 1967.

Smolla, Rodney A. *Suing the Press*. Oxford: Oxford University Press, 1986.

Sorensen, Theodore C. *Kennedy*. New York: Harper & Row, 1965.

Spada, James. *Grace: The Secret Lives of a Princess*. Garden City, N.Y.: Doubleday, 1987.

Sparks, Fred. *The $20,000,000 Honeymoon: Jackie and Ari's First Year*. New York: Dell, 1970.

Spender, Stephen. *Journals 1935-1983*. New York: Random House, 1986.

Speriglio, Milo. *The Marilyn Conspiracy*. New York: Pocket Books, 1986.

Stack, Robert with Mark Evans. *Straight Shooting*. New York: Macmillan, 1980.

Stassinopoulos, Arianna. *Maria Callas, The Woman Behind the Legend*. New York: Simon & Schuster, 1981.

Steel, Ronald. *Walter Lippmann and the American Century*. Boston: Little, Brown, 1980.

Stein, Jean and George Plimpton. *American Journey: The Times of Robert Kennedy*. New York: Harcourt Brace Jovanovich, 1970.

————. *Edie: An American Biography*. New York: Knopf, 1983.

Steinem, Gloria. *Outrageous Acts and Everyday Rebellions*. New York: Holt, Rinehart and Winston, 1983.

Storm, Tempest, with Bill Boyd. *Tempest Storm: The Lady Is a Vamp*. Atlanta, GA.: Peachtree, 1987.

Stoughton, Cecil. *The Memories of Cecil Stoughton, the President's Photographer, and Major General Chester V. Clifton, the President's Military Aide*. New York: Norton, 1973.

Straignt, N.A. *Ariabella: The First*. New York: Random House, 1981.

Strait, Raymond. *The Tragic Secret Life of Jayne Mansfield*. Chicago: Henry Regnery Co., 1974.

Sullivan, William C. *The Bureau: My Thirty Years in Hoover's FBI*. New York: Norton, 1979.

Sulzberger, C.L. *Fathers and Children*. New York: Arbor House, 1987.

————. *The Last of the Giants*. New York: Macmillan, 1970.

Sulzberger, Iphigene Ochs. *Iphigene*. New York: Times Books, 1987.

Summers, Anthony. *Conspiracy*. New York: McGraw-Hill, 1980.

————. *Goddess: The Secret Lives of Marilyn Monroe*. New York: Macmillan, 1985.

Susann, Jacqueline. *Dolores*. New York: William Morrow, 1976.

Swanberg, W.A. *Luce and His Empire*. New York: Scribners, 1972.

Swanson, Gloria. *Swanson on Swanson*. New York: Random House, 1980.

Sykes, Christopher. *Nancy: The Life of Lady Astor*. London: William Collins Sons, 1972.

Taki. *Princes, Playboys & Highclass Tarts*. Princeton; New York: Karz-Cohl, 1984.

Taylor, Robert. *Marilyn Monroe in Her Own Words*. New York: Delilah, 1983.

Teltscher, Henry O. *Handwriting—Revelation of Self: A Source Book of Psychographology*. New York: Hawthorn Books, 1971.

Ten Year Report 1966-1967 to 1976-1977. Boston: The Institute of Politics, John Fitzgerald Kennedy School of Government, Harvard University, 1977.

ter Horst, J.F. and Ralph Albertazzie. *The Flying White House*. New York: Coward, McCann & Geoghegan, 1979.

Teti, Frank. *Kennedy, The New Generation*. New York: Delilah, 1983.

Thayer, Mary Van Rensselaer. *Jacqueline Bouvier Kennedy*. Garden City, N.Y.: Doubleday, 1961.

_____. *Jacqueline Kennedy, The White House Years*. Boston: Little, Brown, 1967.

Thomas, Helen. *Dateline: White House*. New York: Macmillan, 1975.

Thompson, Jim. *The Grifters*. Berkeley, Calif.: Creative Arts, 1985.

Thompson, Josiah. *Six Seconds in Dallas: A Microstudy of the Kennedy Assassination*. New York: Bernard Glass, 1968.

Thompson, Lawrence and R.H. Winnick. *Robert Frost: The Later Years 1938-1963*. New York: Holt, Rinehart and Winston, 1976.

Thompson, Nelson. *The Dark Side of Camelot*. Chicago: Playboy Press, 1976.

Thorndike, Joseph J., Jr. *The Very Rich: A History of Wealth*. New York: American Heritage, 1976.

Tierney, Gene with Mickey Herskowitz. *Self Portrait*. New York: Simon & Schuster, 1979.

Travell, Janet. *Office Hours: Day and Night, The Autobiography of Janet Travell, M.D.* New York: World, 1968.

Trewhitt, Henry L. *McNamara*. New York: Harper & Row, 1971.

Troy, Ann A. *Nutley: Yesterday—Today*. Nutley, N.J.: The Nutley Historical Society, 1961.

Truman, Margaret. *Harry S. Truman*. New York: William Morrow, 1972.

United States Senate. *Final Report of the Select Committee to Study Governmental Operations With Respect to Intelligence Activities. Book V. The Investigation of the Assassination of John F. Kennedy: Performance of the Intelligence Agencies.* U.S. Government Printing Office, April 23, 1976.

Valentine, Tom and Patrick Mahn. *Daddy's Duchess, The Unauthorized Biography of Doris Duke.* Secaucus, N.J.: Lyle Stuart, 1987.

vanden Heuvel, William and Milton Gwirtzman. *On His Own: Robert F. Kennedy 1964-1968.* Garden City, N.Y.: Doubleday, 1970.

Van Riper, Frank. *Glenn: The Astronaut Who Would Be President.* New York: Empire Books, 1983.

Vickers, Hugo. *Cecil Beaton, A Biography.* Boston; Toronto: Little, Brown, 1985.

Vidal, Gore. *The Best Man.* New York: Dramatists Play Service, 1960.

——————. *Homage to Daniel Shays: Collected Essays 1952-1972.* New York: Random House, 1972.

——————. *Julian.* Boston: Little, Brown, 1964.

Vreeland, Diana. *Allure.* Garden City, N.Y.: Doubleday, 1980.

——————. *D.V.* New York: Knopf, 1984.

Walker, John. *Self-Portrait With Donors: Confessions of an Art Collector.* Boston: Little, Brown, 1974.

Wallace, Irving. *The Sunday Gentleman.* New York: Simon & Schuster, 1965.

Wallace, Mike and Gary Paul Gates. *Close Encounters: Mike Wallace's Own Story.* New York: William Morrow, 1984.

Warhol, Andy. *Andy Warhol's Exposures.* Photographs by Andy Warhol; text by Andy Warhol with Bob Colacello. New York: Andy Warhol Books/Grosset & Dunlap, 1979.

The Warren Report. New York: Associated Press, 1964.

Watney, Hedda Lyons. *Jackie.* North Hollywood, CA.: Leisure Books, 1971.

Weatherby, W.J.: *Conversations With Marilyn.* New York: Ballantine, 1977.

Weisberg, Harold. *John F. Kennedy Assassination Post Mortem.* Self-published, 1969.

——————. *Whitewash,* Vols. I & II. New York: Dell, 1966. *Whitewash,* Vols. III & IV. Self-published, 1967.

West, J.B., with Mary Lynn Kotz. *Upstairs at the White House: My Life with the First Ladies.* New York: Coward, McCann & Geoghegan, 1973.

Whalen, Richard J. *The Founding Father: The Story of Joseph P. Kennedy and the Family He Raised to Power*. New York: Signet Books, 1964.

White House Historical Association. *The White House: An Historical Guide*. Washington, D.C., 1967.

White, Ray Lewis. *Gore Vidal*. New York: Twayne, 1968.

White, Theodore H. *In Search of History: A Personal Adventure*. New York: Warner Books, 1978.

_____. *The Making of the President 1960*. New York: Atheneum, 1961.

White, William S. *The Professional Lyndon B. Johnson*. Boston: Houghton Mifflin, 1964.

Wicker, Tom. *On Press*. New York: Viking, 1975.

Wills, Gary. *The Kennedy Imprisonment, A Meditation on Power*. Boston: Little, Brown, 1981.

Wilroy, Mary Edith and Lucie Prinz. *Inside Blair House*. Garden City, N.Y.: Doubleday, 1982.

Wilson, Earl. *Show Business Laid Bare*. New York: G.P. Putnam's Sons, 1974.

_____. *The Show Business Nobody Knows*. New York: Cowles, 1971.

_____. *Sinatra: An Unauthorized Biography*. New York: Macmillan, 1976.

Winter-Berger, Robert N. *The Washington Pay-Off*. New York: Dell, 1972.

Wirth, Conrad L. Parks. *Politics and the People*. Norman, OK: University of Oklahoma Press, 1980.

The Witnesses. Selected and edited from The Warren Commission's Hearings by *The New York Times* with an Introduction by Anthony Lewis. New York: McGraw-Hill, 1964.

Wofford, Harris. *Of Kennedys and Kings: Making Sense of the Sixties*. New York: Farrar, Straus & Giroux, 1980.

Wolff, Perry. *A Tour of the White House With Mrs. John F. Kennedy*. Garden City, N.Y.: Doubleday, 1962.

Youngblood, Rufus W. *20 Years in the Secret Service: My Life With Five Presidents*. New York: Simon & Schuster, 1973.

Ziegler, Philip. *Diana Cooper: A Biography*. New York: Knopf, 1982.

Acknowledgments

A Woman Named Jackie would not have been possible without the help of countless individuals and institutions. First acknowledgment must go to Lyle and Carole Stuart, the original publishers of this book. Then I would like to thank my editor Allan Wilson as well as David Goodnough for their careful reading of the manuscript. I also tip my hat to literary agent Georges Borchardt and public relations specialist-literary agent Marianne Strong for their encouragement and advice. In addition I am indebted to Steven Schragis, Bruce Bender, Maryl Earl, and Sandy Bodner for their help and support in this project.

I am particularly grateful to a fine staff of researchers and interviewers that included Tracey Dewart, Sean Kelly, Pat Maniscalco, Linda McCurdy, Madeleine Nicklin, Mark Padnos, Luis Rivera, Patricia Schaefer, Mary Lynn Soini and Pat Vasquez. Roberta Fineberg was in charge of research in Europe, and to this end logged thousands of miles and conducted scores of interviews. I am especially indebted to Anthony J. Mazzaschi, who not only helped conduct and coordinate the research and interviews in the United States but gave unstinting moral support when it was most needed. I should also thank Patricia Stareck and Marilyn Tamielewicz for their assistance in transcribing hundreds of hours of interview tapes.

A number of individuals were helpful in providing information or putting me in touch with prospective interviewees. Along these lines, I wish to acknowledge the following: Joseph Alsop; Rachel Phillips Balash (Head of the School, Miss Porter's School), Terry L. Birdwhistell (Director, Oral History Program, University of Kentucky Library), Peter Brennan, Cissy Cahan (Metropolitan Museum of Art), Margaret Carson, President Jimmy Carter, Frank Como, Fleur Cowles, Kenneth Davis, Philippe de Gaulle, Angier Biddle Duke (for permission to read the Angier Biddle Duke papers at William R. Perkins Library, Duke University), Peter Edelman, Lois Gilman, Jim Haynes, Paul B. Hensley (Winterthur Museum and Gardens), Nancy Horne (I. M. Pei & Partners), Burke Marshall, Judith McNally, Larry Nathan, Esq., Richard E. Neustadt, James E. O'Neill (Presidential Libraries, National Archives), Dan Rapoport, Mario Sartori, Lillian Smith (Phil Donahue Show), Stephen E. Smith, Jeanne Toomey, Charles E. Treman, Jr., Diana Trilling, John Walters, Elizabeth Webber, and David S. Van Tassel (Presidential Libraries, National Archives).

Numerous organizations and institutions provided documents, correspondence, oral history and written material of every description. While it is not possible to thank the individuals associated with each organization, I would like to express my gratitude to the following institutions: Amherst College Library; The Amistad Research Center; The Archdiocese of Boston; The University of Arkansas Libraries; The George Arents Research Library (Syracuse University); Assassination Archives and Research Center (Washington, D.C.); Associated Press and UPI offices (Athens, Greece); Regional Oral History Office, The Bancroft Library (University of California, Berkeley); Baylor University Institute for Oral History; Bentley Historical Library (The University of Michigan); Boston Public Library; British Broadcasting Corporation; Brown University Library; Jimmy Carter Presidential Center; Central Intelligence Agency; Columbia University Oral History Collection; Cornell University Libraries; Ministère de la Culture (Paris, France); Dartmouth College Library; East Hampton Free Library (Long Island Collection); Dwight D. Eisenhower Library; Emory University; Federal Bureau of Investigation; Gerald R. Ford Library.

The Gelman Library (George Washington University); Georgetown University Library; Harvard Law School Library; The Jean and Alexander Heard Library (Vanderbilt University); Herbert Hoover Presidential Library; The Houghton Library (Harvard University); Illinois State Historical Society; The University of Iowa Libraries; Lyndon Baines Johnson Library; John F. Kennedy Library; Kent State University Library; University of Kentucky Libraries; Library of Congress (Manuscript Division); University of California, Los Angeles (The University Library, Department of Special Collections); Maryland Historical Society; Maysles Films, Inc.; The Andrew Mellon Library (Choate Rosemary Hall); Metropolitan Museum of Art; Minnesota Historical Society; University of Minnesota Libraries; Miss Porter's School; Mugar Memorial Library (Boston University); The Karl E. Mundt Historical and Educational Foundation; National Archives; National Gallery of Art; National Geographic Society; Department of the Navy (Naval War College and Naval Intelligence Command); New York Genealogical and Biographical Society; New York Public Library; New York Society Library; North Texas State University Libraries.

Ohio Historical Society; Alexander S. Onassis Public Benefit Foundation; University of Oregon Library; Pennsylvania Historical and Museum Collection; William R. Perkins Library (Duke University); Phillips Memorial Library (Providence College); Princeton University Library; Harry Ransom Humanities Research Center (The University of Texas at

Austin); Redwood Library and Athenaeum (Newport, R. I.); Walter P. Reuther Library (Wayne State University); Franklin D. Roosevelt Library; Richard B. Russell Memorial Library (University of Georgia); The Arthur and Elizabeth Schlesinger Library on the History of Women in America (Radcliffe College); Smithsonian Institution; Somerset County (New Jersey) Library; Bibliothèque de la Sorbonne (Paris, France); The Stanford University Libraries; The University of Texas at Arlington Library; University of Toronto Library; Department of the Treasury, United States Secret Service; Harry S. Truman Library; U.S. Department of State; U.S. Naval Institute; Vassar College Library; Veterans Administration, Department of Medicine and Surgery; University of Virginia Library; University of Washington Libraries; Washoe County (Nevada) Clerk's Office; The Western Reserve Historical Society; West Virginia and Regional History Collection (West Virginia University); The White House Curator's Office; Winterthur Museum and Gardens; The State Historical Society of Wisconsin; University of Wisconsin at Stevens Point Library; Robert W. Woodruff Library (Emory University); Yale University Library.

Finally I must mention the 825 individuals who agreed to be interviewed for this book or who answered questions in writing. While some requested anonymity, many did not. Among the latter are:

George Allen ("Slim") Aarons; Bess Abell; Joe Acquaotta; Cindy Adams; Charles Addams; Bill Adler; Jerome Agel; Lois K. Alexander; Alexandre (Louis Robert Alexandre Rimon); Hervé Alphand; Cleveland Amory; Paul Anastasi; Claudia Anderson; Jack Anderson; James J. Angleton; Jean-Paul Ansellem; Beny Aristea; Agnes Ash; Brooke Astor; Mrs. Ray Atherton; Hugh Dudley Auchincloss III; Jamie Auchincloss; Janet Lee Bouvier Auchincloss.

Carlos Baker; Letitia ("Tish") Baldridge; Richard ("Dick") Banks; Donald Barnes; Helen Barry; Charles Bartlett; Allen Bassing; Nancy Bastien; Betty Beal; Bouvier Beale; Mrs. Bouvier Beale; Edith ("Edie") Beale; Peter Beard; Orren Beaty; Samuel H. Beer; Lee Belser; Roger F. Bentley; Brigit Berlin; Richie Berlin; Rosamond Bernier; Leonard Bernstein; Yvette Bertin; Lillian Biko; Dr. F. Tremane Billings; K. LeMoyne ("Lem") Billings; Adriana Scalamandré Bitter; Sally Bitterman; Earl Blackwell; William McCormack Blair; Sylvia Whitehouse Blake; G. Robert Blakey; Peter Bloom; Beverly ("Bev") Bogert; Joseph Robert Bolker; Bernard Bosque; Bernard Boutin; Michel ("Miche") Bouvier III; Frank Bowling; Mrs. J. Boyer; Joan Braden; Toni

Bradlee; Frank Brady; James Brady; Muffie Brandon; Susan Braudy; Robert L. Breeden; John Bross; David Brown; Jerry Bruno; Lewis Buck; Barbara Burn; Ed Byrne.

Gordon Caldwell; Maia Calligas; Cass Canfield, Jr.; Anthony Cangiolosi; Laurie Cannon; Marian Cannon; Cornell Capa; Mortimer M. Caplin; Truman Capote; Ari Caratsas; Thomas R. Carney; George Carpozi, Jr.; Igor Cassini; Oleg Cassini; Nash Castro; Joseph Cerrell; Sharon Churcher; Countess Marina Cicogna; Craig Claiborne; Blair Clark; Ramsey Clark, Esq.; Clark M. Clifford, Esq.; Mrs. Garry Clifford; Maj. Gen. Chester V. ("Ted") Clifton; Roy Cohn, Esq.; Margaret Louise Coit; Barbara Coleman; Nancy Tenney Coleman; Thomas Collier; Charles Collingwood; Frank Comerford; Clement E. Conger; Peter Conrad; Lady Diana Cooper; Senator John Sherman Cooper; Newton Cope; Edward J. Costello; Mel Cottone; Roderick Coupe; Countess Consuelo Crespi; Count Rudi Crespi; Jason Croy; Donald J. Crump; Eloise Cuddeback; Halter Cunningham; Audrey Cunow; Kent Cunow; Charlotte Curtis.

Herman Darvick; Lester David; Bob Davidoff; Jules Davids; Deborah Davis; John H. Davis; Emile de Antonio; Philippe De Bausset; Richard de Combray; John W. Dee; Jean-Louis de Faucigny-Lucinge; Steven DeFelice; Hubert de Givenchy; Mary DeGrace; Ormande de Kay; Audrey del Rosario; Ovid Demaris; John Dempsey; Couve de Murville; Robert DeNesha; Linda Grant DePauw; Robin Derby; Baron Alexis de Rédé; Countess Claude de Renty (Mme Bernard de Bigault du Granrut); Countess Guyot de Renty; Jan DeRuth; Count Adalbert de Segonzac; Dorothy Desjardins; Janet DesRosiers; Leslie ("Dawn") Devereax; Tracey Dewart; Nancy Dickerson; Wyatt Dickerson; C. Douglas Dillon; Gladys Dise; Jim Divine; Marjorie Housepian Dobkin; Gregg Sherwood Dodge; Franklin d'Olier, Jr.; Winifred d'Olier; Mary Woolworth Donahue; Sam Donaldson; Humphrey ("Hop") Donnelly; Jack Donnelly; Shannon Donnelly; Isabelle D'Orléans et Bragance; Hebe Dorsey; Elisabeth Draper; Noreen Drexel; Jacqueline Duhème; Angier Biddle Duke; William L. Dunfey; Ralph Dungan.

Louis Ehret; Gerald Ehrlich; Gloria Emerson; John F. English; Edward Jay Epstein; Peter Evans; Rowland Evans, Jr.; George-Michael Evica.

Douglas Fairbanks, Jr.; Paul B. ("Red") Fay, Jr.; Ronald Feldman; Janet Felton; Bernard Fensterwald, Jr.; José V. Ferrer; Roger Fessaguet; John Ficke; Candace Fischer; James Fleming; Edward Folger; Doris Ford; Molly Fowler; Sanford ("Sandy") Fox; Judith Frame; Doris Francisco; Suzanne Freedman; Orville Freeman; Susan French; Elizabeth McNamara Fretz; Grace Lee Frey; Sanford ("Sandy") Friedman, M.D.

Helene Gaillet; Estelle Gaines; Alice Gaither; John Kenneth Galbraith; Betty Galella; Ron Galella; Mary Gallagher; Barbara Gamarekian; Fanny Gardiner; Robert David Lyon Gardiner; George Gardner; Joseph Gargan, Esq.; Romain Gary; Wilson R. Gathings; Louise Gault; George Gazis; Nissarion Gazis; Peter Gazis; Cecilia Parker Geyelin; Mary Bass Gibson; Rod Gibson; Madelin Gilpatric; Roswell Gilpatric, Esq:; Mary Gimbel; Angele Gingras; Eugene Girden, Esq.; Carson Glass, Esq.; Michel Glotz; Arthur Goldberg, Esq.; Christina Goodman; Richard N. Goodwin; Niki Goulandris; George Goulart; Steven Gramkowski; Joseph Grandmaison; Robert Granger; Lucy Grant; Constantine ("Costa") Gratsos; Robert Green; Roosevelt ("Rosey") Grier; Anthony ("Tony") Gronowicz, Jr.; Joy Gross; Thomas H. Guinzburg.

Tom Hailey; David Halberstam; Kay Halle; Halston; Ila Schenck Hamilton; Alfred Hantman, Esq.; Linda Harrell; W. Averell Harriman; Jacques Harvey; Mrs. Anthony Hass; Ellen Hawkes; Ken Hechler; Russell D. Hemenway; Deirdre Henderson; Thomas T. Hendrick; Samuel Herman, Esq.; Nye Heron; John Hersey; Lloyd Hezekiah; Jacqueline Hirsch; Gerri Hirshey; Fletcher Hodges; Bryan Holme; Nora Horan; David Horowitz; Horst P. Horst; Casey Hughes; Conover Hunt; Louisa Hunter; John G. W. Husted, Jr.

Susan Imhoff; Walter Isaacson; Jonathan T. Isham; Franklyn Ives; Hugh Jacobsen; Ruth Jacobson; Thomas E. Jacobson, M.D.; Michael James; Morton L. Janklow, Esq.; Senator Jacob K. Javits; Philip Johnson; Colonel Cloyce H. Johnston; Ted H. Jordan; William Joyce, Esq.; Larry Juris.

James Kalafatis; John Karavlas; Stanley Karnow; Blair Karsch; Jack Kassowitz; Angelo Katopodis; Michael Kay; Mimi Kazon; David Kennedy; Iris Kessler; James Ketchum; Judy Bowdoin Key; Malcolm ("Mac") Kilduff; Carl Killingsworth; Arthur Kirson; Jon Klingensmith; Suzanne Perrin Kloman; Elizabeth I. Knight; Judge James Knott; Nicholas ("Nick the Greek") Kominatos; Mary Lynn Kotz; Jay Kramer, Esq.; Charles Kriss; Paul Oskar Kristeller; Richard A. Kurnit, Esq.; Jonathan Kwitny.

Eleanor Lambert; Mrs. Bernard Lamotte; Paul Landis; Lester Lanin; Lew Laprade; Francis Lara; Ida Large; Mary Lasker; Kwan Lau; Peter Lawford; Lilly Lawrence; Wayne Lawson; Timothy Leary; Jane T. Lee; General Curtis LeMay; Kay Lepercq; Samuel Lester; David Lev; Russell Levine;

Francis ("Frank") Levy; Mort R. Lewis; Doris Lilly; Anne H. Lincoln; Evelyn Lincoln; Thomas R. Lincoln, Esq.; Anne Morrow Lindbergh; Henry C. Lindner; Henry Cabot Lodge, Jr.; Elaine Lorillard; Clare Boothe Luce; Milton Lunin; Nettie Lunin; J.M.A.H. Luns; Ivo Lupis; Renee Luttgen.

Phyllis Brooks Macdonald; Norman Mailer; William Manchester; Lucio Manisco; Irving Mansfield; Senator Mike Mansfield; Peter Manso; George Markham; Jim Marley; John Marquand, Jr.; Bill Martin; John Bartlow Martin; Louis E. Martin; Ralph G. Martin; Susan Martins; Langdon P. Marvin, Jr.; Christina Mason; Paul Mathias (Mathias Polakowitz); Harold Matson; Peter Matthiessen; David Maysles; Dennis V. N. McCarthy; Senator Eugene McCarthy; Helen McCauley; Sarah McClendon;

David Blair McCloskey; Frank McGee; Senator Gale McGee; Senator George McGovern; Mrs. Earl McGrath; Godfrey McHugh; F. Kenneth McKnight; Marianne McLane; Betty McMahon; Robert S. McNamara; Aileen ("Suzy") Mehle; Jonas Mekas; Louise Melhado; Richard Meryman; Cord Meyer, Jr.; Bess Meyerson; Flora Whitney Miller; Hope Ridings Miller; Scott Milne; Alexis Miotis; James H. Mitchell; Cheryl Moch; Ruth Montgomery; Admiral Thomas Moorer; Robert Morey; Peter H. Morrison, Esq.; Ruth Mosse; Maura Moynihan; Lewis C. Murdock; Bess Myerson; Al Nault; Larry Newman; Philip Nobile; Noël Noël.

Lawrence F. ("Larry") O'Brien; Chris O'Donnell; Kenneth P. O'Donnell; Christina Onassis; James E. O'Neill; Ambassador Alejandro Orfilia; Sir David Ormsby-Gore (Lord Harlech); Howard Oxenberg.

Susan Panopoulos; Maria Papastamou; Providencia ("Provi") Parades; Mrs. Henry ("Sister") Parish, II; Estelle Parker; Herbert S. Parmet; Governor Endicott ("Chubb") Peabody; Lorraine Pearce; Senator Claiborne Pell; Mrs. Nuala Pell; Senator Claude Pepper; Lester Persky; Charles Peters; Ezio Petersen; Donald Peterson; Martha Phillips; Robert ("Bob") Phillips; George Plimpton; Edgar Poe; Dave Powers; Walter I. ("Bill") Pozen; Polly Pritchie; Hester Provenson; Alan Pryce-Jones; Victoria ("Tory") Pryor; Michelle Bouvier Putnam.

Susan Radmer; Harrison Rainie; Ben Reed; Peter Reed; Cary Reich; Janine Reiss; Edmund Remington; Barbara Reynolds; Stewart ("Sandy") Richardson; John Rigas; Governor Dennis J. Roberts; Eleanor Roberts; Hélène Rochas; Franklin D. Roosevelt, Jr., Esq.; Ambassador Selwa ("Lucky") Roosevelt; Vincent Roppatte; Carol Rosenwald; Mike Rotando; Philip Roth; Baroness Marie-Hélène Rothschild;

Dovey Roundtree, Esq.; James A. Rousmaniere; Lilly Pulitzer Rousseau; Noreen Rowse; Alan Rubenstein; Dean Rusk; Jay Rutherford.

Pierre Salinger; Michael J. ("Mike") Samek; Mary Sanford; Brent Saville; Edward Savwoir; Raymond Lewis Scherer; Fifi Fell Schiff; Arthur M. Schlesinger, Jr.; Richard Schotter; Judy Schrafft; Rose Schreiber; Charles M. Schwartz; Carol Selig; Tom Seligson; Carolyn Hagner Shaw; Patricia Shea; Scott Shea; Walter Sheades; Tony Sherman; Aaron Shikler; Hugh Sidey; Martin Simmonds; Queenie Simmonds-Nielsen; Eilene Slocum; Senator George Smathers; Earl E. T. Smith; Liz Smith; Lyn Alpha Smith; Oliver Smith; Ron Smith; Sandy Snaty; Theodore ("Ted") Sorensen, Esq.; Rosemary Sorrentino; Thomas L. Souder; Charles ("Chuck") Spalding; Helen Bowdoin Spaulding; Helen Speronis; Purette Spiegler; Chris Spirou; Nikki Sporadis; John Springer; Baroness Garnett Stackleberg; Jessie Stearns; Newton Steers; Gloria Steinem; John Sterling; Mrs. Sandy Stewart; Cecil Stoughton; Nina Auchincloss Steers Straight; Phil Strider; Marianne ("Mimi") Strong; Lyle Stuart; David Susskind; Jane Suydam; Pat Suzuki; Herbert B. Swope.

Senator Robert Taft, Jr.; Taki (Taki Theodoracopoulos); George Tames; Garvin Tankersley; Jonathan Tapper; Roslyn Targ; Gladys Tartiere; Michael Teague; John Theodoracopoulos; Evan Thomas; Evan W. Thomas; Phillip Thomas; Gert Thorne; Mary Tierney; Kathy Tollerton; Robert Tracy; Aileen Bowdoin Train; Janet G. Travell, M.D:; Marietta Tree; Stanley Tretick; Susanna Tschanz; Esther Van Wagoner Tufty; Alice Tyne.

Stewart L. Udall; Fred Ullman; Jesse M. Unruh; Renee K. Vago; Jack Valenti; William J. vanden Heuvel, Esq.; Jeanne Murray Vanderbilt; Jean Van-Egroo; Peter Van Ness; Monique Van Vooren; Martin ("Marty") Venker; Michael Ventresca; René Verdon; Roger Viard; Gore Vidal; Alejo Vidal-Quadros; Marie Charlotte Vidal-Quadros; George Vigouroux; Helen Vlachos; Susan Vogelsinger; Diana Vreeland.

Helga Wagner; Phyllis Cerf Wagner; Frank Waldrop; Gillian Walker; John Walker; Beverly ("Bev") L. Walter; Frank Wangler; Fanny Warburg; Andy Warhol; John Carl Warnecke; Alexandra Webb; Joan Weekly; Mary deLimur Weinmann; S. Cary Welch; Zella West; John B. White; Judy White; Theodore H. ("Teddy") White; Les Whitten; Conrad Wirth; David Wise; Harris Wofford; Perry Wolff; Lois Wright.

Jane Yeoman; Elmer L. ("Rusty") Young; Apostolos Zabelas; Louis Zanelotti; Jerome Zerbe; Henry Zerman; Richard Zoerink; Angelo Zucotti.

*   *   *

My ultimate love and gratitude go to the ladies in my life: Renee, Jeanne and Chloe.

C. David Heymann
January 14, 1989

Index

ABOUT THE AUTHOR

C. DAVID HEYMANN is the author of *Ezra Pound; The Last Rower; American Aristocracy: The Lives and Times of James Russell, Amy and Robert Lowell;* and *Poor Little Rich Girl: The Life and Legend of Barbara Hutton.*

Both the Pound and Lowell biographies were nominated for Pulitzer Prizes and were listed among the Most Notable Books of the Year by *The New York Times Book Review.*

Heymann's writings have appeared in a wide variety of periodicals including *Redbook, Cosmopolitan, Vanity Fair, The New York Times,* the *Washington Post, Paris Match, Stern* (Germany), *Epoca* (Italy), *Encounter* (England), *Partisan Review,* the *Chicago Tribune, New Republic, Saturday Review* and the *International Herald-Tribune.*

He is married, has one child and lives in New York City.